Lecture Notes of the Institute for Computer Sciences, Social Informatics and Telecommunications Engineering 226

More information about this series at http://www.springer.com/series/8197

Xuemai Gu · Gongliang Liu
Bo Li (Eds.)

Machine Learning and Intelligent Communications

Second International Conference, MLICOM 2017
Weihai, China, August 5–6, 2017
Proceedings, Part I

Springer

Editors
Xuemai Gu
Harbin Institute of Technology
Harbin, Heilongjiang
China

Bo Li
Shandong University
Weihai, Heilongjiang
China

Gongliang Liu
Harbin Institute of Technology
Weihai, Heilongjiang
China

ISSN 1867-8211   ISSN 1867-822X (electronic)
Lecture Notes of the Institute for Computer Sciences, Social Informatics
and Telecommunications Engineering
ISBN 978-3-319-73563-4   ISBN 978-3-319-73564-1 (eBook)
https://doi.org/10.1007/978-3-319-73564-1

Library of Congress Control Number: 2017963764

This Springer imprint is published by the registered company Springer Nature Switzerland AG
The registered company address is: Gewerbestrasse 11, 6330 Cham, Switzerland

Preface

We are delighted to introduce the proceedings of the second edition of the 2017 European Alliance for Innovation (EAI) International Conference on Machine Learning and Intelligent Communications (MLICOM). This conference brought together researchers, developers, and practitioners from around the world who are leveraging and developing machine learning and intelligent communications.

The technical program of MLICOM 2017 consisted of 141 full papers in oral presentation sessions at the main conference tracks. The conference tracks were: Main Track, Machine Learning; Track 1, Intelligent Positioning and Navigation; Track 2, Intelligent Multimedia Processing and Security; Track 3, Intelligent Wireless Mobile Network and Security; Track 4, Cognitive Radio and Intelligent Networking; Track 5, Intelligent Internet of Things; Track 6, Intelligent Satellite Communications and Networking; Track 7, Intelligent Remote Sensing, Visual Computing and Three-Dimensional Modeling; Track 8, Green Communication and Intelligent Networking; Track 9, Intelligent Ad-Hoc and Sensor Networks; Track 10, Intelligent Resource Allocation in Wireless and Cloud Networks; Track 11, Intelligent Signal Processing in Wireless and Optical Communications; Track 12, Intelligent Radar Signal Processing; Track 13, Intelligent Cooperative Communications and Networking. Aside from the high-quality technical paper presentations, the technical program also featured three keynote speeches. The three keynote speeches were by Prof. Haijun Zhang from the University of Science and Technology Beijing, China, Prof. Yong Wang from Harbin Institute of Technology, China, and Mr. Lifan Liu from National Instruments China.

Coordination with the steering chairs, Imrich Chlamtac, Xuemai Gu, and Gongliang Liu, was essential for the success of the conference. We sincerely appreciate their constant support and guidance. It was also a great pleasure to work with such an excellent Organizing Committee who worked hard to organize and support the conference, and in particular, the Technical Program Committee, led by our TPC co-chairs, Prof. Xin Liu and Prof. Mingjian Sun, who completed the peer-review process of technical papers and created a high-quality technical program. We are also grateful to the conference manager, Katarina Antalova, for her support and to all the authors who submitted their papers to MLICOM 2017.

We strongly believe that the MLICOM conference provides a good forum for researchers, developers, and practitioners to discuss all the science and technology aspects that are relevant to machine learning and intelligent communications. We also hope that future MLICOM conferences will be as successful and stimulating, as indicated by the contributions presented in this volume.

December 2017

Xuemai Gu
Gongliang Liu
Bo Li

Organization

Steering Committee

Steering Committee Chair

Imrich Chlamtac   University of Trento, Create-Net, Italy

Steering Committee

Xin-Lin Huang   Tongji University, China

Organizing Committee

General Chairs

Xuemai Gu   Harbin Institute of Technology, China
Z. Jane Wang   The University of British Columbia, Canada
Gongliang Liu   Harbin Institute of Technology (Weihai), China

General Co-chairs

Jianjiang Zhou   Nanjing University of Aeronautics and Astronautics, China
Xin Liu   Dalian University of Technology, China

Web Chairs

Xuesong Ding   Harbin Institute of Technology (Weihai), China
Zhiyong Liu   Harbin Institute of Technology (Weihai), China
Xiaozhen Yan   Harbin Institute of Technology (Weihai), China

Publicity and Social Media Chair

Aijun Liu   Harbin Institute of Technology (Weihai), China

Sponsorship and Exhibits Chair

Chenxu Wang   Harbin Institute of Technology (Weihai), China

Publications Chairs

Xin Liu   Dalian University of Technology, China
Bo Li   Harbin Institute of Technology (Weihai), China

Posters and PhD Track Chair

Xiuhong Wang   Harbin Institute of Technology (Weihai), China

Local Chair

Bo Li   Harbin Institute of Technology (Weihai), China

Conference Manager

Katarina Antalova   EAI - European Alliance for Innovation

Technical Program Committee

Technical Program Committee Chairs

Z. Jane Wang   University of British Columbia, Canada
Xin Liu   Dalian University of Technology, China
Mingjian Sun   Harbin Institute of Technology (Weihai), China

TPC Track Chairs

Machine Learning
Xinlin Huang   Tongji University, China
Rui Wang   Tongji University, China

Intelligent Positioning and Navigation
Mu Zhou   Chongqing University of Posts
                              and Telecommunications, China
Zhian Deng   Dalian Maritime University, China
Min Jia   Harbin Institute of Technology, China

Intelligent Multimedia Processing and Security
Bo Wang   Dalian University of Technology, China
Fangjun Huang   Sun Yat-Sen University, China

Wireless Mobile Network and Security
Shijun Lin   Xiamen University, China
Yong Li   Tsinghua University, China

Cognitive Radio and Intelligent Networking
Yulong Gao   Harbin Institute of Technology, China
Weidang Lu   Zhejiang University of Technology, China
Huiming Wang   Xi'an Jiaotong University, China

Intelligent Internet of Things
Xiangping Zhai   Nanjing University of Aeronautics and Astronautics,
                              China
Chunsheng Zhu   The University of British Columbia, Canada
Yongliang Sun   Nanjing Tech University, China

Intelligent Satellite Communications and Networking
Kanglian Zhao   Nanjing University, China
Zhiqiang Li   PLA University of Science and Technology, China

Intelligent Remote Sensing, Visual Computing, and Three-Dimensional Modeling

Jiancheng Luo	Institute of Remote Sensing and Digital Earth, Chinese Academy of Sciences, China
Bo Wang	Nanjing University of Aeronautics and Astronautics, China

Green Communication and Intelligent Networking

Jingjing Wang	Qingdao University of Science and Technology, China
Nan Zhao	Dalian University of Technology, China

Intelligent Ad-Hoc and Sensor Networks

Bao Peng	Shenzhen Institute of Information Technology, China
Danyang Qin	Heilongjiang University, China
Zhenyu Na	Dalian Maritime University, China

Intelligent Resource Allocation in Wireless and Cloud Networks

Feng Li	Zhejiang University of Technology, China
Jiamei Chen	Shenyang Aerospace University, China
Peng Li	Dalian Polytechnic University, China

Intelligent Signal Processing in Wireless and Optical Communications

Wei Xu	Southeast University, China
Enxiao Liu	Institute of Oceanographic Instrumentation, Shandong Academy of Sciences, China
Guanghua Zhang	Northeast Petroleum University, China
Jun Yao	Broadcom Ltd., USA

Intelligent Radar Signal Processing

Weijie Xia	Nanjing University of Aeronautics and Astronautics, China
Xiaolong Chen	Naval Aeronautical and Astronautical University, China

Intelligent Cooperative Communications and Networking

Deli Qiao	East China Normal University, China
Jiancun Fan	Xi'an Jiaotong University, China
Lei Zhang	University of Surrey, UK

Contents – Part I

Machine Learning

An Effective QoS-Based Reliable Route Selecting Scheme
for Mobile Ad-Hoc Networks.................................... 3
    Jiamei Chen, Yao Wang, Xuan Li, and Chao Gao

Space Encoding Based Compressive Tracking with Wireless
Fiber-Optic Sensors.. 12
    Qingquan Sun, Jiang Lu, Yu Sun, Haiyan Qiao,
    and Yunfei Hou

Moving Object Detection Algorithm Using Gaussian Mixture Model
and SIFT Keypoint Match....................................... 22
    Hang Dong and Xin Zhang

Low-Complexity Signal Detection Scheme Based on LLR for Uplink
Massive MIMO Channel... 30
    Xifeng Chen, Liming Zheng, and Gang Wang

Accurate Scale-Variable Tracking............................. 40
    Xinyou Li, Wenjing Kang, and Gongliang Liu

Sparse Photoacoustic Microscopy Reconstruction Based on Matrix
Nuclear Norm Minimization.................................... 49
    Ying Fu, Naizhang Feng, Yahui Shi, Ting Liu, and Mingjian Sun

Clustering Analysis Based on Segmented Images................ 57
    Hongxu Zheng, Jianlun Wang, and Can He

Channel Estimation Based on Approximated Power Iteration Subspace
Tracking for Massive MIMO Systems............................ 76
    Liming Zheng, Donglai Zhao, Gang Wang, Yao Xu, and Yue Wu

BER Performance Evaluation of Downlink MUSA over Rayleigh
Fading Channel... 85
    Yao Xu, Gang Wang, Liming Zheng, Rongkuan Liu,
    and Donglai Zhao

Intelligent Positioning and Navigation

Privacy Protection for Location Sharing Services in Social Networks....... 97
    Hui Wang, Juan Chen, Xianzhi Wang, Xin Liu, and Zhenyu Na

A Non-line-of-Sight Localization Method Based on the Algorithm
Residual Error Minimization.   103
   Sunan Li, Jingyu Hua, Feng Li, Fangni Chen, and Jiamin Li

WLAN Indoor Localization Using Angle of Arrival   112
   Zengshan Tian, Yong Li, Mu Zhou, and Yinghui Lian

Defect Detection of Photovoltaic Modules Based on Convolutional
Neural Network   122
   Mingjian Sun, Shengmiao Lv, Xue Zhao, Ruya Li,
   Wenhan Zhang, and Xiao Zhang

An Effective BLE Fingerprint Database Construction Method
Based on MEMS   133
   Mu Zhou, Xiaoxiao Jin, Zengshan Tian, Haifeng Cong,
   and Haoliang Ren

Intelligent Multimedia Processing and Security

A New Universal Steganalyzer for JPEG Images.   145
   Ge Liu, Fangjun Huang, Qi Chen, and Zhonghua Li

Double JPEG Compression Detection Based on Fusion Features.   158
   Fulong Yang, Yabin Li, Kun Chong, and Bo Wang

Complexity Based Sample Selection for Camera Source Identification   168
   Yabin Li, Bo Wang, Kun Chong, and Yanqing Guo

Wireless Mobile Network and Security

Lattice Reduction Aided Linear Detection for Generalized
Spatial Modulation   181
   Chungang Liu, Chen Wang, and Wenbin Zhang

Radio Frequency Fingerprint Identification Method
in Wireless Communication   195
   Zhe Li, Yanxin Yin, and Lili Wu

Cognitive Radio and Intelligent Networking

Short Term Prediction Models of Mobile Network Traffic Based
on Time Series Analysis   205
   Yunxue Gao, Liming Zheng, Donglai Zhao, Yue Wu,
   and Gang Wang

Calculation Method of Field Strength in the Case of Side Obstacles   212
   Lu Chen, Fusheng Dai, Yonggang Chi, and Ji Zhou

Variable Dimension Measurement Matrix Construction for Compressive
Sampling via m Sequence   221
    Jingting Xiao, Ruoyu Zhang, and Honglin Zhao

Signal Quality Assessment of Wireless Signal Based
on Compressed Sensing.   231
    Fei An and Fusheng Dai

Distributed Compressive Sensing Based Spectrum Sensing Method   239
    Yanping Chen, Yulong Gao, and Yongkui Ma

Recent Advances in Radio Environment Map: A Survey   247
    Jingming Li, Guoru Ding, Xiaofei Zhang, and Qihui Wu

Elimination of Inter-distract Downlink Interference Based on
Autocorrelation Technique   258
    Hui Kang, Hongyang Xia, and Fugang Liu

Intelligent Internet of Things

Application of Cooperative Communications with Dual-Stations
in Wireless Mobile Environments   271
    Ershi Xu, Xiangping Zhai, Weiyi Lin, and Bing Chen

Design for Attendance System with the Direction Identification
Based on RFID.   282
    Hongyuan Wang

A Geo-Based Fine Granularity Air Quality Prediction Using
Machine Learning and Internet-of-Things.   291
    Hang Wang, Yu Sun, and Qingquan Sun

Research on Key Technology in Traditional Chinese Medicine (TCM)
Smart Service System   300
    Yongan Guo, Tong Liu, Xiaomin Guo, and Ye Yang

Application of Wireless Sensor Network in Smart Buildings.   315
    Mingze Xia and Dongyu Song

Distributed System Model Using SysML and Event-B   326
    Qi Zhang, Zhiqiu Huang, and Jian Xie

Intelligent Satellite Communications and Networking

A Full-Protocol-Stack Testbed for Space Network Protocol Emulation   339
    Xiaoqin Ni, Kanglian Zhao, and Wenfeng Li

Application Layer Channel Coding for Space DTN   347
  Dongxu Hou, Kanglian Zhao, and Wenfeng Li

Routing Optimization of Small Satellite Networks Based
on Multi-commodity Flow   355
  Xiaolin Xu, Yu Zhang, and Jihua Lu

Modeling of Satellite-Earth Link Channel and Simulating in Space-Ground
Integrated Network   364
  Beishan Wang and Qi Guo

A Deep Learning Method Based on Convolutional Neural Network
for Automatic Modulation Classification of Wireless Signals   373
  Yu Xu, Dezhi Li, Zhenyong Wang, Gongliang Liu, and Haibo Lv

Modeling and Performance Analysis of Multi-layer Satellite Networks
Based on STK   382
  Bo Li, Xiyuan Peng, Hongjuan Yang, and Gongliang Liu

Artificial-Neural-Network-Based Automatic Modulation Recognition
in Satellite Communication.   394
  Yumeng Zhang, Mingchuan Yang, and Xiaofeng Liu

Licklider Transmission Protocol for GEO-Relayed Space Networks.   405
  Wenrui Zhang, Chenyang Fan, Kanglian Zhao, and Wenfeng Li

Intelligent Remote Sensing, Visual Computing and Three-Dimensional Modeling

Design of LED Collimating Optical System   417
  Yihao Wang, Yuncui Zhang, Xufen Xie, and Yuxuan Zhang

Global Depth Refinement Based on Patches   423
  *Xu Huang, Yanfeng Zhang, Gang Zhou, Lu Liu,
  and Gangshan Cai*

3D Surface Features Scanning System with UAV-Carried Line Laser   434
  *Yilang Sun, Shuqiao Sun, Zihao Cui, Yanchao Zhang,
  and Zhaoshuo Tian*

Contourlet Based Image Denoising Method Combined Recursive
Cycle-Spinning Algorithm   444
  Hongda Fan, Xufen Xie, Yuncui Zhang, and Nianyu Zou

Green Communication and Intelligent Networking

RETRACTED CHAPTER: A Resource Allocation Algorithm Based on
Game Theory in UDN....................................... 453
    Changjun Chen, Jianxin Dai, Chonghu Cheng, and Zhiliang Huang

Optimal Relay Selection Algorithm for Combining Distance and Social
Information in D2D Cooperative Communication Networks............. 463
    Kaijian Li, Jianxin Dai, Chonghu Cheng, and Zhiliang Huang

Linear Massive MIMO Precoding Based on Nonlinear
High-Power Amplifier...................................... 475
    Xudong Yin, Jianxin Dai, Chonghu Cheng, and Zhiliang Huang

Linear Precoding for Massive MIMO Systems with IQ Imbalance......... 484
    Juan Liu, Jianxin Dai, Chonghu Cheng, and Zhiliang Huang

Research on Insurance Data Analysis Platform Based on the
Hadoop Framework....................................... 494
    Mingze Xia

SNR Analysis of the Millimeter Wave MIMO with Lens Antenna Array.... 505
    Min Zhang, Jianxin Dai, Chonghu Cheng, and Zhiliang Huang

Cross-Entropy Optimization Oriented Antenna Selection for Clustering
Management in Multiuser MIMO Networks....................... 516
    Xinyu Zhang, Jing Guo, Qiuyi Cao, and Nan Zhao

Subcarrier Allocation-Based Simultaneous Wireless Information
and Power Transfer for Multiuser OFDM Systems 524
    Xin Liu, Xiaotong Li, Zhenyu Na, and Qiuyi Cao

Intelligent Ad-Hoc and Sensor Networks

A 100 MHz SRAM Design in 180 nm Process...................... 535
    Zhuangguang Chen and Bei Cao

A Modified AODV Protocol Based on Nodes Velocity 545
    Tong Liu, Zhimou Xia, Shuo Shi, and Xuemai Gu

RSA Encryption Algorithm Design and Verification Based
on Verilog HDL.. 555
    Bei Cao, Tianliang Xu, and Pengfei Wu

A Novel High Efficiency Distributed UEP Rateless Coding Scheme
for Satellite Network Data Transmission 564
    *Shuang Wu, Zhenyong Wang, Dezhi Li, Qing Guo,
and Gongliang Liu*

A New Class of Unequal Error Protection Rateless Codes with Equal
Recovery Time Property 574
    Shuang Wu, Zhenyong Wang, Dezhi Li, Gongliang Liu,
    and Qing Guo

Stochastic Geometry Analysis of Ultra Dense Network
and TRSC Green Communication Strategy....................... 584
    Guoqiang Wang and Bai Sun

Reputation-Based Framework for Internet of Things 592
    Juan Chen, Zhengkui Lin, Xin Liu, Zhian Deng,
    and Xianzhi Wang

Gain-Phase Error Calculation in DOA Estimation for Mixed
Wideband Signals.. 598
    Jiaqi Zhen, Yong Liu, and Yanchao Li

Mutual Coupling Estimation in DOA Estimation for Mixed
Wideband Signals.. 606
    Jiaqi Zhen, Yong Liu, and Yanchao Li

Efficient Data Gathering with Compressed Sensing Multiuser Detection
in Underwater Wireless Sensor Networks........................ 614
    Rui Du, Wenjing Kang, Bo Li, and Gongliang Liu

An Efficient Data Collection and Load Balance Algorithm in Wireless
Sensor Networks... 626
    Danyang Qin, Ping Ji, Songxiang Yang, and Qun Ding

RFID Based Electronic Toll Collection System Design
and Implementation....................................... 635
    Yang Li and Peidong Zhuang

Design and Implementation of Survey Vehicle Based on VR 641
    Weiguang Zhao and Peidong Zhuang

Development of the Embedded Multi Media Card Platform
Based on FPGA 648
    Songyan Liu, Ting Chen, Shangru Wu,
    and Cheng Zhang

An Implementation of Special Purpose SSD Device 657
    Songyan Liu, Shangru Wu, Ting Chen, and Cheng Zhang

Performance Evaluation of DTN Routing Protocols in Vehicular
Network Environment 666
    Yongliang Sun, Yinhua Liao, Kanglian Zhao, and Chenguang He

Benefits of Compressed Sensing Multi-user Detection
for Spread Spectrum Code Design.   675
  Yan Wu, Wenjing Kang, Bo Li, and Gongliang Liu

Application of Time-Varying Filter in Time-Frequency
Resource Allocation   682
  Zhongchao Ma, Liang Ye, and Xuejun Sha

Secure Communication Mechanism Based on Key Management
and Suspect Node Detection in Wireless Sensor Networks   692
  Danyang Qin, Songxiang Yang, Ping Ji, and Qun Ding

Research on the Pre-coding Technology of Broadcast Stage
in Multi-user MIMO System   701
  Guoqiang Wang and Shangfu Li

Retraction Note to: A Resource Allocation Algorithm Based on Game
Theory in UDN C1
  Changjun Chen, Jianxin Dai, Chonghu Cheng, and Zhiliang Huang

Author Index   711

Contents – Part II

Intelligent Resource Allocation in Wireless and Cloud Networks

The Application of Equivalent Mean Square Error Method in Scalable
Video Perceptual Quality.................................... 3
  Daxing Qian, Ximing Pei, and Xiangkun Li

Spectrum Allocation in Cognitive Radio Networks by Hybrid Analytic
Hierarchy Process and Graph Coloring Theory..................... 8
  *Jianfei Shi, Feng Li, Xin Liu, Mu Zhou, Jiangxin Zhang,
  and Lele Cheng*

Spectrum Pricing in Condition of Normally Distributed User Preference 15
  Li Wang, Lele Cheng, Feng Li, Xin Liu, and Di Shen

Allocation Optimization Based on Multi-population Genetic
Algorithm for D2D Communications in Multi-services Scenario 23
  *Xujie Li, Xing Chen, Ying Sun, Ziya Wang, Chenming Li,
  and Siyang Hua*

Agricultural IoT System Based on Image Processing
and Cloud Platform Technology 33
  Yaxin Zheng and Chungang Liu

Extension of 2FSK Signal Detection Utilizing Duffing Oscillator 43
  Dawei Chen, Enwei Xu, Shuo Shi, and Xuemai Gu

An Efficient DOA Estimation and Network Sorting Algorithm
for Multi-FH Signals....................................... 53
  *Xin-yong Yu, Ying Guo, Kun-feng Zhang, Lei Li, Hong-guang Li,
  and Ping Sui*

Study on Correlation Properties of Complementary Codes and the
Design Constraints of Complementary Coded CDMA Systems........... 61
  Siyue Sun, Guang Liang, and Kun Wang

A Novel Structure Digital Receiver............................. 71
  Zijian Zhang, Dongxuan He, and Yulei Nie

Analysis of Passive Intermodulation Effect
on OFDM Frame Synchronization.............................. 79
  Yi Wang, Xiangyuan Bu, Xiaozheng Gao, and Lu Tian

Variable Tap-Length Multiuser Detector for Underwater
Acoustic Communication   87
  Zhiyong Liu, Yinghua Wang, and Yinyin Wang

Two-Phase Prototype Filter Design for FBMC Systems   96
  *Jiangang Wen, Jingyu Hua, Zhijiang Xu, Weidang Lu,
  and Jiamin Li*

A Fine Carrier Phase Recovery Method for 32APSK   106
  Yulei Nie, Zijian Zhang, and Peipei Liu

Intelligent Radar Signal Processing

Interferometric-Processing Based Small Space Debris Imaging   117
  Yuxue Sun, Ying Luo, and Song Zhang

Sparse Representation Based SAR Imaging Using Combined Dictionary   124
  Han-yang Xu and Feng Zhou

Parametric Sparse Recovery and SFMFT Based M-D Parameter Estimation
with the Translational Component   132
  Qi-fang He, Han-yang Xu, Qun Zhang, and Yi-jun Chen

A New Radar Detection Effectiveness Estimation Method Based
on Deep Learning   142
  Feng Zhu, Xiaofeng Hu, Xiaoyuan He, Kaiming Li, and Lu Yang

A Novel Parameter Determination Method for Lq Regularization Based
Sparse SAR Imaging   150
  Jia-cheng Ni, Qun Zhang, Li Sun, and Xian-jiao Liang

Downward-Looking Sparse Linear Array Synthetic Aperture Radar 3-D
Imaging Method Based on CS-MUSIC   160
  Fu-fei Gu, Le Kang, Jiang Zhao, Yin Zhang, and Qun Zhang

Adaptive Scheduling Algorithm for ISAR Imaging Radar
Based on Pulse Interleaving   169
  Di Meng, Han-yang Xu, Qun Zhang, and Yi-jun Chen

Direction of Arrive Estimation in Spherical Harmonic Domain Using Super
Resolution Approach   179
  Jie Pan, Yalin Zhu, and Changling Zhou

Adaptive Mainlobe Interference Suppression in Sparse Distributed Array
Radar Based on Synthetic Wideband Signal   188
  Jian Luo, Honggang Zhang, and Yuanyuan Song

Wideband MIMO Radar Waveform Optimization Based on Dynamic
Adjustment of Signal Bandwidth.   198
    Yi-shuai Gong, Qun Zhang, Kai-ming Li, and Yi-jun Chen

Learning Algorithm for Tracking Hypersonic Targets in Near Space   206
    Luyao Cui, Aijun Liu, Changjun Yv, and Taifan Quan

Coherent Integration Algorithm for Weak Maneuvering Target Detection
in Passive Radar Using Digital TV Signals.   215
    Ying Zhou, Weijie Xia, Jianjiang Zhou, Linlin Huang,
    and Minling Huang

High-Resolution Sparse Representation of Micro-Doppler Signal in Sparse
Fractional Domain.   225
    Xiaolong Chen, Xiaohan Yu, Jian Guan, and You He

Estimating of RCS of Ionosphere for High Frequency Surface
Wave Radar   233
    Yang Xuguang, Yu Changjun, Liu Aijun, and Wang Linwei

Intelligent Cooperative Communications and Networking

Joint Mode Selection and Beamformer Optimization for Full-Duplex
Cellular Systems.   243
    Fangni Chen, Jingyu Hua, Weidang Lu, and Zhongpeng Wang

Construction of Emergency Communication Network with Multi
Constraints Based on Geographic Information.   254
    Yuan Feng, Fu-sheng Dai, and Ji Zhou

Design of Turntable Servo Control System Based on Sliding Mode
Control Algorithm.   263
    Zongjie Bi, Zhaoshuo Tian, Pushuai Shi, and Shiyou Fu

Joint Power Allocation and Relay Grouping for Large MIMO Relay
Network with Successive Relaying Protocol   273
    Hong Peng, Changran Su, Yu Zhang, Linjie Xie, and Weidang Lu

The Second Round

Generation of Low Power SSIC Sequences   285
    Bei Cao and Yongsheng Wang

Intrusion Detection with Tree-Based Data Mining Classification
Techniques by Using KDD   294
    Mirza Khudadad and Zhiqiu Huang

Night Time Image Enhancement by Improved Nonlinear Model   304
Yao Zhang, Chenxu Wang, Xinsheng Wang, Jing Wang,
and Le Man

Research on Non-contact Heart Rate Detection Algorithm   316
Chenguang He, Yuwei Cui, and Shouming Wei

Lorentzian Norm Based Super-Resolution Reconstruction
of Brain MRI Image   326
Dongxing Bao, Xiaoming Li, and Jin Li

A Virtual Channel Allocation Algorithm for NoC   333
Dongxing Bao, Xiaoming Li, Yizong Xin, Jiuru Yang, Xiangshi Ren,
Fangfa Fu, and Cheng Liu

A Two-Layered Game Approach Based Relay's Source Selection
and Power Control for Wireless Cooperative Networks   343
Yanguo Zhou, Hailin Zhang, Ruirui Chen, and Tao Zhou

A Novel Method of Flight Target Altitude Attributes
Identification for HFSWR   351
Shuai Shao, Changjun Yu, and Kongrui Zhao

A Minimum Spanning Tree Clustering Algorithm Inspired by P System   361
Xiaojuan Guo and Xiyu Liu

Transfer Learning Method for Convolutional Neural Network in Automatic
Modulation Classification.   371
Yu Xu, Dezhi Li, Zhenyong Wang, Gongliang Liu, and Haibo Lv

Pulse Compression Analysis for OFDM-Based Radar-Radio Systems   381
Xuanxuan Tian, Tingting Zhang, Qinyu Zhang, Hongguang Xu,
and Zhaohui Song

Implementation of Video Abstract Algorithm Based on CUDA.   391
Hui Li, Zhigang Gai, Enxiao Liu, Shousheng Liu, Yingying Gai,
Lin Cao, and Heng Li

Realization of Traffic Video Surveillance on DM3730 Chip   402
Xin Zhang and Hang Dong

Fertilization Forecasting Algorithm Based on Improved BP
Neural Network   410
Tong Xue and Yong Liu

Green Resource Allocation in Intelligent Software Defined
NOMA Networks   418
   Baobao Wang, Haijun Zhang, Keping Long, Gongliang Liu,
   and Xuebin Li

An Algorithm for Chaotic Masking and Its Blind Extraction of Image
Information in Positive Definite System   428
   Xinwu Chen, Yaqin Xie, Erfu Wang, and Danyang Qin

Instruction Detection in SCADA/Modbus Network Based
on Machine Learning.   437
   Haicheng Qu, Jitao Qin, Wanjun Liu, and Hao Chen

A Joint Source-Channel Error Protection Transmission Scheme
Based on Compressed Sensing for Space Image Transmission   455
   Dongqing Li, Junxin Luo, Tiantian Zhang, Shaohua Wu,
   and Qinyu Zhang

Local Density Estimation Based on Velocity and Acceleration Aware
in Vehicular Ad-Hoc Networks.   463
   Xiao Luo, Xinhong Wang, Ping Wang, Fuqiang Liu,
   and Nguyen Ngoc Van

Research on Millimeter Wave Communication Interference Suppression
of UAV Based on Beam Optimization.   472
   Weizhi Zhong, Lei Xu, Xiaoyi Lu, and Lei Wang

Global Dynamic One-Step-Prediction Resource Allocation Strategy
for Space Stereo Multi-layer Data Asymmetric Scale-Free Network.   482
   Weihao Xie, Zhigang Gai, Enxiao Liu, and Dingfeng Yu

Machine Learning Based Key Performance Index Prediction Methods
in Internet of Industry   490
   Haowei Li, Liming Zheng, Yue Wu, and Gang Wang

An Auction-Gaming Based Routing Model for LEO Satellite Networks   498
   Ligang Cong, Huamin Yang, Yanghui Wang, and Xiaoqiang Di

Parameters Estimation of Precession Cone Target Based
on Micro-Doppler Spectrum   509
   MingFeng Wang, AiJun Liu, LinWei Wang, and ChangJun Yu

Automated Flowering Time Prediction Using Data Mining
and Machine Learning.   518
   Runxuan Li, Yu Sun, and Qingquan Sun

Spatial Crowdsourcing-Based Sensor Node Localization in Internet
of Things Environment   528
    Yongliang Sun, Yejun Sun, and Kanglian Zhao

Influence of Inter-channel Error Distribution on Mismatch
in Time-Interleaved Pipelined A/D Converter   537
    Yongsheng Wang, Chen Yin, and Xunzhi Zhou

Distributed Joint Channel-Slot Selection for Multi-UAV Networks:
A Game-Theoretic Learning Approach.   546
    Jiaxin Chen, Yuhua Xu, Yuli Zhang, and Qihui Wu

Ship Detection in SAR Using Extreme Learning Machine   558
    Liyong Ma, Lidan Tang, Wei Xie, and Shuhao Cai

Obtaining Ellipse Common Tangent Line Equations by the Rolling Tangent
Line Method.   569
    Naizhang Feng, Teng Jiang, Shiqi Duan, and Mingjian Sun

On Sampling of Bandlimited Graph Signals   577
    Mo Han, Jun Shi, Yiqiu Deng, and Weibin Song

Data Association Based Passive Localization in Complex
Multipath Scenario   585
    Bing Zhao and Ganlin Hao

Design and Implementation of Multi-channel Burst Frame Detector.   595
    Bing Zhao

Research on Cache Placement in ICN   603
    Yu Zhang, Yangyang Li, Ruide Li, and Wenjing Sun

The Digital Chaos Cover Transport and Blind Extraction
of Speech Signal.   612
    Xinwu Chen, Yaqin Xie, and Erfu Wang

A Multi-frame Image Speckle Denoising Method Based on Compressed
Sensing Using Tensor Model   622
    Ruofei Zhou, Gang Wang, Wenchao Yang, Zhen Li, and Yao Xu

Frequency-Hopped Space-Time Coded OFDM over Time-Varying
Multipath Channel.   634
    Fangfang Cheng, Jiyu Jin, Guiyue Jin, Peng Li, and Jun Mou

Dynamic Characteristic Analysis for Complexity of Continuous Chaotic
Systems Based on the Algorithms of SE Complexity and C_0 Complexity. . . .   647
    Xiaolin Ye, Jun Mou, Zhisen Wang, Peng Li, and Chunfeng Luo

Design and Implemention of an Emulation Node for Space Network
Protocol Testing   658
    Sichen Zhao, Yuan Fang, Wenfeng Li, and Kanglian Zhao

Optimization Spiking Neural P System for Solving TSP   668
    Feng Qi and Mengmeng Liu

Author Index   677

Machine Learning

An Effective QoS-Based Reliable Route Selecting Scheme for Mobile Ad-Hoc Networks

Jiamei Chen[1(✉)], Yao Wang[2], Xuan Li[1], and Chao Gao[2]

[1] College of Electrical and Information Engineering,
Shenyang Aerospace University, Shenyang 110136, China
chenjiamei5870@163.com
[2] Communication Department, Shenyang Artillery Academy,
No. 31 Dongdaying Avenue, Shenhe Area, Shenyang 110161, China

Abstract. In mobile ad-hoc networks, the random mobility of nodes will result in unreliable connection. In addition, the bandwidth resource limit will affect the quality of service (QoS) critically. In this paper, an effective QoS-based reliable route selecting scheme (QRRSS) is proposed to alleviate the above problems. The route reliability can be estimated by received signal strength and the control packet overhead can be decreased by selecting more reliable link that satisfies the QoS requirements. Simulation results indicate that the reliable route selecting scheme presented in this paper shows obvious superiority to the traditional ad-hoc QoS on-demand routing (AQOR) in the packet successful delivery rate, the control packet overhead and the average end-to-end delay.

Keywords: Mobile ad-hoc networks · Quality of service (QoS) · QRRSS
Reliability · AQOR

1 Introduction

This instruction file for Word users (there is a separate instruction file for LaTeX users) may be used as a template. Kindly send the final and checked Word and PDF files of your paper to the Contact Volume Editor. This is usually one of the organizers of the conference. You should make sure that the Word and the PDF files are identical and correct and that only one version of your paper is sent. It is not possible to update files at a later stage. Please note that we do not need the printed paper.

We would like to draw your attention to the fact that it is not possible to modify a paper in any way, once it has been published. This applies to both the printed book and the online version of the publication. Every detail, including the order of the names of the authors, should be checked before the paper is sent to the Volume Editors.

With the development of mobile ad-hoc networks and continuous improvement of user demands, the limited bandwidth resource becomes difficult to guarantee high QoS for users [1]. Although such issues can get some improvement by a serial of QoS routing algorithms [2, 3] recently, no effective discussion of link reliability is available. Due to the link breakage caused by random mobility of nodes, source nodes need continue to trigger the route discovery process, which will lead to sharp increase in the

© ICST Institute for Computer Sciences, Social Informatics and Telecommunications Engineering 2018
X. Gu et al. (Eds.): MLICOM 2017, Part I, LNICST 226, pp. 3–11, 2018.
https://doi.org/10.1007/978-3-319-73564-1_1

control overhead, the probability of packet discard, and average end-to-end delay. Therefore, it will have a serious impact on the QoS. We can see that under the precondition of urgent QoS requirement, to establish a reliable end-to-end route for nodes is very important and necessary [4].

Many pertinent researches of route in mobile ad-hoc networks have been proposed. Nodes in Associative-Based Routing Protocol (ABR) measure the route reliability by sending pilot signal periodically, and meanwhile, ABR supposes that it must exist a stable period after an unstable period. During the stable time all nodes restart to move after experiencing an immobile time [5]. Obviously, this supposition is opposite to the real situation because of the random mobility of nodes in mobile ad-hoc networks. Link Life Based Routing Protocol (LBR) attains link lifetime by estimating the distance and maximum speed of the nodes. When link fails, proactive maintenance is started up to recover the route. However, estimating route lifetime is invalidation owing to the link failure. Consequently, the reliability of backup route may be hard to guarantee [6]. Entropy-Based Long-Life Distributed QoS Routing Protocol (EBLLD) algorithm proposes an idea of using entropy metric to weigh the route reliability and select the longer lifetime path, where the entropy for a route is a function about the relative positions, velocities, and the transmission ranges of the nodes [7]. Although these algorithms can be applied to the mobile ad-hoc networks better than the statistical models, they need the premise of assumption that the relative positions all nodes are known accurately, which is not realistic in most of the mobile ad-hoc networks.

With the gradual maturation of the signal strength measurement technology, the application of signal strength has come to the top in domains of the control of wireless networks [8], measuring distance and orientation [9]. Considering that the signal strength can reflect the connection state of the link indirectly, this paper proposes a method of estimating route reliability based on received signal strength and establishes an effective QoS-based reliable route selecting scheme QRRSS. QRRSS selects more reliable link that satisfies QoS requirement by adding relative information to (Route Request, RREQ)/(Route Reply, RREP), So that it can decrease control packet overhead by reducing frequent route discovery.

2   Effective Qos-Based Reliable Route Estimation Algorithm

A mobile ad-hoc network can be depicted as an undirected graph $G = (V, E)$. Where, V is the set of nodes and E is the set of bidirectional links between the nodes. Any link $l(i, j) \in E$ can be given by residual Bandwidth $B(l)$, Delay $D(l)$ and Link Reliability $LR(l)$. The path from one node s to another node d can be described as $P(s, d) = (s, l(s, x), x, l(x, y), y, \ldots, l(z, d), d)$, where $x, y, \ldots, z$ are some points in the path. The connection between any two nodes is made up of a serial of all possible paths, which is $P(s, d) = \{P_0, P_1, P_i, \ldots, P_n\}$. Accordingly, we can define a certain path P_i between s and d, whose delay, bandwidth and reliability satisfy the requirements as (1),

$$\begin{cases} Delay(P_i) = \sum_{l \in P_i} D(l) \\ Band(P_i) = \min\{B(l_0), B(l_1), B(l_i), \ldots, B(l_n)\} \\ Reliability(P_i) = \prod_{l \in Pi} LR(l) \end{cases} \quad (1)$$

Where, $l_0, l_1, l_i, \ldots, l_n$ are the links that make up the path [10]. Thus, the question can be described as searching the most reliable path P_m which satisfies QoS requirement for nodes. Furthermore, we can depict the question as (2),

$$\begin{cases} Reliability(P_m) = \max\{Reliability(P_0), Reliability(P_1), \\ \qquad\qquad Reliability(P_m), \ldots, Reliability(P_n)\} \\ \forall Band(P_m) \geq \Delta b \\ \forall Delay(P_m) \leq \Delta b \end{cases} \quad (2)$$

Now, for the sake of expression convenience, we introduce the parameters as Table 1.

With the above parameter assumptions, the steps of QRRSS proposed in this paper based on (Decision Rules, DR) can be provided as follows:

DR1: If $SS_{1i,j} \geq Thr_1$, then it means that nodes i and j are close enough, and the link is very reliable. In that case, we set $LR_{i,j} = 1$ and $LU_{i,j} = 0$;

DR2: If $SS_{1i,j} \geq Thr_2$ and node j is a new neighbor node of i, then we set $LU_{i,j} = 1$;

DR3: If $SS_{1i,j} \geq Thr_2$ and $SS_{2i,j} \geq RxThr$, it indicates that the situation of nodes i and j is not sure. If $DSS_{i,j} = SS_{2i,j} - SS_{1i,j}$, we set $LU_{i,j} = 0$; if $DSS_{i,j} \leq m_1$, we set $LR_{i,j} = 1$; if $DSS_{i,j} > m_1$ and $DSS_{i,j} \leq m_2$, we set $LR_{i,j} = (m_2 - DSS_{i,j})/(m_2 - m_1)$; if $DSS_{i,j} > m_2$, we set $LR_{i,j} = 0$.

Table 1. The parameters and meanings in this paper

Parameters	Meanings
$RxThr$	Reception threshold of received signal strength, we assume it is same for all nodes
$SS_{1i,j}$	Current received signal strength for the link between nodes i and j
$SS_{2i,j}$	The received signal strength stored in neighbor information table for the link between nodes i and j, periodically updated by $SS_{1i,j}$
Thr_1	If a node receives signal with strength $\geq Thr_1$, then the link can be assumed to be very reliable
Thr_2	If a node receives signal with strength $< Thr_2$, then the link can be assumed to be unreliable to transfer the data
$DSS_{i,j}$	The difference of signal strength between nodes i and j to indicate the changes of the signal strength
m_1, m_2	m_1 is a threshold for DSS to indicate small environment variations in signal strength, and that m_2 ($>m_1$) is used to detect whether two nodes are leaving away from each other fast
$LR_{i,j}$	Link reliability between nodes i and j, and $LR_{i,j} \in [0, 1]$
$LU_{i,j}$	Link uncertainty between nodes i and j, means that the link's reliability cannot be determined due to lack of $SS_{2i,j}$ in neighbor information table

As a consequence, nodes can obtain the relative parameters from received packets, and estimate route reliability with DR. The packet, whose signal strength is less than or equal to Thr_2, is discarded. We define the route reliability and uncertainty as (3),

$$\begin{cases} RR_r = \prod_{l \in r} LR_l \\ RU_r = \sum_{l \in r} LU_r \end{cases} \tag{3}$$

If RR_r is increasingly big and RU_r is increasingly small, then the route is increasingly reliable.

3   Route Establishment of QRRSS

On the base of satisfying the QoS requirements, QRRSS proposed in this paper estimates route reliability by received signal strength. Every node estimates the route reliability depending on DR, and selects more reliable route to establish end-to-end connection by setting the route reply latency mechanism at the destination node. For the convenience of analysis, we suppose that all RREQ/RREP packets satisfy the QoS requirements. The process of route establishment is shown as Fig. 1. In this figure we

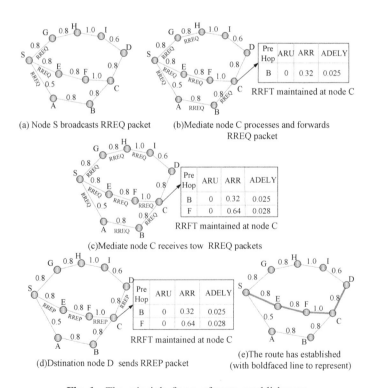

Fig. 1. The principle figure of route establishment

can see that the numbers above the links represents the current reliability of the links. The detailed route discovery process is shown as following:

(1) Firstly, the source node S broadcasts the RREQ packet (including the information of bandwidth and delay requirements), which is shown in Fig. 1(a), and sets the initiate value of parameters as: Accumulated Delay of route, ADELY = 0; Accumulated Route Reliability, ARR = 1; Accumulated Route Uncertainty, ARU = 0. After sending the RREQ packet, S starts a timer of $3 \times Dmax$ to wait the RREP packet.

(2) As shown in Fig. 1(b), mediate node C estimates the route reliability and updates the RREQ packet after receiving the RREQ packet. Before forwarding this received RREQ packet, node C sets the reverse route timer to $3 \times Dmax$ and stores relative information of RREQ into the Route Request Forward Table (RRFT). RRFT of mediate node C has: ADELAY = 0.025, ARR = 0.32, ARU = 0. For the sake of selecting more reliable route, the RREQ packets are also disposed during a certain time, as shown in Fig. 1(c). Mediate node C receives another RREQ packet from node F and registers the information as below: ADELAY = 0.028, ARR = 0.64, ARU = 0. Obviously, we can see that this route reliability is higher.

In summary, if a mediate node receives an RREP packet, it firstly finds out the RRFT of relevant RREQ packet and selects a most reliable route. Secondly, it estimates the route reliability and updates ARR and ARU of RREP packet, since ARR and ARU can represent the current route reliability. Finally, before forwarding the RREP packet, it sets the RRFT timer to $3 \times Dmax$ and stores relative information into the route table

(3) The destination node D may receive many RREQ packets from different paths, like the mediate node C. And it also estimates the route reliability with the same DR. On receiving the first RREQ packet, node D waits a period time, called Route Reply Latency (RRL), to receive other RREQ packets and find a more reliable route to satisfy the QoS requirements. Next, node D copies the value of QoS, ARR, and ARU to the RREP packet. Simultaneously, node D sets the RRFT timer to $3 \times Dmax$ and stores relative information into the route table, which is shown in Fig. 1(d). Eventually, node D will select the route including node F to send the RREP packet via route selecting algorithm. As a consequence, the route from source node S to destination node D that can guarantee the QoS requirements has been established, as shown in Fig. 1(e).

4   Performance Evaluation

In this section, we compare our reliable route selecting scheme to a traditional real-time-flow based QoS routing protocol, AQOR, which is constrained by bandwidth and delay. Then, we give out the performance evaluation from packet successful delivery rate, control packet overhead and average end-to-end delay. Packet successful delivery rate is the ratio of the data packets successfully received at the destinations and the total data packets that are actually sent to the network. Control packet overhead is the ratio of the control packets sent to the network and the total data packets successfully delivered at the destinations. Average end-to-end delay is the average time of delivered time that all data packets have successfully arrived destinations. NS2 based simulation gives the performance evaluation to QRRSS. The simulation results are shown in Figs. 2, 3, 4 and the detailed simulation parameters are shown in Table 2.

Table 2. The parameters and values in the simulation

Parameters	Values
Network topology	1000 m × 1000 m
Number of nodes	40
Maximum mobility speed of nodes (m/s)	0, 2, 5, 10, 15, 20
Pause time (s)	0
Simulation time (s)	300
Minimum bandwidth (kbps)	40
Thr_1, Thr_2	$1.4 \times RxThr$, $1.1 \times RxThr$
m_1, m_2	$0.04 \times RxThr$, $0.3 \times RxThr$
RRL (msec)	$0.3 \times RxThr$
RRL (msec)	70

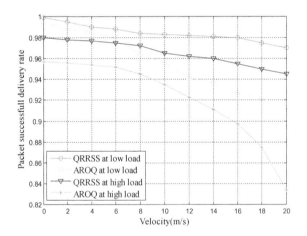

Fig. 2. Packet successful delivery rate

The route failure is one of the most important factors affecting the packet successful delivery rate. When the route fails, upriver nodes will store the data packets in buffers and wait until the route is established again. During this time, the buffers of nodes are filled in quickly, which will result in the subsequently discarding of the received data packets. Figure 2 shows the packet successful delivery rate performance of AQOR and our QRRSS at low/high load respectively. We can see that QRRSS can increase the packet successful delivery rate about 10% when the nodes move quickly, and also significantly improve the delivery performance of the whole network. The reason is that by establishing reliable end-to-end route connection, QRRSS can effectively avoid the data packets discarded extensively due to the route failure, no matter in low or high load environment.

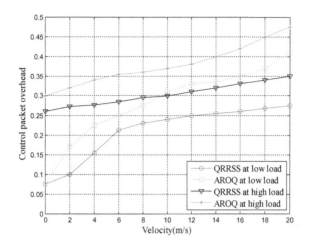

Fig. 3. Control packet overhead

From Fig. 3, it can be seen that the packet control overhead in QRRSS has reduces and especially in high load and nodes moving fast it reduces nearly 12%. The reason seems to be obvious, destination node in AQOR will send many RREP replies so that source node can select a most optimization route, but at the same time it will lead to the control overhead increasing. With contrast to the AQOR, QRRSS not only increases

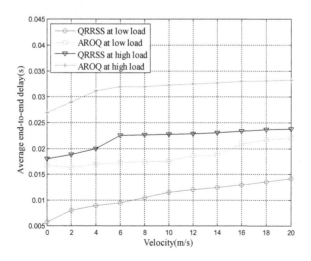

Fig. 4. Average end-to-end delay

the route reliability and reduces the ratio of route failure, but also reduces the route overhead indirectly from some kind of degree.

From Fig. 4, we can observe that the average end-to-end delay of AQOR and QRRSS are both not up to 0.04 s, and obviously, QRRSS has better delay performance than AQOR. That is because the algorithm sets the link uncertainty $(LU_{i,j})$ and other parameters to different values under different conditions, which makes QRRSS can guarantee the route reliability to some extent and decrease the probability of route rediscovery.

5 Conclusion

QRRSS proposed in this paper selects more reliable route connection that can guarantee the QoS requirements by adding relative information to RREQ/RREP. The scheme does not depend on the orientation equipments like GPS and the mobility model of network nodes. Simulation results indicate that QRRSS shows obvious performance improvements with contrast to traditional AQOR in packet successful delivery rate, control overhead and average end-to-end delay.

Acknowledgments. This research was supported by National Natural Science Foundation of China (Grant No. 61501306), Liaoning Provincial Education Department Foundation (Grant No. L2015402).

References

1. Smith, T.F., Waterman, M.S.: Identification of common molecular subsequences. J. Mol. Biol. **147**, 195–197 (1981)
2. May, P., Ehrlich, H.-C., Steinke, T.: ZIB structure prediction pipeline: composing a complex biological workflow through web services. In: Nagel, W.E., Walter, W.V., Lehner, W. (eds.) Euro-Par 2006. LNCS, vol. 4128, pp. 1148–1158. Springer, Heidelberg (2006). https://doi.org/10.1007/11823285_121
3. Foster, I., Kesselman, C.: The Grid: Blueprint for a New Computing Infrastructure. Morgan Kaufmann, San Francisco (1999)
4. Czajkowski, K., Fitzgerald, S., Foster, I., Kesselman, C.: Grid information services for distributed resource sharing. In: 10th IEEE International Symposium on High Performance Distributed Computing, pp. 181–184. IEEE Press, New York (2001)
5. Foster, I., Kesselman, C., Nick, J., Tuecke, S.: The physiology of the grid: an open grid services architecture for distributed systems integration. Technical report, Global Grid Forum (2002)
6. National Center for Biotechnology Information. http://www.ncbi.nlm.nih.gov
7. Zhai, C., Zhang, W., Mao, G.: Cooperative spectrum sharing between cellular and ad-hoc networks. IEEE Trans. Wirel. Commun. **13**(7), 4025–4037 (2014)
8. Song, Y., Xie, J.: BRACER: a distributed broadcast protocol in multi-hop cognitive radio ad-hoc networks with collision avoidance. IEEE Trans. Mob. Comput. **14**(3), 509–524 (2015)

9. Laursen, A.L., Mousten, B., Jensen, V., Kampf, C.: Using an Ad-Hoc corpus to write about emerging technologies for technical writing and translation: the case of search engine optimization. IEEE Trans. Prof. Commun. **57**(1), 56–74 (2014)
10. Rios, M.: Variable route expiration time based on a fixed probability of failure for ad-hoc networks routing applications. IEEE Latin Am. Trans. **13**(1), 383–389 (2015)
11. Conti, M., Giordano, S.: Mobile ad-hoc networking: milestones, challenges, and new research directions. IEEE Commun. Mag. **52**(1), 85–96 (2014)
12. Khalili-Shoja, M.R., Amariucai, G.T., Wei, S., Deng, J.: Secret common randomness from routing metadata in ad-hoc networks. IEEE Trans. Inf. Forensics Secur. **11**(8), 1674–1684 (2016)
13. Haque, I.T.: On the overheads of ad-hoc routing schemes. IEEE Syst. J. **9**(2), 605–614 (2015)
14. Bello, L., Bakalis, P., Rapajic, P., Anang, K.A.: Optimised adaptive power on-demand routing protocol for mobile ad-hoc wireless network. IET Netw. **3**(4), 245–251 (2014)
15. Celimuge, W., Ji, Y., Liu, F., Ohzahata, S., Kato, T.: Toward practical and intelligent routing in vehicular ad-hoc networks. IEEE Trans. Veh. Technol. **64**(12), 5503–5519 (2015)
16. Wang, Z., Chen, Y., Li, C.: PSR: a lightweight proactive source routing protocol for mobile ad-hoc networks. IEEE Trans. Veh. Technol. **63**(2), 859–868 (2014)
17. Tang, F., Guo, M., Guo, S., Cheng-Zhong, X.: Mobility prediction based joint stable routing and channel assignment for mobile ad-hoc cognitive networks. IEEE Trans. Parallel Distrib. Syst. **27**(3), 789–802 (2016)

Space Encoding Based Compressive Tracking with Wireless Fiber-Optic Sensors

Qingquan Sun[1(✉)], Jiang Lu[2], Yu Sun[3], Haiyan Qiao[1], and Yunfei Hou[1]

[1] California State University, San Bernardino, CA 92407, USA
quanqian12345@gmail.com, {hqiao,yunfei.hou}@csusb.edu
[2] University of Houston at Clear Lake, Houston, TX 77058, USA
luj@uhcl.edu
[3] California State Polytechnic University, Pomona, Pomona, CA 91768, USA
yusun@cpp.edu

Abstract. This paper presents a distributed, compressive multiple target localization and tracking system based on wireless fiber-optic sensors. This research aims to develop a novel, efficient, low data-throughput multiple target tracking platform. The platform is developed based on three main technologies: (1) multiplex sensing, (2) space encoding and (3) compressive localization. Multiplex sensing is adopted to enhance sensing efficiency. Space encoding can convert the location information of multi-target into a set of codes. Compressive localization further reduces the number of sensors and data-throughput. In this work, a graphical model is employed to model the variables and parameters of this tracking system, and tracking is implemented through an Expectation-Maximization (EM) procedure. The results demonstrated that the proposed system is efficient in multi-target tracking.

Keywords: Human tracking · Multiplex sensing
Compressive sensing · Space encoding

1 Introduction

Indoor environments monitoring has been demanded in many areas. The applications include human counting, tracking, identification, activity recognition, and situation perception, etc. The purposes are to provide secure and intelligent working and living spaces to users through the surveillance of the environments. Among these applications, human tracking is a very challenging but interesting application, and is receiving more and more attentions. Traditional human tracking systems in indoor environments are based on video cameras. Such systems have been widely applied due to its visual characteristic [1]. Nowadays, some wireless sensor based human tracking systems have been developed and demonstrated with a satisfied performance especially under severe conditions such as poor illumination, low computation, disguise, and so on.

The wireless sensor based human tracking systems are advantageous in (1) large surveillance area; (2) low data throughput; (3) robustness; (4) multiple

© ICST Institute for Computer Sciences, Social Informatics and Telecommunications Engineering 2018
X. Gu et al. (Eds.): MLICOM 2017, Part I, LNICST 226, pp. 12–21, 2018.
https://doi.org/10.1007/978-3-319-73564-1_2

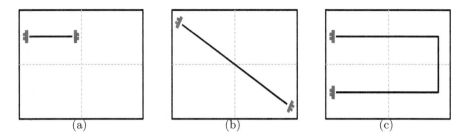

Fig. 1. (a) Simplex fiber-optic sensing; (b) duplex fiber-optic sensing; (c) multiplex fiber-optic sensing.

sensing modalities. Radar, sonar, acoustic sensor based tracking systems are proposed in [3,4]. Radar-based systems demand a large amount of power supply, therefore, they are usually applied in military fields [2]; while acoustic sensor based systems are prone to be interfered by noise, and their performance is limited in silent environments. The pyroelectric infrared (PIR) sensor is able to detect the infrared irradiation of human motions, it is appropriate to be used in human tracking. A typical work is proposed in [5], which uses wireless distributed pyroelectric sensors to achieve multi-human tracking and identification.

Whatever sensor is used to form a human tracking system, the goals are to implement low-data-throughput and energy-efficient sensing. Recently compressive sensing technology has been proposed and applied in image processing and information retrieval [6,7]. It has been proved that compressive sensing can further reduce the data samples but still guarantee the successful reconstructions. Inspired by this technique, we propose a wireless sensor based human tracking platform using compressive sensing. Furthermore, we extend compressive sensing concept from data processing to sensing mode and sampling geometry, namely, we start compress measurements in sensing and sampling phases.

Other than the typical wireless sensor based human tracking systems, mainly the PIR sensor based systems, in this paper, we propose to use a new sensing modality, fiber-optic sensors to implement human tracking. Compared with PIR sensors, fiber-optic sensors are more suitable to human tracking. By adopting multiplex sensing, space encoding and compressive localization, the sensing efficiency and data compression are enhanced. The multi-target tracking is achieved through a graphical model and expectation-maximization (EM) approach.

2 System Model

2.1 Multiplex Fiber-Optic Sensing

As we know, sensing is the process that converting physical information into signals that can be read and observed by an instrument. The fiber-optic sensors can be used to convert the presence and pressure information of targets into light intensities to enable localization and tracking. Multiplex sensing technique is inspired by the antenna of insects which is able to increase the utilization ratio of single sensor cells. Here, in our system, we employ multiplex sensing to enable each fiber-optic sensor to detect multiple regions rather than just one region. In this way, all the sensors can be fully utilized and the number of sensors needed can be reduced dramatically. Such a method can improve the sensing efficiency but at a price of increasing ambiguities in localization. The fiber-optic sensing formats are shown in Fig. Compared with simplex sensing (Fig. 1(a)), multiplex sensing (Fig. 1(b), (c)) consumes less sensors to cover the same size regions.

2.2   Space Encoding Schemes

Space encoding is to segment the monitored area into different blocks and use a certain sensors to encode each block. Thus, when a target appears in a certain block, the corresponding code indicates the target's location. The purpose of using space encoding technology is to enhance the feasibility and efficiency of monitoring. Fiber-optic sensors are appropriate for space encoding due to its flexibility and detection modality. There are multiple space encoding schemes suitable for fiber-optic sensors. The ideal encoding scheme is named decimal encoding, in which a single block is encoded by only one sensor. Apparently, this encoding scheme is able to get a high accuracy with a minimum of ambiguity. The number of sensors, however, could be very large for a wide area. In comparison, binary encoding scheme can reduce the sensor consumption dramatically. For example, encoding a 4 blocks area, decimal encoding scheme needs 4 sensors, while binary encoding scheme only needs 2 sensors, as shown in Fig. 2.

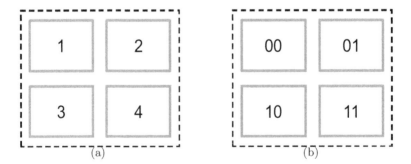

Fig. 2. Space encoding for a 4-blocks region. (a) Decimal encoding scheme; (b) binary encoding scheme.

2.3   Distributed Binary Space Encoding

Suppose n fiber-optic sensors are available in the system, and they are used to monitor a space which is divided into m blocks $\boldsymbol{\gamma} = \{\gamma_1, \gamma_2, \cdots, \gamma_m\}$. Each block

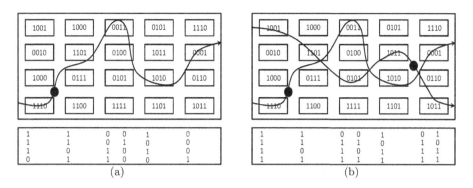

Fig. 3. Illustrations of space encoding for (a) one target case; (b) two targets case.

γ_i is encoded by n fiber-optic sensors, and the corresponding code will be a n-bit binary string, represented by $C_i = \{c_{i1}, \cdots, c_{in}\}$, as shown in Fig. 3. c_{ij} is generated when a target presents in j_{th} block, so

$$c_{ij} = I(\Omega_i \cap \varphi(\gamma_j)) \tag{1}$$

where $I(\cdot)$ is a logic function whose output is "0" or "1"; Ω is the sampling geometry of sensor i; $\varphi(r)$ is the target at location r; and $\cap$ represents bit-wise AND operation. Therefore, with n fiber-optic sensors deployment, the observation area is encoded into a set of n-bit codes.

When only one target presents within the observation area, the measurement y, which is a $n \times 1$ vector, is given by

$$y = Cx_1 \tag{2}$$

where $C = [c_{ij}]^T$, which is a $n \times m$ matrix, and $x_1 = I(r \in \gamma)$, which is a $m \times 1$ binary vector with only one '1' element.

When K targets present within the observation area, the measurement $n \times 1$ vector, y becomes

$$y = \overset{K}{\underset{k=1}{\cup}} Cx_k = C \odot x \tag{3}$$

where $\cup$ denotes the bit-wise OR operation, x_k is the measurement vector for the k_{th} target, $\odot$ denotes the saturation multiplication, i.e., $A \odot x = I(Ax \geq 1)$ if the upper bond is 1 and I is a matrix with only '1's. The example of the binary measurement sequence for one and two targets cases are shown in Fig. 3.

2.4   Compressive Localization

The complexity of the compressive localization for multiple targets comes from the bit-wise OR operation in Eq. 3. To localize K targets with small errors, it requires a high degree of independence among the codes. However, an increase of the independence will lead to an increase of sensors.

Given the space codes matrix H, the binary compressive localization problem is solved by [8]

$$\hat{x} = \operatorname*{argmin}_{x} \|x\|_1 \ s.t. \ y = H \odot x \tag{4}$$

where y is the binary measurement. For simplicity purpose, the nonlinear constraint, $y = H \odot x$, can be replaced by a linear constraint, $y = HX$ by rounding the real number valued solution to a binary vector. Alternatively, the constraint can be further replaced by the binary compressive sensing constraint, $y = H \oplus x$. The original problem is finalized as

$$\hat{x} = \operatorname*{argmin}_{x} \|x\|_1 \ s.t. \ y = [H2I][x; z] \tag{5}$$

where I is the identity matrix and $z > 0$ is an auxiliary vector.

The selection of two solutions is determined by the number of targets and the code matrix.

3 Graphical Model Based Space Decoding and Multi-target Tracking

3.1 Graphical Model

Multiple target tracking is a challenging issue due to the involvement of a bunch of unknown variables and complex conditions. With different characteristics of these variables in multi-target tracking systems, the system models under various conditions can be summarized to:

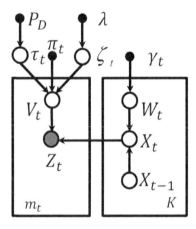

Fig. 4. Multi-target tracking model with unknown number of false alarms.

Case 1 - known data-to-target association
Case 2 - unknown data-to-target association
Case 3 - unknown tracker-to-tracker association
Case 4 - unknown detection failures
Case 5 - unknown false alarms
Case 6 - varying number of targets.

Let $X_t = (x_t^1, x_t^2, \cdots, x_t^k)$ denote the states of k trackers, X_{t-1}^k is the previous state of the k_{th} tracker. $Z_t = (z_t^1, z_t^2, \cdots, z_t^m)$ denotes m observations at time t, which are related and dependent upon X_t. The hidden variables are given as follows:

V_t data-to-tracker association matrix
W_t tracker-to-tracker association matrix
κ_t number of targets
τ_t number of detectable targets
ζ_t number of false alarms.

The first case is the simplex tracking model, in which correct data-to-tracker association can be achieved. Specifically, the k_{th} tracker X_t^k is associated with measurement Z_t^k correctly, and the current states of trackers can be associated with previous states of the same trackers correctly. As for such cases, the multiple targets can be tracked with a high accuracy. While for other cases, if the data-to-tracker association, tracker-to-tracker association, or detection failure is unknown, then the tracking model becomes more complicated and correspondingly the tracking error will be larger. In this work, we establish a more complicated tracking model to investigate the case that the false alarms are unknown.

The system model is shown in Fig. 4. For the cases of unknown false alarms, the number of false alarms is denoted as ζ_t, which is a Poisson random variable with an average value of λ. The location of false alarms yields a uniform distribution with a density value of $\frac{1}{O}$, where O is the volume of the observation space. All the false alarms belong to a clutter tracker X^0; hence, the dimension of the association matrix V becomes $m_t \times (K+1)$. Assuming the measurements are reordered such that

$$z_j| \in [m_t - \zeta(V_t) + 1, m_t] \tag{6}$$

where z_j is a false alarm, then the clutter tracker model is given by

$$p(Z_t|X_t^0, V_t) = \prod_{j=m_t-\zeta(V_t)+1}^{m_t} (\frac{1}{O})^{V_{j0}} \tag{7}$$

Given that $p(\zeta|\lambda)\frac{\lambda^\zeta e^{-\lambda}}{\zeta!}$, $p(\zeta_t)$ could be represented by

$$p(\zeta_t) = \prod_{m=1}^{m_t} [p(\zeta_t|\lambda)]^{\delta(\zeta_t - m)} \tag{8}$$

then

$$p(V_t|\tau_t, \zeta_t) = \prod_{j=1}^{m_t-\zeta_t} \prod_{k=1}^{K} (\pi_t^k)^{V_t^{jk}} \tag{9}$$

and

$$p(Z_t|X_t, V_t) = \prod_{j=1}^{m_t-\zeta(V_t)} \prod_{k=1}^{K} p(z_t^j|x_t^k)^{V_t^{jk}} p(Z_t|X_t^0, V_t) \tag{10}$$

where $K - \tau_t$ columns of the association matrix, V, are all-zero vectors.

The joint probability density function of X, Z, V, W, τ, ζ is given by

$$p(X_{1:t}, Z_{1:t}, V_{1:t}, W_{1:t}, \tau_{1:t}, \zeta_{1:t}) \equiv p_{1:t}^{X,Z,V,W,\tau,\zeta}$$
$$= p_{1:t-1}^{X,Z,V,W,\tau,\zeta} p(Z_t|X_t, V_t) p(X_t|X_{t-1}, W_t) p(W_t)$$
$$p(V_t||\tau_t, \zeta_t) p(\tau_t) p(\zeta_t) \tag{11}$$

3.2   Multiple Target Tracking

The challenge of multi-target tracking is that some hidden variables exist in the sequential estimation and prediction process such as the number of detected targets, the number of trackers, the number of false alarms, and data-to-target association. Let $\mathcal{H}$ represent all the hidden variables, then the general solution can be obtained by using Expectation-Maximization (EM) optimization.

1. **E-step:** estimate the distribution of hidden variables from the predicted target state, $\hat{x}_t$, and measurements, z, by conditioning the joint distribution, $p(\mathcal{H}, x, z)$, which is represented by

$$p(\mathcal{H}|\hat{x}, z) = \frac{p(\mathcal{H}), \hat{x}, z}{\Sigma_{\mathcal{H}} p(z|\hat{x}, \mathcal{H}) p(\hat{x}|z, \mathcal{H}) p(\mathcal{H})} \tag{12}$$

2. **M-step:** estimate the distribution of the target state, x, from measurements, z, by marginalizing hidden variables, $\mathcal{H}$, that is

$$p(x|z) = \sum_{\mathcal{H}} p(x|z, \mathcal{H}) p(\mathcal{H}|\hat{x}, z) \tag{13}$$

4   Performance Analysis

To test the proposed system, the observation area is segmented into 64 blocks. The detection probability is $P_d = 0.825$. In order to achieve the best compression rate, a binary encoding scheme is developed. However, this encoding scheme can only guarantee each block code is unique. If a target triggers two blocks simultaneously, then the obtained code will be the combination of the two codes that represented these two blocks. Thereby the result will be a repetition of a single code. Obviously, the encoding scheme itself brings in false alarms. Technically, it is easy to remove the false alarms introduced by the scheme itself. Although

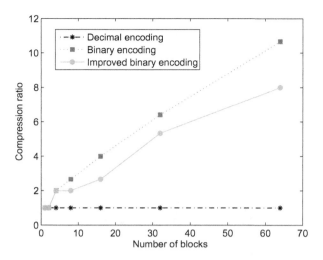

Fig. 5. Measurement compression ratio of various space encoding schemes.

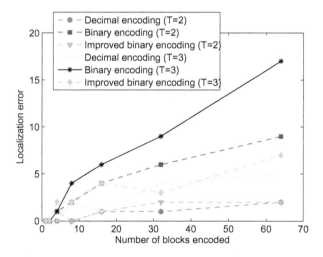

Fig. 6. Compressive localization for two-target and three-target cases.

the price is to increase the number of sensors, the number of sensors added is very small. Compared with decimal encoding, the number of sensors is still much smaller. Therefore, we can still guarantee a high compression rate. As shown in Fig. 5, for a 64-block area, the compression ratio of improved binary encoding is 8, which is close to the compression ratio of binary encoding 10.67 (ideal rate). The compression ratio of decimal encoding is 1, since there is no any compression in this encoding scheme.

Figure 6 shows the localization errors using various space encoding schemes for two targets case and three targets case, respectively. Although binary

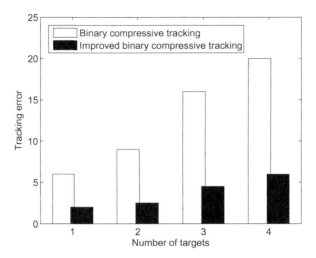

Fig. 7. Multi-target tracking performance.

encoding scheme can achieve the best compression rate, it has highest localization errors due to the ambiguities generated by the repetition of code patterns. In contrast, the improved binary encoding scheme has much lower errors. For the 64-block area, its localization error is just 2, which is much lower than that of binary encoding scheme at 9 for two targets case. When the number of targets increases to 3, the localization errors for all the encoding schemes become larger. It is reasonable since the data-target association becomes more difficult and complicated.

With multiplex sensing and space encoding, it is able to implement effective compressive multi-target tracking. Figure 7 shows the tracking performance of multiple targets via binary compressive tracking. It can be seen that (1) the binary compressive tracking errors are too large for real application, but the improved binary compressive tracking is acceptable with the average tracking errors at 4 and 6 for tracking three targets and four targets; (2) the increase of number of targets degrades the tracking performance of both schemes; (3) the improved binary compressive tracking scheme is more stable and scalable, with the growing of number of targets, its tracking error increases slightly and remains acceptable.

5   Conclusion

This work presents a new modality for wireless sensor based multi-target tracking tasks. The main feature of such a system is compressive tracking, which is easily achieved by using fiber-optic sensors. More specifically, compressive measurement is achieved by using multiplex sensing and space encoding technologies. Compressive tracking is implemented based on compressive localization and graphical model enabled tracking. The presented system is able to deal with complex tracking tasks in terms of false alarms, unknown data-target associations. The results demonstrate a good performance in tracking a small number of humans. The future work will be focusing on sampling geometry optimization and varying targets investigation.

References

1. Benezeth, Y., Emile, B., Laurent, H., et al.: Vision-based system for human detection and tracking in indoor environment. Int. J. Soc. Robot. **2**(1), 41–52 (2010)
2. Anderson, R., Krolik, J.: Track association for over-the-horizon radar with a statistical ionospheric model. IEEE Trans. Signal Process. **50**(11), 2632–2643 (2002)
3. Orton, M., Fitzgerald, W.: A Bayesian approach to tracking multiple targets using sensor arrays and particle filters. IEEE Trans. Signal Process. **50**(2), 216–223 (2002)
4. Gu, D.: A game theory approach to target tracking in sensor networks. IEEE Trans. Syst. Man Cybern. Part B: Cybern. **41**(1), 2–13 (2011)
5. Hao, Q., Hu, F., Xiao, Y.: Multiple human tracking and identification with wireless distributed pyroelectric sensor systems. IEEE Syst. J. **3**(4), 428–439 (2009)
6. Amini, A., Marvasti, F.: Deterministic construction of binary, bipolar, and ternary compressed sensing matrices. IEEE Trans. Inf. Theory **57**(4), 2360–2370 (2011)
7. Li, S., Gao, F., Ge, G., Zhang, S.: Deterministic construction of compressed sensing matrices via algebraic curves. IEEE Trans. Inf. Theory **58**(8), 5035–5041 (2012)
8. Liu, X.-J., Xia, S.-T.: Reconstruction guarantee analysis of binary measurement matrices based on girth. In: Proceedings of IEEE International Symposium on Information Theory, Istanbul, pp. 474–478 (2013)

Moving Object Detection Algorithm Using Gaussian Mixture Model and SIFT Keypoint Match

Hang Dong[(✉)] and Xin Zhang

College of Electronics and Information Engineering,
Tongji University, Shanghai 201804, China
{dh,mic_zhangxin}@tongji.edu.cn

Abstract. In the field of image processing, Gaussian mixture model (GMM) is always used to detect and recognize moving objects. Due to the defects of GMM, there are some error detections in the final consequence. In order to eliminate the defects of GMM in moving objects detections, this paper has studied a moving object detection algorithm, combining GMM with scale-invariant feature transform (SIFT) keypoint match. First, GMM is built to obtain the distributions of background image pixels. Then, morphological processing method is applied to improve the quality of binary segmentation image and extract segmentation images of moving objects. Finally, SIFT keypoint match algorithm is used to eliminate misjudgment segmentation images by judging whether the segmentation image matches with the background template or not. Compared with original GMM, the results show that the accuracy of moving object detection has been improved.

Keywords: Moving object detection · GMM · SIFT keypoint match

1 Introduction

In the field of visual analysis, moving object detection is an important and popular research topic, which consists of classification of moving objects, tracking of moving objects and understanding of moving objects. There are some classical methods for dealing with problems of moving object detection, such as the optical flow method, the inter-frame difference method and the background subtraction method [1, 2].

GMM is one of the background subtraction method. Through training a part of the video data frames, GMM can generate a background image. With input video data, the background image can also be dynamically updated. Then, the foreground image can be separated by comparing the trained background image with each original image [3, 4]. However, with the influence of illumination variation, shaking of cameras and so on, the final moving objects are mixed with the static objects which should be classified into the background image. Thus, in the process of generating a background image using trained video data frames, the accuracy of moving object detection is low.

SIFT keypoint match algorithm can extract the feature of some key points in each image. These features which are invariant to image scale and rotation, have strong

© ICST Institute for Computer Sciences, Social Informatics and Telecommunications Engineering 2018
X. Gu et al. (Eds.): MLICOM 2017, Part I, LNICST 226, pp. 22–29, 2018.
https://doi.org/10.1007/978-3-319-73564-1_3

adaptability to the change of illumination and the deformation of the image [5, 6]. Thus, these features can distinguish with each other and can be used as a basis to match two images.

This article combines GMM method with SIFT keypoint match algorithm to recognize the moving objects. First, the GMM method is used to extract moving objects in a traffic video roughly. Then, the morphological processing method which includes the opening operation and the closing operation is studied in each dynamic pixel in order to form the connected region of pixels of moving objects. Finally, the SIFT keypoint match algorithm is used to process the connected region and match them with the previous background template. The new combined method can reduce the error probability of recognizing moving objects and improve the performance of the whole system to extract moving objects in the traffic video. The improved GMM method combing with SIFT keypoint match can complete the extraction of moving vehicles in a complicated traffic video.

2 Conventional Method

In this part, the theories and functions of three conventional methods including GMM method, morphological processing method and SIFT keypoint match algorithm are briefly introduced as follows.

2.1 GMM Method

GMM is a combination of multiple Gaussian distributions [3, 4], which is used to describe the distributions of background pixel value in this paper. The sample is obtained by the Eq. (1):

$$\{X_1, X_2, \cdots, X_t\} = \{I(x_0, y_0, i); 1 \le i \le t\}. \tag{1}$$

In Eq. (1), X_t is the pixel value of the t frame, $(x_0, y_0,)$ is the position of pixel. X_t obeys the mixed distribution whose probability density function is shown in Eq. (2).

$$P(X_t) = \sum_{i=1}^{K} \omega_{i,t} \times \eta(X_i, \mu_{i,t}, \Sigma_{i,t}). \tag{2}$$

In Eq. (2), K is the number of distribution in the GMM, which depends on the complexity of the background. In this paper, we consider the change of background of video frame as the result of superposition of multiple Gaussian distributions. The value of K are set as 3 in our model, $\omega_{i,t}$, $\mu_{i,t}$, $\Sigma_{i,t}$ are the weight, the mean and the covariance matrix of the i distribution in t moment respectively. $\eta(X_i, \mu_{i,t}, \Sigma_{i,t})$ is a corresponding probability density function, which is shown in the Eq. (3).

$$\eta(X_i, \mu, \Sigma) = \frac{1}{(2\pi)^{n/2}|\Sigma|^{1/2}} e^{-1/2(X_t-\mu)^T\Sigma^{-1}(X_t-\mu)}. \tag{3}$$

In Eq. (3), n is the dimension of X_t, and Σ is the covariance matrix of each dimension of X_t. The probability density function of the mixed distribution is shown in the Fig. 1.

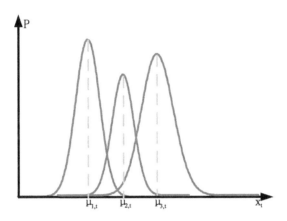

Fig. 1. The probability density function of the mixed distribution.

According to [3, 4], each distribution parameter will be updated as shown in Eq. (4) after the initialization of the GMM.

$$\begin{cases} \hat{\omega}_{i,t} = (1 - \alpha)\omega_{i,t} + \alpha P(k|X_i, \mu_{i,t}, \sigma_{i,t}) \\ \hat{\mu}_{i,t} = (1 - \rho)\mu_{i,t} + \rho X_i \\ \hat{\sigma}^2_{i,t} = (1 - \rho)\sigma^2_{i,t} + \rho(X_i - \mu_{i,t})^T(X_i - \mu_{i,t}) \end{cases} \tag{4}$$

In Eq. (4), in the t moment, $\hat{\omega}_{i,t}$ is the estimated value of $\omega_{i,t}$, $\hat{\mu}_{i,t}$ is the estimated value of $\mu_{i,t}$, and $\hat{\sigma}^2_{i,t}$ is the estimated value of $\sigma^2_{i,t}$. Those estimated values are regarded as the value of $\omega_{i,t}$, $\mu_{i,t}$, $\hat{\sigma}^2_{i,t}$ in the $t+1$ moment. α is the rate of learning, which determines the updating speed. $\rho = \alpha/\omega_{i,t}$ is the learning rate of parameter. The judgment of matching X_t with the k distribution is shown in Eq. (5).

$$|X_t - \mu_{k,t}| < D\delta_{k,t}. \tag{5}$$

If the matching can be satisfied well, $P(k|X_i, \mu_{i,t}, \sigma_{i,t}) = 1$, or the value would be 0. The general value of D is 2.5. After Gaussian distribution is updated, the weight should be normalized according to $\sum_{i=1}^{K} \omega_{i,t} = 1$, and then the weight should be sorted by size of

ω/σ. Finally, first B Gaussian distributions can be selected to describe the background image in Eq. (6).

$$B = \arg\min_{b} \left(\sum_{i=1}^{b} \omega_{i,t} > T \right). \tag{6}$$

2.2   Morphological Processing Method

The morphological processing method contains the opening operation and the closing operation. They both consist of corrosion and expansion. The only difference between them is the order.

Corrosion is a process of eliminating boundary points and contracting the boundary inward. It can be used to eliminate small and meaningless pixel objects. On the other hand, expansion is the process of merging all the background points. It can be used to fill holes in objects.

Opening operation is a process of expansion after corrosion. It can eliminate small objects, separate the objects in the fine points and smooth the boundary of the large object. Meanwhile, it doesn't significantly change the area. Closing operation is a process of corrosion after expansion. It can fill the body with tiny holes, connect nearby objects and smooth its boundaries. It doesn't significantly change the area either.

2.3   SIFT Keypoint Match Algorithm

The SIFT key point match algorithm was proposed by Lowe in 1999 and perfected in 2004 [5, 6]. The SIFT feature is based on the interest points of some local appearance on the object and has nothing to do with the size and rotation of the image. The SIFT feature also has a high tolerance of light, noise, and micro vision changes.

The algorithm consists of following six steps. (1) Generate Gaussian difference pyramid and construct scale space. (2) Detect the spatial extreme points. (3) Locate the key points precisely. (4) Allocate the direction information of stable key points. (5) Describe the key points. (6) Match the key points. The flowchart of SIFT keypoint match algorithm is shown in Fig. 2.

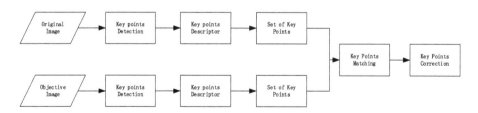

Fig. 2. The flowchart of SIFT keypoint match algorithm.

3   Method Combined GMM with SIFT Keypoint Match

The GMM is used to model the video image, which can generate the background image. The foreground image can be generated by subtracting from the original image. However, there are still misjudgments in obtaining the foreground influenced by illumination variation, partial occlusions and shaking of camera. The pixels judged to be the foreground is under the morphological processing, which means that the connected region is obtained by opening operation and closing operation. As a result, these pixels become a whole object rather than the scattered pixels. The background image of the previous GMM is regarded as a static graphic template.

Then the connected domain is surrounded by the minimum area of the rectangle, which represents the moving object. However, there are some background images in it, and the SIFT keypoint match algorithm is used to find out the right foreground by matching the background template. Through extracting rectangular image I_1, we can obtain its location, length and width. These information can be used to locate the rectangle in background template which is called I_2. The number of SIFT key points in rectangular image I_1 is N_1 and the number of SIFT key points in rectangular image I_2 is N_2. The number of matching points in rectangular image I_1 and rectangular image I_2 is M. If the relationship between N_1 and M satisfies that as shown in Eq. (7),

$$P = \frac{M}{N_1} > R, \; R = 0.7 \,. \tag{7}$$

then, the rectangular image I_1 and the rectangular image I_2 will be considered as matching successfully, which means that the rectangular image I_1 is a static image rather than a moving object. Thus, the rectangular image I_1 should be removed from the foreground. The flowchart of the method is shown in Fig. 3.

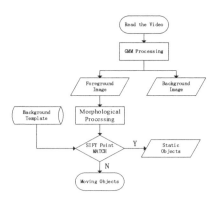

Fig. 3. The flowchart of the method.

4   Results and Analysis

The improved algorithm is compiled by using the image processing toolkit from MATLAB software. We select two videos as the testing videos [8]. Comparing with the original GMM algorithm, the experimental results show that the moving object detection accuracy rate has a great improvement when applying the improved GMM algorithm combined SIFT keypoint matching algorithm. For the video of crossroads, the compared results are as follows (Figs. 4, 5, 6 and 7).

Fig. 4. The result of the detection of original GMM algorithm in video 1.

Fig. 5. The result of the binarization of foreground and background in video 1.

Fig. 6. The result of the improved algorithm in video 1.

In the case of time complexity, the proposed algorithm takes more time to deal with the video per frame than the original GMM algorithm. However, it can satisfy the need of video analysis better. Figure 8 shows the detection results of moving objects using

Fig. 7. The result of the binarization of foreground and background in video 1.

Fig. 8. The result of the improved algorithm in video 2.

the improved GMM algorithm combined with SIFT keypoint match algorithm. In the video of roads, the number of video frame is 5258 and the total number of moving objects is 85. Using the traditional algorithm, the number of wrong detection moving objects is 21 and the correct rate of detection moving objects is 72%. While using the improved algorithm, the correct number of detection moving objects is 74 and the correct detection rate of moving objects is 87%. Thus, one can find the improved algorithm has a better performance than the traditional algorithm.

5   Conclusion

In this paper, a moving object detection algorithm combined GMM algorithm with SIFT keypoint match algorithm is studied. First, the basic GMM was used to obtain the moving pixels in each video frame. The morphological processing was applied to group the rectangular image from moving pixels. Second, the SIFT keypoint match algorithm was used to obtain moving objects by distinguishing the foreground and background. Finally, the algorithm was evaluated on two different videos. It is shown that the performance of the moving objects detection algorithm is better than the traditional algorithm. Our future work will focus on how to reduce the computational complexity.

References

1. Pietikäinen, M., Hadid, A., Zhao, G., et al.: Background subtraction. Surf. Sci. **461**(1–3), 1–15 (2011)
2. Piccardi, M.: Background subtraction techniques: a review. In: IEEE International Conference on Systems, Man and Cybernetics, vol. 4, pp. 3099–3104. IEEE (2005)
3. Stauffer, C., Grimson, W.E.L.: Adaptive background mixture models for real-time tracking. In: IEEE Computer Society Conference on Computer Vision and Pattern Detection, vol. 2, pp. 246–252. IEEE Xplore (1999)
4. KaewTraKulPong, P., Bowden, R.: An improved adaptive background mixture model for real-time tracking with shadow detection. In: Remagnino, P., Jones, G.A., Paragios, N., Regazzoni, C.S. (eds.) Video-Based Surveillance Systems, pp. 135–144. Springer, Boston (2002). https://doi.org/10.1007/978-1-4615-0913-4_11
5. Lowe, D.G.: Distinctive Image Features from Scale-Invariant Keypoints. Kluwer Academic Publishers, Dordrecht (2004)
6. Lowe, D.G.: Object detection from local scale-invariant features. In: The Proceedings of the 7th IEEE International Conference on Computer Vision. IEEE (2002)
7. Zivkovic, Z.: Improved adaptive Gaussian mixture model for background subtraction. In: Proceedings of the 17th International Conference on Pattern Detection, ICPR 2004, vol. 2. IEEE (2004)
8. Wang, X., Ma, X., Grimson, W.E.: Unsupervised activity perception in crowded and complicated scenes using hierarchical Bayesian models. IEEE Trans. Pattern Anal. Mach. Intell. **31**(3), 539–555 (2009)

Low-Complexity Signal Detection Scheme Based on LLR for Uplink Massive MIMO Channel

Xifeng Chen, Liming Zheng, and Gang Wang$^{(\boxtimes)}$

Communication Research Center, Harbin Institute of Technology,
Harbin 150001, China
chenxf_hit@163.com, {zheng,gwang51}@hit.edu.cn

Abstract. This paper proposes low-complexity detection algorithms for Massive MIMO system: Multiple Dominant Eigenvector Detection Algorithm (MDEDA) and Antenna Selection Scheme (ASS). Both the schemes calculate the log likelihood ratios (LLRs). Based on the Single Dominant Eigenvector Detection (SDEDA), MDEDA searches transmitted signal candidates in multiple dominant eigenvector directions. For one thing, combined multiple eigenvectors, MDEDA attains better BER performance, for another, it greatly reduces the number of transmitted signal candidates. The ASS contains Single Antenna Selection Scheme (SASS) and Multiple Antenna Selection Scheme (MASS), focus on channel error modeling, the ASS assumes the signal of some antennas corresponding to the constellation points in order to minimize the channel error. SASS searches all transmit antennas, nevertheless, MASS chooses multiple antennas based on the eigenvalue. Finally, SASS gains better BER performance but more complexity. Finally, SASS provides an excellent trade-off between performance and complexity.

Keywords: Massive MIMO · Signal detection · Dominant eigenvector search
Antenna selection · LLR

1 Introduction

Massive MIMO is one of the promising technologies for next-generation wireless communication system with a large number of antennas at the base-station (BS) serving a large number of users concurrently and within the same frequency band [1–3]. The price to pay are the increased complexity of signal processing with the increase of the number of antennas. The optimal signal detection for the system is the maximum likelihood detection (MLD) [4] which can achieve the minimum bit error rate (BER). However, MLD requires a prohibitively large amount of computational complexity that exponentially increases with both the number of data streams and that of constellations.

Linear detection can decrease the complexity greatly, especially when the number of BS antennas is much larger than the number of the uplink users (i.e., the low system loading factors), linear detectors like the minimum mean square error (MMSE) detector are appropriate in terms of both complexity and performance [5]. Unfortunately, for the massive MIMO system whose number of BS antennas and number of the uplink user are approximate, a single linear detection may result in more loss of performance. The system is exactly our object of study. Hence, the balance of complexity and performance of detection schemes in massive MIMO system have attracted lots of attention.

To reduce such complexity, an iterative receiver based on the turbo principle has been proposed [6]. The iterative receiver can improve reliability of signal detection by exchanging log likelihood ratio (LLR) of coded bits between soft demodulator and soft channel decoder parts. The method in [7] first employs a low complexity in order to find the transmitted signal candidate that maximizes the log likelihood function, that is the maximum likelihood sequence (MLS). Then, the method applies another low complexity algorithm in order to find the transmitted signal candidate that maximize the log likelihood function under a constraint that a coded bit be inverse to that of the estimated MLS, which is referred to as inverse-bit MLS (IB-MLS). Thus, this conventional method needs to apply the low-complexity algorithm for all the coded bits so as to find IB-MLS, which requires high complexity. A one-dimensional algorithm, named plural projection method (PM) was proposed in [8], which can simultaneously find MLS and IB-MLS in the direction of significance eigenvector with MMSE detection as stating point. However, one-dimension search algorithm suffers a severe degradation in BER performance over spatially correlated MIMO channels, because multiple dominant directions of eigenvector are likely to appear [9].

This paper proposes a low-complexity algorithm that can find MLS and IB-MLS in multi-dimensional direction of eigenvector. Based on channel error modeling, this paper also proposes a stream search scheme. Computer simulations demonstrate that the proposed scheme can maintain excellent receiver performance while reducing the complexity drastically.

2 System Model

Consider an uplink massive MIMO system with N_T transmit antennas and N_R receive antennas. Then the associate massive MIMO transmission can be model as

$$y = Hs + n \qquad (1)$$

where H is a $N_R \times N_T$ complex channel matrix and is assumed to be flat Rayleigh fading channel and known perfectly at the receiver. At the transmitter side, the information bit s is generated in the source and is first encoded by a convolutional encoder and then mapped to symbols of different constellation points. The mapped complex symbols are divided into N_T separate independent parallel streams with a transmitted signal vector $s = [s_1, s_2, \cdots s_{N_T}]^T \in \vartheta^{N_T}$, where ϑ stands for the complex constellation and $|\vartheta| = 2^Q = M$ with M stands for the modulation order, (e.g., for QPSK, $M = 4$), as a result, each transmit vector s is associated with $N_T \times Q$ binary values $x_{i,b} \in \{0, 1\}$, $i = 1, \cdots N_T$, $b = 1, \cdots Q$, corresponding to the bth bit of symbols of s_i, y is a $N_R \times 1$ received signal vector $y = [y_1, \cdots y_{N_R}]^T$, and n is a $N_R \times 1$ vector of independent zero-mean complex Gaussian distributed noise vector with variance $\sigma^2 = N_0$ per complex entry (Fig. 1).

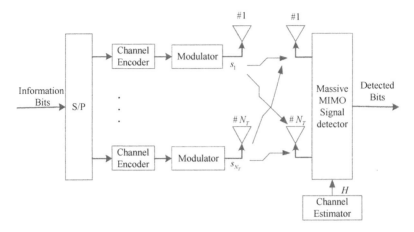

Fig. 1. Massive MIMO system

3 Search in Direction of Dominant Eigenvector Based on MMSE

3.1 Analysis of MMSE Detection

The MMSE detection multiplies y by the weigh matrix and the resultant $\hat{x}$ is given by

$$\hat{x} = PH^H y, \tag{2}$$

$$P = \left(H^H H + \sigma^2 I_{N_T}\right)^{-1}, \tag{3}$$

where P is the inverse matrix to be considered and I_{N_T} is the N_T-by-N_T identity matrix. The derivation assumed that $\langle ss^H \rangle = I_{N_T}$, and the detected signal is equal to a hard decision of $\hat{x}$.

According to (2) and (3), we have

$$\left\langle (s - \hat{x})(s - \hat{x})^H \right\rangle = \sigma^2 P, \tag{4}$$

then, the difference between s and $\hat{x}$ can be expressed as

$$s - \hat{x} = P^{1/2} \tilde{n}, \tag{5}$$

where $\tilde{n}$ is a N_T-by-1 zero-mean complex Gaussian distributed noise vector of with variance $\sigma^2 = N_0$.

Next, since $H^H H$ is an Hermite matrix and is assumed to be positive definite, the eigenvalue deposition of P^{-1} yields

$$P = \left(H^H H + \sigma^2 I_{N_T}\right)^{-1} = VDV^H, \tag{6}$$

where V is an N_T-by-N_T unitary matrix and is given by

$$V = [v_1, v_2, \cdots v_{N_T}], \tag{7}$$

$v_k, k \in [1, N_T]$ is the k-th N_T-by-1 normalized eigenvector. D is an N_T-by-N_T diagonal matrix and is given by

$$D = \mathrm{diag}[\lambda_1, \lambda_2, \cdots \lambda_{N_T}], \tag{8}$$

where $\lambda_k(>0)$ is the eigenvalue of the k-th eigenvector v_k. Without loss of generality, $\lambda_1 \leq \lambda_2 \leq \cdots \leq \lambda_{N_T}$ is assumed.

According to (7) and (8),

$$P^{1/2} = VD^{1/2}V^H, \tag{9}$$

$$P^{1/2}\tilde{n} = \sum_{k=1}^{N_T} \sqrt{\lambda_k} v_k^H n v_k . \tag{10}$$

Finally, (5) and (10) imply that the decision errors by the MMSE detection are likely to occur in the direction of v_{k_0} when λ_{k_0} is very large. The direction coincide with eigenvector of P having dominant eigenvalues.

3.2 Conventional Single Dominant Eigenvector Detection Algorithm (SDEDA)

With $\hat{x}$ as a starting point, the one-dimensional search, performs one-dimensional search in the direction of v_p to find MLS and IB-MLS. Suppose that a hard decision of $x_{k,m,p}(1 \leq k \leq N_T, 1 \leq m \leq M, 1 \leq p \leq N_P)$, where N_P is the number of dominant eigenvalue and $1 \leq N_P \leq N_T$.

$$x_{k,m,p} = \hat{x} + \mu(k, m)v_p, \tag{11}$$

$\mu(k, m)$ is a complex number which determines the distance between $x_{k,m,p}$ and $\hat{x}$. $\mu(k, m)$ is obtained so that the k-th element of the hard decision of $x_{k,m,p}$ can be equal to one of constellations $a(m)(1 \leq m \leq M)$, and is given by

$$\mu(k, m) = \rho \frac{\eta_{k,m}}{(v_p)_k}, \tag{12}$$

$$\eta_{k,m} = a(m) - (\hat{x})_k \tag{13}$$

In the case of rectangular QAM, ρ is set as

$$
\rho = \begin{cases} 1.0 & \text{for } a(m) = \text{Dec}[(\hat{x})_k] \\ 1 + \frac{\xi d_{\min}}{2|\text{Re}(\eta_{k,m})|} & \begin{aligned} & \text{for } a(m) \neq \text{Dec}[(\hat{x})_k] \\ & |\text{Re}(\eta_{k,m})| > |\text{Im}(\eta_{k,m})| \end{aligned} \\ 1 + \frac{\xi d_{\min}}{2|\text{Im}(\eta_{k,m})|} & \begin{aligned} & \text{for } a(m) \neq \text{Dec}[(\hat{x})_k] \\ & |\text{Re}(\eta_{k,m})| \leq |\text{Im}(\eta_{k,m})| \end{aligned} \end{cases} \tag{14}
$$

where Dec[ ] denotes the hard decision operation and ξ is a real number to satisfy $|\xi| \leq 1$. $d_{\min}$ is the minimum distance between the constellations; $d_{\min} = \sqrt{2}$ for QPSK modulation.

MLS and IB-MLS are selected from $\text{Dec}[x_{k,m,p}]$ plus $\text{Dec}[\hat{x}]$ on the basis of the matric. Since the number of $x_{k,m,p}$ is less than or equal to $N_T M N_P$, the number of the hard decisions called transmitted signal candidates is at most $N_T M N_P + 1$.

3.3 Proposed Multiple Dominant Eigenvector Detection Algorithm (MDEDA)

Transmitted signal may get performance degradation in several directions. So compared with the one-dimensional search scheme above, the multi-dimension search scheme searches transmitted signal in multiply dominant directions of eigenvector. The detail is as following.

Compared with (11), transmitted signal candidates are given by

$$
x_{k,m} = \hat{x} + \sum_{p=1}^{N_P} \mu_p(k,m)v_p , \tag{15}
$$

where $\mu_p(k,m)$ is step size at the p-th dominant direction of eigenvector.

Let us assume that the k-th element of the candidate is equal to $a(m)$, where $m(1 \leq m \leq M)$ is an integer and $a(m)$ is one of the constellation point. So we have

$$
\sum_{p=1}^{N_P} \mu_p(k,m)(v_p)_k = a(m) - (\hat{x})_k, \tag{16}
$$

where $(\cdot)_k$ denotes the k-th element of a vector. The equation can be rewritten in a vector format as

$$
a(m) - (\hat{x})_k = \tilde{v}_k^H \mu, \tag{17}
$$

$$
\tilde{v}_k^H = [(v_1)_k, (v_2)_k, \cdots (v_{N_P})_k], \tag{18}
$$

$$\mu^H = \left[\mu_1(k,m), \mu_2(k,m), \cdots \mu_{N_P}(k,m) \right], \tag{19}$$

where $\tilde{v}_k^H$ and μ are N_P-by-1 vectors.

Log likelihood function can be transformed into

$$L(s) = \left\| (y - H\hat{x}) - H(s - \hat{x}) \right\|^2$$
$$= L(\hat{x}) + \sigma^2 \left(\|\hat{x}\|^2 - \|s\|^2 \right) + (s - \hat{x})^H P^{-1}(s - \hat{x}). \tag{20}$$

When SNR is high, the second term can be neglected. Substituting (6) and (8) into (20) result in

$$L(x_{k,m}) \approx L(\hat{x}) + \sum_{p=1}^{N_p} \left(\lambda_p \right)^{-1} \left| v_p^H(s - \hat{x}) \right|^2. \tag{21}$$

The equation can be rewritten in a vector format as

$$L(x_{k,m}) \approx L(\hat{x}) + \left\| \tilde{D}^{-1/2} \mu \right\|^2, \tag{22}$$

$$\tilde{D}^{-1} = \mathrm{diag}[\lambda_1, \lambda_2, \cdots \lambda_{N_P}]. \tag{23}$$

The proposed algorithm performs the maximum likelihood estimation of μ for obtaining candidate of s. The minimization of $L(x_{k,m})$ under the constraint of (16) can be solved by the method of Lagrange multiplier. Thus, the estimation becomes equivalent to finding μ that minimizes the following cost function $f(\mu)$:

$$f(\mu) = \mu^H \tilde{D}^{-1} \mu + \omega \left[a(m) - \hat{x}_k - \tilde{v}_k^H \mu \right] + \omega^* \left[a^*(m) - \hat{x}_k^* - \mu^H \tilde{v}_k \right], \tag{24}$$

where ω is the complex Lagrange multiplier. By calculation, the desired step size μ is obtained as

$$\mu = \left[a(m) - (\hat{x})_k \right] \tilde{D} \left(\tilde{v}_k^H \tilde{D} \tilde{v}_k \right)^{-1} \tilde{v}_k. \tag{25}$$

MLS and IB-MLS are selected from the set C, whose element is $\mathrm{Dec}[x_{k,m}]$ plus $\mathrm{Dec}[\hat{x}]$ on the basis of the matric. Since the number of $x_{k,m}$ is less than or equal to $N_T M$, the number of the hard decisions called transmitted signal candidates is at most $N_T M + 1$. Finally, calculate the LLR [9] of these candidates.

4   Antenna Selection Scheme (ASA) Based on Decision Errors Modeling

According to (4), we may as well assume $d = s - \hat{x}$ and e follows complex Gaussian distribution, thus we have

$$\langle dd^H \rangle = \sigma^2 P, \tag{26}$$

$$p[d] = \frac{1}{(\pi\sigma^2)^{N_T} \det P} \exp\left(\frac{d^H P^{-1} d}{\sigma^2}\right), \tag{27}$$

Next, we propose the single antenna selection scheme (SASS), which chooses the k-th $(1 \leq k \leq N_T)$ antenna, assume that s_k is equal to a modulation constellation point $b(m)$ $(1 \leq m \leq M)$, the decision error of the k-th antenna is

$$d_k = b(m) - \hat{x}_k = d(m, k). \tag{28}$$

Under the constraint of (28), apply the Lagrange multipliers in terms of decision error e:

$$L[d] = d^H P^{-1} d + \alpha\left(R_k^H d - d(m, k)\right) + \alpha^*\left(d^H R_k - d^*(m, k)\right), \tag{29}$$

where α is a complex Lagrange multiplier, and R_k is an N_T-by-1 unit vector of which the k-th element is 1 and the others are 0.

Finally,

$$\alpha^* = -\left(R_k^H P R_k\right)^{-1} d(m, k), \tag{30}$$

$$\hat{d} = \left(R_k^H P R_k\right)^{-1} d(m, k) P R_k = \frac{P_k}{P_{kk}} d(m, k), \tag{31}$$

where P_k and P_{kk} are the k-th column vector and the (k, k)-th. Let $\hat{s}(m, k)$ denotes detected signal s. So $\hat{s}(m, k)$ can be given by

$$\hat{s}(m, k) = \hat{x} + \frac{P_k}{P_{kk}}[b(m) - \hat{x}_k], \tag{32}$$

When $\hat{s}(m, k)$ are obtained with all combinations of m and k, the number of candidate is $1 + N_T M$, then the final detected signal $\hat{s}$ is selected as the one according to log likelihood ratio.

In the scheme above, we choose just one antenna, to obtain more performance gain, we extend the number of antenna to plural l, which has $C_{N_T}^l$ antenna selection in total. There is no doubt that the number of candidate vectors is increased greatly, which results in high computation complexity. So select just one set of antenna based on some principle is essential, which is named as Multiple Antenna Selection Scheme (MASS).

The antennas of which transmission performance is degraded owing to the MMSE should be selected. Combined with Multi-Dimensional Search scheme above, we can choose l antennas of which eigenvalue is relatively small. Then the number of candidate transmitted vector is $1 + M^l$, which increases exponentially with the number of antennas we choose. So if we choose too many antennas, there's no doubt that the complexity is unacceptable.

5   Simulation Results and Analysis

Computer simulations were conducted to verify performance of the proposed algorithms. The simulation conditions are listed in Table 1, in the following, we simulated six kinds of detection schemes, including SASS, MDEDA, SDEDA, MASS, MMSE-OSIC, MMSE-PIC.

Table 1. Simulation conditions

Number of transmit antennas N_T	32
Number of transmit antennas N_R	32
Number of dominant eigenvector $N_P = l$	2
Modulation	QPSK
Channel coding	Convolution code
Decoding	LLR
Range of SNR	0–20 dB
Channel model	Rayleigh fading $\left(\sqrt{\frac{\pi}{2}}, 2 - \frac{\pi}{2}\right)$

Observing from Figs. 2 and 3, BER of SASS and MDEDA is superior to that of other schemes. Furthermore, SASS outperforms MASS, and MDEDA is better than SDEDA, corresponding to the theory above. MMSE-OSIC and MMSE-PIC have poor detection performance, and the former's complexity increases with transmitted

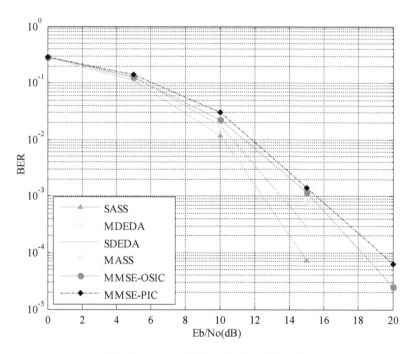

Fig. 2. Average BER with $N_T = N_R = 32$

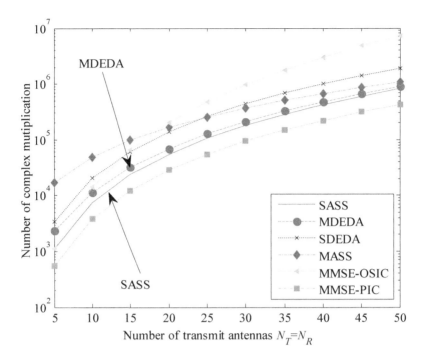

Fig. 3. Computational complexity with $N_T = N_R = 32$

antennas rapidly, however, MMSE-PIC has the least complexity to adapt to system of which detection performance requirements are not high. Fortunately, SASS and MDEDA get a superior trade-off between performance and complexity. In the condition of Fig. 2, MLD has complexity of 2.0×10^{22}, SASS reduce the complexity to about 10^{-18} of that of MLD. Compared with the other schemes, SASS achieves low-complexity detection algorithm and ensures the BER performance.

6   Conclusion

This paper has proposed low-complexity signal detection algorithms for Massive MIMO system, including MDEDA, SASS and MASS. MDEDA combined the effect of several eigenvector, thus attaining better BER performance and less complexity. Focusing on error modeling, SASS and MASS are proposed. SASS searched all transmit antennas, and MASS just choose several antennas. SASS got less complexity and superior BER performance, compared with MDEDA. In the system of Massive MIMO, SASS obtained a superior trade-off between performance and complexity.

References

1. Marzetta, T.L.: Noncooperative cellular wireless with unlimited numbers of base station antennas, 3590–3600 (2010). IEEE Press, New York
2. Vardhan, K., Mohammed, S.K., Chockalingam, A., et al.: A low-complexity detector for large MIMO systems and multicarrier CDMA systems. IEEE J. Sel. Areas Commun. **26**, 473–485 (2008)
3. Rusek, F., Persson, D., Lau, B.K., et al.: Scaling up MIMO: opportunities and challenges with very large arrays. J. IEEE Sig. Process. Mag. **30**, 40–60 (2012)
4. Yin, B., Wu, M., Wang, G., et al.: A 3.8 Gb/s large-scale MIMO detector for 3GPP LTE-Advanced. In: IEEE International Conference on Acoustics, Speech and Signal Processing, Florence, Italy, pp. 3879–3883 (2014)
5. Hoydis, J., Brink, S.T., Debbah, M.: Massive MIMO in the UL/DL of cellular networks: how many antennas do we need? IEEE J. Sel. Areas Commun. **31**, 160–171 (2013)
6. Dovillard, C., Jezequel, M., Berrov, C., Picart, A., Dider, P., Glavieux, A.: Iterative correction of intersymbol interference: turboequalization. Eur. Trans. Telecommun. Mag. **80**, 505–511 (1995)
7. Higashinaka, M., Motoyoshi, K., Nagayasu, T., et al.: Likelihood estimation for reduced-complexity ML detectors in a MIMO system. IEICE Trans. Commun. **91**, 837–847 (2008)
8. Zheng, L., Woo, J., Fukawa, K., et al.: Low-complexity algorithm for log likelihood ratios in coded MIMO-OFDM communications. IEEE Trans. Commun. **94**, 1–5 (2009)
9. Zheng, L., Fukawa, K., Suzuki, H., et al.: Low-complexity signal detection by multi-dimensional search for correlated MIMO channels. In: IEEE ICC, pp. 1–5 (2011)

Accurate Scale-Variable Tracking

Xinyou Li, Wenjing Kang[(⊠)], and Gongliang Liu

School of Information and Electrical Engineering,
Harbin Institute of Technology, Weihai, China
13115416536@163.com, {kwjqq,liugl}@hit.edu.cn

Abstract. In recent years, several correlation tracking algorithms have been proposed exploiting hierarchical features from deep convolutional neural networks. However, most of these methods focus on utilizing the CNN features for target location and neglect the changes of target scale, which may import error to the model and lead to drifting. In this paper, we propose a novel scale-variable tracking algorithm based on hierarchical CNN features, which learns correlation filters to locate the target and constructs a target pyramid for scale estimation. To evaluate the tracking algorithm, extensive experiments are conducted on a benchmark with 100 video sequences, which demonstrate features exploited from different CNN layers are well fit to estimate the object scale. The evaluation results show that our tracker outperforms the state-of-the-art methods by a huge margin (+14.6% mean OS rate and +14.3% mean DP rate).

Keywords: Correlation tracking · Scale estimation · CNN features

1 Introduction

Object tracking is a fundamental problem in computer vision with several applications such as video surveillance, medical diagnosis and human-computer interactions. However, the interference factors like illumination, occlusion, scale variations and abrupt motion make visual tracking still a challenging problem.

Many exiting tracking algorithms utilize hand-crafted features as target descriptors [1, 2], but recent years deep Convolutional Neural Networks (CNNs) features have demonstrated great success on object presentation. Thus recent algorithms utilize CNNs features to train correlation filters to predict target position [3, 4]. However, these algorithms do not take object scale variation into account and the error would stimulate when the target undergoes scale changes, which would eventually lead to drifting or tracking failure. This issue is the well-known stability-plasticity dilemma. In this paper, we effectively alleviate this dilemma by integrating target location and scale estimation. We generate a translation template using correlation filters for target location and scale models to construct a target pyramid for scale estimation. The scale model utilizes the predicted target position to search for the optimal scale, and the estimated target size in return helps to generate a more stable translation model for target location.

Except for scale variation, there are other video attributes would affect tracking performance. However, most of the existing methods using HOG features to construct the target pyramid, while CNN features are prevailing in high-level visual recognition

© ICST Institute for Computer Sciences, Social Informatics and Telecommunications Engineering 2018
X. Gu et al. (Eds.): MLICOM 2017, Part I, LNICST 226, pp. 40–48, 2018.
https://doi.org/10.1007/978-3-319-73564-1_5

problems because of the robustness against attributes like motion blur or illumination variation. We also find that hierarchical CNN features retain semantic information and spatial details, which are both needed in modeling the target. With these observations, we propose to utilize hierarchical CNN features to build the target pyramid. Moreover, we conceive a new approach to extract scale features in the target pyramid by using a CNN to scan the image computing a large feature map, which effectively reduce computational load and demonstrate great success.

We make the following three contributions. First, we alleviate the stability-plasticity dilemma by integrating target location with object scale estimation. A target pyramid is constructed centered around predicted target location to determine the object scale, and the translation template is updated considering estimated object size to locate the target position. The integrating tracking strategy effectively reduces tracking drifts and remarkably improves the performance in videos with scale variation. Second, we innovatively propose to utilize hierarchical CNN features to generate the target pyramid. We extract every scale features in target pyramid with a scan from the CNN. Features from different layers of a CNN retain spatial details and sematic information, which are both helpful to encode scale models robust against motion blur and illumination variation. Third, we conduct extensive experiments on a large-scale benchmark dataset with 100 video sequences [5]. The tracking results demonstrate the effectiveness of our proposed accurate scale-variable tracking algorithm (AST).

2   Related Work

Heriques et al. first exploit circulant structure of training samples and propose to transfer correlation filters into the Fourier domain with CSK method, which reaches a speed of about 250 frames per second [6]. Furthermore, the KCF tracking algorithm uses HOG features other than illumination intensity features and improves the performance of CSK [7]. In [8], Bolme et al. learn a minimum output sum of squared error filter on gray-scale images, using intensity features to represent the object.

Recent years deep CNNs have improved state-of-the-art performance in many computer vision tasks, and some researchers attempt to explore the usage of CNNs in visual tracking. Ma et al. develop a correlation tracker based on hierarchical features from a deep CNN. Due to its coarse-to-fine translation estimation strategy, the HCF tracker can locate the target precisely. Qi et al. combine weak CNNs based trackers into a single stronger tracker [4]. However, these trackers do not take target scale changes into account and cannot perform well when target undergoes scale variation.

For scale estimation, Danelljan et al. propose to construct target pyramid around the object, and their fast scale tracking algorithm with HOG features performs well in overlap success rate with a considerable speed [9]. Ma et al. learns a multi-level correlation filters to estimate target scale, but they do not use estimated scale to improve positioning accuracy [10]. In this paper, we exploit hierarchical features for different CNN layers to build a target pyramid and train two models separately for predicting position and scale estimation. We conduct extensive experiments on large-scale benchmark datasets, and the results demonstrate the effectiveness of our algorithm, especially when tracking sequences with scale variation, motion blur and deformation.

3 Proposed Algorithm

3.1 Correlation Tracking

Let $x \in \mathbb{R}^{M \times N}$ denotes feature vector of size $(M \times N)$. Each shifted sample $x_{m,n}$, $(m, n) \in \{0, 1, \cdots, M - 1\} \times \{0, 1, \cdots, N - 1\}$ has a Gaussian Function label of $y(m, n) = exp\left(-\left((m - M/2)^2 + (n - N/2)^2\right)/2\sigma^2\right)$, where σ is the kernel width. A correlation filter w is generated by solving following minimization problem:

$$w = \arg \min_{w} \sum_{m,n} \|w \cdot \varphi(x_{m,n}) - y(m, n)^2\| + \lambda \|w\|_2^2 \tag{1}$$

where $\varphi(x_{m,n})$ denotes the mapping to a kernel and λ is a regularization parameter.

Henriques et al. [6] exploit the circulant structure of training samples $x_{m,n}$ and transform the minimization problem in (2) to compute the coefficient α in $w = \sum_{m,n} \alpha(m, n) \cdot \varphi(x_{m,n})$. And α can be computed in frequency domain:

$$A = \mathcal{F}(\alpha) = \frac{\mathcal{F}(y)}{\mathcal{F}(\varphi(x) \cdot \varphi(x)) + \lambda} \tag{2}$$

$\mathcal{F}(\cdot)$ indicates the Fourier transform. The position of target in new frame is determined by searching for the location of the maximal value of correlation response map.

3.2 Scale Estimation

According to [9], let N be the number of scales with a scale factor of a. For every $n \in \{-(N - 1)/2, \cdots, (N - 1)/2\}$ we extract image patch I_n of size $S_n = \alpha^n \cdot [h, w]$ centered around the target, where $[h, w]$ is the target size in previous frame. For each image patch I_n we extract CNNs features then compute response map p_n and find the maximal value of each p_n. The optimal target scale for currant frame is determined by:

$$S = S_n = \underset{n}{argmax}(p_n) \tag{3}$$

Note that we train two correlation filter R_t and R_s separately for target location and scale estimation. And R_t incorporates both target and surrounding context information because this information can effectively discriminate the target from background [11]. In contrast, R_s only depend on the target size for robust scale estimation.

3.3 Deep CNN Features

Several CNN models, such as AlexNet, R-CNN, CaffeNet and VGG-Net have been designed and demonstrate great success in large-scale image classification and object recognition tasks. According to Ma et al. [3], the features learned from latter CNNs layers encode more semantic information and earlier layers retain higher spatial resolution, which are both needed in tasks of target location and scale estimation.

Therefore, we propose to utilize hierarchical features from VGG-NET-19 [12] for translation template and scale models.

According to traditional method, we must first crop out windows of every scale in target pyramid and then obtain hierarchical features using a CNN. It means that we need to repeat extracting CNN features every frame. Since the process of forward propagation of a CNN requires large amount computing time, and these scale features retain many repeating information. Based on these observations, we propose to use CNN to scan the whole image and then gain all scale features at once. We first use target pyramid to compute the size of searching window adjusted by previous target size, then we crop out a window from the image and gain its CNN feature maps, finally we extract features of every scale in target pyramid from the large feature maps at once.

3.4   Model Update

In our proposed algorithm, we train two models R_t and R_s separately for target location and scale estimation. Since the target appearance would change throughout a sequence, we update the models every frame by a learning rate η:

$$\tilde{x} = \tilde{x}^{t-1} + \eta\tilde{x}^t \tag{4}$$

$$A = A^{t-1} + \eta A^t \tag{5}$$

where t is the frame index. Notice that we update R_t and R_s every frame using (4) and (5) with the same learning rate. We predefine a threshold ξ_s and stably update models only when the difference between the response map's maximal value of previous frame and current frame is less than ξ_s.

Algorithm 1 Proposed tracking algorithm: iterate at frame t

Input   : Previous target position p_{t-1} and scale s_{t-1},
Output: Estimated target position p_t and scale s_t
Repeat:
    Crop out the searching window in frame t according to (p_{t-1}, s_{t-1}) and extract features;
    Compute the correlation map yt using R_t to estimate the new position p_t;
    Build the target pyramid according to (p_{t-1}, s_{t-1}) and compute the correlation map ys using R_s;
    if $|\max(ys_t) - \max(ys_{t-1})| < \xi_s$
        Estimate the optimal scale s_t using (3);
    else
        $s_t = s_{t-1}$;
    end
    Updated R_t and R_s use (4) and (5);
Until *End of the video sequences*

---

4   Experiments

4.1   Implemental Details

The main steps of the proposed algorithm are presented in Algorithm 1. We set the regulation parameter of (1) to $\lambda = 10^{-4}$. The number of scale space in target pyramid is set to $S = 21$ with scale factor of 1.03. The learning rate in (4) is set to 0.01. The threshold of updating target scale is set to $\xi_s = 0.1$. We run our implementations in Matlab on HP OMEN 15-AX000 with an Intel I5-6700HQ 2.6 MHz CPU, 4 GB RAM and a GeForce GTX960 GPU card. The GPU card is only used to extract CNN features.

4.2   Comparisons with State-of-the-Art Trackers

We compare our tracker with top 5 state-of-the-art tracking algorithms that are provided in OTB-100 [5]. These algorithms can be divided into three typical categories, (i) correlation tracker (CSK [6], KCF [7]), (ii) tracking by single classifier (MIL [13], Struck [14]), (iii) tracking by multiple online classifier (TLD [15]).

Quantitative evaluation. Figure 1 and Table 1 presents the tracking results on OTB-100. We highlight the best value in Table 1 by bold. Among all 5 trackers, the KCF tracker achieves the highest DP rate of 69.0%, OS rate of 54.6% and CLE of 44.6. And our algorithm outperforms KCF with raises of 14.3% DP rate, 14.6% OS rate and reduction of 21.2 CLE. Note that our tracker runs in a speed of 3.8 frames per second on OTB-100 [5], because the forward propagation process of CNNs has a high computation load.

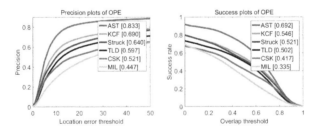

Fig. 1. Distance precision and overlap success plot over OTB-100 using one-pass evaluation (OPE)

Table 1. Comparisons with the state-of-the-art trackers on 100 benchmark sequences

	Ours	CSK [6]	Struck [14]	MIL [13]	TLD [15]	KCF [7]
DP rate (%)	**83.3**	52.1	64.0	44.7	59.7	69.0
OS rate (%)	**69.2**	41.7	52.1	33.5	50.2	54.6
CLE (pixel)	**23.4**	305	47.1	72.1	60.0	44.6
SPEED (FPS)	3.77	**248**	9.84	28.0	23.3	207

Attribute-based evaluation. To further analyze robustness of the proposed algorithm when tracking in various scenes, we evaluate the performance of our algorithm under different video attributes and show the results in Fig. 2. As revealed in Fig. 2, our approach outperforms other methods in all the six tracking challenges. Especially, AST shows its great superiority when tracking the sequences with scale variation, motion blur and illumination variation. The hierarchical features from CNN retain spatial details and semantics, which are both useful for discriminating target from background in fast motion and motion blur sequences. Meanwhile, target pyramid constructed centered around the object effectively predict target scale and stable update strategy helps to generate robust models in videos with scale variation.

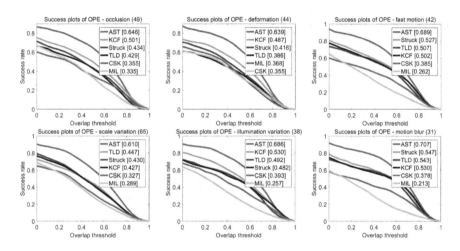

Fig. 2. Overlap success plots over six tracking challenges

Qualitative evaluation. We report tracking results of 5 sequences from 6 trackers in Fig. 3. The CSK tracker learns a kernelized correlation filter for tracking, but the intensity features make the tracker drift when target undergoes rotation, fast motion and partial deformation (Toy, Tiger1, DragonBaby and Skiing). The KCF tracker improve the performance of CSK by using HOG features, but HOG features cannot well discriminate targets in cluttered background and fast motion (DragonBaby and Skiing). The Struck method use structure output to alleviate sample ambiguity, but the HOG features cannot handle large appearance changes and it does not perform well in rotation, deformation and background clutter (Tiger1, DragonBaby and Skiing). The MIL method use multiple instance learning to find positive samples to train the detector. But the insufficient positive samples result in tracking drift caused by fast motion, illumination variation and partial deformation (Toy, Car4, Tiger1, DragonBaby and Skiing). Meanwhile, the TLD method cannot sufficiently exploit semantic information and spatial details, and it prone to drift or even fail to re-detect when comes to fast motion, deformation and partial occlusion (Toy, Tiger1, DragonBaby and Skiing).

There are mainly 3 reasons why the proposed AST tracker performs favorably against the other 5 algorithms. First, we exploit features from different CNN layers to build a target pyramid. The hierarchical features retain both spatial details and semantic information, which are both necessary for target description. Second, we combine correlation tracking with scale changes to alleviate the stability-plasticity dilemma and effectively improve tracking performance. Third, we stably update target scale to gain a robust model and effectively alleviate tracking drifts. As a result, our proposed algorithm effectively handle all the 5 videos.

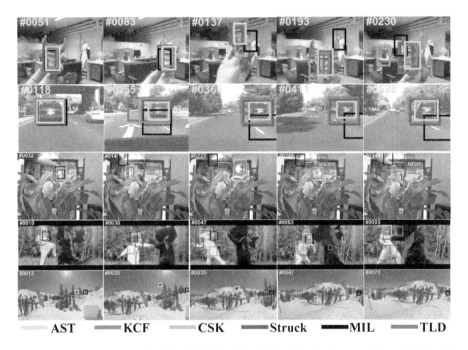

Fig. 3. Qualitative results of AST, KCF [7], MIL [13], CSK [6], Struck [14] and TLD [15] methods on five challenging sequences (Toy, Car4, Tiger1, DragonBaby and Skiing)

4.3   Component Analysis

We further implement three algorithms on benchmark dataset [16] with 50 videos to demonstrate the effectiveness of the proposed algorithm. Except the AST, we generate the ATCNN tracker training correlation filters for target location like AST but remove the target pyramid. Also, we implement the ATHOG tracker training correlation filters and target pyramid both using HOG features. The results are reported in Fig. 4.

As shown in Fig. 4, ATHOG preforms the worst among 3 trackers. Because the target pyramid is constructed centered around the predicted target position, the effectiveness of scale estimation does closely depend on the accuracy of target location. And HOG cannot well describe target appearance in different scenarios. Compared with AST, the ATCNN tracker neglects target scale changes and trains correlation filters with a fixed- size window. AST uses hierarchical CNN features generating target models with the consideration of scale variation, raising the DP rate to 89.4% and OS rate to 76.9%.

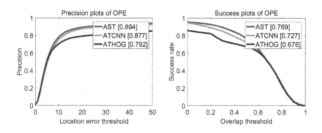

Fig. 4. Comparisons of component effectiveness features

5 Conclusion

In this paper, we propose an effective algorithm for accurate scale-variable tracking. The integrating of target location and scale estimation successfully alleviates the stability-plasticity dilemma caused by scale variation. Meanwhile, scale models trained by hierarchical CNN features remarkably improves the performance in tracking videos with motion blur and illumination variation. Extensive experiment results on a large-scale benchmark demonstrate the great success of the AST tracker.

Acknowledgments. This work was supported by the National Natural Science Foundation of China (Grant No. 61501139, 61371100), and the Natural Scientific Research Innovation Foundation in Harbin Institute of Technology (HIT.NSRIF.2013136).

References

1. Jia, X., Lu, H., Yang, M.-H.: Visual tracking via adaptive structural local sparse appearance model. In: CVPR, pp. 1822–1829. IEEE Press, Plantations (2012)
2. Zhang, J., Ma, S., Sclaroff, S.: MEEM: robust tracking via multiple experts using entropy minimization. In: Fleet, D., Pajdla, T., Schiele, B., Tuytelaars, T. (eds.) ECCV 2014. LNCS, vol. 8694, pp. 188–203. Springer, Cham (2014). https://doi.org/10.1007/978-3-319-10599-4_13
3. Ma, C., Huang, J.-B., Yang, X., Yang, M.-H.: Hierarchical convolutional features for visual tracking. In: ICCV, pp. 3074–3082. IEEE Press, Santiago (2015)
4. Qi, Y., Zhang, S., Qin, L., Yao, H., Huang, Q., Lim, J., Yang, M.-H.: Hedged deep tracking. In: CVPR, pp. 4303–4311. IEEE Press, Las Vegas (2016)
5. Wu, Y., Lim, J., Yang, M.-H.: Object tracking benchmark. IEEE Trans. Pattern Anal. Mach. Intell. **37**(9), 1834–1848 (2015)

6. Henriques, J.F., Caseiro, R., Martins, P., Batista, J.: Exploiting the circulant structure of tracking-by-detection with kernels. In: Fitzgibbon, A., Lazebnik, S., Perona, P., Sato, Y., Schmid, C. (eds.) ECCV 2012. LNCS, vol. 7575, pp. 702–715. Springer, Heidelberg (2012). https://doi.org/10.1007/978-3-642-33765-9_50

7. Henriques, J.F., Caseiro, R., Martins, P., Batista, J.: High-Speed tracking with kernelized correlation filters. TPAMI **37**(3), 583–596 (2015)

8. Bolme, D.S., Beveridge, J.R., Draper, B.A., Lui, Y.M.: Visual object tracking using adaptive correlation filters. In: CVPR, pp. 2544–2550. IEEE Press, San Francisco (2010)

9. Danelljan, M., Hager, G., Khan, F.S., Felsberg, M.: Accurate scale estimation for robust visual tracking. In: BMVC, pp. 583–596. BMVA Press, Nottingham (2014)

10. Ma, C., Yang, X., Zhang, C., Yang, M.H.: Long-term correlation tracking. In: CVPR, pp. 5388–5396. IEEE Press, Boston (2015)

11. Zhang, K., Zhang, L., Liu, Q., Zhang, D., Yang, M.-H.: Fast visual tracking via dense spatio-temporal context learning. In: Fleet, D., Pajdla, T., Schiele, B., Tuytelaars, T. (eds.) ECCV 2014. LNCS, vol. 8693, pp. 127–141. Springer, Cham (2014). https://doi.org/10.1007/978-3-319-10602-1_9

12. Simonyan, K., Zisserman, A.: Very deep convolutional networks for large-scale image recognition. arXiv:1409.1556 [cs.CV]

13. Babenko, B., Yang, M.-H., Belongie, S.: Robust object tracking with online multiple instance learning. TPAMI **33**(8), 1619–1632 (2011)

14. Hare, S., Saffari, A., Torr, P.H.S.: Struck: structured output tracking with kernels. In: ICCV, pp. 263–270. IEEE Press, Barcelona (2011)

15. Kalal, Z., Mikolajczyk, K., Matas, J.: Tracking-learning-detection. TPAMI **34**(7), 1619–1632 (2012)

16. Wu, Y., Lim, J., Yang, M.-H.: Online object tracking: a benchmark. In: CVPR, pp. 2411–2418. IEEE Press, Portland (2013)

Sparse Photoacoustic Microscopy Reconstruction Based on Matrix Nuclear Norm Minimization

Ying Fu[1], Naizhang Feng[1], Yahui Shi[1], Ting Liu[2],
and Mingjian Sun[1(✉)]

[1] Department of Control Science and Engineering,
Harbin Institute of Technology at Weihai, Weihai 264209, China
fu_ying_hit@163.com, fengnz@yeah.net,
295182727@qq.com, sunmingjian@hit.edu.cn
[2] Department of Measurement and Control Technology and Instrumentation,
Dalian Maritime University, Dalian 116026, China
liuting15348@126.com

Abstract. As a high-resolution deep tissue imaging technology, photoacoustic microscopy (PAM) is attracting extensive attention in biomedical studies. PAM has trouble in achieving real-time imaging with the long data acquisition time caused by point-to-point sample mode. In this paper, we propose a sparse photoacoustic microscopy reconstruction method based on matrix nuclear norm minimization. We use random sparse sampling instead of traditional full sampling and regard the sparse PAM reconstruction problem as a nuclear norm minimization problem, which is efficiently solved under alternating direction method of multiplier (ADMM) framework. Results from PAM experiments indicate the proposed method could work well in fast imaging. The proposed method is also be expected to promote the achievement of PAM real-time imaging.

Keywords: Sparse photoacoustic microscopy reconstruction
Real-time imaging · Matrix completion · Nuclear norm minimization

1 Introduction

Photoacoustic microscopy (PAM) has been considered as an effective tool for high-resolution deep tissue imaging in biomedical studies, such as imaging of tumor microenvironments, brain functions and gene activities [1–5]. In PAM, the lateral resolution is defined by the overlap of both optical excitation and ultrasound detection's foci, which are focused on the same spot, while the axis resolution is defined by the acoustic time of fight. According to the sizes of optical excitation and ultrasound detection's foci, PAM is divided into optical-resolution PAM (OR-PAM) and acoustic-resolution PAM (AR-PAM) [6]. In conventional PAM, the measured data X is detected by point-to-point mechanical scanning of ultrasound and optical components on the target surface to obtain high resolution of deep tissue. This sampling of PAM is one kind of oversampling (Fig. 1(a)). More sampling points are necessary for higher

© ICST Institute for Computer Sciences, Social Informatics and Telecommunications Engineering 2018
X. Gu et al. (Eds.): MLICOM 2017, Part I, LNICST 226, pp. 49–56, 2018.
https://doi.org/10.1007/978-3-319-73564-1_6

resolution. However, it leads to consuming more sampling time, larger data size and more requirements for system hardware. The most common way to enhance the resolution is to improve the performances of objective and ultrasound transducer, which will increase the system cost. For example, to increase optical numerical aperture (NA) of objective can improve resolution for OR-PAM, but it also means that the penetration depth will be decreased at the same time and the optical scanning devices should have higher performance indexes [4, 5]. Thus, it's significant for PAM to improve the scanning speed with no influence to resolution under limited experiment condition.

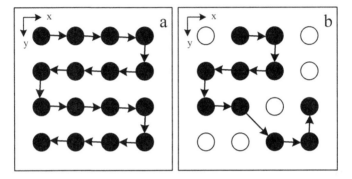

Fig. 1. (a) Scanning path of the traditional full-sampling mode; (b) scanning path of the sparse sampling mode

In many studies, it's shown that most medical images are sparse by themselves or proper transformation including photoacoustic images [7, 8]. The sparsity of photoacoustic imaging has been proven and fully utilized to obtain highest-resolution photoacoustic image by the least amount of sampling data [9, 10]. In particular, the application of compressive sensing (CS) technology in photoacoustic tomography (PAT) has achieved remarkable success and received excellent experiment results [11], but CS application in PAM is rare. What's more, the conventional sampling of PAM is one kind of oversampling. We can achieve fast data acquisition by decreasing measurement numbers with sparse sampling method, whose scanning path is shown in Fig. 1(b). In sparse sampling mode, the random sampling mask A can be generated if sampling rate (SR) k and sampling point numbers m, n in direction of x, y respectively are known. Here assume $A \in \mathbb{R}^{m \times n}$ as a 0, 1 matrix, where 1 means the point's data needs to be collected while 0 means not. According to the sampling mask A, computer can plan shortest scanning path to achieve sparse scanning and minimize sampling time. Therefore, the sparse PAM measured data $b \in \mathbb{R}^p$ is defined as

$$b_l = X_{i,j} \text{ if } A_{i,j} = 1, \ 1 \leq i \leq m, \ 1 \leq j \leq n, \ 1 \leq l \leq p, \ p < m \times n, \quad (1)$$

where $X \in \mathbb{R}^{m \times n}$ is final PAM image what we want to recover i.e. the measured data of conventional PAM and $A \in \mathbb{R}^{m \times n}$ is sparse sampling mask.

In this paper, we propose a method to solve a sparse photoacoustic microscopy reconstruction problem, which is to acquire the real images from fast-scanning data, i.e. recover PAM image $X \in \mathbb{R}^{m \times n}$ from compressive measured data $b \in \mathbb{R}^p$.

2   Method

According to sparse PAM reconstruction problem, we attempt to recover complete matrix $X \in \mathbb{R}^{m \times n}$ from measured matrix $b \in \mathbb{R}^p$ which can be approximately regarded as a part of X. It can be described as a matrix recovery problem, also known as a matrix completion problem. Recht et al. proved that most matrices $X \in \mathbb{R}^{m \times n}$ which has low-rank property can be recovered from $b \in \mathbb{R}^p$ if the entries of A are suitably random e.g., i.i.d. Gaussian [12, 15]. Fortunately, as a result that the low-rank property of photoacoustic imaging has been verified in recent studies [13], sparse PAM reconstruction problem can be transformed to the completion problem of low-rank matrix, which takes low-rank property for a constraint. Thus, sparse photoacoustic microscopy reconstruction problem is defined as:

$$
\begin{aligned}
&\min \ \mathrm{rank}(X) \\
&\text{s.t. } \mathcal{A}(X) = b
\end{aligned} \tag{2}
$$

where $X \in \mathbb{R}^{m \times n}$ is the decision variable, $\mathcal{A}: \mathbb{R}^{m \times n} \to \mathbb{R}^p$ is the sampling map, and vector b is measured.

Due to the problem (1) is a NP-hard problem in general, we can replace rank (X) with the nuclear norm of X, which is the tightest convex relaxation of rank(X) [14, 15]. Approximating nuclear norm to the rank function, the problem (1) can be transformed into the form as below [16]:

$$
\begin{aligned}
&\min \ \|X\|_* \\
&\text{s.t. } \mathcal{A}(J) = b, \ X = J
\end{aligned} \tag{3}
$$

where $\|X\|_* := \sum_{i=1}^{r} \sigma_i(X)$ is the nuclear norm of X which has r positive singular values of $\sigma_1 \geq \sigma_2 \geq \ldots \geq \sigma_r > 0$.

To solve the problem conveniently, the problem (3) is transformed to the form of corresponding augmented Lagrangian function

$$
\begin{aligned}
L_\mu(X, J, x, j) =\ &\|X\|_* - \langle x, X - J \rangle - \frac{\mu_1}{2} \|X - J\|_F^2 - \langle j, \mathcal{A}(J) - b \rangle \\
&+ \frac{\mu_2}{2} \|\mathcal{A}(J) - b\|_2^2,
\end{aligned} \tag{4}
$$

where $x \in \mathbb{R}^{m \times n}$, $j \in \mathbb{R}^p$ is the Lagrangian multiplier, and $\mu_1 > 0$ and $\mu_2 > 0$ are the penalty parameters for the linear constraint.

The solution can be obtained by solving the problem (3) under ADMM [17], described as follows:

$$X_{k+1} = \arg\min_X \|X\|_* + \frac{\mu_1}{2}\left\|X - (J_k + \frac{1}{\mu_1}x_k)\right\|_F^2, \tag{5}$$

$$J_{k+1} = \arg\min_J -\langle x_k, X_{k+1} - J\rangle + \frac{\mu_1}{2}\|X_{k+1} - J\|_F^2 - \langle j_k, \mathcal{A}(J) - b\rangle \\ + \frac{\mu_2}{2}\|\mathcal{A}(J) - b\|_2^2, \tag{6}$$

$$x_{k+1} = x_k - \gamma_1(X_{k+1} - J_{k+1}), \tag{7}$$

$$j_{k+1} = j_k - \gamma_2(\mathcal{A}(J_{k+1}) - b), \tag{8}$$

where γ_1 and γ_2 are the penalty parameters for the linear constraint.

Assume $X \in \mathbb{R}^{m \times n}$ and the SVD of X is $X = U\text{Diag}(\sigma)V^T$, $U \in \mathbb{R}^{m \times r}$, $\sigma \in \mathbb{R}_+^r$, $V \in \mathbb{R}^{n \times r}$. For any $v > 0$, the matrix shrinkage operator $\mathcal{S}_v(\cdot)$ is defined as [15]

$$\mathcal{S}_v(X) := U\text{Diag}(\bar{\sigma})V^T, \text{ with } \bar{\sigma} := \begin{cases} \sigma - v, & \sigma - v > 0 \\ 0, & \text{o.w.} \end{cases}, \tag{9}$$

Obviously, the closed solution of X-subproblem (4) can be described as

$$J_{k+1} = \mathcal{S}_{\frac{1}{\mu_1}}(J_k + \frac{1}{\mu_1}x_k)J_k \text{ and } x_k, \tag{10}$$

On the other hand, nothing the right value of J-subproblem (5) as $f(J)$, a unique solution of it can obtained by taking partial derivatives with respect to J, i.e., $\partial f(J)/\partial J = 0$, described as

$$(\mu_1 I + \mu_2(\mathcal{A}^*\mathcal{A}))J = \mu_1 X_{k+1} - x_k - \mathcal{A}^*(\mu_2 b + j_k), \tag{11}$$

where I is an identity matrix, and $\mathcal{A}^*$ is the adjoint of $\mathcal{A}$. The linear operator equation can be solved easily by the conjugate gradient method.

Based on the discussion above, we summarize the algorithm for sparse photoacoustic microscopy reconstruction problem based on matrix nuclear norm minimization via ADMM in Table 1, where *maxiter* is maximum number of iterations, *tol* is termination criterion for iteration.

3   Experimental Results

In this section, experiment results on several PAM images for solving sparse PAM reconstruction problem are reported, which show the efficiency of the proposed method (Algorithm 1). In order to evaluate the performances of proposed method qualitatively and quantitatively, four performance indexes are utilized. They are: peak signal-to-noise

Table 1. Reconstruction algorithm based on matrix nuclear norm minimization via ADMM.

Reconstruction algorithm based on matrix nuclear norm minimization via ADMM
Input: b, μ_1, μ_2, γ_1, γ_2, *maxiter*, *tol*, $k=0$, $X_0 = 0$, $J_0 = 0$, $x_k = 0$, $j_k = 0$
for $k=0,1,\ldots,maxiter$
1. Compute X_{k+1} via (9) with fixed J_k and x_k;
2. Compute J_{k+1} via (10) with fixed X_{k+1}, x_k and j_k;
3. Update x_k and j_k with fixed J_{k+1} and X_{k+1};
4. If $\left\| X_{k+1} - X_k \right\| \leq tol$, stop and return X_{k+1};
5. End if;
6. End for;
Output: $X = X_{k+1}$

ratio (PSNR), structural similarity (SSIM) index, relative error (Rerr) and mean square error (MSE), respectively.

$$PSNR = 10 * \log_{10} \frac{mn}{\sum\limits_{i=1}^{m}\sum\limits_{j=1}^{n} (X_{ij} - Y_{ij})^2}, \tag{12}$$

$$SSIM(X, Y) = \frac{(2\mu_X\mu_Y + C_1)(\sigma_{XY} + C_2)}{(\mu_X^2 + \mu_Y^2 + C_1)(\sigma_X^2 + \sigma_Y^2 + C_2)}, \tag{13}$$

$$Rerr = \frac{\|X^K - X\|_2}{\|X\|_2}, \tag{14}$$

$$MSE = \frac{\sum\limits_{i=1}^{m}\sum\limits_{j=1}^{n} (X_{ij} - Y_{ij})^2}{mn}, \tag{15}$$

where X is the approximate optimal solution of problem (3), i.e. restored image, and Y is the reference image. μ_X, μ_Y are respectively mean of X and Y, σ_X and σ_Y are respectively variance of X and Y and σ_{XY} is covariance of image X and Y. C_1 and C_2 are constants to prevent denominator from being zero [18].

In our experiments, we obtain two groups of PAM images by full-sampling and random-sampling PAM system. The first group is PAM images of mouse brain (resolution: 211×211), whose sample rates (SR) are respectively 1.0, 0.6, 0.5, 0.4, 0.3, 0.2, 0.1; another group is of mouse ear (resolution: 954×954), whose sample rates are same to the first group. Figures 2(a)–(d) and Figs. 3(a)–(d) show two groups of typical experimental results from the method described above. The values of Rerr, MSE, PSNR and SSIM obtained in different sampling rate by the proposed method are summarized in Table 2. As can be seen, when the sampling rate is 0.4, the recovered images of both two groups have already having relatively good resolution. The PSNRs between the recovered images and the reference images are over 40 dB and the SSIMs are 1, which indicate the proposed method has a great effectiveness. It is also worth noting that less sampling rate means less sampling time.

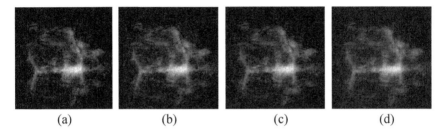

| (a) | (b) | (c) | (d) |

Fig. 2. Results from mouse brain images. (a) Full sampling image. (b)–(d) Recovered images by our method which sampling rates are 0.6, 0.4, 0.2, respectively.

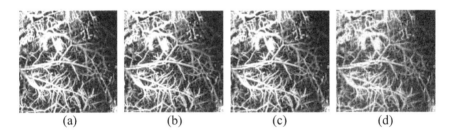

| (a) | (b) | (c) | (d) |

Fig. 3. Results from mouse ear images. (a) Full sampling image. (b)–(d) Recovered images by our method which sampling rates are 0.6, 0.4, 0.2, respectively.

Table 2. The results in different sampling rate by the proposed method

	SR	0.6	0.5	0.4	0.3	0.2	0.1
Group 1	Rerr	0.0379	0.0608	0.0927	0.1340	0.1930	0.3060
	MSE	0.0047	0.0075	0.0114	0.0165	0.0237	0.0376
	PSNR	47.3873	45.3329	43.5004	41.3871	40.3105	38.3176
	SSIM	1.0000	1.0000	1.0000	1.0000	1.0000	0.9999
Group 2	Rerr	0.0379	0.0608	0.0927	0.1340	0.1930	0.3060
	MSE	0.0112	0.0150	0.0263	0.0493	0.0944	0.1761
	PSNR	43.5818	42.3096	40.0256	37.1342	34.3135	31.6086
	SSIM	1.0000	1.0000	1.0000	0.9998	0.9993	0.9970

4 Conclusion

In conclusion, we present a sparse photoacoustic microscopy reconstruction method to recover complete PAM images from parts of images. It aims to reduce data acquisition time and reconstruct the real images from fast-scanning data from fast-scanning data. An efficient matrix completion algorithm has been proposed to solve the associated optimization problem. The results from PAM experiments demonstrate the proposed method could work well in fast imaging, so we expect that the study can be applied in actual operation and provide a way for the achievement of PAM real-time imaging. For further study, the case that the image is not sparse at all will be considered.

Acknowledgments. This work is partially supported by the National Natural Science Foundation of China (Grant No. 61371045), Science and Technology Development Plan Project of Shandong Province, China (Grant No. 2015GGX103016, 2016GGX103032) and the China Postdoctoral Science Foundation (Grant No. 2015M571413).

References

1. Wang, L.V., Hu, S.: Photoacoustic tomography: in vivo imaging from organelles to organs. Science **335**(6075), 1458 (2012)
2. Yao, J., Wang, L.V.: Photoacoustic Microscopy. Laser Photonics Rev. **7**(5), 758–778 (2013)
3. Zhang, H.F., Maslov, K., Stoica, G., Wang, L.V.: Functional photoacoustic microscopy for high-resolution and noninvasive in vivo imaging. Nat. Biotechnol. **24**, 848–851 (2006)
4. Zhang, C., Maslov, K., Hu, S., et al.: Reflection-mode submicron-resolution in vivo photoacoustic microscopy. J. Biomed. Opt. **17**(2), 020501 (2012)
5. Wu, Z.H., Sun, M.J., Wang, Q., et al.: Photoacoustic microscopy image resolution enhancement via directional total variation regularization. Chin. Opt. Lett. **12**, 104–108 (2014)
6. Zhou, Y., Wang, L.V.: Translational photoacoustic microscopy. In: Olivo, M., Dinish, U.S. (eds.) Frontiers in Biophotonics for Translational Medicine. POSP, vol. 3, pp. 47–73. Springer, Singapore (2016). https://doi.org/10.1007/978-981-287-627-0_2
7. Provost, J., Lesage, F.: The application of compressed sensing for photo-acoustic tomography. IEEE Trans. Med. Imaging **28**(4), 585–594 (2009)
8. Liang, D., Zhang, H.F., Ying, L.: Compressed-sensing photoacoustic imaging based on random optical illumination. Int. J. Funct. Inf. Personal. Med. **2**(4), 394–406 (2009)
9. Guo, Z., Li, C., Song, L., et al.: Compressed sensing in photoacoustic tomography in vivo. J. Biomed. Opt. **15**(2), 021311 (2010)
10. Sun, M., Feng, N., Shen, Y., et al.: Photoacoustic imaging method based on arc-direction compressed sensing and multi-angle observation. Opt. Express **19**(16), 14801–14806 (2011)
11. Wu, Z.H., Sun, M.J., Wang, Q., et al.: Compressive sampling photoacoustic tomography based on edge expander codes and TV regularization. Chin. Opt. Lett. **12**(10), 41–45 (2014)
12. Recht, B., Fazel, M., Parrilo, P.A.: Guaranteed minimum-rank solutions of linear matrix equations via nuclear norm minimization. SIAM Rev. **52**(3), 471–501 (2007)
13. Liu, T., Sun, M., Feng, N., et al.: Sparse photoacoustic microscopy based on low-rank matrix approximation. Chin. Opt. Lett. **9**, 62–66 (2016)
14. Fazel, M.: Matrix rank minimization with applications. Ph.D. thesis, Stanford University (2002)

15. Ma, S., Goldfarb, D., Chen, L.: Fixed point and Bregman iterative methods for matrix rank minimization. Math. Program. **128**(1), 321–353 (2011)
16. Jin, Z., Wan, Z., Jiao, Y., Lu, X.: An alternating direction method with continuation for nonconvex low rank minimization. J. Sci. Comput. **66**(2), 849–869 (2016)
17. He, B.S., Liao, L.Z., Han, D.R., et al.: A new inexact alternating directions method for monotone variational inequalities. Math. Program. **92**(1), 103–118 (2002)
18. Sreelekha, G., Koparde, P.G.: Perceptual video coder incorporating wavelet based Intra frame coder. In: International Conference on Computer and Communication Technology, p. 188193. IEEE Press, Allahabad (2010)

Clustering Analysis Based on Segmented Images

Hongxu Zheng, Jianlun Wang[(⊠)], and Can He

College of Information and Electrical Engineering,
China Agricultural University, Beijing 100083, China
496326832@qq.com, wangjianlun@cau.edu.cn,
348506582@qq.com

Abstract. Image segmentation plays an important role in the field of digital production management. Image resolution is an important factor affecting the size of its segmentation and segmentation efficiency, and the physical characteristics of the image capturing device is another important factor. With high-resolution segmentation algorithm in image segmentation, we often find that the edge contour image segmentation is difficult to accurately determine, more complex image arithmetic operation efficiency is not high and images taken with a different device in response to segmentation algorithms are very different. In this paper, the plant leaf image collected from different cameras was used as the object of study, and the feature quantity was extracted. The appropriate segmentation boundary was determined by cluster analysis. The leaf image was pretreated with the resolution adjustment, and the leaf image was in the appropriate segmentation feature range. After the clustering domain processing of the feature range in this paper, it solves the problem that the real edge of the leaf area information is too difficult to distinguish, and effectively solves the problem of complex image algorithm and ordinary pc machine in the process of complex image processing Efficiency issues. The appropriate segmentation feature range of the devices is established for different devices, which effectively solves the different response of different devices to the segmentation algorithm.

Keywords: Image segmentation · Resolution adjustment
Gray-level co-occurrence matrix · Clustering analysis

1 Introduction

Image segmentation is related to the resolution properties of the device and the image. Under the condition of natural light, the result is different from the plant leaves under different resolutions. In the field of image segmentation, the universality of a single algorithm is higher, such as Otsu [1], Canny algorithm [2], watershed algorithm [3], regional growth algorithm [4], mean drift clustering [5], Threshold [6], but when dealing with the same or different devices under different environmental conditions, the single segmentation operator is affected by factors such as physical condition, optical radiation environment, image noise, image complexity, threshold selection and so on. The image difference is mainly reflected in the complexity of the image, the resolution and the size of the image memory, and thus make its image segmentation efficiency and

© ICST Institute for Computer Sciences, Social Informatics and Telecommunications Engineering 2018
X. Gu et al. (Eds.): MLICOM 2017, Part I, LNICST 226, pp. 57–75, 2018.
https://doi.org/10.1007/978-3-319-73564-1_7

effect are different. The complex composite algorithm effectively solves the influence of factors such as image noise, complexity and threshold selection when image segmentation is carried out. However, there is still no general segmentation algorithm for image acquisition devices under different environmental conditions to solve all the segmentation problems. And the existing segmentation algorithm is for different specific environmental conditions, specific equipment and the subject of the segmentation problem, so the division of the universal effect is low. With the improvement of various segmentation algorithms, the universal effect and efficiency of the composite segmentation algorithm for image segmentation of different specific subjects have been improved, such as Wang et al. [7] proposed an adaptive segmentation algorithm OTSU algorithm and Canny edge detection of plant leaf segmentation algorithm, you can get a better segmentation contour effect, the success rate to achieve a higher. The success rate is higher than the accuracy requirements, because in natural light conditions, the plant blade environment is complex, resulting in high image complexity. Not only requires a class of objects to accurately extract the edge, but also requires the algorithm. The segmented object has a certain degree of adaptability, that is, the same segmentation accuracy for objects with different environmental conditions. Dhalia Sweetlin et al. [8] proposed a method for segmenting CT images of lung disease based on patient-specific automated models, and also obtained a very high segmentation accuracy. However, this article only studies the accuracy of segmentation without involving success rates.

At present, all kinds of algorithm programs can solve the problem of incomplete and incomplete information when dealing with the complex images with high natural light and high resolution. At the same time, complex images with large amounts of information also slow down the image processing speed. So some scholars have made improvements. Such as Kim et al. [9], Frucci et al. [10], Liao et al. [11], Wang et al. [12], Zhu et al. [13]. In the high-resolution image segmentation, because of the large amount of image information, the high complexity of the factors is not conducive to the image of fast and accurate segmentation, but by adjusting the image resolution, Low resolution conditions, making the texture structure changes, to avoid excessive division, you can get the contours of the image, with better details to retain the characteristics and better anti-noise performance, thereby improving efficiency.

Some scholars have studied the problem of poor efficiency of segmentation image function algorithm in dealing with natural light image. Such as Moallem et al. [14], Delibasis et al. [15], Huang et al. [16], Saksa et al. [17], Zhang et al. [18]. The use of appropriate segmentation algorithm for a single device to obtain the image segmentation, can get a better segmentation effect. But for many devices to obtain the image, but rarely on the image segmentation effect is expressed. The study of multi-device image segmentation involves accuracy, but the efficiency of image segmentation is rarely mentioned. It can be seen that in the natural light state, the segmentation efficiency of the same segmentation algorithm for multi-device is still urgent to be solved, namely, the universality and efficiency of the algorithm. Natural light images of plant leaf images, not only by its complex background, shadow, light radiation and other factors, and different devices produce natural light conditions images, the same algorithm for them also have very different segmentation effect. The same type of camera and lens, because the impact of processing factors are not exactly the same, the imaging can not be exactly the same, but more than the different models to be closer. Therefore, the same algorithm in the different equipment image segmentation must effectively eliminate the impact of these factors, in order to make the image segmentation algorithm universality and efficiency is improved. In this paper, the plant leaf images obtained from three different cameras under natural light conditions are clustered according to the classification boundary formed by the sample base, and then the clustering is processed and then segmented to prove the versatility and goodness of the proposed method. The efficiency of image segmentation.

Some scholars have studied the attribute adjustment of clustering data and the effect of different clustering methods on clustering results. Such as Meged and Gelbard [19], Dee Miller et al. [20], Ji et al. [21], Hong et al. [22]. For the clustering of attribute data, the general research is to adapt the attributes by adjusting the algorithm, but there is little research on the algorithm to adapt the attributes by adjusting the attributes. Our approach is to adjust the raw data attributes so that the adjusted data can meet the attribute requirements processed by the segmentation algorithm and generate new raw data clusters. We have two requirements: 1. Attribute adjustment is appropriate; 2. Method adjustment appropriate.

For attribute data clustering, its attribute value, clustering algorithm will affect the effect of clustering. Through the adjustment of the attribute value can make the effect of clustering better, to achieve higher classification accuracy. Different clustering algorithms often get different clustering results for the same data, and the clustering results of the data can be obtained by comparing the different clustering algorithms. However, there is little research on the relationship between image attributes and segmentation effects and efficiency. In this paper, we find that the method can easily and effectively judge the segmentation effect and efficiency, and adjust the image attributes to achieve the purpose of improving the segmentation effect and efficiency. The research of this paper focuses on the segmentation effect and efficiency of the different images obtained by different devices in the process of plant leaf segmentation. When the complex image is segmented by complex algorithm, the complex features of the image are complex background, the leaf overlap, the difference between the veins and the leaf brightness, and the leaf edge gradient change is not obvious, which causes the image foreground and background separation difficult.

In this paper, a leaf adaptive image segmentation algorithm [7] is used to segment the plant leaves collected by different devices under natural light, and the attribute feature data are obtained. Through analysis, we select the three-dimensional feature Quantity, memory ratio, unit pixel entropy ratio, energy than the characteristics of the parameters of the amount of three-dimensional structure, on the basis of clustering. By comparing the clustering boundary obtained by different clustering methods, the optimal three-dimensional feasible domain boundary is selected. The boundary provides the basis for rapid classification of newly acquired image data and, on this basis, performs resolution adjustment. So that different image sources and different resolution images can be separated from the complete foliage edge contours, for the subsequent plant leaf domain biological characteristics of identification, three-dimensional reconstruction and other biomass calculation work pave the way. We apply the clustering method to the image attribute data of different segmentation results, which proves the simplicity and efficiency of the method.

2 Method

2.1 Materials

As the different models and manufacturers of camera features may be different, so this paper in the completion of the experiment used in the shooting equipment selected three different manufacturers and different models of the camera, they are: 10 million pixel CCD Nikon color camera, 2 megapixel CCD Canon color camera and 8 million pixel CCD Sony color camera; use of these three cameras were in the same shooting environment conditions collected plant leaf image.

In this paper, the quality of the image picture has a strict request, the camera equipment to capture the image content to keep the natural, real and clear texture, the actual life applications, the impact of camera image imaging factors are many, such as outdoor light direct, Jitter, focal length adjustment, noise interference, overlapping blade morphology and large reflection surface interference, so when shooting plant leaves, to avoid the interference described above, select the appropriate natural light shooting environment, try to ensure that the image clarity.

2.2 General Natural Light Image Segmentation Results

In the natural light condition, the plant leaf image collected in farmland has large information volume, high resolution, complicated background, overlapping leaves, poor leaf blade and leaf brightness, and no obvious change of edge gradient. The background is difficult to separate. All kinds of segmentation algorithm to process the segmentation of the contour is difficult to accurately determine the split efficiency is poor. For the same object different devices to shoot the image of a large difference, and the precise division, the different equipment, the efficiency of the division is also different. So a single algorithm can not accurately segment the blade contour. Artificial light adopts the adaptive binarization of the subject to obtain the binary map with small amount of information, but it is not conducive to the analysis of biomass and other plant image texture features. A large number of studies are now effective in solving this problem. In this paper, a blade adaptive image segmentation algorithm is used, as shown in Fig. 1. However, regardless of which kind of segmentation algorithm, will face the natural light, plant blade image high resolution, segmentation efficiency is not high, the difference between different devices caused by the impact of such issues. Therefore, we analyze the feature quantity of the reaction image information to find a solution to these problems.

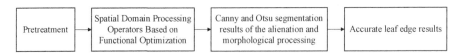

Fig. 1. The introduction of adaptive image segmentation algorithm

2.3   Analysis of Factors Affecting Image Segmentation

It is found that the image equipment and image information content have a great influence on the segmentation result, and it is necessary to carry out quantitative analysis.

2.3.1   Image Device on the Image Segmentation

The influence of image device and image information on image segmentation is as follows. First of all, different models and manufacturers of different physical characteristics of the camera, which CCD size, pixel size and processing accuracy, optical lens construction and processing accuracy and so on factors will cause imaging differences. Second, the same manufacturers of the same model of the physical characteristics of the camera can not be exactly the same, can also cause imaging differences. Again, the existing segmentation and other image algorithms and ordinary PC computing power is limited. In addition, the large amount of information on the leaf image is likely to cause the image processing function of the output is complicated, can not determine the real edge of the blade.

These problems are bound to result in the existing segmentation program can not be fully ideal for efficient and efficient segmentation. In this paper, the adaptive segmentation algorithm is based on the natural light conditions of the blade segmentation algorithm, the single blade of the success rate of about 70%. But the actual work of different camera equipment found different resolution of the blade image segmentation success rate is very different, but there are some centralized laws, as shown in Fig. 4.

In order to enable the segmentation algorithm to efficiently segment different images and images of different devices under natural light conditions, it is necessary to process the images taken by different devices so that they can be in an ideal divisible Resolution domain and information domain, and establish the clustering and clustering threshold of the domain. On this basis, it is necessary to determine the three-dimensional boundary which is suitable for segmentation of different devices in order to solve the above four problems.

2.3.2   Image Resolution on the Segmentation of the Impact

The resolution of the image affects the segmentation effect of the image. High-resolution images are smooth edges, rich in detail and texture, giving a soft feel. However, when the high-resolution plant leaves are divided, there is a problem that the success rate of the equipment is high, the division time is too long, and the contour of the appropriate division is obtained. The edge of the low-resolution image will have obvious grain and jaggedness, the image's sharpness is poor, affecting the quality of the image. In the segmentation, + segmented contour is more smooth, loss of detail information, can not be a good response to plant leaf area and so on.

Resolution Adjust the experiment to be used in the steps: First, the resolution adjustment, access to different resolution images; Second, the image will be adjusted after the split experiment; Thirdly, the clustering threshold of the feature quantity of the image segmentation result of each experimental camera is analyzed.

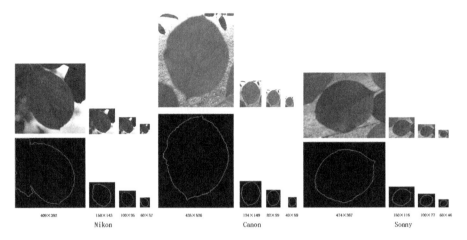

Fig. 2. The segmentation effect of the leaves taken by Nikon camera.

Table 1. The resolution range of single blade image which adapts segmentation algorithm.

Camera equipment	Image label	Suitable for segmentation of the resolution area	Suitable for segmentation of the pixel area
Nikon	Nikon (221)	80 * 77–210 * 201	6160–42210
Canon	Canon (15)	37 * 45–433 * 525	1685–227325
Sonny	Sonny (37)	35 * 26–525 * 404	945–212575

Through the experiment shown in Fig. 2, the resolution of the vane image affects the effect of dividing the edge contour.

Table 1 summarizes the range of suitable resolution and the number of suitable pixels for the monolithic images nikon (221), canon (15) and sonny (37) from the three camera devices.

Since each of the blade images has a different resolution domain that is suitable for segmentation, the resolution of the resolution range of the 90 monolithic leaf image samples of each group of camera devices is defined as the resolution spatial domain library of the device.

Through the observation and analysis, we found that the characteristics of the plant leaves obtained by different devices under natural light conditions also have important influence on the segmentation of the images. The success rate of the different resolution images obtained by different camera devices is very different. There are some centralized laws, through the analysis of the amount of features, you can effectively obtain the different camera equipment to capture the appropriate image of the plant blade area.

3   Image Feature Analysis

The energy of the image is the square sum of the elements of the gray covariance matrix. It can measure the stability of the gray scale of the texture. The larger the value is, the more stable the gray scale is, and the gray distribution of the image is more uniform. The entropy of the image belongs to the inherent attribute of the image. Entropy can not only reflect the density of the gray distribution in the image, but also reflect the spatial characteristics of the gray spatial distribution. The resolution of the image, that is, the resolution of the image, reflects the amount of information and detail stored in the digital image, usually expressed in terms of the number of pixels per unit inch.

3.1   Feature Selection

The resolution of the plant leaves with different complexity obtained under different natural conditions was analyzed. The resolution, pixel entropy, memory and gray covariance were selected as parameters to study the suitable segmentation of plant leaves.

3.1.1   Unit Pixel Entropy, Resolution and Memory

The higher the entropy of the image, the greater the detail in brightness and the conversion, the need for higher compression; otherwise, you need less compression. The unit pixel entropy reflects the size of the image on the unit pixel. Pixel is the abbreviation of the image element. In the computer operation analysis, if the image is magnified several times, the human eye can find that these continuous regions and texture are concatenated by a lot of squares with similar color or similar color, Square small area element is the smallest unit of pixels that make up the computer digital image, the pixel is also called the pixel or pixel element, the pixel is the resolution of the size unit. The larger the pixel, the higher the resolution, the clearer the picture, and the larger the output photo size. The size of the memory of the image file is proportional to the square of its image resolution, and the pixel of the image is proportional to the resolution of the image.

In this experiment, the unit pixel entropy, pixel ratio and memory ratio of 90 single leaf images of Nikon camera are used to obtain the ratio of the corresponding feature of the corresponding image by adjusting the resolution to select the characteristic parameter quantity suitable for clustering.

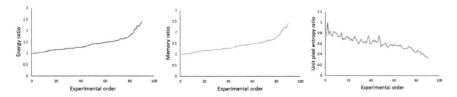

Fig. 3. Ratio of parameters before and after compression taken by Nikon camera.

As shown in Fig. 3, the abscissa order is sorted in ascending order according to the pixel ratio of the image before and after the resolution is adjusted. The memory ratio is proportional to the pixel ratio. The memory ratio and pixel ratio are independent of the unit pixel entropy ratio.

3.1.2   Gray Covariance Moment

The gray-level co-occurrence matrix [23] can describe the texture by studying the spatial correlation properties of the gray scale, and transform the spatial distribution information of the gray level into texture information. Haralick et al. [24] proposed 14 methods of texture quantization based on texture features such as uniformity, energy, variance, contrast, entropy, and inverse moment. In the boundary analysis, the energy parameters are used to construct the harmonic function boundary. Therefore, the energy ratio is chosen as the third dimension parameter.

3.2   Dimensional Space

Through the pixel ratio and the memory ratio of Fig. 3 is proportional to the ratio, with the associated nature, so these two parameters can only choose a participant in the data analysis; unit pixel entropy ratio is independent of the other two parameters. Therefore, this paper chooses the memory ratio, the unit pixel entropy ratio, and the energy ratio as the parameters to construct the clustering space.

Taking the Nikon camera as an example, the upper boundary vane image, which is suitable for segmentation, is suitable for segmentation of the blade image, and the resolution, unit pixel entropy of the image is extracted for each blade image and the appropriate segmented upper blade image after adjusting the resolution. Energy, adjust the resolution of these parameters and the appropriate division is the ratio of plant leaf parameters, constitute a three-dimensional space, as shown in Fig. 4.

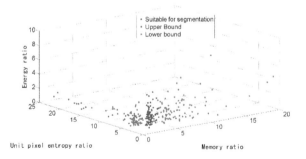

Fig. 4.   Three dimensional data distribution map taken by Nikon camera.

4   Cluster Analysis

Cluster analysis itself is based on data to explore the data object and its relationship information, and the data grouping. The objects within each group are similar, and the objects between the groups are irrelevant. The higher the similarity in the group, the higher the heterogeneity between groups, the better the clustering. In general, the clustering method is divided into hierarchical clustering method, hierarchical clustering algorithm, density-based clustering algorithm, model-based clustering algorithm and grid-based clustering algorithm. The clustering algorithm based on the partitioning method requires the number of given clusters K, and the number of classes based on the user-defined hope in the hierarchical partitioning method is usually the end condition. The clustering algorithm based on density, the clustering algorithm based on the model and the grid-based clustering algorithm can not determine the number of clustering clusters in advance. The data studied in this paper are clustered by the upper and lower bounds of the appropriate segmentation of the plant leaf image, and the number of clustering clusters is known in advance. In order to obtain the most suitable segmentation region, K-Means [25], BIRCH and K-Medoids were used for comparative analysis.

4.1 Clustering Experiments

By analyzing the data in Fig. 4, it is found that the data space domain effect is ideal, but the threshold of the appropriate segmentation space domain is obtained. Through the calculation of clustering parameters, it is possible to obtain the appropriate spatial domain parameters of plant leaves, which can give the threshold of quantization adjustment resolution and other feature quantity.

The clustering analysis of the data points in the three-dimensional space is carried out. The Nikon camera uses the k-means algorithm as an example to cluster the data points of different colors respectively. Figure 5 is a Nikon camera three-dimensional data clustering map. According to this can be summarized Nikon camera image clustering data information, as shown in Table 2.

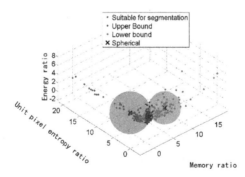

Fig. 5. Clustering space of three dimensional data taken by Nikon camera (ASM ratio). (Color figure online)

Table 2. Three dimensional data clustering information by Nikon camera.

Clustering algorithm	Spherical			
		Suitable for segmentation	Upper bound	Lower bound
K-Means	Coordinates	1.4073	0.3044	5.4744
		0.6145	4.6680	0.1865
		2.3564	1.7188	2.8003
	Radius	1.07	4.11	3.20
BIRCH	Coordinates	1.6388	0.4364	8.9659
		0.6603	9.0446	0.23
		2.8889	2.1712	4.3599
	Radius	3.55	9.12	6.32
K-Medoids	Coordinates	1.3769	0.3066	5.1053
		0.6148	3.6632	0.1777
		2.2725	1.6797	2.6835
	Radius	1.05	3.29	3.11

Similarly, Canon and Sony camera image clustering of data information, as shown in Tables 3 and 4.

Table 3. Three dimensional data clustering information by Canon camera.

Clustering algorithm	Spherical			
		Suitable for segmentation	Upper bound	Lower bound
K-Means	Coordinates	1.2723	0.2567	4.7749
		0.7913	6.4207	0.2667
		1.9610	1.4624	2.3417
	Radius	0.73	5.51	2.88
BIRCH	Coordinates	1.3633	0.2722	7.7996
		0.8764	10.9753	0.3356
		2.205	1.5037	2.4728
	Radius	2.7	10.49	5.65
K-Medoids	Coordinates	1.2642	0.2724	4.3015
		0.7911	4.8999	0.2560
		1.9121	1.4253	2.2711
	Radius	0.73	4.13	2.55

Table 4. Three dimensional data clustering information by Sonny camera.

Clustering algorithm	Spherical			
		Suitable for segmentation	Upper bound	Lower bound
K-Means	Coordinates	1.2548	0.2010	5.2534
		0.8328	10.0731	0.2198
		0.7834	0.6178	0.9291
	Radius	1.94	9.29	2.35
BIRCH	Coordinates	1.4507	(0.2503	8.7385
		0.8222	14.0611	0.2611
		1.112	0.7685	1.3843
	Radius	1.84	13.31	6.08
K-Medoids	Coordinates	1.2225	0.2089	4.9716
		0.8390	7.3437	0.2151
		0.7746	0.5997	0.8991
	Radius	1.94	6.84	2.30

Through the data from Tables 2, 3 and 4, we can see the clustering results, and provide the basis for improving the efficiency of blade segmentation.

(1) Through the analysis of the feature range, it is found that the leaf image has different feature quantity attributes with its resolution.

(2) Different camera equipment its suitable segmentation threshold range is different.

(3) Through the analysis of the appropriate threshold of different equipment, you can get the appropriate segmentation feature range of the device.

4.2 Clustering Results Analysis

Cluster analysis take Nikon camera as an example, select any single-leaf image, and adjust it to the three resolution fields shown in Fig. 5. Then, the image data points falling in the three clustering domains are selected, and their corresponding images are segmented edge contours to obtain three leaf edge contours as shown in Fig. 6.

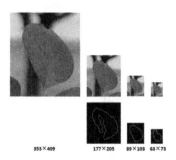

Fig. 6. The segmentation effect of new leave image by Nikon, Sonny and Canon camera.

From the edge of the camera segmentation effect, as shown in Figs. 5 and 6, the main process and the results are as follows.

(1) The three different sets of original resolution images of different cameras through the program automatically traverse cut to obtain a number of monolithic plant leaves of the image;

(2) According to the proportion of adjustment rules, the different equipment of the image group, adjust the resolution of the blade image and split its outline until the appropriate segmentation of the blade contour;

(3) Filtering the feature quantity of the adjusted image, and obtaining the appropriate resolution domain and the corresponding other feature range for each leaf image;

(4) For three-dimensional feature quantity clustering. The resolution field and the feature range of each segment are clustered according to their segmentation results. The image texture energy ratio of the gray level co-occurrence matrix based on the image is used as the third dimension data volume of the clustering space, and the three-dimensional data is clustered to obtain the appropriate segmentation feature. The range of gravity and the clustering radius of the upper bound of the feature quantity and the boundary of the appropriate segmentation feature;

(5) The clustering of each group is taken into the intersection to obtain the appropriate resolution of each device and the threshold of the eigenvalue clustering domain.

The resolution of the original image is adjusted by the clustering domain with the resolution ratio and the eigenvalue ratio, and the edge segmentation is carried out, which greatly improves the success rate and running efficiency of the existing segmentation algorithm. But because of its part of the data can not distinguish between its scope, therefore, need a reasonable boundary, in order to better define its appropriate segmentation of the region.

5 Three-Dimensional Harmonic Boundary

Aiming at the attribution problem of sample data points in overlapping regions of different camera clusters, this paper constructs the boundary function of overlapping clustering space, and divides the clustering space. And the three-dimensional clustering information of three camera devices is combined with Laplace equation and Gibbs free energy to reconcile the boundary function of clustering overlapping region.

5.1 Harmonic Boundary Function

The harmonic function equation is a second order continuous derivative function (which is an open subset) on the domain of the definition. The harmonic function satisfies the Laplace equation, that is, satisfies the Eq. (1):

$$\frac{\partial^2 f}{\partial x_1^2} + \frac{\partial^2 f}{\partial x_2^2} + \ldots + \frac{\partial^2 f}{\partial x_n^2} = 0 \tag{1}$$

Equations (1) can also be written or, where the symbol is called the Laplacian operator. The Laplace operator is defined as the divergence of the gradient and can represent the transport of matter due to the uneven distribution of matter. On the Riemannian manifold, the harmonic function has another definition. The Laplacian operator is called the Laplacian-Drumm operator. In this case, the harmonic function is satisfied.

Gibbs free energy is defined as:

$$G = U - TS + \rho V \tag{2}$$

Where G is Gibbs free energy, U is the internal energy of the whole system, T is the temperature of the system, S is the entropy of the system, ρ is the pressure, V is the volume, and $H = U + \rho V$ is the enthalpy of the system. At room temperature and pressure system, Gibbs free energy can be completely determined by the system's internal energy.

By constructing the surface satisfying the harmonic function Eq. (1), we can determine the boundary between the "complete segmentation" and the "lower bound" medium clustering domain. The Laplace pressure between the two clusters is used to obtain the curve equation. Together, the formula for the Laplace pressure can be deduced from the Young-Laplacian formula:

$$\Delta P \equiv P_{in} - P_{out} = \gamma \left(\frac{1}{R_1} + \frac{1}{R_2} \right) \tag{3}$$

Where R_1 and R_2 are the radius of curvature and γ is the tension coefficient of the surface. In general, the convex surface can be represented by a positive curvature radius, and the concave surface is represented by a negative curvature radius. By the definition of the surface tension coefficient, it can be seen that the surface tension coefficient γ can be obtained by the partial derivative of the area A of Gibbs free energy G in the case where the temperature T and the pressure P remain constant:

$$\gamma = \left(\frac{\partial G}{\partial A} \right)_{T,P} \tag{4}$$

The Gaussian free energy G of the sphere can be substituted into the Eq. (4) by calculating the sum of the sum of the squares of the elements of the normalized image and the second order moments in the angular direction. The curve equation fits the desired set of points.

5.2 The Construction of 3D Boundary Function and the Correctness

The attribution of sample data points in overlapping regions of different camera clusters requires the use of Gibbs free energy as the basis for constructing the harmonic boundary.

The two spherical domains are modeled into two different media, and the data fitting points of the three cameras are obtained by calculating their free energy, and then the harmonic boundary equation is found.

The steps to obtain three fitting points include:

First, calculate the Laplace pressure difference:

Gibbs free energy expression for the $G = U - TS + \rho V$, due to the system at room temperature and pressure, so the free energy changes only by the system's own energy. The total value G_1 of the image energy value after the compression resolution of 90 data points in the "complete segmentation" sphere, the surface area S_1 of the "complete segmentation" sphere, and the compression resolution of 90 data points in the "lower bound" sphere The total value of the image energy after the value of G_2, the "lower bound" sphere surface area S_2. The surface tension γ_1 and γ_2 of "complete segmentation" and "lower bound" are obtained by using the surface tension formula $\gamma = G/S$, then the difference between the energy per unit area of the "suitable segmentation" and the "lower bound" cluster sphere is $\Delta\gamma = \gamma_1 - \gamma_2$. Into the formula (2) can be obtained between the two spheres of the Laplace pressure difference ΔP;

Second, the boundary fixed:

The pressure difference is projected onto the two core wires, and the boundary vertices of the harmonic function are obtained.

Third, calculate the two fitting points:

With the energy of the ball on the distance from the two spherical distance from the farthest point as a fitting point.

Fourth, calculate the boundary parameters:

According to the vertex and two fitting points can be determined to determine the center of the boundary and radius.

According to the above steps, the boundary functions are determined as shown in Table 5.

The results show that the efficiency of the segmentation of the plant leaves in the boundary is shown in Table 6 by analyzing the results of 90 suitable segmentation resolution domains.

Through the above comparison, the boundary obtained by K-Means clustering algorithm is the best, because the boundary obtained by this algorithm can adjust the blade image segmentation.

5.3 Segmentation Success Rate of Three-Dimensional Limit Function

Under natural light, the obtained leaf image of the plant was selected and 30 leaflets were selected for validation. The experimental flow is shown in Fig. 7. The efficiency of the plant leaves before and after the adjustment of the equipment is shown in Table 7. The results show that there is no adjustment of the resolution directly on the split edge of the edge of the edge of the success rate is relatively low, the average running time is longer.

Table 5. Three dimensional harmonic boundary function.

Clustering algorithm	Camera equipment	Dimensional harmonic boundary function	Domain
K-Means	Nikon	$(x - 0.25)^2 + (y - 4.87)^2$ $+ (z - 1.69)^2 = 4.19^2$ $(x - 5.6)^2 + (y - 0.17)^2$ $+ (z - 2.81)^2 = 3.29^2$	$(4.19 * x - 0.44 * y$ $+ 0.46 * z - 24.66 < 0)$ $(1.16 * x - 4.26 * y$ $+ 0.67 * z - 19.3 > 0)$
	Canon	$(x - 0.14)^2 + (y - 7.05)^2$ $+ (z - 1.41)^2 = 6.11^2$ $(x - 7.85)^2 + (y + 0.19)^2$ $+ (z - 2.68)^2 = 6^2$	$(1.13 * x - 6.25 * y$ $+ 0.55 * z + 43.12 > 0)$ $(6.58 * x - 0.98 * y$ $+ 0.71 * z - 53.73 < 0)$
	Sonny	$(x - 0.18)^2 + (y - 10.28)^2$ $+ (z - 0.61)^2 = 9.3^2$ $(x - 5.37)^2 + (y - 0.2)^2$ $+ (z - 0.93)^2 = 2.36^2$	$(1.08 * x - 9.45 * y$ $+ 0.17 * z + 96.82 > 0)$ $(4.11 * x - 0.63 * y$ $+ 0.15 * z - 22.08 < 0)$
BIRCH	Nikon	$(x - 0.33)^2 + (y - 9.79)^2$ $+ (z - 2.11)^2 = 9.15^2$ $(x - 9.75)^2 + (y - 0.18)^2$ $+ (z - 4.52)^2 = 6.38^2$	$(1.31 * x - 9.13 * y$ $+ 0.78 * z + 87.22 > 0)$ $(8.11 * x - 0.48 * y$ $+ 1.63 * z - 86.42 < 0)$
	Canon	$(x - 0.23)^2 + (y - 11.33)^2$ $+ (z - 1.48)^2 = 10.49^2$ $(x - 8.34)^2 + (y - 0.3)^2$ $+ (z - 2.5)^2 = 5.68^2$	$(1.13 * x - 10.52 * y$ $- 0.73 * z + 117.82 > 0)$ $(6.98 * x - 0.52 * y$ $+ 0.29 * z - 58.74 < 0)$
	Sonny	$(x - 0.24)^2 + (y - 14.19)^2$ $+ (z - 0.77)^2 = 13.31^2$ $(x - 8.87)^2 + (y - 0.25)^2$ $+ (z - 1.39)^2 = 6.09^2$	$(1.21 * x - 13.37 * y$ $+ 0.35 * z + 189.15 > 0)$ $(7.42 * x - 0.57 * y$ $+ 0.28 * z - 66.09 < 0)$
K-Medoids	Nikon	$(x - 0.2)^2 + (y - 3.96)^2$ $+ (z - 1.62)^2 = 3.44^2$ $(x - 5.33)^2 + (y - 0.15)^2$ $+ (z - 2.71)^2 = 3.25^2$	$(1.17 * x - 3.34 * y$ $+ 0.65 * z + 11.95 > 0)$ $(3.96 * x - 0.46 * y$ $+ 0.44 * z - 22.2 < 0)$
	Canon	$(x - 0.01)^2 + (y - 6)^2$ $+ (z - 1.29)^2 = 5.21^2$ $(x - 10.97)^2 + (y - 0.92)^2$ $+ (z - 3.06)^2 = 9.33^2$	$(1.26 * x - 5.21 * y + 0.62 * z$ $+ 30.48 > 0)$ $(9.7 * x - 1.71 * y$ $+ 1.15 * z - 111.53 < 0)$
	Sonny	$(x - 0.16)^2 + (y - 7.64)^2$ $+ (z - 0.59)^2 = 6.85^2$ $(x - 5.19)^2 + (y - 0.18)^2$ $+ (z - 0.91)^2 = 2.32^2$	$(1.06 * x - 6.8 * y$ $+ 0.18 * z + 51.61 > 0)$ $(3.96 * x - 0.66 * y$ $+ 0.13 * z - 20.56 < 0)$

Table 6. The correctness of the constructor.

Clustering algorithm	Camera equipment	Correct rate %
K-Means	Nikon	92.22
	Canon	97.78
	Sonny	94.44
BIRCH	Nikon	78.89
	Canon	80
	Sonny	77.5
K-Medoids	Nikon	80
	Canon	84.44
	Sonny	58.89

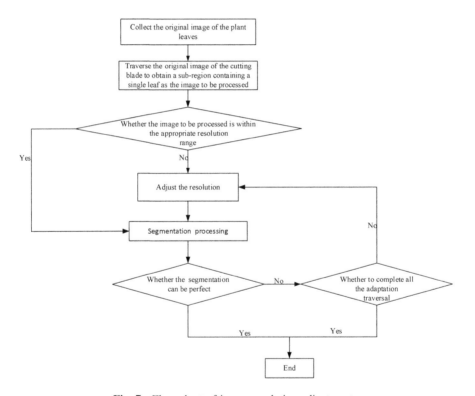

Fig. 7. Flow chart of image resolution adjustment.

Table 7. The segmentation efficiency changes between the leave images before and after the characteristic parameters.

Camera equipment	Before adjustment		After adjustment	
	The rate of segmentation/%	Time/m	The rate of segmentation/%	Time/m
Nikon	26.67	>20	73.33	1.14
Sonny	23.33	>20	66.67	1.26
Canon	33.33	>20	70	1.05

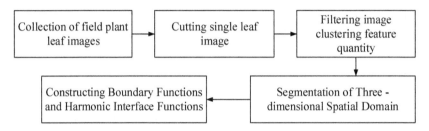

Fig. 8. The process of obtaining the spatial domain of image features and spatial resolution

6 Conclusion

In this paper, the plant leaf images collected from different cameras (Nikon, Canon and Sony, respectively) were used as the object of study. After a large number of feature information were extracted and sorted, the clustering analysis was carried out, and the leaf image was pretreated by resolution adjustment. The image is in a reasonable feature range based on clustering analysis. Which effectively prevents the computer from consuming too much load operation. At the same time, it effectively solves the problem that the real edge of the leaf area information is too large is difficult to distinguish. After analyzing the feature area of different devices by clustering processing of feature area, the appropriate segmentation feature area of each device is established. And the image based on the domain is adjusted according to the feature size of the image for efficient segmentation.

According to the above experimental and experimental results, the process of leaf image feature and resolution adjustment is shown in Fig. 8.

According to the study of this paper, the resolution size is a factor that affects its segmentation effect and segmentation time. Another factor is the physical characteristics of the image capture device. In order to improve the segmentation success rate of the program and improve the efficiency of the algorithm, this paper obtains the resolution range of each device adapting to the algorithm by comparing the resolution of different cameras and improves the success rate and efficiency of the algorithm. (Image energy, entropy, moment of inertia, correlation), and select the appropriate parameters to do the clustering analysis, to find out the resolution of the image (the number of pixels), the memory, the unit pixel entropy and the image grayscale covariance matrix texture feature vector. The center of gravity of the clustering domain and the radius and feasible domain, and the boundary of the resolution adjustment feature corresponding to the segmentation algorithm for the captured image of the device is determined.

Acknowledgments. This work was supported by the Beijing 'The agricultural technology promotion information project in Hebei Province' program and was undertaken by China Agricultural University.

References

1. Zhou, Y., Gao, M., Fang, D., Zhang, B.: Unsupervised background-constrained tank segmentation of infrared images in complex background based on the Otsu method. SpringerPlus. **5**(1), 1–15 (2016)
2. Jiang, W., Zhou, H., Shen, Y., Liu, B., Fu, Z.: Image segmentation with pulse-coupled neural network and Canny operators. Comput. Electr. Eng. **46**, 528–538 (2015)
3. Wang, M., Wang, Y., Chai, L.: Application of an improved watershed algorithm in welding image segmentation. Russ. J. Nondestr. Test. **47**(5), 352–357 (2011)
4. Frulla, L., Lira, J.: An automated region growing algorithm for segmentation of texture regions in SAR images. Int. J. Remote Sens. **19**(18), 3595–3606 (1998)
5. Wu, G., Zhao, X., Luo, S., Shi, H.: Histological image segmentation using fast mean shift clustering method. Biomed. Eng. Online **14**(1), 1–12 (2015)
6. Chen, M.F., Zhu, H.S., Zhu, H.J.: Segmentation of liver in ultrasonic images applying local optimal threshold method. Imaging Sci. J. **61**(7), 579–591 (2013)
7. Wang, J., He, J., Han, Y.: An adaptive thresholding algorithm of field leaf image. Comput. Electron. Agric. **2013**(96), 23–39 (2013)
8. Dhalia Sweetlin, J., Khanna Nehemiah, H., Kannan, A.: Patient-specific model based segmentation of lung computed tomographic images. J. Inf. Sci. Eng. **32**(5), 1373–1394 (2016)
9. Kim, B.-G., Shim, J.-I., Park, D.-J.: Fast image segmentation based on multi-resolution analysis and wavelets. Pattern Recogn. Lett. **24**(16), 2995–3006 (2002)
10. Frucci, M., Ramella, G., Sanniti di Baja, G.: Using resolution pyramids for watershed image segmentation. Image Vis. Comput. **25**(6), 1021–1031 (2007)
11. Liao, C.-C., Xiao, F., Wong, J.-M., Chiang, I.-J.: A multiresolution binary level set method and its application to intracranial hematoma segmentation. Comput. Med. Imaging Graph. **33**(6), 423–430 (2009)
12. Wang, W., Qin, J., Chui, Y.P., Heng, P.A.: A multiresolution framework for ultrasound image segmentation by combinative active contours. IEEE Eng. Med. Biol. Soc. **2013**, 1144–1147 (2013)
13. Zhu, H., Cai, L., Liu, H., Huang, W.: Information extraction of high resolution remote sensing images based on the calculation of optimal segmentation parameters. PLoS One **11**(6), 1–15 (2016)
14. Moallem, P., Razmjooy, N., Mousavi, B.S.: Robust potato color image segmentation using adaptive fuzzy inference system. Iran. J. Fuzzy Syst. **11**(6), 47–65 (2014)
15. Delibasis, K.K., Goudas, T., Maglogiannis, I.: A novel robust approach for handling illumination changes in video segmentation. Eng. Appl. Artif. Intell. **49**, 43–60 (2016)

16. Huang, Z., Zhang, J., Li, X., Zhang, H.: Remote sensing image segmentation based on dynamic statistical region merging. Optik - Int. J. Light Electron Optics **125**(2), 870–875 (2014)
17. Saksa, T., Uuttera, J., Kolström, T., Lehikoinen, M., Pekkarinen, A., Sarvi, V.: Clear-cut detection in boreal forest aided by remote sensing. Scand. J. For. Res. **18**(6), 537–546 (2003)
18. Zhang, X., Xiao, P., Song, X., She, J.: Boundary-constrained multi-scale segmentation method for remote sensing images. ISPRS J. Photogramm. Remote Sens. **78**, 15–25 (2013)
19. Meged, A., Gelbard, R.: Adjusting fuzzy similarity functions for use with standard data mining tools. J. Syst. Softw. **84**(12), 2374–2383 (2011)
20. Dee Miller, L., Soh, L.-K., Scott, S.: Genetic algorithm classifier system for semi-supervised learning. Comput. Intell. **31**(2), 201–232 (2015)
21. Ji, J., Pang, W., Zhou, C., Han, X., Wang, Z.: A fuzzy k-prototype clustering algorithm for mixed numeric and categorical data. Knowl.-Based Syst. **30**, 129–135 (2012)
22. Hong, X., Wang, J., Qi, G.: Comparison of semi-supervised and supervised approaches for classification of e-nose datasets: case studies of tomato juices. Chemom. Intell. Lab. Syst. **146**, 457–463 (2015)
23. MacQueen, J.: Soma methods for classification and analysis of multivariate observations. In: Proceedings of the Symposium on Mathematical Statistics and Probability, pp. 281–297. University of California Press, Berkeley (1967)
24. Haralick, R.M., Shanmugam, K., Dinstein, I.H.: Textural features for image classification. IEEE Trans. Syst. Man Cybern. **3**(6), 610–621 (1973)
25. Kim, H.A., Karp, B.: Autograph: toward automated distributed worm signature detection. In: Proceedings of the 13th Usenix Security Symposium (2004)

Channel Estimation Based on Approximated Power Iteration Subspace Tracking for Massive MIMO Systems

Liming Zheng, Donglai Zhao, Gang Wang$^{(\boxtimes)}$, Yao Xu, and Yue Wu

Harbin Institute of Technology, Harbin, China
{zheng, gwang51, wuy}@hit.edu.cn, zd1527@126.com,
1101698146@qq.com

Abstract. Traditional semi-blind channel estimator is based on eigen value decomposition (EVD) or singular value decomposition (SVD), which effectively reduces the interference through dividing the observed signal into signal subspace and noise subspace. Due to the large computation, Massive MIMO systems could not afford the cost of traditional algorithms in spite of the high performance. In this paper, we propose a channel estimation algorithm based on subspace tracking, in which the signal subspace is obtained by approximating power iteration algorithm. Without sacrificing the estimation performance, the complexity is greatly reduced compared with the traditional semi-blind channel estimation algorithm, which improves the applicability of the estimator.

Keywords: Massive MIMO · Channel estimation · Semi-blind
Subspace tracking

1 Introduction

Massive MIMO technology greatly improves the system capacity and spectrum efficiency [1–4] through installing hundreds or thousands of antennas at BSs. It has become one of the key technologies of 5G now. The dimension of the channel state matrix increases with the number of antennas, which results in higher requirements for the channel estimation algorithm. Pilot contamination is particularly prominent in Massive MIMO system, so it's a serious problem to seek low complexity and anti-pilot contamination channel estimation algorithm.

The pilot-based channel estimation algorithms can't completely eliminate the effects of pilot contamination [5–7], while full-blind or semi-blind channel estimation algorithms don't require pilots or transmit fewer short pilots, thus avoiding pilot contamination. The subspace based channel estimation algorithm divides observation signal into signal subspace and noise subspace, which effectively reduces the interference and obtains the excellent estimation performance. Ngo. B. Q proposed a EVD based channel estimation algorithm to transform the channel estimation problem into the problem of ambiguous matrix. Through the eigenvalue decomposition of the received vector covariance matrix, the channel vector can be expressed as a corresponding eigenvector multiplying a scalar ambiguous factor, and the ambiguous factors constitute an ambiguous diagonal matrix [8]. The estimation performance and error

© ICST Institute for Computer Sciences, Social Informatics and Telecommunications Engineering 2018
X. Gu et al. (Eds.): MLICOM 2017, Part I, LNICST 226, pp. 76–84, 2018.
https://doi.org/10.1007/978-3-319-73564-1_8

term of EVD based algorithm are theoretically deduced and analyzed in [9], then the generalized linear (WL) algorithm is proposed. Dr. Hu proposed a semi-blind channel estimation algorithm based on SVD for Massive MIMO systems, like the method in [8], singular value decomposition of the received vector covariance matrix is needed. The ambiguity matrix of SVD based channel estimator is not a diagonal matrix, but a square matrix, which reduces the error caused by the non-orthogonal channel [10].

EVD and SVD algorithm have a large computational complexity $O(M^3)$, where M is the dimension of the received vector. When the number of antennas in the BS reaches hundreds, the huge complexity of EVD or SVD based algorithm is unacceptable in Massive MIMO systems. In this paper, a subspace tracking based channel estimation algorithm is proposed, which uses the approximation power iteration algorithm to obtain the signal subspace with fast convergence and low complexity, the computational complexity to solve signal subspace of each iteration is $O(MK^2)$ using API algorithm, FAPI algorithm needs only $O(MK)$ operations for each update [11], K is the number of users in each cell.

2 System Model

Consider a multiuser Massive MIMO system with L cells that share the same band of frequencies, each cell contains K single-antenna users and one central BS equipped with M antennas. The system works in time-division duplex, so the uplink channel matrix is just the transpose of the downlink matrix because of the channel reciprocity. We consider the uplink where the users in the system synchronously send signals to BSs, the received signal vector at the BS of the jth cell can be expressed as

$$\mathbf{y}_j = \sqrt{p_\mathrm{u}} \sum_{i=1}^{L} \mathbf{G}_{ji}\mathbf{x}_i + \mathbf{w}_j \tag{1}$$

$$\mathbf{G}_{ji} = \mathbf{H}_{ji}\mathbf{D}_{ji}^{1/2} \tag{2}$$

where $\mathbf{x}_i$ is the transmitted symbols by the K users from the ith cell. p_u is the average power used by each user. $\mathbf{H}_{ji}$ is the $M \times K$ matrix of fast fading coefficients between K users in the ith cell and the jth BS. $\mathbf{D}_{ji}^{1/2}$ is a $K \times K$ diagonal matrix representing the geometric attenuation and shadow fading, diagonal elements are $\left[\mathbf{D}_{ji}\right]_{kk} = \beta_{jik}.\mathbf{w}_j$ is additive Gaussian white noise with zero mean and unit variance.

3 Traditional Semi-blind Channel Estimation

In this section, EVD and SVD based semi-blind channel estimator will be introduced.

3.1 EVD Based Estimator

The covariance matrix of the received vector $\mathbf{y}_j$ can be expressed as

$$\mathbf{R}_y \triangleq E\{\mathbf{y}_j\mathbf{y}_j^H\} = p_u \sum_{i=1}^{L} \mathbf{H}_{ji}\mathbf{D}_{ji}\mathbf{H}_{ji}^H + \mathbf{I}_M \tag{3}$$

The channel vectors are approximately orthogonal in the Massive MIMO systems. multiplying (3) from the right by $\mathbf{H}_{jj}$, then we can obtain

$$\mathbf{R}_y\mathbf{H}_{jj} \approx \mathbf{H}_{jj}(Mp_u\mathbf{D}_{jj} + \mathbf{I}_K) \tag{4}$$

When M trends to infinity, the columns of $\mathbf{H}_{jj}$ are approximately orthogonal, and $Mp_u\mathbf{D}_{jj} + \mathbf{I}_K$ is a diagonal matrix. So Eq. (4) can be considered as a characteristic equation for the covariance matrix $\mathbf{R}_y$, the kth column of $\mathbf{H}_{jj}$ is the eigenvector corresponding to the eigenvalue $Mp\beta_{jjk} + \sigma_w^2$ of $\mathbf{R}_y$. Each column of $\mathbf{H}_{jj}$ can be expressed as a corresponding eigenvector multiplying a scalar ambiguous factor, which is

$$\hat{\mathbf{H}}_{jj}^{EVD} = \mathbf{U}_j\mathbf{C} \tag{5}$$

where $\mathbf{U}_j$ is the $M \times K$ eigenvector matrix. Ambiguity matrix $\mathbf{C}$ is K-order diagonal matrix, the ambiguity can be solved by using a short pilot sequence.

In practice, this covariance matrix is unavailable. Instead, we use the sample data covariance matrix $\hat{\mathbf{R}}_y$ as the estimate of $\mathbf{R}_y$,

$$\hat{\mathbf{R}}_y \triangleq \frac{1}{N_d} \sum_{n=1}^{N_d} \mathbf{y}_j(n)\mathbf{y}_j(n)^H \tag{6}$$

The EVD-based channel estimation algorithm is as follows,

(1) Given the number of samples N_d, compute $\hat{\mathbf{R}}_y$.
(2) Perform EVD of $\hat{\mathbf{R}}_y$, then obtain $\mathbf{U}_j$.
(3) Obtain the estimate $\hat{\mathbf{C}}$ of ambiguity matrix using a short pilot sequence.
(4) Obtain the channel estimate as $\hat{\mathbf{H}}_{jj}^{EVD} = \mathbf{U}_j\hat{\mathbf{C}}$.

3.2   SVD Based Estimators

The channel estimation based on EVD algorithm utilizes orthogonality of the channel vectors, However, the antenna number M in the actual system is not infinite, The channel vectors are not perfectly orthogonal. The ambiguity matrix of SVD based channel estimator is not a diagonal matrix, but a square matrix, which reduces the error caused by the non-orthogonal channel.

The channel matrix can be expressed as

$$\mathbf{H}_{ji} = \tilde{\mathbf{H}}_{ji}\mathbf{\Gamma}_i \tag{7}$$

where $\Gamma_i \in \mathbb{C}^{K \times K}$ represents the error between the real channel matrix $\mathbf{H}_{ji}$ and the orthogonal channel matrix $\tilde{\mathbf{H}}_{ji}$. Substituting into (3), then $\mathbf{R}_y = p_u \sum\limits_{i=1}^{L} \tilde{\mathbf{H}}_{ji} \mathbf{A}_{ji} \tilde{\mathbf{H}}_{ji}^{\mathrm{H}} + \mathbf{I}_M$, where the k-order normal matrix $\mathbf{A}_{ji} = \Gamma_i \mathbf{D}_{ji} \Gamma_i^{\mathrm{H}}$ and its SVD form $\mathbf{A}_{ji} = \mathbf{V}_i \tilde{\Sigma}_i \mathbf{V}_i^{\mathrm{H}}$, $\mathbf{V}_i \in \mathbb{C}^{K \times K}$ is the left-singular matrix. Therefore, $\mathbf{R}_y$ can be expressed as

$$\mathbf{R}_y = p_u \sum_{i=1}^{L} \tilde{\mathbf{H}}_{ji} \mathbf{V}_i \tilde{\Sigma}_i \mathbf{V}_i^{\mathrm{H}} \tilde{\mathbf{H}}_{ji}^{\mathrm{H}} + \mathbf{I}_M \tag{8}$$

$\mathbf{R}_y$ is also a normal matrix and its SVD can be expressed as

$$\mathbf{R}_y = \mathbf{Q}_j \Sigma_j \mathbf{Q}_j^{\mathrm{H}} \tag{9}$$

where $\mathbf{Q}_j$ contains M singular vectors; Σ_j is a real diagonal matrix which contains M singular values with descending order. $\mathbf{Q}_j = \left[\mathbf{Q}_j^s, \mathbf{Q}_j^n \right]$, where $\mathbf{Q}_j^s \in \mathbb{C}^{M \times K}$, $\mathbf{Q}_j^n \in \mathbb{C}^{M \times (M-K)}$. The columns of $\frac{1}{\sqrt{M}} \tilde{\mathbf{H}}_{ji} \mathbf{V}_i$ are the left-singular vectors that correspond to the largest KL singular values of $\mathbf{R}_y$. Assuming $\beta_{jjk} \gg \beta_{jik}$, $\mathbf{Q}_j^s$ can be denoted as $\mathbf{Q}_j^s = \frac{1}{\sqrt{M}} (\tilde{\mathbf{H}}_{jj} + \mathbf{F}_j) \mathbf{V}_j \mathbf{B}_j$. $\mathbf{F}_j = \sqrt{M} \mathbf{O}_j \mathbf{V}_j^{\mathrm{H}}$ corresponds to the ICI in the received data symbols, $\mathbf{B}_j$ is a permutation matrix. Despite $\mathbf{F}_j$, we obtain

$$\mathbf{Q}_j^s = \frac{1}{\sqrt{M}} \mathbf{H}_{jj} \mathbf{E}_j \tag{10}$$

where $\mathbf{E}_j = \Gamma_j^{-1} \mathbf{V}_j \mathbf{B}_j$, ambiguity matrix $\mathbf{E}_j$ is approximately a unitary matrix, the estimate of $\mathbf{E}_j$ can be resolved by pilot,

$$\hat{\mathbf{E}}_j = \frac{1}{\sqrt{M}} (\hat{\mathbf{H}}_{jj}^{\mathrm{LS}})^{\mathrm{H}} \mathbf{Q}_j^s \tag{11}$$

From (10) and (11), we obtain the channel estimate,

$$\hat{\mathbf{H}}_{jj}^{\mathrm{SVD}} = \mathbf{Q}_j^s (\mathbf{Q}_j^s)^{\mathrm{H}} \hat{\mathbf{H}}_{jj}^{\mathrm{LS}} \tag{12}$$

The SVD-based channel estimation algorithm is as follows,

(1) Given the number of samples N_d, compute $\hat{\mathbf{R}}_y$.
(2) Perform SVD of $\hat{\mathbf{R}}_y$, then obtain $\mathbf{Q}_j^s$.
(3) Compute the pilot-based channel estimate $\hat{\mathbf{H}}_{jj}^{\mathrm{LS}}$.
(4) Obtain the channel estimate as $\hat{\mathbf{H}}_{jj}^{\mathrm{SVD}} = \mathbf{Q}_j^s (\mathbf{Q}_j^s)^{\mathrm{H}} \hat{\mathbf{H}}_{jj}^{\mathrm{LS}}$.

4   Subspace Tracking Based Channel Estimation

Although EVD and SVD-based algorithms effectively reduce the interference, but the complexity is too large to apply to Massive MIMO system.

The subspace tracking based channel estimation algorithm is similar to the principle based on SVD, except that the method of obtaining the signal subspace is different. The algorithm steps are as follows,

(1) Given the number of samples N_d.
(2) Obtain the signal subspace estimate $\tilde{\mathbf{Q}}_j^s$ using subspace tracking algorithm.
(3) Compute the pilot-based channel estimate $\hat{\mathbf{H}}_{jj}^{LS}$.
(4) Obtain the channel estimate as $\hat{\mathbf{H}}_{jj}^{ST-CE} = \tilde{\mathbf{Q}}_j^s (\tilde{\mathbf{Q}}_j^s)^H \hat{\mathbf{H}}_{jj}^{LS}$.

4.1   API Subspace Tracking Algorithm

The approximated power iteration subspace algorithm is an improvement to the power iteration algorithm. Firstly, we introduce the idea of the power iteration subspace tracking algorithm.

The covariance matrix of the received vector $\mathbf{y}(n)$ can be expressed as

$$\mathbf{R}_{yy}(n) = \sum_{m=-\infty}^{n} \tau^{n-m} \mathbf{y}(n) \mathbf{y}(n)^H \tag{13}$$

where τ is the forgetting factor. The covariance matrix can be recursively updated according to the following scheme,

$$\mathbf{R}_{yy}(n) = \tau \mathbf{R}_{yy}(n-1) + \mathbf{y}(n) \mathbf{y}(n)^H \tag{14}$$

Let the $M \times K$ orthogonal matrix $\mathbf{Q}(n)$ be transformed into the dominant subspace of $\mathbf{R}_{yy}(n)$, then the compressed received vector $\mathbf{r}(n) = \mathbf{Q}(n-1)^H \mathbf{y}(n)$. The power iteration method tracks the dominant subspace by the following compression step and orthonormalization step,

$$\mathbf{R}_{yr}(n) = \mathbf{R}_{yy}(n) \mathbf{Q}(n-1) \tag{15}$$

$$\mathbf{Q}(n)\Psi(n) = \mathbf{R}_{yr}(n) \tag{16}$$

where $\Psi(n)$ a non-negative Hermitian matrix, and satisfying $\Psi(n)^H \Psi(n) = \mathbf{R}_{yr}(n)^H \mathbf{R}_{yr}(n)$. If $\mathbf{R}_{yy}(n)$ remains constant and its first K eigenvalues are strictly larger than the M-K others, the power iteration method converges globally and exponentially to the dominant subspace.

By introducing the compensation matrix and the auxiliary matrix, the API algorithm makes $\mathbf{Q}(n)$ and $\mathbf{R}_{yr}(n)$ independent recursive operations, and avoids the complicated process of solving $\Psi(n)$. The steps of the API algorithm are shown in Table 1.

Table 1. API algorithm

Step	Complexity
Initialization: $\mathbf{Q}(0) = [\mathbf{I}_k; \mathbf{0}_{(M-k)\times k}]$, $\mathbf{Z}(0) = \mathbf{I}_k$	
FOR $n = 1, 2, \cdots, N_d$	
$\mathbf{r}(n) = \mathbf{Q}(n-1)^{\mathrm{H}}\mathbf{y}(n)$	MK
$\mathbf{h}(n) = \mathbf{Z}(n-1)\mathbf{r}(n)$	K^2
$\mathbf{g}(n) = \frac{\mathbf{h}(n)}{\tau + \mathbf{r}(n)^{\mathrm{H}}\mathbf{h}(n)}$	$2K$
$\mathbf{e}(n) = \mathbf{y}(n) - \mathbf{Q}(n-1)\mathbf{r}(n)$	MK
$\mathbf{\Theta}(n) = (\mathbf{I}_k + \|\mathbf{e}(n)\|^2 \mathbf{g}(n)\mathbf{g}(n)^{\mathrm{H}})^{-\frac{1}{2}}$	$M + \mathrm{O}(K^3)$
$\mathbf{Z}(n) = \frac{1}{\tau}\mathbf{\Theta}(n)^{\mathrm{H}}(\mathbf{I}_k - \mathbf{g}(n)\mathbf{y}(n)^{\mathrm{H}})\mathbf{Z}(n-1)\mathbf{\Theta}(n)^{-\mathrm{H}}$	$\mathrm{O}(K^3)$
$\mathbf{Q}(n) = (\mathbf{Q}(n-1) + \mathbf{e}(n)\mathbf{g}(n)^{\mathrm{H}})\mathbf{\Theta}(n)$	$MK^2 + MK$
End	

4.2 FAPI Subspace Tracking Algorithm

The fast approximated power iteration algorithm optimizes the solution process of the compensation matrix, thus speeding up the convergence. The steps of the FAPI algorithm are shown in Table 2.

Table 2. FAPI algorithm

Step	Complexity
Initialization: $\mathbf{Q}(0) = [\mathbf{I}_k; \mathbf{0}_{(M-k)\times k}]$, $\mathbf{Z}(0) = \mathbf{I}_k$	
FOR $n = 1, 2, \cdots, N_d$	
$\mathbf{r}(n) = \mathbf{Q}(n-1)^{\mathrm{H}}\mathbf{y}(n)$	MK
$\mathbf{h}(n) = \mathbf{Z}(n-1)\mathbf{r}(n)$	K^2
$\varepsilon^2(n) = \|\mathbf{y}(n)\|^2 - \|\mathbf{r}(n)\|^2$	$M + K$
$\vartheta(n) = \frac{\varepsilon^2(n)}{1 + \varepsilon^2(n)\|\mathbf{g}(n)\|^2 + \sqrt{1 + \varepsilon^2(n)\|\mathbf{g}(n)\|^2}}$	K
$\eta(n) = 1 - \vartheta(n)\|\mathbf{g}(n)\|^2$	1
$\mathbf{r}'(n) = \mathbf{r}(n)\eta(n) + \mathbf{g}(n)\vartheta(n)$	$2K$
$\mathbf{h}'(n) = \mathbf{Z}(n-1)^{\mathrm{H}}\mathbf{r}'(n)$	K^2
$\varepsilon(n) = \frac{\vartheta(n)}{\eta(n)}(\mathbf{Z}(n-1)\mathbf{g}(n) - \mathbf{h}'(n)^{\mathrm{H}}\mathbf{g}(n)\mathbf{g}(n))$	$K^2 + 3K$
$\mathbf{Z}(n) = \frac{1}{\tau}(\mathbf{Z}(n-1) - \mathbf{g}(n)\mathbf{h}'(n)^{\mathrm{H}} + \varepsilon(n)\mathbf{g}(n)^{\mathrm{H}})$	$2K^2$
$\mathbf{e}'(n) = \mathbf{y}(n)\eta(n) - \mathbf{Q}(n-1)\mathbf{r}'(n)$	$MK + M$
$\mathbf{Q}(n) = \mathbf{Q}(n-1) + \mathbf{e}'(n)\mathbf{g}(n)^{\mathrm{H}}$	MK
End	

4.3 Complexity Analysis

API algorithm has a computational complexity $MK^2 + O(MK)$ for each update, FAPI algorithm needs only $3MK + O(M)$ operations for each update. The number of samples is N_d, the complexity to obtain $K \times K$-dimensional signal subspace based on different algorithms is shown in Table 3.

Table 3. Algorithm complexity

Algorithm	Complexity
SVD	$O(M^3) + N_d M^2$
API-CE	$N_d MK^2 + N_d O(MK)$
FAPI-CE	$3N_d MK + N_d O(M)$

Obviously, the FAPI based channel estimation algorithm greatly reduces the complexity of the SVD based algorithm, and the simulation analysis based on the subspace tracking channel estimation algorithm will be introduced in the next section.

5 Simulation Results

Let $M = 128$, $K = 4$, $L = 3$. The large scale fading of the main cell take the random value of 0.6–1, and the large scale fading of the adjacent cells take the random value of 0.1–0.4. The modulation mode is BPSK. The estimation accuracy of the various algorithms is measured by the normalized mean square error (NMSE), which is defined as follows,

$$\text{NMSE} = \frac{\left\| \hat{\mathbf{H}} - \mathbf{H} \right\|_F^2}{\left\| \mathbf{H} \right\|_F^2} \tag{10}$$

where $\hat{\mathbf{H}}$ is the channel estimate of $\mathbf{H}$.

The simulation results of the channel estimation algorithm based on subspace tracking are shown in Fig. 1, and the performance curves of EVD and SVD are also given for comparative analysis.

As the simulation shown, the API-CE and FAPI-CE channel estimation algorithms approach to the estimation performance of the SVD-based algorithm, and outperform the EVD-based algorithm. When SNR is 10 dB, the performance of the proposed algorithm is improved by nearly 10 dB compared with EVD algorithm. With the increase of SNR, the estimation accuracy of the proposed algorithm is higher, but the performance of EVD algorithm is not improved significantly because of the nonorthogonality part of the channel vectors.

As shown in Fig. 2, with the increase of antenna number, the estimation accuracy of API-CE and FAPI-CE algorithm both improve. When M grows from 100 to 300, the NMSE curve decreased significantly, the main source of error at this time is the channel

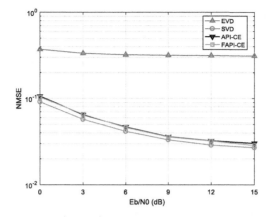

Fig. 1. NMSE versus Eb/N0 for $M = 128$, $k = 4$, $L = 3$, $N_d = 100$.

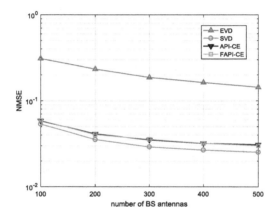

Fig. 2. NMSE versus M for Eb/N0 = 5 dB, k = 4, L = 3, Nd = 100.

nonorthogonality. When M is 300 to 500, the decrease of NMSE is gentle, the main factor that limits the performance is the error between the sample data covariance matrix and the real covariance matrix.

6   Conclusion

In this paper, we propose a channel estimation algorithm based on approximation power iteration subspace tracking. The computational complexity to solve signal subspace of each iteration is $MK^2 + O(MK)$ using API algorithm, $3MK + O(M)$ using FAPI algorithm. The proposed channel estimation algorithms approach to the estimation performance of the SVD based algorithm, and outperform the EVD based algorithm in terms of the normalized mean square error, while greatly reduce the computational complexity. As the number of antennas increases, the estimation accuracy of API-CE and FAPI-CE algorithm improves. Therefore, the low complexity subspace tracking based channel estimation algorithm is very suitable for Massive MMO systems.

Acknowledgment. This work is supported in part by National Natural Science Foundation of China (No. 61671184, No. 61401120, No. 61371100), National Science and Technology Major Project (No. 2015ZX03001041).

References

1. Wang, C.X., Haider, F., Gao, X., et al.: Cellular architecture and key technologies for 5G wireless communication networks. IEEE Commun. Mag. **52**(2), 122–130 (2014)
2. Juho, L., Younsun, K., Yongjun, K., et al.: LTE-advanced in 3GPP Rel-13/14: an evolution toward 5G. IEEE Commun. Mag. **54**(3), 36–42 (2016)
3. Bhushan, N., Li, J., Malladi, D., et al.: Network densification: the dominant theme for wireless evolution into 5G. IEEE Commun. Mag. **52**(2), 82–89 (2014)
4. Liu, W., Han, S., Yang, C.: Energy efficiency comparison of massive MIMO and small cell network. In: IEEE Global Conference on Signal and Information Processing, pp. 617–621. IEEE Press, Atlanta (2014)
5. Sorensen, J.H., De, C.E.: Pilot decontamination through pilot sequence hopping in massive MIMO systems. In: IEEE GLOBECOM, pp. 3285–3290. IEEE Press, Austin (2014)
6. Yin, H., Gesbert, D., Filippou, M.C., et al: Decontaminating pilots in massive MIMO systems. In: 2013 IEEE International Conference on Communications, pp. 3170–3175. IEEE Press, Budapest (2013)
7. Zhang, J., Zhang, B., Chen, S., et al.: Pilot contamination elimination for large-scale multiple-antenna aided OFDM systems. IEEE J. Sel. Top. Sig. Process. **8**(5), 1–14 (2014)
8. Ngo, B.Q., Larsson, E.G.: EVD-based channel estimation in multicell multiuser MIMO systems with very large antenna arrays. In: 2012 IEEE International Conference on Acoustics, Speech and Signal Processing, pp. 3249–3252. IEEE Press, Kyoto (2012)
9. Guo, K., Guo, Y., Ascheid, G.: On the performance of EVD-based channel estimations in MU-Massive-MIMO systems. In: 2013 IEEE 24th International Symposium on Personal Indoor and Mobile Radio Communications. pp. 1376–1380. IEEE Press, London (2013)
10. Hu, A., Lv, T., Lu, Y.: Subspace-based semi-blind channel estimation for large-scale multi-cell multiuser MIMO systems. In: IEEE 77th Vehicular Technology Conference, pp. 1–5. IEEE Press, Dresden (2013)
11. Badeau, R., David, B., Richard, G.: Fast approximated power iteration subspace tracking. IEEE Trans. Sig. Process. **53**(8), 2931–2941 (2005)

BER Performance Evaluation of Downlink MUSA over Rayleigh Fading Channel

Yao Xu, Gang Wang[(✉)], Liming Zheng, Rongkuan Liu,
and Donglai Zhao

Harbin Institute of Technology, Harbin, China
xuyao_hit@sina.com,
{gwang51, zheng, liurongkuan}@hit.edu.cn,
zdl527@126.com

Abstract. Downlink multi-user shared access (MUSA) is a non-orthogonal multiple access scheme (NOMA) based on the traditional power domain superposition and uses a mirror constellation to optimize the modulated symbol mapping of the paired users. In this paper, bit error ratio (BER) performance of MUSA with successive interference cancellation (SIC) is investigated in a cellular downlink scenario over Rayleigh fading channel. Firstly, we elaborate downlink MUSA system based on NOMA and spreading sequences in detail. Then, we compare the BER performance of MUSA with pure NOMA under different power allocation schemes. On this basis, we further study the system average BER performance in downlink MUSA and NOMA with respect to the power difference of the users, respectively. In addition, BER performance of MUSA with different spreading sequences is evaluated. Finally, the simulation results show that MUSA with appropriate spreading sequences is able to obtain better BER performance than NOMA under the same simulation conditions, and a reasonable power allocation is the key to improve BER performance of MUSA and NOMA.

Keywords: MUSA · NOMA · SIC · BER performance · 5G communication
Rayleigh fading channel

1 Introduction

The rapid growth of wireless communication technology and smart Internet of Things (IoT) brings many challenges to the fifth generation (5G) mobile communications, such as higher user experience rates, higher spectral efficiency, higher connection density, and lower handover latency, etc. To meet these requirements, enhanced or innovative technologies are required. A promising technology which can increase the system throughput and provide massive connections is non-orthogonal multi-user superposition and shared access among the potential candidates. Non-orthogonal access enables several users to utilize time and frequency resources through simple linear superposition or power domain multiplexing. At present, the non-orthogonal access schemes proposed by the industry and academia mainly include sparse code multiple access (SCMA) [1] technology based on multi-dimensional modulation and sparse

© ICST Institute for Computer Sciences, Social Informatics and Telecommunications Engineering 2018
X. Gu et al. (Eds.): MLICOM 2017, Part I, LNICST 226, pp. 85–94, 2018.
https://doi.org/10.1007/978-3-319-73564-1_9

code spreading, patterning division multiple access (PDMA) [2] based on non-orthogonal feature pattern, non-orthogonal multiple access (NOMA) [3–11] based on power superposition, and multi-user shared access (MUSA) [12, 13] based on complex spreading sequence and enhanced superposition coding, etc.

In the past, the performance of NOMA has been evaluated in many research works. In [3], the authors discussed the outage performance and the ergodic sum rates of a downlink NOMA with randomly distributed users. The authors in [4] considered the outage probability and the ergodic sum rates of a NOMA based relay cooperative communication networks over Nakagami-m fading channels. For instance, the authors of [5] have provided an analysis of NOMA performance gains from both link-level and system-level perspectives. It has been shown that NOMA can provide higher gains compared to OFDMA. In [6], system-level throughput of a NOMA which assumes proportional fair based radio resource allocation and uses a successive interference canceller in the cellular downlink have been studied. In order to study a more realistic analysis of SIC in downlink NOMA, the study in [7] has given the numerical results in terms of BER when the receiver uses both perfect and imperfect SIC. In [8], a NOMA constellation rotation scheme has been proposed to enhance the link-level performance for NOMA with ML receiver, and the symbol error rate (SER) simulations have been conducted. For uplink NOMA, the authors in [9] proposed an uplink NOMA strategy that removes the resource allocation exclusivity to achieve higher capacity and provided the link-level performance evaluation in terms of BER. The work in [10] analyzes the uplink spectral efficiency of NOMA in Rayleigh fading environment. An uplink power control scheme has been developed for NOMA to achieve diverse arrived power in [11]. The outage performance and the achievable sum rate for the scheme proposed in this paper have been theoretically analyzed. Additionally, MUSA scheme has been first proposed in [12], and the authors studied the link-level and system-level performance in terms of block error rate (BLER) compared to orthogonal systems.

In this paper, we focus on downlink MUSA over Rayleigh fading channel with two goals. The first is to compare BER performance of MUSA with NOMA in a two users scenario when they use different power allocation strategies, and then investigate the relationship between BER performance and users' power difference. The second is to evaluate BER performance of MUSA using various spreading sequences in the downlink scenario. The numerical results derive that MUSA outperform NOMA in terms of BER performance under the same conditions.

2 System Model

2.1 Basic Notation

Consider a downlink transmission scenario in which a base station (BS) serving M randomly distributed single-antenna users, U_m, with $m \in M = \{1, ..., M\}$. And we assume the total available transmitted power of the base station is P and the power allocation coefficient for m-th user is c_m, with $\sum_{m \in M} c_m = 1$. The channel between the user and the BS can be described as independent and identically distributed (i.i.d.) Rayleigh block flat fading with additive white Gaussian noise (AWGN) which is a random complex variable with zero mean and σ_n^2 variance. The channel coefficients and gains can be denoted by h_m (for BS $\rightarrow U_m$ link), and $|h_m|^2$, respectively. According to the Rayleigh fading property, h_m can be written as $h_m = v_m / \sqrt{1 + d_m^\alpha}$, where v_m is the small-scale Rayleigh fading gains with $v_m \sim CN(0, \sigma_v^2)$, d_m denotes the distance between the BS and m-th user and α denotes the pass loss factor. Without loss of generality, we assume that $0 < |h_1|^2 \leq |h_2|^2 \leq \cdots \leq |h_m|^2$ and the power allocation coefficients should satisfy $c_1 \geq c_2 \geq \cdots \geq c_M$.

2.2 Principle of Downlink NOMA

The BS can make multi users share the same radio resources, either in time, frequency or code via the NOMA scheme, which uses superposition coding at the transmitter and SIC at the receiver. Based on the protocol of NOMA, ransmitted signal from the BS can be given as $x_{\text{NOMA}} = \sum_{i=1}^{M} \sqrt{c_i P} x_i$, where x_i denotes one information bit for m-th user. Therefore, the received signal at m-th user can be written by

$$y_{m,\text{NOMA}} = h_m \sum_{i=1}^{M} \sqrt{c_i P} x_i + n_m \tag{1}$$

Where n_m denotes the Gaussian noise at receiver. SIC will be carried at m-th user receiver and the user can decode the information bits for i-th user with $i < m$. As a result, the user can remove all inter-user interference from the weaker users and its achievable data rate is given by

$$R_{m,\text{NOMA}} = \log\left(1 + \frac{c_m P |h_m|^2}{P |h_m|^2 \sum_{i=m+1}^{M} c_i + \sigma_n^2}\right) \tag{2}$$

2.3 Principle of Downlink MUSA

NOMA scheme based on power superposition allows the BS send a linear superposition of multi user's data flows directly in the power domain by using the same time-frequency resources. A reasonable power allocation strategy and user pairing should be considered to achieve good performance but a wrong choice of power allocation scheme will lead to greater multiple access interference. In order to make the SIC process at the receiver more robust, complex spreading sequences are used in downlink MUSA to ensure low correlation among users and improve system performance.

According to the principle of MUSA, the BS will send $\mathbf{x}_{\text{MUSA}} = \sum_{i=1}^{M} \sqrt{c_i P}(x_i \mathbf{w}_i)$, where $\mathbf{w}_{i(1 \times L)}$ denotes a short normalized complex spreading sequence with the size of L for i-th user. Therefore, the observation at m-th user is given by

$$\mathbf{y}_{m,\text{MUSA}} = h_m \sum_{i=1}^{M} \sqrt{c_i P}(x_i \mathbf{w}_i) + \mathbf{n}_m \tag{3}$$

Similarly, each receiver also employs a SIC technique and the achievable data rate of m-th user is given by

$$
\begin{aligned}
R_{m,\text{MUSA}} &= \log\left(1 + \frac{c_m P |h_m|^2 \|\mathbf{w}_m\|^2}{P|h_m|^2 \sum_{i=m+1}^{M} c_i \|\mathbf{w}_i\|^2 + \sigma_n^2}\right) \\
&= \log\left(1 + \frac{c_m P |h_m|^2}{P|h_m|^2 \sum_{i=m+1}^{M} c_i + \sigma_n^2}\right)
\end{aligned}
\tag{4}
$$

In Fig. 1, a more specific transceiver structure for the BS to m-th user link is illustrated. And the detailed step descriptions are provided as follows.

Step1: The information bit flow $\mathbf{I}_i$ for i-th user is encoded using a turbo code with code rate R, and the output of encoder is coded bit vector $\mathbf{IC}_{i(1 \times N)}$, where N denotes the length of $\mathbf{IC}_m$.

Step2: $\mathbf{IC}_i$ is modulated by a QPSK modulator, generating the modulated symbols vector $\mathbf{ICM}_{i(1 \times N/2)}$.

Step3: $\mathbf{ICM}_i$ is spread with a short complex spreading sequence $\mathbf{w}_{i(1 \times L)}$, producing the spread symbols vector $\mathbf{ICMS}_{i(1 \times NL/2)}$.

Step4: $\mathbf{ICMS}_i$ is transmitted over Rayleigh fading channel.

Step5: At the receiver side, linear detection and SIC are used to decode the information bits for m-th user and the vector form of the received signal is given by

$$
\mathbf{r}_{m,\text{MUSA}} = h_m \sum_{i=1}^{M} \sqrt{c_i P}\,\mathbf{ICMS}_i + \mathbf{n}_m
\tag{5}
$$

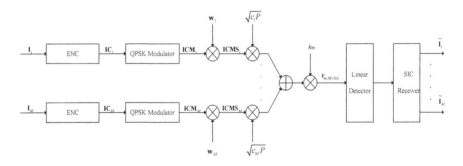

Fig. 1. Downlink MUSA system structure

3   Detection and Spreading Sequences

Compare with the spreading sequences used by traditional direct sequence CDMA, the modulated symbols of users are spread by specially designed complex spreading sequences which can promote the implementation of robust SIC. Additionally, detection algorithm at receiver is the key to ensure the good performance of downlink MUSA. This section is dedicated to the details of the complex spreading sequences design and minimum mean squared error based on SIC (MMSE-SIC) algorithm.

3.1 MMSE-SIC

One way to boost the performance of SIC receiver is to use in conjunction with liner detection algorithms such as zero forcing (ZF) and MMSE. For MMSE algorithm, the optimization goal is to minimize the mean squared error between the estimated values of transmit data based on received data and the target data, and the filter coefficient matrix of the linear detector can be described as following

$$\mathbf{W}_{\text{MMSE}} = (\mathbf{H}^H \mathbf{H} + \sigma^2 \mathbf{I})^{-1} \mathbf{H}^H \tag{6}$$

In addition, the SIC receiver performs data detection in descending order of users' signal to interference plus noise ratio (SINR). For the sake of analysis, the matrix form of Eq. (5) can be further expressed by

$$
\begin{aligned}
\mathbf{R}_{m,\text{MUSA}} &= \sum_{i=1}^{M} \sqrt{c_i P} h_m (\mathbf{w}_i^{\text{T}} \times \mathbf{ICM}_i) + \mathbf{N} \\
&= \sum_{i=1}^{M} \tilde{\mathbf{H}}_i \times \mathbf{ICM}_i + \mathbf{N}
\end{aligned}
\tag{7}
$$

Where $\tilde{\mathbf{H}}_i = \sqrt{c_i P} h_m \mathbf{w}_i^{\text{T}}$ is the equivalent channel coefficient matrix of i-th user. The steps of MMSE-SIC in downlink MUSA are summarized in Algorithm 1.

Algorithm 1 MMSE-SIC detection in downlink MUSA(for BS→m-th user link)

1: Initialize k, m, i, number of users M, SINR of i-th user $SINR_i$, detection coefficient matrix of i-th user ξ_i, ID of user with maximum $SINR$ $j\leftarrow 0$, estimated value of j-th user's modulated symbols $\hat{\mathbf{ICM}}_j$ and information bits $\hat{\mathbf{I}}_j$, encoding and modulation operator $\mathbf{Q}(.)$, de modulation and decoding operator $\mathbf{Q}^{-1}(.)$, set of user IDs $U=\{1,2,\ldots,M\}$.

2: **while** $j \neq m$ **do**

3: $\forall i \in U$, compute $\xi_i = (\tilde{\mathbf{H}}_i^H \tilde{\mathbf{H}}_i + \sigma^2 \mathbf{I})^{-1} \tilde{\mathbf{H}}_i^H$, $SINR_i = \dfrac{\| \tilde{\mathbf{H}}_i \xi_i \|^2}{\| \tilde{\mathbf{H}}_i \|^2 \sum\limits_{k \in U, k \neq i} \| \xi_k \|^2 + N_i}$

4: Search user ID with maximum $SINR$, $\max\limits_{i \in U}\{SINR_i\} = SINR_j, j \in U$

5: Compute $\hat{\mathbf{ICM}}_j = \xi_j \mathbf{R}_{m,\text{MUSA}}$, $\hat{\mathbf{I}}_j = \mathbf{Q}^{-1}(\hat{\mathbf{ICM}}_j)$

6: Update $\mathbf{R}_{m,\text{MUSA}} = \mathbf{R}_{m,\text{MUSA}} - \sqrt{c_j P} \mathbf{H}_m (\mathbf{W}_j \times \mathbf{Q}(\hat{\mathbf{I}}_j))$, $U = U - \{j\}$

7: **end**

8: $\hat{\mathbf{I}}_m \leftarrow \hat{\mathbf{I}}_j$

9: **Return**: $\hat{\mathbf{I}}_m$

3.2   Spreading Sequences Design

The complex spreading sequences used by downlink MUSA is the same as that used in uplink MUSA. The design of short complex spreading sequences can not only achieve the low correlation between the user data but reduce the complexity of transceiver. The complex spreading sequences consists of a series of complex values in which the real and imaginary parts are taken from the same set including multiple real numbers. The available number of q-ary complex codes with the code length of L is q^{2L}. For instance, the complex spreading sequence constellations with $q = 2$ and $q = 3$ are shown in the Fig. 2, and each complex value of the spreading sequences corresponds to the point on the constellations.

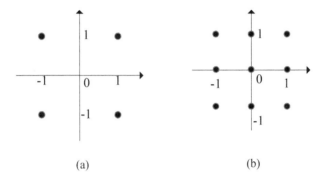

(a)   (b)

Fig. 2.   Complex spreading sequence. (a) $q = 2$. (b) $q = 3$.

4   Numerical Results

For the sake of simplicity, numerical results are provided to explain the BER performance of downlink MUSA and NOMA in a two users scenario. In addition, we assume that UE_1 is the near user, UE_2 denotes the far user and power allocation difference between UE_1 and UE_2 is $\Delta P = c_2 - c_1$. The detailed parameters of simulation are summarized in Table 1.

Table 1.   Simulation parameters

Parameters	Assumptions
Coding scheme	Turbo coding with code rate 1/2
Modulation scheme	QPSK
spreading sequences	PN codes, binary and tri-level complex spreading sequences
Transmitted power	$P = 1$
Power allocation scheme	Fixed power allocation algorithm, $c_1 + c_2 = 1$
Channel condition	Non-frequency selective and slow fading Rayleigh channel, $\alpha = 2$
Antenna configuration	1Tx, 1Rx
Channel estimation	Ideal
Cellular radius	$R_D < 30$ m
Receiver	MMSE-SIC

Figure 3 demonstrates the BER performance of near user with different power allocation schemes in downlink NOMA and MUSA. And the length of tri-level complex spreading sequence used in MUSA scheme is 4. As expected, the BER performance of MUSA is better than NOMA under the same conditions. Interestingly, the BER performance of NOMA becomes better firstly and then turn into worse with the increase of c_1, because BER of UE_1 is jointly decided by c_1 and ΔP., BER of NOMA decreases with the increase of UE_1's power when c_1 is less than 0.25, but when the c_1 is greater than 0.25, the power difference becomes smaller, which makes cross-correlation between users larger and results in higher bit error rates. However, the complex spreading sequences are used in MUSA to ensure the low cross-correlation between users so good BER performance is able to be obtained even if ΔP is small.

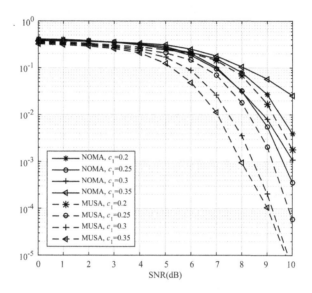

Fig. 3. BER performance comparison of UE_1.in downlink MUSA and NOMA

For a clearer explanation of the results in Figs. 3, 4 shows the relationship between the system average BER performance and the power allocation difference in downlink MUSA and NOMA scenario, respectively. And we assume SNR at UE_1 side is 12 dB and SNR at UE_2 is 8 dB. From the numerical results, it can be showed that the trend of system BER curves go down at first and then rise as well as UE_1, and the performance of UE_2 becomes better continuously with the increase of ΔP. The reason is that ΔP is the main influencing factor of UE_1's BER performance when ΔP is small, but c_1 becomes the main influence when c_1 is small enough. Additionally, BER of NOMA and MUSA becomes almost the same when c_1 is extremely small. Therefore, reasonable selection of power allocation scheme for downlink MUSA and NOMA is significant to gain good BER performance.

Figure 5 compares the BER performance of UE1 in downlink MUSA with various lengths of binary complex spreading sequences. As can be seen, the BER performance of receiver with different lengths binary spreading sequences are almost the same when the size of sequence is more than 8. However, BER performance is improved as the sequence length increase when the length of binary spreading sequence is less than 8. It is because longer spreading sequences can guarantee lower cross-correlation between users so that superior BER performance can be obtained by using longer complex spreading sequences when the length of sequences is not very long.

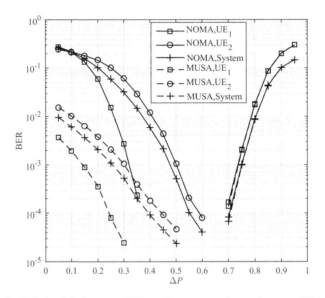

Fig. 4. Relationship between BER performance and users' power difference

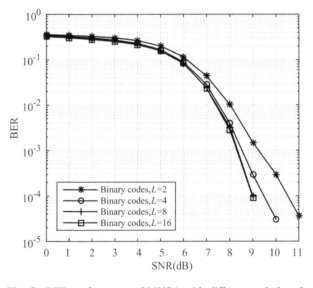

Fig. 5. BER performance of MUSA with different code length

As shown in Fig. 6, BER performance of downlink MUSA with various kinds of spreading sequences such as PN codes, binary complex spreading sequences and tri-level complex spreading sequences. We can find that complex spreading sequences are used in downlink MUSA, especially tri-level spreading sequences, can obtain better system BER performance compared with the PN codes. Because the cross-correlation between complex spreading sequences is lower than PN codes.

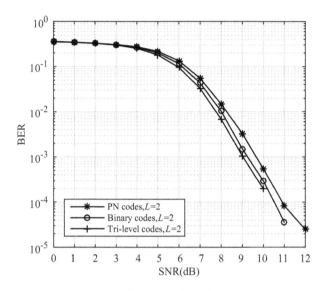

Fig. 6. BER performance of MUSA with different spreading sequences

5   Conclusion

In this paper, we have first proved that downlink MUSA can achieve better BER performance than NOMA over Rayleigh fading channel. Additionally, we have shown that system BER is a concave function of power difference in downlink MUSA and NOMA with two users, therefore the power allocation scheme should be chosen carefully to ensure their performance. And we have found great performance can be obtained by utilizing tri-level complex spreading sequences in downlink MUSA compared with binary PN codes. However, analysis for error propagation of SIC receiver and implementation complexity of MUSA is subject to further study.

Acknowledgement. This work is supported in part by National Natural Science Foundation of China (No. 61671184, No. 61401120, No. 61371100) and National Science and Technology Major Project of China (No. 2015ZX03001041).

References

1. Yan, C., Kang, G., Zhang, N.: A dimension distance-based SCMA codebook design. IEEE Access **5**, 5471–5479 (2017)
2. Chen, S., Ren, B., Gao, Q., Kang, S., Sun, S., Niu, K.: Pattern division multiple access-a novel nonorthogonal multiple access for 5th-generation radio networks. IEEE Trans. Veh. Technol. **66**(4), 3185–3196 (2017)
3. Ding, Z., Yang, Z., Fan, P., Poor, H.V.: On the performance of non-orthogonal multiple access in 5G systems with randomly deployed users. IEEE Sig. Process. Lett. **21**(12), 1501–1505 (2014)
4. Men, J., Ge, J., Zhang, C.: Performance analysis of nonorthogonal multiple access for relaying networks over Nakagami-m fading channels. IEEE Trans. Veh. Technol. **66**(2), 1200–1208 (2017)
5. Benjebbour, A., Saito, K., Li, A., Kishiyama, Y., Nakamura, T.: Nonorthogonal multiple access (NOMA): concept, performance evaluation and experimental trials. In: 10th IEEE International Conference on Wireless Networks and Mobile Communications, pp. 1–6. IEEE Press, Morocco (2015)
6. Otao, N., Kishiyama, Y., Higuchi, K.: Performance of non-orthogonal access with SIC in cellular downlink using proportional fair-based resource allocation. In: 9th IEEE International Symposium on Wireless Communication Systems, pp. 476–480. IEEE Press, Paris (2012)
7. Usman, M.R., Khan, A., Usman, M.A., Seong, J.Y., Shin, S.Y.: Performance of perfect and imperfect SIC in downlink non orthogonal multiple access (NOMA). In: 2016 IEEE International Conference on Smart Green Technology in Electrical and Information Systems, pp. 102–106. IEEE Press, Bali (2016)
8. Zhang, J., Wang, X., Tsuyoshi, H., Tokuro, K.: Downlink non-orthogonal multiple access (NOMA) constellation rotation. In: IEEE 84th Vehicular Technology Conference, pp. 1–5. IEEE Press, Montreal (2016)
9. Mohammed, A., Pei, X., Mohammed, A.I., Rahim, T.: Uplink non-orthogonal multiple access for 5G wireless networks. In: 11th IEEE International Symposium on Wireless Communication Systems, pp. 781–785. IEEE Press, Barcelona (2014)
10. Pongsatorn, S., Tatcha, C.: Uplink spectral efficiency for non-orthogonal multiple access in Rayleigh Fading. In: 18th IEEE International Conference on Advanced Communication Technology, pp. 751–754. IEEE Press, Pyeongchang (2016)
11. Zhang, N., Wang, J., Kang, G., Liu, Y.: Uplink nonorthogonal multiple access in 5G systems. IEEE Commun. Lett. **20**(3), 458–461 (2016)
12. Yuan, Z., Yu, G., Li, W., Yuan, Y., Wang, X., Xu, J.: Multi-user shared access for internet of things. In: IEEE 83rd Vehicular Technology Conference, pp. 1–5. IEEE Press, Nanjing (2016)
13. Yuan, Y., Yuan, Z., Yu, G., Hwang, C., Liao, P., Li, A., Takeda, K.: Non-orthogonal transmission technology in LTE evolution. IEEE Commun. Mag. **54**(7), 68–74 (2016)

Intelligent Positioning and Navigation

Privacy Protection for Location Sharing Services in Social Networks

Hui Wang[1], Juan Chen[2(✉)], Xianzhi Wang[3], Xin Liu[4], and Zhenyu Na[2]

[1] National Computer Network Emergency Response Technical Team/Coordination Center of China, Beijing 100029, China
wh@cert.org.cn
[2] School of Information Science and Technology,
Dalian Maritime University, Dalian 116026, China
juanchencs@gmail.com
[3] School of Computer Science and Engineering,
University of New South Wales, Sydney, NSW 2052, Australia
[4] School of Information and Communication Engineering,
Dalian University of Technology, Dalian 116024, China

Abstract. Recently, there is an increase interest in location sharing services in social networks. Behind the convenience brought by location sharing, there comes an indispensable security risk of privacy. Though many efforts have been made to protect user's privacy for location sharing, they are not suitable for social network. Most importantly, little research so far can support user relationship privacy and identity privacy. Thus, we propose a new privacy protection protocol for location sharing in social networks. Different from previous work, the proposed protocol can provide perfect privacy for location sharing services. Simulation results validate the feasibility and efficiency of the proposed protocol.

Keywords: Privacy protection protocol · Location sharing
Wireless social network

1 Introduction

Social networks are widely used for various applications. With the ubiquitous use of mobile devices and a rapid shift of technology accessing to social networks, people are able to exchange real-time information such as idea, current status and location with their friends conveniently. With the wide spread of GPS and Mobile Internet, mobile social network applications such as Weibo and Twitter with location-based service (LBS) are very popular.

Location sharing services which helps people to share their locations with their nearby friends is one significant building block to implement LBSs over social networks. However, behind the convenience brought by location sharing in social networks, there comes an indispensable security risk of privacy. Most location sharing applications need update user location information to provide better services despite the possibility of user privacy violation [1]. The leak of user

© ICST Institute for Computer Sciences, Social Informatics and Telecommunications Engineering 2018
X. Gu et al. (Eds.): MLICOM 2017, Part I, LNICST 226, pp. 97–102, 2018.
https://doi.org/10.1007/978-3-319-73564-1_10

identity and location information will increase the risk of adversary tracking the daily life of the user or will receive customized advertisements which is unwilling or even revealing his private activities such as visiting a bank or going to a hospital [2].

Privacy protection for location sharing services over social network [3–7] has received much attention in recent years. However, they are not suitable for social network. Furthermore, little research so far can provide identity privacy, location privacy and user relationship privacy at the same time.

In order to deal with the above challenges, we propose a **P**rivacy-preserving **P**rotocol for location **S**haring in social networks (PPS). Different from existing work, the proposed protocol can support perfect privacy for location sharing services in social networks.

The rest paper is organized as follows. Section 2 introduces the system. Section 3 proposes PPS, the privacy-preserving protocol in detail. The simulation results are given in Sect. 4. Finally, we conclude the paper in Sect. 5.

2   System Initialization

The system consists of Location Server (LS), mobile users and Social Network Server (SNS). In order to protect the user privacy, the user identities, relationship (also known as users friends list) and locations are separately stored in SNS and LS. Thus, LS cannot infer the users relationship and user identity while SNS cannot obtain the users current locations. Specifically, we make the following configuration of the three components.

- Each user, say v generates his own public/private key pair (puk_v, prk_v). The public key puk_v is shared with LS and SNS. In addition, v shares its symmetric key sk_v, named 'friend key' with his friends.
- SNS is pre-loaded a hash function H, a public/private key pair (puk_S, prk_S) and a bloom filter BF. SNS shares its puk_S with all the registered users and LS. The hash function H is used to compute the real/fake location tags and fake IDs. We use BF to conceal the user relationship.
- LS is pre-loaded its asymmetric key pair (puk_L, prk_L). Then, LS shares its public key, say puk_L with SNS.

3   Privacy-Preserving Protocol

A privacy-preserving protocol, named PPS is presented for location sharing services in social network. The purpose of PPS are (a) to manage users' relationships and user identities by SNS while proting users' locations from; (b) to manage users' locations by LS while preventing users' identities and user relationships from inferring by LS. Specifically, PPS includes three processes: user registration, location management, nearby friends query.

3.1   User Registration

Before using the location sharing service, a mobile user, say v has to register at the SNS. Then, SNS stores vs personal profile and his friends' information into SNS. The user registration process is as follows:

(a) User v sends a registration request to SNS.
(b) SNS replies a message $<MR, ID_v, puk_S>$ to v, where MR is the message type field, ID_v is the unique ID generated for v by SNS.
(c) v sends the message $<MR, puk_v, FS, df_v, ds_v>$ to SNS, where $FS = \{ID_{v,i} | 1 \le i \le M\}$ is the set of v's friend. M is the total number of vs friends. $ID_{v,i}$ denotes the ID of vs i-th friends. ds_v stands for the distance within which v would like to share his location with strangers. df_v is the distance within which v would like to share his location with his friends.
(d) v exchanges his friend key with each of his friends.
(e) SNS inserts v's friend information FS and his personal profile into user information table (as can be seen in Fig. 1) and friend information table (as can be seen in Fig. 1) respectively.

Personal information		...
User ID	**User fake ID**	**...**
ID_1	FID_1	...
...	...	...
ID_v	FID_v	...
...	...	...

Friend information of v	
User ID	**Friend ID**
ID_v	$PID_{v,1}$
ID_v	$PID_{v,2}$
...	...
ID_v	...

Fig. 1. Data storage structure of SNS.

3.2   Location Management

Once a user moves to some new place, he has to submit his location into LS. Take note that the user doesnt want to send his real location directly to LS as LS can infer his identity through his sensitive location or his path.

In order to update the users location privately, v firstly sends his encrypted location *spot* other than his real location l_v to SNS, where $spot = E_{puk_L}(l_v, E_{sk_v}(l_v))$. Then, SNS anonymizes the vs identity. Finally, in order to hide vs location, SNS generates $k-1$ fake locations and sends k locations to LS. Particularly, $k-1$ fake locations are randomly generated which are far away from v and scattered throughout a large area, say the city. Take note that since each location update relates with a new and different fake ID, the location information table in LS cannot meet the storage requirement resulted by the infinitely increasing location updates. Thus, LS deletes old entries from the location information table after a period of time. Specifically, this sub-protocol performs the following seven steps.

(a) Once v moves to a new place l_v, v sends SNS a location update notification message $<MU, spot, t, sig_v>$, where MU, $spot$, t and sig_v stand for the message type, encrypted location, timestamp and signature respectively. Specifically, $spot$ is of the form $E_{puk_L}(l_v, E_{sk_v}(l_v))$. The timestamp is used to defend against replay attack. The signature is of the form $E_{prk_v}(ID_v, t)$.

(b) SNS verifies the signature sig_v.

(c) SNS generates a unique fake ID, $FID_v = H(ID_v \oplus t_c)$ for user v, where t_c denotes the current time.

(d) SNS generates $k - 1$ scattered fake locations randomly which are far away from v.

(e) SNS generates k location tags, $\{tag_i | 1 \le i \le k\}$ which is used to identify real location from fake ones. If $tag_i = H(ID_v)$, the location related with tag_i is real. If $tag_i = H(ID_v \oplus i)$, the related location is fake.

(f) SNS sends the message $<MU, FID_v, \{spot_i, tag_i | 1 \le i \le k\}, df_v, ds_v, t, sig_S>$ including k locations to LS, where $spot_i$ and tag_i are the i-th location and its corresponding location tag respectively. Specifically, $spot_i = E_{puk_L}(loc_i, E_{sk_v}(loc_i))$ and $sig_S = E_{prk_S}(FID_v, t)$.

(g) By decrypting $\{spot_i | 1 \le i \le k\}$ from the received message, LS obtains k locations $\{(loc_i, E_{sk_v}(loc_i)) | 1 \le i \le k\}$.

3.3   Nearby Friends Query

In order to query the users friends nearby in a privacy-preserving way, the following steps are performed.

- v sends the request message $<MNFQ, ID_v, t, sig_v>$ to SNS, where $MNQF$ denotes the message type field.
- SNS verifies the signature sig_v.
- SNS generates the bloom filter BF including vs friends information.
- SNS sends the query message $<MNFQ, FID_v, BF, t, sig_S>$ to LS.
- LS retrieves k locations of FID_v, say $\{l_i | 1 \le i \le k\}$.
- For each location, say l_i, LS finds v's friends around l_i through BF and obtains the set N_i. Each element of N_i has the form $(FID_{v'}, E_{sk_{v'}}(l_{v'}), tag_{v'})$ satisfying that the distance between $l_{v'}$ and l_i is no more than $min\{df_v, df_{v'}\}$.
- LS sends all its nearby friends $<MNFQ, FID_v, \{N_i | 1 \le i \le k\}, t, sig_L>$ to SNS, where $sig_L = E_{prk_L}(FID_v, t)$.
- SNS removes the element with fake location from N_i.
- Considering the false positive results resulted by the bloom filter, SNS has to remove the strangers from N_i according to vs friend information table (see Fig. 1). Then, SNS can obtain the real friends set N_i''.
- For $\{N_i'' | 1 \le i \le k\}$, SNS replaces each fake ID with real ID and obtains $N_v = \{ID_j, E_{sk_j}(l_j) | 1 \le j \le q\}$, where q is the number of vs nearby friends.
- SNS sends N_v to v.
- v decrypts N_v and obtains the real locations of vs nearby friends.

4   Simulation

Since mobile devices are much more resource constrained compared with wired device, we examine the acceptability and feasibility of PPS on mobile devices. AES and RSA are chosen by us for symmetric cryptography and asymmetric

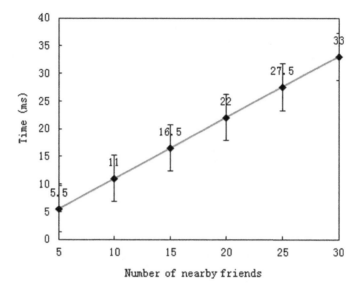

Fig. 2. Decryption by AES

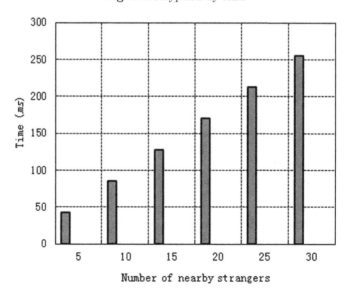

Fig. 3. Decryption by RSA

cryptography respectively. All simulation is executed on Huawei NEM-AL10 smartphone running Android 6.0 operation system.

Figures 2 and 3 show the average execution time for data decryption by AES and RSA respectively. It is observed from Fig. 2 that AES takes more time for decryption as the users nearby friends increases. We can also observe that even though there are as many as 30 friends around the user, no more than 35 ms is needed by AES. Obviously, it is acceptable for current mobile devices. Similarly, we can see from Fig. 3 that the time RSA takes for decryption grows with the increasing number of the user's nearby strangers. When the number of strangers around the user is as many as 30, the time cost for RSA is less than 300 ms which is acceptable.

5   Conclusion

In this paper, we firstly propose a privacy protection protocol for social network location sharing services (PPS). Extensive experimental results demonstrate that, different from previous research, not only execution is possible but also convenient on the mobile device that requests location sharing over social network.

Acknowledgement. This research is supported in part by the Natural Science Foundation of China under grants No. 61300188 and 61601221; by the Fundamental Research Funds for the Central Universities No. 3132016024; by Scientific Research Staring Foundation for the Ph.D in Liaoning Province No. 201601081; by Scientific Research Projects from Education Department in Liaoning Province No. L2015056.

References

1. Shin, K.G., et al.: Privacy protection for users of location-based services. In: IEEE Wirel. Commun. **19** (2012)
2. Karim, W.: The privacy implications of personal locators: why you should think twice before voluntarily availing yourself to GPS monitoring. Wash. UJL and Pol'y **14** (2004)
3. Wei, W., Xu, F., Li, Q.: Mobishare: flexible privacy-preserving location sharing in mobile online social networks. In: 2012 IEEE Proceedings of INFOCOM, pp. 2616–2620. IEEE Press (2012)
4. Liu, Z., Li, J., Chen, X., et al.: N-mobishare: new privacy-preserving location-sharing system for mobile online social networks. Int. J. Comput. Math. **93** (2016)
5. Li, J., Li, J., Chen, X., et al.: MobiShare+: security improved system for location sharing in mobile online social networks. J. Internet Serv. Inf. Secur. **4**, 25–36 (2014)
6. Shen, N., Yang, J., Yuan, K., et al.: An efficient and privacy-preserving location sharing mechanism. Comput. Stan. Interfaces **44**, 102–109 (2016)
7. Li, J., Yan, H., Liu, Z., Chen, X., et al.: Location-sharing systems with enhanced privacy in mobile online social networks. In: IEEE Syst. J. (2015)

A Non-line-of-Sight Localization Method Based on the Algorithm Residual Error Minimization

Sunan Li[1], Jingyu Hua[1(✉)], Feng Li[1], Fangni Chen[1,2], and Jiamin Li[3]

[1] College of Information Engineering, Zhejiang University of Technology,
Hangzhou 310023, China
eehjy@163.com
[2] College of Information Science and Electrical Engineering,
Zhejiang University of Science and Technology, Hangzhou 310023, China
[3] National Mobile Communication Research Lab, Southeast University,
Nanjing 210096, China

Abstract. Wireless localization has become a key technology location based services, and the non-line-of-sight (NLOS) propagation is one of the most important error source in the localization. Therefore, this paper defines a novel algorithm residual error (ARE) in NOLS environment, and estimates the position of mobile station (MS) by minimizing this ARE, where the quadratic programming is employed to solve the minimization problem. The simulation results show that the proposed algorithm produces significant performance improvements in NLOS environments.

Keywords: Wireless localization · Non-line-of-sight error
Algorithm residuals · Quadratic programming

1 Introduction

The wireless localization technology is one of the key techniques in the future internet of things, and therefore has attracted widely attentions. For example, in early 1990's, the FCC announced emergency call standard which requires a localization accuracy within 125 m [1]. So far, the localization parameters usually utilized the time-of-arrival (TOA/TDOA), angle-of-arrival (AOA) and received-signal-strength (RSS) or other information [2–5], and the positioning algorithms might include CHAN algorithm, Taylor series method, FANG algorithm, Friedlander algorithm, spherical interpolation algorithm (SI) and SX algorithm [6–10]. However, in non-line of sight (NLOS) environments, these previous algorithms could not achieve good performance, since the NLOS error in a real-world cellular network may approach 500–700 m. Meanwhile, the NLOS error cannot be statistically modeled. Therefore, the NLOS error suppression had become one of the key issues to the practical localization applications.

There are three kinds of NLOS mitigation methods. The first attempted to accurately model the NLOS environment, followed a position estimator exploiting this model [11, 12]. However, it is difficult in practice to obtain an accurate model to describe the complicated NLOS propagating environments. Thus, this kind of method was difficult to be widely used. The second kind of algorithm identified the NLOS base

X. Gu et al. (Eds.): MLICOM 2017, Part I, LNICST 226, pp. 103–111, 2018.
https://doi.org/10.1007/978-3-319-73564-1_11

stations (BS), and then employed only the LOS BSs to estimate the MS position [13, 14]. Such algorithms required a certain number of LOS BSs, but the NLOS BS identification performance could not be controlled, resulting in the positioning performance degradation sometimes. The third class of algorithm tried to weight the ranging measurements or intermediate estimations, and the weights were usually derived from the geometric and algebraic relationship between the BSs and the MSs [15–17]. The advantage of this kind of algorithm was that the MS could always be positioned, while its disadvantage was the limited estimation accuracy.

In order to tackle the above issues, this paper defines a novel residual error, i.e., the ARE, and then an optimization model is constructed. In detail, the optimization objective function is defined as the residual error of two conventional algorithms, and the constraints come from the relationships between measurements and corresponding true distances. Finally, a quadratic programming is employed to solve the optimization problem and achieve the position estimation. Computer simulations show that the proposed algorithm is superior to conventional localization algorithms in NLOS environments.

2 Range Based and Range-Inverse Based Localizations

Let (x_i, y_i) and (x, y) denote the coordinate of the i-th BS and MS, we have the BS-MS distance as

$$r_i = \sqrt{(x - x_i)^2 + (y - y_i)^2} \tag{1}$$

After some mathematical transformations, we rewrite (1) as

$$r_i^2 - K_i = -2x_i x - 2y_i y + R \tag{2}$$

where $K_i = x_i^2 + y_i^2$ and $R = x^2 + y^2$. Equation (2) can be written in the matrix form, i.e.

$$\mathbf{P} = \mathbf{AX} \tag{3}$$

where $\mathbf{P} = \begin{bmatrix} r_1^2 - K_1 \\ r_2^2 - K_2 \\ \vdots \\ r_N^2 - K_N \end{bmatrix}$, $\mathbf{A} = \begin{bmatrix} 2x_1, & 2y_1, & -1 \\ 2x_2, & 2y_2, & -1 \\ & \vdots & \\ 2x_N, & 2y_N, & -1 \end{bmatrix}$, $\mathbf{X} = \begin{bmatrix} x \\ y \\ R \end{bmatrix}$.

It is easy to derive the least squares (LS) solution from (3)

$$\hat{\mathbf{X}} = (\mathbf{A}^T \mathbf{A})^{-1} \mathbf{A}^T \mathbf{P} \tag{4}$$

Next, we define the reciprocal of r_i, i.e.

$$R_i = \frac{1}{r_i} = \frac{1}{\sqrt{(x - x_i)^2 + (y - y_i)^2}} \tag{5}$$

Squaring both sides of (5), we have

$$R_i^2 = \frac{1}{K_i - 2x_i x - 2y_i y + R} \tag{6}$$

After some maths operations, we have

$$R_i^2 K_i - 1 = (2x_i x - 2y_i y - R)R_i^2 \tag{7}$$

Similarly, we can turn (7) into a matrix form, namely

$$\mathbf{Y} = \mathbf{CX} \tag{8}$$

where $\mathbf{Y} = \begin{bmatrix} R_1^2 K_1 - 1 \\ R_2^2 K_2 - 1 \\ \vdots \\ R_N^2 K_N - 1 \end{bmatrix}$, $\mathbf{C} = \begin{bmatrix} 2x_1 R_1^2, & 2y_1 R_1^2, & -R_1^2 \\ 2x_2 R_1^2, & 2y_2 R_1^2, & -R_1^2 \\ & \vdots & \\ 2x_N R_1^2, & 2y_N R_1^2, & -R_1^2 \end{bmatrix}$, $\mathbf{X} = \begin{bmatrix} x \\ y \\ R \end{bmatrix}$.

Thus, the LS solution can be found as

$$\widehat{\mathbf{X}} = (\mathbf{C}^T \mathbf{C})^{-1} \mathbf{C}^T \mathbf{Y} \tag{9}$$

3   The ARE Based Localization Algorithm

As said in Sect. 1, this section will detailed introduce the ARE based localization by utilizing the quadratic programming model, where the objective function, the constraints and the final optimization problem are investigated next.

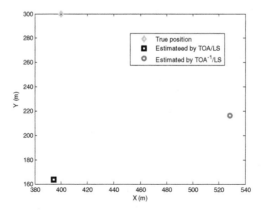

Fig. 1. Positioning results for different algorithms

3.1   The Object Function

In the NLOS environment, the above two position estimates will be different, which indicates that the residual error of different positioning algorithms is reasonable. Figure 1 shows that when the BS number is five, the above two position estimates, i.e., $\hat{\mathbf{X}}_1 = \hat{\mathbf{X}}$ and $\hat{\mathbf{X}}_2 = \bar{\mathbf{X}}$, will deviate from each other significantly. Accordingly, we can define an object function based on the ARE as

$$F(v) = norm(\mathrm{P}(\hat{\mathbf{X}}_1 - \hat{\mathbf{X}}_2))^2 \tag{10}$$

where $norm(\bullet)$ represent the l_2-norm and $\mathbf{P} = \begin{bmatrix} 1 & 0 & 0 \\ 0 & 1 & 0 \end{bmatrix}$. Moreover, the relation between the range inverse and its true value can be written as

$$R_i^0 = \frac{1}{\alpha_i} R_i \tag{11}$$

where α_i represents the scaling factor. Then, formula (7) can be rewritten as

$$R_i^2 K_i - \alpha_i^2 = (2x_i x - 2y_i y - R) R_i^2 \tag{12}$$

From (12), we have the LS solution as

$$\hat{\mathbf{X}}_2 = (\mathbf{C}^T \mathbf{C})^{-1} \mathbf{C}^T (\mathbf{C} - \mathbf{v}) \tag{13}$$

where $\mathbf{B} = [R_1^2 K_1, R_2^2 K_2, \cdots, R_N^2 K_N]^T$, $\mathbf{v} = [\alpha_1^2, \alpha_2^2, \cdots, \alpha_N^2]^T$. Similarly, the range based position estimation can be rewritten as

$$\hat{\mathbf{X}}_1 = (\mathbf{A}^T \mathbf{A})^{-1} \mathbf{A}^T \mathbf{Y} = (\mathbf{A}^T \mathbf{A})^{-1} \mathbf{A}^T (\mathbf{T} \mathbf{v} - \mathbf{Y}') \tag{14}$$

where $\mathbf{T} = diag\{r_1^2, r_2^2, \cdots, r_N^2\}$, $\mathbf{Y}' = [K_1, K_2, \cdots, K_N]^T$. Finally, the objective function (10) can be rewritten as

$$F(\mathbf{v}) = norm(\mathbf{P}((\mathbf{A}^T \mathbf{A})^{-1} \mathbf{A}^T (\mathbf{T} \mathbf{v} - \mathbf{Y}') - (\mathbf{C}^T \mathbf{C})^{-1} \mathbf{C}^T (\mathbf{B} - \mathbf{v}))) \tag{15}$$

Next, we can turn the location estimation into an optimization problem, i.e.,

$$\text{minimize}\quad F(\mathbf{v}) \tag{16}$$

3.2   The Constraints

The constraint is the rule that object parameters need to follow, and the optimization algorithms is to meet these constraints and find an expected value of the objective function to achieve the optimal solution. The proposed algorithm present in this paper has two main constraints, the first one derived from [15].

At first we should ensure the lower bound of vector $\mathbf{v}$

$$\mathbf{V}_{min} = [\alpha_{1,min}^2, \alpha_{2,min}^2, \cdots, \alpha_{N,min}^2] \tag{17}$$

where $\alpha_{i,min} = \max\left\{ \frac{L_{i,j}-d_i}{d_i} \middle| j \neq i, j \in [1,N], i \in [1,N] \right\}$. Note $L_{i,j}, i \neq j$ refers the distance between the i-th BS and j-th BS, and $\max\{\bullet\}$ denotes the maximum element of a vector (or set). Finally the first constraint can be expressed as $\mathbf{V}_{min} \leq \mathbf{v} \leq \mathbf{V}_{max}$ with $\mathbf{V}_{max} = [1, 1, \cdots, 1]^T$.

The second constraint comes from a fact that in the NLOS environment, the distance between MS and BS must be smaller than the measured distance. Hence, the MS must lie in the public areas, namely the feasible region. This constraint can be written as

$$\tilde{\mathbf{R}} \leq \mathbf{D}_{meas} \tag{18}$$

where $\tilde{\mathbf{R}} = \begin{bmatrix} norm(\mathbf{X} - BS_1) \\ norm(\mathbf{X} - BS_2) \\ \vdots \\ norm(\mathbf{X} - BS_N) \end{bmatrix}$, $\mathbf{D}_{meas} = \begin{bmatrix} r_1^2 \\ r_2^2 \\ \vdots \\ r_N^2 \end{bmatrix}$.

3.3   The Optimization Problem

According to Sects. 3.1 and 3.2, we can put the NLOS weight search into an optimization problem as follows

$$\begin{array}{ll} \min & F(\mathbf{v}) \\ subject & to \\ \left\{ \begin{array}{l} \mathbf{V}_{min} \leq \mathbf{v} \leq \mathbf{V}_{max} \\ \tilde{\mathbf{R}} \leq \mathbf{D}_{meas} \end{array} \right. \end{array} \tag{19}$$

Equation (19) can be solved by quadratic programming [18], and by substituting obtained vector into (10), we can obtain the optimal MS position estimate.

4   Simulation and Analysis

This paper exploits the classical BS topology as $(0,0)$, $(\sqrt{3}r,0)$, $(\frac{\sqrt{3}r}{2},\frac{3}{2}r)$, $(-\frac{\sqrt{3}r}{2},\frac{3}{2}r)$ and $(-\sqrt{3}r,0)$, where r denotes the radius of a cellular cell, 1000 m in our study. In simulations, the measured noise will be modeled as a zero-mean Gaussian noise with its standard deviation of 10 m if unspecified. By contrast, the NLOS error cannot be accurately modeled, thus it is assumed as a uniformly distributed random variable ranging from 0 to MAX [19]. In addition, there are four algorithms compared in simulations, including the proposed algorithm, the CLS algorithm [20], the LLOP algorithm [21] and the TS-WLS algorithm [19].

4.1   Effects of NLOS Error

Figure 2 shows the NLOS error effect on the accuracy of tested algorithms, in which the MS is located in [400, 400]. From Fig. 2, we clearly see that all algorithms will produce higher RMSE with rising NLOS errors. Although the proposed algorithm differs from the CLS algorithm trivially for MAX less than 300 m, the performance advantage of the proposed method is obviously for a larger NLOS error scenario, i.e., MAX > 300 m.

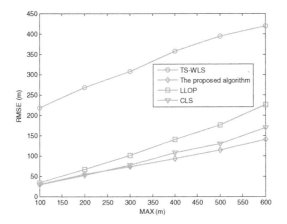

Fig. 2. NLOS error effect

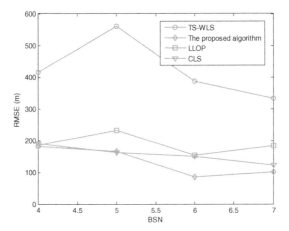

Fig. 3. BS number effect

4.2   Effects of the BS Number

Figure 3 shows the effects of BS number under the typical seven-BS topology, where the maximum value of NLOS error is 400 m and the MS randomly distributed within the cellular cell. From it, we explicitly find that the increase of BS number has improved the accuracy of all algorithms. It is also easy to see that for the proposed algorithm and CLS algorithm, they produce similar performance so long as the BS number is less than five, while the proposed algorithm significantly outperforms the CLS method with a higher BS number. From Figs. 2 and 3, the performance order of above algorithms must be, the proposed algorithm > CLS > LLOP > TS-WLS.

4.3   Effects of the LOS-BS Number

Figure 4 shows the effects of different LOS-BS numbers. As can be seen from this figure, the increasing LOS-BS number will increase the accuracy of the proposed algorithm. For instance, when the LOS-BS number is 1, the probability of accuracy of 120 m is 85%, but when the number reaches 2, the probability is 92%.

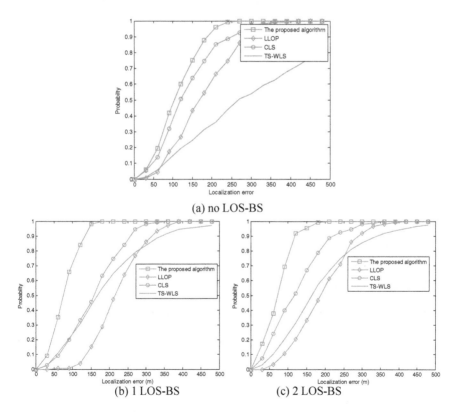

(a) no LOS-BS

(b) 1 LOS-BS   (c) 2 LOS-BS

Fig. 4. Effect of LOS-BS number

In summary, the proposed algorithm is superior to the traditional location algorithm on accuracy, and the increase of the BS number will make accuracy of the proposed algorithm increase significantly. Simultaneously, since the LOS-BS will narrow the scope of feasible region, it also improves the accuracy of the proposed algorithm.

5 Conclusions

The NLOS error is a key and difficult point in wireless localization. Therefore it is important to study the localization under the NLOS corrupts. In this paper, we propose a new concept of residual error based on the positioning difference of different localization algorithms, and then we employ the optimization theory to reach a NLOS suppression localization, in which the estimation model is transferred into an optimum weights search. The quadratic programming is exploited to solve it and significantly improves the performance. Simulations prove that the proposed method is superior to some conventional algorithms.

Acknowledgement. This paper is sponsored by National Natural Science Foundation of China (Grant No. 61601409 and Grant No. 61471322).

References

1. FCC Docket No. 94-102, Revision of Commission's Rules to Ensure Compatibility with Enhanced 911 Emergency Calling System. RM-8143, 26 July 1996
2. Sayed, A.H., Taright, A., Kgajehnouri, N.: Network-based wireless location. IEEE Signal Process. Mag. **22**(4), 24–40 (2005)
3. Gustafsson, F., Gunnarsson, F.: Mobile positioning using wireless networks: possibilities and fundamental limitations based on available wireless network measurements. IEEE Signal Process. Mag. **22**(42), 41–53 (2005)
4. Hui, H., Darabi, H., Banerjee, P., Liu, J.: Survey of wireless indoor positioning techniques and systems. IEEE Trans. Syst. Man Cybern. Part C Appl. Rev. **37**(6), 1067–1080 (2007)
5. Patwari, N., Ash, J.N., Kyperountas, S., Hero, A.O., Moses, R.L., Correal, N.S.: Locating the nodes: cooperative localization in wireless sensor networks. IEEE Signal Process. Mag. **22**(4), 54–69 (2005)
6. Fang, B.T.: Simple solutions for hyperbolic and related fixes. IEEE Trans. Aerosp. Electron. Syst. **26**(5), 748–753 (1990)
7. Chan, Y.T., Ho, K.C.: K. C. HO. A simple and efficient estimator for hyperbolic location. IEEE Trans. Signal Process. **42**(8), 1905–1915 (1994)
8. Foy, W.H.: Position-location solutions by Taylor-series estimation. IEEE Trans. Aerosp. Electron. Syst. **12**(3), 187–194 (1976)
9. Friedlander, B.: A passive location algorithm and its accuracy analysis. IEEE J. Ocean. Eng. **12**(1), 234–244 (1987)
10. Schau, H.C.: Passive source location employing intersecting spherical surfaces from time of arrival different. IEEE Trans. Acoust. Speech Signal Process. **25**(8), 1223–1225 (1987)
11. Al-Jazzar, S., Caffery, J.J., You, H.R.: A scattering model based approach to NLOS mitigation in TOA location systems. In: Proceedings of the 2002 IEEE Vehicular Technology Conference, Birmingham, UK, pp. 861–865. IEEE (2002)

12. Al-Jazzar, S., Caffery, J.J.: ML and Bayesian TOA location estimators for NLOS environments. In: Proceedings of the 2002 IEEE Vehicular Technology Conference, Birmingham, UK, pp. 856–860. IEEE (2002)
13. Guvenc, I., Chong, C.C., Wantanable, F., Inamura, H.: NLOS identification and weighted least squares localization for UWB systems using multipath channel statistics. EURASIP J. Adv. Signal Process. 36(1), 1–14 (2008)
14. Cong, L., Zhuang, W.H.: Non-line-of-sight error mitigation in mobile location. IEEE Trans. Wirel. Commun. 4(2), 560–573 (2004)
15. Venkatraman, S., Caffery, J.J., You, H.R.: A novel TOA location algorithm using LOS range estimation for NLOS environments. IEEE Trans. Veh. Technol. 53(5), 515–1524 (2004)
16. Khajehnouri, N., Sayed, A.H.: A non-line-of-sight equalization scheme for wireless cellular location. In: Proceedings of the 2003 IEEE International Conference on Acoustics, Speech and Signal Processing, Hongkong, pp. 549–552. IEEE (2003)
17. Chen, P.P.: A non-line-of-sight error mitigation algorithm in location estimation. In: Proceedings of the 1999 IEEE Wireless Communications and Networking Conference, New Orleans, LA, USA, pp. 316–320. IEEE (1999)
18. Gong, C., Wang, Z.L.: Optimizing Computation Using Matlab, 3rd edn. Publishing House of Electronics Industry, Beijing (2014)
19. Chan, Y.T., Tsui, W.Y., So, H.C., Ching, P.C.: Time-of-arrival based localization under NLOS conditions. IEEE Trans. Veh. Technol. 55(1), 17–24 (2006)
20. Wang, X., Wang, Z., Odea, B.: TOA-based location algorithm reducing the errors due to non-line-of-light propagation. IEEE Trans. Veh. Technol. 52(1), 112–116 (2003)
21. Zheng, X., Hua, J., Jiang, B., Lu, W., Wen, H., Yu, X.: A novel NLOS mitigation and localization algorithm exploiting the optimization method. Chin. J. Sens. Actuators 2013(5), 722–727 (2013)

WLAN Indoor Localization Using Angle of Arrival

Zengshan Tian, Yong Li$^{(\boxtimes)}$, Mu Zhou, and Yinghui Lian

Chongqing Key Lab of Mobile Communications Technology,
Chongqing University of Posts and Telecommunications,
Chongqing 400065, People's Republic of China
{tianzs,zhoumu}@cqupt.edu.cn, ly94ong@163.com,
lianyinghui321@foxmail.com

Abstract. With the development of information technology and the rising of demanding for location-based services, indoor localization has obtained great attentions. Accurate estimation of Angle of Arrival (AoA) of signals make it possible to achieve a high precision location. So as to resolve multipath signals effectively and then extract AoA of the direct path, in this paper we first use the existing three-antenna commercial Wi-Fi Network Interface Card (NIC) to collect radio Channel Frequency Response (CFR) measurements and then jointly estimate AoA and Time of Arrival (ToA). Second, we propose a sensing algorithm to distinguish Line-of-Sight (LoS) and Non-Line-of-Sight (NLoS) propagation and therefore obtain finer localization. Our experiments in a rich multipath indoor environment show that the AoA-based the proposed localization system can achieve a median accuracy of 0.8 m and 1.3 m in LoS environment and NLoS environment, respectively.

Keywords: Indoor localization · Wi-Fi · CFR · AoA

1 Introduction

Recent years have witnessed a great interest in developing indoor localization system that can enable clients to navigate indoor spaces. Location-based service has become more and more important with the rapid development of Internet of Thing (IoT) and smart home. Outdoors, users can share a robust and accurate localization from Global Positioning System (GPS) and BeiDou Navigation Satellite System (BDS) while indoor localization is unavailable since signals of satellite are faded severely due to obstacle. Thus, providing a high accuracy indoor location is significant important.

Many high accuracy indoor localization systems have been developed recently, such as radio frequency identification (RFID) [1], RSSI based, and AoA based. RFID is limited by power and can only be used for short-range localization. Fingerprint based localization system in WLAN is labor and time consuming. At the same time, this system is difficult to deploy since they require

© ICST Institute for Computer Sciences, Social Informatics and Telecommunications Engineering 2018
X. Gu et al. (Eds.): MLICOM 2017, Part I, LNICST 226, pp. 112–121, 2018.
https://doi.org/10.1007/978-3-319-73564-1_12

an expensive and recurring fingerprinting operation when there are changes in the environment. AoA of multipath computation with conventional MUSIC algorithm [2] requires that the antenna number must greater than multipath components. But typically in an indoor environment there are around 6–8 significant reflectors [3], so it is impossible for current commodity Wi-Fi device. Indoor localization using AoA based on WiFi signal is a well studied problem and there are many prior works in AoA. Niculescu and Nath [4] emulate AoA-based localization in an ad hoc mesh network. AoA has been proposed in CDMA mobile cellular systems, especially as a hybrid approach between AoA and TDoA [5], and also in concert with interference cancellation and ToA estimation [6]. Patwari and Kasera [7] propose a system that uses the channel impulse response and channel estimates of probe tones to detect when a device has moved, but it does not address localization problem. Geo-fencing [8] utilizes directional antennas and a frame coding approach to control APs indoor coverage boundary. SpotFi have been proposed in [16] to obtain centimeter-level localization, but the coherent signals are not considered.

In this paper we propose a novel indoor localization system that can be deployed on commodity Wi-Fi infrastructure. The system incorporates spatial smoothing algorithm that can accurately estimate AoA of multipath components even when the access point (AP) has only three antennas. Then, we use clustering algorithm to classify multipath components in indoor multipath environment. After that, we use weighting factor to identify the direct path among multiple paths, moreover we can discern identify LoS and NLoS propagation. Finally, the target can be localized by least squares (LS) algorithm with several direct path AoA.

The organization of this paper as follows: the system design is presented in Sect. 2. Our experimental evaluation is presented in Sect. 3. Then, we conclude this paper in Sect. 4.

2   System Design

In this section, we detail three techniques: super-resolution AoA estimation algorithm, direct path identification and propagation recognition algorithm. The super-resolution AoA estimation algorithm mainly solves the problem of limitation of the number of physical antennas by using a spatial smoothing technique, and then we can realize precise AoA estimation of indoor multipath signals with commodity AP equipped with only three antennas. The direct path recognition algorithm uses the AoA and ToA computed by the super-resolution algorithm to classify the path with clustering algorithm and then selects the direct path by means of weighting analysis method.

2.1   Channel Model Description

The Wi-Fi signal in 802.11n standard use orthogonal frequency division multiplexing (OFDM) modulation. OFDM is an encoding method using multiple carriers and widely used in wireless communication. It divides the channel into many orthogonal sub-channels in the frequency domain and then transmit data with subcarriers in parallel. For OFDM modulation signal, channel frequency response (CFR) can be used to describe the channel parameters including attenuation and delay of multipaths. It can be denoted as

$$Y\left(e^{jw}\right) = H\left(e^{jw}\right) X\left(e^{jw}\right) + \mathbf{N} \tag{1}$$

where $Y\left(e^{jw}\right)$ and $X\left(e^{jw}\right)$ are the received and transmitted signal in frequency domain, respectively. $H\left(e^{jw}\right)$ denotes CFR, $\mathbf{N}$ denotes white Gaussian noise. At the transmitter, the original data is converted into symbol sequence and inverse fast Fourier transform (IFFT) algorithm is used to realize the orthogonal subcarrier modulation and the cyclic prefix is added to the radio frequency (RF) emission. At the receiver, the frequency conversion of the RF signal is carried out first, after removes cyclic prefix fast Fourier transform (FFT) algorithm is used to demodulation the orthogonal sub-carrier. Next, system carries on channel estimation according to the incoming leading signal (Pilot), the obtained value is the CFR measured value for each sub-carrier. According to the IEEE 802.11n standard, the 40 MHz bandwidth uses 114 subcarriers, and the corresponding subcarrier measurements are outputted during signal processing.

2.2 Super-Resolution AoA Estimation Algorithm

MUSIC algorithm [9] requires that the number of array antennas is greater than the number of multipath components or the signal and noise subspace cannot be separated. Moreover, the performance of MUSIC algorithm degraded severely in indoor environment because of the signal subspace diffusing into the noise subspace when the source is coherent.

Super-resolution AoA estimation algorithm uses spatial smoothing technology to create a virtual antenna array. The CFR in different subcarrier is written as

$$\text{CFR}\left[f_n\right] = \sum_{k=1}^{K} \alpha_k e^{-j2\pi(f_0 + n\Delta f)\tau_k} \tag{2}$$

where K is the number of propagation paths, α_k is the complex attenuation of the kth path, τ_k is the time delay of the kth path, and $f_n = f_0 + n\Delta f$ is carrier frequency of subcarrier, Δf is the subcarrier spacing. We implemented our system on Intel 5300 commodity Wi-Fi card, which can measure CFR at 30 of the subcarriers while data is sent on 114 subcarriers for 40 MHz bandwidth.

We assume there are K paths arriving at receiver, so CFR measurement matrix of 30 subcarriers on three antennas can be expressed as follows:

$$\mathbf{H} = [h_{1,1}, \ldots, h_{1,N}, h_{2,1}, \ldots, h_{2,N}, \ldots, h_{M,1}, \ldots, h_{M,N}]^{\mathrm{T}} \tag{3}$$

where $h_{m,n}$ is the CFR of nth subcarrier at m^{th} antenna. And then, $\mathbf{H}$ is given by

$$\mathbf{H} = \mathbf{A}\mathbf{X} + \mathbf{N} \tag{4}$$

where matrix $\mathbf{N}$ is additive white Gaussian noise of zero mean and covariance $\sigma^2 \mathbf{I}_{MN}$ can be write as $\mathbf{N} = [n_{1,1}, \ldots n_{1,30}, n_{2,1}, \ldots n_{2,30}, n_{3,1}, \ldots n_{3,30}]^{\mathrm{T}}$, and attenuation coefficient vector X is given by

$$\mathbf{X} = [\alpha_1, \alpha_2, \ldots \alpha_K]^{\mathrm{T}} \tag{5}$$

The matrix $\mathbf{A}$ is a steering matrix which can be written as:

$$\mathbf{A} = [\mathbf{a}(\theta_1, \tau_1), \mathbf{a}(\theta_2, \tau_2), \ldots, \mathbf{a}(\theta_k, \tau_k)] \tag{6}$$

where $\mathbf{a}(\theta, \tau)$ expressed as:

$$\mathbf{a}(\theta, \tau) = [\alpha_1(\theta, \tau), \alpha_2(\theta, \tau), \ldots, \alpha_m(\theta, \tau)]^{\mathrm{T}} \tag{7}$$

where $\alpha_m(\theta_k, \tau_k) = [\alpha_{m,1}(\theta_k, \tau_k), \ldots, \alpha_{m,n}(\theta_k, \tau_k)]^{\mathrm{T}}$ is the steering vector of the kth subcarrier at m^{th} antenna, $a_{m,n}(\theta_k, \tau_k) = e^{-j2\pi[(n-1)\Delta f \tau_k + d(m-1)\sin\theta_k/\lambda]}$ and Δf is subcarrier frequency spacing, τ_k and θ_k are the TOA and AOA of the kth path, respectively, d is antenna spacing.

The covariance matrix of measured CFR is given by

$$R = E\{H \times H^\dagger\} \tag{8}$$

where $(.)^\dagger$ represent the transpose-conjugate operator. A prior work [17] has noted that the minimal eigenvectors are orthogonal to the steering matrix $\mathbf{A}$. So, the spatial spectrum of multipath components, which respect to AoA and ToA is written as:

$$P_{\mathrm{music}} = \frac{1}{\alpha^{\mathrm{H}}(\theta, \tau) E_N E_N{}^{\mathrm{H}} \alpha(\theta, \tau)} \tag{9}$$

where E_N is the noise subspace eigenvector of covariance matrix R.

MUSIC algorithm can determine AoA only when the received signals are incoherent with each other. But the received signals include many coherent signals that can degrade the performance of MUSIC in indoor environment. Prior work [16] propose a novel method to get several dependent snapshots by reconstructing CFR measurements, but the coherent signals are not be considered. In order to decorrelate the coherent signals, we propose a two-dimensional spatial smoothing algorithm.

Indeed, one could check that the total number of overlapping subarrays is equal to $L_1 \times L_2$, where $L_1 = M - M_{sub} + 1$ and $L_2 = N - N_{sub} + 1$. The CFR measurement $N_{sub1} = 2$ and $N_{sub2} = 15$, and therefore a total of $L_1 \times L_2 = 32$ subarrays. The 2D spatial smoothed covariance matrix is given by

$$\overline{R} = \frac{1}{L_1 \times L_2} \sum_{m=1}^{L_1} \sum_{n=1}^{L_2} R_{m,n} \tag{10}$$

where $R_{m,n}$ is the CFR covariance matrix of subarray $\{(i,j)\}_{j=n\ldots N_{sub}+n-1}^{i=m\ldots M_{sub}+m-1}$. Plug Eq. (9) into MUSIC algorithm to estimate each path AoA and ToA.

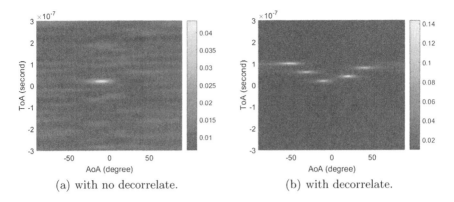

(a) with no decorrelate.   (b) with decorrelate.

Fig. 1. (a) Plots the AoA and ToA of five coherent signals in typical algorithm and (b) plots the AoA and ToA of five coherent signals in spatial smoothing.

Simulation results are presented to show the validity of 2D spatial smoothing. Simulations have been done with $M = 3$ antennas and $N = 30$ subcarriers. The antenna spacing d is half a wavelength. The subcarrier spacing is chosen 1.25 MHz and carrier frequency is 5.2 GHz.

We have fixed $s = 5$ coherent signals, where there corresponding angles and times of arrival are $(\theta_1, \tau_1) = (-10°, 20\,\text{ns})$, $(\theta_2, \tau_2) = (20°, 40\,\text{ns})$, $(\theta_3, \tau_3) = (40°, 80\,\text{ns})$, $(\theta_4, \tau_4) = (-50°, 100\,\text{ns})$, $(\theta_5, \tau_5) = (-30°, 60\,\text{ns})$. Figure 1 shows the determine result of no spatial smoothing and spatial smoothing. It is shown that the 2D spatial smoothing technology can accurately estimate AoA and ToA.

2.3   Identifying Direct Path AoA

Phase Correction: In multipath propagation indoor environment, the spatial spectral function calculated by the MUSIC algorithm has more than one peak which stands for the existence of the multipath signal. According to triangulation principle, it is necessary to determine the direct path for each LoS AP. To the best of knowledge, there are some conventional direct path identification using the shortest ToA or biggest spectral peak to determine the direct path. The signal with shortest ToA is treated as the direct path in [11,12] since the sender and receiver are time synchronization and the accuracy of ToA estimation is nanosecond level. But for the current Wi-Fi network cannot achieve so high accuracy. Moreover, in Wi-Fi networks each received packet introduces a random packet detection delay (PDD) which introduces an additional delay for all multipath components.

The PDD is different for each received data packets and the additional phase shift at subcarrier caused by PDD is $-2\pi\Delta f (n - 1) \tau$ presented in [13]. Usually, τ is the additional delay with 3 to 6 sample times. For 20 MHz bandwidth Wi-Fi signal, the signal is sampled once every 50 ns. Thus, τ is 75 to 150 ns which is much larger than the normal ToA of WiFi signal in indoor environment. Consequently, the CSI phases between subcarriers are approximately linear. However, all the RF channels in the same Wi-Fi chip are fully synchronized, so the phase shift at a particular subcarrier is same across all antennas. We use least squares linear fit algorithm to estimate and then eliminate the effect of PDD on CFR phase for each subcarrier. Assuming $\Phi_i(m, n)$ is the nth subcarrier CFR phase in the ith packet received at m^{th} antenna. The least squares fit using CFR phases of 30 subcarriers at 3 antennas is given by

$$\hat{\tau}_i = \arg\min_{\tau_i} \sum_{n=1}^{30} \sum_{m=1}^{3} (\Phi_i(m, n) + 2\pi\Delta f(n-1)\tau_i + \beta)^2 \tag{11}$$

Then, we correct the CFR phase as following:

$$\overset{\wedge}{\underset{i}{\Phi}}(m, n) = \Phi_i(m, n) + 2\pi\Delta f(n-1)\overset{\wedge}{\underset{i}{\tau}} \tag{12}$$

Identifying Direct Path and NLoS/LoS Environment: After obtain several clusters corresponding to each physical paths [14,15], we need to identify the clustering belongs to direct path. In this paper, we use a weight based direct path identification scheme proposed in [16]. We assign weights for each path as:

$$w_k = f(\omega_c C_k - \omega_\theta \sigma_{\theta_k} - \omega_\tau \sigma_{\tau_k} - \omega_s \tau_k) \tag{13}$$

where f is an increment function, C_k, σ_{θ_k}, σ_{τ_k} and τ_k are the number of extreme points, angle variance, time variance and mean time of the kth clustering, respectively. And ω_c, ω_θ, ω_τ and ω_s are weight factor of extreme points, angle variance, time variance and time mean, respectively. Then, we select path with the largest weights as the direct path and the average angle of the clustering as the direct path AoA.

Usually there is no direct path between target and APs due to obstacle blocking in complex indoor environment. So the selected direct path by the foregoing step is incorrect, so as to avoid this case we need to distinguish LoS and NLoS condition before locating the target. We conduct data collection campaign in LoS and NLoS environment, respectively. The maximum weights calculated by the Eq. (15) were extracted from LoS and NLoS environment respectively, and then we calculate a threshold which can class LoS and NLoS environment. In fact, LoS/NLoS identification can be formulated as a class binary hypothesis test with LoS condition and NLoS condition as following:

$$\begin{cases} H_0 : w \leq w_{th} \\ H_1 : w > w_{th} \end{cases} \tag{14}$$

where w_{th} is the optimal threshold.

2.4 Localizing the Target

We use the AoA of direct paths of multiple APs to locate the target and we assume there are R receivers in which receivers are in LoS environment. We measure the deviation using standard least squares cost. Mathematically, we find the location that minimizes the following objective function:

$$\text{location} = \min \sum_{i=1}^{R_{\text{los}}} \left(\hat{\theta}_i - \theta_i \right)^2 \tag{15}$$

where θ_i is the true direct path AoA of ith AP, and $\hat{\theta}_i$ is the estimated direct path AoA at i^{th} AP.

3   Experimental Evaluation

We implemented our system in a typical indoor environment, and we deploy four ProBox23 MS-B083 mini PCs equipped with Intel 5300 commodity Wi-Fi cards which act as access points and one PC in tester act as the target. Each AP possesses an antenna array consisting of three omnidirectional antennas with spaced by half a wavelength and no further hardware modification. The locations of every access points are measured accurately using laser range finder when we install APs on the wall. We use Linux CSI toolkit [10] to collect CFR measurements and then ship the measurement to the localization engineer acted by a computer and Fig. 2 shows our testbed.

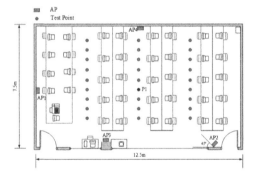

Fig. 2. Experiment tested showing the target locations (red spots) and the AP locations (blue rectangles). The region covering 12.5 m × 7.5 m area, represents typical indoor office environment. (Color figure online)

Estimating direct path AoA: Figure 3 shows the clustering and spatial spectrum at one AP and the test point P1. The data collected at test point P1 is transmitted to the central server. The performance of AoA estimation our algorithm is shown in Fig. 4. From this figure, we can find that our algorithm outperforms the conventional MUSIC algorithm used by SpotFi. Our algorithm is able to achieve the median angle error 5° better than that achieved by SpotFi in the actual static indoor environment. Since our algorithm can resolve more coherent signals comparing to the SpotFi, so the multipath components have lower interference on the AoA estimation of direct path.

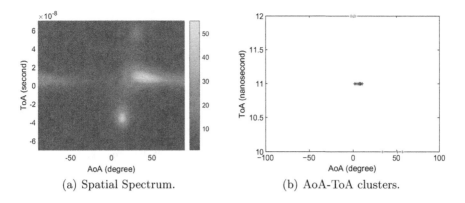

(a) Spatial Spectrum.   (b) AoA-ToA clusters.

Fig. 3. Plots spatial spectrum and AoA-ToA clusters respectively.

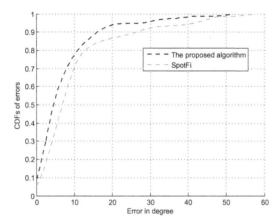

Fig. 4. Plots CDFs of AoA estimation error achieved by proposed algorithm and SpotFi in this paper for the same data.

Identifying LOS/NLOS environment: We create a NLoS environment between AP4 and the target at test point P1. Figure 5 shows the result of path clustering with the AP4 at test point P1 in LOS environment and NLoS environment respectively. The clustering result present that the angle clustering map is concentrated in LOS environment while dispersed in NLoS environment.

Localizing the target: Figure 6 shows the localization error accumulation curve in LOS environment and NLOS environment respectively. We can see that in LOS environment median location errors is 0.8 m with proposed super-resolution angle estimation algorithm and the location accuracy reaches sub-meter level while 1.7 m with typical MUSIC algorithm. In NLOS environment, the median location error is 1.3 m with proposed environment recognition algorithm while 2.7 m with typical algorithm.

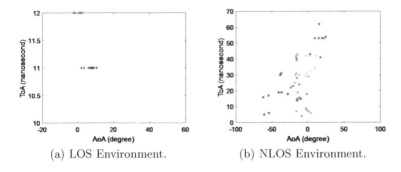

(a) LOS Environment.   (b) NLOS Environment.

Fig. 5. AoA-ToA clusters in LOS environment and NLOS environment respectively.

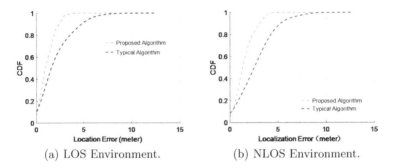

(a) LOS Environment.   (b) NLOS Environment.

Fig. 6. The CDFs of localization error by proposed algorithm and compare with location error by typical algorithm for the same data in LOS environment and NLOS environment respectively.

4   Conclusion

We have presented a sub-meter accuracy indoor localization system only use commodity AP with three antennas. The system firstly provides an OFDM signal based super-resolution AOA estimation algorithm. The algorithm can accurately estimate AoA of multipath signal with no additional hardware modification. And then using a clustering based direct path detection algorithm to pick out direct path. We also expand the direct path information to the scene recognition that can improve the robustness of the localization system. Since the system using multiple antennas and the characteristics of the OFDM signal, such that the algorithm of the present system is readily ported to the LTE system and the upcoming 5G communication system.

References

1. Ni, L.M., Liu, Y., Lau, Y.C.: LANDMARC: indoor location sensing using active RFID. Wirel. Netw. **10**, 701–710 (2004)
2. Gezici, S., Poor, H.V.: Position estimation via Ultra-Wide-Band signals. Proc. IEEE **97**, 386–403 (2009)

3. Gjengset, J., Xiong, J., Mcphillips, G.: Phaser: enabling phased array signal processing on commodity WiFi access points. In: MobiCom, pp. 6–9 (2009)

4. Niculescu, D., Nath, B.: Ad-hoc positioning system (APS) using AoA. In: Proceedings of IEEE INFOCOM (2003)

5. Xie, Y., Wang, Y., Zhu, P., You, X.: Grid search-based hybrid ToA/AoA location techniques for NLOS environments. IEEE Commun. Lett., 254–256 (2009)

6. Tarighat, A., Khajehnouri, N., Sayed, A.: Improved wireless location accuracy using antenna arrays and interference cancellation. IEEE (2003)

7. Patwari, N., Kasera, S.: Robust location distinction using temporal link signatures. In: Proceedings of the ACM MobiCom Conference, pp. 111–122 (2007)

8. Sheth, A., Seshan, S., Wetherall, D.: Geo-fencing: confining Wi-Fi coverage to physical boundaries. In: Tokuda, H., Beigl, M., Friday, A., Brush, A.J.B., Tobe, Y. (eds.) Pervasive 2009. LNCS, vol. 5538, pp. 274–290. Springer, Heidelberg (2009). https://doi.org/10.1007/978-3-642-01516-8_19

9. Laxmikanth, P., Surendra, L., Ratnam, D.V.: Enhancing the performance of AOA estimation in wireless communication using the MUSIC algorithm. In: IEEE SPACES, pp. 448–452 (2015)

10. Halperin, D., Hu, W., Sheth, A.: Tool release: gathering 80211.n traces with channel state information. ACM SIGCOMM Comput. Commun. Rev. **41**, 53 (2011)

11. Rabbachin, A., Oppermann, I., Denis, B.: ML Time-of-Arrival estimation based on low complexity UWB energy detection. In: IEEE 2006 International Conference on Ultra-Wideband, pp. 1–5 (2009)

12. Xie, Y., Li, Z., Li, M.: Precise power delay profiling with commodity WiFi. In: MobiCom, pp. 53–64 (2015)

13. Wang, K., Zhang, J., Li, D.: Adaptive affinity propagation clustering. Acta Autom. Sin. **33**, 1242–1246 (2007)

14. Cheng, Z., Zhao, L., Tao, H.: An intrusion detection approach based on affinity propagation clustering. Radio Eng., 4–7 (2013)

15. Wang, J., Jiang, H., Xiong, J.: LiFS: low human-effort, device-free localization with fine-grained subcarrier information. In: MobiCom, pp. 243–256 (2016)

16. Kotaru, M., Joshi, K., Bharadia, D., Katti, S.: SpotFi: decimeter level localization using WiFi. In: SIGCOMM 2015, pp. 269–282 (2015)

17. Venkatraman, S., Caffery, J., You, H.-R.: A novel ToA location algorithm using LoS range estimation for NLoS environments. IEEE Trans. Veh. Technol. **53**, 1515–1524 (2004)

Defect Detection of Photovoltaic Modules Based on Convolutional Neural Network

Mingjian Sun[✉], Shengmiao Lv, Xue Zhao, Ruya Li, Wenhan Zhang, and Xiao Zhang

Department of Control Science and Engineering,
Harbin Institute of Technology at Weihai,
Weihai 264209, Shandong, People's Republic of China
sunmingjian@hit.edu.cn

Abstract. Deep learning is employed to detect defects in photovoltaic (PV) modules in the thesis. Firstly, the thesis introduces related concepts of cracks. Then a convolutional neural network with seven layers is constructed to classify the defective battery panels. Finally, the accuracy of the validation set is 98.35%. Besides, the thesis introduces a method in which a single battery cell can be extracted from the Electro Luminescence (EL) image of the PV module. This method is very suitable for automatic inspection of photovoltaic power plants.

Keywords: Convolutional Neural Network · PV module cracks
Defect detection · Deep learning

1 Introduction

Photovoltaic power generation has become the most widely used way of generating new energy. In December 2016, National Energy Administration of China announced that by the end of 2016, cumulative installed capacity of photovoltaic power of China had reached 77.42 million kilowatts. In accordance with national requirements, China's photovoltaic power capacity will reach more than 150 million kilowatts in 2020 (see [1]). The core component of the whole photovoltaic power plant is the solar panel. The inevitable defects in the production and installation process will affect the efficiency of the plant. Thus, it is necessary to carry out defect detection for solar panels. The existing detection methods which are relatively mature in application are Infrared Thermal Imaging (ITI) and Electro Luminescence (EL). Infrared thermal imaging is suitable for a wide range of detection, but generally this approach only detects hot spot defects. The Electroluminescence method is suitable for detecting defects in a single PV module. Compared with infrared thermal imaging, it can show the details of the defects more clearly. It is generally used for the detection of the hidden cracks in the single module. At present, for large-scale photovoltaic power plants, manual sampling method is generally adopted, which costs a lot of labor and time. In terms of the current method of manual sampling, this paper proposes a kind

© ICST Institute for Computer Sciences, Social Informatics and Telecommunications Engineering 2018
X. Gu et al. (Eds.): MLICOM 2017, Part I, LNICST 226, pp. 122–132, 2018.
https://doi.org/10.1007/978-3-319-73564-1_13

of automatic detection method based on deep learning, which can realize the automatic detection and classification of the hidden cracks of PV modules.

Convolutional Neural Network is a classic deep learning framework inspired by the biological perception of natural visual perception. Convolutional neural networks, characterized by translational invariance, shared values and pooling, are effective in reducing network parameters, which renders it outstanding performance in many areas like image processing, video and voice (see [4]). In this paper, a CNN with seven layers is established to identify and classify the hidden flaws. The final classification accuracy reaches 98.35%.

The thesis introduces related concepts of cracks and the hazards and classification of hidden cracks in the Sect. 2. The theory of CNN, including the establishment of data set, the structure of neural network, the algorithms and so on, is introduced and the obtained results are shown in the Sect. 3. Section 4 describes how to extract a single battery cell from a single PV module.

2   Cracks

When the battery cell (component) is subjected to greater mechanical or thermal stress, the invisible crack probably comes into being, which is difficult to detect (see [10]). Different from hot spots, cracks only lead to battery disconnection, thus affecting the power output. Different types of cracks have different effects on the panels. As the hidden crack is difficult to directly observe with eyes, EL test is necessary for observation.

2.1   The Hazards and Classification of Cracks

The current flow path in the battery is that the collected current is transmitted to the main grid line by the fine grid line and is led out through the bus bar and the junction box. The current of the battery chip is proportional to the area of the power generation. If part of the current can not be transmitted to the main grid line due to cracks, the power output of the PV module will be affected. Thus, the main hazard of crack is forming failure area and affecting the output power (see [11,12]). Figure 1(a) shows that the hidden crack runs through the battery unit, but does not form a failure area, so the impact on the power output

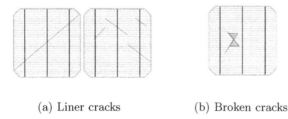

(a) Liner cracks   (b) Broken cracks

Fig. 1. Different cracks.

Fig. 2. From left to right, the types of cracks are normal, linear, cross, flaky and broken. The impact on output power is from weak to strong.

is less. Figure 1(b) shows that the battery cell has a failure area, therefore there is a worse impact on the power of the PV module.

   Therefore, according to the magnitude of hazards, the cracks are divided into five categories, respectively: normal, linear, cross, flaky and broken cracks, based on the impact on power output from weak to strong, as is shown in Fig. 2.

2.2   Electroluminescence Mechanisms

When the crystalline silicon cell is applied with a forward bias voltage, the carrier traverses the PN junction so that the carrier concentration exceeds the thermal equilibrium value to form an excess carrier. Excessive carrier recombines and the energy is released in the form of heat and light (photon). In the photon emission, the electrical energy is transformed into light, which is called injection electroluminescence (see [9]). Emission spectrum is mainly concentrated between 1000 nm–1300 nm. The brightness of electroluminescence is proportional to the total number of minority unbalanced carrier, the minority-carriers diffusion length and the current density. The minority diffusion length is lower where there is a defect, so the image is dark relatively. Thus, the defect can be judged from the light and shade. Figure 3 shows the EL mechanisms of test equipment. The camera used for the experiment is OPT-M311, the main chip of which is Sony EXPEED4, 24 million pixels. Figure 4 shows the image acquired by the EL detector.

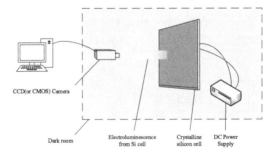

Fig. 3. Electroluminescence mechanisms.

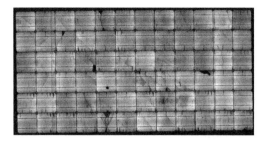

Fig. 4. Images acquired by EL detector. Defects can be judged from the light and shade.

3   Convolutional Neural Network

3.1   Image Data Set

The dataset includes the EL images acquired during the practical process. The EL image of each component is divided into images of single battery cell and processed to grayscale images with a size of 100 × 100. The original data can not be directly input to the neural network. Standardization is required and the method is as follows:

$$y = \frac{(x - mean)}{stddev} \tag{1}$$

where x, y are the pixel values at any point of the original image before and after the transformation. $mean$ is the mean of the image. $stddev$ is the standard deviation of the image.

It should be noted that the input image can not be uniform, otherwise there will be a division by 0 error. The entire data set storage structure is shown in Fig. 5.

Fig. 5. The storage structure of data set

The establishment of the data set refers to the format of the MNIST database of handwritten digits (see [14]), consisting of file headers, labels, pictures. The headers record the number and the ranks of images. In this way, the labels and images are combined together. Although the establishment process is slightly cumbersome compared to the data sets where labels and pictures are separated, this way has its own advantages. Firstly, data sets can be read into the memory block by block, avoiding the lack of memory when the data set is too large and avoiding the waste of time by reading pictures one by one. Secondly, it can facilitate the expansion of data. Comparatively speaking, data sets where labels and pictures are separated can only be read into memory all at once, and it is difficult to expand the data set.

3.2   Data Augmentation

Small data sets easily lead to over-fitting, while large data sets are difficult to obtain. Regarding this, data augmentation is quite essential (see [3]). The main methods include rotating the images, adjusting the brightness, conducting horizontal transformation and blurring the images. Rotating the images once every $5°$ from $-10° \sim 10°$ can enhance the effect from the slight tilt of the captured image. In addition, it is necessary to rotate $90°, 180°$ and $270°$ in turn. This will reduce the influence of the main grid lines on the classification accuracy, as the main line is easily recognized as a defect. Brightness and blurring are adopted to simulate the common situations of capturing images with cameras in order to enhance the generalization ability of neural network. Different methods of data augmentation are shown in Fig. 6. Finally, the entire data set has a total of 6120 pictures, of which 5120 images are used as training set and 1000 images are for validation.

Fig. 6. The methods of data augmentation. From left to right: original image, rotating $90°$, increasing brightness, mirror transformation, rotating $5°$.

3.3   Network Architecture

The CNN constructed in this paper is a multi-layer structure referring to [5], including two convolutional layers (C1, C3), two pooling layers (S2, S4), and a fully connected network. The overall network structure is shown in Fig. 7. As is shown, this network is relatively simple. It is mainly because the features of hidden cracks are obvious and easy to identify. This shallow network can achieve better results and effectively reduces the amount of calculation and the difficulty of training, thus this network is of engineering practicability.

The input image is a 100×100 grayscale image. After convolving with sixteen 5×5 kernels, sixteen 96×96 feature maps (C1) are obtained. After 2×2 max-pooling, sixteen 48×48 maps (S2) are acquired. Next, sixteen 46×46 feature maps (C3) are obtained with sixteen 3×3 kernels and then with max-pooling, layer S4 is produced. Finally, followed is a three-layer structure of fully connected network with 128 neurons in C5 layer and F6 layer. The last layer is the output layer with five neurons meaning five categories.

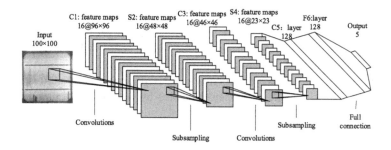

Fig. 7. The structure of CNN

Apart from the last layer using the Sigmoid activation function, the network uses the ReLU activation function (see [4]). The advantages are:

1. The essence of ReLU is a piecewise linear model. Forward calculation is very simple without calculation like exponent calculation.
2. ReLU is easy to calculate partial derivatives in back propagation.
3. ReLU is easy to train. The derivative will not tend to zero like Sigmoid activation function.
4. When input is less than 0, ReLU outputs 0. Thus many neurons output is 0, making the network become sparse, which can reduce the over-fitting phenomenon.

As the total output value of Softmax is 1, which means that the growing probability of one term will inevitably lead to the reduction of others, that is, output results of softmax are exclusive, the last layer does not use the Softmax function. However, a variety of defects may exist on the same cell of the battery. Softmax may lead to that the probabilities of different defects are all very small. Assuming that there are three defects on the battery chip, the output probabilities of defects may be 0.3, 0.3 and 0.4. Then it is not easy to judge what flaws are.

3.4   Training and Results of Neural Network

As mentioned earlier, increasing the training samples is one way to reduce over-fitting. Another is L2 normalization (weight decay). The idea of L2 normalization is to add an additional item to the loss function (see [13]). The regularization term shown in Eq. 2 is added to the cross entropy loss function which is used in this thesis.

$$C = -\frac{1}{n} \sum_{xj} \left[y_j \ln a_j^L + (1 - y_j) \ln(1 - a_j^L) \right] + \frac{\lambda}{2n} \sum_w w^2 \qquad (2)$$

where x is the input sample, a is the actual output vector of the neural network, y is the desired output vector for the neural network, w is the weight. The first term in Eq. 2 is just the usual expression for the cross-entropy. The second term, namely the sum of the squares of all the weights in the network is added to the cross-entropy. This is scaled by a factor $\frac{\lambda}{2n}$, where $\lambda > 0$ is known as the regularization parameter.

In the practical training process, the dropout method is also applied [3]. The dropout rate is 50%, which means that the connection layer neuron output is set to 0 randomly. In this way, the corresponding weight will not be updated, which can help reduce over-fitting. The training method applies the Nesterov gradient acceleration (NAG) method, which is slightly different from the momentum update and stochastic gradient descent and has become more popular now [2]. Nesterov can guarantee a stronger theoretical convergence for convex function and the practical performance is better than momentum and stochastic gradient descent. The core idea of Nesterov is to accelerate in the same gradient direction and decelerate in the changing gradient. The momentum update formula is Eq. 3.

$$\Delta V_t = \rho \Delta V_{t-1} - \eta \left[\nabla C \left(V_{t-1} \right) \right]^T \tag{3}$$

The momentum update includes two parts: one is the updated value $\rho \Delta V_{t-1}$, which has been calculated at last moment and is known at this moment; the other is calculated gradient $\eta \left(\nabla C \right)^T$ based on the current position. Nesterov accelerated gradient points out: since it is known that the update at this time will go $\rho \Delta V_{t-1}$, then go $\rho \Delta V_{t-1}$ first and correct according to the gradient there. Therefore, the gradient calculated in this method is not on a basis of old position, but is forward-looking.

$$\Delta V_t = \rho \Delta V_{t-1} - \eta \left[\nabla C \left(V_{t-1} - \rho \Delta V_{t-1} \right) \right]^T \tag{4}$$

The NAG update formula is shown in Eq. 4. In Eq. 4, the learning rate is set to 0.005, the momentum factor is set to 0.9, the batch size is set to 64, with a total of 2000 steps, that is 25 epochs.

Figure 8 shows the relationship between the accuracy of the classification and the number of training steps. The solid line indicates the accuracy rate of the training set. The test is to extract 1000 images randomly from the training set

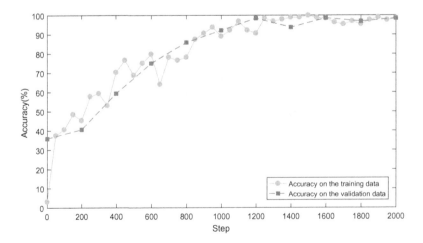

Fig. 8. Accuracy on the training and validation data set.

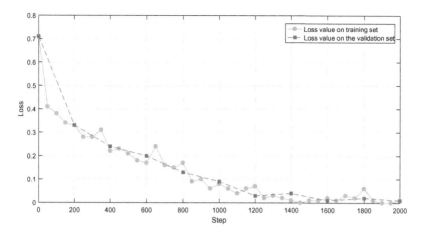

Fig. 9. The loss function is changing with the number of steps on the training and validation data set. The value of the loss function is small, indicating that the neural network has achieved better performance.

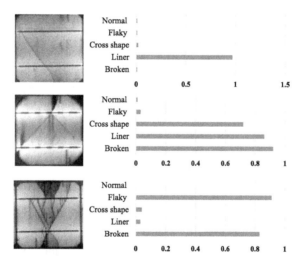

Fig. 10. Testing a single picture. The horizontal coordinate represents the probabilities predicted by the neural network and vertical coordinate represents the types of cracks.

to test the accuracy every 50 training steps. At Step 2000, the accuracy of the training set is 98.40%. The dotted line indicates the accuracy of the validation set. During the training process, there is validation on validation set every 200 steps. The final accuracy is 98.35%. As is shown, the network have achieved relatively good results on the test set and the validation set. The results indicate that the network is reasonable and is of strong generalization ability without over-fitting. This point can be seen from Fig. 9. The loss function finally reached a very small value of 0.2. Figure 10 shows the probabilities of different defects when testing a single image.

4   Acquirement of the Battery Unit EL Images

As is shown in Fig. 3, the first thing is to obtain crack images from the camera, and then use the neural network to identify the crack. The camera captures the EL image of the entire PV module, but the neural network requires an image of a single cell. So it is necessary to pre-process the acquired EL images. The processing steps are shown in Fig. 11.

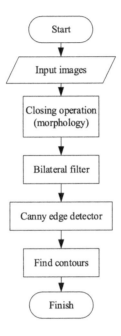

Fig. 11. The process of images processing

First, the morphological closed operation is used to fill the small voids in the foreground, especially reducing the effect of the two main grid lines on each cell. Otherwise, the two main grid lines will cause negative effects on border extraction. Second, use the bilateral filter algorithm to filter the pictures (see [8]). Bilateral filtering algorithm is a nonlinear filtering method, the advantage of which is to retain the edge information when filtering. This is favorable for the edge extraction. Next, use Canny edge detection to extract the edges (see [6]). Finally, adopt the method in literature [10] to extract the boundaries of each cell. The whole result is shown in the Figs. 12 and 13.

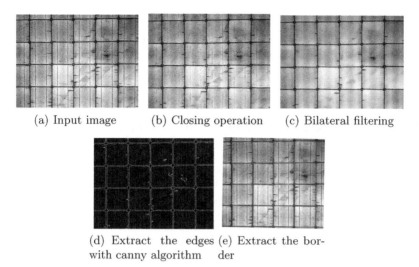

(a) Input image   (b) Closing operation   (c) Bilateral filtering

(d) Extract the edges (e) Extract the bor-
with canny algorithm   der

Fig. 12. The images (a)–(e) in turn show the results obtained after each step of image processing

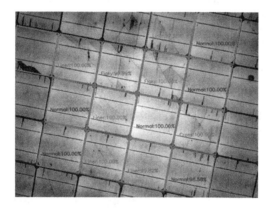

Fig. 13. Final recognition of results. To show clearer images and results, the images above are clipped from the input images. Thus, part information is missing and some cracks in the image are not detected.

5 Conclusion

The system first obtains the image data of each battery cell through a series of image processing algorithms, and then puts it into a well-trained neural network for classification. The accuracy of recognition reaches 98.40%. The characteristic of the whole system is that the algorithm can accurately extract the corresponding information and accurately identify the defects in the EL image collected from the camera no matter how much angle the PV modules rotate or when the modules tilt in the range of $-20° \sim 20°$. Thus, the system is very suitable for auto-inspecting the photovoltaic power plant, such as using a unmanned aerial vehicle (UAV) equipped with cameras to inspect power station.

References

1. China National Energy Administration: 13th five year plan for solar energy development. Solar Energy **12**, 5–14 (2016)
2. Bengio, Y., Boulanger-Lewandowski, N., Pascanu, R.: Advances in optimizing recurrent networks. In: 2013 IEEE International Conference on Acoustics, Speech and Signal Processing (ICASSP), pp. 8624–8628. IEEE (2013)
3. Krizhevsky, A., Sutskever, I., Hinton, G.E.: ImageNet classification with deep convolutional neural networks. In: Advances in neural information processing systems, pp. 1097–1105 (2012)
4. LeCun, Y., Bengio, Y., Hinton, G.: Deep learning. Nature **521**(7553), 436–444 (2015)
5. LeCun, Y., Bottou, L., Bengio, Y., Haffner, P.: Gradient-based learning applied to document recognition. Proc. IEEE **86**(11), 2278–2324 (1998)
6. Rong, W., Li, Z., Zhang, W., Sun, L.: An improved canny edge detection algorithm. In: 2014 IEEE International Conference on Mechatronics and Automation (ICMA), pp. 577–582. IEEE (2014)
7. Suzuki, S., et al.: Topological structural analysis of digitized binary images by border following. Comput. Vis. Graph. Image Process. **30**(1), 32–46 (1985)
8. Zhang, B., Allebach, J.P.: Adaptive bilateral filter for sharpness enhancement and noise removal. IEEE Trans. Image Process. **17**(5), 664–678 (2008)
9. Fuyuki, T., Kitiyanan, A.: Photographic diagnosis of crystalline silicon solar cells utilizing electroluminescence. Appl. Phys. A **96**, 189–196 (2009)
10. Wu, Z., Huang, H.: Research on the effects of PV modules' transformation on the performance. Mech. Eng. Autom. **4**, 107–109 (2011)
11. Xu, Z., Wang, H., et al.: Research progress in crack features of PV modules: part 1. Solar Energy **10**, 47–51 (2015)
12. Kajari-Schröder, S., Kunze, I., Eitner, U., Köntges, M.: Spatial and orientational distribution of cracks in crystalline photovoltaic modules generated by mechanical load tests. Solar Energy Mater. Solar Cells **95**, 3054–3059 (2011)
13. Krogh, A., Hertz, J.A.: A simple weight decay can improve generalization. In: NIPS, vol. 4, pp. 950–957 (1991)
14. MNIST database of handwritten digits. http://yann.lecun.com/exdb/mnist/

An Effective BLE Fingerprint Database Construction Method Based on MEMS

Mu Zhou[✉], Xiaoxiao Jin, Zengshan Tian, Haifeng Cong, and Haoliang Ren

Chongqing Key Lab of Mobile Communications Technology,
Chongqing University of Posts and Telecommunications, Chongqing 400065, China
{zhoumu,tianzs}@cqupt.edu.cn, jxxcq_836235528@foxmail.com,
18008382985@163.com, 13108970732@163.com

Abstract. In indoor positioning system based on fingerprint, the traditional fingerprint database construction method consumes much manpower and time cost. To solve this problem, we propose an effective method for constructing fingerprint database by using Microelectro Mechanical System (MEMS) to assist Bluetooth Low Energy (BLE), which overcomes the low efficiency of traditional methods. Meanwhile, the method achieves the comparable positioning accuracy and reduces workload more than 70%. In the optimization procedure, we use affine propagation clustering, outlier detection and filtering of Received Signal Strength Indication (RSSI) to optimize fingerprint database. Finally, the BLE positioning error conducted by the effective database is about 2 m.

Keywords: Indoor positioning
Fingerprint database construction method · BLE

1 Introduction

With the development of wireless positioning technology, the demand for Location Based Service (LBS) is becoming popular. At present, the Global Positioning System (GPS) technology can not meet the needs of indoor positioning accuracy [1]. Aiming at the complex signal propagation environment, many indoor positioning technologies have been proposed, such as Bluetooth [2], MEMS sensor [3] and Wire Local Area Networks (WLAN) [4]. The cost of equipment, scalability and accuracy limit the development of WLAN positioning technology. Meanwhile, the traditional fingerprint database constructing method receives RSSI at Reference Points (RPs), which is not suitable for large indoor scenes. The BLE technology is of low power consumption, low cost and short delay, which greatly reduces the cost of the BLE anchor. And compared with WLAN signal, the BLE signal is more stable.

To solve the inefficiency of traditional database constructing method, we propose an effective BLE fingerprint database constructing system based on MEMS. Firstly, the test staff holds the mobile phone and goes along the designated path, RSSI and MEMS data are uploaded to the server. The server tracks the change

© ICST Institute for Computer Sciences, Social Informatics and Telecommunications Engineering 2018
X. Gu et al. (Eds.): MLICOM 2017, Part I, LNICST 226, pp. 133–141, 2018.
https://doi.org/10.1007/978-3-319-73564-1_14

of heading angle and signal peak of RSSI propagation model to determine the
coordinate of the beacons, which are used for correcting Pedestrian Dead Reckoning (PDR). Then, we use affinity propagation clustering, outlier detection and
RSSI filter to eliminate noise and generate fingerprint sub-database. Thus in
positioning phase, we firstly determine the sub-database and then do fingerprint
positioning, which also reduces the server load.

The remainder of the paper is organized as follows. Section 2 reviews some
related work about effective construction methods of fingerprint database. In
Sect. 3, we introduce the proposed algorithm in detail. Section 4 shows the experimental results. Finally, the conclusion is provided in Sect. 5.

2   Related Work

In recent years, the effective construction methods of fingerprint database have
been widely concerned. An automatic database construction system based on
crowdsourcing is introduced in [5]. In the system, fixed landmark nodes, invisible landmarks and particle filtering technology are used to correct crowdsourcing
path. However, the system does not filter low quality data, which can not guarantee that all fingerprints are valid. In order to reduce the labor cost of the
off-line phase, a method is proposed to solve fingerprint identification in [6].
The off-line analytical fingerprint database is generated automatically by the
server, which avoids the link of the actual survey and construction. However,
this method requires a low SNR in environment, and the data from MATLAB
simulation experiments are not verified by the actual project. In [7], the system
uses a relative RSSI value vector group to replace the absolute RSSI value as the
fingerprint data, but failed to solve the problem of low efficiency of traditional
method. The main contribution of this paper is that we construct a more effective and accurate fingerprint database by using beacons to constantly correct
the PDR trajectory, which reduces the error of the fingerprint coordinate. At
the same time, we also use clustering, sub-database generating and filtering algorithm to further optimize the fingerprint database, which improves the efficiency
of online fingerprint matching.

3   Algorithm Description

3.1   Algorithm Overview

The overall framework of the system is shown in Fig. 1, which includes the speed
and heading reckoning module, the fingerprint database generation module and
the fingerprint database optimization module. Firstly, based on the accelerometer, gyroscope and magnetometer data from MEMS sensor, gait detection and
pedestrian attitude heading reckoning are used to get the speed and heading
of the target. Secondly, the beacons are determined by observing the change
of heading angle and the peak of signal propagation model. The beacons are
used to correct PDR trajectory, and then the fingerprint coordinates and RSSI

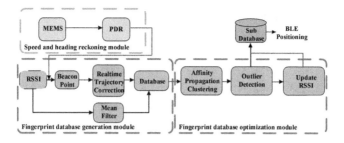

Fig. 1. The BLE fingerprint database construction method block.

are successively stored into the fingerprint database. Thirdly, the optimization steps include affinity propagation clustering, outlier detection and RSSI filter. In the BLE positioning phase, we firstly compare the real-time RSSI with all sub-database, and then position the target.

3.2 Speed and Heading Angle Estimation

The system uses 3-axis accelerometer, 3-axis magnetometer and 3-axis gyroscope in smartphone to estimate the speed and heading angle of the target.

Speed estimation. In order to avoid additional error caused by the difference of equipments, we firstly calculate the total acceleration of the 3-axis acceleration as once smoothing filter, $a_i^{total} = \sqrt{(a_i^x)^2 + (a_i^y)^2 + (a_i^z)^2}$, (a_i^x, a_i^y, a_i^z) are accelerometer value at point i. From [8], the acceleration is of sinusoidal variation, so we judge the pedestrian step by comparing the peak of a_i^{total} with the given threshold. The sampling frequency of the MEMS sensor is f_s, the number of sampling points between adjacent peaks is ΔN, the time required for pedestrian step k is $t_k = \Delta N / f_s$, P_k is the step size of pedestrian step k, the corresponding average velocity is

$$v_k = \frac{P_k}{t_k} = \frac{P_k f_s}{\Delta N} \tag{1}$$

Heading angle estimation. To estimate the heading angle, we update the attitude angle matrix through quaternion [9]. The mutual relation between the quaternion and attitude angle is in [10], so we estimate the parameters of quaternion and then solve the corresponding attitude angle matrix. Thus, we can get the real-time attitude angle of the carrier. The attitude information of gyro is corrected by the observation data of the gravity vector and the geomagnetic vector of the geomagnetic sensor. Finally, the quaternion is updated by EKF model [11], the target heading angle is

$$\varphi = \arctan(-\frac{2(q_1 q_2 + q_0 q_3)}{q_0^2 + q_1^2 - q_2^2 - q_3^2}) \tag{2}$$

3.3   BLE Fingerprint Database Generation

Standard fingerprint database generation. At the beginning of database constructing phase, standard fingerprint coordinates are generated

$$\begin{cases} X_i = x_0 + i * L_{step\_x} \\ Y_i = y_0 + i * L_{step\_y} \end{cases} (i \in 1, 2, ..., \frac{|x_{end} - x_0|}{L_{step\_x}}) \tag{3}$$

In the formula, (x_0, y_0) and (x_{end}, y_{end}) are starting coordinate and ending coordinate of each trajectory. L_{step_x} and L_{step_y} are interval constant between two RPs. In our system, the interval constant is 0.6 m.

Location estimation and correction. In the process of dynamic acquisition of fingerprint data, PDR algorithm is used to calculate corresponding coordinates of each RSSI. With the increase of time, PDR trajectory will be offset, which leads to the error of the estimated coordinate, so its necessary to correct the error

$$\begin{cases} x_i = x_0 + \sum_{n=1}^{i} vx_n + \sum_{n=1}^{i} \varepsilon x_n \\ y_i = y_0 + \sum_{n=1}^{i} vy_n + \sum_{n=1}^{i} \varepsilon y_n \end{cases} \tag{4}$$

In the formula, (x_i, y_i) is the corrected coordinates at point i, vx_n and vy_n are the estimated velocity at point n, ε_{xn} and ε_{yn} are respectively the coordinate correction of x and y at point n.

$$\begin{cases} \varepsilon_{xi} = \frac{vx_i}{\sum_{n=1}^{end} vx_n}(L_x - L_{xpdr}) \\ \varepsilon_{yi} = \frac{vy_i}{\sum_{n=1}^{end} vy_n}(L_y - L_{ypdr}) \end{cases} \tag{5}$$

In the formula, (L_x, L_y) is the coordinate of beacon, $L_{xpdr} = \sum_{n=1}^{end} vx_n$ and $L_{ypdr} = \sum_{n=1}^{end} vy_n$ are respectively the projection of the PDR trajectory on the X axis and Y axis, vx_i and vy_i are respectively the projection of velocity at point i on the X axis and Y axis

$$\begin{cases} vx_i = v_i \sin(head_i) \\ vy_i = v_i \cos(head_i) \end{cases} \tag{6}$$

Standard fingerprint database generation. By formula (4), we get the estimated coordinate and perform Nearest Neighbor (NN) algorithm between the estimated coordinate and the standard coordinate. RSSI is stored in standard database at each second and then we seek the mean value of RSSI.

$$RSSI_n = \frac{\sum_{i=1}^{M} rssi_i}{M} \tag{7}$$

In the formula, $RSSI_n$ represents the RSSI at point n, $rssi_i$ is the RSSI received at point n, at the i time, we store the fingerprint data M times at point n.

3.4   Optimization of the Fingerprint Database

The fingerprint positioning method includes offline and online phases. The offline phase includes database construction and optimization, which includes affinity propagation clustering, outlier detection and RSSI filter, the online phase mainly determines the coordinate of the target. To save the time cost of fingerprint matching, we use the affine propagation clustering algorithm [12] to separate the fingerprint database into sub-database. In the online phase, we match the real-time RSSI with each sub-database center and select the optimal sub-database for position calculation. The RSSI collected by the effective construction method is easily affected by factors such as signal jitter and environmental noise, so we filter the fingerprint. The specific process is: traverse each fingerprint sub-database for outlier detection [13], when the outlier factor of a certain point is greater than a given threshold, we judge that the point is a outlier. And update the RSSI of the point according to the k adjacent RSSI. The flowchart for separating fingerprint sub-database is shown in Fig. 2.

Assuming that $density(x, k)$ and $rel\_density(x, k)$ indicate the density and relative density of point x about their adjacent points

$$density(x, k) = \left(\frac{\sum\limits_{y \in N(x,k)} distance(x, y)}{|N(x, k)|} \right)^{-1} \tag{8}$$

$$rel\_density(x, k) = \frac{density(x, k)}{\sum\limits_{y \in N(x,k)} \frac{density(y,k)}{|N(x,k)|}} \tag{9}$$

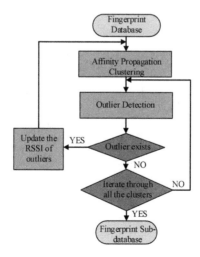

Fig. 2. The fingerprint sub-database separating flowchart.

In the formula, distance(x, y) is the Euclidean distance between x and y, $N(x, k)$ is a collection of k nearest neighbor points of point x, $|N(x, k)|$ indicates the number of elements of $N(x, k)$.

4   Performance Evaluation

4.1   Experimental Setup

To investigate the performance of the proposed approach, we conducted experiments in a real indoor environment with the size of 62 m by 62 m on the third floor of an office building, as shown in Fig. 3. The shadow section is the test area, and 10 Anchors are arranged in the whole location area. We design the BLE Anchor independently, which contains a Bluetooth signal transmitting antenna and is powered by a lithium battery. We select TI company's CC2540 as its built-in chip and HUAWEI mate9 mobile phone as terminal equipment, in which integrates BLE, accelerometer, gyroscope and magnetometer module. At the same time, we design an application for the acquisition of RSSI and MEMS data, and the application uploads data to the server periodically. The hardware platform of the system is shown in Fig. 4.

Figure 5 shows the change curve of RSSI within 30 min from an Anchor 1.5 m, it is clear that in such a long time, the BLE signal floats in a fixed range, so the stability of BLE signal is good. However, from previous analysis, the WLAN signal is likely to hop because of the pedestrian interference and other factors, so the stability is not as good as BLE signal. Figure 6 is a test of the signal strength and distance change of a BLE Anchor, the abscissa represents the distance between the test terminal and Anchor, the ordinate indicates the signal strength of Anchor received by terminal. We can find that the signal

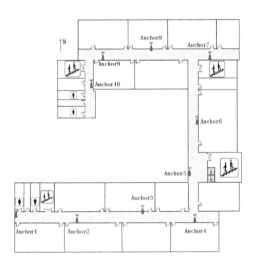

Fig. 3. Physical layout of target environment.

(a) The BLE Anchor   (b) The Android APP interface

Fig. 4. The system hardware platform.

is attenuated obviously in the range of 10 m, and accords with the propagation model of the theoretical signal. Therefore, the BLE signal is reliable and suitable in RSSI estimation at each point. Above all, we use the BLE signal for fingerprint database construction and positioning.

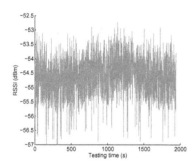
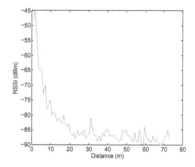
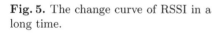

Fig. 5. The change curve of RSSI in a long time.

Fig. 6. The test result about the signal strength and distance change of the same Anchor.

Figures 7 and 8 show the clustering results before and after the original database denoising, respectively. Obviously, after removing singular points, the fingerprints of each region are comparatively pure. Therefore, denoising is beneficial to get the physical neighborhood RPs into a same cluster, which improves the efficiency of fingerprint matching in the online phase.

In view of the fingerprint database based on traditional fingerprint database construction method and the effective construction method proposed in this

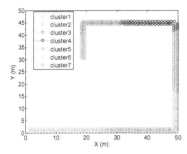

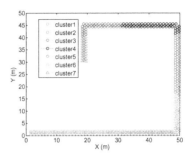

Fig. 7. Fingerprint database clustering result before de-noising.

Fig. 8. Fingerprint database clustering result after de-noising.

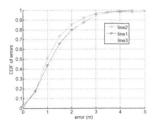

Fig. 9. The CDF of BLE positioning error with the traditional fingerprint database.

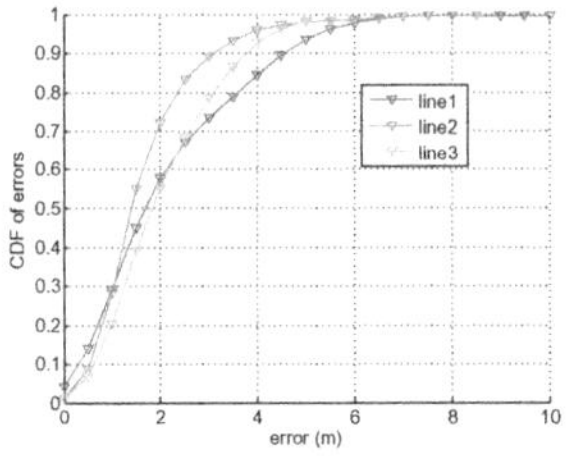

Fig. 10. The CDF of BLE positioning error with the effective fingerprint database.

paper, we research the accuracy and time cost in BLE positioning. We select three tracks for BLE positioning test, Figs. 9 and 10 are cumulative distribution function (CDF) based on two kinds of database. We can find that the BLE positioning accuracy based on effective fingerprint database has declined, but the 2.5 m accuracy under the condition of confidence rate of 70% is still able to meet the needs of indoor pedestrian positioning. Figure 11 shows the time cost on two methods of constructing fingerprint database in two test areas. Obviously, the effective BLE fingerprint database construction method saves a lot of time, and greatly improves the efficiency of database construction phase.

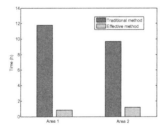

Fig. 11. The time cost of two kinds of database construction methods in different areas.

5   Conclusion

In order to solve the inefficiency of the traditional database construction method, an effective BLE fingerprint database construction method based on MEMS is proposed. In the process of constructing fingerprint database, we use the beacon point to correct PDR trajectory, which avoids the error caused by the large offset of PDR in a long time and improves the accuracy of fingerprint database. Then we use affine propagation clustering, outlier detection and RSSI filter to optimize the fingerprint database, and the sub-database saves much time on fingerprint matching. According to the experimental results, the effective fingerprint database construction method saves about 70% of the time cost and keeps the BLE positioning accuracy without significant decline, so the effective method is of great application prospect.

References

1. Agarwal, N., Basch, J., Beckmann, P.: Algorithms for GPS operation indoors and downtown. GPS Solutions **6**(3), 149–160 (2002)
2. Hallberg, J., Nilsson, M., and Synnes, K.: Positioning with Bluetooth. In: 10th IEEE International Conference on Telecommunications, pp. 954–958 (2003)
3. Judd, T.: A personal dead reckoning module. ION GPS **97**, 1–5 (1997)
4. Li, B., Salter, J., Dempster, A.G.: Indoor positioning techniques based on wireless LAN. In: LAN, First IEEE International Conference on Wireless Broadband and Ultra Wideband Communications (2006)
5. Huang, Z.Y., Xia, J., Yu, H.: Automatic collecting of indoor localization fingerprints: an crowd-based approach. In: 3rd IEEE/CIC International Conference on Communications in China(ICCC), pp. 769–774 (2014)
6. LLiu, J.L., Wan, Y.H., Xu, B.G.: A novel indoor positioning method based on location fingerprinting. In: 2013 International Conference on Communications, Circuits and Systems (ICCCAS), vol. 2, pp. 239-242. IEEE (2013)
7. Dong, G., Lin, K., Li, K.: FMA-RRSS: fingerprint matching algorithm based on relative received signal strength in indoor wi-fi positioning. In: 2014 IEEE 17th International Conference on Computational Science and Engineering (CSE), pp. 1071–1077. IEEE (2014)
8. Shin, S.H., Park, C.G., Kim, J.W.: Adaptive step length estimation algorithm using low-cost MEMS inertial sensors. In: SAS 2007 Sensors Applications Symposium, pp. 1–5. IEEE (2007)
9. Kuipers, J.B.: Quaternions and Rotation Sequences. Princeton University Press, Princeton (1999)
10. Barshan, B., Durrant-Whyte, H.F.: Inertial navigation systems for mobile robots. IEEE Trans. Robot. Autom. **11**(3), 328–342 (1995)
11. Kraft, E.: A quaternion-based unscented Kalman filter for orientation tracking. In: Proceedings of the Sixth International Conference of Information Fusion, vol. 1, pp. 47–54 (2003)
12. Bodenhofer, U., Kothmeier, A., Hochreiter, S.: APCluster: an R package for affinity propagation clustering. Bioinformatics **27**(17), 2463–2464 (2011)
13. Ramaswamy, S., Rastogi, R., Shim, K.: Efficient algorithms for mining outliers from large data sets. In: ACM Sigmod Record, vol. 29, no. 2, pp. 427–438. ACM (2000)

Intelligent Multimedia Processing and Security

A New Universal Steganalyzer for JPEG Images

Ge Liu[1], Fangjun Huang[2,3(✉)], Qi Chen[2], and Zhonghua Li[1]

[1] School of Electronics and Information Technology,
Sun Yat-Sen University, Guangzhou 510006, China
[2] School of Data and Computer Science, Sun Yat-Sen University,
Guangzhou 510006, China
huangfj@mail.sysu.edu.cn
[3] State Key Laboratory of Information Security,
Institute of Information Engineering, Chinese Academy of Sciences,
Beijing 100093, China

Abstract. The JPEG (Joint Photographic Experts Group) file format is currently one of the most widely used image formats. The study on JPEG steganography and steganalysis is a hotspot in the field of information hiding. With the matrix coding and some new adaptive embedding strategies having been put forward, the detection of stego images is becoming more and more difficult. In recent years, a series of new feature extraction methods have been proposed in the field of steganalysis. However, the detection accuracy rate can only be increased by 1–2% points or even less. Based on those existing steganalytic algorithms, a new feature merging method is proposed in this paper. Via merging features extracted from different domains, the detection accuracy rate of those existing JPEG steganalytic algorithms can be improved by 3% points or even higher. Considering about that the feature dimension is so high after feature merging and thus it may bring difficulties in the feature extraction, training and classification process, a new feature selection method is also proposed in this paper. Experimental results demonstrate that it can not only achieve reduction of the dimensionality, but also maintain a high detection accuracy rate.

Keywords: Steganography · Steganalysis · JPEG · Feature merging
Feature selection

1 Introduction

Steganography is a technique for invisible communication. Its purpose is to embed secret messages into digital covers, such as digital images, for covert communication through public communication channels [1]. Conversely, steganalysis is a technique for detecting the presence of hidden messages in cover objects.

Due to the common use of JPEG images in recent years, JPEG image steganography has been proposed one by one, e.g., YASS [2, 3], NPQ [4], DF-US [5], UED [6], UERD [7], J-UNIWARD [8]. Therefore, how to effectively detect the JPEG steganographic algorithms is one of the most urgent practical problems. Currently, researches

© ICST Institute for Computer Sciences, Social Informatics and Telecommunications Engineering 2018
X. Gu et al. (Eds.): MLICOM 2017, Part I, LNICST 226, pp. 145–157, 2018.
https://doi.org/10.1007/978-3-319-73564-1_15

on steganalysis can be divided into two classes: special steganalysis and universal steganalysis. Special steganalysis [9–11] is designed for a specific hiding technique, while universal steganalysis [12–21] is generally designed for a series of steganographic methods simultaneously. Due to the diversity of the current steganographic techniques, universal steganalysis is more adaptable in practical applications. Accordingly, the universal steganalysis has attracted extensive attention.

The universal steganalysis is based on machine learning and therefore, the key issue is to find distinguishing features that can classify cover images and stego images. This process has two important aspects. The first one is the design of feature extraction. The selected features should react sensitively to the embedding changes but insensitive to the image content. The second one is to propose an effective classifier with low computational complexity. This paper focuses on the first one, namely the design of feature extraction. In terms of feature extraction, it is believed in [13] that the best (most sensitive) features for steganalysis are obtained when they are calculated directly in the embedding domain. Thus, for JPEG images, the features were generally chosen from the quantized discrete cosine transform (DCT) domain for classification in the early study. For example, an effective Markov process (MP) based JPEG steganalysis scheme proposed in [14] utilized both the intrablock and interblock correlations among DCT coefficients; Fridrich et al. extended the 23 DCT features vector [15] to form a 274-dimensional feature vector [16] by merging Markov and DCT features and later, this 274-dimensional feature vector was extended to twice its size by Cartesian calibration [17]; Kodovský et al. extracted a 7850-dimensional feature vector [18] and used a rich model of DCT coefficients to form a 22510-dimensional feature vector [19]. Recently, in addition to extracting features from the DCT domain directly, some new steganalytic methods extracted features from the other domains were also studied. For example, Fridrich extracted a 34671-dimensional feature vector [20] from the spatial domain to attack the JPEG steganographic algorithms. Besides, features can be extracted from the undecimated DCT domain. For example, in [21], Holub et al. introduced a novel feature vector of which features were engineered as first-order statistics of quantized noise residuals obtained from the decompressed JPEG image using 64 kernels of the DCT coefficient matrix (the so-called undecimated DCT). Obviously, the features of these universal steganalyzers above are selected from a single domain, such as the DCT domain, the spatial domain, the undecimated DCT domain.

Based on those existing steganalytic algorithms, a new feature merging method is proposed in this paper. In recent years, though a series of new feature extraction methods have been introduced in the field of steganalysis, the detection accuracy rate can only be increased by 1–2% points or even less compared with those previously proposed methods. In this paper, we firstly propose that those features extracted in different domains can be merged together to form a more powerful steganalyzer, and the experimental results demonstrate the detection accuracy rate can be improved by 3% points or even higher. However, considering about that the feature dimension is so high after feature merging and thus it may bring difficulties to the feature extraction, training and classification, a new feature selection method is also proposed according to some properties introduced in [22]. Our experimental results demonstrate that this new feature selection strategy can not only reduce the dimensionality of the feature vector, but also maintain a high detection accuracy rate.

This paper is organized as follows. In Sect. 2, we present how to merge features extracted from different domains, such as the DCT domain, the spatial domain and the undecimated DCT domain. The new feature selection method is also proposed in Sect. 2. Experiments and results are then given in Sect. 3. Finally, we summarize this paper in Sect. 4.

2 Feature Merging and Feature Selection

2.1 Characteristics of Difference Images in Different Domains

Due to the intrusion characteristics of steganography, some distortion must be introduced to the cover image. In this place, one image randomly selected from BOSSbase ver. 1.01 [23] is exemplified to illustrate the influence of message embedding on the statistical distribution of the JPEG image. First, the image coming from the BOSSbase is compressed with JPEG quality factor (QF) 75, and then used as the cover as shown in Fig. 1(a). The stego image is generated via using the most representative J-UNIWARD JPEG steganographic algorithm [8]. The embedding rate is 0.4 *bpnc* (bits per non-zero DCT coefficients)and the stego image is shown in Fig. 1(b).

(a)   (b)

Fig. 1. The cover image and the stego image corresponding to the J-UNIWARD algorithm. (a) The cover image. (b) The stego image with the embedding rate of 0.4 *bpnc*.

Figure 2(a)–(c) illustrate the difference images between the stego image and the cover image in spatial domain, DCT domain, and undecimated DCT domain, respectively. The white points indicate that in these positions the elements (pixels/ coefficients) have been modified, whereas the black points represent in those positions the elements keep untouched in the embedding process. It is observed from Fig. 2 that even if the same steganographic algorithm is applied, the obtained difference images have different statistical distribution characteristics. As we all know, the steganalytic features are extracted to discriminate the difference between the cover and stego images. In general, the features extracted from different domains may complement and reinforce each other. Thus, the detection accuracy rate can be improved via merging features extracted in different domains, such as the DCT domain, the spatial domain, and the undecimated DCT domain.

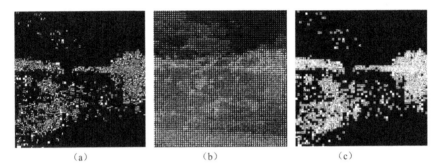

(a)   (b)   (c)

Fig. 2. The difference images between the cover and stego image obtained in different domains with the J-UNIWARD algorithm. (a) The spatial domain. (b) The DCT domain. (c) The undecimated DCT domain.

2.2 Characteristics of Feature Vector

As introduced in our previous work [22], the difference between cover and stego images should consistently increase with the increase of embedding rate. Some experimental results corresponding to the steganographic scheme J-UNIWARD are illustrated in Fig. 3. The cover image is shown in Figs. 1(a) and 3(a)–(d) show the modifications that have been made by using the J-UNIWARD algorithm with different embedding rates.

As seen in Fig. 3, even if embedding rates are different, most of the modifications are made in the same edge areas or complex texture regions. And the difference between cover and stego images will become greater with the increase of embedding rate. As is known, the most basic principle of steganalytic features is to capture the difference between cover and stego images. Via extracting the appropriate features, these two types of images can be classified. In our opinion, if the extracted feature value changes in one direction (consistently decrease or increase) with the increase of embedding rate, this extracted feature should be selected for classification. On the contrary, if the extracted feature presents a randomly decreasing or increasing characteristic, this kind of extracted feature may confuse the classifier and should be excluded from the original feature vector in the steganalytic process. The specific selection method of effective features will be detailed in Sect. 2.3.

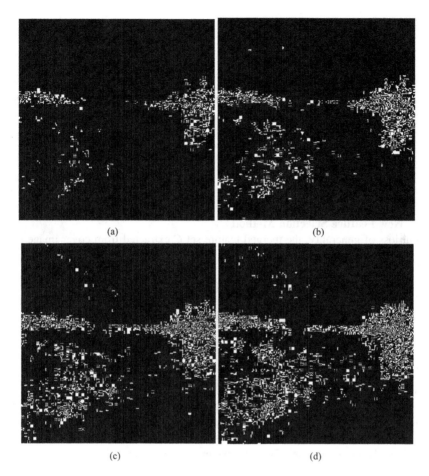

Fig. 3. Difference images between the cover and stego images regarding to different embedding rates. (a) The difference image with the embedding rate of 0.1 *bpnc*. (b) The difference image with the embedding rate of 0.2 *bpnc*. (c) The difference image with the embedding rate of 0.3 *bpnc*. (d) The difference image with the embedding rate of 0.4 *bpnc*.

2.3 Feature Merging and Feature Selection

Based on the characteristic described in Sects. 2.1 and 2.2, it is obvious that the modifications introduced by embedding messages present different characteristics in different domains and thus steganalysis features in different domains may have different detection ability. The detailed realization of our proposed feature merging method and feature selection method are given in the following.

2.3.1 Merging Features Extracted in Different Domains

Suppose that there are $A_t(t = 1, 2, \ldots)$ feature extracted domains. According to our previous analysis, today's modern steganalytic algorithms generally extract features from one of the domains. Assume that $F_{t,j}(t = 1, 2, \ldots)$ denotes the value of the jth

dimensional feature which is extracted from an image in domain A_t. F_t which denotes the feature vector extracted from the image in domain A_t is defined as

$$F_t = \{F_{t,j} | 1 \leq j \leq N_t\}, \tag{1}$$

where the parameter N_t denotes the total number of features extracted from an image in domain A_t.

And F which denotes the new feature vector obtained by merging features extracted in different domains is represented as

$$F = [F_1 \, F_2 \ldots]. \tag{2}$$

2.3.2   New Feature Selection Method

Without loss of generality, the merged feature set C extracted from cover image set is defined as

$$C = \{C_{i,j} | 1 \leq i \leq M, 1 \leq j \leq N\}. \tag{3}$$

And the merged feature set S^α extracted from stego images is defined as

$$S^\alpha = \{S_{i,j}^\alpha | 1 \leq i \leq M, 1 \leq j \leq N\}. \tag{4}$$

In Eqs. (3) and (4), M denotes the number of images in the image set, N denotes the total number of features after merging features extracted from an image in different domains. The parameter α represents the embedding rate.

Then we can obtain P_j as follows, which denotes mean value of all the jth dimensional features extracted from images in the image set.

$$P_j = \left(\sum_{i=1}^{i=M} C_{i,j} \right) / M, \quad (1 \leq j \leq N). \tag{5}$$

And a new variable is defined as

$$T_j^\alpha = \sum_{i=1}^{M} f\left(S_{i,j}^\alpha - P_j \right), \tag{6}$$

where

$$f(x) = \begin{cases} 0, & x \leq 0 \\ 1, & x > 0 \end{cases}. \tag{7}$$

According to our previous analysis in Sect. 2.2, if the value of T_j^α in Eq. (6) consistently decreases or increases with the increase of embedding rate α, the jth dimensional feature will be selected as effective feature.

Some experimental results corresponding to the steganalysis scheme JRM are shown in Table 1. We randomly select 5000 images from BOSSbase ver. 1.01, which are compressed as the cover images with QF = 75. Then 5000 stego images are created by using the most representative steganographic algorithm J-UNIWARD with different embedding rates. The cover feature set and stego feature set are extracted from cover and stego images using JRM steganalytic algorithm. We calculate T_j^α using Eqs. (5) and (6), where the parameters M and N are equal to 5000 and 22500 respectively. The three $T_j^\alpha (j = 6, 11, 19)$ values (i.e., the 6th dimensional feature, the 11th dimensional feature and the 19th dimensional feature) extracted by JRM from 5000 stego images with different embedding rates are shown in Table 1.

Table 1. characteristic of the same feature of difference images with different embedding rates

Embedding rates	T_j^α values		
	$j = 6$	$j = 11$	$j = 19$
$\alpha = 0.1bpnc$	2290	2387	2302
$\alpha = 0.2bpnc$	2278	2393	2315
$\alpha = 0.3bpnc$	2275	2368	2325
$\alpha = 0.4bpnc$	2271	2400	2346

It is observed from Table 1 that T_6^α corresponding to the 6th dimensional feature (T_{19}^α corresponding to the 19th dimensional feature) consistently decrease (increase) with the increase of embedding rate α. Whereas for T_{11}^α corresponding to the 11th dimensional feature, it may decrease or increase randomly with the increase of embedding rate α. According to our previous analysis, these kinds of features (e.g., the 6th dimensional feature and 19th dimensional feature) may be effective and should be selected in the steganalytic process. However, those kinds of features (e.g., the 11th dimensional feature) may confuse the classifier and can be excluded from the original feature set in the steganalytic process.

As a result, if T_j^α value consistently decreases or increase with the increase of embedding rate α, this extracted j^{th} dimensional feature may be effective and should be selected. Thus, in our proposed method, the extracted feature may be selected as an effective feature in these two cases as follows. Here, a parameter δ is introduced to control the number of selected features.

Case 1: T_j^α values consistently decrease with the increase of embedding rate α. The extracted features from the original high dimensional feature set must satisfy the following two conditions.

(1) For any given image set to be tested, the stego images are obtained with different embedding rates, i.e., $\alpha_1, \alpha_2, \ldots, \alpha_n$. For $0 < \alpha_1 < \alpha_2 < \cdots < \alpha_n (n = 1, 2, 3, \ldots)$, if the jth dimensional feature is considered as the effective feature and can be selected for classification, the T_j^α values should consistently decrease with the increase of embedding rate α, namely the following inequality (8) must be satisfied, i.e.,

$$T_j^{\alpha_1} > T_j^{\alpha_2} > \cdots > T_j^{\alpha_n} \tag{8}$$

(2) For any given embedding rate, if the jth dimensional $(1 \leq j \leq N)$ feature is effective, the following inequalities must be satisfied to control the number of selected features.

$$0 \leq T_j^{\alpha_1} \leq M \times \delta$$
$$0 \leq T_j^{\alpha_2} \leq M \times \delta$$
$$\vdots$$
$$0 \leq T_j^{\alpha_n} \leq M \times \delta$$

The parameter δ $(0 < \delta < 1)$ is used to control the number of selected valid classification features. In this paper, we can select $\delta = 0.45$–0.50. Generally, the number of effective features may increase with the increase of δ.

Case 2: T_j^{α} values consistently increase with the increase of embedding rate α. The extracted feature from the original high dimensional feature set must satisfy the following two conditions.

(1) For any given image set to be tested, the stego images are obtained with different embedding rates, i.e., $\alpha_1, \alpha_2, \ldots, \alpha_n$. For $0 < \alpha_1 < \alpha_2 < \cdots < \alpha_n (n = 1, 2, 3, \ldots)$, if the jth dimensional feature is considered as the effective feature and can be selected for classification, the T_j^{α} values should consistently increase with the increase of embedding rate α, namely the following inequality (9) must be satisfied, i.e.,

$$T_j^{\alpha_1} < T_j^{\alpha_2} < \cdots < T_j^{\alpha_n} \tag{9}$$

(2) For any given embedding rate, if the jth dimensional $(1 \leq j \leq N)$ feature is effective, the following inequalities must be satisfied to control the number of selected features.

$$M \times (1 - \delta) \leq T_j^{\alpha_1} \leq M$$
$$M \times (1 - \delta) \leq T_j^{\alpha_2} \leq M$$
$$\vdots$$
$$M \times (1 - \delta) \leq T_j^{\alpha_n} \leq M$$

Similarly, we can select $\delta = 0.45$–0.50.

3 Experimental Results

3.1 Experiment Setup

In this paper, we utilize the BOSSbase ver. 1.01 [23] image data set for all of our experiments. It consists of 10000 gray-scale images with the size 512×512, which are compressed as the cover images with QF = 75. The stego images are generated by using the most representative JPEG steganographic algorithm J-UNIWARD with different embedding rates. Four different embedding rates, i.e., 0.1 *bpnc*, 0.2 *bpnc*, 0.3 *bpnc* and 0.4 *bpnc*, are selected in our testing. The ensemble classifier [18] is used for classification. We randomly select 5000 images for training and the remaining 5000 images are used for testing.

3.2 Experiment #1

In this experiment, algorithm SRM [20] is applied to extract features from JPEG stego images in A_1 domain (the spatial domain). The dimension of the SRM feature vector is $N_1(N_1 = 34671)$. Algorithm JRM [19] is applied to extract features from JPEG stego images in A_2 domain (the DCT domain). The dimension of the JRM feature vector is $N_2(N_2 = 22510)$. Algorithm DCTR [21] is applied to extract features from JPEG stego images in A_3 domain (the undecimated DCT domain). The dimension of the DCTR feature vector is $N_3(N_3 = 8000)$. A new feature vector is obtained by merging features extracted in two or three different domains. The ensemble classifier [18] is used for classifying JPEG cover images and JPEG stego images. The efficiency of our proposed feature merging method is shown in the Table 3. In comparison, the efficiency of the features extracted in a single domain is shown in the Table 2. In this case, three different steganalysis schemes, i.e., SRM, JRM and DCTR and four different embedding rates, i.e., 0.1 *bpnc*, 0.2 *bpnc*, 0.3 *bpnc*, 0.4 *bpnc* are tested.

Table 2. Features dimension and testing error for four different embedding rates in different single domain

Embedding rates (*bpnc*)	Testing error		
	SRM	JRM	DCTR
Dimension	34671	22510	8000
0.1	0.4514	0.4725	0.4383
0.2	0.3797	0.4177	0.3408
0.3	0.2857	0.3411	0.2368
0.4	0.1988	0.2585	0.1504

From the Tables 2 and 3, it is obvious that the detection accuracy rate can be improved via merging features extracted from different domains. For example, when the embedding rate is 0.4 *bpnc*, the testing error of the steganalysis scheme SRM is

Table 3. Features dimension and testing error of merging features

Embedding rates (*bpnc*)	Testing error			
	SRM + JRM	SRM + DCTR	JRM + DCTR	SRM + JRM + DCTR
Dimension	57181	42671	30510	65181
0.1	0.4464	0.4445	0.4385	0.4385
0.2	0.3585	0.3395	0.3370	0.3378
0.3	0.2664	0.2344	0.2309	0.2214
0.4	0.1667	0.1397	0.1402	0.1320

0.1988 with the feature dimension of 34671, while the testing error of the steganalysis scheme JRM is 0.2585 with the feature dimension of 22510, and the testing error of the steganalysis scheme DCTR is 0.1504 with the feature dimension of 8000. However, when combines SRM features and JRM features together, the testing error works out to be 0.1667 with the feature dimension of 57181. This indicates that the new feature merging method achieves to a higher classification rate by 3% points or even higher compared to the JPEG steganalytic algorithms SRM and JRM. Furthermore, when combines the SRM features, JRM features and DCTR features simultaneously, the testing error can be decreased to 0.1352 with the feature dimension of 65181. That is to say, its detection accuracy rate can be improved by 2–3% points or even more.

3.3   Experiment #2

Based on experiment 1 presented in Sect. 3.2, this experiment is to demonstrate the efficiency of our new method for dimensionality reduction, and the results are shown in Table 4. In this experiment, four different embedding rates, i.e., 0.1 *bpnc*, 0.2 *bpnc*, 0.3 *bpnc*, 0.4 *bpnc* are tested. In the training process, the effective features are selected according to the control parameter δ (δ is selected as 0.45, 0.46, 0.47, 0.48 or 0.49 in our testing) and a series of classifiers can be obtained. Then these obtained classifiers are used for testing.

As shown in Table 4, the proposed feature selection method can not only reduce the dimensionality of the merged feature vector, but also maintain a high detection accuracy rate. For example, when $\delta = 0.49$ and the embedding rate is 0.4 *bpnc*, for the merged feature set "SRM + JRM", the dimension can be reduced from 57181 to 13482. Though the testing error is increased from 0.1667 to 0.1717, the detection accuracy rate is still better than using SRM (the testing error is 0.1988) and JRM (the testing error is 0. 2585) separately. When $\delta = 0.49$ and the embedding rate is 0.4 *bpnc*, for the merged feature set"SRM + JRM + DCTR", the dimension can be reduced from 65181 to 16518. Though the testing error is increased from 0.1320 to 0.1340, the detection accuracy rate is still better than SRM (the testing error is 0.1988), JRM (the testing error is 0. 2585) or DCTR (the testing error is 0. 1504) separately.

Table 4. Features dimension and testing error of effective features

Embedding rates (*bpnc*)			Testing error			
			SRM + JRM	SRM + DCTR	JRM + DCTR	SRM + JRM + DCTR
0.1	$\delta = 0.49$	Dimension	13482	10406	9148	16518
		Testing error	0.4510	0.4393	0.4357	0.4356
	$\delta = 0.48$	Dimension	11557	8661	8382	14300
		Testing error	0.4510	0.4417	0.4358	0.4358
	$\delta = 0.47$	Dimension	9890	7122	7604	12308
		Testing error	0.4513	0.4418	0.4428	0.4367
	$\delta = 0.46$	Dimension	8348	5780	6940	10534
		Testing error	0.4515	0.4465	0.4446	0.4407
	$\delta = 0.45$	Dimension	7092	4742	6392	9113
		Testing error	0.4527	0.4467	0.4509	0.4419
0.2	$\delta = 0.49$	Dimension	13482	10406	9148	16518
		Testing error	0.3562	0.3287	0.3358	0.3278
	$\delta = 0.48$	Dimension	11557	8661	8382	14300
		Testing error	0.3588	0.3368	0.3369	0.3307
	$\delta = 0.47$	Dimension	9890	7122	7604	12308
		Testing error	0.3611	0.3418	0.3500	0.3421
	$\delta = 0.46$	Dimension	8348	5780	6940	10534
		Testing error	0.3646	0.3534	0.3570	0.3461
	$\delta = 0.45$	Dimension	7092	4742	6392	9113
		Testing error	0.3670	0.3599	0.3711	0.3492
0.3	$\delta = 0.49$	Dimension	13482	10406	9148	16518
		Testing error	0.2566	0.2279	0.2285	0.2189
	$\delta = 0.48$	Dimension	11557	8661	8382	14300
		Testing error	0.2592	0.2360	0.2317	0.2225
	$\delta = 0.47$	Dimension	9890	7122	7604	12308
		Testing error	0.2604	0.2407	0.2455	0.2310
	$\delta = 0.46$	Dimension	8348	5780	6940	10534
		Testing error	0.2683	0.2514	0.2527	0.2389
	$\delta = 0.45$	Dimension	7092	4742	6392	9113
		Testing error	0.2754	0.2609	0.2745	0.2442
0.4	$\delta = 0.49$	Dimension	13482	10406	9148	16518
		Testing error	0.1717	0.1398	0.1432	0.1340
	$\delta = 0.48$	Dimension	11557	8661	8382	14300
		Testing error	0.1722	0.1463	0.1459	0.1385
	$\delta = 0.47$	Dimension	9890	7122	7604	12308
		Testing error	0.1746	0.1524	0.1579	0.1452
	$\delta = 0.46$	Dimension	8348	5780	6940	10534
		Testing error	0.1820	0.1596	0.1686	0.1534
	$\delta = 0.45$	Dimension	7092	4742	6392	9113
		Testing error	0.1912	0.1733	0.1862	0.1565

4   Conclusions

In this paper, we propose a new universal JPEG steganalyzer. The contributions of this paper are as follows.

(1) A new feature merging method is proposed in this paper. Via merging features extracted from different domains, the detection accuracy rate of those existing JPEG steganalytic algorithms can be improved by 3% points or even higher.

(2) Considering about that the feature dimension is so high, a new feature selection method is also proposed in this paper. Experimental results demonstrate that it can not only achieve reduction of the dimensionality, but also maintain a high detection accuracy rate.

Acknowledgements. This work is partially supported by National Natural Science Foundation of China (61772572), Natural Science Foundation of Guangdong Province of China (2017A030313366), and the Fundamental Research Funds for the Central Universities (17lgjc45).

References

1. Cheddad, A., Condell, J., Curran, K., Kevitt, P.M.: Digital image steganography: survey and analysis of current methods. Sig. Process. **90**(3), 727–752 (2010)
2. Solanki, K., Sarkar, A., Manjunath, B.S.: YASS: yet another steganographic scheme that resists blind steganalysis. In: Furon, T., Cayre, F., Doërr, G., Bas, P. (eds.) IH 2007. LNCS, vol. 4567, pp. 16–31. Springer, Heidelberg (2007). https://doi.org/10.1007/978-3-540-77370-2_2
3. Sarkar, A., Solanki, K., Manjunath, B.S.: Further study on YASS: steganography based on randomized embedding to resist blind steganalysis. In: Proceedings of the SPIE Security, Steganography, and Watermarking of Multimedia Contents X, San Jose, pp. 16–31. SPIE (2008)
4. Huang, F., Huang, J., Shi, Y.Q.: New channel selection rule for JPEG steganography. IEEE Trans. Inf. Forensics Secur. **7**(4), 1181–1191 (2012)
5. Huang, F., Luo, W., Huang, J., Shi, Y.Q.: Distortion function designing for JPEG steganography with uncompressed side-image. In: Proceedings of the First ACM Workshop on Information Hiding and Multimedia Security, Montpellier, France, 17–19 June 2013
6. Guo, L., Ni, J., Shi, Y.Q.: Uniform embedding for efficient JPEG steganography. IEEE Trans. Inf. Forensics Secur. **9**(5), 814–825 (2014)
7. Guo, L., Ni, J., Su, W., Tang, Ch., Shi, Y.Q.: Using statistical image model for JPEG steganography: uniform embedding revisited. IEEE Trans. Inf. Forensics Secur. **10**(12), 2669–2680 (2015)
8. Holub, V., Fridrich, J., Denemark, T.: Universal distortion function for steganography in an arbitrary domain. EURASIP J. Inf. Secur. **2014**, 1–13 (2014)
9. Li, B., Shi, Y.Q., Huang, J.: Steganalysis of YASS. In: Proceedings of the 10th ACM Multimedia & Security Workshop, Oxford, pp. 139–148. ACM (2008)
10. Fridrich, J., Goljan, M., Hogea, D.: Steganalysis of JPEG images: breaking the F5 algorithm. In: Petitcolas, F.A.P. (ed.) IH 2002. LNCS, vol. 2578, pp. 310–323. Springer, Heidelberg (2003). https://doi.org/10.1007/3-540-36415-3_20

11. Kodovsky, J., Fridrich, J.: Quantitative steganalysis of LSB embedding in JPEG domain. In: Proceedings of the 12th ACM Workshop on Multimedia and Security, pp. 187–198. ACM (2010)
12. Liu, G., Huang, F., Li, Z.: Universal steganalysis against adaptive steganographic algorithms. J. Appl. Sci. **34**(5), 598–604 (2016). (in Chinese)
13. Goljan, M., Fridrich, J., Holotyak, T.: New blind steganalysis and its implications. In: Proceedings of the SPIE Security Steganography and Watermarking of Multimedia Contents VIII, vol. 6072, pp. 1–13 (2006)
14. Chen, C., Shi, Y.: JPEG image steganalysis utilizing both intrablock and interblock correlations. In: IEEE International Symposium on Circuits and Systems (ISCAS), pp. 3029–3032 (2008)
15. Fridrich, J.: Feature-based steganalysis for JPEG images and its implications for future design of steganographic schemes. In: Fridrich, J. (ed.) IH 2004. LNCS, vol. 3200, pp. 67–81. Springer, Heidelberg (2004). https://doi.org/10.1007/978-3-540-30114-1_6
16. Pevny, T., Fridrich, J.: Merging Markov and DCT features for multiclass JPEG steganalysis. In: Proceedings of the SPIE, Electronic Imaging, Electronic Imaging, Security, Steganography, and Watermarking of Multimedia Contents IX, pp. 301–314 (2007)
17. Kodovsky, J., Fridrich, J.: Calibration revisited. In: Proceedings of 11th ACM Multimedia & Security Workshop, pp. 7–8 (2009)
18. Kodovský, J., Fridrich, J., Holub, V.: Ensemble classifiers for steganalysis of digital media. IEEE Trans. Inf. Forensics Secur. **7**(2), 432–444 (2012)
19. Kodovsky, J., Fridrich, J.: Steganalysis of JPEG images using rich models. In: Proceedings of SPIE, Electronic Imaging, Media Watermarking, Security, and Forensics of Multimedia XIV, San Francisco, CA, vol. 8303, 22–26 January 2012
20. Fridrich, J., Kodovsky, J.: Rich models for steganalysis of digital images. IEEE Trans. Inf. Forensics Secur. **7**(3), 868–882 (2012)
21. Holub, V., Fridrich, J.: Low complexity features for JPEG steganalysis using undecimated DCT. IEEE Trans. Inf. Forensics Secur. **10**(2), 219–228 (2015)
22. Tan, Y., Huang, F., Huang, J.: Feature selection for high dimensional steganalysis. In: Shi, Y.-Q., Kim, H.J., Pérez-González, F., Echizen, I. (eds.) IWDW 2015. LNCS, vol. 9569, pp. 134–144. Springer, Cham (2016). https://doi.org/10.1007/978-3-319-31960-5_12
23. Bas, P., Filler, T., Pevný, T.: "Break our steganographic system": the ins and outs of organizing BOSS. In: Filler, T., Pevný, T., Craver, S., Ker, A. (eds.) IH 2011. LNCS, vol. 6958, pp. 59–70. Springer, Heidelberg (2011). https://doi.org/10.1007/978-3-642-24178-9_5

Double JPEG Compression Detection Based on Fusion Features

Fulong Yang, Yabin Li, Kun Chong, and Bo Wang[(✉)]

School of Information and Communication Engineering,
Dalian University of Technology, Dalian 116024, People's Republic of China
{201081534,zhongkun}@mail.dlut.edu.cn, yabinli_dlut@foxmail.com,
bowang@dlut.edu.cn

Abstract. Detection of double JPEG compression plays an increasingly important role in image forensics. This paper mainly focuses on the situation where the images are aligned double JPEG compressed with two different quantization tables. We propose a new detection method based on the fusion features of Benford features and likelihood probability ratio features in this paper. We believe that with the help of likelihood probability ratio features, our fusion features can expose more artifacts left by double JPEG compression, which lead to a better performance. Comparative experiments have been carried out in our paper, and experimental result shows our method outperforms the baseline methods, even when one of the quality factors is pretty high.

Keywords: Double compression detection · DCT coefficients
Likelihood probability ratio features · Benford features

1 Introduction

With the development of technology and the popularity of the digital image editing softwares, people can arbitrarily tamper, repair and adjust images with different purposes, which brings significant concern over the integrity of digital images, especially in the field of image forensics. Therefore, how to guarantee the authenticity and reliability of digital images is of great importance. As a digital image compression standard, JPEG is now widely used in digital cameras. Considering the essential positions of JPEG compression in image capturing and processing, the JPEG image forensic has been attracting more and more attention recently. In this paper, we focus on the research of double JPEG compression detection.

According to whether the two compressed blocks are aligned, double JPEG compression can be divided into aligned double JPEG compression (A-DJPG) and non aligned double JPEG compression (NA-DJPG). This paper considers the case of aligned double JPEG compression with two different quantization tables. Now there are already numerous methods to detect aligned double JPEG compression with different quantization tables. Fu *et al.* [1] noted that the first

© ICST Institute for Computer Sciences, Social Informatics and Telecommunications Engineering 2018
X. Gu et al. (Eds.): MLICOM 2017, Part I, LNICST 226, pp. 158–167, 2018.
https://doi.org/10.1007/978-3-319-73564-1_16

digit of the DCT coefficients follows the Benford's law and the characteristics of the image will be destroyed after compression. Li *et al.* [2] made an improvement on this basis, and proposed a special model to measure the first digital distribution. Feng and Doerr [3] observed the periodicity and discontinuity contained in the double compressed JPEG images and extracted these features from the pixel histograms to detect the aligned double JPEG compression. Popescu and Farid [4] and Popescu [5] had experimentally found that double JPEG compressed images show periodic characteristic on JPEG coefficients, which can be considered as a clue to distinguish single compressed images from double compressed images.

After further analysis of double JPEG compression, Ramesh *et al.* [6] found that the JPEG coefficients histograms would show a double peak obviously when the two JPEG compression quantization tables are different. Lukáš and Fridrich [7] extracted the features according to this phenomenon for double JPEG detection. However, since the high frequency components of the JPEG coefficients have a large number of zeros, the algorithm only extracts the histogram features from the nine positions in the low frequency AC coefficients, which includes 144-D features. Chen *et al.* [8] calculated the difference matrix of the JPEG coefficients in four directions, and then extracted features from the Markov transition probability of the difference matrix. In their work, a total of 243-D Markov features were extracted and a decent detection result of double JPEG compression was achieved. A recent work is [9], Shang *et al.* improved the traditional first-order Markov transition probability algorithm and proposed a method based on content analysis and high order statistic features, which obtain a higher detection accuracy. It is worth mentioning that double JPEG compression with the same quantization matrix can also be detected nowadays [10], but this situation is not within the scope of this study.

In this paper, we propose a double JPEG compression detection method based on the fusion features of Benford features and likelihood probability ratio features. The likelihood probability ratio features are based on the distribution of the DCT coefficient, which show the probability of each image block of being doubly compressed, and the Benford features are based on the digital statistical properties of the DCT coefficients. We believe that the combination of this two kinds of features can expose more artifacts left by double JPEG compression, and therefore lead to a better performance.

The rest of this paper is organized as follows. In Sect. 2, we give a brief review of the process of single and double JPEG compression and model the DCT coefficients after double compression. In Sect. 3, we introduce how to extract the two kinds of features used in our experiments in detail. And several comparative experiments are carried out in Sect. 4 to show the effectiveness of our proposed method. Conclusions are drawn in Sect. 5.

2   Aligned Double JPEG Compression

In this section, we briefly review the process of JPEG compression and introduce the statistical model used to characterize A-DJPG artifacts.

2.1   The Process of JPEG Compression

JPEG, Joint Photographic Experts Group, is a widely used image compression standard for grayscale images and color images. JPEG compression can be divided into lossy compression and lossless compression. Where lossless compression means that the decompressed image is the same as the original image in a single scan, and lossy compression generally uses a DCT transform and obtain a JPEG image with higher compression rate based on the Huffman encoding. The JPEG image has high compression ratio and small memory, which makes it widely used in digital cameras. The JPEG image compression can be modeled by four basic steps: the conversion of color space, 8×8 sub-block DCT transformation of the image pixels, quantization of DCT coefficients according to a certain quantization table, and encoding of the quantized values. The process of decompression of JPEG images is just the opposite of the above process. First, the JPEG compressed image is decoded according to the coding table, and then the image of YCbCr mode is obtained by inverse quantization and inverse DCT transformation. The image is transformed into a true color image of RGB mode at last. We generally consider that quantization is achieved by dividing each DCT coefficient by a proper quantization step Q and rounding the result to the nearest integer, whereas inverse quantization is achieved by simply multiplying by Q. This process can be modeled as follows:

$$D_i = \left\lfloor \left\lfloor \frac{d_i}{Q} \right\rfloor Q \right\rfloor \tag{1}$$

where d_i denotes the DCT coefficients of the original image, D_i is the DCT coefficients after inverse quantization, and Q is the quantization step used for JPEG compression. Since the quantized DCT coefficients are obtained by rounding, it is only the approximate value of the original value. We can not recover the original DCT coefficients accurately.

2.2   The Process of Aligned Double JPEG Compression

This paper considers the case of aligned double JPEG compression with two different quantization tables. Given an uncompressed image I, the single compressed image I_1 is obtained by compression of image I with quality factor Q_1. Then I_1 is decompressed, and compressed again by another quality factor $Q2$, where the corresponding block DCT is perfectly aligned. The DCT coefficients after double compression can be modeled as:

$$C_2 = Q_2 \left(D_{00} I_1 \right) = Q_2 \left(D_1 \left(Q_1 \left(U \right) \right) + D_{00} E_1 \right) \tag{2}$$

where $U = D_{00} I$ are the unquantized DCT coefficients of I, Q_1 and Q_2 denotes different quantization tables used in compression, and E_1 is the error introduced by rounding and truncating.

3   Proposed Method

Based on the above analysis, we propose a detection method for double JPEG compression based on the fusion features in this section, which consist of Benford features and likelihood probability ratio features. The block diagram of our method is shown in Fig. 1. The method mainly consists of three parts: DCT coefficients calculation, fusion features extraction and classification. Firstly, the DCT coefficients are calculated from the given images, and then the likelihood probability ratio features and the Benford feature are extracted. The two features are fused into a SVM classifier to train a model to detect double JPEG compression. In the following, we will introduce the features used and their extraction methods in detail.

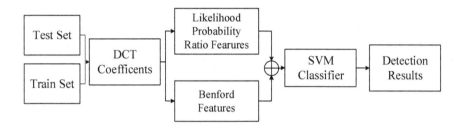

Fig. 1. The block diagram of the proposed method.

3.1   Benford Features

The fusion features consist of two parts: Benford features and likelihood probability ratio features. First, Benford law is a well-known natural statistical phenomenon, it is mainly used to count the frequency of occurrence of natural numbers from 1 to 9 and can be expressed as:

$$P\left(d\right) = \log_{10}\left(1 + \frac{1}{d}\right) \tag{3}$$

where $P(d)$ is the probability of the occurrence of the number d. The distribution of digital statistics follows an interesting law called Benford Law, where the frequency of 1 appears about one-third, and the probability of occurrence of $2, 3, 4, \ldots, 9$ decreases in turn.

Fu *et al.* [1] found that the first digit of the JPEG image before the quantization of the DCT coefficients follow the Benford rule. For a JPEG compressed image, the first digital distribution of the quantized DCT coefficients do not follow the Benford rule strictly, while the first digital distribution of the DCT coefficients is similar to the logarithmic distribution of the Benford rule. They referred to this phenomenon as generalized Benford distribution, which can be expressed as follows:

$$P\left(x\right) = N\log_{10}\left(1 + \frac{1}{s + x^q}\right), x = 1, 2, \ldots, 9 \tag{4}$$

where N is the normalization parameter, s and q is the parameters of Benford rule model that changes with the JPEG compression quality factor. For a double JPEG compressed image, the first digit of the DCT coefficients will no longer satisfy the generalized Benford distribution. Based on the difference of distribution, Fu *et al.* [1] took the first digital distribution of the DCT coefficients as features to detect double JPEG compression. Amerini *et al.* [11] used Benford features to detect whether an image is locally compressed. In this paper, the Benford feature vector from [11] is used.

3.2   Likelihood Probability Ratio Features

The likelihood probability ratio features are based on the variation of the DCT coefficients distribution. Bianchi and Piva [12] proposed likelihood probability ratio to generate likelihood map to detect image forgery localization. The ratio shows the probability of each image block of being doubly compressed, which can be used in double JPEG compression detection. Assuming I is an uncompressed image, I_1 is a single JPEG compressed image with quality factor Q_1, then I_1 can be expressed as follows:

$$I_1 = D_{00}^{-1} D \left(Q \left(D_{00} I \right) \right) + E_1 = I + R_1 \tag{5}$$

where Q_{00} represents the DCT transform of 8×8 block in the upper left corner, $Q(\bullet)$ and $D(\bullet)$ represents the quantization and inverse quantization respectively, E_1 is the error introduced by rounding and truncation, and R_1 is the total error in the whole JPEG compression process.

When image I_1 is compressed again with another quality factor Q_2, we can get a double JPEG compressed image. The DCT coefficients after double compression can be modeled as:

$$C_2 = Q_2 \left(D_{00} I_1 \right) = Q_2 \left(D_1 \left(Q_1 \left(U \right) \right) + D_{00} E_1 \right) \tag{6}$$

where $U = D_{00} I$ are the unquantized DCT coefficients of image I, Q_1 and Q_2 denote the different quantization tables used in the process of double JPEG compression. Since JPEG compression tables contain 64 quantization steps, the above formula Eq. (6) can be expressed as follows:

$$p_{DQ} \left(x; q_1, q_2 \right) = \sum_{\nu = q_2 x - q_2/2}^{q_2 x + q_2/2} p_1 \left(\nu; q_1 \right) * g_{DQ} \left(\nu \right) \tag{7}$$

where q_1 and q_2 are the first and second quantization steps respectively, $g_{DQ} \left(\nu \right)$ is the rounding and truncation error in DCT domain, and $*$ means convolution. And the following formula models the distribution of the DCT coefficients after quantization and inverse quantization by Q_1:

$$p_1 \left(\nu; q_1 \right) = \begin{cases} \sum_{\mu = \nu - q_1/2}^{\nu + q_1/2} p_0 \left(\mu \right) & \nu = k q_1 \\ 0 & elsewhere \end{cases} \tag{8}$$

where $p_0(\mu)$ represents the distribution of the unquantized coefficients. The rounding and truncation error in the spatial domain is a independent and identically distributed random variable. According to the central-limit theorem, satisfies the Gaussian distribution as shown in Eq. (9):

$$g_{DQ}(\nu) = \frac{1}{\sigma_e\sqrt{2\pi}}e^{-(\nu-\mu_e)^2/\sigma_e^2} \tag{9}$$

If the JPEG image is not double compressed, the Eq. (7) shall be expressed as follows:

$$p_{NDQ}(x; q_2) = \sum_{\nu=q_2 x-q_2/2}^{q_2 x+q_2/2} p_{0(\nu)} \tag{10}$$

Now, given an image I, if x is the pixel value of I in spatial domain, then its conditional assumption probability distribution can be expressed as follows respectively:

$$\begin{cases} p(x|H_0) = p_{NDQ}(x; q_2) \\ p(x|H_1) = p_{DQ}(x; q_1, q_2) \end{cases} \tag{11}$$

where $p(x|H_0)$ and $p(x|H_1)$ denotes the probability distributions of x conditional to the hypothesis of being singly and doubly compressed. Thus, the likelihood ratio can be obtained as : $\Gamma(x) = p(x|H_1)/p(x|H_0)$. And if the likelihood ratio is greater than 1, then x is double-compressed, otherwise it is not.

4   Experiments and Results

4.1   Image Database

To prove the effectiveness of our proposed method, we carried our experiments on a public database BOSSBase [13], which consists of 10,000 uncompressed grayscale images with size of 512 × 512. We randomly select 500 images to conduct our experiment, some of the image samples used in the experiment are shown in Fig. 2.

These images are firstly compressed into JPEG images with quality factor Q1 vary from 50 to 95 with a step of 5. Thus we get 5000 single compressed images. Then these 5000 single compressed images are compressed again with quality factor Q2 = 50, 55, 60 ..., 95, respectively, to form the set of double JPEG compressed images.

We randomly select 300 images with quality factor Q1 of single compressed images and 300 double compressed images with quality factor Q1 followed by quality factor Q2 to form the training set, and the remaining 200 images of the single and double compressed images are aggregated into testing set. In our experiment, we only consider the situation when Q1 ≠ Q2. In this way, we can get 90 groups of training and testing sets.

Fig. 2. Six image samples in BOSSBase dataset.

4.2   Performance Evaluation

To have a fair comparison, Benford method [11], GLDH method [14], and our proposed method are carried out with the same database and experimental environment mentioned above. The experimental results are listed in tables below.

Table 1 shows the result of GLDH method. We can see that the detection accuracy is pretty high nearly 100% when $Q_2 > Q_1$, and the accuracy is higher than 99.25% in most case when $Q_2 < Q_1$, except for some special case when $Q_1 = 50, Q_2 = 55$ or $Q_1 = 55, Q_2 = 50$.

Table 1. Detection results based on GLDH features [14].

Q_1	Q_2									
	50	55	60	65	70	75	80	85	90	95
50	–	50	100	100	100	100	100	100	100	100
55	69	–	99.5	100	100	100	100	100	100	100
60	100	95.25	–	99.5	100	100	100	100	100	100
65	100	100	99.25	–	97.75	100	100	100	100	100
70	100	100	99.5	97.25	–	100	100	100	100	100
75	97	99.5	100	100	99.5	–	100	100	100	100
80	99.5	99.25	96.75	100	100	97.25	–	100	100	100
85	97.25	94.5	99.75	99.25	98.5	100	98.5	–	100	100
90	99	99.75	97.25	96.75	99	99.75	95.75	99.25	–	100
95	99.75	99.75	99.75	99	98.75	99	99.25	96	99.25	–

Table 2. Detection results based on Benford features [11].

Q_1	Q_2									
	50	55	60	65	70	75	80	85	90	95
50	–	100	100	100	100	98.25	100	99.25	99.25	98
55	100	–	100	100	100	100	100	99.25	78.75	95.25
60	100	99.5	-	100	100	100	97.25	98.5	97.25	95.75
65	100	100	100	–	100	100	100	100	100	97.75
70	100	100	100	100	–	100	100	100	99.75	99.5
75	100	100	100	100	100	–	100	100	100	97.75
80	99.75	100	100	100	100	100	–	100	99.75	99.5
85	100	100	100	100	100	100	100	–	100	100
90	100	100	100	100	100	100	100	100	–	99.5
95	100	100	100	100	100	100	100	100	100	–

Table 3. Detection results based on fusion features.

Q_1	Q_2									
	50	55	60	65	70	75	80	85	90	95
50	–	100	100	100	100	100	100	99.75	100	100
55	100	–	99.5	100	100	100	100	99.25	100	99.75
60	100	99.75	–	100	100	100	99.75	100	100	100
65	100	100	100	–	100	99.75	100	100	100	100
70	100	100	100	100	–	100	100	100	100	100
75	100	100	100	100	100	–	100	100	100	100
80	100	100	99.75	100	99.75	100	–	100	100	100
85	100	100	100	100	100	100	100	–	99.5	100
90	100	100	100	100	100	100	100	100	–	100
95	100	100	100	100	100	100	100	99.5	100	–

Also, to prove the effectiveness of our fusion features, the detection accuracy of Benford feature alone is listed in Table 2. Contrary to Table 1, the method performs quite well when $Q_2 < Q_1$, but when Q_2 is higher, the detection accuracy decreases a little bit. The reason is that when the images are recompressed with a higher quality factor Q_2, the artifact left by double compression is much more difficult to track by Benford features.

Table 3 shows the detection results of our proposed method, which outperforms that of work [11,14]. The detection accuracy is 100% in most case, and most others higher than 99.75%. The lowest detection accuracy is 99.25% when $Q_1 = 60, Q_2 = 80$. Figure 3 shows the detection results of the three methods with different Q_1 when $Q_2 = 95$, while Fig. 4 shows the detection results of the three

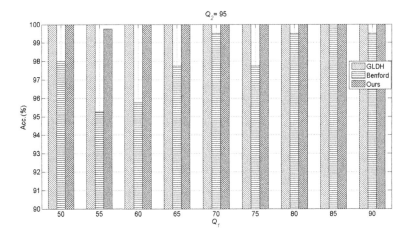

Fig. 3. Detection accuracy with different Q_1 when $Q_2 = 95$.

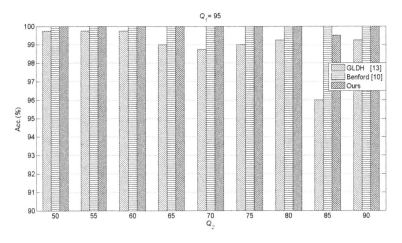

Fig. 4. Detection accuracy with different Q_2 when $Q_1 = 95$.

methods with different Q_2 when $Q_1 = 95$. It is quite obvious that the method proposed in this paper outperforms the baselines, Benford based [11] and GLDH based [14] methods.

5   Conclusion

In this paper, a set of effective fusion features combined Benford features and likelihood probability ratio features are proposed to detect double JPEG compression. Likelihood probability ratio features show the probability of each image block of being doubly compressed, and thus our fusion features can expose more artifacts left by double JPEG compression and therefore lead to a better performance. Comparative experiments show that our method outperforms that of work [11,14], even when the first quality factor or the second quality factor is pretty high.

Acknowledgments. This work is supported by the National Science Foundation of China (No. 61502076) and the Scientific Research Project of Liaoning Provincial Education Department (No. L2015114).

References

1. Fu, D., Shi, Y.Q., Su, W.: A generalized Benford's law for JPEG coefficients and its applications in image forensics. In: Security, Steganography, and Watermarking of Multimedia Contents IX, pp. 65051L–65051L-11. SPIE, San Jose (2007)
2. Li, B., Shi, Y.Q., Huang, J.: Detecting doubly compressed JPEG images by using mode based first digit features. In: 10th Workshop on Multimedia Signal Processing, pp. 730–735. IEEE Press, New York (2008)
3. Feng, X., Doerr, G.: JPEG recompression detection. In: Media Forensics and Security II, pp. 75410J–75410J-12. SPIE, San Jose (2010)
4. Popescu, A.C., Farid, H.: Statistical tools for digital forensics. In: Fridrich, J. (ed.) IH 2004. LNCS, vol. 3200, pp. 128–147. Springer, Heidelberg (2004). https://doi.org/10.1007/978-3-540-30114-1_10
5. Popescu, A.C.: Statistical tools for digital image forensics. Ph.D. theses, Department of Computer Science, Dartmouth College, NH (2004)
6. Prasad S., Ramakrishnan K.R.: On resampling detection and its application to detect image tampering. In: International Conference on Multimedia and Expo, pp. 1325–1328. IEEE Press, New York (2006)
7. Lukás, J., Fridrich, J.: Estimation of primary quantization matrix in double compressed JPEG images. In: Digital Forensic Research Workshop, pp. 5–8, Cleveland (2003)
8. Chen, C., Shi, Y.Q., Su, W.: A machine learning based scheme for double JPEG compression detection. In: 19th International Conference on Pattern Recognition, pp. 1–4. IEEE Press, New York (2008)
9. Shang, S., Zhao, Y., Ni, R.: Double JPEG detection using high order statistic features. In: International Conference on Digital Signal Processing, pp. 550–554. IEEE Press, New York (2016)
10. Huang, F., Huang, J., Shi, Y.Q.: Detecting double JPEG compression with the same quantization matrix. IEEE Trans. Inf. Forens. Secur. **5**(4), 848–856 (2010)
11. Amerini, I., Becarelli, R., Caldelli, R., Andrea, D.M.: Splicing forgeries localization through the use of first digit features. In: International Workshop on Information Forensics and Security, pp. 143–148. IEEE Press, New York (2014)
12. Bianchi, T., Piva, A.: Image forgery localization via block-grained analysis of JPEG artifacts. IEEE Trans. Inf. Forens. Secur. **7**(3), 1003–1017 (2012)
13. Bas, P., Filler, T., Pevný, T.: "Break our Steganographic System": the Ins and Outs of organizing BOSS. In: Filler, T., Pevný, T., Craver, S., Ker, A. (eds.) IH 2011. LNCS, vol. 6958, pp. 59–70. Springer, Heidelberg (2011). https://doi.org/10.1007/978-3-642-24178-9_5
14. Dong, L., Kong, X., Wang, B., You, X.: Double compression detection based on Markov model of the first digits of DCT coefficients. In: 6th International Conference on Image and Graphics, pp. 234–237. IEEE Press, New York (2011)

Complexity Based Sample Selection for Camera Source Identification

Yabin Li, Bo Wang$^{(\boxtimes)}$, Kun Chong, and Yanqing Guo

School of Information and Communication Engineering,
Dalian University of Technology, Dalian 116024, People's Republic of China
yabinli_dlut@foxmail.com, {bowang,guoyq}@dlut.edu.cn,
zhongkun@mail.dlut.edu.cn

Abstract. Sensor patter noise (SPN) has been proved to be an unique fingerprint of a camera, and widely used for camera source identification. Previous works mostly construct reference SPN by averaging the noise residuals extracted from images like blue sky. However, this is unrealistic in practice and the noise residual would be seriously affected by scene detail, which would significantly influence the performance of camera source identification. To address this problem, a complexity based sample selection method is proposed in this paper. The proposed method is adopted before the extraction of noise residual to select image patches with less scene detail to generate the reference SPN. An extensive comparative experiments show its effectiveness in eliminating the influence of image content and improving the identification accuracy of the existing methods.

Keywords: Camera source identification · Sensor pattern noise
Sample selection · Image complexity

1 Introduction

With the continuous advancement of technology, it is very convenient to get access to various image acquisition devices, and digital images make an important role of lives. However, the emergence and prevalence of a variety of image editing softwares makes it easier than ever before to temper and forge digital images. In recent years, the tampering and forging events have risen a concern about the authenticity and originality of digital images, which is called digital image forensics. As an important branch of digital image forensic, camera source identification focus on the originality of digital images, which can be divided into two branches: (1) model-based, and (2) device-based camera source identification. In this paper, we mainly discuss the latter.

In last decade, several methods were proposed to solve the problem of camera-based source camera identification, such as sensor patter noise [1], sensor dust characteristics [2], and defects in CCDs [3]. The key idea of these methods is to extract unique characteristic features introduced by the hardware of image

© ICST Institute for Computer Sciences, Social Informatics and Telecommunications Engineering 2018
X. Gu et al. (Eds.): MLICOM 2017, Part I, LNICST 226, pp. 168–177, 2018.
https://doi.org/10.1007/978-3-319-73564-1_17

acquisition devices. Among them, SPN has been widely considered as a reliable fingerprint because of its universality and stability.

Lukas *et al.* [1] first extracted SPN from digital images using a wavelet-based Wiener de-noising filter. To reduce the false acceptance probability, Goljan *et al.* [4] proposed the Peak to Correlation Energy ratio (PCE) instead of the normalized correlation to estimate the correlation between the reference and test SPN. Considering computational cost, Hu *et al.* [5] proposed a new method only taking the large components of SPN into account. Recently, Li *et al.* [6] proposed an effective feature extractor based on the Principal Component Analysis (PCA) de-noising algorithm [7] to reduce the size of camera fingerprint and significantly improve the performance of several existing methods.

However, the reference SPN extracted through the methods above will be unavoidably affected by scene details, which would significantly influence the accuracy of source camera identification. To solve this problem, Wu *et al.* [8] introduced an edge adaptive SPN predictor to reduce the influence of images content residual based on content adaptive interpolation, and also proved that the reference SPN with less scene noise could achieve a higher identification accuracy. Recently, Li *et al.* [9] proposed a framework based on random subspace method (RSM) and majority voting (MV) to suppress the interference of image content.

Different from the methods discussed above, we propose a complexity based sample selection method to obtain more accurate reference SPN. Firstly, we adopted image complexity as the representation of amount of scene details. Then, the sample selection method is used before the extraction of noise residual to select image pathes with less scene detail to generate reference SPN. After the construction of reference SPN, different methods are performed to verify the effectiveness of the proposed method.

The rest of this paper is organized as follows. Section 2 firstly introduce the measurement of image complexity, and then propose the sample selection method based on image complexity. In Sect. 3, experimental results show the effectiveness and applicability of the proposed method, and finally, conclusion is drawn in Sect. 4.

2   Proposed Method

Previous works suggested that SPN should be extracted in several pure images, such as a dark or white one [8]. They insisted that the noise residual extracted from those images with less scene detail is much more pure and reliable. As shown in Fig. 1, the image scene detail obviously differs in different area of an image. In most cases, there are always some regions containing less image content, which means lower image complexity, and the SPN generated from these regions is much more reliable. Inspired by this, a new complexity based sample selection method is proposed in this section, by quantitatively analyzing the image complexity.

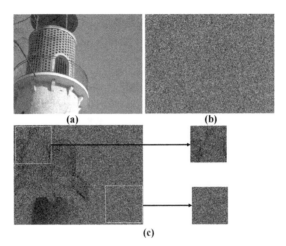

Fig. 1. (a) An image taken by Canon_Ixus70. (b) Reference SPN of Canon_Ixus70. (c) The noise residual extracted from (a).

2.1   Image Complexity Measurement

There are many kinds of image complexity measurements, in which texture features are widely used and quite effective. Textures are characterized by the relationship of the intensities of neighboring pixels ignoring their color, which means they are a representative pattern of spatial distribution of image intensities. They contain fatal information about the structural arrangement of surfaces and their relationship to the surrounding environment. Since the textural properties of images appear to carry useful information of image content, it is reasonable to consider texture features as the representation of image complexity.

In various methods of texture analysis, the gray level co-occurrence matrix (GLCM) proposed by Haralick and Shanmugam [10] is considered as the most widely used algorithm because of its adaptability and robustness in different scenes. In our paper, the GLCM is adopted to analyze the texture features of the image, considering as the complexity of the image patches.

The co-occurrence matrix is defined over an image according to the distribution of co-occurring values for a given offset. More specifically, GLCM calculates how often a specified pixel with gray-level value occurs either horizontally, vertically, or diagonally to the adjacent pixels. Mathematically, the co-occurrence matrix C, defined over an $m \times n$ image I and parameterized by an offset $(\Delta x, \Delta y)$, is calcultated as:

$$C_{\Delta x, \Delta y}(p, q) = \sum_{i=1}^{m} \sum_{j=1}^{n} \begin{cases} 1, & \text{if } I(i, j) = p \text{ and } I(i + \Delta x, j + \Delta y) = q \\ 0, & \text{otherwise} \end{cases} \tag{1}$$

where p and q are pixel values of the image, and i, j is the spatial positions in the given image I. What's more, the offset $(\Delta x, \Delta y)$ depends on the direction adopted and the distance at which the matrix is computed. Haralick *et al.* extracted 14 parameters form GLCM to describe the textural properties of a given image, but some of them show redundancies, and the commonly used parameters are energy, contrast, entropy, homogeneity and correlation coefficients.

As discussed above, the texture features of the whole image can be expressly represented by the combination of those GLCM parameters. However in this paper, our goal is to simply measure the complexity of image patches and find the patch of smallest complexity to extract more pure SPN, rather than precisely describe the sharpness and depth of the texture. So we just select correlation coefficient as the representation of image complexity. The definition of correlation in GLCM is given by:

$$cov = \sum_{i,j} \frac{(i - \mu_i)(j - \mu_j) G(i,j)}{\sigma_i \sigma_j} \tag{2}$$

where μ_i, μ_j is the mean of the GLCM elements along the horizontal and vertical direction respectively, and σ_i, σ_j is the variance matrix of ith row and jth column.

Correlation coefficient measures the consistency of image textures. Usually, the patch with less scene detail will has a high correlation coefficient. In other words, the higher the correlation coefficient, the lower image complexity. As shown in Fig. 2, it is obvious that the upper left patch of the image, whose correlation coefficient is highest, has less scene detail.

14.9606	11.7036	8.6227	9.4348
2.1603	0.1516	4.3974	0.4487
0.1999	0.1249	0.1335	0.2457
0.0858	0.0821	0.0443	0.0951

(a)   (b)

Fig. 2. (a) An image taken by Canon_Ixus70. (b) The image complexity of each patch.

2.2   Image Complexity Based Sample Selection

Lukas et al. [1] firstly proposed to extract the reference SPN from digital image by averaging noise residuals. They adopted a wavelet-based Wiener de-noising filter to extract the residual signals from the wavelet high frequency coefficients:

$$r_i = I_i - F(I_i) \tag{3}$$

where I_i is the original image and F is the de-noising filter. Then the reference SPN is given by:

$$R = \frac{\sum\limits_{i=1}^{N} r_i}{N} \tag{4}$$

where N is the number of images to generate reference SPN. But the averaging method has an limitation, the image to generate reference SPN are mostly blue sky, which is not realistic in practice.

To address this problem, image patch selection is adopted before the extraction of noise residual. Assuming there are n images denoted by I_i ($i = 1, 2, 3, ..., n$) taken by the same camera. Firstly, every image is segmented into several non-overlapping blocks with the size of 256×256 pixels. Then, the complexity coefficient cov is calculated using Eq. 2 of each image block to form a complexity matrix, as shown in Fig. 2. For all images in the experiment database, complexity coefficients of the same location are then added together to form a new complexity matrix N. For the purpose of using the region with less scene detail to generate the reference SPN, the block with maximum value in N is selected to extract noise residual for construction of reliable reference SPN using method in [1]. The block diagram of complexity-based SPN generation is shown in Fig. 3.

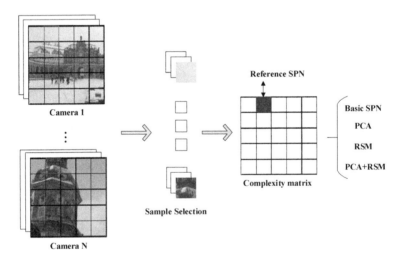

Fig. 3. The block diagram of complexity based sample selection.

3   Experimens and Results

3.1   Experimenal Setting

In order to evaluate the performance of the proposed method, we carry out our experiments on the Dresden mage Database [11]. A total of 1200 images from

10 cameras are considered in the experiments, which are all taken indoors and outdoors with variety of natural scene sight. The 10 cameras devices belong to four camera models, and each model has 2–3 different devices. Table 1 lists the details of the 10 cameras used in the experiments.

Table 1. Camera used in the experiments.

Cameras	Size	Abbr.
Canon_Ixus70_0	3072×2304	C1
Canon_Ixus70_0	3072×2304	C1
Canon_Ixus70_1	3072×2304	C2
Canon_Ixus70_2	3072×2304	C3
Nikon_CoolPixS710_0	4352×3264	N1
Nikon_CoolPixS710_1	4352×3264	N2
Samsung_L74wide_0	3072×2304	S1
Samsung_L74wide_1	3072×2304	S2
Samsung_L74wide_2	3072×2304	S3
Olympus_mju_1050SW_0	3648×2734	O1
Olympus_mju_1050SW_1	3648×2734	O2

For each camera, 120 images are divided into two subsets for training and testing, of which 50 images are used to construct the reference SPN, and the test set is consisted of the remaining 70 images. For a fair comparison, the basic SPN [1], PCA [6]and RSM [9] method mentioned above are respectively performed with and without the proposed sample selection method. Considering the computational cost, the experiments without sample selection are performed on the central block with the size of 256×256 cropped from the original image.

3.2 Performance Evaluation

As described in Sect. 2, the image complexity based sample selection method is performed before the extraction of SPN. We first cut the images into the size of 2048×2048 from the upper left corner of the original images. Then, the cropped images are segmented into 64 patches with size of 256×256. For all images in the experiment database, correlation coefficients of the same locations are then added together to form the complexity matrix of whole database, which is shown in Table 2.

As we can see from Table 2, the patch of $1st$ row and $2nd$ column has the largest correlation coefficient, which also means minimum image complexity and less scene detail. So, we select this patch as the representation of images to extract SPN. In order to verify the effective of the proposed method, we carried out several comparative experiments with and without sample selection, and the experimental results are shown in tables below.

Table 2. Correlation coefficients of image database.

Corrlation coefficient($\times 10^4$)							
1.3610	1.5925	1.4586	1.2352	1.4163	1.2155	1.5770	1.3235
1.4200	1.2593	0.9244	1.2302	0.9442	1.2868	1.5716	1.3474
1.0984	0.8087	0.7612	1.0199	1.2054	1.0570	1.2178	1.1123
1.1353	0.6064	0.5761	0.6027	0.8489	0.7015	0.5064	0.7193
0.5969	0.4425	0.3381	0.6384	0.4943	0.3305	0.2352	0.7417
0.4119	0.4034	0.4896	0.4890	0.2098	0.1629	0.2229	0.2415
0.4419	0.5472	0.7511	0.5914	0.3907	0.3329	0.3395	0.3156
0.6491	0.5252	0.7422	0.6516	0.7076	0.5305	0.4543	0.4978

The basic SPN method of image source identification is to directly extract noise residual from several images to form reference SPN by averaging. Then, the correlation coefficient between the reference and test noise residual is calculated. The test image is belong to the origin whose correlation coefficient is highest. The experimental results are shown in Tables 3 and 4. When adopted the proposed sample selection method, the average identification accuracy of basic SPN method has an improvement of 0.42% from 87.29% to 87.71%. The average identification accuracy of three other methods are also listed in Table 3.

Table 3. Average identification accuracy with and without sample selection.

Method	Basic SPN	PCA	RSM SPN	PCA RSM SPN
Without SS	87.29	86.87	87.01	87.41
With SS	87.71	87.62	87.85	87.96

Table 4. Identification accuracy of basic SPN with and without sample selection (%).

Method	C1	C2	C3	N1	N2	S1	S2	S3	O1	O2	Ave.
Basic SPN	98.57	98.57	100	65.71	92.86	91.43	77.14	88.57	77.14	82.86	**87.29**
SS SPN	95.71	94.29	98.57	81.43	88.57	84.29	88.57	85.71	77.14	72.86	**87.71**

PCA is a widely used method to reduce the dimension of camera fingerprint while represent the original data as well as possible. When selecting an appropriate proportion of principal components, there should be a certain extent improvement of identification accuracy. The results of the experiment are shown in Table 5. It is easy to find that the identification accuracy of SS PCA has an obvious improvement compared with the PCA without sample selection, especially when the proportion of principal components G(T) is smaller. When G(T) = 0.99, the SS PCA shows its highest accuracy of 88.14%, and the average improvement of identification accuracy is 0.78%. Table 5 also lists the identification accuracy of each device respectively when G(T) = 0.99.

Table 5. Identification accuracy of PCA SPN with and without sample selection (%).

G(T)	0.91	0.92	0.93	0.94	0.95	0.96	0.97	0.98	0.99	1.0	Ave.
PCA	85.86	85.86	86.43	86.29	87.00	87.14	87.43	87.86	**88.00**	87.43	**86.84**
SS PCA	87.29	87.29	87.57	87.57	87.43	87.29	87.71	88.14	**88.14**	88.14	**87.62**
Method	C1	C2	C3	N1	N2	S1	S2	S3	O1	O2	Ave.
PCA	98.57	98.57	100	67.14	94.29	92.86	77.14	90.00	77.14	84.29	**88.00**
SS PCA	97.14	84.29	98.57	80.00	88.57	84.29	88.57	97.14	77.14	75.14	**88.14**

In work [9], random subspace method and majority voting is used to improve the identification accuracy. There are two parameters which would affect the identification performance: the dimension of each random subspaces M and the number of random subspaces L. According to [9], we empirically set $L = 600$ while M/d various from 0.1 to 1, where d is the size of entire feature space. It is worth mentioning that the performance of RSM method is the same as that of basic SPN method when $M/d = 1$, which has been proved by the results shown in Table 6. The highest identification accuracy of RSM method and SS RSM method is 87.29% and 88.14% respectively, and the average improvement is 0.84%. Similar with Table 5, the improvement is more obvious when M/d is smaller. Also, Table 6 shows the identification accuracy of each device with highest average identification accuracy when $M/d = 0.6$ (for RSM) and 0.3 (for SS RSM).

Table 6. Identification accuracy of RSM SPN with and without sample selection (%).

M/d	0.1	0.2	0.3	0.4	0.5	0.6	0.7	0.8	0.9	1.0	Ave.
RSM	87.00	85.93	86.64	87.21	87.36	**87.29**	87.14	87.00	87.29	87.29	**87.01**
SS RSM	87.93	88.07	**88.14**	87.64	87.79	88.07	87.64	87.79	87.71	87.71	**87.85**
Method	C1	C2	C3	N1	N2	S1	S2	S3	O1	O2	Ave.
RSM	98.57	98.57	100	65.00	92.14	91.43	78.57	89.29	76.43	82.86	**87.29**
SS RSM	96.43	95.00	98.57	80.71	88.57	83.57	90.00	95.71	77.14	75.71	**88.14**

Then another experiment combining sample selection, PCA and RSM with $L = 600$ and $G(T) = 0.99$ is performed to see whether the identification accuracy would be further improved. Table 7 shows the experimental results. The highest

Table 7. Identification accuracy of PCA RSM with and without sample selection (%).

M/d	0.1	0.2	0.3	0.4	0.5	0.6	0.7	0.8	0.9	1.0	Ave.
PCA RSM	86.00	87.00	87.07	87.50	87.71	**87.79**	87.64	87.64	87.79	87.68	**87.38**
SS PCA RSM	88.00	88.00	87.57	87.79	88.07	88.07	87.71	**88.14**	88.07	88.10	**87.95**
Method	C1	C2	C3	N1	N2	S1	S2	S3	O1	O2	Ave.
PCA RSM	98.57	98.57	100	65.00	93.57	92.14	78.57	90.71	76.43	84.29	**87.79**
SS PCA PSM	97.14	94.29	98.57	80.00	88.57	84.29	88.57	97.14	77.14	75.71	**88.14**

accuracy of SS PCA RSM method is 88.14%, whose average accuracy improvement is 0.57%. Table 7 also shows the identification accuracy of each device with highest average identification accuracy when $M/d = 0.6$ (for PCA RSM) and 0.8 (for SS PCA RSM).

4   Conclusion

An effective complexity based sample selection method for camera source identification is proposed in this paper. Considering the noise residual extracted from natural images may be seriously affected by scene details, we adopt a sample selection method based on image complexity to select image patches with less image content to generate reference SPN, which could significantly enhance the credibility of reference SPN. An extensive comparative experiments are carried out to prove the effectiveness of the proposed method. And the experimental results show that the proposed method can eliminate the influence of image content and improve the identification accuracy of the existing methods.

Acknowledgments. This work is supported by the National Science Foundation of China (No. 61502076) and the Scientific Research Project of Liaoning Provincial Education Department (No. L2015114).

References

1. Lukas, J., Fridrich, J., Goljan, M.: Digital camera identification from sensor pattern noise. IEEE Trans. Inf. Forensics Secur. **1**(2), 205–214 (2006)
2. Dirik, A.E., Sencar, H.T., Memon, N.: Source camera identification based on sensor dust characteristics. In: IEEE Workshop on Signal Processing Applications for Public Security and Forensics, pp. 1–6. IEEE Press, New York (2007)
3. Geradts, Z.J., Bijhold, J., Kieft, M., Kurosawa, K., Kuroki, K., Saitoh, N.: Methods for identification of images acquired with digital cameras. In: Enabling Technologies for Law Enforcement, pp. 505–512. SPIE, San Jose (2001)
4. Goljan, M.: Digital camera identification from images – estimating false acceptance probability. In: Kim, H.-J., Katzenbeisser, S., Ho, A.T.S. (eds.) IWDW 2008. LNCS, vol. 5450, pp. 454–468. Springer, Heidelberg (2009). https://doi.org/10.1007/978-3-642-04438-0_38
5. Hu, Y., Yu, B., Jian, C.: Source camera identification using large components of sensor pattern noise. In: IEEE International Conference on Computer Science and its Applications, pp. 1–5. IEEE Press, New York (2009)
6. Li, R., Li, C.T., Guan, Y.: A compact representation of sensor fingerprint for camera identification and fingerprint matching. In: IEEE International Conference on Acoustics Speech and Signal Processing, pp. 1777–1781. IEEE Press, New York (2015)
7. Zhang, L., Lukac, R., Wu, X., Zhang, D.: PCA-based spatially adaptive denoising of CFA images for single-sensor digital cameras. IEEE Trans. Image Process. **18**(4), 797–812 (2009)
8. Wu, G., Kang, X., Liu, K.J.R.: A context adaptive predictor of sensor pattern noise for camera source identification. In: 19th IEEE International Conference on Image Processing, pp. 237–240. IEEE Press, New York (2012)

9. Li, R., Kotropoulos, C., Li, C.T., Guan, Y.: Random subspace method for source camera identification. In: 25th International Workshop on Machine Learning for Signal Processing, pp. 1–5. IEEE Press, New York (2015)
10. Haralick, R.M., Shanmugam, K.: Textural features for image classification. IEEE Trans. Syst. Man Cybern. **3**(6), 610–621 (1973)
11. Gloe, T., Böhme, R.: The dresden image database for benchmarking digital image forensics. J. Dig. Forensic Pract. **3**(2–4), 150–159 (2010)

Wireless Mobile Network and Security

Lattice Reduction Aided Linear Detection for Generalized Spatial Modulation

Chungang Liu, Chen Wang, and Wenbin Zhang[✉]

Communication Research Center, Harbin Institute of Technology,
Harbin 150080, China
{cgliu, zwbgxyl973}@hit.edu.cn, 417682268@qq.com

Abstract. For reducing the complexity of equalization, linear equalization can be adopted for generalized spatial modulation (GSM) which is a special case of multiple-input-and-multiple-output (MIMO). However, because of its inferior performance, linear equalization may be infeasible for practical GSM systems which has large number of antennas and constellation. On the other hand, lattice-reduction (LR) is an effective method to improve the performance of linear equalization. The lattice reduction can't be utilized by GSM directly, because signals on some antennas don't exist. For tackling this problem, we propose a compatible 8-QAM constellation scheme integrating LR-aided linear equalization with GSM effectively. Next, we prove that LR-aided linear equalizers collect the same diversity order as that exploited by the ML detector under Rayleigh fading channels, and implement some simulations. Simulation results show the superior of the proposed 8-QAM over traditional 4-QAM and 8-QAM under Rayleigh fading channel. Moreover, our scheme obtains the full receive diversity under correlated channel.

Keywords: Generalized spatial modulation · Lattice reduction
Linear detection · 8-QAM

1 Introduction

Spatial modulation (SM) has been recognized as a promising MIMO transmission technology to develop energy-efficient, low-complexity solutions that satisfy target throughput requirements in future mobile networks [1]. Comparing with traditional MIMO scheme, SM only activates one antenna according to the information bits per channel use. So only one RF chain is needed, corresponding results are that the hardware implementation cost reduces, inter-channel interference is avoided, and inter-antenna problem doesn't exist. These merits make the SM become the research focus of MIMO.

The spectral efficiency of SM is increased logarithmically with the number of transmit antenna, which cannot satisfy the demand for higher throughput under the fixed transmit antenna number. For tackling this problem, generalized spatial modulation (GSM) activating more than one antenna during each transmission is introduced [2–4]. Now, there exists two types of GSM, One is that all active antennas send the same modulated symbol simultaneously [2, 3], and the other is that different active

© ICST Institute for Computer Sciences, Social Informatics and Telecommunications Engineering 2018
X. Gu et al. (Eds.): MLICOM 2017, Part I, LNICST 226, pp. 181–194, 2018.
https://doi.org/10.1007/978-3-319-73564-1_18

antennas send different modulated symbol independently [4]. For convenience, we call the former single symbol generalized spatial modulation (SS-GSM), the latter multiple symbol generalized spatial modulation (MS-GSM). It is worth to notice that GSM eliminates the demand that the transmit antenna number must be a power of two. Moreover, SS-GSM completely keep the advantages of single RF chain obviously, and MS-GSM have a higher spectral efficiency. However, ICI and IAS problems still exist in MS-GSM.

For MIMO receiver, maximum likelihood (ML) detection can obtain the best bit-error rate (BER). However, the huge computation complexity make ML infeasible in practical system. At the same time, linear equalization has an inferior performance while low complexity. Considering the important factors impacting the linear receiver is column coherence of channel matrix, and lattice reduction can reduce the dependency among column effectively, some researchers propose LR-aided linear equalization for Vertical Bell Laboratories Layered Space-Time (V-BLAST) architecture [5]. However, LR is not suitable for GSM, because only a portion of antennas are activating during each transmission, and receiver cannot obtain the consecutive integer lattice point in I-Q constellation diagram. For tacking this problem, we propose a compatible 8-QAM constellation scheme for SS-GSM and MS-GSM, which meets the requirement of lattice reduction. Sequentially, we prove that LR-aided linear equalizers can collect the same diversity order as that exploited by the ML detector and the simulations are implemented to corroborate our theoretical claims.

The remainder of this paper is organized as follows. Section 2 describes system and signal models. Section 3 extends the proposed equalizations to GSM and proposes a compatible 8-QAM constellation. Section 4 gives performance analyze. Section 5 shows the simulation results, followed by concluding remarks in Sect. 6.

2 GSM System Model

Consider a GSM system with N_t transmit antennas and N_r receive antennas. For each symbol time, only N_a transmit antennas is activated to send symbols, where $2 \leq N_a \leq N_t$. Obviously, there are $C_{N_t}^{N_a}$ kinds of possible active antennas combinations, among them, at most N kinds of combinations can be used to transmit $\log_2 N$ bits information, where $N = 2^{\lfloor \log C_{N_t}^{N_a} \rfloor}$ and $\lfloor \bullet \rfloor$ is the floor function. In the context of this paper, we call the N kinds of combinations a spatial constellation and any one of them a spatial symbol. The transmitted symbol vector can be written as

$$\mathbf{X} = \mathbf{E}_i \mathbf{s}, \tag{1}$$

where $\mathbf{E}_i$ is a $N_t \times N_a$ matrix which contains N_a columns chosen from the $N_t \times N_t$ identity matrix and is the matrix form expression for a spatial symbol. Definitely, the spatial symbol can also be represented in combination indices form as $I_j = \{j_1, j_2, \cdots, j_{N_a}\}$, where every element j_k, $k \in [1, 2, \cdots, N_a]$ denotes the antenna index which is arranged in ascending order for convenience. As a result, the spatial constellation in combination indices form can be written as $\mathcal{I} = \{I_1, I_2, \cdots, I_N\}$.

The ordinals of columns in $\mathbf{E}_i$ are chosen according to the antenna indices in each spatial symbol, so there are totally N kinds of $\mathbf{E}_i$ that make up of the spatial constellation in matrix form ε, where $\varepsilon = \{E_1, E_2, \cdots, E_N\}$. $\mathbf{s} = [s_1, \cdots, s_{N_a}]^T$ is the power-normalized $N_a \times 1$ signal symbol vector namely $\mathrm{E}[\mathbf{s}\mathbf{s}^H] = \mathbf{I}_{N_a}$. For SS-GSM, the N_a signal symbols are the same, namely $s_1 = s_2 = \cdots = s_{N_a} \in \mathcal{S}$, where $\mathcal{S}$ is the conventional QAM constellation. As to MS-GSM, the N_a signal symbols are independent, which means $\mathbf{s} \in \mathcal{S} \times \mathcal{S} \cdots \mathcal{S} = \mathcal{S}^{N_a}$. Definitely for M-QAM, in each symbol time, SS-GSM can transmit $\log_2 N + \log_2 M$ bits whereas MS-GSM can transmit $\log_2 N + N_a \log_2 M$ bits.

Assume that the channel is flat-fading quasi-static, where the channel matrix is invariant during a frame and changes independently among frames, and each entry of the channel matrix $\mathbf{H}$ follows an independent and identically distributed (i.i.d) complex Gaussian distribution $\mathcal{CN}(0, 1)$ with mean 0 and variance 1. The received signal vector can be represent as

$$\mathbf{y} = \mathbf{H}\mathbf{E}_i\mathbf{s} + \mathbf{n} = \mathbf{H}\mathbf{X} + \mathbf{n}, \tag{2}$$

where $\mathbf{n} \in \mathbb{C}^{N_r \times 1}$ is the additive noise vector following complex Gaussian distribution with mean zero and covariance matrix $\mathrm{E}[\mathbf{n}\mathbf{n}^H] = \sigma^2 \mathbf{I}_{N_r}$. Let $\mathbf{H}_{E_i} = \mathbf{H}\mathbf{E}_i$ and it is easy to know that $\mathbf{H}_{E_i} \in \mathcal{H} = \{\mathbf{H}_{E_1}, \mathbf{H}_{E_2}, \cdots, \mathbf{H}_{E_N}\}$ is sub-channel matrix including N_a columns chosen from the channel matrix $\mathbf{H}$. Equation (2) can be rewritten as:

$$\mathbf{y} = \mathbf{H}_{E_i}\mathbf{s} + \mathbf{n}. \tag{3}$$

At the receiver, the ML detector provides the optimal performance by exhaustively searching through spatial constellation and signal constellation. The output for SS-GSM can be written as

$$\left(\hat{\mathbf{E}}_i, \hat{\mathbf{s}}\right) = \arg \min_{\mathbf{H}_{E_i} \in \mathcal{H}, s_1 = s_2 = \cdots s_{N_a} \in \mathcal{S}} \left\| \mathbf{y} - \mathbf{H}_{E_i}\mathbf{s} \right\|_2^2, \tag{4}$$

and

$$\left(\hat{\mathbf{E}}_i, \hat{\mathbf{s}}\right) = \arg \min_{\mathbf{H}_{E_i} \in \mathcal{H}, \mathbf{s} \in \mathcal{S}^{N_a}} \left\| \mathbf{y} - \mathbf{H}_{E_i}\mathbf{s} \right\|_2^2 \tag{5}$$

for MS-GSM.

3   LR-Aided Linear Equalization for GSM MIMO System

3.1   Lattice Reduction

Considering that the problems involved in wireless communications are mostly complex valued, we only introduce the complex lattice and complex lattice reduction here [6, 7]. A complex-valued lattice of rank m in the n-dimension complex space $\mathbb{C}^n$ is defined as

$$\mathcal{L} \triangleq \left\{ x \middle| x = \sum_{l=1}^{m} z_l b_l, z_l \in \mathbb{Z}_j \right\}, \tag{6}$$

where $b_l \in \mathbb{C}^n$ are complex basis vectors and $\mathbb{Z}_j = \mathbb{Z} + j\mathbb{Z}$ is the set of complex integers that are also called Gausses integers. The complex basis vectors can be arranged into an $n \times m$ complex matrix $\mathbf{B}$ which can be simply called the basis of the lattice, thus any element $\mathbf{x}$ in the lattice can be represent as $\mathbf{x} = \mathbf{B}\mathbf{z}$. It can be show that there exist infinitely bases which can be chosen for a specific lattice. For different bases, the same lattice can have different orthogonality defect, which defined as

$$\xi(\mathbf{B}) = 1 - \frac{\det(\mathbf{B}^H \mathbf{B})}{\prod_{n=1}^{N_t} \|\mathbf{b}_n\|^2}. \tag{7}$$

There is $0 \leq \xi(\mathbf{B}) \leq 1$ for all $\mathbf{B}$. $\xi(\mathbf{B}) = 1$ if $\mathbf{B}$ is singular and $\xi(\mathbf{B}) = 0$ if the columns of $\mathbf{B}$ are orthogonal to each other. Lattice reduction algorithms are to reduce the orthogonality defect of a lattice by column swaps and size reductions, while hold the same lattice. The implementation process of these algorithms is using a unimodular matrix to multiply the original basis, the corresponding equation is given as:

$$\mathcal{L}(\mathbf{B}_{LR}) = \mathcal{L}(\mathbf{B}) \Leftrightarrow \mathbf{B}_{LR} = \mathbf{B}\mathbf{T}, \tag{8}$$

where all elements of $\mathbf{T}$ are Gausses integers, $\det(\mathbf{T}) = \pm 1$, and $\xi(\mathbf{B}_{LR}) < \xi(\mathbf{B})$.

A powerful and famous reduction criterion for arbitrary lattice dimensions is introduced by Lenstra et al. [8], and the algorithm they proposed is known as the LLL (or L^3) algorithm. Since the signal and channel matrix are complex valued, we use complex LLL algorithm (CLLL) provided in [9].

3.2   LR-Aided Linear Equalization

With the channel matrix after lattice reduction $\mathbf{H}_{LR} = \mathbf{H}\mathbf{T}$, the received signal can be written as

$$\mathbf{y} = \mathbf{H}\mathbf{X} + \mathbf{n} = \mathbf{H}\mathbf{T}\mathbf{T}^{-1}\mathbf{X} + \mathbf{n} = \mathbf{H}_{LR}\mathbf{Z} + \mathbf{n}. \tag{9}$$

The idea of LR-aided linear equalization is to apply linear equalization to $\mathbf{Z}$ instead of $\mathbf{X}$ and calculate $\mathbf{X}$ by $\mathbf{X} = \mathbf{T}\mathbf{Z}$. The estimation of $\mathbf{Z}$ are obtained as:

$$\hat{\mathbf{Z}}_{ZF} = \mathcal{Q}_1 \left(\left(\left(\mathbf{H}_{LR}^H \mathbf{H}_{LR} \right)^{-1} \mathbf{H}_{LR}^H \right) \mathbf{y} \right), \tag{10}$$

$$\hat{\mathbf{Z}}_{MMSE} = \mathcal{Q}_1 \left(\left(\left(\mathbf{H}_{LR}^H \mathbf{H}_{LR} + \sigma^2 \mathbf{I}_{N_t} \right)^{-1} \mathbf{H}_{LR}^H \right) \mathbf{y} \right), \tag{11}$$

where $\mathcal{Q}_1(\bullet)$ denotes the component-wise rounding operation. The estimation of $\mathbf{X}$ is given as:

$$\hat{\mathbf{X}}_{\text{ZF}} = \mathcal{Q}_2\big(\mathbf{T}\hat{\mathbf{Z}}_{\text{ZF}}\big) = \mathcal{Q}_2\Big(\mathbf{T}\mathcal{Q}_1\Big(\big((\mathbf{H}_{\text{LR}}^{\text{H}}\mathbf{H}_{\text{LR}})^{-1}\mathbf{H}_{\text{LR}}^{\text{H}}\big)\mathbf{y}\Big)\Big), \tag{12}$$

$$\hat{\mathbf{X}}_{\text{MMSE}} = \mathcal{Q}_2\big(\mathbf{T}\hat{\mathbf{Z}}_{\text{MMSE}}\big) = \mathcal{Q}_2\Big(\mathbf{T}\mathcal{Q}_1\Big(\big((\mathbf{H}_{\text{LR}}^{\text{H}}\mathbf{H}_{\text{LR}} + \sigma^2\mathbf{I}_{N_t})^{-1}\mathbf{H}_{\text{LR}}^{\text{H}}\big)\mathbf{y}\Big)\Big), \tag{13}$$

where $\mathcal{Q}_2(\bullet)$ restricts the symbols to lie in the constellation. If we extend the original channel matrix and received signal vector as

$$\tilde{\mathbf{H}} = \begin{bmatrix} \mathbf{H} \\ \sigma\mathbf{I}_{N_t} \end{bmatrix}, \tilde{\mathbf{y}} = \begin{bmatrix} \mathbf{y} \\ \mathbf{0}_{N_t \times 1} \end{bmatrix}, \tag{14}$$

the result of MMSE can also be written in the ZF form:

$$\hat{\mathbf{X}}_{\text{MMSE}} = \mathcal{Q}\Big(\big(\tilde{\mathbf{H}}^{\text{H}}\tilde{\mathbf{H}}\big)^{-1}\tilde{\mathbf{H}}^{\text{H}}\tilde{\mathbf{y}}\Big), \tag{15}$$

For V-BLAST MIMO system, formula (12) and (13) represent the whole detection. However, for SM system, the spatial symbol and signal symbol must be separated according to estimated vector $\hat{\mathbf{X}}_{\text{ZF}}$ or $\hat{\mathbf{X}}_{\text{MMSE}}$. For the brevity, we use $\hat{\mathbf{X}}$ to stand for $\hat{\mathbf{X}}_{\text{ZF}}$ or $\hat{\mathbf{X}}_{\text{MMSE}}$.

Considering the entries corresponding to inactive antennas in estimated vector should approach zero, we choose the largest N_a entries in $\hat{\mathbf{X}}$: $(\hat{x}_{i_1}, \hat{x}_{i_2}, \cdots, \hat{x}_{i_{N_a}}), |\hat{x}_{i_k}| \geq |\hat{x}_m|,$ $i_k \in \tilde{I} = \{i_1, i_2, \cdots, i_{N_a}\}, m \in (U - \tilde{I}), U = \{1, \cdots, N_t\}$ and arrange the corresponding antennas indices combination in ascending order: $i_1 < i_2 < \cdots < i_{N_a}$. The estimation of spatial symbol is given as

$$\hat{I}_j = \mathcal{Q}_3(\tilde{I}) = \mathcal{Q}_3(\{i_1, i_2, \cdots, i_{N_a}\}), \tag{16}$$

where $\mathcal{Q}_3(\bullet)$ forces the $\hat{I}_j$ to lie in the spatial constellation. After estimating the spatial symbol, choose the entry of $\hat{\mathbf{X}}$ corresponding to the first active antenna index as the estimation of signal symbol for SS-GSM:

$$\hat{s}_1 = \hat{s}_2 = \cdots = \hat{s}_{N_a} = \hat{x}_{i_1}, \tag{17}$$

As to MS-GSM, choose the entries of $\hat{\mathbf{X}}$ corresponding to the entire antenna index of the spatial symbol $\hat{I}_j$ as the estimation of signal symbol:

$$\hat{\mathbf{s}} = \big[\hat{x}_{i_1}, \hat{x}_{i_2}, \cdots, \hat{x}_{i_{N_a}}\big]. \tag{18}$$

Considering that the MMSE equalizer is equal to the ZF equalizer in the form of the extended system (15), we summarize the main steps of the LR-aided ZF equalization to represent the LR-aided linear equalization detector for GSM systems in Table 1.

Table 1. The main steps of LR-aided ZF equalization detector for MIMO GSM system.

S1	At the receiver, perform the CLLL algorithm to get the more orthogonal channel matrix and the unimodular matrix: $[\mathbf{H}_{LR}, \mathbf{T}] = CLLL(\mathbf{H})$
S2	In formula (10), use ZF equalization to equalize the received signal vector, and obtain $\hat{\mathbf{Z}}$
S3	In formula (12), recover the transmitted symbol vector $\mathbf{X}$
S4	In formula (16), estimate the spatial symbol $\hat{I}_j$ from $\hat{\mathbf{X}}$
S5	According to $\hat{I}_j$, estimate the signal symbol $\hat{s}$ for SS-GSM or MS-GSM. in formula (17) or (18)

3.3 A Compatible 8-QAM Constellation for GSM

Based on the theory of lattice, $\mathbf{X}$ should stem from the infinite integer space [10]. Considering the necessary condition of the lattice reduction is consecutive integers lattice, in [10, 11], square M-QAM constellation is translated into a finite consecutive integers set by proper scaling and shifting for V-BLAST MIMO system. However, the general expression of GSM which includes zero entries in transmitted vector don't satisfy this condition. For example, a 4-QAM constellation in GSM as shown in Fig. 1, which includes the original point, and scaling and shifting operation cannot turn points of constellation into consecutive integers. So the lattice reduction isn't suitable for GSM. For tacking this problem, we propose an 8-QAM constellation which can satisfy the complex consecutive integer requirement for $\mathbf{X}$, as depicted in Fig. 2. The proposed 8-QAM constellation is made up of two orthogonal real integers set: $\Lambda \times \Lambda$, where $\Lambda = \{-1, 0, 1\}$ (Fig. 3).

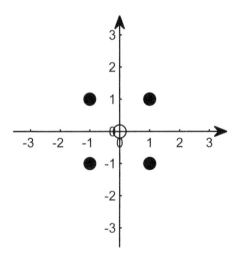

Fig. 1. A 4-QAM constellation in GSM.

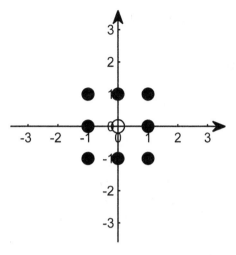

Fig. 2. Proposed 8-QAM constellation.

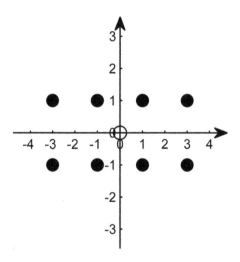

Fig. 3. Contrasting 8-QAM constellation

4 Performance Analyze

The LR-aided linear detectors for MIMO V-BLAST system can collect the same diversity order as that exploited by the ML detector [13], based on this, the diversity order of LR-aided linear detectors for MIMO GSM system is analyzed here.

Proposition 1: Given the signal model in (1), system model in (2), the proposed 8-QAM constellation in Sect. 4.2, channels consisting of i.i.d complex Gaussian distributed entries with zero mean and unit variance, the diversity order collected by LR-aided ZF equalization for GSM is N_r.

Proof: Substitute (9) for **y** in (10), the equalization result in step S2 of Table 1 can be rewritten as:

$$\hat{\mathbf{Z}}_{ZF} = \mathcal{Q}_1\left(\mathbf{H}_{LR}^{\dagger}\mathbf{y}\right) = \mathcal{Q}_1\left(\mathbf{H}_{LR}^{\dagger}\mathbf{H}_{LR}\mathbf{Z} + \mathbf{H}_{LR}^{\dagger}\mathbf{n}\right) = \mathbf{Z} + \mathcal{Q}_1\left(\mathbf{H}_{LR}^{\dagger}\mathbf{n}\right). \tag{19}$$

As a result, the estimation of transmitted symbol vector can be expressed as:

$$\hat{\mathbf{X}}_{ZF} = \mathcal{Q}_2\left(\mathbf{T}\hat{\mathbf{Z}}_{ZF}\right) = \mathcal{Q}_2\left(\mathbf{T}\left(\mathbf{Z} + \mathcal{Q}_1\left(\mathbf{H}_{LR}^{\dagger}\mathbf{n}\right)\right)\right) = \mathbf{X} + \mathcal{Q}_2\left(\mathbf{T}\mathcal{Q}_1\left(\mathbf{H}_{LR}^{\dagger}\mathbf{n}\right)\right). \tag{20}$$

Definitely, there will be $\hat{\mathbf{X}}_{ZF} = \mathbf{X}$ if $\mathcal{Q}_1\left(\mathbf{H}_{LR}^{\dagger}\mathbf{n}\right) = 0$. The correct estimation of **X** will lead to correct estimate of I_j and **s** according to the method described in Sect. 4.1. Therefore, the symbol error probability for a given **H** is upper-bounded by

$$P_{e|\mathbf{H}} \leq 1 - P\left(\mathcal{Q}_1\left(\mathbf{H}_{LR}^{\dagger}\mathbf{n}\right) = 0|\mathbf{H}\right) \tag{21}$$

$\tilde{\mathbf{H}}^{\dagger}$ can be represented as $[\mathbf{a}_1, \mathbf{a}_2, \ldots, \mathbf{a}_{N_t}]^{T}$, where $\mathbf{a}_i^{T}$, $i \in [1, N_t]$ is the ith row of $\tilde{\mathbf{H}}^{\dagger}$. The upper bound can be rewritten as

$$P_{e|\mathbf{H}} \leq P\left(\max_{1 \leq i \leq N_t}\left|\mathbf{a}_i^{T}\mathbf{n}\right| \geq \frac{1}{2}\bigg|\mathbf{H}\right). \tag{22}$$

According to Lemma 1 in [12], we obtain the inequality:

$$\max_{1 \leq i \leq N_t}\left\|\mathbf{a}_i^{T}\right\| \leq \frac{1}{\sqrt{1 - \xi(\mathbf{H}_{LR})} \cdot \min\limits_{1 \leq i \leq N_t}\left\|\tilde{\mathbf{h}}_i\right\|}, \tag{23}$$

where $\tilde{\mathbf{h}}_i$, $i \in [1, N_t]$ is the i th column of $\mathbf{H}_{LR}$. Consider that

$$\max_{1 \leq i \leq N_t}\left|\mathbf{a}_i^{T}\mathbf{n}\right| \leq \max_{1 \leq i \leq N_t}\left\|\mathbf{a}_i^{T}\right\| \cdot \|\mathbf{n}\| \leq \frac{\|\mathbf{n}\|}{\sqrt{1 - \xi(\mathbf{H}_{LR})} \cdot \min\limits_{1 \leq i \leq N_t}\left\|\tilde{\mathbf{h}}_i\right\|}, \tag{24}$$

$P_{e|\mathbf{H}}$ is further bounded by

$$P_{e|\mathbf{H}} \leq P\left(\frac{\|\mathbf{n}\|}{\sqrt{1 - \xi(\mathbf{H}_{LR})} \cdot \min\limits_{1 \leq i \leq N_t}\left\|\tilde{\mathbf{h}}_i\right\|} \geq \frac{1}{2}\bigg|\mathbf{H}\right) \tag{25}$$

Since $\mathbf{H}_{LR}$ is derived from **H** by using the CLLL algorithm with parameter δ, and **H** is full rank with probability one, we can obtain the following inequality according to Lemma 1 in [9]:

$$\sqrt{1 - \xi(\mathbf{H}_{\mathrm{LR}})} \geq 2^{\frac{N_{\mathrm{col}}}{2}} \left(\frac{2}{2\delta - 1}\right)^{-\frac{N_{\mathrm{col}}(N_{\mathrm{col}}+1)}{4}} := c_\delta, \tag{26}$$

where N_{col} is the number of columns of $\mathbf{H}$. Use $\mathbf{h}_{\min}$ to stand for the minimum non-zero norm vector in the lattice generated by $\mathbf{H}$. Because $\mathbf{H}_{\mathrm{LR}}$ spans the same lattice as $\mathbf{H}$, we have

$$\|\mathbf{h}_{\min}\| \leq \min_{1 \leq i \leq N_t} \|\tilde{\mathbf{h}}_i\|. \tag{27}$$

Substitute (26) and (27) into (25), and the (25) can be simplified as:

$$P_{e|\mathbf{H}} \leq P\left(\|\mathbf{n}\| \geq \frac{c_\delta \|\mathbf{h}_{\min}\|}{2} \bigg| \mathbf{H}\right). \tag{28}$$

Average (28) with respect to the random matrix $\mathbf{H}$, we have

$$\begin{aligned}
P_e = E_{\mathbf{H}}\left[P_{e|\mathbf{H}}\right] &\leq E_{\mathbf{H}}\left[P\left(\|\mathbf{n}\|^2 \geq \frac{c_\delta^2 \|\mathbf{h}_{\min}\|^2}{4} \bigg| \mathbf{H}\right)\right] \\
&= E_{\mathbf{n}}\left[P\left(\|\mathbf{h}_{\min}\|^2 \leq \frac{4\|\mathbf{n}\|^2}{c_\delta^2}\right) \bigg| \mathbf{n}\right].
\end{aligned} \tag{29}$$

$\|\mathbf{n}\|^2$ is a central Chi-square random variable with $2N_r$ degrees of freedom and mean $N_r\sigma^2$ since $\mathbf{n}$ is an $N_r \times 1$ complex white noise vector with zero mean and covariance matrix $\sigma^2 \mathbf{I}_{N_r}$. According to Lemma 2 in [12], we have

$$P\left(\|\mathbf{h}_{\min}\|^2 \leq \varepsilon\right) \leq c_{N_r N_t} \varepsilon^{N_r}, \tag{30}$$

where $c_{N_r N_t}$ is a finite constant depending on N_r and N_t. Then P_e can be further bounded as:

$$P_e \leq E_{\mathbf{n}}\left[c_{N_r N_t} \left(\frac{4}{c_\delta^2}\right)^{N_r} \|\mathbf{n}\|^{2N_r}\right]. \tag{31}$$

Calculate the N_r th moment of Chi-square random variable $\|\mathbf{n}\|^2$, we get the final result:

$$P_e \leq c_{N_r N_t} \left(\frac{4}{c_\delta^2}\right)^{N_r} \frac{(2N_r - 1)!}{(N_r - 1)!} \left(\frac{1}{\sigma^2}\right)^{-N_r}. \tag{32}$$

Therefore, the diversity order of the LR-aided ZF detector for GSM is greater than or equal to N_r. Since the maximum diversity order for the GSM MIMO system is N_r, the LR-aided ZF detector for GSM collects diversity N_r. The result is easy to extend for LR-aided MMSE detector. ∎

5 Simulation Results

In this section, we will testify three conclusion by Monte Carlo method with MATLAB: (1) under the condition that GSM system adopts the LR-aided linear detector, compared with the contrasting 8-QAM constellation depicted in Fig. 5 and the 4-QAM constellation depicted in Fig. 2, the proposed 8-QAM constellation has inherent performance superiority; (2) the proposed detector obtains full receive diversity order; (3) simulation results with Kronecker Model show that the proposed method still can collect receive diversity on correlated channel. Except (3), all simulations are implemented under the channel described in Sect. 2.

Figures 4 and 5 show the simulation results of BER performance among three kinds of signal constellation using MMSE or LR-aided MMSE detector for SS-GSM and MS-GSM system. The antenna configuration for these two system is $N_t = 4, N_a = 2, N_r = 6$. It is easy to know that the spectral efficiencies are $R_{SS-4-QAM} = 4\,\text{bit/s/Hz}$, $R_{SS-8-QAM} = 5\,\text{bit/s/Hz}$ for SS-GSM system and $R_{MS-4-QAM} = 6\,\text{bit/s/Hz}$, $R_{MS-8-QAM} = 8\,\text{bit/s/Hz}$ for MS-GSM system. We can see that the simulation results of SS-GSM is nearly the same as those of MS-GSM. While under the condition that the spectral efficiency of three schemes are identical, the proposed 8-QAM have superior BER at lower Signal Noise Ratio (SNR) compared with the contrasting 8-QAM: the improvement stage starts at 10 dB for the proposed 8-QAM while lattice reduction takes effect from 15 dB for the contrasting 8-QAM. Although the BER improvement of the proposed 8-QAM adopting lattice reduction is merely 0.5 dB, the spectral efficiency of 8-QAM is apparently higher than 4-QAM. In summary, the proposed 8-QAM constellation is superior to the contrasting 8-QAM and the contrasting 4-QAM when using the LR-aided MMSE detector.

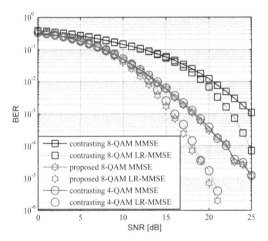

Fig. 4. BER performance of MMSE and LR-MMSE detector among three kinds of constellations for SS-GSM MIMO system.

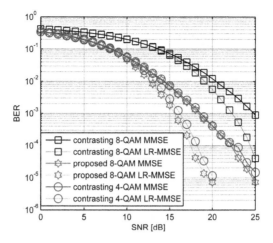

Fig. 5. BER performance of MMSE and LR-MMSE detector among three kinds of constellations for MS-GSM MIMO system.

Figures 6 and 7 compare the performance of LR-aided linear detector with the joint ML detector for SS-GSM and MS-GSM system while using the proposed 8-QAM constellation. The antenna configuration is $N_t = 4, N_a = 2, N_r = 6$. As we can see from the figures, regardless of the SS-GSM or MS-GSM system, the advantage lattice reduction presenting appears when SNR is higher than 10 dB and finally collect receive diversity. Compared with SS-GSM MIMO system, LR-aided linear detector works better on MS-GSM: the performance gap between the LR-aided linear detector and the optimal detector is about 6 dB for SS-GSM while nearly 3 dB for MS-GSM. It also should be noted that lattice reduction faster the unification of ZF and MMSE equalization at high SNR [11].

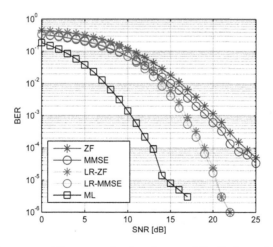

Fig. 6. BER performance of linear equalization detector, LR-aided equalization detector and ML detector employing the proposed 8-QAM constellation for SS-GSM MIMO system.

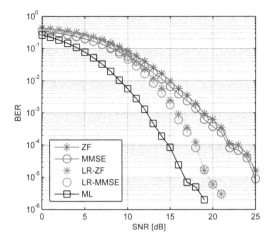

Fig. 7. BER performance of linear equalization detector, LR-aided equalization detector and ML detector employing the proposed 8-QAM constellation for MS-GSM MIMO system.

Figure 8 compares the BER performance under uncorrelated fading channel and correlated channel generated according to Kronecker Model. The antenna configuration of the MS-GSM system adopting the proposed 8-QAM constellation is $N_t = 5, N_a = 2, N_r = 6$. The correlation coefficient among the transmitting antennas and receiving antennas is 0.2, namely $r_{transmiter} = r_{receiver} = 0.2$. As we can see from the Fig. 8, the LR-aided MMSE detector can effectively alleviate the impact of channel correlation: the SNR gap between uncorrelated and correlated channel is nearly 8 dB for MMSE detector while merely 3 dB for LR-aided MMSE detector. Moreover, the LR-aided MMSE detector still can collect the receive diversity under the correlated channel.

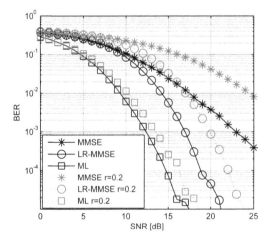

Fig. 8. BER performance under uncorrelated fading channel and correlated channel that employ the Kronecker Model.

6   Conclusion

In this paper, we introduce the LR-aided linear detector into GSM modulation and prove the method can collect the full receive diversity. Considering the characteristic of the transmit vector of GSM system, a compatible 8-QAM constellation is proposed to meet the LR requirement that the coefficient of the lattice base should be consecutive integers. Compared with the contrasting 4-QAM and 8-QAM, simulation results verify the superiority of the proposed 8-QAM on BER performance. At last, we also find that the LR-aided detector is more robust when dealing with the correlated channel.

In this paper, there are still some inadequacies to be study further. First, the theoretical analysis only proves that the LR-aided linear detector can collect the full receive diversity and does not further reveal how to affect the BER of GSM. Second, the performance gap between the LR-aided linear detector and ML detector is considerable, which need more effort to further promote the performance of linear detector for GSM system under the constraints of low complexity requirement.

References

1. Mesleh, R.Y., Haas, H., Sinanovic, S., Ahn, C.W., Yun, S.: Spatial modulation. IEEE Trans. Veh. Technol. **57**(4), 2228–2241 (2008)
2. Younis, A., Serafimovski, N., Mesleh, R., Haas, H.: Generalised spatial modulation. In: Proceedings of 2010 Asilomar Conference on Signals, Systems and Computers, pp. 1498–1502 (2010)
3. Fu, J., Hou, C., Wei, X., Yan, L., Hou, Y.: Generalised spatial modulation with multiple active transmit antennas. In: Proceedings of 2010 IEEE Globecom Workshop on Broadband Wireless Access, pp. 839–844 (2010)
4. Wang, J., Jia, S., Song, J.: Generalised spatial modulation system with multiple active transmit antennas and low complexity detection scheme. IEEE Trans. Wirel. Commun. **11**(4), 1605–1615 (2012)
5. Yao, H., Wornell, G.W.: Lattice-reduction-aided detectors for MIMO communication systems. In: Proceedings of IEEE Global Communications Conference (GLOBECOM), Taipei, Taiwan (2002)
6. Gan, Y.H., Ling, C., Mow, W.H.: Complex lattice reduction algorithm for low-complexity full-diversity MIMO detection. IEEE Trans. Signal Process. **57**(7), 2701–2710 (2009)
7. Mow, H.W.: Universal lattice decoding: a review and some recent results. In: Proceedings of IEEE International Conference on Communications (ICC), Paris, France, vol. 5, pp. 2842–2846 (2004)
8. Lenstra, A.K., Lenstra, H.W., Lovász, L.: Factoring polynomials with rational coefficients. Math. Ann. **261**(4), 515–534 (1982)
9. Ma, X., Zhang, W.: Performance analysis for MIMO systems with lattice-reduction aided linear equalization. IEEE Trans. Commun. **56**(2), 309–318 (2008)
10. Wübben, D., Böhnke, R., Kühn, V., Kammeyer, K.D.: MMSE-based lattice reduction for near-ML detection of MIMO systems. In: Proceedings of ITG Workshop Smart Antennas (WSA), Munich, Germany, March 2004
11. Bai, L., Choi, J.: Low Complexity MIMO Detection. Springer Science+Business Media, New York (2012). https://doi.org/10.1007/978-1-4419-8583-5

12. Taherzadeh, M., Mobasher, A., Khandani, A.K.: Lattice-basis reduction achieves the precoding diversity in MIMO broadcast systems. In: Proceedings of 39th Conference on Information Sciences and Systems. Johns Hopkins University, Baltimore, 15–18 March 2005
13. Tse, D., Viswanath, P.: Fundamentals of Wireless Communication. Cambridge University Press, Cambridge (2004)

Radio Frequency Fingerprint Identification Method in Wireless Communication

Zhe Li[✉], Yanxin Yin, and Lili Wu

Research and Development Center,
China Academy of Launch Vehicle Technology, Beijing, China
zheli@163.com, xinye624@163.com, shsqulili@163.com

Abstract. The Radio frequency fingerprinting (RFF) generation mechanism is analyzed in this paper. It is proved to be a secure means for network security access. At the same time, the method of RFF extraction is also given. The characteristics of RFF are analyzed theoretically. Then, a high-precision fingerprint feature identification method based on Kalman filter is proposed. The results of the experiments show that the proposed system can work effectively in the environment where the signal-to-noise ratio (SNR) is higher than 10 dB, and the achieved identification rate is higher than 90%.

Keywords: Radio frequency fingerprinting · Identification method
Identity authentication

1 Introduction

With the constantly emerging information countermeasure in the complex electro-magnetic environment, soft attack can be achieved to deceive, disruption, and even control the enemy's information space by using open air interface. Accordingly, the advanced information security technology has become increasingly prominent in wireless communications. At present, there is still flaw in the security protocol. It is very important to study the new physical layer security technology on the theoretical basis of security, which is of urgent military demand and military application value.

Radio frequency fingerprinting (RFF) is derived from the inconsistency in the production process of the components in wireless transmitters, which is reflected by a subtle feature in the launch signal. This subtle difference identifies the different characteristics of the transmitters, similar to human fingerprints, with the uniqueness. RFF can be used for physical layer authentication to protect against replicating, tampering, forgery and other attacks. It can support large-scale concurrent security access authentication and seamless security switch. It can guarantee that the node identity is maintained credibly and the service is maintained continuously.

2 Uniqueness of RFF

The tolerance in the production of the components of radio transmitters is the main cause of RFF. The possible sources of the tolerance include internal electrical components, printed circuit boards, power amplifiers, antennas and other transmitter components.

© ICST Institute for Computer Sciences, Social Informatics and Telecommunications Engineering 2018
X. Gu et al. (Eds.): MLICOM 2017, Part I, LNICST 226, pp. 195–202, 2018.
https://doi.org/10.1007/978-3-319-73564-1_19

Even the components with the same standard values have different actual values. The actual value is generally distributed within the tolerance range centered on the standard value and subjects to a certain probability distribution. Due to the presence of component tolerances, the transmitter output signal is different even with the same input excitation. Thus the RFF is formed.

Since the tolerance is slow time-varying, the actual value can be modeled as a random variable, with a mean value of the standard value and subjecting to a certain probability distribution within the tolerance, expressed as m_i, $i = 1, 2, 3, \cdots$.

The baseband signal is translated into an intermediate frequency (IF) signal by quadrature modulation. Then it is converted to an radio frequency (RF) signal via the up-conversion module and the power amplifier. Finally it is eradiated into the radio environment through the antenna. The RFF identification system receives the RF signal from the radio channel, and then is transformed into two baseband signals, namely the in-phase (I) and the quadrature (Q) components, through filtering, amplification and demodulation processing. Then the recognition algorithm will deal with the I and Q components.

The part between the transmitted signal $f(t)$ and the received signal $y(t)$ can be modeled as a constant invariant continuous system with an impulse response of $h(t)$. Since $h(t)$ is determined by the internal electronic components, it is equivalent to RFF [1].

The transmitter element m_i is a random variable, and the recognition system is the same for different transmitters. So the recognition system component value is modeled as a constant invariant quantity. At any time t, $h(t)$ is a definite function of the random variable m_i, expressed as $h(m_i|t)$, which subjects to the determined probability distribution, whose probability density function is $pdf(h(m_i|t))$

The uniqueness of the RFF is equivalent to the uniqueness of $h(t)$, that is, the probability of $\Delta h(m_i|t) = 0$.

$$
\begin{aligned}
P &= p\{\Delta h(m_i|t) = 0\} \\
&= \int_{\Delta h(m_i|t)=0} pdf(h(m_i|t))dh(m_i|t) = 0
\end{aligned}
\tag{1}
$$

That is, at any time, the RFF of arbitrary wireless transmitter is unique.

3 Extraction Method and Feature of RFF

3.1 Extraction Method

The procedure of RFF extraction is as follows: Firstly, the demodulated baseband signal is preprocessed and the signal is processed by the coarse synchronization module to obtain the frequency offset of the received signal roughly. Then the frequency offset of the received baseband signal is corrected coarsely. Afterwards, the frequency offset of the received baseband signal is corrected accurately through the precise synchronization module. Finally, the baseband signal is compensated by the sampling rate offset estimation module.

The signal is then compensated with the estimated phase shift by carrier phase synchronization module after the synchronization of the frequency offset and the sampling rate. After a series of synchronization and compensation operations described above, a stable baseband signal is obtained. The constellation trajectory feature, time domain feature and frequency domain feature are obtained from the constellation trajectory, the time-domain waveform and the frequency-domain of the baseband signal. The wireless target identification is carried out in multiple dimensions and multiple time resolutions [2, 3] (Fig. 1).

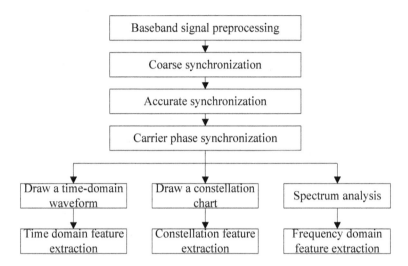

Fig. 1. RFF extraction workflow

3.2 Fingerprint Features

Offset Quadrature Phase Shift Keying (OQPSK) is a kind of high efficiency constant envelope digital modulation technique which is suitable for band-limited nonlinear channels. It is widely used in wireless communication systems. In this paper, OQPSK is used to analyze the characteristics of RFF.

After preprocessing and frequency/phase offset correction, the constellation trajectory is shown in Fig. 2.

It can be seen from Fig. 2 that although the frequency offset has been estimated and compensated, there is still residual frequency offsets. Accordingly, the directly received constellation is blurred. But we can take a split circle to extract the coordinates of the circle in the trajectory of the constellation. Using this method, the results are shown in Fig. 3.

As can be seen from Fig. 3, we can identify two devices very well through the analysis of the constellation. At the same time, the device has been repeatedly measured with the results of a high degree of consistency. The time domain waveform contains three dimensional information, the time axis, I axis and Q axis, as shown in Fig. 4.

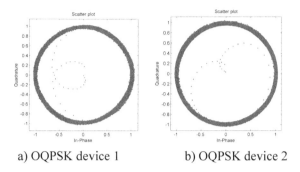

a) OQPSK device 1   b) OQPSK device 2

Fig. 2. Collected OQPSK constellation trajectory map

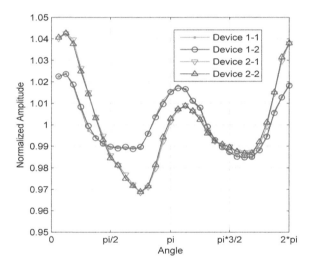

Fig. 3. Analysis of distortion degree of circular for two devices

The time domain feature can also be used to construct a feature extraction method for wireless objects with multiple temporal resolution to accommodate different symbol rates and different channels.

The frequency domain power spectrum is drawn by segmenting the received signal according to a certain length and then the Fourier transform. The spectrum can be analyzed after the Fourier transform, to extract the feature in the frequency domain (Fig. 5).

The spectrum feature is mainly to collect the characteristics of the received signal inside the signal bandwidth and outside the signal bandwidth, so as to obtain the auxiliary wireless target identifying feature.

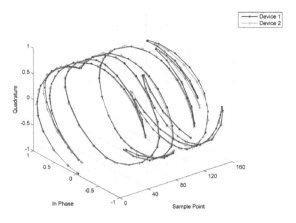

Fig. 4. Time-domain waveform which contains three dimensional information

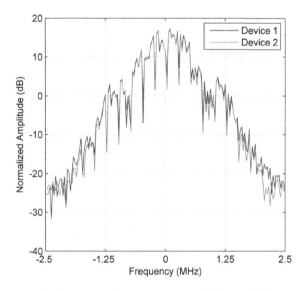

Fig. 5. Frequency-domain spectrum of the two devices

4 High Precision Identification Method for RFF

In the second section, the extraction method of the RFF is given. The next step is to select the appropriate identification algorithm to realize the correct identification of the RFF for different devices. Since the RF characteristics collected in practice are affected by the distortion of the amplifier and the distortion of the channel multipath effect, it is necessary to establish an easily recognizable identification model, to estimate the non-linear characteristics of the amplifier and the channel transmission characteristics, and select the appropriate identification vector, in order to achieve a higher identification rate.

According to the definition of RFF in [4, 5], the identification vector of RFF features is modeled as follows.

$$RFF = \left(\left| \frac{h_b^2}{h_b^1} \right|, \left| \frac{h_b^3}{h_b^1} \right|, \cdots, \left| \frac{h_b^M}{h_b^1} \right| \right)^T \tag{2}$$

Since the extended channel is time invariant, that is

$$\mathbf{h}_{bn} = \mathbf{h}_{b(n-1)} \tag{3}$$

Kalman filter is designed to calculate $\mathbf{h}_b$, and then we can obtain RFF. The state equation and the measurement equation are as follows.

$$\begin{cases} \mathbf{h}_{bn} = \mathbf{h}_{b(n-1)} \\ y_n = \mathbf{\Phi}_n \mathbf{h}_b + v_n \end{cases} \tag{4}$$

The Kalman filter algorithm can be decomposed. The decomposition formula of optimal predictive value is as follows.

$$\hat{\mathbf{h}}_{b(n/n-1)} = \hat{\mathbf{h}}_{b(n-1)} \tag{5}$$

The decomposition formula of the predictive error covariance is:

$$\mathbf{P}_{n/n-1} = \mathbf{P}_{n-1} \tag{6}$$

The decomposition formula of the filter gain is:

$$\mathbf{K}_n = \mathbf{P}_{n/n-1} \mathbf{\Phi}_n^H (\mathbf{\Phi}_n \mathbf{P}_{n/n-1} \mathbf{\Phi}_n^H + \mathbf{R})^{-1} \tag{7}$$

The decomposition formula of the estimated error covariance is:

$$\mathbf{P}_n = (1 - \mathbf{K}_n (\mathbf{\Phi}_n \mathbf{P}_{n/n-1} \mathbf{\Phi}_n^H + \mathbf{R})) \mathbf{P}_{n/n-1} \tag{8}$$

The decomposition formula of the optimal filter value is:

$$\hat{\mathbf{h}}_{bn} = \hat{\mathbf{h}}_{b(n/n-1)} + \mathbf{K}_n \cdot \left(y_n - \mathbf{\Phi}_n \cdot \hat{\mathbf{h}}_{b(n/n-1)} \right) \tag{9}$$

where $\mathbf{\Phi}_n$ is the measurement matrix and $\mathbf{R}$ is the correlation matrix of measurement noise. According to the observed value y_n obtained at the nth time, the nth state estimation $\hat{\mathbf{h}}_{bn}$ can be estimated. When the extended channel $\mathbf{h}_b$ is estimated, the RFF can be calculated and classified.

A software radio platform is used to establish the experiment system. The Zigbee wireless modules are used as target to be identified. In this experiment, different CC2530 Zigbee templates were used to simulate different wireless targets. The software radio platform receives the modulation signals transmitted by different CC2530 modules and identifies the different CC2530 modules.

A channel simulator is used for the simulation of the wireless channel. The recommended parameters of ITU-R M.1225 are used. The equivalent multipath delay parameter is: [0, 50, 110, 170, 290, 310] (ns). The amplitude parameter is: [0, −3, −10, −18, −26, −32] (ns).

Using the identification vector given by Eq. (2), $\mathbf{h}_b$ can be recursively calculated with the Kalman filter method. Then the identification vectors of different CC2530 devices can be calculated.

By adding different sizes of white noise, the performance of the algorithm can be evaluated. The results of the measurement are shown in Fig. 6.

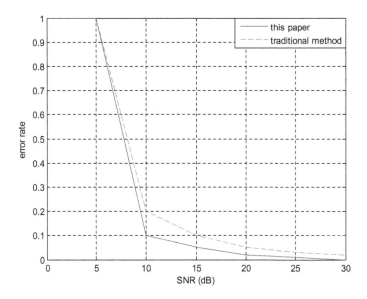

Fig. 6. Error recognition rate with the changes of the signal to noise ratio

As can be seen, the system can work effectively in the environment where the signal-to-noise ratio (SNR) is higher than 10 dB. And the identification rate is higher than 90%. The identification rate approaches 100% when the SNR reaches 28 dB. The traditional method is to draw the constellation map with the normalization process, and look for the appropriate threshold for device identification. When the SNR is higher than 15 dB, the identification rate of the system is up to 90%.

5 Conclusion

In this paper, the RFF extraction method is given, and the uniqueness of the fingerprint feature is verified from the results of the experiments. A high precision identification method of RFF is proposed and verified by experiments. RFF identification technology in military communications has broad application prospects, and can be combined with protocol layer security mechanism to greatly improve the wireless communication network security performance. Besides, fingerprint features of wireless transmitter can be used to distinguish between different transmitters, which can also be used to determine the equipment production process consistency.

References

1. Yuan, L.: Mathematical model of RF fingerprint recognition system. J. Commun. Technol. **42**, 113–117 (2009)
2. Xu, D.: Radiation source fingerprint mechanism and identification method. Ph.D. National University of Defense Technology. Changsha, China (2008)
3. Padilla, P., Padilla, J.L., Valenzuela-Valdes, J.F.: Radio frequency identification of wireless devices based on RF fingerprinting. Electron. Lett. **49**, 1409–1410 (2013)
4. Tang, Z.L., Yang, X.N., Li, J.D.: Fingerprint feature extraction method for narrowband communication radiation source based on sequential statistics. J. Electron. Inf. Technol. **33**, 1224–1228 (2011)
5. Liu, M.W., Doherty, J.F.: Nonlinearity estimation for specific emitter identification in multipath channels. IEEE Trans. Inf. Forensics Secur. **6**, 1076–1085 (2011)

Cognitive Radio and Intelligent Networking

Short Term Prediction Models of Mobile Network Traffic Based on Time Series Analysis

Yunxue Gao[1], Liming Zheng[1], Donglai Zhao[1], Yue Wu[2(✉)],
and Gang Wang[1]

[1] School of Electronic Information Engineering, Harbin Institute of Technology,
Harbin 150028, China
gaoyunxue@hotmail.com, {zheng,gwang51}@hit.edu.cn,
zdl527@126.com
[2] School of Management, Harbin Institute of Technology, Harbin 150028, China
wuy@hit.edu.cn

Abstract. In the mobile network, building a prediction based network traffic model is of great significance for mobile network optimization, so that the operators is able to schedule the resources adaptively. In the paper, multiplicative seasonal Autoregressive Integrated Moving Average model (ARIMA) and Holt-Winters model are proposed for modeling of traffic predication, where the historical traffic series of a typical tourist area are utilized to verify the performance. The two methods analyze the trend of mobile network traffic per hour, build and validate models. Then predict mobile network traffic within a given period of time. The error rate of different models predictions is analyzed to provide certain decision basis for the allocation of network resources.

Keywords: Traffic model · Multiplicative seasonal ARIMA · Holt-Winters
Short term prediction

1 Introduction

With the continuous development and popularization of mobile communication technology and intelligent terminals, the demand of extracting dynamic information whenever and wherever possible is increasing. Keeping wireless networks with good and stable performance and reducing the occurrence of wireless network failures are becoming more important. Massive user groups increase the difficulty of operation and maintenance, and operators must allocate network resources reasonably to ensure the user experience. Low network load settings in hot spots may lead to increased congestion, decreased call quality and even paralysis of the system. Excessive network load will waste network resources. Therefore, the prediction of traffic in hot spots can provide a reasonable basis for decision-making and optimize the allocation of network resources.

Through the signaling analysis platform of both radio access network (RAN) and the core network that carriers deployed to collect mobile network signaling. The network and terminal data is intercepted from the signaling, and the data are cleaned and structured, and finally the data is acquired as time series. Researches on time series and

© ICST Institute for Computer Sciences, Social Informatics and Telecommunications Engineering 2018
X. Gu et al. (Eds.): MLICOM 2017, Part I, LNICST 226, pp. 205–211, 2018.
https://doi.org/10.1007/978-3-319-73564-1_20

prediction have been discussed in [1]. In [2] authors proposed ARIMA model to process historical data of cells in mobile networks and generate reliable forecasting results. Traffic characterization is analyzed in [3] to be used to build models. In [4] authors proposed traffic prediction technique relies on analysis of traffic data on cells by using Holt-Winter's exponential smoothing. The traffic prediction accuracy of machine learning techniques - Multi-Layer Perception (MLP), Multi-Layer Perception with Weight Decay (MLPWD) and Support Vector Machines (SVM) are investigated in [5]. A hybrid traffic prediction model is introduce to forecasts the workload of base stations by utilizing historic traffic traces in [6]. In this paper, Holt-Winters and multiplicative seasonal ARIMA are used to model and validate the user data, and then traffic in the next period is predicted. The two models are popular models based on mathematic theory for time series short-term prediction. This article takes a typical tourist area as an example to build models and verify the performance.

2 Research Models

Time series is a sequence of data in equal intervals which mainly include long-term trend, seasonal variation and irregular change. The main purpose of time series analysis is to predict the future based on existing historical data. This section explains the principle of ARIMA and Holt-Winters.

2.1 ARIMA Model

ARIMA model doesn't consider the influence of other factors. It only explores the change rule of the sequence itself. The model can be conducted to predict short-term and long-term data. But the precision of short-term forecast is higher [7]. The ARMA formula is:

$$\phi(B)\nabla^d x_t = \theta(B)e_t, \tag{1}$$

where $\{x_t\}$ is the observed time series, $\{e_t\}$ is a white noise sequence that satisfies a mean of zero and constant variance, B is the backward shift operator, and d is order of the difference. $\nabla = 1 - B$. $\phi(B) = 1 - \sum_{i=1}^{p} \phi_i B^i$, $\theta(B) = 1 - \sum_{j=1}^{q} \theta_j B^j$ where p and q is the order of AR and MA model, $\{\phi_j\}$, $\{\theta_j\}$ is the coefficients of AR and MA model.

The seasonality of time series is a common pattern that repeat over S time period. Multiplicative seasonal ARIMA is designed to fit model that has trends, seasonal characteristics and adjacent sequence correlation. Multiplicative seasonal ARIMA $ARIMA(p, d, q) \times (P, D, Q)_S$ includes seasonal and non-seasonal factors where P, D, Q are order of seasonal AR, seasonal difference and seasonal MA respectively. The formula is:

$$\phi(B)\Phi(B^s)\nabla^d \nabla_s^D x_t = \theta(B)\Theta(B^s)e_t, \tag{2}$$

where $\Phi(B) = 1 - \sum_{i=1}^{p} \Phi_i B^{iS}$, $\Theta(B) = 1 - \sum_{j=1}^{q} \Theta_j B^{jS}$ and $\{\Phi_j\}$, $\{\Theta_j\}$ is the coefficients of AR and MA model.

2.2 Holt-Winters Model

Seasonal Holt-Winters smoothing fits data with trends and seasonality. The model can be applied to linear, exponential and damped trend. Holt-Winters includes the additive seasonal model and the multiplicative seasonal model. The additive seasonal model implies that seasonality and other trends are additive relation. Assume that α, β, $\gamma \in [0, 1]$ are smoothing parameters, a_t is the smoothed level, b_t is the trend, c_t is the seasonal smooth, and x'_{t+k} is k steps ahead forecasted value. The formulas [8, 9] are:

$$
\begin{aligned}
a_t &= \alpha(x_t - c_{t-s}) + (1 - \alpha)(a_{t-1} + b_{t-1}) \\
b_t &= \beta(a_t - a_{t-1}) + (1 - \beta)b_{t-1} \\
c_t &= \gamma(y_t - a_t) + (1 - \gamma)c_{t-s} \\
x'_{t+k} &= a_t + b_t k + c_{t+1+(k-1)\bmod S}
\end{aligned}
\tag{3}
$$

The multiplicative seasonal model is used to fit data have multiplicative seasonality. The formulas [8, 9] are:

$$
\begin{aligned}
a_t &= \alpha(x_t/c_{t-s}) + (1 - \alpha)(a_{t-1} + b_{t-1}) \\
b_t &= \beta(a_t - a_{t-1}) + (1 - \beta)b_{t-1} \\
c_t &= \gamma(y_t/a_t) + (1 - \gamma)c_{t-s} \\
x'_{t+k} &= (a_t + b_t k)c_{t+1+(k-1)\bmod S}
\end{aligned}
\tag{4}
$$

Holt-Winters is based on recursive relations, which suggests that start values need to be set before using. But start values have little effect on future calculations. For seasonal models, start values are detected by performing a simple decomposition in trend and seasonal component using moving averages.

3 Research Results

This section selects traffic data from 0:00 July 15, 2015 to 8:00 August 14, 2015 per hour as modeling data to explain the process of modeling. Forecast traffic data between 9:00 and 17:00 August 14, 2015. The experimental environment is R language with the version of 3.3.3.

3.1 ARIMA Modeling

The first step of model identification is to study the stationarity of time series. Stationary time series usually have a random fluctuation near a constant value, and the range of fluctuation is bounded with no obvious trend or seasonal characteristics. Non-stationary sequences tend to have different mean values at different time periods. The autocorrelation of stationary sequences decrease rapidly. The paper uses ADF (Augmented Dickey-Fuller Unit Root Test) to confirm whether time series are stationary. Null hypothesis forecasts the existence of unit root. If P value is smaller than 5%, the model test result reject the null hypothesis, and it can be assumed that time series satisfy stationarity. The function adf.test in R package tseries is used to run the

ADF test. The p value is less than 0.01, so the null hypothesis is rejected and the sequence is stable.

The second step is to determine the order of the model. Model order estimation is not only considering the fitting degree of the model to the original data, but also taking the number of undetermined parameters in the model into account, and take a reasonable tradeoff between the two. AIC (Akaike information criterion) is applicable to the order determination. Try to choose the minimum AIC value within a certain range. And Try to avoid over fitting as much as possible. Several excellent models and their AIC values are shown in Table 1. According to the simulation results, the Θ_2 parameter of $ARIMA(1,0,2) \times (1,0,2)_{24}$ is 0.0680 approximately zero, the t value is not significant, and the AIC value is close to $ARIMA(1,0,2) \times (1,0,1)_{24}$. In order to simplify the complexity, $ARIMA(1, 0, 2) \times (1, 0, 1)_{24}$ is applied. Model identification is completed.

Table 1. Several models and their AIC values

Model	AIC
ARIMA(1, 0, 2)(1, 0, 2)[24]	4107.25
ARIMA(1, 0, 2)(1, 0, 1)[24]	4108.32
ARIMA(2, 0, 1)(1, 0, 1)[24]	4109.03
ARIMA(1, 0, 1)(1, 0, 2)[24]	4112.04

Using MLE (Maximum Likelihood Estimation) to estimate parameters of the model. These parameters are shown in Table 2.

Table 2. Parameters of $ARIMA(1, 0, 2) \times (1, 0, 1)_{24}$

φ_1	θ_1	θ_2	ϕ_1	Θ_1	Intercept
0.7424	0.5933	0.1113	1	−0.9854	21.4832

After the completion of model identification, order determination and parameter estimation, next step is to estimate the validity of the chosen model. The validity test of the model is essentially to examine whether the residual sequence is a white noise sequence. The time series diagram of residuals should be a rectangular scatter plot without any trend around zero. The mean value of residuals is calculated to be about 0.09. And residual sequence meets the requirements according to Fig. 1. The auto-correlation function (ACF) of residual sequence is calculated. The correlation coefficients of the residuals are small except the zeroth order in Fig. 1, which means the residuals satisfy the independence. ACF only considers the existence of a certain lag order. The Ljung-Box test is based on a series of lags to determine the correlation of the sequence. The p values in Fig. 1 are all greater than 0.05, so the null hypothesis cannot be rejected, which means the residual sequence is a white noise sequence.

Once the model is identified, future values can be predicted from past and present values of the time series. Minimum mean square error estimation is commonly used in prediction. Confidence intervals, predictive values and actual values are displayed in Fig. 2.

3.2   Holt-Winters Modeling

The additive Holt-Winters model is used to analysis data. This section analysis and predict the same period of time series as previous section.

The model uses following parameters: 0.102 for a, 0.004 for b, and 0.231 for c. The value of B is approximately 0, indicating that the slope of the estimated trend component is essentially constant. The value of 'a' and 'c' indicate that the level and seasonality based on recent observations and historical observations. The ACF of residual sequence is calculated in Fig. 2. Based on the additive Holt-Winters model, the prediction of time series is calculated and displayed in Fig. 3.

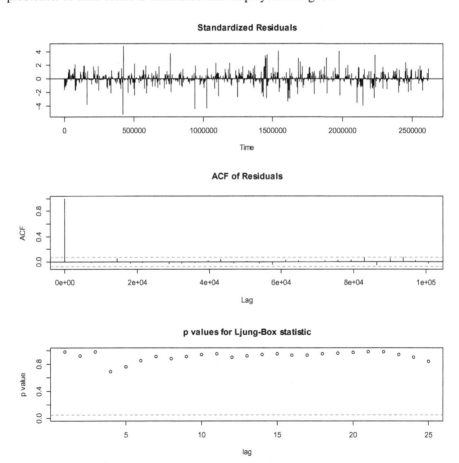

Fig. 1. This shows three figures consisting of *standardized residuals (first), ACF of residuals (second)*, and *p value for Ljung-Box statistic (third)*.

ACF of Residuals

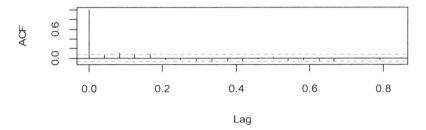

Fig. 2. *ACF* of residuals

Predictive value

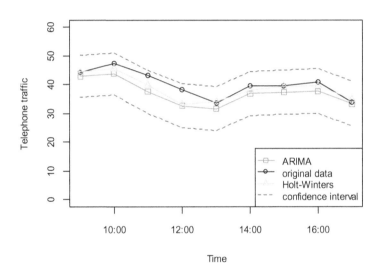

Fig. 3. *Predictive value* of ARIMA and Holt-Winters

4 Conclusion

Accurate traffic prediction is beneficial to balance the resources of mobile network according to the different characteristics of busy and idle time. Prediction helps to avoid excessive network load or waste of network resources. Depending on the data structure, different approaches can be tried. The paper presented the analysis of mobile network traffic. Multiplicative seasonal ARIMA model and Holt-Winters model are provided. The two models build and validate models and predict future values respectively. The forecast error of Holt-Winters model is lower than ARIMA in this situation. The order determination of ARIMA is more complex. Holt-Winters model is better than multiplicative seasonal ARIMA model in this situation. However, the model adopted in reality is decided by the different characteristics of the specific data, and a model can not always be the optimal model.

Acknowledgement. This work was supported by the National Natural Science Foundation of China under Grant No. 61401120.

References

1. Brockwell, P.J., Davis, R.A.: Introduction to Time Series and Forecasting. Springer, New York (2002). https://doi.org/10.1007/b97391
2. Guo, J., Peng, Y., Peng, X.: Traffic forecasting for mobile networks with multiplicative seasonal ARIMA models. In: 2009 9th International Conference on Electronic Measurement & Instruments (2009)
3. Khedher, H., Valois, F.: Traffic characterization for mobile networks. In: IEEE 56th Vehicular Technology Conference, pp. 1485–1489 (2008)
4. Tikunov, D., Nishimura, T.: Traffic prediction for mobile network using Holt-Winter's exponential smoothing. In: 15th International Conference on Software, Telecommunication and Computer Networks, pp. 310–314 (2007)
5. Nikravesh, A.Y., Ajila, S.A., Lung, C.-H.: Mobile network traffic prediction using MLP, MLPWD, and SVM. In: BigData Congress (2016)
6. Dawoud, S., Uzun, A., Göndör, S.: Optimizing the power consumption of mobile networks based on traffic prediction. In: Computer Software and Applications Conference (COMPSAC) (2014)
7. Mladenović, J., Lepojević, V., Janković-Milić, V.: Modelling and prognosis of the export of the Republic of Serbia by using seasonal Holt-Winters and ARIMA method. J. Econ. Themes **54**, 233–260 (2016)
8. Koehler, A., Snyder, R., Ord, J.K.: Forecasting models and prediction intervals for the multiplicative Holt-Winters method. Int. J. Forecast. **17**, 269–286 (2001)
9. Lepojevic, V., Andjelkovic-Pesic, M.: Forecasting electricity consumption by using Holt-Winters and seasonal regression models. Econ. Organ. **8**(4), 421–431 (2011). Facta Universitatis, Series

Calculation Method of Field Strength in the Case of Side Obstacles

Lu Chen[1,3], Fusheng Dai[2,3(✉)], Yonggang Chi[1], and Ji Zhou[2,3]

[1] Harbin Institute of Technology, Harbin 150001, China
[2] Harbin Institute of Technology at Weihai, Weihai 264209, China
dfs7113@126.com
[3] Science and Technology on Communication Networks Laboratory,
Shijiazhuang 050081, China

Abstract. Aiming at the problem of side obstacles on the transmission path, an algorithm for more accurate prediction of field strength has been proposed. The algorithm uses the slant profile which is determined by the antenna line and the minimum Fresnel radius to gather the information of the side obstacles, determine the Fresnel clearance and calculate the diffraction loss. The simulation results show that the side obstacles can produce the diffraction loss in the radio wave propagation as same as the vertical obstacle can, and verify the correctness and rationality of the attenuation calculated by the method in the case of the side obstacle.

Keywords: Radio wave propagation · Field strength prediction
Side obstacles · Propagation attenuation

1 Introduction

In free space, the propagation of electromagnetic waves is a relatively simple natural phenomenon, but the propagation prediction of surface electromagnetic waves is a relatively complicated process because of the diversity of the surface environment. The propagation of electromagnetic waves in different ground environment also has a different process [1]. The ITU-R P.526 model [2] mainly calculates the loss of radio wave propagation based on the vertical profile of the ground, but can not obtain the information of the side obstacles. However, the propagation of electromagnetic waves in space is not just presented in the vertical section, which leads to deviation of propagation prediction. In view of this problem, this paper considers the existence of side obstacles on the transmission path, and provides a better way to predict the wireless communication field strength.

Supported by: Science and Technology on Communication Networks Laboratory.

© ICST Institute for Computer Sciences, Social Informatics and Telecommunications Engineering 2018
X. Gu et al. (Eds.): MLICOM 2017, Part I, LNICST 226, pp. 212–220, 2018.
https://doi.org/10.1007/978-3-319-73564-1_21

2 Basic Theory

2.1 The Spatial Fresnel Zones of Wave Propagation

The main channel of the radio wave propagation is not a straight line, but a rotating ellipsoid. Thus, even though the obstacle does not block the geometric rays between the two points, they have entered the first Fresnel zone. At this point, the field strength of the receiving point has been affected, so the propagation cannot be regarded as free space propagation between the two points [3]. In practical engineering applications, it can be assumed that the waves propagate freely between the two points as long as at least 55% of the first Fresnel zone, which is called the minimum Fresnel zone, is not blocked.

First Fresnel radius:

$$R_1 = 550[\frac{d_1 d_2}{(d_1 + d_2)f}]^{1/2} \tag{1}$$

Minimum Fresnel radius:

$$R_0 = 0.577 R_1 \tag{2}$$

In the formula, f is the frequency (MHz); d_1 and d_2 are the distance (km) from the point to the transmitter and the receiver on the elliptical radius.

2.2 ITU-R P.526 Model

The distance between the straight line connecting the two ends of the path and the highest point of the ground obstacle is defined as the Fresnel clearance h (Fig. 1). When the line is below the obstacle, h is positive ((a) on Fig. 1) and the radio has a large diffraction loss. When the line is above the obstacle, h is negative ((b) on Fig. 1). When $-1 < h / R_0 \leq 0$, part of the minimum Fresnel zone is blocked, but it still generates a large diffraction loss. When $h / R_0 < -1$, the minimum Fresnel zone is not blocked, so the receiving point receives the free space field strength [4, 5].

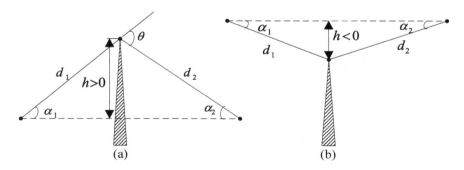

Fig. 1. Single knife-edge diffraction

V is the normalized geometric parameter of the marker obstacle:

$$v = 0.0316h \left[\frac{2(d_1 + d_2)}{\lambda d_1 d_2} \right]^{1/2} \tag{3}$$

In the formula, h is the Fresnel clearance (m); d_1 and d_2 is the distance (m) between the top of the obstacle and the ends of the path; λ is the wavelength (m) (Fig. 2). The relationship between the diffraction loss $J(v)$ and v is [6]:

$$J(v) = \begin{cases} 6.9 + 20\log\left(\sqrt{(v - 0.1)^2 + 1} + v - 0.1 \right) & v > -0.78 \\ 0 & v \leq -0.78 \end{cases} \tag{4}$$

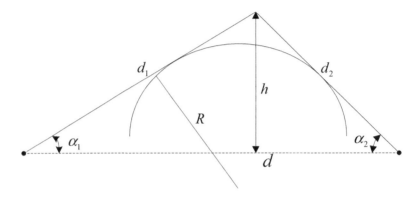

Fig. 2. Single rounded diffraction

The diffraction loss for a single rounded obstacle is [8]:

$$\begin{cases} L_v = v_0(a - H_c/H_0) \\ v_0 = 14.42 + A_v|u - 1.4|^{1.5} - 20\lg u \\ H_0 = -F_1/\sqrt{3} \end{cases} \tag{5}$$

Where:

L_v is the diffraction loss (dB) for the single rounded obstacle.
v_0 is the diffraction loss (dB) when $h = 0$.
F_1 is the first Fresnel radius (m).
H_c is the Fresnel clearance (m).
u is the terrain parameter.

Table 1. A_v relationship with u

u	0.6–0.79	0.8–1.09	1.1–1.9	1.91–2.2	2.21–2.9
Av	5.5	3.3	2.0	1.8	1.6

2.3   Side Obstacle

As shown in Fig. 3, there is an obstacle on the side of the transmitter T and the receiver R's connection path, which is adjacent to the vertical profile of the propagation path, causing interference to the propagation of the side waves. The wave produces a diffraction attenuation when it travels on the side of the path. So the obstacle is called the side obstacle (Table 1).

3   Calculation Method of Wave Diffraction Loss in the Presence of Side Obstacles

Radio waves are propagated in a three-dimensional space, not only in the transmitter and receiver path profiles. On both sides of the path of the transmitting and receiving antenna, there may be obstacles in the first Fresnel zone, which affect the propagation of the radio waves. The vertical profile on the propagation path does not contain information about the side obstacles. Therefore, the calculation of the attenuation of the side obstacles is required to analyze the geographic information on the slant profile [7].

3.1   Analysis of Ground Type

The ground type analysis mainly determines whether there is an obstacle in the vertical cross section of the transmission path by comparing the terrain irregularity parameter Δh with the first Fresnel radius maximum value R_{max} in the propagation path. Specific steps:

1. Calculate Δh. The terrain irregularity parameter Δh is a parameter that characterizes the change of part or all of the ground height on the propagation path. It is usually defined as the difference between more than 90% of the terrain height and more than 10% of the terrain height when the path specified part is sampled at equal intervals.
2. When $\Delta h > 0.1R_{max}$, it is consumed that one or more isolated obstacles in the terrain profile of the propagation path. In this case, it should be calculated according to the ITU-R P.526 model. At this point the impact of side obstacles is small. Even if $\Delta h \leq 0.1R_{max}$, the propagation path could not simply be thought as the smooth earth. Because it is not possible to determine whether there is an obstacle in the first Fresnel zone, it is necessary to decide whether there are side obstacles [9].

3.2   Determination of Side Obstacles

The main channel of the wave propagation is an ellipsoid whose focuses are the transmitting and receiving antenna. β is a flat in the ellipsoid that contains the straight line connecting the two ends of the path and has the largest projection of the ellipsoid on the ground. Combined the geographic information on the vertical profile of the propagation path with the slope β to determine whether there is an obstacle in the first Fresnel zone. There are many sampling points on the propagation path of the transmitter and the receiver. The set of all points with the minimum Fresnel radius from the sampling points make the projection of the minimum Fresnel zone boundary. Since the minimum Fresnel zone is the extreme distance of the obstacle occlusion, it is stipulated that there is a side obstacle in the smallest Fresnel zone when the elevation value of the boundary projection coordinates is larger than the antenna's connection height of the corresponding sampling point. Specific steps:

1. Take the same interval sampling method to get the coordinates of each point on the path when we know the location of the transmitter T and receiver R. Take a point a, and we can get the coordinates of the point b whose vertical distance from a is R_0. It is indicated that there is an obstacle in ab's section when b's elevation value H_b is larger than the height of the antenna connection T_a at point a, as shown in Fig. 3.

2. We can get the ab's profile data, when we know the location coordinates of point a and point b. According to the analysis of the ground type, there are no obstacles in the vertical section of TR, so the elevation data of the point a is smaller than the antenna height T_a. There must be a point on the ab's section with the same height of T_a because of the continuity of the elevation value of the terrain. And the distance from this point to point a is the Fresnel clearance h of the point. Or else $h = 0$, if there are no obstacles.

3. And so on, we can calculate the Fresnel clearances corresponding to each point on the path. The set of all Fresnel clearances make the projection of the side obstacle on surface β, as shown in Fig. 4. Thus, the path profile analysis for the side obstacle can be equivalent to the analysis on the vertical profile.

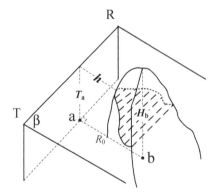

Fig. 3. Side obstacles diffraction

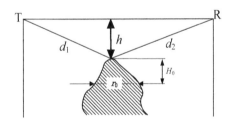

Fig. 4. Analysis of side obstacles profile

3.3   The Shape and Number of Side Obstacles

As the ITU-R P.526 model, isolated obstacles are divided into two types: blade shape and circle. The obstacle type is determined by the terrain parameter u. If $u \geq 3$, it is the ideal blade shape. If $u < 3$, it is a circular obstacle [10]. The mathematical expression for terrain parameter u calculation is:

$$u = 2.02[\frac{d_1 d_2}{(d_1 + d_2)r_0}]^{\frac{2}{3}} \tag{6}$$

In the formula, d_1 and d_2 are the horizontal distance from the vertex of the obstacle to the transmitter and the receiver. The meaning of the parameter r_0 is the width of the obstacle, which is at the distance H_0 below the vertex of the obstacle, in the direction of the connection path of the transmitting and receiving antenna, where $H_0 = R_1/\sqrt{3}$ (R_1 is the first Fresnel radius).

Unlike the vertical obstacle, since the side obstacle does not have continuity between various obstacles, it does not have to take into account the multimodal situation. As long as the minimum Fresnel zone in the propagation path is not blocked, it can be considered as free space propagation. However, the superposition of obstacles on both sides of the antenna will be considered. Specific steps:

1. Find the maximum position of the path in the lateral section, that is, the maximum position of the Fresnel clearance ($h < 0$, h is the largest distance from the obstacle recently, and the diffraction loss is the largest) as the main peak of the topographic profile curve.
2. Extend H_0 horizontally in the main peak. And do a vertical section paralleling to the antenna connection over the point. Compare the height to the antenna connection height, and take the higher part to determine the width r_0 and type of obstacle (Fig. 4).
3. Look for obstacles on both sides of the antenna connection. Calculate and sum the diffraction loss.

3.4   Loss Calculation of Various Situations

The wave propagation attenuation includes both the free space attenuation L_{bf} and the side obstacle diffraction attenuation L_s. Total attenuation L is:

$$L = L_{bf} + L_s \tag{7}$$

The Free Space Attenuation. The free space attenuation can be calculated by the free space attenuation formula, which is modified by the empirical data in the COST-231 model [11]:

$$L_{bf} = 42.6 + 20 log f + 26 log d \tag{8}$$

In the formula, f is the frequency (MHz); d is the transmission path distance (km).

The Side Obstacle Diffraction Attenuation. Calculate the Fresnel clearance h of the main peak of the side obstacle and the terrain parameter u to determine the type of obstacle. The formulas (3) and (4) are for the single knife-edge obstacle and the formula (5) is for the circular obstacles. Finally, calculate the total propagation attenuation.

4 Simulation Verification

Construct two simulation terrains which are in the case of the vertical obstacle and side obstacle respectively. Their profiles are the single peak blade obstacle, whose Fresnel clearance is 5 m and locate in the midpoint of the propagation path. Initialize parameters: set the transmission antenna's height h_t and receive antenna's height h_r to 15 m, frequency f to 460 MHz, and the transceiver antenna distance to 1500 m. The minimum Fresnel radius at the midpoint is calculated to be 9.42 m, so diffraction attenuation is bound to occur. Compare the wave propagation attenuation of the vertical and the lateral obstacle respectively.

The wave propagation attenuation of the vertical obstacle based on the ITU-R P.526 model and the lateral obstacle based on the proposed algorithm are shown in Table 2. Compare them with free space attenuation. It can be seen from Fig. 5:

1. In the vicinity of 800 m, the attenuation of radio waves increases dramatically because of the presence of obstacles nearby, resulting in diffraction loss. On the whole, the attenuation of the radio waves increases with the increase of the path distance, and the change trend is in accordance with the actual attenuation's characteristics.
2. When the vertical obstacle and side obstacle have the same Fresnel clearance, the two attenuation curves are basically consistent. It is shown that, in the process of the radio wave propagation, the side obstacle will block the first Fresnel zone and produce diffraction loss as the vertical obstacle will do.
3. The Fresnel clearance of the vertical obstacle calculated by the ITU-R P.526 model and the Fresnel clearance of the lateral obstacle calculated by the method are −4.9682 m and −4.9364 m, when the ideal Fresnel clearance is 5 m, and the resulting diffraction loss are 2.3092 dB and 2.3311 dB. The data of the two groups and the attenuation curve are basically consistent, which proves the correctness of the method.

Table 2. Path parameters and attenuation prediction results

Name	In vertical case	In lateral case
Transmission path length d (m)	1500	1500
Fresnel clearance h (m) at the vertex of the obstacle	−4.9682	−4.9364
Obstacle diffraction attenuation L_s (dB)	2.3092	2.3311
Path propagation in the vertical direction L_{bf} (dB)	115.1781	115.1781
Total attenuation of radio wave propagation L (dB)	117.4872	117.5091

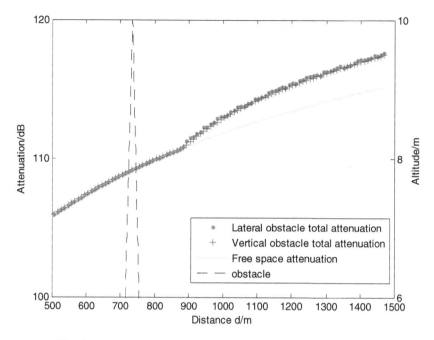

Fig. 5. Contrast of total attenuation under three kinds of conditions

5 Conclusion

On the basis of ITU-R P.526 model, this paper presents an algorithm to calculate the diffraction attenuation of side obstacles. By analyzing the geographic information of the obstacle on the oblique section, we can determine the type and number of the side obstacle, and then calculate the diffraction attenuation. Simulation results show that the algorithm is feasible and reasonable. In the process of radio wave transmission, especially under the condition of irregular terrain, this method can accurately analyze and predict the loss of electromagnetic wave.

References

1. He, J.H., Feng, J.F., Li, Y.X.: Analysis of wave propagation. Model Radio TV Broadcast Eng. **33**(12), 57–59 (2006)
2. Recommendation ITU-R P.526–11: Propagation by diffraction. International Telecommunication Union (2009)
3. Hu, H.B., Jiang, Y.J., Fu, W.B.: Study on prediction of attenuation characteristics of radio propagation in irregular terrain. J. Air Force Radar Acad. **22**(4), 271–274 (2008)
4. Ou, Y.J.: Research and application of communication model in mobile communication system (2011)
5. Cheng, R.T.: Study on propagation of multi-blade radiation and the ITU-R P.526 Model. China Radio **10**, 51–53 (2006)

6. Liu, Y., Zong, X.Z., Ke, H.F.: Effect of the roughness of the ground-surface on the line-of-sight propagation. Telecommun. Eng. **43**(5), 103–106 (2003)
7. Xu, X.Q.: Tactical network planning based on 3D visualization of geographic information. Harbin Institute of Technology, pp. 40–50 (2015)
8. Jin, M.Y., Sang, L.: Analysis of diffraction loss algorithm in wireless network planning. Mod. Sci. Technol. Telecommun. **7**, 32–37 (2012)
9. Sun, Y.: Radio wave propagation prediction based on electronic map. Xidian University, pp. 41–45 (2010)
10. Yang, D.: Wave propagation prediction based on electronic map. Inf. Commun. **2**, 11–12 (2013)
11. Li, D.W.: Research on modeling and simulation technology based on wireless mobile channel. Radio Commun. Technol. **2**, 32–35 (2013)

Variable Dimension Measurement Matrix Construction for Compressive Sampling via m Sequence

Jingting Xiao[(⊠)], Ruoyu Zhang, and Honglin Zhao

Communication Research Center, Harbin Institute of Technology,
Harbin 150001, China
hitxjting@163.com, hitzhangruoyu@163.com
hlzhao@hit.edu.cn

Abstract. Signal acquisition in ultra-high frequency is a challenging problem due to high cost of analog-digital converter. While compressed sensing (CS) provides an alternative way to sample signal with low sampling rate, the construction of measurement matrix is still challenging due to hardware complexity and random generation. To address this challenge, a variable dimension deterministic measurement matrix construction method is proposed in this paper based on cross-correlation characteristics of m sequences. Specifically, a lower bound of the spark of measurement matrix is derived theoretically. The proposed measurement matrix construction method is applicable to compressive sampling system to improve the quality of signal reconstruction, especially for modulated wideband converter (MWC) architecture. Simulation results demonstrate that the proposed measurement matrix is superior to random Gauss matrix and random Bernoulli matrix.

Keywords: Measurement matrix · Compressed sensing
Modulated wideband converters · M sequence optimum pairs

1 Introduction

Signal processing and communication technology will inevitably involve the sampling process. Nyquist sampling theorem is recognized as basic theory in sampling theory, and it reveals that the required sampling frequency must be greater than or equal to twice the highest frequency sampling signal.

Communication signals always have certain structures and characteristics. For sparse signal processing, compressed sensing (CS) [1] is a revolutionary technology in recent years. It is a kind of effective signal acquisition method that sample signal at a much lower frequency than the Nyquist sampling frequency if signal is sparse in some domain. According to small amount of observations, the original signal can be recovered with high accuracy.

Designing measurement matrix is an important research direction. In order to ensure that the signal is not lost in the process of observation, measurement matrix needs to satisfy certain properties. RIP (Restricted Isometry Property) [2] is a sufficient condition for measurement matrix to be satisfied. However, it is proved that

© ICST Institute for Computer Sciences, Social Informatics and Telecommunications Engineering 2018
X. Gu et al. (Eds.): MLICOM 2017, Part I, LNICST 226, pp. 221–230, 2018.
https://doi.org/10.1007/978-3-319-73564-1_22

measurement matrix satisfies RIP property is a combinatorial problem, and there is no effective method to verify whether measurement matrix satisfies RIP property in polynomial time. A feasible alternative is to evaluate mutual coherence of measurement matrix. It is proved that the smaller cross-correlation value of the measurement matrix is, the more likely the measurement matrix satisfies RIP. The widely used measurement matrix are random Gauss matrix, Bernoulli matrix, partial Fourier matrix, partial Hadamard matrix, Toeplitz matrix and so on. Random matrix such as random Gauss matrix and Bernoulli matrix, their dimension can be arbitrarily generated and their performance are good. It requires large storage space and high complexity of hardware implementation, which limit CS using in practical application. Partial orthogonal matrix such as partial Fourier matrix, partial Hadamard matrix and structured matrix such as Toeplitz matrix, their hardware complexity are greatly reduced compared with random matrix. However, the dimension of these measurement matrix is fixed, which limits actual engineering application in signal acquisition. Moreover, the accurate probability of signal recovery needs to be improved.

In this paper, a variable dimension deterministic measurement matrix construction method is proposed based on cross-correlation characteristics of m sequences. Firstly, the proposed method can sample signal with variable dimension compared with existing methods [3]. Then, it reduces hardware complexity especially in the block diagram of MWC system. Meanwhile, the signal reconstruction performance can be further improved by using proposed method, so as to alleviate the number of required measurements.

2 Compressed Sensing Overview

If $\mathbf{x} \in \mathbb{R}^N$ can be sparsely represented in orthonormal basis $\boldsymbol{\Psi} \in \mathbb{R}^{N \times N}$, $\mathbf{f} \in \mathbb{R}^N$ can be recovered from $\mathbf{y} \in \mathbb{R}^M$ which is a small number of data $M(M \ll N)$.

The sampled signal via compressive sensing can be expressed as:

$$\mathbf{y} = \boldsymbol{\Phi}\mathbf{f} + \mathbf{z} = \boldsymbol{\Phi}\boldsymbol{\Psi}\mathbf{x} + \mathbf{z} \tag{1}$$

If the N dimensional time domain signal $\mathbf{f} \in \mathbb{R}^{N \times 1}$ can be expanded in a linear group $\boldsymbol{\psi} = \{\psi_i\}_{i=1}^N$, we can get formula (2).

$$\mathbf{f} = \sum_{i=1}^N \psi_i x_i = \boldsymbol{\psi}\mathbf{x} \tag{2}$$

where $\mathbf{x}$ is coefficient of the N dimensional vector, $K(K \ll N)$ is the number of nonzero elements. The measurement matrix $\boldsymbol{\Phi}_{M \times N}$ is used to observe $\mathbf{x}$ in time domain.

$$\mathbf{y} = \boldsymbol{\Phi}\mathbf{f} = \boldsymbol{\Phi}\boldsymbol{\Psi}\mathbf{x} = \boldsymbol{\Theta}\mathbf{x} \tag{3}$$

where $\boldsymbol{\Phi}\boldsymbol{\Psi} = \boldsymbol{\Theta}$.

Because $\mathbf{x}$ is K-sparse, the process of recovering $\mathbf{x}$ through observations $\mathbf{y}$ can be transformed into solving the following linear programming problem:

$$\min_{\mathbf{x}} \|\mathbf{x}\|_0 \quad \text{s. t. } \mathbf{y} = \boldsymbol{\Theta}\mathbf{x} \tag{4}$$

where $\min_{\mathbf{x}} \|\mathbf{x}\|_0 \triangleq |\{i \ : \ x_i \neq 0\}|$ denotes l_0 -norm of $\mathbf{x}$. l_0 -minimization problem is a NP hard problem. In CS, it is usually transformed into l_1 -minimization problem which is tractable.

$$\min_{\mathbf{x}} \|\mathbf{x}\|_1 \quad \text{s. t. } \mathbf{y} = \boldsymbol{\Theta}\mathbf{x} \tag{5}$$

where $\min_{\mathbf{x}} \|\mathbf{x}\|_1 \triangleq |\{i \ : \ x_i \neq 0\}|$ denotes l_1 -norm of $\mathbf{x}$. (5) is l_1 -norm optimization to solve $\mathbf{x}$, and we can get reconstruction signal $\widehat{\mathbf{f}}$ at the same time. In order to obtain the accurate reconstruction of $\mathbf{f}$, measurement matrix should satisfy RIP.

Definition 1. If and only if a given constant $\varepsilon \in (0, 1)$ meet:

$$(1 - \varepsilon)\|\mathbf{f}\|_2^2 \leq \|\boldsymbol{\Phi}\mathbf{f}\|_2^2 \leq (1+\varepsilon)\|\mathbf{f}\|_2^2 \tag{6}$$

If K-sparse signal $\mathbf{f}$ satisfies (6), we call matrix $\boldsymbol{\Phi}$ satisfies RIP (N, K, ε). It is quite difficult to judge whether a matrix satisfies RIP. In addition to RIP, mutual correlation can be utilized to measure the ability of measurement matrix $\boldsymbol{\Phi}$ for reconstructing sparse signal [4], which is defined as follows:

$$\rho = \max_{s \neq t} \frac{|\langle \boldsymbol{\Phi}(s), \boldsymbol{\Phi}(t)\rangle|}{\|\boldsymbol{\Phi}(s)\|_2 \, \|\boldsymbol{\Phi}(t)\|_2} \tag{7}$$

where $\boldsymbol{\Phi}(s)$, $\boldsymbol{\Phi}(t)$ is column s and column t of $\boldsymbol{\Phi}$ respectively, $\langle \bullet, \bullet \rangle$ is inner product of two column vectors. The smaller ρ is, the stronger non-correlation of $\boldsymbol{\Phi}$ is.

The RIP condition is consistent with the uncorrelated constraint condition in the physical sense. (6) requires that sub matrix composed of arbitrary K columns should be approximately orthogonal. That is to say, correlation coefficient of $\boldsymbol{\Phi}$ is small [5].

Definition 2. The spark of $\boldsymbol{\Phi}$ is

$$Spark(\boldsymbol{\Phi}) \stackrel{def}{=} \min\{\|\boldsymbol{\xi}\|_0 \colon \boldsymbol{\xi} \in \boldsymbol{\Phi}_{Nullsp\mathbf{R}*}\} \tag{8}$$

where $\boldsymbol{\Phi}_{Nullsp\mathbf{R}*} \stackrel{def}{=} \{\boldsymbol{\xi} \in \mathbf{R}^N : \boldsymbol{\Phi}\boldsymbol{\xi} = 0, \boldsymbol{\xi} \neq \mathbf{0}\}$. It can be proved that if and only if $Spark(\boldsymbol{\Phi}) > 2k$, k sparse signal $\mathbf{x}$ can be obtained by solving l_0- minimization problem with exact approximation [6].

3   Variable Dimension CS Matrix Construction and Analysis

The m sequence is also called the longest linear feedback shift register sequence, which is pseudo randomness, sharp autocorrelation and small cross-correlation. In the construction of CS measurement matrix, we mainly use the good correlation property. The cross-correlation function of a sequence is defined as follows:

$$R_{a,b}(\tau) = \sum_{i=0}^{M-1} a_i b_{i+\tau} \tag{9}$$

where the cycle of $a(a_0, a_1, \cdots, a_{M-1})$ and $b(b_0, b_1, \cdots, b_{M-1})$ are M. The cross-correlation coefficient is defined as:

$$\rho_{a,b}(\tau) = \frac{1}{n} \sum_{i=0}^{M-1} a_i b_{i+\tau} \tag{10}$$

3.1   Construction Process of CS Matrix

The construction process of measurement matrix in this paper is shown in Fig. 1.

According to the actual length of signal is N, appropriate sub matrix dimension $P \times P$ is selected which satisfies $N/2 \leq P \leq N$.

On the basis of signal cycle P, m sequence optimum pairs $\mathbf{a} = \{a_1\, a_2\, a_3\, \cdots\, a_{P-1}\}$ and $\mathbf{b} = \{b_1\, b_2\, b_3\, \cdots\, b_{P-1}\}$ are generated by correlation verifying. Where $P = 2^r - 1$ and, r is the number of shift registers.

The following Toeblitz matrix A and B are achieved by circular shift of m sequence optimum pairs $\mathbf{a} = \{a_1\, a_2\, a_3\, \cdots\, a_{P-1}\}$ an $\mathbf{b} = \{b_1\, b_2\, b_3\, \cdots\, b_{P-1}\}$ respectively.

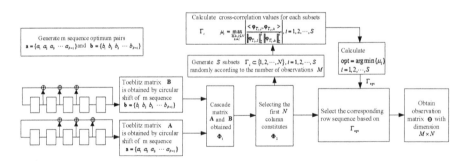

Fig. 1. Construction process of measurement matrix

$$\mathbf{A}=\begin{bmatrix} a_0 & a_1 & a_2 & \cdots & a_{P-1} \\ a_1 & a_2 & a_3 & \cdots & a_0 \\ a_2 & a_3 & a_4 & \cdots & a_1 \\ \vdots & \vdots & \vdots & \ddots & \vdots \\ a_{P-1} & a_0 & a_1 & \cdots & a_{P-2} \end{bmatrix}, \mathbf{B}=\begin{bmatrix} b_0 & b_1 & b_2 & \cdots & b_{P-1} \\ b_1 & b_2 & b_3 & \cdots & b_0 \\ b_2 & b_3 & b_4 & \cdots & b_1 \\ \vdots & \vdots & \vdots & \ddots & \vdots \\ b_{P-1} & b_0 & b_1 & \cdots & b_{P-2} \end{bmatrix}, \quad (11)$$

Cascade matrix A and B in the following manner to form $\mathbf{\Phi}_1$. The dimension of Matrix $\mathbf{\Phi}_1$ is $P \times 2P$.

$$\mathbf{\Phi}_1 = [\mathbf{A}|\mathbf{B}] = \left[\begin{array}{ccccc|ccccc} a_0 & a_1 & a_2 & \cdots & a_{P-1} & b_0 & b_1 & b_2 & \cdots & b_{P-1} \\ a_1 & a_2 & a_3 & \cdots & a_0 & b_1 & b_2 & b_3 & \cdots & b_0 \\ a_2 & a_3 & a_4 & \cdots & a_1 & b_2 & b_3 & b_4 & \cdots & b_1 \\ \vdots & \vdots & \vdots & \ddots & \vdots & \vdots & \vdots & \vdots & \ddots & \vdots \\ a_{P-1} & a_0 & a_1 & \cdots & a_{P-2} & b_{P-1} & b_0 & b_1 & \cdots & b_{P-2} \end{array}\right] = [\boldsymbol{\varphi}_1\ \boldsymbol{\varphi}_2\ \boldsymbol{\varphi}_3\ \cdots\ \boldsymbol{\varphi}_{2P}] \quad (12)$$

Selecting the first N column constitutes $\mathbf{\Phi}_2$.

$$\mathbf{\Phi}_2 = [\boldsymbol{\varphi}_1\ \boldsymbol{\varphi}_2\ \boldsymbol{\varphi}_3\ \cdots\ \boldsymbol{\varphi}_N]. \quad (13)$$

If we have sampled M observations, we can randomly generate S subsets $\Gamma_i \subset \{1, 2, \cdots, N\}, i = 1, 2, \cdots, S$ that meet $|\Gamma_i| = M$. Calculate μ_i:

$$\mu_i = \max_{\substack{1 \le k, l \le N \\ k \ne l}} \left| \frac{<\boldsymbol{\varphi}_{\Gamma_i,l}, \boldsymbol{\varphi}_{\Gamma_i,k}>}{\|\boldsymbol{\varphi}_{\Gamma_i,l}\|_2^2 \|\boldsymbol{\varphi}_{\Gamma_i,k}\|_2^2} \right|, i = 1, 2, \cdots, S. \quad (14)$$

Then, choose opt $= \arg \min\{\mu_i\}, i = 1, 2, \cdots, S$, and Γ_{opt} is the optimal subset. Selecting the corresponding line in $\mathbf{\Phi}_2$ on the basis of Γ_{opt}, measurement matrix is constructed.

$$\mathbf{\Theta} = \mathbf{\Phi}_2(\Gamma_{\text{opt}}, :). \quad (15)$$

3.2 Analysis of the Proposed CS Matrix

It is easily got that m sequence optimum pairs has three cross-correlation values by theory analysis.

$$R_{a,b}(\tau) \in \left\{ -1, -1 - 2^{\lfloor \frac{(r+2)}{2} \rfloor}, -1 + 2^{\lfloor \frac{(r+2)}{2} \rfloor} \right\} \quad (16)$$

where r is an even number that cannot be divisible by 4. $\lfloor \bullet \rfloor$ is rounding down the objective. The maximum cross-correlation value of the measurement matrix can be obtained. [7]

$$\mu(\boldsymbol{\Phi}_r)_{max} = \max_{1 \le l \neq k \le N} \frac{|<\boldsymbol{\varphi}_l, \boldsymbol{\varphi}_k>|}{\|\boldsymbol{\varphi}_l\|_2^2 \|\boldsymbol{\varphi}_k\|_2^2} = \max\left(\frac{1}{n}, \frac{1+2^{\lfloor\frac{(r+2)}{2}\rfloor}}{n}, \frac{-1+2^{\lfloor\frac{(r+2)}{2}\rfloor}}{n}\right)$$

$$= \frac{1+2^{\lfloor\frac{(r+2)}{2}\rfloor}}{n} \tag{17}$$

The lower bound of the spark value of the constructed measurement matrix can be calculated.

$$S(\boldsymbol{\Phi}) \ge 1 + \frac{1}{\mu(\boldsymbol{\Phi})_{max}}, \tag{18}$$

where r cannot be divisible by 4.

We can obtain $S(\boldsymbol{\Phi})/2 \ge k$ from the previous theoretical analysis, then

$$k < \frac{1}{2}\left(1 + \frac{n}{1+2^{\lfloor\frac{(r+2)}{2}\rfloor}}\right). \tag{19}$$

If (18) is satisfied, signal can be reconstructed exactly. For variable dimensional matrices $\boldsymbol{\Theta}$, rows with small cross correlation values are selected based on M, so that the upper bounds may be reduced.

$$k < \frac{1}{2}\left(1 + \frac{n}{1+2^{\lfloor\frac{(r+2)}{2}\rfloor}}\right) \text{ or } \frac{1}{2}\left(1 + \frac{n}{-1+2^{\lfloor\frac{(r+2)}{2}\rfloor}}\right). \tag{20}$$

4   Performance Evaluation

In this section, we use MWC to show the performance of the proposed measurement matrix described in the previous section. MWC for sub-Nyquist sampling system [8] is shown in Fig. 2. The sampled signal passes through m parallel channels, and each row of measurement matrix corresponds to each parallel channel. Signals are multiplied in each channel with modulation sequence. Then, they pass through low pass filter, and finally it sample at a low rate. These is the signal acquisition process.

Suppose function expression of the original analog signal is:

$$x(t) = \sum_{n=1}^{N/2} \sqrt{E_n B_n} sinc(B_n(t - \tau_n)) cos(2\pi f_n(t - \tau_n)). \tag{21}$$

The energy coefficient E_n and the time delay τ_n are randomly set. Signal bandwidth is $B_n = 50$ MHz, and the carrier frequency f_n is randomly distributed in $[0, 5]$ GHz, which means that Nyquist sampling frequency of the signal is $f_N = 10$ GHz at least. According to the number of parallel channels MWC is 50, the original analog signal

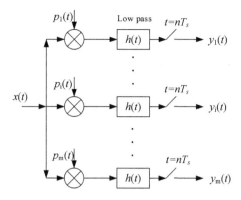

Fig. 2. Block diagram of modulated wideband converter (MWC)

spectrum can be divided into 195 equivalent blocks, and this sets cutoff bandwidth for low-pass filter in each channel and sampling frequency for low speed analog-to-digital converter. Therefore, the total sampling rate of MWC is $50 \times 51.3 \approx 2.565$ GHz, and the dimension of measurement matrix needed for MWC is 50×195. The m sequence cycle is $P = 127 = 2^7 - 1$, which means requiring 7 stage shift registers. Select m sequence optimum pairs $x^7 + x^3 + x^2 + x + 1$ and $x^7 + x^3 + 1$. Then $\Theta \in \mathbb{R}^{50 \times 195}$ is constructed based on the steps of Sect. 3. In this paper, measurement matrix construction requires only two pairs of cyclic shift registers to obtain m sequences. The mixing sequences of other channels can be obtained by cyclic shifts of the generated m sequences. Compared with the traditional random measurement matrix, measurement matrix constructed in this paper greatly reduces the required storage space and is easy to implement by hardware.

In this article, all simulations are based on MWC for sub-Nyquist sampling system. Reconstruction algorithm is Orthogonal Matching Pursuit (OMP) algorithm [9] (Fig. 3).

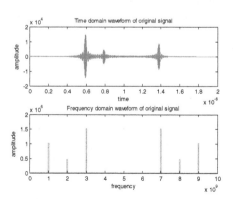

Fig. 3. Original signal waveform

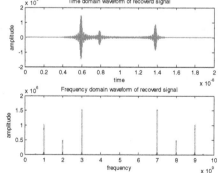

Fig. 4. Reconstructed signal waveform

Figure 4 shows the time domain and frequency domain waveform of reconstructed signal which uses the measurement matrix constructed in this paper. The measurement matrix constructed in this paper is used as mixed function $P_i(t)$. When the sampling frequency is only 1/4 of Nyquist frequency, the original analog signal can be restored almost without distortion.

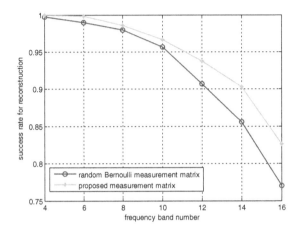

Fig. 5. Performance comparison between proposed measurement matrix and Bernoulli matrix

Figure 5 compares the probability of successful recovery of the signal under different frequency band between the proposed measurement matrix and the Bernoulli measurement matrix for signal acquisition. It can be seen clearly that when frequency band number of analog signals is 6, the signals can still recover almost 100% using the proposed measurement matrix. When frequency band of original analog signal continues to increase, success rate of analog signal restoration using the proposed measurement matrix is still higher than that of Bernoulli measurement matrix. Compared with Bernoulli measurement matrix, the designed measurement matrix occupies less storage and hardware resources. At the same time, it shows better performance, high recovery probability and high reliability in practical applications.

The recovery probability of Gauss signal and 0–1 signal under different sparsity is conducted. Figures 6 and 7 are comparisons of success reconstruction ratio of the proposed measurement matrix and the random Gauss measurement matrix under Gauss signal and 0–1 signal respectively. The dimension of measurement matrix is 50 × 195. For Gauss signal, random Gauss measurement matrix cannot guarantee accurate reconstruction of the signal when sparsity is 40. However, the measurement matrix designed in this paper still guarantee success rate of reconstruction approaching 100%. For 0–1 signal, performance of signal reconstruction is worse than Gauss signal. However, compared with the random Gauss measurement matrix, the maximum reconstruction probability gain is 45% if using the proposed measurement matrix in this paper.

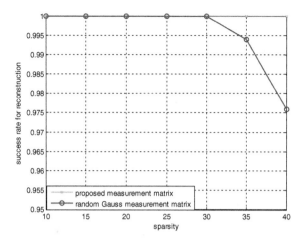

Fig. 6. Recovery probability comparison under Gauss signal

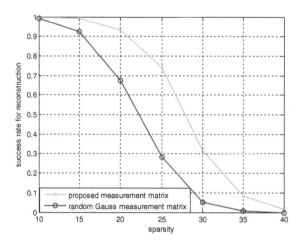

Fig. 7. Recovery probability comparison under 0–1 signal

5 Conclusion

To alleviate the hardware complexity of random measurement matrix. A variable dimension measurement matrix construction method is proposed in this paper based on characteristics of m sequences. A lower bound of the spark for the proposed matrix is obtained by theoretical derivation, which shows the proposed matrix is feasible for signal measurement. Additionally, the method of measurement construction can be extended to partial orthogonal matrices and Toeplitz matrices to realize variable dimension measurement matrix, which is a variable dimension construction framework for measurement matrix. Simulation results demonstrate that the proposed measurement matrix is superior to random Gauss measurement matrix and random Bernoulli matrix for both Gaussian and 0–1 signals in terms of the probability of success reconstruction. For sub-Nyquist sampling architecture MWC, it saves hardware storage resources significantly due to high reconstruction probability.

Acknowledgments. This work was supported by the Fundamental Research Funds for the Center Universities (Grant No. HIT.MKSTISP.2016 13).

References

1. Candes, E.J., Romberg, J., Tao, T.: Robust uncertainty principles: exact signal reconstruction from highly incomplete frequency information. J. IEEE Trans. Inf. Theory. **52**, 489–509 (2006)
2. Candes, E.J., Tao, T.: Decoding by linear programming. J. IEEE Trans. Inf. Theory **51**, 4203–4215 (2005)
3. Sun, R., Zhao, H., Xu, H.: The application of improved Hadamard measurement matrix in compressed sensing. In: International Conference on Systems and Informatics, pp. 1994–1997. IEEE, Yantai (2012)
4. Donoho, D.L., Elad, M.: Optimally sparse representation in general (nonorthogonal) dictionaries via ℓ1minimization. J. Proc. Natl. Acad. Sci. U.S.A. **100**, 2197–2202 (2003)
5. Xia, S.T., Liu, X.J., Jiang, Y., Zheng, H.T.: Deterministic constructions of binary measurement matrices from finite geometry. J. IEEE Trans. Sig. Process. **63**, 1017–1029 (2013)
6. Tropp, J.A.: Greed is good: algorithmic results for sparse approximation. J. IEEE Trans. Inf. Theory **50**, 2231–2242 (2004)
7. Dang, K., Ma, L., Tian, Y., Zhang, H., Ru, L., Li, X.: Construction of the compressive sensing measurement matrix based on m sequences. J. Xian Dianzi Keji Daxue Xuebao/J. Xidian Univ. **42**, 186–192 (2015)
8. Mishali, M., Eldar, Y.: From theory to practice: sub-nyquist sampling of sparse wideband analog signals. J. IEEE J. Sel. Top. Sig. Process. **4**, 375–391 (2010)
9. Karahanoglu, N.B., Erdogan, H.: A* orthogonal matching pursuit: best-first search for compressed sensing signal recovery. J. Digit. Sig. Process. **22**, 555–568 (2012)

Signal Quality Assessment of Wireless Signal Based on Compressed Sensing

Fei An[1,2] and Fusheng Dai[1,2(✉)]

[1] Harbin Institute of Technology at Weihai, Weihai 264209, China
anfei19931220@163.com
[2] Science and Technology on Communication Networks Laboratory,
Shijiazhuang 050081, China
dfs7113@126.com

Abstract. Detecting signal interference and assessing signal quality are essential tasks to ensure the normal communication within an area. As for traditional methods, we have to take field measurements after setting up a base station which needs to obtain huge data in low efficiency. Aiming at this particular problem, this paper proposed to assess signal quality by compressed sensing. Method of compressed sensing used in signal quality assessment is firstly discussed. After that, we introduced the specific process when assessing. At last the results of reconstructing the measured data and the predicted data separately shows that it could met the accuracy requirements of signal quality assessment.

Keywords: Wireless communication · Signal quality assessment
Compressed sensing · Field measurements

1 Introduction

Whether for military network or civil network, with the increase of network equipments, factors on interference of signal quality is more and more, especially in the complex electromagnetic environment, thus ensure the quality of wireless signals within range of base station has become a key problem [1]. In many complex environment, it is unrealistic for assessing signal quality with field measurement everywhere. In addition, before the erection of base station, if not predict the signal quality within range of it in advance, it may result in the risk of demolition and reerection because of a terrible erection position. Therefore we need to assess signal quality in advance until find out a good erection position. Thus, consider to sample sparse point and look for an appropriate algorithm to recover the signal quality of whole area. Compressed sensing theory has broken the traditional Nyquist Sampling Theorem. It does not consider the frequency characteristics of signals, but using the sparsity of signal in a transform domain,

---

F. An and F. Dai—Supported by: Science and Technology on Communication Networks Laboratory.

© ICST Institute for Computer Sciences, Social Informatics and Telecommunications Engineering 2018
X. Gu et al. (Eds.): MLICOM 2017, Part I, LNICST 226, pp. 231–238, 2018.
https://doi.org/10.1007/978-3-319-73564-1_23

project the signal to a low dimensional space by using a measurement matrix irrelated with basis matrix, to reconstruct the signal by solving a convex optimization problem [2,3]. The reason of choosing this method is that nobody has used compressed sensing to assess signal quality through the literature retrieval, aimed to solve the contradiction between large amount of signal data and limited resources in complex network environment. Considering the detected signal strength is sparse under natural conditions, collecting a small number of signal strength data can recover the high-precision signal quality map by using reconstruction algorithm based on compressed sensing theory. This paper will introduce the key problems of compressed sensing and the method of detecting electromagnetic interference, then combine these two term, and construct a sparse model of signals to realize the signal quality assessment.

2   Signal Quality Assessment Method Based on Compressed Sensing

2.1   Construct Regional Sparse Model

The premise of compressed sensing is that signal can express sparsely under the selected basis matrix, so how to select a reasonable basis matrix makes the original signal become sparse after transformation is the key problem. For a one-dimensional signal $X \in R^N$, which can be linear representation as $X = \Psi S$ on the basis matrix $\Psi^T = [\Psi_1, \Psi_2, \ldots, \Psi_N]$, where S is called the sparse coefficient [4,5].

In the actual situation, assuming an area is grid distribution, then divide it into $I \times J$ homogeneous areas. Due to the electromagnetic wave signal has a spatial correlation, so each area after divided is considered as a sample point. After that, convert $I \times J$ regional matrix into one-dimensional $N \times 1$ matrix $X(N = I \times J)$, to facilitate the measurement matrix to measure. Considering the sparsity of electromagnetic wave signal, we chose the Fast Fourier Transform as a basis matrix. Specifically, if S is the two-dimensional Fourier Transform of X, it can get $s = Wx$, with $s = vec(S)$, $x = vec(X)$. (If V is a $k \times 1$ matrix, then $vec(V)$ means the $kl \times 1$ vector stacked by columns of V, that is $vec(V) = [v_{11}, \ldots, v_{l1}, \ldots, v_{1k}, \ldots, v_{kl}]^T$). W is the Discrete Fourier Transform matrix $W[m, k] = e^{-j2\pi mk/l}$, s is sparse.

2.2   Construction of the Unit Measurement Matrix

The construction of measurement matrix is the core problem of compressed sensing. One of the focuses is to measure and preserve most of the useful information of original signal, so that the reconstruction and recovery are meaningful. Otherwise once the information is missing while doing measurement, we can foresee the recovery signal must be far from the original signal. Another focus of constructing measurement matrix is to ensure it is not related with the vast majority of basis matrix, and can be used for the majority of compressed signal [6,7].

Currently, the measurement matrix which satisfy these conditions and has been widely applied includes Fourier matrix, Bernoulli random matrix, Gaussian random matrix, etc.

Combined with the previously constructed sparse model, this paper uses a special measurement matrix transformed by the unit matrix [8], specific steps are as follows:

1. Ramdomly disturbing a unit matrix of $N \times N$ and extract M rows, get a ϕ matrix of $M \times N$ (a subset of unit matrix), 1 only shows up one time in each row with others are all 0.
2. Multiplying ϕ by X, then get the matrix Y of $M \times 1$ after measurement. Due to the characteristics of ϕ, its each row multiplied by X makes only one value be retained, the others are 0. It means we only select one area from X, and the characteristics of ϕ would determine the selection will not be repeated later.

2.3 Signal Reconstruction Algorithm

When reconstruct the signal, the length of measurement value M is far less than the length of original signal N, thus the reconfiguration problem is essentially a problem of solving underdetermined equations, that is the minimum 0 norm problem [9]. Such as shown in formula (1).

$$min\|\Psi^T X\|_0 \qquad s.t.\, AX = \phi\Psi X = Y \qquad (1)$$

Superficially, it seems to be a NP hard problem. But because the signal is compressible and it has been proved that if the measurement matrix meet the property of RIP(Restricted Isometry Property), this L0 problem can be transformed to L1 problem by Candes, Tao and Donoho, such as formula (2) shows.

$$min\|\Psi^T X\|_1 \qquad s.t.\, AX = \phi\Psi X = Y \qquad (2)$$

Based on the above problems, new reconstruction methods are proposed continually. Now it mainly including greed tracking algorithm, convex optimization algorithm and reconstruction algorithm based on bayesian framework, etc. [10].

Considering the greedy tracking algorithm has characteristics of high recovery rate and it is easy to implement, OMP (Orthogonal Matching Pursuit), as the reconstruction algorithm, is chosen to prove the validity of the project [11,12]. According to the selected areas of the observation matrix we can get these Y signal strength values, then reconstruct the signal of $I \times J$ by OMP.

3 Signal Quality Assessment

For a large scale of communication network, there may be multiple base stations, radios and other communication equipments in an area. In this complex electromagnetic environment, as the communication network topological structure and spectrum allocation been finished, there may not have a good communication quality within the scope of cover. Thus, assessing the quality to ensure the rationality of the communication network construction is necessary.

3.1 Electromagnetic Wave Propagation Attenuation Analysis

In actual communication, considering the attenuation between transmitting end and receiving end because of complex terrain, the transmission process is more complex. Thus the electromagnetic wave model of free space transmission must be modified based on these factors. According to the result of field measurement, compared the predicted results of deterministic model (ITU-RP.526) with the semi empirical and semi deterministic model (Longley-Rice), it shows that the predicted result of ITU-RP.526 model is closer to the actual result as shown in Fig. 1. So ITU-RP.526 model can take the place of field measurement to compare with reconstructed signal. Specific steps are as follows:

1. To start with, analyze the ground type and determine the irregularity of the terrain with Δh. The terrain is smooth if $\Delta h \leq 0.1 \times R_{max}$, otherwise exists obstacles, where Δh is the height difference between transmitter and receiver, R_{max} is the maximum radius of the first Fresnel region on the propagation path.
2. Suppose the terrain is smooth, then judge whether the horizon is blocked with $d_{los} = \sqrt{2a_e}(\sqrt{h_1} + \sqrt{h_2})$. If the distance between transmitter and receiver $d \geq d_{los}$, so calculate the diffraction attenuation by out of horizon path, otherwise using the horizon path.
3. If there are obstacles on the terrain, then judging the type of obstacle firstly, which is divided into blades and circles. After that, calculate the number of obstacles.
4. Finally, for the different types of obstacle models, calculate the diffraction attenuation L_p of electromagnetic wave refer to the ITU-RP.526 proposal [13].

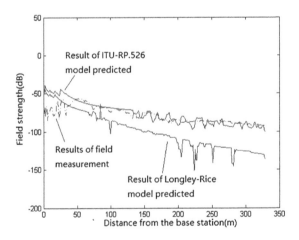

Fig. 1. The result of comparison between field measurements and prediction of simulation models.

3.2 Frequency Deviation Inhibitory Factor

For a large scale of communication network, multiple base stations are usually set up in an area. Because of the limitation of frequency resources, different base stations may be assigned to different working frequencies. It may cause interference signals to fall into the receiver's frequency band which can affect the signal quality that can hardly communicate. Therefore, it is neccessary to introduce the frequency deviation inhibitory factor(OCR), which is used to measure the suppression of the receiver's selective curve to the interference spectrum [14]. It is defined as formula (3):

$$OCR(\Delta f) = -10 \log \frac{\int_{-\infty}^{\infty} P(f)|H(f + \Delta f)|^2 \, df}{\int_{-\infty}^{\infty} P(f) \, df} \tag{3}$$

Then, the signal quality can be assessed by formula (4).

$$SNR = P_d - \sum_{i=1}^{n} P_i \quad (dB) \tag{4}$$

The P_d and P_i are according to formula (5) to calculate.

$$\begin{cases} P_i = P_t + G_t + G_r - L_p - OCR(\Delta f) \\ P_d = P_t + G_t + G_r - L_p \end{cases} \tag{5}$$

where the P_i is interfering signal strength, P_d is useful signal strength, P_t is transmitting power, G_t is transmitter antenna gain, G_r is receiver antenna gain, L_p is attenuation values, OCR is frequency deviation inhibitory factor.

4 Experiment and Simulation Analysis

4.1 Simulation of Field Measurements Data

In order to verify the correctness of the proposed signal quality assessment scheme based on compressed sensing, the actual data measured by a certain area is used to take experimental comparison.

In Table 1, the base station is located at $80.94219° E$, $41.07261° N$, with the antenna basic parameters of the down-tilt angle is $2°$, the azimuth is $150°$, the height is 58 m, and the carrier power is 150 W. The original data and the reconstructed result are shown in Fig. 2.

Because the data of field measurements is useful signal strength, thus it can be used to reconstruct the SNR. From the Fig. 3, it can be seen that as the number of samples increases, the error of the reconstruction decreases, although there are some cusps on the curve caused by bad samples. When the sampling point is more than 80%, the original signal is basically perfectly reconstructed, but at the cost of time and resource.

Table 1. Part of signal strength of field measurements

Longitude (°E)	Latitude (°N)	Distance from the base station (m)	Signal strength (dB)	Predicted results (dB)	Reconstructed results (dB)
80.94202000	41.07396167	151	−80.13	−79.50	−77.43
80.94194667	41.07422833	182	−59.69	−56.71	−62.85
80.94190500	41.07436333	197	−57.63	−58.37	−54.71
80.94185667	41.07450333	214	−57.00	−59.58	−56.53
80.94174167	41.07479167	247	−59.50	−62.20	−61.88
80.94167333	41.07494167	265	−63.67	−61.74	−66.04
80.94159833	41.07509333	284	−72.13	−74.51	−74.85
80.94151500	41.07524833	302	−78.64	−77.98	−75.90
80.94132667	41.07556667	342	−67.29	−70.21	−71.60
80.94122333	41.07573000	363	−65.00	−66.14	−63.53

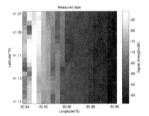 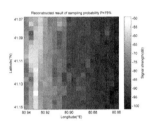

Fig. 2. Reconstructed result with 75% sampling point, Pe = 0.0287.

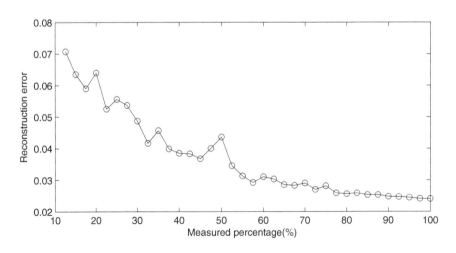

Fig. 3. Sampling proportion versus reconstruction error.

4.2   Simulation of Predicted Data by ITU-RP.526 Model

In order to ensure the practicality of the scheme, the signal quality of the surrounding area can be estimated before set up the base station, and verify it by the ITU-RP.526 model. The result shows as Fig. 4.

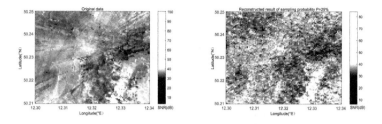

Fig. 4. Reconstructed result of prediction of ITU-RP.526 model, Pe = 0.0737.

The jammers are located at

1. $12.31342° E$, $50.23786° N$, frequency is 150.42 MHz, power is 40 W.
2. $12.30368° E$, $50.24468° N$, frequency is 150.61 MHz, power is 30 W.
3. $12.30154° E$, $50.22156° N$, frequency is 150.35 MHz, power is 20 W.

The useful receiver is located at $12.33161° E$, $50.23611° N$, frequency is 150.55 MHz, power is 30 W.

The results show that when sampling points are 25%, it is already clear to distinguish the area of high SNR from low SNR. It meets actual demand and proves the correctness of the scheme.

5   Conclusion

The paper introduced an estimate method based on compressed sensing. The method can solve the enormous data problems benefits from the advantage of compressed sensing, which works well on data reconstruction and compression. The results show that the new algorithm meets our demand both in field measurement and model prediction. The future work is to solve the problem of the reconstruction error caused by terrain mutation.

References

1. Sharma, S.K., Lagunas, E., Chatzinotas, S., Ottersten, B.: Application of compressive sensing in cognitive radio communications: a survey. IEEE Commun. Surv. Tutor. **18**(3), 1838–1860 (2016)
2. Donoho, D.L.: Compressed sensing. IEEE Trans. Inf. Theory **52**(4), 1289–1306 (2006)

3. Tsaig, Y., Donoho, D.L.: Extensions of compressed sensing. Sig. Process. **86**(3), 549–571 (2006)
4. Dai, Q.H., Fu, C.J., Ji, X.Y.: Research on compressed sensing. Chin. J. Comput. **34**(3), 425–435 (2011)
5. Bougher, B.: Introduction to compressed sensing. Lead. Edge **34**(10), 1256–1257 (2015)
6. Baraniuk, R.G.: Compressive sensing [lecture notes]. IEEE Sig. Process. Mag. **24**(4), 118–121 (2007)
7. Candes, E.J., Wakin, M.B.: An introduction to compressive sampling. IEEE Sig. Process. Mag. **25**(2), 21–30 (2008)
8. Zheng, H., Yang, F., Tian, X., et al.: Data gathering with compressive sensing in wireless sensor networks: a random walk based approach. IEEE Trans. Parallel Distrib. Syst. **26**(1), 35–44 (2015)
9. Shi, G.M., Liu, D.H., Gao, D.H., Liu, Z., Lin, J., Wang, L.J.: Advances in theory and application of compressed sensing. Acta Electron. Sin. **5**(37), 1070–1081 (2009)
10. Li, S., Ma, C.W., Li, Y., Chen, P.: Survey on reconstruction algorithm based on compressive sensing. Infrared Laser Eng. **42**(s1), 225–232 (2013)
11. Baraniuk, R., Davenport, M., Devore, R., et al.: A simple proof of the restricted isometry property for random matrices. Constr. Approx. **28**(3), 253–263 (2008)
12. Liu, F., Wu, J., Yang, S.Y., Jiao, L.C.: Research advances on structured compressive sensing. Acta Autom. Sin. **39**(12), 1980–1995 (2013)
13. ITU-RP.526-11: ITU International Telecommunication Union (2007)
14. ITU-R SM.337-6: ITU International Telecommunication Union (2008)

Distributed Compressive Sensing Based Spectrum Sensing Method

Yanping Chen[1], Yulong Gao[2(✉)], and Yongkui Ma[2]

[1] School of Computer and Information Engineering,
Harbin University of Commerce, Harbin, China
yanping1009@163.com
[2] Department of Communications Engineering,
Harbin Institute of Technology, Harbin, China
{ylgao,yk_ma}@hit.edu.cn

Abstract. For multi-antenna system, the difficulties of preforming spectrum sensing are high sampling rate and hardware cost. To alleviate these problems, we propose a novel utilization of distributed compressive sensing for the multi-antenna case. The multi-antenna signals first are sampled in terms of distributed compressive sensing, and then the time-domain signals are reconstructed. Finally, spectrum sensing is performed with help of energy-based sensing method. To evaluate the proposed method, we do the corresponding simulations. The simulation results proves the proposed method.

Keywords: Distributed compressive sensing · Spectrum sensing
Joint sparse model · Time-domain detection

1 Introduction

Spectrum sensing is the base of cognitive radio. At present, some known methods mainly conclude Energy-based algorithm, cyclostationary detection and eigenvalue-based algorithm [1, 2]. Generally speaking, these methods are applied in the individual antenna case. However, with the growing requirements of date rate and the improvement of wireless communication technologies, multi-antenna technologies have already been applied in many wireless communication systems. Subsequently, spectrum sensing under the multi-antenna circumstances become a problem to be solved. Currently, some multi-antenna based spectrum sensing methods were proposed, such as random matrix based methods and GLRT (generalized likelihood ratio test) methods [3–7]. For random matrix based methods, the signals sampled from multiple antennas are comprised of a random matrix, and then some parameters, such as eigenvalue, are extracted to perform spectrum sensing.

GLRT-based methods are a kind of technologies as solving the problem of multi-antenna spectrum sensing. In [4–6], some eigenvalues of sampled covariance matrix are used as test statistic. In literature [7], GLRT is exploited directly as test statistic, and the idea is evaluated in OFDM and MIMO system. It is well known that multi-antenna technology bring some advantages for the wireless communication. On the other hand, some disadvantages have also been introduced inevitably, such as too much data and high sampled frequency. Fortunately, compressed sensing provides a practical idea to deal with these difficulties. In 2006, compressed sensing is proposed [8], and then it has been fast applied to many fields, including the wireless communication, signal processing and image processing. In the view of compressed sensing, sample and compression are performed simultaneously, and the signal is sampled based on the signal sparsity but not the bandwidth used in the Nyquist sampling theorem, which can alleviate the computational complexity and hard cost. Meanwhile, in order to fully exploit the correlation of inter-signal and intra-signal, the framework of distributed compressed sensing is built on the base of the joint sparse model [9, 10], which bridge between multi-antenna based wireless communication and compressed sensing. More importantly, computational complexity is further reduced because of the correlation structure.

In this paper, we obtain the sampled signals in terms of distributed compressed sensing, which can reduce the hard cost and further decrease the subsequent computational complexity, and then the energy-based spectrum sensing is adopted. Because of the utilizing of the correlation of multiple antennas, the sparsity in single antenna case is extended to the multiple antenna case by virtue of joint sparse model. It follows that higher reconstruction probability is obtained with the constriction of the same sensing measurement.

2 The Description of the Proposed Method

2.1 Distributed Compressive Sensing

We suppose that the number of antennas is J, and the received signal ensemble can be expressed as $X = [x_1 \quad x_2 \quad \cdots \quad x_J]^T$, where $x_i \in R^N$. In the framework of distributed compressive sensing, the compressed measurements are written as

$$Y = \Phi X \tag{1}$$

where $Y = [y_1 \quad y_2 \quad \cdots \quad y_J]^T$, $\Phi = \begin{bmatrix} \Phi_1 & 0 & \cdots & 0 \\ 0 & \Phi_2 & \cdots & 0 \\ \vdots & \vdots & \ddots & \vdots \\ 0 & 0 & \cdots & \Phi_J \end{bmatrix}$. For the individual sig-

nal, $y_i = \Phi_i x_i$, where $y_i \in R^M$, $\Phi_i \in R^{M \times N}$.

It is well known that the concept of common sparsity is built on the single signal. For multiple antennas, however, the multiple signals possess intra-signal and inter-signal correlation. Joint sparse models (JSM), called common/innovation component JSMS, were introduced to describe these characteristics, which includes three specific models, named JSM-1, JSM-2 and JSM-3. Therefore, in the framework of distributed compressive sensing, JSM is written uniformly as

$$X_j = Z_C + Z_j, \ j \in \{1, \ 2 \cdots J\} \tag{2}$$

where Z_C denotes the common component, and Z_j is the innovation component. Specifically, they can be sparsely represented as

$$Z_C = \Psi_C \cdot \Theta_C, \quad \|\Theta_C\|_0 = K_C$$
$$Z_j = \Psi_j \cdot \Theta_j, \quad \|\Theta_j\|_0 = K_j$$

$$(3)$$

where $\|\cdot\|_0$ denotes the l_0-norm, e.g., the number of nonzero values of signal vector. In this setting, the signal ensemble X can be rewritten as

$$X = \Psi\Theta \tag{4}$$

where $\Psi = \begin{bmatrix} \Psi_C & \Theta_j & 0 & \cdots & 0 \\ \Psi_C & 0 & \Theta_j & \cdots & 0 \\ \vdots & \vdots & \vdots & \ddots & \vdots \\ \Psi_C & 0 & 0 & \cdots & \Theta_j \end{bmatrix}, \Theta = \begin{bmatrix} \Theta_C^T & \Theta_1^T & \Theta_2^T & \cdots & \Theta_J^T \end{bmatrix}^T.$

The different sparsity assumptions regarding the common and innovation component correspond to different models. When both of the common and innovation components are sparse, we call it JSM-1 model. When there exist no common components in the signal ensemble, we refer to it as JSM-2 model. In this model, each innovation component of signal ensemble is sparse, and all the signals possess the same sparse support but have different nonzero values in the same locations. A practical scenario well-modeled by JSM-2 model is MIMO communication system we often encounter in this paper. If the common component is not factorized sparsely, we name the model as JSM-3 model. It is widely recognized that the signal ensemble from multiple antennas of MIMO satisfy the condition of the common and innovation component. It follows that we restrict out attention on JSM-2 model. Currently, the recovery algorithms in the framework of JSM model are categorized into trivial pursuit and iterative greedy pursuit, such as DCS-SOMP arisen from conventional OMP algorithm.

2.2 The Proposed Algorithm

In order to interpret the proposed method, we first show the block diagram in Fig. 1. We can find from Fig. 1 that the proposed method consists of DCS, DCS-JOMP and energy-based detection algorithm. We will introduce them in the following section, respectively.

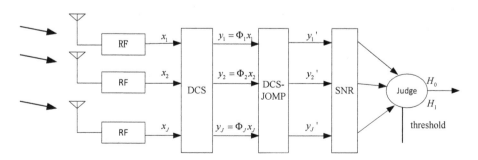

Fig. 1. The block diagram of the proposed method

For multi-antenna signals, the received signals fit with JSM-2 model. Therefore, distributed compressed sensing can be applied to sample the multi-antenna signals. Supposed that the sparsity of signal is K, the sampled signals in the framework of compressed sensing can be expressed as

$$\begin{cases} y_1 = \Phi_1 x_1 = \Phi_1 \Psi \theta_1 \\ y_2 = \Phi_2 x_2 = \Phi_2 \Psi \theta_2 \\ \cdots \\ y_J = \Phi_J x_J = \Phi_J \Psi \theta_J \end{cases} \tag{5}$$

where x_i, $i = 1, \cdots, J$ denotes the received signal from i^{th} antenna. Φ_i, $i = 1, \cdots, J$ is measurement matrix, Ψ is the sparse basis, and θ_1 is sparse representation in the sparse basis.

Joint reconstruction of distributed compressed sensing (DCS-JOMP) is described as follows:

(1) Initialize. k is the times of iteration, Ω is the space spanned by coefficients vector to be reconstructed. $r_{j,k}$ is the residual error. Let $\Omega = []$, $r_{j,0} = y_j$.

(2) Judgment of the correlation. The column corresponding to the biggest correlation with $r_{j,k-1}$ is picked out from $\Phi_j \Psi$, i.e., $\xi_k = \arg \max_{n \in \{1,2...N\}} \sum_{j=1}^{J} |\langle r_{j,k-1}, \phi_{j,n} \rangle|$. Then the space Ω is be updated to $\Omega = [\Omega \ \xi_k]$.

(3) Updating of residual base, $\Lambda_{j,k} = \Phi_{j,\Omega}$. Where $\Phi_{j,\Omega}$ is the group of the selected column of measurement matrix based on $\Omega = [\Omega \ \xi_k]$.

(4) Updating of the residual error. The sparse representation after the each iteration is denoted as $\theta_{j,k} = (\Lambda'_{j,k} \Lambda_{j,k})^{-1} \Lambda'_{j,k} y_j$, so the residual error is expressed as $r_{j,k} = y_j - \Lambda_{j,k} \theta_{j,k}$.

(5) Stopping the iteration. When $k > K$, we stop the iteration.

By exploiting DCS-JOMP algorithm, we obtain the time-domain signals. And then the error and noise are estimated to compute the SNR, further set the threshold. Finally, energy-based method is employed to perform spectrum sensing. Specific process is described in the following section.

For the conventional energy-based method, the test statistic is $Z = \sum_{n=1}^{2TW} x^2(n)$. Where $2TW$ is the length of the received signals, T is the time interval, and W is the bandwidth. The received signal is $x(n) = s(n) + w(n)$.

For simplification, but without loss of generality, we normalize the received signal by the noise covariance, i.e., $w'(n) = w(n)/\sigma_w$, $s'(n) = s(n)/\sigma_w$. Therefore, the test statistic reduces to $Z = \sum_{n=1}^{N} y'(n)^2$. In this situation, the binary hypothesis test can be expressed in the form

$$Z = \begin{cases} \sum_{n=1}^{2TW} w'(n)^2, & H_0 \\ \sum_{n=1}^{2TW} (s'(n) + w'(n))^2, & H_1 \end{cases} \quad (6)$$

By analyzing (6), we can conclude that the received signal follows the central chi-square distribution when no signal exists. Inversely, the received signal follows the non-central chi-square distribution with the non-central parameter

$$\delta = \sum_{n=1}^{2TW} s'(n)^2 = \sum_{n=1}^{2TW} \left(\frac{s(n)}{\sigma_w}\right)^2 = \frac{\sum_{n=1}^{2TW} s(n)^2}{\sigma_w^2} = \frac{2TWP_s}{P_n} = 2TW\gamma \quad (7)$$

Correspondingly, we can compute the detection probability and the false-alarm probability

$$P_d = P(Z > \lambda | H_1) = Q_u(\sqrt{\delta}, \sqrt{\lambda}) \quad (8)$$

$$P_f = P(Z > \lambda | H_0) = \frac{\Gamma(u, \frac{\lambda}{2})}{\Gamma(u)} \quad (9)$$

where $\Gamma(.)$ is Gamma function, $\Gamma(.,.)$ is the incomplete gamma function, $Q_u(.,.)$ is the generalized Marcum Q function, the λ is the predetermined threshold. $u = TW$ is the production of time and bandwidth. Generally speaking, we refer to the false-alarm probability as constant, i.e., constant false-alarm probability, and then compute the decision threshold. Finally, substitution of threshold into (8) yields the detection probability.

3   Numerical Simulation and the Corresponding Analyzing

We first analyze the reconstruction error of compressed sensing and distributed compressed sensing for the various number of antennas. In the simulation, we assume that the signal is spare in the discrete cosine base, the length $N = 64$, the sparsity K is 4. The noise follows the Gaussian distribution, SNR = 10 dB. The times of Monte Carlo is 500. The reconstruction algorithm of compressed sensing and distributed compressed sensing are OMP algorithm and DCS-JOMP algorithm. The results are shown in Fig. 2.

It can be seen that the reconstruction error reduces with the increasing of the number of sensing measurements, which fit with the theoretical analysis. Additionally, for distributed compressed sensing, the reconstruction error is inversely proportional to the number of antennas. For example, for $M = 20$, the reconstruction error is 33.8% when compressed sensing is adopted, the reconstruction error is 10.6% and 7.4% for 2 antennas and 4 antennas when we exploit distributed compressed sensing.

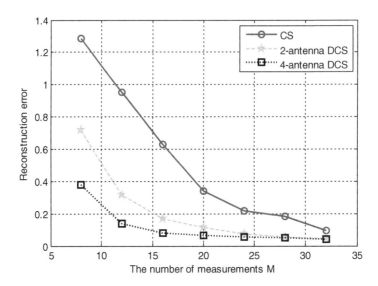

Fig. 2. The relationship between the number of measurements and the reconstruction error

To further evaluate the performance of the proposed method under the different antennas, we as before take 2 antennas and 4 antennas as the example. SNR is 3 dB. In the simulation, we use the detection probability under constant false-alarm probability to measure the performance of the proposed algorithm. The simulation results are illustrated in Fig. 3.

It is obviously observed that the detection probability of multi-antenna distributed compressed is higher than that of compressed sensing, and the detection probability varies with the number of antennas. For example, when $M = 20$, the detection probability is 82.1% when compressed sensing is adopted, the reconstruction error is 97.3% and 99.4% for 2 antennas and 4 antennas.

In the following, we evaluate the detection probability under the different SNR. The SNR varies from −15 dB to 10 dB. In addition, to compare with the conventional energy-based detection algorithm, its detection probability is also provided. In this simulation, the false-alarm probability is 0.05, the number of antenna J is 4. The number of sensing measurements is $M = 16$, and the sparsity is 4. We compute the threshold using (8), and then obtain the detection probability illustrated in Fig. 4.

It can been seen from Fig. 4 that the detection probability increases with the increasing of SNR. Generally, the performance of the conventional time-domain detection algorithm outperforms that of the proposed method. This is because that compressed sensing leads to the wastage of the signal energy. For example, when the detection probability reaches 100% for the conventional time-domain detection, SNR is 5 dB, and the sampled number is 64. For the proposed method, however, the number of antennas and sensing measurements are 4 and $M = 13$ respectively when the detection probability reaches 100%.

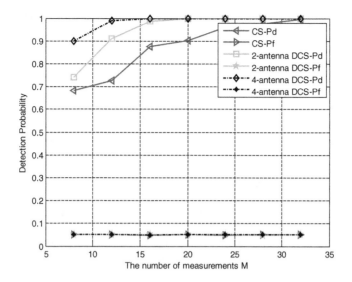

Fig. 3. The relationship between the number of measurements and the detection probability

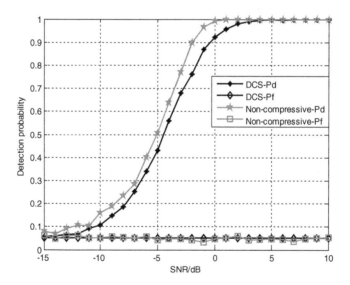

Fig. 4. The relationship between SNR and the detection probability

4 Conclusions

To solve the problem of high sampling rate and hardware cost, we exploit the intra-signal and inter-signal to sample the MIMO multi-antenna signals, which obviously decrease the sampling rate and hardware cost. Combining with energy-based sensing method, we proposed a novel spectrum sensing. The proposed method perform the nearly similar to the conventional time-domain spectrum sensing.

Acknowledgments. This work is supported by National Natural Science Foundation of China (NSFC) (61671176).

References

1. Haykin, S.: Cognitive radio: brain-empowered wireless communications. IEEE J. Sel. Areas Commun. **23**(2), 201–220 (2005)
2. Axell, E., Leus, G., Larsson, E.G., et al.: Spectrum sensing for cognitive radio: state-of-the-art and recent advances. IEEE Sig. Process. Mag. **29**(3), 101–116 (2012)
3. Wang, L., Zheng, B., Cui, J., Meng, Q.: Cooperative MIMO spectrum sensing using free probability theory. In: The 5th International Conference on Wireless Communications, Networking and Mobile Computing (WiCom 2009), pp. 1–4 (2009)
4. Wang, P., Fang, J., Han, N., Li, H.: Multi antenna-assisted spectrum sensing for cognitive radio. IEEE Trans. Veh. Technol. **59**(4), 1791–1800 (2010)
5. Taherpour, A., Nasiri-Kenari, M., Gazor, S.: Multiple antenna spectrum sensing in cognitive radios. IEEE Trans. Wirel. Commun. **9**(2), 814–823 (2010)
6. Zhang, R., Lim, T.J., Liang, Y.-C., Zeng, Y.: Multi-antenna based spectrum sensing for cognitive radios: a GLRT approach. IEEE Trans. Commun. **58**(1), 84–88 (2010)
7. Font-Segura, J., Wang, X.: GLRT-based spectrum sensing for cognitive radio with prior information. IEEE Trans. Commun. **58**(7), 2137–2146 (2010)
8. Donoho, D.L.: Compressed sensing. IEEE Trans. Inf. Theory **52**(4), 1289–1306 (2006)
9. Duarte, M.F., Sarvotham, S., Baron, D., Wakin, M.B., Baraniuk, R.G.: Distributed compressed sensing of jointly sparse signals (2005)
10. Baron, D., Duarte, M.F., Wakin, M.B., Sarvotham, S., Baraniuk, R.G.: Distributed compressive sensing (2009). https://arxiv.org/abs/0901.3403v1

Recent Advances in Radio Environment Map: A Survey

Jingming Li[1(✉)], Guoru Ding[2,3], Xiaofei Zhang[1], and Qihui Wu[1]

[1] Department of Electronics and Information Engineering,
Nanjing University of Aeronautics and Astronautics, Nanjing 211100, China
lijingmingjlu@163.com, zhangxiaofei@nuaa.com,
wuqihui2014@sina.com
[2] College of Communications Engineering,
PLA University of Science and Technology, Nanjing 210007, China
dr.guoru.ding@ieee.org
[3] National Mobile Communications Research Laboratory,
Southeast University, Nanjing 210018, China

Abstract. Electromagnetic spectrum, the main medium of wireless communication has been over-crowded. Accompanied by the arrival of big data era, the problem of the spectrum scarcity has received people's attention. The emergence of cognitive radio improves the utilization of the spectrum and provides an effective solution to break the limitations of the traditional static allocation. Radio Environmental Maps (REM) is an enabling technology of cognitive radio which can be intuitive, multi-dimensional display of spectrum information. It provides a visual basis while accessing dynamic spectrum and sharing spectrum. In this paper, the various aspects of REM are studied from the perspective of cognitive radio. Based on the concept of REM, the recent research progress of REM is summarized, and a series of challenges in the construction of spectrum pattern are also highlighted.

Keywords: Cognitive radio · Radio environment map · Spectrum trend
Spectrum dynamic access · Spectrum sharing

1 Introduction

With the rapid development of radio technology and business, the demand for radio spectrum resources is exploding. The mobile traffic is expected to increase by a factor of 1,000 over the next decade. In order to meet the huge traffic growth, the next generation mobile network is expected to achieve 1,000 times the capacity growth compared with the current wireless network deployment [1]. So the work of radio spectrum resource management is becoming complicated. National radio management departments have been fully aware of the important resources of spectrum, the economic and social development, and national defense construction. The Federal Communications Committee (FCC) established the Spectrum Task Force in 2003 and formally approved the use of dynamic spectrum access equipment in 2010. The Next Generation (XG), funded by the Defense Advanced Research Project Agency

© ICST Institute for Computer Sciences, Social Informatics and Telecommunications Engineering 2018
X. Gu et al. (Eds.): MLICOM 2017, Part I, LNICST 226, pp. 247–257, 2018.
https://doi.org/10.1007/978-3-319-73564-1_25

(DARPA), studies dynamic spectrum management through flexible spectrum policies. In addition, DARPA has introduced an advanced radio map to achieve real-time sensing of the radio spectrum in frequency, space and time [2].

At present, the existing spectrum allocation mechanism is static which is at the division of the partition. Each segment of the spectrum is fixedly assigned to different authorized users. Most of the spectrum resources have been exhausted. It is difficult for new business to provide a large section of available spectrum resources. So, the dynamic sharing of spectrum resources and promoting the integration of heterogeneous networks of cognitive wireless technology are considered to improve the spectrum utilization of promising ways [3]. The term Cognitive Radio (CR) is proposed by Dr. Joseph Mitola in 1990. In general, CR allows unauthorized sub-users to access the unoccupied spectrum of the authorized primary user [4]. The core purpose of cognitive radio is to detect the free spectrum of the radio environment and use these idle spectrums intelligently without affecting the main user system to achieve the effect of improving the spectrum utilization. Therefore, we need to build and manage the spectrum database to obtain time, space and other multi-dimensional spectrum availability information [5]. Radio Environmental Maps (REM) is a promising tool for the realization of cognitive radio network (CRN). REM is an integrated database that includes information about the radio frequency (RF) signal environment, the relevant laws and regulations, the strategy, the physical location of the equipment, the available services and relevant historical experience [6]. With REM, the primary user and the secondary user can better understand their radio environment, help secondary users access the main user free frequency band, reduce the hidden node problem, improve the overall network performance. In this paper, we summarize the recent research progress of REM, and we elaborate the various aspects of REM in detail through the whole view in order to provide a comprehensive framework for how to use REM for spectrum dynamic access and spectrum management.

As shown in Fig. 1, the structure of this paper is as follows: The second part defines REM and generalizes the application scenario of REM. The third part introduces the theory and method of spectrum trend from several key technologies of spectrum trend,

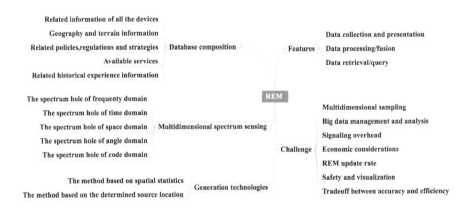

Fig. 1. Various aspects of REM

and introduces the application of spectrum potential perception, spectrum trend generation and spectrum trend respectively. Part four provides guidelines and research challenges for future work. Finally, we make a conclusion in part five.

2   Various Aspects of REM

2.1   Definition of REM

The concept and model of REM was first proposed in 2006 [7]. By using geographic location database multi-domain information, spectrum usage characteristics, geographic terrain model, propagation environment and rules, it builds a cognitive radio network integrated map. The vision is to design a cognitive radio network (CRN) that makes simple devices without advanced cognitive functions can be perceived and operated in an efficient manner by REM. The simulation results in [8] show that the utilization rate of idle spectrum can be increased by more than 50% in the case of REM support. Spectrum analysis based on radio environment map has become the main research direction of dynamic spectrum management. As shown in Fig. 2, REM is considered to be an integrated database for characterizing real-world radio scenarios.

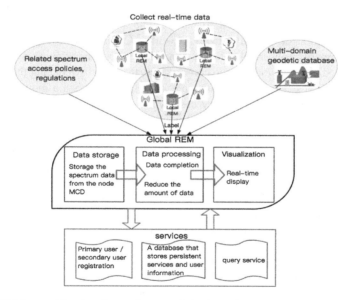

Fig. 2. REM is considered to be an integrated database for characterizing real-world radio scenarios.

In Fig. 2, REM can be divided into local REM and global REM. Global REM provides a wide range of processing capabilities, while local REM improves system responsiveness. More dynamic parameters of the radio environment will preferably be stored in the local REM, as this will facilitate REM updates. Mainly including radio propagation related information, such as propagation loss, signal strength, mobile terminal/monitoring node location information. The information stored in the global REM includes Quality of Service (QoS) metrics, information about available WiFi access networks, and so on. Local REM is synchronized with global REM, and REM synchronization is critical to the accuracy and reliability of the information provided.

It is impractical to acquire the spectrum data from the node MCD having the spectral sensing capability, since the measurement is performed at each position in the entire operation area. So the data is subjected to completion processing so as to estimate interference level at the position without measurement data, implement the data storage, processing/integration and ultimate visualization, and provide users with the radio environment information intuitively [9]. The REM database consists of three services: a primary user/secondary user registration, a database that stores persistent services and user information, and a query service. The data query service means that the secondary user obtains the best and allowed operating parameters by submitting a query to the REM manager. Because the historical data and current spectrum occupancy information are stored in the REM, the secondary user can query to obtain the current/historical state and some statistics.

2.2 REM Application Scenario

TV White Spectrum (TVWS) is a part of the UHF and VHF bands that appear after the digital shift from analog to digital. It has become an effective catalyst for the first practical application of cognitive radio networks (CRNs) [10]. As the broadcasting industry is primarily concerned with the protection of existing television services, the rules developed by regulators are too conservative, thus greatly reducing the utilization of television white space [11]. For example, the FCC developed a monitoring signal strength of −114 dBm for the primary user, which makes the primary user's channel protection threshold too conservative that is not conducive to the dynamic sharing of the spectrum and the loss of a large number of spectral resources. At present, the database-based white spectrum equipment trial operation has been taken into consideration by the United States and the relevant departments of the United Kingdom. In November 2009, the FCC issued a call for the regulatory authorities of the database. And it passed 10 companies to operate in 2010, of which four in 2013 completed the trial operation of the test. So the application of cognitive radio network in the white band of television has a very high practical significance.

The radar band is also a potential candidate band for real-time sharing of spectrum sharing. Because the radar band currently occupies a large part of the radio spectrum below 6 GHz, these bands provide better propagation conditions and reduce the cost of semiconductor devices. However, due to the wide application of radar systems, different types of radar are used in aviation, astronomy, military, weather and law enforcement and many other areas. So different radar systems require different technologies, different operating modes and different interference protection standards [12]. Therefore, a single method cannot be used to share spectrum with all the different radar systems. From the perspective of radar system spectrum sharing, the existing shared model can be divided into two categories:

1. A spatial dimension-based sharing model: Geo-restricted (GEZ) model and dynamic frequency selection (DFS) model.
2. A region-based sharing model: looking for potential sharing opportunities in space and time dimensions. There are a around the rotary radar is divided into three areas. In zone 1, the secondary user access is prohibited, because it will cause interference to the radar system. In zone 2, time sharing occurs where the secondary user can transmit each time the primary beam of the radar is pointing in the other direction. In zone 3, the secondary user is free to use the spectrum.

In [13], the radar-based radar band shared spectrum access innovation framework is introduced in detail, and the sharing details and the challenges are summarized through the actual measurement activities. In the literature [14], further proposed three different types of rotary radar system and the Internet of things to achieve the spectrum sharing framework. It can be seen that the radar band has great potential for the realization of spectrum sharing, so some countries have opened part of the S and C frequency band, contribute to the rational use of spectrum resources.

3   The Main Research Stage of Spectrum Situation

At present, the research of spectrum situation is mainly focused on three aspects: spectrum situation sensing, spectrum situation generation, and spectrum situation application.

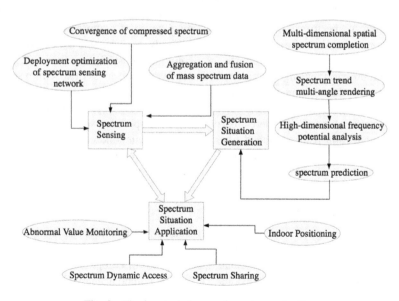

Fig. 3. The key techniques of spectrum situation

As shown in Fig. 3, spectrum sensing is the premise of spectrum situation generation and application. It is mainly responsible for obtaining the current state of spectrum space, including spectral cavity information, spectral radiated power information, spectrum modulation mode, and spectrum access protocol. Spectrum situation generation is based on the spectrum of the situation, the analysis, forecasting the comprehensive situation of the spectrum space and the future development trend. Spectrum situation application is our ultimate goal, is an important part of the spectrum of the overall situation. Through the dynamic allocation of spectrum resources, spectrum sharing, abnormal value monitoring, indoor positioning and other fields of application of the spectrum of the situation more practical significance.

3.1 Spectrum Sensing

Spectrum sensing, in which the current state of the time slot spectrum and spectrum hole can be obtained, is the essential factor to implement dynamic spectrum access. In Cognitive Radio Networks (CRN), users can be divided into two categories according to whether they have authorization: primary users (PU) and secondary users. Primary users have the priority right to use the authorized frequency band, while the secondary users need to monitor the spectrum information in the surrounding environment via spectrum sensing to share the spectrum with primary users. The spectrum cavity can be obtained in frequency domain, time domain, airspace, angle domain, code domain, etc., leading to multi-dimensional spectrum perception. As a result, multi-dimensional information is exploited to increase the efficiency of spectrum access. A detailed review of methods and challenges in cognitive radio spectrum sensing is illustrated in [15].

Wide-area spectrum situational perception includes three aspects: deployment optimization of spectrum sensing network, convergence of compressed spectrum and aggregation and fusion of mass spectrum data. Firstly, we optimize the deployment of spectrum sensing network to minimize the deployment cost of the network. Then we use the compression sensing technology to improve the robustness of spectrum sensing. Finally, we use the efficient convergence theory to converge and fuse the massive data in data center to ensure the transmission capacity and reliability, and reduce the delay of aggregation transmission. There are several types of spectrum sensing methods, such as energy detection (ED), matched filter detection, cyclic smoothing, and eigenvalue detection. Energy detection method is widely used in dynamic spectrum access, because it is easy to achieve and easy to calculate the cost [16].

3.2 Spectrum Situation Generation

Spectrum situation generation is to further analyze and predict the comprehensive situation and future development trends of spectrum based on the spectrum perception. The content includes multi-dimensional spatial spectrum completion, spectrum trend multi-angle rendering, high-dimensional frequency potential analysis, spectrum prediction and so on.

The spectral spectrum graph can collect the spectral data of the monitoring nodes in the network, collect data from the monitoring equipment regularly and make decisions based on the spectrum trend graphs to achieve reliable data fusion. However, if we want to get spectral data for each location in a cognitive radio network, it is impractical to estimate the remaining unknown nodes by known nodes. At present, the main construction method of the spectrum can be divided into two categories: based on spatial statistics and based on the determined source location.

1. The method based on spatial statistics is to characterize the characteristics of a given region by mining the spatial correlation. Using spatial statistics and spectral data at a specific location, the missing data is estimated from the function of known data. Table 1 lists the more commonly used interpolation method [17]. Recently, in the literature [18], the authors proposed a data recovery method by combining a fixed point continuation algorithm (FPCA) with a popular k-nearest neighbor (KNN) algorithm. Simulation results show that the proposed approach has a better performance in the TVWS database recovery than the traditional FPCA.

Table 1. There are several commonly used interpolation techniques.

Method	Description
1. Kriging [19]	The key to the Kriging method is the determination of the weighting factor. The method dynamically determines the value of the variable according to an optimization criterion function in the interpolation process, so that the interpolation function is in the best condition
2. Nearest neighbor [20]	This method is to find the k nearest neighbors of the unknown sample point, and obtain the attribute of the unknown sample point by assigning the weight of the attribute of these neighbors
3. Inverse distance weighted [21]	This method assumes that each input point has a local effect, and this effect is weakened as the distance increases
4. Trend surface	Trend surface uses polynomial to represent lines or surfaces, carrys out data fitting according to the least squares principle, which can be used to estimate the value of other points
5. Thin plant splines [22]	The surface of the control point is established by the sheet spline function and the slope of all points is minimized. That is, the minimum curvature surface fitting control point
6. Discrete smooth interpolation [23]	A network of interconnected networks is established between discretized data points. If the known node value on the network satisfies a certain constraint, the value on the unknown node can be obtained by solving the linear equation
7. Joint tensor completion [24]	Model the multi-dimensional spectrum data from the perspective of a spectrum tensor. Improve the low rank tensor completion algorithm, and evaluate it by comparing the improved spectrum tensor completion, the original one, and the spectrum matrix completion scheme

2. The method based on the determined source location can infer its performance by a priori information such as the location of the source, and then estimate the signal strength value for each location by applying the propagation model. Since the

method based on the location of the transmission source is based on the main user location data, the required spectral data is greatly reduced as compared with the spatial statistics-based method. In the literature [25], the existing algorithms are compared and a new method based on the determined source location is proposed. In the literature [26], the spectrum of the spectrum of the generation method were compared and summarized.

After the situation is completed, the data will be presented at multiple angles, which can be divided into the following four steps: 1. The data is unified and normalized. 2. For the time, empty dimension of the property to reduce the dimension and projection. 3. The spectral data are aggregated and depolymerized according to the time dimension, the spatial dimension and the frequency dimension. 4. Design is different from the visual model, to achieve high-dimensional trend of visual presentation. Finally, we can visually analyze the current radio environment by visualizing the spectrum trend, and through the analysis of historical data and evolution laws, we can predict the trend of complex multidimensional spectrum environment.

3.3   Spectrum Situation Application

Spectrum is widely used in the cognitive radio network. Carrying out the observation and analysis of the spectrum situation can achieve the dynamic allocation of spectrum resources, obtain the effective management of spectrum resources, improve the spectrum utilization, and guide the realization of spectrum sharing between primary users and secondary users or among various primary users [27]. As the spectral trend graph directly characterizes the mapping between the physical position and the signal energy, a signal strength database corresponding to the known position is established. Therefore, the spectrum of the map can also be applied to indoor positioning.

In addition, with the rapid development of Internet of things, the electromagnetic spectrum environment is also increasingly complex, malicious users also increased, such as: "black radio", eavesdropping, radio cheating and other illegal equipment is harmful to people's normal life, the use of spectrum, the monitoring of abnormal values, positioning, as an effective means to protect the spectrum of security. The spectrum trend has different applications in different scenarios. In [28], the application of spectrum profiles in different scenarios is described in detail.

4   Challenges

In the 5G era and the Internet of Things (IoT) environment, the intensive use of networks and the use of network heterogeneous technologies require a deeper understanding of the radio environment. REM provides a multi-dimensional, visual radio environment map, intuitive to provide users with spectrum occupancy information. In this section, we discuss a series of challenges in the construction of REM.

1. Multidimensional Sampling: It is necessary to design samples carefully on multiple dimensions, such as time, frequency, and space, to obtain the required data at the same time when measuring activity on an area with multiple devices.

2. Big data management and analysis: Multidimensional sampling challenges the real-time processing of data storage, the management and measurement of data. Big data problems and associated large computationally analyzed loads are being addressed by advances in computer technology, so it is necessary to make plans for rational storage of spectral data and data size.

3. Tradeoff between accuracy and efficiency: Increasing the resolution of any dimension will improve the accuracy of the results, but will also reduce the efficiency of the calculations. Therefore, it is necessary to dynamically balance the accuracy and efficiency based on the available computing resources.

4. Signaling overhead: In a dynamic scenario with a mobile transmission device, the data needs to be transmitted more frequently than in a fixed scene. And the local database needs to be synchronized with each other in order to keep the information in each data fresh and accurate. So in REM, signaling overhead is also a meaningful challenge.

5. Economic considerations: The number of MCDs is the main cause of high costs associated with the deployment and maintenance of REM, and is directly related to the resolution and reliability of the spatial spectrum occupancy of REM. So optimizing the MCD deployment will help reduce costs. In the literature [18], in order to determine the optimal position for sensing the main activity, an iterative clustering technique using tree structured vector quantization is used.

6. REM update rate: The REM update rate defines the granularity level of the spectrum occupancy rate in the time domain. It is necessary to frequently update the REM and the resulting spectrum occupancy change needs to be propagated to the SU with the lowest delay. This will impose a strong demand on the REM server processing speed and the MCD server interface channel quality.

7. Safety and visualization: In order to ensure the results to be accurately and successfully communicated to people who need different backgrounds of information, we need a safe, reliable and standardized database to provide users with better service. So the standardization of REM is also an important challenge.

5 Conclusion

This paper reviews various aspects of REM in the field of spectral cognition. Firstly, proposed the definition of REM and application scenarios. And then analyzed the spectrum sensing, spectrum situation generation, spectrum situation application of the various stages in detail. Finally, a series of challenges in REM construction are given, which provide a research direction for further research.

Acknowledgements. This work is supported by the National Natural Science Foundation of China (No. 61631020 and No. 61501510).

References

1. Li, Q.C., Niu, H., Papathanassiou, A.T.: 5G network capacity: key elements and technologies. IEEE Veh. Technol. Mag. **9**(1), 71–78 (2014)
2. Advanced RF Mapping (Radio Map). http://www.darpa.mil/program/advance-rf-mapping
3. Huang, X., Hu, F., Wu, J., Chen, H., Wang, G., Jiang, T.: Intelligent cooperative spectrum sensing via hierarchical Dirichlet process in cognitive radio networks. IEEE J. Sel. Areas Commun. **33**(5), 771–787 (2015)
4. Mitola, J., Maguire, G.Q.: Cognitive radio: making software radios more personal. IEEE Pers. Commun. **6**(4), 13–18 (1999)
5. Ding, G., Wang, J., Wu, Q., Yao, Y., Song, F., Tsiftsis, T.A.: Cellular-base-station-assisted device-to-device communications in TV white space. IEEE J. Sel. Areas Commun. **34**(1), 107–121 (2016)
6. Hoyhtya, M., Mammela, A., Eskola, M., Matinmikko, M., Kalliovaara, J., Ojaniemi, J., Roberson, D.: Spectrum occupancy measurements: a survey and use of interference maps. IEEE Commun. Surv. Tutor. **18**(4), 2386–2414 (2016)
7. Zhao, Y., Reed, J.H., Mao, S.: Overhead analysis for radio environment mapenabled cognitive radio networks. In: 1st IEEE Workshop on Networking Technologies for Software Defined Radio Networks, SDR 2006, pp. 18–25. IEEE (2006)
8. Murty, R., Chandra, R., Moscibroda, T., Bahl, P.: SenseLess: a database-driven white spaces network. IEEE Trans. Mob. Comput. **11**(2), 189–203 (2012)
9. Yilmaz, H.B., Tugcu, T., Alagöz, F., Bayhan, S.: Radio environment map as enabler for practical cognitive radio networks. IEEE Commun. Mag. **51**(12), 162–169 (2013)
10. White Space Database Administrators. http://www.fcc.gov/encyclopedia/white-space-database-administrators-guide
11. How Much White Space has the FCC Opened Up? http://www.eecs.berkeley.edu/~sahai/Papers/CommLetters09.pdf
12. Griffiths, H., Cohen, L., Watts, S., Mokole, E.L., Baker, C., Wicks, M.C., Blunt, S.D.: Radar spectrum engineering and management: technical and regulatory issues. Proc. IEEE **103**(1), 85–102 (2015)
13. Paisana, F., Khan, Z., Lehtomaki, J., Dasilva, L.A., Vuohtoniemi, R.: Exploring radio environment map architectures for spectrum sharing in the radar bands. In: International Conference on Telecommunications, pp. 1–6 (2016)
14. Khan, Z., Lehtomaki, J.J., Iellamo, S.I.: IoT connectivity in radar bands: a shared access model based on spectrum measurements. IEEE Commun. Mag. **55**(2), 88–96 (2017)
15. Yucek, T., Arslan, H.: A survey of spectrum sensing algorithms for cognitive radio applications. IEEE Commun. Surv. Tutor. **11**(1), 116–130 (2009)
16. Liang, Y., Zeng, Y., Peh, E., Hoang, A.T.: Sensing-throughput tradeoff for cognitive radio networks. IEEE Trans. Wirel. Commun. **7**(4), 1326–1337 (2008)
17. Angjelicinoski, M., Atanasovski, V., Gavrilovska, L.: Comparative analysis of spatial interpolation methods for creating radio environment maps. In: Proceedings of the TELFOR, Belgrade, Serbia, pp. 334–337 (2011)
18. Tang, M., Zheng, Z., Ding, G., Xue, Z.: Efficient TV white space database construction via spectrum sensing and spatial inference. In: Computing and Communications Conference, pp. 1–5 (2015)
19. Grimoud, S., Jemaa, S.B., Sayrac, B., Moulines, E.: A REM enabled soft frequency reuse scheme. In: Global Communications Conference, pp. 819–823 (2010)

20. Zhang, H., Berg, A.C., Maire, M., Malik, J.: SVM-KNN: discriminative nearest neighbor classification for visual category recognition. In: Computer Vision and Pattern Recognition, pp. 2126–2136 (2006)
21. Lu, G.Y., Wong, D.W.: An adaptive inverse-distance weighting spatial interpolation technique. Comput. Geosci. **34**(9), 1044–1055 (2008)
22. Miller, R.L.: Trend surfaces: their application to analysis and description of environments of sedimentation. J. Geol. **64**(5), 425–446 (2015)
23. Mallet, J.: Discrete smooth interpolation. ACM Trans. Graph. **8**(2), 121–144 (1989)
24. Tang, M., Ding, G., Wu, Q., Xue, Z., Tsiftsis, T.A.: A joint tensor completion and prediction scheme for multi-dimensional spectrum map construction. IEEE Access **4**(99), 8044–8052 (2016)
25. Yilmaz, H.B., Tugcu, T.: Location estimation-based radio environment map construction in fading channels. Wirel. Commun. Mob. Comput. **15**(3), 561–570 (2015)
26. Ureten, S., Yongacoglu, A., Petriu, E.M.: A comparison of interference cartography generation techniques in cognitive radio networks. In: International Conference on Communications, pp. 1879–1883 (2012)
27. Perezromero, J., Zalonis, A., Boukhatem, L., Kliks, A., Koutlia, K., Dimitriou, N., Kurda, R.: On the use of radio environment maps for interference management in heterogeneous networks. IEEE Commun. Mag. **53**(8), 184–191 (2015)
28. De Beek, J.V., Cai, T., Grimoud, S., Sayrac, B., Mahonen, P., Nasreddine, J., Riihijarvi, J.: How a layered REM architecture brings cognition to today's mobile networks. IEEE Wirel. Commun. **19**(4), 17–24 (2012)

Elimination of Inter-distract Downlink Interference Based on Autocorrelation Technique

Hui Kang[(⊠)], Hongyang Xia, and Fugang Liu

School of Electronic and Information Engineering,
Heilongjiang University of Science and Technology, Harbin 150022, China
qihang1601@sina.com, xhy0454045l@163.com,
15846589756@163.com

Abstract. In order to eliminate downlink interference and improve system performance, we proposed a method to eliminate inter-distract downlink interference based on the non-overlapping nature of the signal in autocorrelation domain. In this method, multi-antenna technology was used and spectrum resource was not additionally occupied, without requiring channel conditions. The simulation result showed that this method is suitable for the removal of strong downlink interference in the mobile station at the edge of the distract.

Keywords: Downlink interference · Autocorrelation · Mobile station

1 Introduction

The main purpose of signal processing is to identify and separate the useful signals and the interferences in the special transform domain. The typical transform domains are time domain, frequency domain, code domain, and spatial domain. There is an obvious advantage in the method of distinguishing signals based on the non-overlapping nature in the autocorrelation domain, i.e., the interfering signal may be eliminated no matter how strong it is, and the channel state information is not necessary to be supplied to the receiver. In this paper, the correlation function matching algorithm was applied to the downlink cellular system. The non-overlapping nature of the signal in the autocorrelation domain was achieved by preprocessing the autocorrelation function of signals that transmitted by the base station [1–7]. In the receiver, the inter-distract downlink Interference may be eliminated after passing through the autocorrelation matching filter.

2 Design of System

2.1 System Model

In this paper, each of the base stations is equipped with a single transmitting antenna, and each of the mobile stations is equipped with N_r receiving antennas, thus the downlink channel may be seen to be a SIMO channel model. The typical system model is given in Fig. 1.

© ICST Institute for Computer Sciences, Social Informatics and Telecommunications Engineering 2018
X. Gu et al. (Eds.): MLICOM 2017, Part I, LNICST 226, pp. 258–267, 2018.
https://doi.org/10.1007/978-3-319-73564-1_26

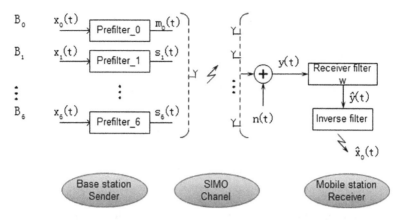

Fig. 1. System model

At the base station sender, the original signal to be transmitted is processed by a prefilter, so the autocorrelation function of the transmitted signal is linearly independent. At the mobile station receiver, the inter-distract downlink interference in the received signal was eliminated after passing through the receive filter W, and then the original signal was recovered by inverse filter. The receiver filter W was designed according to the autocorrelation function of the transmitted signal and the received signal. This is a blind algorithm, and the channel state information is not involved.

2.2 Signal Model

Both large scale fading and small scale fading are considered in the channel parameters. Assuming that the receiving antenna is properly placed, so that the large scale fading is of the same and the small scale fading is different between transmitting antenna and each receiving antenna of the base station. According to the system model of Fig. 1, the received signal of a mobile station in this distract B0 can be expressed to be,

$$y(t) = \sqrt{P_0}h_0m_0(t) + \sum_{i=1}^{6}\sqrt{P_i}f_is_i(t) + n(t) \tag{1}$$

In formula (1),

P_0 is large scale fading power between the mobile station and the base station of this local distract;

P_i is large scale fading power between the mobile station in this local distract and the base station in adjacent distract;

h_0 is the N_r-dimensional small scale fading power vector between the mobile station and the base station in this local distract;

f_i is the N_r-dimensional small scale fading power vector between the mobile station in this local distract and the base station in adjacent distract;

$m_0(t)$ is the L-dimensional transmitted signal vector of the base station in this local distract;

$s_i(t)$ is the L-dimensional transmitted signal vector of base station in the adjacent distract;

$n(t)$ is N_r-dimensional complex vector of white Gauss noise that obeys $N(0, 1)$;

The sum on the right side of formula (1) represents the downlink interference received by the mobile station in this local distract.

Assume $\mathbf{F} = [\mathbf{f_1}, \cdots, \mathbf{f_6}]$; $\mathbf{P} = \text{diag}[\sqrt{P_1}, \cdots, \sqrt{P_6}]$; $\mathbf{S}(t) = \text{diag}[s_1(t), \cdots, s_6(t)]^T$, then the received signal in formula (1) can be expressed as,

$$y(t) = \sqrt{P_0}\mathbf{h_0}m_0(t) + \mathbf{FPS}(t) + \mathbf{n}(t) \tag{2}$$

Assume the channel matrix $[\mathbf{h_0}\ \ \mathbf{F}]$ is a matrix of full column rank, then channel estimation is not needed for the receiver to obtain the channel parameters. At the receiver of the base station, based on the autocorrelation function of the transmitted signal and the received signal, the filter W, as a N_r-dimensional complex vector, was designed, in which the downlink interference may be eliminated. The output signal of the filter W is,

$$\hat{y}(t) = \sqrt{P_0}\mathbf{W}^*\mathbf{h_0}m_0(t) + \mathbf{W}^*\mathbf{FPS}(t) + \mathbf{W}^*\mathbf{n}(t) \tag{3}$$

If the filter meets $\mathbf{W}^*\mathbf{F} = 0$, the inter-distract downlink interference may be completely eliminated.

2.3   Design of Transmitted Signal

In this paper, different autocorrelation functions were used to distinguish signals. If the N autocorrelation sequences are linearly independent, the N signals may not overlap in the autocorrelation domain, then they can be transmitted at the same time with the same frequency and the same spreading spectrum sequence, and they can not be confused. The original signals were processed through the prefilter in Fig. 1, so that the transmitted signal of the base station in this local distract and the signals from the adjacent distract are linearly independent. The following FIR filters are used as prefilter.

$$H(z) = 1 + z^{-\zeta} \tag{4}$$

In formula (4), $H(z)$ is the system function of the filter. Different ζ corresponds to different FIR filters. For the same filter, if the input signal is a white random signal, the output signal has the same autocorrelation sequence. If the mean value of the input signal is 0, the output signal has autocorrelation function values ($\neq 0$) when $\tau = \zeta$, otherwise the autocorrelation function of the output signal is 0. For different filters, the autocorrelation sequence of the output signal is linearly independent. Substitute $\zeta_6 \geq \ldots \geq \zeta_1 \geq \zeta_0 \geq 1$ into the formula (4), and seven filters were designed for $B_i(i = 0, 1, \ldots, 6)$ in Fig. 1, which was used as a prefilter on the sending end of the base station. Both signal $m_0(t)$ and $s_i(t)$ outputted by the prefilter are not overlapped in autocorrelation domain.

Define their autocorrelation sequences and the autocorrelation matrix,

$$\mathbf{r}_{m_0} = [r_{m_0}(\zeta_0), \ldots, r_{m_0}(\zeta_6)]^T \tag{5}$$

$$\mathbf{r}_{s_i} = [r_{s_i}(\zeta_0), \ldots, r_{s_i}(\zeta_6)]^T \tag{6}$$

$$\mathbf{T} = [\mathbf{r}_{m_0}\mathbf{r}_{s_1}\ldots\mathbf{r}_{s_6}] = \begin{bmatrix} r_{m_0}(\zeta_0) & r_{s_1}(\zeta_0) & \cdots & r_{s_6}(\zeta_0) \\ \vdots & \vdots & \ddots & \vdots \\ r_{m_0}(\zeta_6) & r_{s_1}(\zeta_6) & \cdots & r_{s_6}(\zeta_6) \end{bmatrix} \tag{7}$$

Assume that the original signal $x_i(t)$ is a white random signal with a mean value of 0 and a variance of 1, then the autocorrelation matrix can be further simplified,

$$\mathbf{T} = \begin{bmatrix} r_{m_0}(\zeta_0) & 0 & \cdots & 0 \\ 0 & r_{s_1}(\zeta_1) & \cdots & 0 \\ \vdots & \vdots & \ddots & \vdots \\ 0 & 0 & \cdots & r_{m_6}(\zeta_6) \end{bmatrix} \tag{8}$$

In matrix (8), T is a diagonal matrix of 7 * 7. Obviously, T is also a matrix of full column rank. So r_{m_0} and r_{s_i} are independent linearly. Therefore, the transmitted signal $m_0(t)$ of base station in this local distract and the transmitted signal $s_i(t)$ of base station in the adjacent distract are not overlapped in the autocorrelation domain.

2.4   Design of Receive Filter

Assume that $\mathbf{m}_0(t)$, $\mathbf{s}(t)$ and $n(t)$ are uncorrelated each other. Given $\tau \geq 0$, the auto-correlation function of the received signal in formula (2) can be obtained,

$$\mathbf{R}_y(\tau) = P_0 r_{m_0}(\tau)\mathbf{h}_0\mathbf{h}_0^* + \mathbf{FPR}_s(\tau)\mathbf{P}^*\mathbf{F}^* + \mathbf{R}_n(\tau) \tag{9}$$

In formula (9), $\mathbf{R}_y(\tau) = E[y(t)y^*(t-\tau)]$, $\mathbf{R}_s(\tau) = E[s(t)s^*(t-\tau)]$, $\mathbf{R}_n(\tau) = E[n(t)n^*(t-\tau)]$. $n(t)$ is white Gauss noise. $\mathbf{R}_n(\tau) = 0$ when $\tau > 0$. Since the transmitted signals were uncorrelated each other, the co-variance matrix of $s(t)$ can be further written to be,

$$\mathbf{R}_s(\tau) = \text{diag}[r_{s_1}(\tau) \cdots r_{s_6}(\tau)] \tag{10}$$

Substitute it into formula (9),

$$\mathbf{R}_y(\tau) = P_0 r_{m_0}(\tau)\mathbf{h}_0\mathbf{h}_0^* + \sum_{i=1}^{6} P_i r_{s_i}(\tau)\mathbf{f}_i\mathbf{f}_i^* \quad \tau > 0 \tag{11}$$

By formula (8), $r_{m_0}(\tau) = 0$ when $\tau > \zeta_0$,

$$\mathbf{R}_y(\tau) = \sum_{i=1}^{6} P_i r_{s_i}(\tau) \mathbf{f}_i \mathbf{f}_i^* \quad \tau > \zeta_0 \tag{12}$$

In the autocorrelation function of the received signal, only the downlink interference information is left. In addition, by formula (8),

$$\mathbf{R}_y(\zeta_i) = P_i r_{s_i}(\zeta_i) \mathbf{f}_i \mathbf{f}_i^* \quad 1 \le i \le 6 \tag{13}$$

Construct a $6N_r \times N_r$ matrix R as follows,

$$\mathbf{R} = \begin{bmatrix} \mathbf{R}_y(\zeta_1) \\ \vdots \\ \mathbf{R}_y(\zeta_6) \end{bmatrix} = \mathrm{diag}[P_1 r_{s_1}(\zeta_1) \mathbf{f}_1, \cdots, P_6 r_{s_6}(\zeta_6) \mathbf{f}_6] \mathbf{F}^* \tag{14}$$

Both the diagonal matrix and $\mathbf{F}$ are all matrix of full column rank with rank 6 in formula (14). $\mathbf{F}^* \mathbf{W} = 0$ when $\mathbf{R}^* \mathbf{W} = 0$. If $\mathbf{W}^* \mathbf{F} = 0$, Receiving filter $\mathbf{W}$ can be obtained directly by singular value decomposition of $\mathbf{R}$, as follows,

$$\mathbf{R} = \mathbf{U} \begin{bmatrix} \Sigma & 0 \\ 0 & 0 \end{bmatrix} \begin{bmatrix} \mathbf{V} & \mathbf{V}^\perp \end{bmatrix} \tag{15}$$

In formula (15), Σ is non-zero singular value diagonal matrix. Both $\mathbf{U}$ and $\begin{bmatrix} \mathbf{V} & \mathbf{V}^\perp \end{bmatrix}$ are unitary matrix. Since the rank of matrix $\mathbf{R}$ is 6, it can be computed at last,

$$\mathbf{W} = \mathbf{V}^\perp \mathbf{c} \tag{16}$$

In the formula (16), $\mathbf{V}^\perp$ is a $N_r \times (N_r - 6)$ dimensional matrix, and $\mathbf{c}$ is any one-dimensional vector. Therefore, the filter $\mathbf{W}$ is solvable when the N_r is larger than 6. Therefore, at least 7 receiving antennas are required in the present method. After passing through the filter $\mathbf{W}$, the inter-distract downlink interference was eliminated. The resulting signal was obtained,

$$\hat{x}(t) = \sqrt{P_0} \mathbf{W}^* \mathbf{h}_0 \mathbf{m}_0(t) + \mathbf{W}^* \mathbf{n}(t) \tag{17}$$

Finally, the original signal $x_0(t)$ can be recovered by the inverse filter $F^{-1}(z)$ of formula (4).

3 Eliminate the Downlink Interference Between Two Adjacent Distracts

The necessary condition for the existence of receiving filter is that the number of receiving antenna is larger than six. That is, if the interference from the six adjacent distracts is to be eliminated, the mobile station must be equipped with at least seven receiving antennas. However, this is not realistic for the design of mobile station. The downlink interference received by the mobile station is closely related to the distance between the mobile station and the base station in the adjacent distracts. The distances between the mobile station and the base stations in the six adjacent distracts are different, as a result, the strengths of the six downlink interference are different. A nearer base station has a stronger interference to the mobile station. If the strongest downlink interference is eliminated by using fewer receiving antennas, then the system performance may be greatly improved. Especially for the users at the edge of the distract, the interference from adjacent distract is as strong as the signal transmitted by the base station in its own distract. Therefore, if the downlink interference from the adjacent distract was to be eliminated, the SINR of the mobile station may be greatly improved. Next, an improved method is proposed. By using two receiving antennas, the single strongest downlink interference from adjacent distract may be eliminated. The system model, the signal model and the signal design of transmitter were adopted in the base station in Sect. 2. The receiving filter of the mobile station was redesigned. In order to eliminate the downlink interference when the signal from the adjacent base station B_6 is $s_6(t)$, a new receiver filter should be adopted in the mobile station, meeting the requirements $\mathbf{W}^* f_6 = 0$. When $\tau > 0$, the autocorrelation function of the received signal (2) is,

$$\mathbf{R}_y(\tau) = P_0 r_{m_0}(\tau) h_0 h_0^H + \sum_{i=1}^{5} P_i r_{s_i}(\tau) f_i f_i^* + P_6 r_{s_6}(\tau) f_6 f_6^* \tag{18}$$

Since the autocorrelation sequences of the transmitted signals from each base stations are independent of each other, and meet the requirements of formula (8), then when $\tau = \zeta_6$,

$$\mathbf{R}_y(\zeta_6) = P_6 r_{s_6}(\zeta_6) f_6 f_6^* \tag{19}$$

The $\mathbf{R}_y(\zeta_6)$ is a $N_r \times N_r$-dimensional matrix. $f_6^* w = 0$ when $\mathbf{R}_x(\zeta_6)w = 0$. The receiver filter that meet $\mathbf{W}^* f_6 = 0$ may be obtained directly by making the singular value decomposition of $\mathbf{R}_y(\zeta_6)$ as follows,

$$\mathbf{R}_y(\zeta_6) = \mathbf{U}_1 \begin{bmatrix} \Sigma_1 & 0 \\ 0 & 0 \end{bmatrix} \begin{bmatrix} \mathbf{V}_1 & \mathbf{V}_1^\perp \end{bmatrix} \tag{20}$$

In formula (20), Σ_1 is non-zero singular value diagonal matrix. $\mathbf{U}_1$ and $\begin{bmatrix} \mathbf{V}_1 & \mathbf{V}_1^\perp \end{bmatrix}$ are all unitary matrix.

Since the rank of matrix $f_6 f_6^*$ is 1, then,

$$\mathbf{W} = \mathbf{V}_1^\perp c_1 \tag{21}$$

In formula (21), $\mathbf{V}_1^\perp$ is a $N_r \times (N_r - 1)$-dimensional matrix, and c_1 is any $(N_r - 1)$-dimensional vector. As a result, the filter $\mathbf{W}$ is solvable when N_r is larger than 1. After passing through receiving filter $\mathbf{W}$, the resulting signal is,

$$\hat{y}'(t) = \sqrt{P_0}W^*h_0m_0(t) + \sum_{i=1}^{5} \sqrt{P_i}W^*f_is_i(t) + W^*n(t) \tag{22}$$

In the improved method, the mobile station only needs to be equipped with two receiving antennas, which can eliminate the strongest downlink interference between this local distract and adjacent distract. It is realistic that the mobile station is equipped with two receiving antennas. In fact, the improved method may be used to eliminate the downlink interference from any of the six adjacent distracts. For example, if you were to eliminate the downlink interference s_i from the base station in distract B_i, substitute $\tau = \zeta_i$ into formula (18), then,

$$\mathbf{R}_y(\zeta_i) = P_i r_{s_i}(\zeta_i)f_if_i^* \tag{23}$$

Similarly, a reception filter satisfying $w_i^*f_i = 0$ may be obtained in making the singular value decomposition of $\mathbf{R}_y(\zeta_i)$.

In the two methods in Sects. 2 and 3, the solution of receiving filter is only related to the autocorrelation function of the received signal and the autocorrelation function of the transmitted signal of each base station. The solution of the receiving filter is independent of signal strength and channel parameters. Consequently, the method of eliminating downlink interference based on signal autocorrelation technology is a blind algorithm, the downlink interference may be effectively eliminated no matter how strong its power is.

4 Simulation Analysis

When there is a downlink cellular system in the seven distracts, the system parameters [8] are present in Table 1.

Table 1. System parameters

Distract radius	Path loss constant	Path loss index factor	Shadow fading factor	Noise power	Small-scale fading (Rayleigh fading model)
2 km	−137 dB	4	8 dB	−129 dB	$h \sim CN(0, 1)$

The mobile station is equipped with two receiving antennas, the single strongest downlink interference from adjacent distract is eliminated by using the improved method proposed above. By using Monte and Carlo simulation, the SINR of the signal was compared and analyzed before and after the method was used. In the simulation, the following three SINR parameters are involved:

(1) the SINR of the signal before receiving the filter W:

$$SINR_b = \frac{E\left[P_0|\mathbf{h}_0\mathbf{m}_0(t)|^2\right]}{E\left[\left|\sum_{i=1}^{6}\sqrt{P_i}\mathbf{f}_i\mathbf{s}_i(t)\right|^2\right] + E\left[|\mathbf{n}(t)|^2\right]} \tag{24}$$

(2) the SINR of the signal after being processed by the filter W:

$$SINR_a = \frac{E\left[P_0|\mathbf{w}^H\mathbf{h}_0\mathbf{m}_0(t)|^2\right]}{E\left[\left|\sum_{i=1}^{6}\sqrt{P_i}\mathbf{w}^H\mathbf{f}_i\mathbf{s}_i(t)\right|^2\right] + E\left[|\mathbf{w}^H\mathbf{n}(t)|^2\right]} \tag{25}$$

(3) the SINR of the received signal after a single strongest downlink interference from adjacent distract was theoretically removed:

$$SINR_n = \frac{E\left[P_0|\mathbf{h}_0\mathbf{m}_0(t)|^2\right]}{E\left[\left|\mathbf{x}(t) - \sqrt{P_0}\mathbf{h}_0\mathbf{m}_0(t) - \sqrt{P_6}\mathbf{f}_6\mathbf{s}_6(t)\right|^2\right]} \tag{26}$$

In formula (26), the SINR was used to compare the effectiveness of filter W. When the mobile station was located at the edge of the distract, the SINR of the received signals was compared before and after the improved method was used. As can be seen from Fig. 2, after using the improved method, the SINR of mobile station is obviously improved, no matter how strong the transmitter power is.

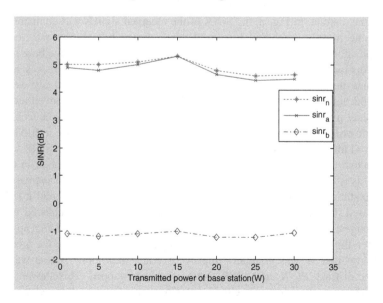

Fig. 2. SINR comparison for different transmit power of the base station

It is apparent that $SINR_a$ is very closed to $SINR_n$ in Fig. 2. This indicated the strongest downlink interference from adjacent distract may be effectively eliminated after passing the filter W.

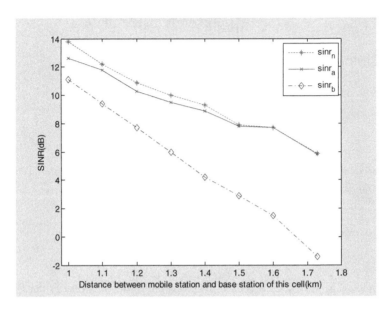

Fig. 3. SINR comparison for different locations of the mobile station in the distract

Assume the transmitting power of the base station was 20 W and the mobile station moved toward the distract edge when the mobile station was 1 km away from the base station in the distract. In Fig. 3, the SINR of the received signals was compared before and after the improved method was used when the mobile station was located in different positions in the distract. When the mobile station is close to the base station in the local distract, the power of useful signal from this base station was relatively stronger and the downlink interference from adjacent distract is relatively weaker, so the downlink interference may be ignored. With the mobile station moved away from the base station in the local distract, the power of useful signal was reduced and the power of downlink interference was increased, resulting in a decrease in SINR. Using the improved method, the SINR was improved and the improvement in SINR was more apparent when the mobile station was farther away from the base station in the local distract. This is because the single strongest downlink interference was increased when the mobile station was near the edge of the distract, and its ratio in total interference was increased. Consequently, a larger improvement in SINR was achieved when the single strongest downlink interference was eliminated. in Fig. 3, $SINR_a$ approaches $SINR_n$ when the mobile station was nearer the edge of the distract, and the precision of the receiving filter W was gradually improved. When the mobile station was on the edge of the distract, $SINR_a$ and $SINR_n$ were nearly overlapped. This showed that the strong interference was effectively eliminated. Consequently, the improved method was very effective in eliminating the interference for the user on the edge of the distract.

5   Conclusion

In this paper, a method of eliminating inter-distract downlink interference based on signal autocorrelation was present. In this method, each base station is equipped with a transmitting antenna, and each mobile station is equipped with a plurality of receiving antennas. The prefilter was used to process the signal at the transmitter of base station. The transmitted signals did not overlap in the autocorrelation domain. Therefore the processed signal can be transmitted at the same time with the same frequency and spreading sequence. In the receiver of mobile station, the received signal passed through the receiving filter, and then recovered to the original signal through the inverse process of prefilter. The receiving filter was designed according to the auto-correlation function of the transmitted signal and the autocorrelation function of the received signal, no channel state information and the intensity of interference were involved. In order to eliminate the downlink interference from the adjacent distracts, the mobile station needed to be equipped with receiving antennas more than those equipped in the adjacent distracts. This makes the design of mobile station more difficult. In the improved method present in this paper, only two receiving antennas are required in the mobile station to eliminate the single strongest downlink interference from the adjacent distract. The simulation result indicated that this method is especially suitable for the mobile station located in the edge of the distract.

Acknowledgments. This work was supported by the Natural Science Foundations of Hei-longjiang Province (F2015019), the Postdoctoral Science Foundations of Heilongjiang Province (LBH-Z16054), and the Science and Technology Research Project Foundations of the education hall of Heilongjiang province (12543070).

References

1. Zeng, H.H., Tong, L.: Blind channel estimation using the second-order statistics algorithms. IEEE Trans. Sig. Process. **45**, 1919–1930 (1997)
2. Hamdi, K.A., Sedtheetorn, P.: On the spectral efficiency of CDMA downlink distractular mobile networks. IEEE Trans. Wireless Commun. **7**, 4133–4141 (2008)
3. Liu, Q., Hu, B.: A modified blink MIMO channel equalization method based on autocorrelation matching principle. Int. Conf. Commun. Circuits Syst. **1**, 215–218 (2005)
4. Luo, H., Liu, R.W.: A close-form solution to blind MIMO FIR channel equalization for wireless communication systems based on autocorrelation matching. In: IEEE International Conference on Accoustics, Speech and Signal Processing, pp. 293–296 (2003)
5. Gomadam, K., Cadambe, V.R., Jafar, S.A.: A diatributed numerical approach to interference alignment and applications to wireless interference networks. IEEE Trans. Inf. Theory **57**, 3309–3322 (2011)
6. Jafar, S.A., Sharnai, S.: Degrees of freedom region of the MIMO X channel. IEEE Trans. Inf. Theory **54**, 151–170 (2008)
7. Foschini, G.J., Gans, M.J.: On limits of wireless communications in a fading environment when using multiple antennas. Wireless Pers. Commun. **6**, 311–335 (1998)
8. Holma, H., Toskala, A.: WCDMA for UMTS: Radio Access for Third Generation Mobile Communications. Wiley, Hoboken (2004)

Intelligent Internet of Things

Application of Cooperative Communications with Dual-Stations in Wireless Mobile Environments

Ershi Xu$^{(\boxtimes)}$, Xiangping Zhai, Weiyi Lin, and Bing Chen

Nanjing University of Aeronautics and Astronautics, Nanjing, China
xeshgd@163.com, {blueicezhaixp,cb_china}@nuaa.edu.cn, linweiyi18@163.com

Abstract. Wireless networks have been widely used in various industries, e.g., the subway communication system. However, there are many technical problems that are still unsolved. One of the most important issues about the problem is the reliability of "train-to-earth" communication. Therefore, to enhance the stability and reliability of the subway wireless communication system, we dispose the dual gateways and stations, and propose a dual-stations collaborative communication scheme. Implementation between dual gateways and dual stations are required to design a state testing scheme. Therefore, the system reliability is improved as it can detect the system malfunctions. There are three kinds of work modes where each mode has been designed to solve the stated problems previously. The experiment results show that the proposed scheme can reach the expected requirements, thus achieving the reliable and secure "train-to-earth" communication.

Keywords: Dual-stations · State testing scheme · Reliability
Communication scheme

1 Introduction

As far as we know, the subway plays an important role of urban transport as a rail transmit system. At the same time, wireless networks with the superior flexibility and convenience get more and more mature in the network applications. Moreover, wireless networks have played an increasingly important role and penetrated into all aspects of human life. Subway communication system is one of the important application [1].

However, although wireless networks are widely used in many industries, there are still many technical problems to be solved for the reliability of the requirements in the subway communication system. This is mainly determined by the particularity of the subway train-to-earth wireless communication environment. The main features are as follows: *(1) Environmental complexity.* Subway communication environment is quite complex, coupled with climate, temperature and other conditions, so the subway wireless communication mechanism in the design and use of the process must be taken into account the signal coverage

© ICST Institute for Computer Sciences, Social Informatics and Telecommunications Engineering 2018
X. Gu et al. (Eds.): MLICOM 2017, Part I, LNICST 226, pp. 271–281, 2018.
https://doi.org/10.1007/978-3-319-73564-1_27

model and the anti-jamming capability. *(2) Reliability.* The data in the subway environment is divided into two kinds, i.e., one is the control command data of the subway, and the other is the subway user access service data. For control commands, it is necessary to achieve high reliability and real-time performance in relation to the safe travel of the train. For users' service data, such as voice over internet protocol, high reliability must be also achieved. However, because of the variety of environmental interferences and noises in the process of the wireless signal transmission, its channel bit error rate is relatively high. Therefore, it is important to achieve the reliability and real-time vehicle communication in the subway communication system. *(3) Security.* Due to the particularity of the data transmission in the subway communication system, it is necessary to ensure that the network has sufficient security, otherwise it will be terrible if the criminals get the data [2–4].

Then, the above characteristics can be combined into the usability, that is, a kind of ability to complete the specified function of a product in a specified period of time, under the specified conditions and at a certain time [5,6]. The key issue that needs to be solved in the current metro traffic is to provide a wireless communication mechanism with strong fault handling capability to achieve high availability [7].

In general, based on the existing wireless networks researches and communication protocols, this paper presents an improved and feasible method which is called dual-stations cooperative communication mechanism to achieve the expected reliability standards for the subway train-to-earth wireless communication environment. The rest of this paper is structured as follows. In Sect. 2, we introduce the design of the dual-Stations communication mechanism. In Sect. 3, we apply our framework to an experiment to show that this scheme can reach the expected requirements. At last, we conclude the paper in Sect. 4.

2 Design of Communication Mechanism with Dual-Stations

In the subway communication system, because of the need to send the train control information, the system requires a high standard of reliability. Therefore, the system has designed a variety of redundant settings [7]. It can achieve high reliability and high availability through the provision of redundant communication gateway, redundant core switches, redundant station, and redundant wireless signal coverage [8].

The dual-stations cooperative communication mechanism runs between dual communication gateways and dual stations. The program is started with the device. It automatically detects the heartbeat information at regular intervals and discovers the system faults in order to improve the reliability of the system. On the basis of the state detection program, this mechanism sets three working modes for the system: hot standby mode (HSM), load balancing mode (LBM) and hot standby redundancy mode (HSRM). Each communication gateway and stations must be set to one of the hot standby mode, the load balancing mode and the hot standby redundancy mode at the same time. The operating mode can be set manually by the manual application according to the actual application requirements [9–11]. Next, we will discuss three modes in detail.

2.1 Hot Standby Mode

Figure 1 shows the hot standby mode. Under normal circumstances, the main communication gateway and the main station (STA) are in the action state. The slave communication gateway and the slave station (STA) are in the standby state and do not provide services. The uplink data is transmitted by the main station and the main communication gateway to the vehicle personal computer, and the downlink data is transmitted through the main communication gateway and the main station too. The main communication gateway and the communication gateway detect each other's working state through the state detection program. When one of the devices detects failure of the other operation of the equipment, it will transfer the main communication gateway's work by the pre-designed strategy so that the system can continue to provide services. Therefore, the user does not feel any problems. The main station and the slave station keep working through the same way.

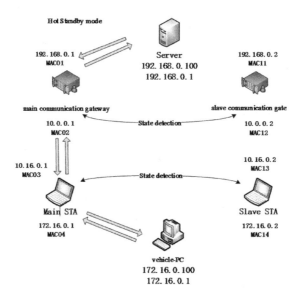

Fig. 1. Hot standby mode.

When the system fails in the hot standby mode, the processing flow of the stations is as follows (the processing flow of the communication gateway can be analogous to the station):

(1) Main stations troubleshooting process: If the interface of application port or communication port fails, we can exchange the IP address and MAC address of the main station (STA) application and the communication port with them of the slave station (STA) application port. Then the next hop routing information of the slave station to application server will be changed to the main communication gateway communication port's address. After the fault processing is completed, the uplink data is transmitted from the slave station and the main communication gateway, and the downlink data is also transmitted through the main communication gateway and the slave station.

(2) Slave stations troubleshooting process: Report the information about failures to the application server, and do not need to deal with anything.

2.2 Load Balancing Mode

Figure 2 shows the function diagram of the load balancing mode. Normally, the main communication gateway, the slave communication gateway and the main or slave stations are all in working condition. In order to achieve the load balancing of the wireless link, the system will divide the network traffic of the main station (STA) and the slave station (STA) into two parts. So the data transmission and reception of the personal computer will be completed through two wireless links to break through the limited bottleneck of the wireless link bandwidth. For the vehicle personal computer, the uplink data is transmitted through the main station and communication gateway, and the downlink data is transmitted

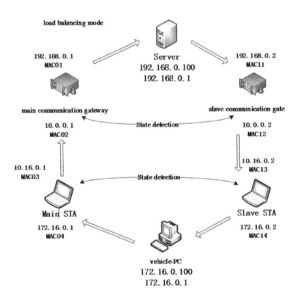

Fig. 2. Load balancing mode.

through the slave station and communication, thereby improving the overall throughput of the system and reducing the possibility of network congestion. The main communication gateway and the communication gateway detect each other's working state through the state detection program. When one of the devices detects failure of the other operation of the equipments, it will transfer the main communication gateway's work by the pre-designed strategy so that the system can continue to provide service. Meanwhile, the user does not feel any problems. Note that the main station and the slave station also through the same way to work.

When the system fails in load balancing mode, the processing flow is as follows (the processing flow of the gateway can be analogous to the station):

(1) Main stations troubleshooting process: If the interface of application port or communication port fails, we exchange the IP address and MAC address of the main station (STA) application and the communication port with them of the slave station (STA) application port. Then the next hop routing information of the slave station to the application server will be changed to the main communication gateway communication port's address. After the fault processing is completed, the uplink data is transmitted from the slave station and the main communication gateway to the vehicle personal computer, and the downlink data is transmitted through the slave communication gateway and the slave station.

(2) Slave stations troubleshooting process: It can be analogous to main stations. If the interface fails, we can exchange the IP address and MAC address. Then the next hop routing information of the slave station to the application server will be changed to the main communication gateway communication port's address. After that, the uplink data is transmitted from the main station and the main communication gateway to the vehicle personal computer. On the other hand, the downlink data is transmitted through the slave communication gateway and the main station.

2.3   Hot Standby Redundancy Mode

Figure 3 shows the hot standby redundancy mode. Under normal circumstances, both the main communication gateway and the slave communication gateway are in the action state. With regard to the vehicle personal computer, the uplink data is transmitted through the main station (STA). When the data arrive at the main station (STA), the main station copies the data to the slave station, and then the data are sent to the application server through both the main and the slave communication gateways respectively. The upper layer of the application server will deal with the repetitive packets. The downlink data will be sent to the main communication gateway through the application server. The main communication gateway will copy the data to the slave communication gateway, and then both the main and the slave communication gateway will send the data to the vehicle personal computer through the main station and the slave station

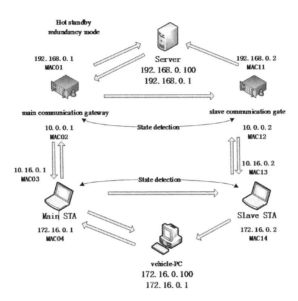

Fig. 3. Hot standby redundancy mode.

respectively. Of course, it will deal with the repetitive packets too. Moreover, the state detection mechanism is analogous to the mode before.

When the system fails in hot standby redundancy mode, the processing flow is as follows (the processing flow of the gateway can be analogous to the station):

(1) Main stations troubleshooting process:
   a. The interface of application port fails. We can exchange the IP address in the same way before. After that, the uplink data is transmitted from the slave station and the communication gateway, and the downlink data is transmitted through the main communication gateway, the slave communication gateway and the slave station.
   b. The interface of communication port fails. Do not need to deal with anymore. The uplink data is transmitted from the slave communication gateway, the slave station, and the main station. The downlink data is transmitted through the main communication gateway, the slave communication gateway and the slave station.
   c. The interface of application port and communication port all fail. The method is same as method in the fails about the interface of application port.
(2) Slave stations troubleshooting process: Report the information about failures, and do not need to deal with anything.

3   Experiments

The network topology shown in Fig. 4 is used to simulate the dual-stations cooperative communication in wireless mobile environment of the subway. Set up dual communication gateways and dual stations, which is distinguished with main and slave, in order to achieve three kinds of related work modes. The two access points' working channel are set as two channels, equipped with two wireless cards. And they are both in the station (STA) mode, using directional antennas, pointing to the vehicle in the two directions, respectively, in the 3-channel and 7-channel.

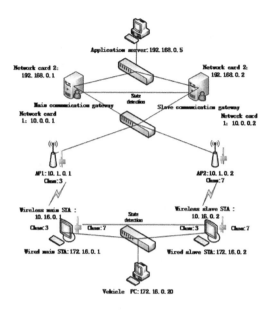

Fig. 4. The experiment network topology.

There are some criteria about the three kinds of working modes proposed in this paper, such as the networks delay, throughput and fault response time. In order to test these criteria, this paper designed four sets of test experiments: throughput comparison experiment of three kinds of work mode under normal or faulty circumstances; response time comparison experiment of three kinds of work mode under normal or faulty circumstances;

By the test conditions, the failure rate of the three working modes is determined by the continuous operation of the system for 12 h. No fault has occurred for each working mode after ten consecutive days of testing. Therefore, the fault rate of the system can be considered as 0 in this case.

Tables 1 and 2 show the throughput and the average response time experiment results (unit: Mbps) under normal circumstances. In each mode, TCP and UDP are tested with 1 KBytes, 10 KBytes and 100 KBytes packets for 30 min.

Figures 5 and 6 show the comparison of the data in Tables 1 and 2. It can be seen from the figures that the mode with the maximum throughput and minimum average response time is the load balancing mode in the use of TCP protocol. Next is the hot standby mode, and hot standby redundancy mode is

Table 1. Comparison of throughput under normal conditions (unit: Mbps)

Packet	HSM-TCP	HSM-UDP	LBM-TCP	LBM-UDP	HSRM-TCP	HSRM-UDP
1K	7.979	6.376	8.275	6.882	7.542	5.833
10K	16.404	11.863	18.524	14.579	15.404	10.863
100K	17.949	16.155	24.949	19.155	15.949	13.155

Table 2. Comparison of average response time under normal conditions (unit: s)

Packet	HSM-TCP	HSM-UDP	LBM-TCP	LBM-UDP	HSRM-TCP	HSRM-UDP
1K	0.001	0.001	0.001	0.001	0.001	0.001
10K	0.003	0.004	0.003	0.005	0.004	0.005
100K	0.031	0.040	0.021	0.038	0.035	0.048

the last. Meanwhile, the UDP protocol also have the same rule. Thus, the load balancing mode uses two links to send and receive data at the same time to achieve a balanced load of the link to improve the system throughput. But the hot standby redundancy mode send same packet twice so that the burden of system increases and the network throughput decreases.

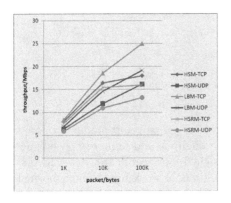

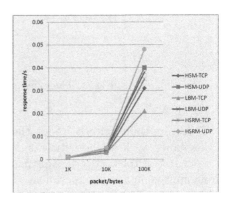

Fig. 5. Throughput comparison under normal condition.

Fig. 6. Response time comparison under normal conditions.

Tables 3 and 4 show the results under faulty circumstances. There is a total of 16 types of faults include the fault of either the communication interface or the application interface in either the communication gateway or the station and the heartbeat overtime fault. The interface failure is manually by closing the corresponding network card, and the heartbeat overtime fault is manually by the machine closed. Each type is completed within one minute.

Figures 7 and 8 show the comparison of the data in table before. It can be seen from the figures that the mode with the maximum throughput and

Table 3. Comparison of throughput under faulty conditions (unit: Mbps)

Packet	HSM-TCP	HSM-UDP	LBM-TCP	LBM-UDP	HSRM-TCP	HSRM-UDP
1K	5.528	5.197	5.890	5.497	5.955	5.429
10K	13.433	8.836	14.021	9.528	14.481	10.563
100K	13.988	10.545	15.236	12.102	15.583	12.799

Table 4. Comparison of average response time under faulty conditions (unit: s)

Packet	HSM-TCP	HSM-UDP	LBM-TCP	LBM-UDP	HSRM-TCP	HSRM-UDP
1K	6.240	6.850	6.331	6.533	4.211	4.311
10K	6.402	6.833	6.890	6.998	4.221	4.821
100K	7.158	8.034	8.513	9.211	5.332	5.522

minimum average response time is the hot standby redundancy mode. Thus, the hot standby redundancy mode can keep at least one package be successfully reached in the event of most of the failure so as to achieve a higher throughput. Load balancing mode and hot standby mode only can continue delivery package when the fault has been completed.

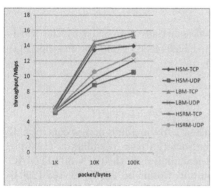

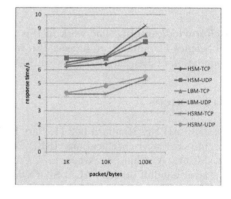

Fig. 7. Throughput comparison under normal condition.

Fig. 8. Response time comparison under normal conditions.

The above experiment results show that the dual communication gateways and dual-stations can be used for cooperative communication.

In the normal case, the load balancing mode can achieve the highest throughput and the lowest average response time. Obviously, it has the best performance, the hot standby mode is the second, and the hot standby redundancy mode is the worst. Transmission delay are controlled within 500 ms, and the uplink and downlink bandwidth are maintained more than 400 Kbps. In the faulty case, the hot standby redundancy mode can achieve the highest throughput and the lowest average response time. Meanwhile, the hot standby mode is the second, and the load balancing mode is the worst. The fault response time is controlled within 10 s and the uplink and downlink bandwidth are maintained more than 400 Kbps. Therefore, the three modes can meet the expected requirements of the subway wireless communication system, and each has its advantages and disadvantages. It can be chosen according to the current system to achieve the performance criteria.

4   Conclusion

This paper makes an in-depth study on the reliable wireless communication mechanism in the subway environment. In order to ensure the stability and reliability of the wireless transmission of the subway control signal, a dual-stations cooperative communication mechanism is proposed. Moreover, by running the state detection program between the dual communication gateways and dual stations, the system reliability is improved. Based on this, the communication gateway and station will be set up in three working modes, i.e., the hot standby mode, the load balancing mode and the hot standby redundancy mode. In the event of system failure, the corresponding methods to solve the problem are provided for the three modes of operation to achieve the dual-stations cooperative communication, which can guarantee the reliability of the wireless communication networks.

Acknowledgement. The work in this paper was partially supported by the Natural Science Foundation of Jiangsu Province (No. BK20140835), and the Postdoctoral Foundation of Jiangsu Province (No. 1401018B).

References

1. IEEE. IEEE Standard 802.11, Part II: Wireless LAN medium access control and physical layer specifications. IEEE Computer Society Press, Washington (1999)
2. Mishra, A., Shin, M., Arbaugh, W.: An empirical analysis of the IEEE 802.11 MAC layer handoff process. ACM SIGCOMM Comput. Commun. **33**(2), 93–102 (2004)
3. IEEE Std. 802.11f, IEEE Trial-Use Recommended Practice for Multi-Vendor Access Point Interoperability via an Inter-Access Point Protocol Across Distribution Systems Supporting. IEEE 802.11 Operation. IEEE Press (2003)
4. Perkins, C. (ed.): IP Mobility Support for IPv4 (2002)
5. Lee, S.H.: Reliability Evaluation of a Flow Network. IEEE Trans. Reliab. **29**, 24–28 (1980)
6. Abraham, J.A.: An improved algorithm for network reliability. IEEE Trans. Reliab. **28**, 58–61 (1979)
7. Ramani, I., Savage, S.: SyncScan: practical fast handoff for 802.11 infrastructure networks. In: 24th Annual Joint Conference of the IEEE Computer and Communications Societies INFOCOM 2005, pp. 675–684 (2005)
8. Issac, B., Hamid, K.A., Tan, C.E.: Pre-authenticated and adaptive IP mobility for WLAN Nodes. In: The 2nd International Conference of Distributed Frameworks for Multimedia Applications, pp. 1–8 (2006)

9. Doulliez, P., Jamoulle, J.: Transportation networks with random arc capacities. Math. Programs Act. Anal. **3**(9), 45–60 (1972)
10. Clancy, D.P., Gross, G., Wu, F.F.: Probabilitic flows for reliability evaluation of multiarea power system interconnections. Int. J. Electr. Power Energy Syst. **5**(2), 101–114 (1983)
11. Fishman, G.S.: Monte Carlo estimation of the maximal flow distribution with discrete stochastic arc capacity levels. Naval Res. Logistrics Q. **36**(6), 829–849 (1989)

Design for Attendance System
with the Direction Identification Based
on RFID

Hongyuan Wang[✉]

School of Information Science and Engineering,
Dalian Polytechnic University, Dalian 116034, China
1096018567@qq.com

Abstract. A direction recognition attendance system based on RFID (Radio Frequency Identification) is designed in the paper. Using multiple card readers (a master and more slave), the system can recognize the direction of the card-holders effectively. Firstly, to read the RFID cards held by passersby and vehicles, multiple card readers must be installed in the region. Secondly, according to reading the difference of recorded time by multiple card readers, the direction of passage can be decided. Synchronism of the master-slave card readers are achieved using the time hack command, which ensure the accuracy of the decided direction. Finally, the access records will be packaged and transmitted to the server by the mobile network from the master card reader. The system can decide the direction of passage and calculate the passing time of the passersby and vehicles, making it a highly intelligent and efficient attendance management system.

Keywords: RFID · Card reader · Direction of passage · Attendance system

1 Introduction

Personnel attendance is one of the most important parts of the Enterprise Management System, and how to fulfill attendance in an easy but efficient way is what the company cares. In previous, staffs were asked to clock in and out or recording manually by the companies. It was inefficient and error-prone. Now, with the development of RFID tech and the enterprises informatization construction, it is being a trend for a company using the RFID tech to deal with the personnel attendance work [1, 2].

RFID is a kind of non-contact, automatic identification technology [3]. It has some advantages, such as lower cost, more stable signals and longer distance for reading. RFID is widely applied in areas such as industrial automation, communication and transportation, etc. [4]. For example, traffic monitoring, item management and checking in/out as well as attendance system are using RFID technology [5, 6].

As we all know, it is common to use RFID in personnel attendance system. Personnel attendance can be completed via a card reader reading a RFID card [7]. But some problems might be occurred in certain occasions like large-scale mine factories. For instance, most systems are using proximity card-reading devices which request our

© ICST Institute for Computer Sciences, Social Informatics and Telecommunications Engineering 2018
X. Gu et al. (Eds.): MLICOM 2017, Part I, LNICST 226, pp. 282–290, 2018.
https://doi.org/10.1007/978-3-319-73564-1_28

staffs to check manually and closely, causing inefficiency if high pass rate needed in the factory. Another instance is that although system of large-scale mine factories can recognize a target, while they cannot tell which direction the target's heading. Thus, the system cannot monitor or manage the staff's clock-in or clock-out automatically. And people need to do statistics and manage the condition of passersby [8].

In order to enhance the efficiency of personnel attendance and solve the problem that the attendance system cannot decide the direction of the passage, a RFID-based direction identification system is designed. We need to install a few of card readers to read the RFID cards on the passersby or vehicles in areas which needed to be decided in this system. According to reading the difference of recorded time by multiple card readers, the direction of passage can be decided. Then the data by the card readers will be transmitted to the server for storage and recording via mobile communication networks. In this system, we adopt the active RFID technology, which is stable with signal and can be read in a long distance with little interference [9]. This design for personnel attendance system based-on RFID technology can tell the direction that people or vehicles are heading. And can calculate the passing time and working time information and so on, which will contribute to more intelligent personnel attendance system for large-scale mine factories.

2 Composition of the System

Figure 1 shows an installation diagram for a large-scale mine factory's personnel attendance system. The volume of the card readers installation is up to the reading distance and the width of the gate of the factory (If the width of the gate is shorter than the distance which the readers can cover, we need a pair of card readers. Otherwise, we need several pairs.). One is the master card reader, others are slave readers. To elaborate easily, 2 pairs of card readers are installed in the paper. The master card reader 1 and the slave card reader 3 are in the front of the gate. Slave card reader 2 and 4 are behind the gate. The master card reader 1 and slave card reader 2 constitute a pair of card readers, slave card reader 3 and 4 become the other pair. With the help of cards working in pairs installed in the front door and back door, the system can calculate the time difference. Card readers are connected with wired Ethernet and data are transmitted by it. The master card reader is connected to the remote servers via mobile communication base station and Internet, then it will send card-reading records and access records to the remote servers.

Slave card readers read RFID information in their covering ranges, then pack the data and transmit it to the master card reader. The master card reader also reads RFID information in its own covering range. At the same time, it accepts information from the slave card readers and analyses them. The system can decide the directions of the RFID cardholders by calculating the time difference from the front/back card readers, the system can decide the directions of the RFID cardholders. And it is requested the master-slave card readers must keep time synchronous.

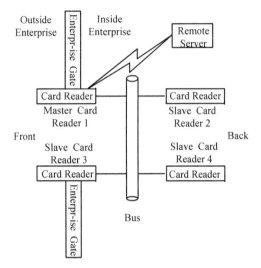

Fig. 1. The installation instruction of attendance system

3 Design of Card Readers

3.1 Composition of a Card Reader

As shown in Fig. 2, the constitution of the card reader includes: power module, MCU, RAM, FLASH, clock module, Long-wave-time-service module, acousto-optic indicating unit, RFID card-reading module, configuration interface, Ethernet interface module, and mobile communication module.

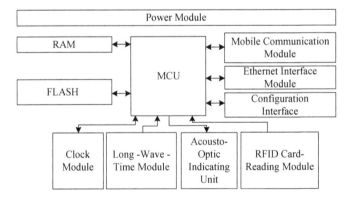

Fig. 2. Circuit diagram of the card reader

Power module: to supply other modules with power.

MCU: control other modules, process data, decide the direction, upload information and other secondary functions.

RAM: cache the to-be-processed data.

FLASH: to preserve data that mustn't be lost when the power is being cut-off, including configuration figures of the card-reader, unsent reading records, unsent access records.

Clock module: to provide card readers standard time, produce card-reading records and access records timestamp. Slave card readers preferentially adopt the clock time from the master card reader to keep in time synchronization.

Long-wave-time-service module: to proofread the clock module of the card readers. Adopting BPL time service [10], this module receives standard signals from long-wave-time-service launcher, then demodulates the time-serving signals, via electric level signals output by the timers' pins. The MCU can synchronize the system clock according to the electric level time periods, then provide card readers with relatively accurate time, thus realizing time synchronization with the master-slave card readers. The key of direction recognizing is to synchronize the time of every card reader, adopting long-wave-time-serving module preferentially [11]. When long wave time serving signal can be received, this system can use the time service to synchronize time of every card reader. When interference appears or owing to the restrictions the environment, the card readers cannot receive the time-serving signals, this system can use the clock module to synchronize time of every card reader by networking synchronization. The master card reader can obtain the standard time by connecting time-serving servers via mobile communication base stations. Then, via Ethernet, the master card reader can give instructions to slave card readers, the slave card readers can keep in time synchronization with the master card reader.

Acousto-optic indicating unit: to indicate the working status of the card reader via LED and buzzers.

RFID card-reading module: to complete reading information of the RFID cards.

Configuration interface: providing standard interface to deploy the working parameters for card readers.

Ethernet interface module: to provide data communication between the master-slave card readers.

Mobile communication module: process the aerial interface between remote servers and card readers, fulfill the data uploading tasks.

3.2 Programming Flow of the Card Reader

The working process of a slave card reader is showed as Fig. 3. Once electrified, this system will decide the current device is a slave card reader from the systematic configuration, then start up the overtime timer.

The processing flow of the slave card reader: the card reader will go to interrupt if it gets data. The serial port will save the data in the UART (Universal Asynchronous Receiver/Transmitter). Then the main loop of the card reader could read and analyze data in the UART queue. If analyzed successfully, the data will be transferred into records by reading the current time using the time module, then the records will be saved in the RAM. If the records fulfill a page of FLASH, it will be saved in the FLASH. And overtime timer will be reset every time the reading record is generated. When the data in the UART queue is finished and no new card-reading data arrival, the

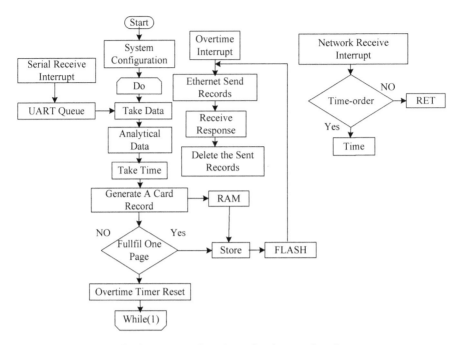

Fig. 3. Program flowchart of a slave card reader

overtime timer will run over because of no reset, then the procedure will jump into the timeout interrupt, timeout interrupt reads card-reading records from the FLASH and sent the records via Ethernet to the master card reader, at the same time, receiving the response from it. If the master card reader receives rightly, the record will be removed from the slave card readers.

During the slave readers working period, if the network receives the interrupt which is the time order from the master card reader, the time checking operation is triggered. If not, the procedure will return to the main loop to continue.

The processing flow of the master card reader is showed as Fig. 4. Once electrified, this system will decide the current device is a master card reader and start the timeout timer.

The working process of the master card reader: it is similar to the slave card readers, the difference is that the program will jump to timeout interrupt to execute, when the overtime timer overflow. The timeout interrupt read the access records from FLASH and send them to server via Mobile communication network, at the same time it will receive the server's response, if the server receives the records of the master card reader rightly, the master card reader should delete the transmitted records.

In the working process of the master card reader, if the network receives an interrupt which is the record of transportation from the slave card readers to the master card reader, the master card reader will receive records and store in the FLASH, otherwise, it will return to the main loop to continue.

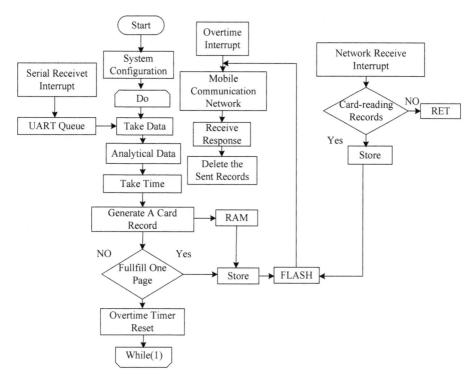

Fig. 4. Program flowchart of the master card reader

4 Direction Recognition Algorithm

In order to decide the direction of the passersby and vehicles, this paper proposed the algorithm of the direction recognition. As shown in Fig. 5.

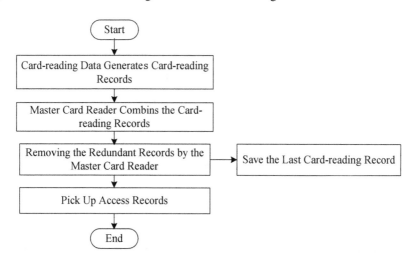

Fig. 5. The flowchart of direction recognition

(1) Card-reading data generates card-reading records

All card readers get data from reading the RFID cards, then sort the data based on the ascending array in the same RFID card. The card-reading data timestamp is the timing of the reader read RFID cards. Because of passersby or vehicles take time to go through a single card-reader area, the same RFID card will be read repeatedly, which will cause the data redundancy, so, the redundancy need to be removed to generate new records.

The redundant data will be processed as below: for the same card (identified with card ID), the first time the card is read, record the card-reading time as t_1, when read the I times, record as t_i. The system will set a overtime as TOT, which should be designed less than the passing time from the front/back (or back/front) card-reader. Then combine the data with this RFID card, if:

$$t_i - t_1 > TOT. \tag{1}$$

The card-reading records will be recorded and saved as t_i, if not, the card-reading data will be considered as redundant data and it will be deleted. The procedure will cycle like this until the card-reading records generated. As shown in Fig. 6.

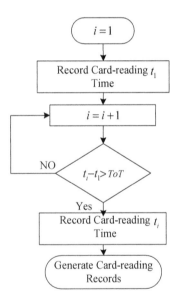

Fig. 6. Flowchart of card reader removing redundant data

(2) Master card reader assembles the card-reading records.

The slave card readers transport the card-reading records via LAN to the master card reader. The master card reader will assemble the records, then assort them based on the card ID and order the records in the ascending rule of timestamp in each part.

(3) Removing the redundant records by the master card reader

For the generation of card-reading records is independent between card readers, one RFID card may be read by different card readers at the same time and saved as card-reading records, so once the records were combined together, there will be repeat records, which should be processed as below: compare every item after summary and make a decision according to the different card readers but with the same RFID card: compare the absolute D-value of the first record with second record, if the D-value is smaller the *TOT*, delete the second record, then compare the third record with the first one, looping like this to remove the redundant records in the same RFID card. This procedure is the same with data redundancy removing, just the difference of data and records.

(4) Pick up access records

Search the trip point (from the front to the back/from the back to the front) according to the ID of RFID card after processing the redundant records. Pick up the records before and after the trip point as one piece of access records, so will decide the direction of accessing. After picking up the position of readers in couple, mark the record in position of "front-back" as "enter", and mark the record in position of "back-front" as "leave".

(5) Save the last card-reading record

Removing the redundant records in the master card reader, pick up and save the last one to be used as accessing records in the next implement.

5   Conclusion

A direction recognition attendance system based on RFID is designed in the paper. Multiple card readers must be installed in the region. With the cooperation of master-slave card readers, the system can decide the direction of the card holders by the time difference from a pair of card-readers. Also calculate the access time and working time. The information by card readers will be recorded and saved in the server via mobile communication module. Compared to the traditional attendance system, this paper can decide the direction of accessing people, increase the efficiency and shorten the passing time.

References

1. Shukla, S.: RFID based attendance management system. Int. J. Electr. Comput. Eng. **3**, 784–790 (2013)
2. Nainan, S., Parekh, R., Shah, T.: RFID technology based attendance management system. Int. J. Comput. Sci. Issues **10**(1) (2013)
3. Pardal, M.L., Marques, J.A.: Towards the internet of things: an introduction to RFID technology. In: Proceedings of the International Workshop on RFID Technology-Concepts,

Applications, Challenges, IWRT 2010, in Conjunction with ICEIS 2010, Funchal, Madeira, Portugal, June 2010, pp. 69–78. DBLP (2010)

4. Rogers, H., Hakam, T.A.E., Hartmann, E., Gebhard, M.: RFID in retail supply chains: current developments and future potential. In: Dethloff, J., Haasis, H.D., Kopfer, H., Kotzab, H., Schönberger, J. (eds.) Logistics Management, pp. 201–212. Springer, Cham (2015). https://doi.org/10.1007/978-3-319-13177-1_16

5. Dasilva, J., Shervey, R.C.: Radio frequency identification based personnel safety system. US 8115650 B2 (2012)

6. Woo, Y.H., Lee, J.H., Kim, J.E.: Method and system for confirming location of product within shelf using RFID. US 8947213 B2 (2015)

7. Chiagozie, O.G., Nwaji, O.G.: Radio frequency identification (RFID) based attendance system with automatic door unit. Acad. Res. Int. **2**(2), 168 (2012)

8. Li, D., Yang, H., Fred, K., et al.: A staff access control system based on RFID technology. Atlantis Press (2016)

9. Jian, Y.U., Yang, W.: Judgment of direction of movement based on active RFID. Sci. Technol. Eng. **32**, 45 (2011)

10. Wen, D.J., Lin, W.Y., Xia, C.A.: Time control method for long wave BPL time service system. J. Time Freq. (2008)

11. Han, B., Zheng, H., Wang, Y., et al.: Research on time synchronization technology of virtual radio. Atlantis Press (2015)

A Geo-Based Fine Granularity Air Quality Prediction Using Machine Learning and Internet-of-Things

Hang Wang[1][(⊠)], Yu Sun[2], and Qingquan Sun[3]

[1] University High School, Irvine, CA 92612, USA
alfred1186381762@gmail.com
[2] Department of Computer Science, California State Polytechnic University,
Pomona, Pomona, CA 91768, USA
yusun@cpp.edu
[3] School of Computer Science and Engineering,
California State University, San Bernardino, San Bernardino, CA 92407, USA
qsun@csusb.edu

Abstract. As the development of economy and industry, air quality decreases as one of the exchanges of our achievements. Although air pollution has already been considered as a global and critical issue over the past decades, there has not been much innovation on the way people monitor and check the quality. Most of the air quality data today is provided by government or professional sensors set up in cities, which does not provide more detailed status in smaller geo locations with finer granularity, such as specific villages, schools, and shopping malls. In this project, we use machine learning to make a mathematical model which could be used to predict the air quality for small geo locations with accuracy and fine granularity. Through series of experiments and comparisons, the most accuracy mathematical model was found, which had a difference percentage less than 20% with the real data.

Keywords: Machine learning · Air quality prediction · Internet-of-Things

1 Introduction

Air quality has received much attention in recent years due to the development of industry and environmental protection sense of people. There is a data said that from 2008 to 2013, the air pollution increased about 8% among the cities around the world. Air pollution perplexes everyone, there are about 5.5 million people died due to the air pollution. According to the report of American Lung Association, half of the American population live in an environment which has the danger of air pollution. 6 of the most polluted cities in the United States are in California. Published by UNICEF on October 31, 2026, "Clear the Air for Children" said there are about 300 million children living in extreme polluted environment.

The standards of measurement in determining the air quality are PM 2.5, PM 10, O_3, NO_2, SO_2. PM 2.5 were Fine particles which were 2.5 μm in diameter or smaller, and can only be seen with an electron microscope. PM 10 were coarse dust particles which

© ICST Institute for Computer Sciences, Social Informatics and Telecommunications Engineering 2018
X. Gu et al. (Eds.): MLICOM 2017, Part I, LNICST 226, pp. 291–299, 2018.
https://doi.org/10.1007/978-3-319-73564-1_29

were 2.5 to 10 micrometers in diameter. O_3 were group of pollutants emitted during the combustion of fossil fuels. Nitrogen dioxide is an important air pollutant because it contributes to the formation of photochemical smog, which can have significant impacts on human health. SO_2 results from the burning of either sulfur or materials containing sulfur. One way to detect air quality is to put professional sensors everywhere around world in every area in every city. However, although the governments and some websites are doing this, the data are not real time and with high cost. In addition, these professional sensors only cover a limited number of big cities, leaving the air quality for most of areas unavailable. For instance, Fig. 1 shows a popular website that displays the PM 2.5 information for various locations in the world. However, the website mostly covers the major big cities, leaving the small regions and areas unprocessed.

Fig. 1. A screenshot from https://waqi.info that displays city PM 2.5

In this paper, we propose to use machine learning to build a mathematical model which could be used to predict the air quality for small geo locations with accuracy and fine granularity. Machine learning is a type of artificial intelligence (AI) that provides computers with the ability to learn without being explicitly programmed [11]. In order to get the real air quality input data, we also built a cost-effective Internet-of-Things (IoT) solution that can monitor air quality data and send the data through the Internet at real-time. Internet of things is the internetworking of items embedded with electronics, software, sensors, actuators, and network connectivity that enable these objects to collect and exchange data [10]. When making the air quality predictions, there are some variables that can affect the result such as the layout of the deployed monitor devices, the number of deployed monitor devices and the layout of the geo location. The goal is to use very few air quality sensors to make accurate predictions using machine learning approaches.

The rest of the paper is organized as follows: Sect. 2 gives the details on how we built the system including the architecture design and the specific components; Sect. 3 focuses on the machine learning experiments and discusses the results; Sect. 4 presents a few related work in this area, following by giving the conclusion remarks in Sect. 5, as well as pointing out the future work.

2   System Overview and Implementation

The system workflow includes building sensor monitors, collecting data and predicting air quality, as well as visualizing the data. This whole system can use the limited measured data from sensors, and through machine learning to find a suitable model to predict real time air quality. Figure 2 shows an overview of the system.

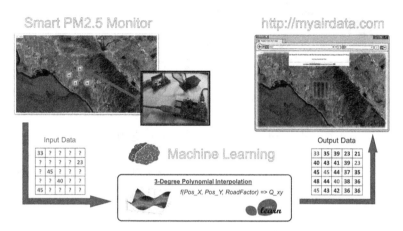

Fig. 2. The system overview

In order to get the most accurate mathematical model, an Internet-of-Things application has been built to collect air quality data, make air quality predictions and display air quality result. The application contains two modules:

Module 1. The hardware device that monitor the data and send those data to database, which allows data to be processed, followed by sending out the data to the cloud server.
Module 2. The web-based server application that receives the data, and fits them in the mathematical model to make air quality predictions in other places using machine learning algorithms. A web-based frontend user interface has been built to visualize the air quality data and periodically refresh it (Fig. 3).

The PM 2.5 sensor used in this project is dfRobot laser dust sensor SEN0177. PM2.5 laser sensor is a digital sensor used to obtain the amount of suspended matter in air with value range from 0.3 to 10 microns. In order to read the sensor data, Arduino [2] is used. It is an electronics platform which can interact with many sensors for different purposes. Arduino is used as a single-board microcontroller programed by C or C++. One of the major limitations of the Arduino is that it is not easy to send and receive data from the Internet. Thus, Raspberry PI [3] is used to upload the data to the database.

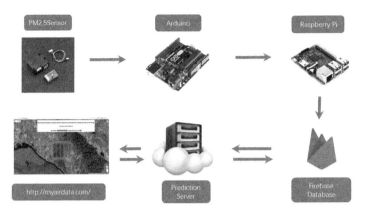

Fig. 3. The system architecture

In this project, Google Firebase is used as the database. It allows the users to upload the data from a device and get access of those data at any devices. Firebase's initial product was a real-time database, which allows developers to store and sync data across multiple clients [4].

Server here plays an important rule; it fits the data into the mathematical model and return the prediction result. The server is implemented using Python Flask [5].

In order to give out a more user-friendly experience, a web site is created to visualize the air quality data result as shown in Fig. 4. The website is based on google map. The color shown in the website represents the magnitude of pollution, red represents bad, and green represent good.

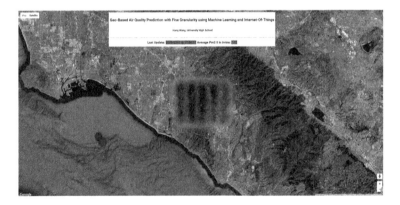

Fig. 4. The web user interface to visualize the air quality data for the city of Irvine, CA

3   Geo-Based Prediction of Air Quality

The core part of the system is to apply machine learning algorithms to predict the air quality for geo locations with fine granularity. The accuracy of the prediction model depends on the following factors:

Factor 1. The machine learning algorithm used to generate the model
Factor 2. The layout of input air quality data for known locations
Factor 3. The usage of special features (e.g. highways, population density).

Thus, to answer the question of what the best model is to predict the air quality data, a series of experiments are conducted to analyze the correlations between these factors and the accuracy.

For each experiment, we use a set of known data set as the input data, followed by running the machine learning algorithm to predict the unknown data set. Then, we compare the predicted data set values with the real actual data set, and calculate the error rate. The error rate will be based on the following formula:

$$E = (|Vexperimental - Vactual|)/((Vexperimental + Vactual)/2)$$

3.1   Experiment 1 - Machine Learning Algorithm Comparison

In this experiment, we chose 3 different common machine learning algorithms – linear regression [7], SVM [6] and polynomial interpolation [8], using the same set of air quality data we obtained from the application, we can calculate the accuracy (i.e., percentage error rate) of each machine learning algorithm.

Table 1. The input matrix with known air quality values (left) and the output matrix with air quality values being predicted (right) using linear regression

8	?	?	?	15
?	?	?	?	?
?	?	?	27	?
?	?	?	?	?
2	?	?	?	7

8	12	14.83	17.167	15
8.42	10.75	13.08	15.41	17.75
6.67	9.0	11.33	27	15.99
4.92	7.03	9.58	11.92	14.03
2	5.5	7.83	10.17	7

The Table 1 shown above is a sample experiment data used to evaluate the accuracy of linear regression. Using only 5 of the input data samples, we are able to predict the rest of the data cells using linear regression. By comparing the predicted data with the actual data values, it shows the percentage error to be: 36.53%. Using the same technique, the other two algorithms have been evaluated as shown in Fig. 5.

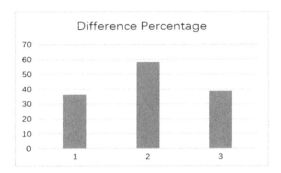

Fig. 5. Comparing the error rate of three different machine learning models

3.2   Experiment 2 - Input Data Layout Comparison

In this experiment, 4 different layouts of input air quality data are used as shown in Fig. 6. Using the best two mathematical model from Experiment 1, we can calculate the difference percentage of each layout.

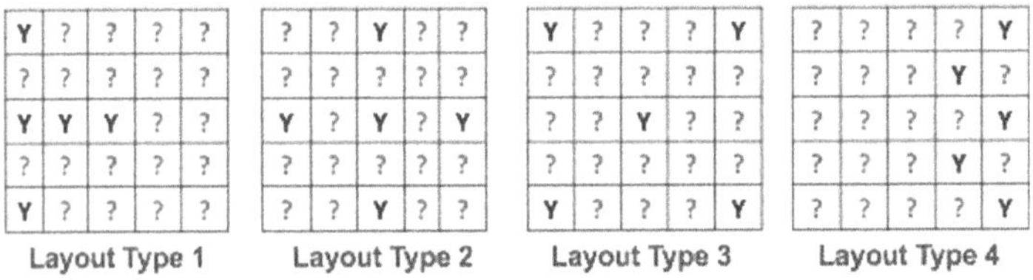

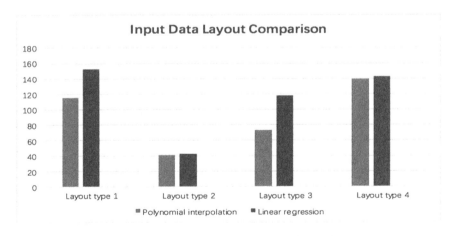

Fig. 6. Different data input layout used for the known data cells

It can be seen from Fig. 7 that the second type of layout with a balanced input data points works better than the others.

Fig. 7. Comparing the error rate of four different layouts

3.3   Experiment 3 – the Impact of Applying Special Features

As we analyze the real data set, it can be found that one factor that affects the air quality data is the highways and traffic, because the areas that are close to highways generally have slightly higher PM2.5 index than the areas without the highways. Therefore, in order to further improve the accuracy of the machine learning algorithm, we decided to add the area factor into the machine learning algorithm. Specifically, for each input data set, we also calculate the distance between the area and the highway, which will be added as the 3rd dimension to the data model. In this experiment, the locations of layouts of input air quality data are being concerned. Using the best two mathematical model from experiment 1, and best layout of air quality data from experiment 2, we can calculate the difference percentage of each model as shown in Fig. 8.

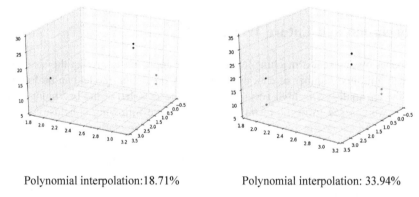

Polynomial interpolation:18.71%   Polynomial interpolation: 33.94%

Fig. 8. Comparing the error rate of applying the special feature or not

From the result in experiment 1, we can conclude that SVM is not an appropriate mathematical method for predicting air data, considering the fact that SVM is typically used to perform classification, rather than the value calculation. As the result shown in experiment 2, a series of comparison are made to get the most accurate layout for predicting air data, and we found that the second one is the most accurate. After two series of experiments, we found out that the percentage difference with actual air data is still very high. So for the third experiment, we think that environment of the predicting place is important, a geo-based perimeters are made and added into the prediction. As the result the third experiment, a mathematical mothed with percentage error of 18.71% was the best mothed that can be used for predicting air quality.

4   Related Works

There are quite a few initiatives by organizations and researchers to perform air quality related model construction and monitoring.

U-Air [11, 12] – "when urban air quality inference meets big data", uses the concept of big data to infer air quality information. They showed the usage of five sensors in Beijing and shanghai, which is a distance about 2 h by plane, and through the data they collected for both the historical and real-time to infer a real-time air quality information. However, we used a more efficient way which only takes the real-time data from the censors and other factors, through machine learning to get a very detailed air-quality data. In addition, building the cost-effective PM 2.5 sensor is another key contribution from our work.

The website waqi.info [13] displays air quality on a google map. The source of the data used by this website is unknown. However, the main limitation of this website is that the granularity of the data is not fine enough to cover most of the small cities and suburb areas. This is the main motivation for our work to predict and present the air quality data in those areas.

5 Conclusion and Future Work

In this paper, we present a machine-learning based approach to predict the air quality value with a limited number of data input points. A prediction model can be found to predict the air quality with high accuracy as hypothesis stated at the beginning of the paper. As we can see from the result shown above, the following conclusions about these different factors can be made: The polynomial interpolation model with concerning of locations and layout of contain both data at corners and center are the best model in the combinations made in the experiments. When comparing the model with the linear regression or SVM model, it turns out that the polynomial interpolation was the best model because the air quality prediction is not a simple linear problem. In addition, when the locations were being concerned, the difference percentage between prediction result and real values changed dramatically, this is because the resources of the pollution were related with these locations.

The experimental design can be improved in the model selecting. We believe that more optimized and similar mathematical model might be found to compare, particularly using deep learning, which will be one of the major works for the near future.

References

1. Kyrkilis, G., Chaloulakou, A., Kassomenos, P.A.: Development of an aggregate air quality index for an urban mediterranean agglomeration: relation to potential health effects. Environ. Int. **33**(5), 670–676 (2007)
2. Schmidt, M.: Arduino: Pragmatic bookshelf (2011)
3. Raspberry Pi 3 Model B (2017). https://www.raspberrypi.org/products/raspberry-pi-3-model-b/
4. Firebase (2017). https://en.wikipedia.org/wiki/Firebase
5. Python Flask (2017). http://flask.pocoo.org/
6. Furey, T., Cristianini, N., Duffy, N., Bednarski, D., Schummer, M., Haussler, D.: Support vector machine classification and validation of cancer tissue samples using microarray expression data. Bioinformatics 2000 **16**(10), 906–914 (2000)

7. Seber, G., Lee, A.: Linear Regression Analysis, vol. 936. Wiley, Hoboken (2012)
8. Michie, D.: Memo functions and machine learning. Nature **218**(5136), 19–22 (1968)
9. Xia, F., Yang, L., Wang, L., Vinel, A.: Internet of things. Int. J. Commun Syst **25**(9), 1101 (2012)
10. Goldberg, D., Holland, J.: Genetic algorithms and machine learning. Mach. Learn. **3**(2), 95–99 (1988)
11. Zheng, Y., Liu, F., Hsieh, H.: U-air: when urban air quality inference meets big data. In: Proceedings of the 19th ACM SIGKDD International Conference on Knowledge Discovery and Data Mining (2013)
12. Devarakonda, S., Sevusu, P., Liu, H., Liu, R., Iftode, L., Nath, B.: Real-time air quality monitoring through mobile sensing in metropolitan areas. In: Proceedings of the 2nd ACM SIGKDD International Workshop on Urban Computing, p. 15 (2013)
13. Air Pollution in the World Real-time Air Quality Index (AQI) (2017). http://waqi.info/

Research on Key Technology in Traditional Chinese Medicine (TCM) Smart Service System

Yongan Guo[1,2(✉)], Tong Liu[2], Xiaomin Guo[1], and Ye Yang[2]

[1] College of Telecommunications and Information Engineering,
Nanjing University of Posts and Telecommunications, Nanjing 210003, China
guo@njupt.edu.cn, 965810248@qq.com
[2] Jiangsu Key Lab of Wireless Communications,
Nanjing University of Posts and Telecommunications, Nanjing 210003, China
782808036@qq.com, 921629128@qq.com

Abstract. This paper studies the combination of information network technologies like Internet of Things (IoT) and big data with traditional Chinese medicine (TCM) to build a system framework oriented to TCM smart service. TCM-oriented knowledge representation technology is also explored so as to realize computer recognition and calculation of TCM health service, the self-learning reasoning technology of system is further studied, and TCM knowledge fuzzy model and modified BP neural network algorithm are introduced into TCM smart service system to conduct machine learning and smart judgment upon various diseases. These technologies will promote the scientific research and artificial intelligence aided diagnosis of TCM.

Keywords: Big data · Traditional Chinese medicine · Self learning
Knowledge representation · Fuzzy processing · System framework

1 Introduction

Due to the problems in TCM like secluded development, lack of innovation and brain drain, a great number of TCM theoretical essences, academic ideas and experience have failed to be promoted [1], hence making TCM walk on a path of rapid decline. Furthermore, the development of internet of things, big data and mobile internet has exerted a profound influence upon society, and also changed our ways of production, living and working, not only promoting the updating of various traditional sectors but also driving the innovative development of society.[1] It serves as a huge opportunity in TCM history of development as to how to utilize information network technology to combine TCM with big data [2] and further develop it.

[1] The work is supported by the national 973 project of China under Grants 2013CB329104, the Natural Science Foundation of China under Grants 61427801, the Natural Science Foundation of the Jiangsu Higher Education Institutions (Grant No. 13KJB520029), the Jiangsu Province colleges and universities graduate students scientific research and innovation program CXZZ13_0477, NUPTSF (Grant No. NY217033).

© ICST Institute for Computer Sciences, Social Informatics and Telecommunications Engineering 2018
X. Gu et al. (Eds.): MLICOM 2017, Part I, LNICST 226, pp. 300–314, 2018.
https://doi.org/10.1007/978-3-319-73564-1_30

The combination of information network technologies and TCM will bring revolutionary changes to the latter, and the development of TCM will step into a new era. It is expected to combine advanced technology like big data, internet of things and internet+ with TCM [3] so as to use a huge database to store previous wealth, integrating and categorizing rich data, timely collecting and processing new information to realize system self learning and reasoning functions, and achieving information transparency and resources sharing with internet [4]. By such a way, the problems like TCM informationization, networking and lack of intelligence will be solved.

Part two of this paper introduces related work on TCM's informationization and networking. Part three presents TCM smart service oriented system framework studies. Part four and five introduce TCM oriented knowledge representation and system reasoning model. The last part brings the summary and expectation.

2 Related Work

Many scholars have done a lot of related work on TCM's informationization, networking and datamation. In 2010, Chen developed a data digging method to study related TCM therapies of clinical cancer cases as well as herbal medicine dosage. It was proposed that scientific research methods of TCM were suitable not only for cancer but also for other diseases [5]. In 2010, Cui expounded that data digging should be regarded as a useful technology that can be applied into the discussion of TCM studies of treatment rules, and used to detect treatment principles through established network as well as relevance between herbal medicine and suitable technologies of TCM [6]. In 2012, Wen developed a development information management system able to satisfy TCM hospital function features when studying the building mode of TCM hospital informationized management system, hence laying data foundation for medical administrative management, medical insurance and TCM treatment based on symptoms. Up-to-date computer and network technology can be effectively utilized to build TCM hospital informationized management system with TCM characteristics to uplift modern management level of TCM hospitals [7]. In 2012, Zhou introduced the concept of fuzzy information granulation into TCM smart diagnosis system and developed a computer-aided smart diagnosis prototype with a combination of database technology. The system had self-learning function, with diagnostic precision of sexual precocity child diseases reaching 96% [8]. In 2016, Li used the collected big data pulse condition features and three-layer forward-type BP network in building TCM pulse condition recognition smart judgment model. Self-adapting learning speed method and momentum factor were introduced to optimize the enormous pulse condition connection weight and threshold; as a result, precise pulse condition recognition judgment results were obtained. Tests showed that using big data pulse conditions could improve the precision in TCM disease recognition judgment [9]. In 2016, Ma proposed a topic model to help capture the relation between symptom and disease, with the view to informationizing it with computer obtained medical knowledge to help doctors for symptom diagnosis [10].

This paper studies the key technology of TCM smart service system, in which the IoT-based four-layer system framework conducts informationized collection of observation, listening, inquiry and pulse feeling (four methods of diagnosis in TCM). This system stores TCM theoretical essences, academic ideas and previous experience into database. For convenience of computer recognition and calculation, TCM disease knowledge is to be expressed through informationization. This system is also equipped with self learning and reasoning ability, which can ensure constant information updating in it, helpful for machine learning, saving cost and improving efficiency, hence convenient for realizing resources sharing through internet. TCM, after combining solid model of western medicine, is no longer a traditional phenomenological model [11], thus solving the issue of TCM westernization.

3   TCM Smart Service Oriented System Framework

By referring to the four-layer system framework of internet of things [12], TCM smart service system framework includes four layers, namely smart perception layer, network transmission layer, information layer and application service layer. As shown in Fig. 1.

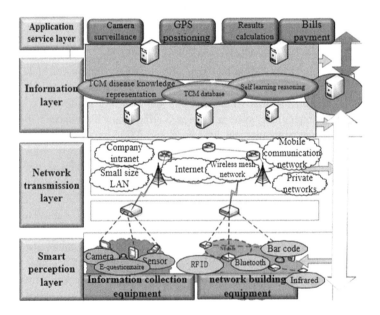

Fig. 1. Architecture of TCM intelligent diagnostic service system

3.1   Smart Perception Layer

Smart perception layer is the foundation of TCM smart service system. It is mainly consisted of information collection equipment and network building equipment. Through collecting relevant information about patient complexion, breath, symptom and pulse with information collection equipment, the four methods of diagnosis of "observation, listening, inquiry and pulse feeling" were realized. Then the collected information will be transmitted to network transmission layer with network building equipment. Information collection equipment recognizes human body and collects data through means like camera, e-questionnaire, and sensor; network building equipment constructs information collection equipment into network and then aggregates and transmits to the next layer with infrared, site bus, bar code, Bluetooth, RFID, etc. [13].

3.2 Network Transmission Layer

Network transmission layer is the "courier" in TCM smart service system for data transmission, conveying the data obtained at smart perception layer. The information can be transmitted through internet, company intranet, mobile communication network, small size LAN, various private networks and wireless mesh network. Data transmission layer works as a bridge by undertaking the data from the smart perception layer below and initiating the information layer above, and thus realizing the precise transmission of data.

3.3 Information Layer

Information layer is the "brain" of the whole TCM smart service system, a database containing enormous resources like TCM theoretical essences, academic ideas and previous experience and formulizing TCM disease knowledge representation. Self learning, self representation and self reasoning can be realized of the enormous data in the database through relevance, perceptibility and traceability. After going through network transmission layer, data will extract relevant information from the database at information layer for representation.

3.4 Application Service Layer

Application service layer is the "envoy" in TCM smart service system, which will realize intelligence and informationization according to patient needs. Application layer can realize the integration of basic data in TCM smart service system and feedback the results to patients. Application service layer provides interface for application interaction between humans and various devices. This layer is responsible for data integration and results feedback, including camera surveillance, GPS positioning, results calculation and bills payment. It serves as further incorporation of IoT and mobile internet technology into TCM smart service system [14].

4   TCM Oriented Knowledge Representation Technology

4.1   Observation for Diagnosis

Observation for diagnosis means using eyes to observe the surface conditions of patients, including complexion, normality of five sense organs, tongue and connection position of different parts. The visual sense involved therein is replaced by computer visual image processing.

Steps are as follows:

Step1: Store all images of face and tongue characterizing TCM diseases into information layer database of smart service system;

Step2: Use camera equipment to take pictures of patient face and tongue;

Step3: Transmit images to main network through short distance transmission technology like RFID, bar code, site bus, Bluetooth and infrared and further to database;

Step4: Process the images at application service layer, and output corresponding face and tongue features based on images with high similarity to patient images.

4.2   Listening for Diagnosis

Listening for diagnosis refers to using ears for diagnosis mainly for patient utterance, breath and coughing sound. According to Inner Canon of Yellow Emperor, the five internal organs of humans can produce five notes like nature [15–17]. Yu proposed a set of five notes frequency decomposition method based mathematical model suitable for any kind of periodic time domain sound signals, which could be used for five notes decomposition of human physiological signals, putting in place a new mathematical model for TCM diagnosis [18]. The five notes are the same as the "gong (do), shang (re), jue (mi), zhi (sol), yu (la)" in ancient times; their difference lies in the tones, which can be shown in a sine cosine function. That is to say, the sounds produced by human body can be decomposed into the expression formula containing five notes frequency components, through which human sounds can be expressed via mathematical formulas and transformed into the language that can be recognized by computer.

First of all, the basic rule of the five notes frequency is given [10–13]. Assuming that one "gong" sound is produced by an ideal object which can be seen as a particle, then the rule of its amplitude changing with time can be expressed with a sine function:

$$f_g(t) = asin(\omega t + \varphi) \tag{1}$$

If the translation can be increased on time, then it can also be expressed with a sine function:

$$f_g(t) = msin\omega t \tag{2}$$

According to the rules of Pythagorean intonation, the object can be divided into three sections. The sound generated by the remaining two sections after abandoning one is "zhi" [10–13]. Then the sound of "zhi" can be expressed as:

$$f_z(t) = msin\frac{3}{2}\omega t \tag{3}$$

The object producing the sound "zhi" is further divided into three parts with another one added, and then the sound will be "shang" [10–13]. Then the sound of "shang" can be expressed as:

$$f_s(t) = n\sin\frac{3}{2} * \frac{3}{4}\omega t \tag{4}$$

If the object producing the sound of "shang" is kept, then the sound produced will be "yu". Then the sound of "yu" can be expressed as:

$$f_y(t) = n\sin\frac{3}{2} * \frac{3}{4} * \frac{3}{2}\omega t \tag{5}$$

If the sound of "yu" is added, then the sound produced will be "jue" [19–21]. Then the sound of "jue" can be expressed as:

$$f_j(t) = n\sin\frac{3}{2} * \frac{3}{4} * \frac{3}{2} * \frac{3}{4}\omega t \tag{6}$$

On the basis of "gong", five notes of "gong, shang, jue, zhi, yu" can be obtained through two times of decrease and three times of increase.

Every kind of periodic sound can be seen as a function of particle amplitude. According to Fourier series expansion rules, this kind of sound is consisted of several sine waves with different frequency. The sine waves of several different frequencies are different five notes frequencies.

The frequency value of a series of five notes produced through the above five notes generation principles is the different powers of the basic frequency fraction as shown below:

$$g_{k1}(t) = m_k\sin\left(\frac{3}{2}\right)^k\left(\frac{3}{4}\right)^{k-1} \tag{7}$$

$$g_{k2}(t) = n_k\sin\left(\frac{3}{2}\right)^k\left(\frac{3}{4}\right)^k \omega t \tag{8}$$

Then based one above rules, the sounds obtained through listening for diagnosis can be expanded by a trigonometric function with a series of five notes frequency:

$$f(t) = \frac{m_0}{2} + m\sin\omega t + n\cos\omega t + \sum_{k=1}^{+\infty}[m_k\sin(\frac{3^{2k-1}}{2^{3k-2}})w_0 t + n_k\sin(\frac{3^{2k}}{2^{3k}})\omega t$$
$$+ p_k\cos(\frac{3^{2k-1}}{2^{3k-2}})\omega t + q_k\cos(\frac{3^{2k}}{2^{3k}})\omega t] \tag{9}$$

To obtain the coefficient of expansions, expand the series to k_0 term and obtain the coefficient for each term:

$$m_k = \frac{1}{\pi} \int_{-\pi}^{\pi} f(t) \sin\left(4 * 3^{2k-1}\right) x * dx$$
$$= \frac{1}{\pi} \int_{-\pi}^{\pi} f\left(\frac{x * 2^{3k_0}}{\omega}\right) \sin\left(4 * 3^{2k-1}\right) x * dx \tag{10}$$

Similarly, we can get

$$n_k = \frac{1}{\pi} \int_{-\pi}^{\pi} f\left(\frac{x * 2^{3k_0}}{\omega}\right) \sin\left(3^{2k}\right) x * dx \tag{11}$$

$$p_k = \frac{1}{\pi} \int_{-\pi}^{\pi} f\left(\frac{x * 2^{3k_0}}{\omega}\right) \cos\left(4 * 3^{2k-1}\right) x * dx \tag{12}$$

$$q_k = \frac{1}{\pi} \int_{-\pi}^{\pi} f\left(\frac{x * 2^{3k_0}}{\omega}\right) \cos\left(3^{2k}\right) x * dx \tag{13}$$

When the series is expanded to k_0 term, the value for the following calculation of the integral:

$$\int_{-\frac{\pi}{\omega}}^{\frac{\pi}{\omega}} f(t)dt = \int_{-\frac{\pi}{\omega}}^{\frac{\pi}{\omega}} \frac{m_0}{2} dt \tag{14}$$

Then:

$$m_0 = \frac{1}{\pi} \int_{-\pi}^{\pi} f\left(\frac{x}{\omega}\right) dx \tag{15}$$

In the same way, the value for the successive multiplication at both sides followed by integral:

$$m = \frac{1}{\pi} \int_{-\pi}^{\pi} f\left(\frac{x}{\omega}\right) sinxdx \tag{16}$$

$$n = \frac{1}{\pi} \int_{-\pi}^{\pi} f\left(\frac{x}{\omega}\right) cosxdx \tag{17}$$

Mathematical language is used to describe the rules of Pythagorean intonation, and formulas for any periodic time domain sound signals decomposed into several five notes frequency signal combinations are given. Through five notes decomposition method, human physiological signals can be analyzed and processed, providing an effective mathematical model conforming to TCM theory for TCM diagnostic equipment and further promoting its development. In this way, in TCM diagnosis diagnostic equipment can collect sounds and transform them into five notes frequency expansions, which are mathematical knowledge formulas recognizable by computers. Hence, the modernization and informationization of TCM knowledge representation can be realized, so as to keep up with the times and promote the development of smart diagnosis.

4.3 Inquiry for Diagnosis

Inquiry for diagnosis means inquiring about patient conditions carefully. TCM smart service system, apart from inquiring about patient conditions orally, can also adopt e-forms or machine language expression for inquiry. In this way, diagnostic equipment voice recognition function can be utilized to transmit keywords of patient conditions into database through network transmission network and use other diagnoses of application service layer to process informationized results, so as to obtain corresponding diagnostic results and treatment methods.

4.4 Pulse Feeling for Diagnosis

Pulse feeling for diagnosis means feeling and examining the pulse. According to the state of pulse condition, it can be divided into eight types, namely surface pulse–floating; internal pulse–sinking, solid and hidden; cold pulse–delay, slow, solid and intense; hot pulse–frequent, moving, rapid and hurried; feeble pulse–feeble, weak, slight, scattered, short; solid pulse–solid, long, slippery; qi pulse–flooding, moist; blood pulse–tiny, elastic, unsmooth, hollow [22].

Pulse feeling for diagnosis is very important in TCM. Factors like human respiration, mental state and disease can all affect the results, so there are many variations for human pulse signals, because using singular spectrogram cannot conduct complete representation for common features of one pulse condition is determined by various spectrograms. Hence, Lei Li chose 8 feature parameters out of three major spectrogram features (power spectrum, cepstrum and transfer function spectrum) as the basis for TCM pulse condition recognition and judgment. Feature parameters included (1) power spectrum fundamental frequency, basic frequency of pulse beating; (2) cepstrum feature RC that can describe the type of pulse cepstrum wave; (3) cepstrum null component that can describe the strength of pulse beat; (4) spectrum energy ratio that can describe the relation between pulse energy and frequency; (5) ratio between cepstrum wave amplitude and cepstrum null component that can describe the smoothness of pulse beat; (6) average distance of formant that can describe the average distance of formant in transfer function; (7) number of formant in transfer function that can describe the features of formant in human pulse conditions; and (8) harmonic wave number in power spectrum that can describe human pulse beat rhythm [24].

5 System Self Learning and Reasoning Model Technology

After completing TCM knowledge representation, TCM self-learning reasoning model is also needed to realize TCM smart service system.

System self learning reasoning model is based on the database containing enormous TCM theoretical essences, academic ideas and previous experience. This model can imitate professional TCM judgment processes and conduct self learning and reasoning based on TCM knowledge and experience to aid human expert judgment to ultimately reach the effect of smart diagnosis. This model regards physiological indexes of patient as input parameters, mobilizes knowledge in database and utilizes reasoning mechanism for diagnosis (Fig. 2).

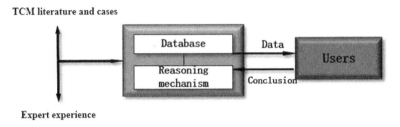

Fig. 2. Self learning and reasoning model

Self-learning and reasoning model of TCM system contains two parts, namely TCM knowledge fuzzy model and modified BP neural network algorithm.

BP neural network adopts self-adapting learning process of external environment, approximates to non-linear relationship with high precision, so it can be used for non-linear system [23]. However, due to the large influence of feature parameters upon neural network layer to be input, the modeling output effect of BP neural network will be affected if feature parameters are fuzzy without extracting fuzzy information therein, so the difference to expectation will be large and precision be affected [23]. Therefore, fuzzy processing has to be conducted of input layer of BP neural network in advance.

5.1   TCM Knowledge Fuzzy Model

(1) Fuzzy Membership Function

Assuming that there is one fuzzy set on the area to be discussed, there is one correct pair of membership for any element there. The mapping relationship is:

$$\mu_A : U \rightarrow [0, 1] \tag{18}$$

$$u \rightarrow \mu_A(u) \tag{19}$$

This mapping is the membership function of the fuzzy set. The evaluation scope is $[0, 1]$, and it shows the membership degree of elements [24]. Larger evaluation of membership indicates that this element has a higher affiliation degree to current fuzzy set.

In this way, TCM knowledge fuzzy set can be characterized by membership function, which can be determined according to the type of TCM diagnosis. For example, before the 8 feature parameters of the above pulse conditions are input in BP neural network, fuzzy processing is needed. Function can be resorted to in obtaining the membership degree of each node.

(2) **Fuzzy Rules**

There are many fuzzy concepts in the expression of TCM knowledge. Fuzzy rules can help understand the fuzzy meaning of TCM knowledge. Rules are effective tools for quantitative modeling of word or sentence in natural or artificial language, in which reasoning based on rules can be used to draw conclusion from one set of fuzzy rule and known facts. There are two parts for fuzzy rules, namely IF, precondition for fuzzy rules, and THEN, conclusion for fuzzy rules [23]. Commonly seen rules have two forms, namely Mamdani fuzzy rules and T-S fuzzy rules [25]. Among them, T-S fuzzy rules are those applied for non-linear system recognition. Given that big data based TCM smart diagnostic service in most cases is non-linear system, T-S fuzzy rules are adopted in our system. The general form of T-S fuzzy rules is:

$$R^j : IF x_1 \text{ is } A_1^j \text{ and } x_2 \text{ is } A_2^j \ldots x_m \text{ is } A_m^j. \tag{20}$$

Then

$$y = c_0^j + c_1^j x_1 + \ldots c_m^j x_m \, j = 1, 2 \ldots r \tag{21}$$

Where, R^j is item of fuzzy rule, and x_m is input and output variables of fuzzy system, A_i^j is output subset of item of ith rule, r is total number of rules, and c_m^j is coefficient of input variables.

It can be seen that one experience of TCM can be seen as a fuzzy rule. That is, when the priori condition of experience is satisfied, it will output in the form of non-linear combination. After the database stores TCM theoretical essences, academic ideas and previous experience, it possesses fuzzy rules for TCM disease reasoning.

5.2 Modified BP Neural Network Algorithm

BP neural network algorithm is one kind of multi-layer feed-forward neural network algorithm, composed of forward propagation and back propagation. Forward propagation is the weight and function calculation from signal input at input layer to hidden layer to be output through output layer. Back propagation is the feedback output error signals with forward propagation to network. Through BP algorithm and based on error signal, when error signal becomes smaller, weight and threshold at each node have to be modified. This solves the problem of difficulty in training inside multi-layer forward and back networks, which can facilitate further expansion of neural network.

BP neural network includes input layer, hidden layer and output layer. Interlayer connection between neurons at each layer is there, but no connection inside layers. The diagram is as shown below (Fig. 3):

Input Layer.   Hidden Layer.   Output Layer.

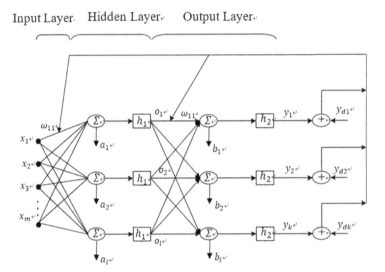

Fig. 3. The three-layer BP network structure diagram

Input vector of input layer is $X = (x_1, x_2, \ldots, x_m)^T$, output vector of hidden layer is $O = (o_1, o_2, \ldots, o_l)^T$, actual output vector of output layer is $Y = (y_1, y_2, \ldots, y_k)^T$, expected output is $Y_d = (y_{d1}, y_{d2}, \ldots, y_{dk})^T$.

$\omega_{ij}$is the connection weight of nodes in mode, ω_{ik} is the connection weight between nodes at different layers in model, a and b are the threshold of nodes between hidden layer and output layer.

Hidden layer:

$$o_j = h(z_j) \tag{22}$$

$$z_j = \sum\nolimits_{i=1}^{m} \omega_{ij} x_i - a_j \tag{23}$$

Output layer:

$$y_k = h(z_k) \tag{24}$$

$$z_k = \sum\nolimits_{j=1}^{i} \omega_{jk} o_j - b_k \qquad k = 1, 2, \ldots, m \tag{25}$$

Where, h is excitation function. The error between actual output and expected output should be kept low, so as to ensure high precision for BP neural network. Error is described through error of mean square:

$$E = E[(y_d - y)^T (y_d - y)] \tag{26}$$

Weight and threshold of each node are adjusted through the steepest descent algorithm. Then the $K+1$ iteration

$$\omega_{jk}(k+1) = \omega_{jk}(k) - \eta \frac{\partial E_k}{\partial \omega_{jk}} \tag{27}$$

$$b_k(k+1) = b_k(k) - \eta \frac{\partial E_k}{b_k} \tag{28}$$

Obtain partial derivative to get output layer results:

$$\omega_{jk}(k+1) = \omega_{jk}(k) + \eta \delta_k o_j \tag{29}$$

$$b_k(k+1) = b_k(k) + \eta \delta_k \tag{30}$$

In the same way, obtain the hidden layer output results:

$$\omega_{ij}(k+1) = \omega_{ij}(k) + \eta \delta_j x_i \tag{31}$$

$$a_j(k+1) = a_j(k) + \eta \delta_j \tag{32}$$

Where, δ_k is inverse transmission error of output layer:

$$\delta_k = (y_{dk} - y_{dk})h'(z_k) \tag{33}$$

δ_j Is inverse transmission error of hidden layer:

$$\delta_j = h'(z_k) \sum_{k=1}^{l} \delta_k \omega_{jk} \tag{34}$$

Although BP neural network enjoys sound precision in seeking optimal solution, we still find out that it also has long convergence time, and the optimal solution obtained is most likely to be the local optimal solution instead of global optimal solution [26]. Therefore, the above BP neural network has to be modified. Hereby the concepts of momentum factor and learning rate are introduced.

The momentum factor γ is introduced when modifying the weight of nodes from input layer to hidden layer.

$$\Delta\omega_{ij}(k+1) = (1-\gamma)\alpha\delta_j x_i + \gamma\Delta\omega_{ij}(k) \tag{35}$$

$$\Delta a_j(k+1) = (1-\gamma)\alpha\delta_j + \gamma\Delta a_j(k) \tag{36}$$

Where, ω_{ij} is connection weight between nodes, γ is momentum factor, α is self adapting learning rate, x_j is error signal, x_j is the input quantity at node, a_i is threshold detected at node.

In the same way, the modification of weight and threshold from hidden layer to output layer is completed.

The following formula can be used to self-adaptingly regulate learning rate:

$$\alpha(k+1) = \begin{cases} 1.05\alpha(k) & E(K+1) < E(k) \\ 0.7\alpha(k) & E(K+1) > 1.04E(k) \\ \alpha(k) & others \end{cases} \qquad (37)$$

To establish formula (35), the following restrictions have to be satisfied.

$$\gamma = \begin{cases} 0.95 & E(k) < E(k-1) \\ 0 & E(k) > 1.04E(k-1) \\ \gamma & others \end{cases} \qquad (38)$$

5.3 Observation for Diagnosis

Neural network processing information scope and ability are expanded through introducing TCM knowledge fuzzy reasoning model into modified BP neural network algorithm. Therefore, the combination of TCM knowledge fuzzy reasoning model and modified BP neural network algorithm constitutes the self learning and reasoning model for TCM smart diagnostic service system.

This model firstly builds T-S fuzzy rules based on TCM theoretical essences, academic ideas and previous experience through conducting fuzzy processing of initial variables to be input to obtain input layer variable and then using modified BP neural network algorithm to establish the neural network between input and output variables. Then it obtains the weight and threshold of each node in network through self learning function of network and ultimately builds self learning and reasoning model. The structure diagram of self learning reasoning model is shown as follows (Fig. 4):

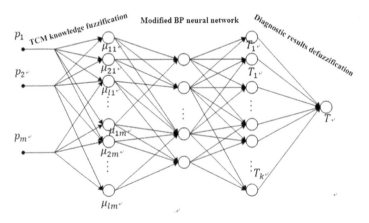

Fig. 4. Self learning and reasoning structure diagram

6   Conclusion

This paper discusses the key technology of TCM smart service system, in which advanced technologies like internet of things, big data and mobile internet are combined with TCM, conducting informationized collection by machine from observation, listening, inquiry and pulse feeling, and storing TCM theoretical essences, academic ideas and previous experience into database. This system can build self learning reasoning model through TCM knowledge fuzzy model and modified BP neural network algorithm, so as to enable it to update information in database and keep up with the times. The updated database resources and informationized expression of TCM knowledge will facilitate machine learning and diagnosis of various diseases. The buildup of TCM database will also provide a shortcut for realizing resources sharing through internet, hence saving cost and improving efficiency. With these technologies, medical equipment can realize more comprehensive, thorough and deeper smart judgment, further promoting development of TCM and providing higher service quality for patients. The informationization, intelligence and networking of the system can solve the problems like TCM westernization and lack of innovation through machine with the philosophy of "high efficiency and supreme quality." These technologies will no doubt realize lasting prosperity and booming development.

Acknowledgement. The work is supported by the Natural Science Foundation of China under Grants 61372124, 61427801, the Natural Science Foundation of the Jiangsu Higher Education Institutions (Grant No. 13KJB520029), the Jiangsu Province colleges and universities graduate students scientific research and innovation program CXZZ13_0477, NUPTSF (Grant No. NY217033).

References

1. Tang, Q., He, Q.: Study on the current situation and modernization of traditional Chinese medicine. Chin. J. Tradit. Chin. Med. **11**(11), 2728–2730 (2011)
2. Tu, S.: Construction and research on bibliographic database of traditional Chinese Medicine. Anhui University of Traditional Chinese Medicine (2015)
3. Dong, Z., Xiang, H., He, W.: Remote diagnosis in traditional Chinese medicine using wireless sensor networks. In: 2010 Third International Symposium on Information Processing, Qingdao, pp. 255–257 (2010)
4. Dai, Y., et al.: The research for digitalization of four great classical literatures of traditional Chinese medicine knowledge for clinic use. In: 2013 IEEE International Conference on Bioinformatics and Biomedicine, Shanghai, p. 26. IEEE Press, New York (2013)
5. Tang, B., Chen, S.S.: A weighted structural model clustering approach for identifying and analyzing core genetic regulatory modules. In: 2010 IEEE International Conference on Bioinformatics and Biomedicine Workshops (BIBMW), Hong Kong, pp. 213–216. IEEE Press, New York (2010)
6. Cui, Z., He, D., Zheng, G., Jiang, M., Wang, Y.: To discover the traditional Chinese medicine techniques applied in diabetes mellitus through data mining. In: 9th International Conference on Computer Science & Education, Vancouver, BC, pp. 672–676 (2014)

7. Wen, H., Wang, Z.: Construction and research on information management system of TCM hospital. Comput. CD - ROM Softw. Appl. **22**(22), 42–43 (2012)
8. Zou, Y., Li, Z., Zhu, X., Yu, J., Gu, Z.: Research on the computer-assisted intelligent diagnosis system of traditional Chinese medicine. In: 9th International Conference on Fuzzy Systems and Knowledge Discovery, pp. 329–333, Sichuan (2012)
9. Li, L.: Traditional Chinese medicine pulse condition recognition intelligent judgment based on large data analysis. Sci. Technol. Bull. **32**(08), 41–45 (2016)
10. Ma, J., Zhang, Y.: Using topic model for intelligent computer-aided diagnosis in traditional Chinese medicine. In: 2016 International Conference on Intelligent Networking and Collaborative Systems (INCoS), pp. 504–507, Ostrawva (2016)
11. Zhang, Z.: Analysis on the methodology of slow development of modern traditional Chinese medicine. A Study Dialectics Nat. **3**(03), 62–66 (2003)
12. Valera, A.J.J., Zamora, M.A., Skarmeta, A.F.G.: An architecture based on internet of things to support mobility and security in medical environments. In: 7th IEEE Consumer Communications and Networking Conference, Las Vegas, NV, pp. 1–5. IEEE Press, New York (2010)
13. Hu, X.: Construction of wisdom medical system architecture model under the framework of internet of things - taking Wuhan wisdom medical as an example. E-government **12**(12), 24–31 (2013)
14. Zheng, G.: The intelligent medical system architecture based on internet of things and its application. Shanxi Electron. Technol. **5**(05), 66–68 (2016)
15. Liang, D., Shi, S., He, J.: A study on the relationship between the theory of "Wu Di Nei Jing" and the age of Women **1**(1), 10–12 (2006)
16. Huang, L.: Historical data analysis of music therapy in Huang Di Nei Jing. Northeast Normal University, Changchun (2010)
17. Yang, J.: Into the world of strings to talk about the past three thousand years of human research on the strings and the thinking. Chin. Nat. Mag. **26**(3), 117–118 (2001)
18. Yu, F., Jin, L.: Developing a new mathematical model for TCM diagnostic equipment: five-tone decomposition. Chin. J. Tradit. Chin. Med. **26**(09), 3799–3802 (2016)
19. Ding, J.: A brief discussion on the harmony of the phonology of the Guqin and the twelve law. Music Stud. **1**(1), 60–69 (1991)
20. Huang, X.: Research on Chinese traditional music. People's Music Publishing House, Beijing (1993)
21. Li, C.: The exploration of the sorcerer and the churches. Archaeology. **20**(1), 56–60 (1974)
22. Zhao, C.: Pulse diagnosis, tongue diagnosis and treatment of the establishment of a database system. University of Traditional Chinese Medicine, Beijing (2008)
23. Zhao, L.: Based on the fuzzy model of expert system reasoning method. Zhejiang University (2013)
24. Klir, G.J., Yuan, B.: Fuzzy sets and fuzzy logic: theory and applications. Possibility Theory versus Probab. Theory. **32**(2) (1996)
25. Wang, L.X.: Fuzzy systems are universal approximators. In: IEEE International Conference on Fuzzy Systems, San Diego, CA, vol. 7, pp. 1163–1170. IEEE Press, New York (1992)
26. Heermann, P.D., Khazenie, N.: Classification of multispectral remote sensing data using a back- propagation neural network. In: IEEE Transactions on Geoscience and Remote Senseng, vol. 30(1), pp. 81–88. IEEE Press, New York (1992)

Application of Wireless Sensor Network in Smart Buildings

Mingze Xia[1]([✉]) and Dongyu Song[2]

[1] Heilongjiang University (HLJU), Harbin, China
hlju_xia@yeah.net
[2] Harbin Institute of Technology (HIT), Harbin, China
songdy.381@qq.com

Abstract. The development of technology in large strides has enabled wireless sensor network to extensively supersede traditional wired sensor network (WSN), which is accompanied with its application to every aspect of life and production. In terms of smart buildings, presently the mainstream direction in the research is combining wireless sensor network with IOT technology and internet technology, etc. In this paper, based on ZigBee wireless sensor network (WSN) combined with Java, Android, etc., developed to monitor building real-time environmental data of intelligent building system, and can achieve the combination of automatic and manual household appliance control platform.

Keywords: WSN · Smart buildings · ZigBee technology · Java Web
MySQL · Android

1 Introduction

So-called smart buildings [1] are product of combining traditional architectural technology with internet technology and communication technology, etc. Mainly oriented towards office buildings, schools, hospitals, traffic, residences, shopping malls, etc., which are outfitted with smart and automatic functions to make our life, work, study and entertainment more comfortable and sustainable.

Wireless sensor network (WSN), a distributed sensing network, is the result of combining sensor with wireless communication technology. Its features of small volume, low power dissipation and a strong ad hoc network capacity, etc. have made it gradually replace traditional wired sensor network and become the mainstream direction for present scientific research and development for use. The sensors are widely or even randomly dispersed over monitored area, and the information collected by sensor is transferred via ad hoc and multiple hop wireless communication modules with low power dissipation to upper computer for related processing. The today's wireless communication technology is extensively applied to military, agricultural, traffic, and medical domains [2], etc. People's demands in everyday life dramatically boosted upgrading of traditional sensors, with multimedia sensor emerging as the times require in such domains as medical treatment and traffic, etc. The collected information is no

© ICST Institute for Computer Sciences, Social Informatics and Telecommunications Engineering 2018
X. Gu et al. (Eds.): MLICOM 2017, Part I, LNICST 226, pp. 315–325, 2018.
https://doi.org/10.1007/978-3-319-73564-1_31

longer traditional temperature and humidity, etc. but is multimedia information such as audios, videos and pictures, etc. Combination of wireless communication modules (GPRS, Bluetooth, ZigBee, etc.) with sensors substituted traditional wired sensor network to save substantive resources. With advantages of high scalability, ad hoc property, low power dissipation, high integration, etc., wireless sensor network is fully applied in monitored regions with sparse population and complicated geologic environment [3].

2 Introduction of ZigBee Technology

ZigBee technology is a LAN wireless communication technology with low power dissipation, low latency, a strong ad hoc network capacity and quick reaction rate. Its communication protocol is based on 802.15.4 standard, and network topological architecture is mainly divided into three types: star topology, tree topology and mesh topology, wherein the star topology consumes the least energy. In ZigBee technology, the primary routing protocol algorithms are Cluster - Tree, AODVjr, and Cluster - Tree + AODVjr. Many scholars improved the three routing protocols to create many new and more efficient routing protocols, which will not be described in details here. The ZigBee network mainly comprises three parts: co-ordinator, router and end device, which are selected according to network topology styles. For example, the star network structure needs no router. The co-ordinator must be a global functional device, while end device allows two-way selection and can be both a global functional device and a device with simplified functions. Compared with Bluetooth and WIFI, notwithstanding relatively shorter transmission distance, this leads to lower dissipation of energy for ZigBee network. Besides, in terms of quantity of network connections, ZigBee network support more than 65,000 nodes [4–7].

3 Application of ZigBee Technology in Smart Building System

The smart building system based on ZigBee technology can realize automation and intellectualization of buildings by dint of low power dissipation, low cost and high integration of ZigBee. Terminal node is integration of sensor and ZigBee module to transfer the collected data to coordinator node which integrates data and submit it to upper computer. In the meanwhile the coordinator node issues the device operation directive of upper computer to control nodes to finish control of home appliances. The general frame is as shown in Fig. 1:

3.1 Acquisition of Sensor Data

The acquisition process of sensor data in intelligent building system is to transfer data collected by sensors to coordinator nodes through ZigBee module for summarization

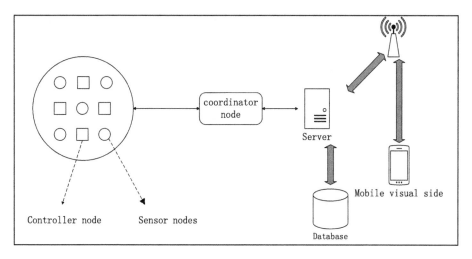

Fig. 1. General frame

and processing. The coordinator sends the processed data through the serial port, WIFI, GPRS and other networks to the designated ports on the server and monitor the start of server of this port starts. The data packets are processed and stored in the database by a communication protocol in advance. Its architecture is mainly divided into 3 parts.

(1) Information acquisition and transmission layer: By using ZigBee network, various environment data information sensors are formed into an information acquisition and transmission network. The sensors are distributed at specific detection points in the monitoring area. The ZigBee module transfers the collected data to the coordinator node.

(2) Information summarization and upload layer: The ZigBee coordinator sends the data uploaded by the lower computer to the ARM chip so that the data can be summarized and processed according to specific network protocols. Finally, it is uploaded to the designated server IP via the serial port, WIFI or GPRS (depending on the environment).

(3) Information analysis and processing layer: The data uploaded by the lower computer is parsed by monitoring the service of designated port server. The analysis is based on the network protocol corresponding to the information summarization and upload layer. The parsed data stream is then stored in the database for the use of the server and visual end.

3.2   Communication Protocol

Communication protocol refers to rule and regulations that both parties must comply with in order to complete communication or service. The protocol defined the format used by data unit, information and meaning that information unit should include, connection mode, sequence of information transmitting and receiving so as to ensure data in the network to be transmitted to a certain place smoothly.

Network protocol in this paper includes message header, data layer and message ending. Message header mainly includes lead code, data length, equipment tag, message type, etc. and represents the beginning of a piece of message. Message ending includes weighted sum verification and ending symbol.

The function of data layer is to cover the type of sensing data of a piece of message and data value so as to form a data package. On the server, it is analyzed into different data flows and saved to different lists in database. Specific network protocol is shown in the Fig. 2:

Lead code	Data length	Device identification	Message type	Data type 1	Data value	......	Checkout	Ending

◄─────────────────Headers──────────────► ◄──────Data acquisition──────► ◄──message ending──►

Fig. 2. Specific network protocol

3.3 Hardware Design

The smart building system based on wireless sensor network adopts ZigBee module on wireless collection transmission terminal. ZigBee chip is CC2530, which supports global free wave band of 2.4 GHz. The network type is star network and mesh network, with the largest network capacity being 65, 535 nodes, transmission range being 800 m and emissive power being 4.5 dbm. The core controller of coordinator adopts STM32F103RBT6 chip, which is a 32-bit microcontroller launched by STMicroelectronics NV, with 64 pins. It has a Flash capacity of 128 k bytes, working temperature of −40 °C–85 °C and is packaged by way of LQFP.

In agricultural detection system based on ZigBee, the simple hardware circuit diagram for coordinator node is as shown in Fig. 3.

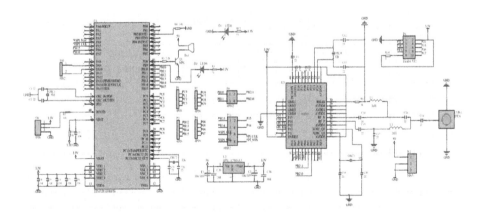

Fig. 3. Coordinator node

The simple hardware circuit diagram for sensor node is as shown in Fig. 4.

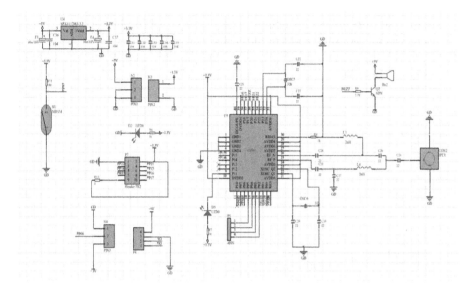

Fig. 4. Sensor node

3.4 Software Design

Software end mainly comprises three aspects: processing and storage of collected data, server of visual terminal, and visual terminal (Android mobile).

Processing and storage of collected data adopt C++ language and MySQL database, with primary functions as follows: hardware unit transfers via network the collected date to daemon written with C++ for resolving using communication protocol commonly defined with hardware unit to get the desired data. The data is not only collected environmental data, but also includes IP address of data source i.e. collection terminal. Lastly the information is stored in MySQL database.

In data processing course, the daemon process filters and screens the data. Data size received by the daemon process is huge, but data error may appear owing to limitation of hardware equipment, network time delay, network capacity, network throughput capacity. The daemon process calculated calculates all data of one type of sensor and gets the average value of sensing data at one time node. When there is great difference between data uploaded by the sensor and average value, the daemon process will abandon such item of data and insert the average value to database. Moreover, the daemon process also makes comparison according to the preset sensing range of sensor in database so as to screen the wrong data.

Visual server is developed using lightweight Java-Web, with three major functions:

(1) Real-time data, history data and equipment status value are issued to visual terminal.
(2) Collect and store the information fed back by the visual terminal. Related control operations for the equipment are finished via the feedback.
(3) Combine real-time data and fixing algorithm (threshold algorithm, etc.) to finish control of equipment.

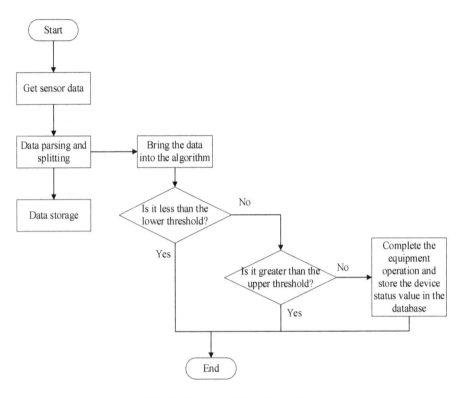

Fig. 5. Data acquisition flow chart

Wherein the priority for (2) and (3) is (3) is higher than (2), i.e. the server terminal makes algorithm evaluation and controls the equipment with priority, then modifies the equipment state via the operational data fed back by visual terminal. The flowchart is as shown in Figs. 5 and 6:

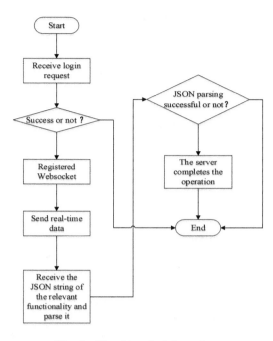

Fig. 6. Visual terminal flow chart

The database mainly comprise five tables: i.e. collector table, collection area table, environmental data table, user information table and equipment state table, etc. Wherein the collector table (collector) stores relevant information of collector, including: ID, IP address, heartbeat frequency, equipment mac address, etc. Table definitions are as shown in Table 1 below:

Table 1. Collector table (collector)

Field name	Data type	Whether is master key	Whether is external key	Description
collectorId	Int	Yes	No	Collector ID
rate	Int	No	No	Heartbeat frequency
last	Datatime	No	No	The last uploading time
mac	Varchar(32)	No	No	Mac address of equipment
binding	Int	No	No	Binding state
areaId	Int	No	No	ID for bound collection area
areaName	Varchar(50)	No	No	Name of bound collection area

Collection area table, also called office area table (area), mainly stores: area ID, area name, area address, area description, ID of bound user, etc. The Table definitions are as shown in Table 2 below:

Table 2. Office area table (area)

Field name	Data type	Whether is master key	Whether is external key	Description
areaId	Int	Yes	No	ID of collection area
areaName	Varchar(50)	No	No	Name of collection area
address	Varchar(12)	No	No	Address of collection area
setTime	Datetime	No	No	Time of creating
userId	Int	No	No	ID of bound user
userName	Varchar(50)	No	No	Name of bound user
unit	Float	No	No	Area

The environmental data table (data) mainly stores relevant information of sensor and collected data, etc., mainly comprising: data ID, collector ID, sensor type, sensor value, time of uploading sensed amount, upper and lower limits of sensed amount, etc. The table definitions are as shown in Table 3 below:

Table 3. Environmental data table (data)

Field name	Data type	Whether is master key	Whether is external key	Description
Id	Int	Yes	No	Data ID
collectorId	Int	No	No	Collector ID
sType	Int	No	No	Sensor type
sValue	Varchar(2)	No	No	Sensor value
Date	Datetime	No	No	Time of uploading sensed amount
rMax	Decimal(8, 2)	No	No	Maxima of measuring range
rMin	Decimal(8, 2)	No	No	Minima of measuring range

User information table (user) mainly comprises all personal information of users, through which, collector can be bound. For example, the user in office block on the second floor is bound with relate sensor and home appliances of the second floor, so he cannot control the equipment on the third floor. The table definitions are as shown in Table 4 below:

Table 4. User information table (user)

Field name	Data type	Whether is master key	Whether is external key	Description
userId	Int	Yes	No	User ID
userName	Varchar(50)	No	No	User name
type	Int	No	No	User type
pwd	Varchar(32)	No	No	User code
realName	Varchar(50)	No	No	Real name
tele	Varchar(12)	No	No	Tel.
email	Varchar(30)	No	No	Email
userAddress	Varchar(20)	No	No	Address

Equipment table is similar to collector table, mainly storing: equipment ID, equipment name, current state of equipment (0, 1), ID of bound office area, etc. The table definition is as shown in Table 5 below:

Table 5. Equipment table (equipment)

Field name	Data type	Whether is master key	Whether is external key	Description
equipmentId	Int	Yes	No	ID of home appliance
rate	Int	No	No	Heartbeat frequency
last	Datatime	No	No	The last uploading time
mac	Varchar(32)	No	No	Mac address of equipment
state	Int	No	No	Current state value
areaId	Int	No	No	ID for bound collection area
areaName	Varchar(50)	No	No	Name of bound collection area

The visual terminal is App software developed based on Android OS, which runs on mobile and tablet computer, with major functions of: checking real-time data; checking history data; checking equipment status and control equipment. The user cannot only check real-time data of current sensor on the visual terminal, but also can obtain history data via history data interface, and get the current state of home appliances, thereby making secondary regulation according to actual condition.

3.5 Test of Smart Building System

Test showed that the fundamental functions of wireless smart building system based on ZigBee can be realized. Test of networking and communication succeeded, environmental data was successfully inserted into database, the database data is shown in

Fig. 7. The visual terminal displays normally. The issuing time of data is averagely 2 s. The time interval between issuing of control directive and finishing of actual control operation is averagely 3 s, indicating functions of wireless smart building system are basically enabled.

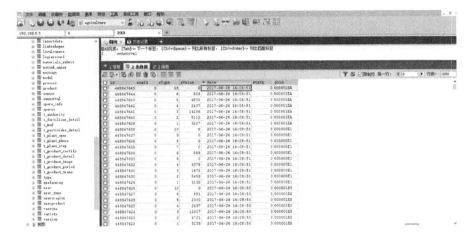

Fig. 7. Database data

4   Conclusion

The increasingly higher economic level is coupled with increasing of people's demands for life quality. The rise of IOT and development of e-technology provide a better foundation for smart home and smart buildings, etc. via use of sensors, server and other electronic devices clustered in a large scale, the smart buildings provide convenience for people in entertainment and work, etc. The paper introduces a wireless smart building system which combines ZigBee wireless networks and mobile development technology and is applicable to office environment. Next, the author will continue to research networking communication of wireless sensor network, data transfer, and practical application and expanding, etc. to underpin technically the smart building domains such as building automation and office automation in a better way.

References

1. Minoli, D., Sohraby, K., Occhiogrosso, B.: IoT considerations, requirements, and architectures for smart buildings-energy optimization and next-generation building management systems. IEEE Internet Things J. **4**, 269–283 (2017). IEEE Press
2. Zhang, Z., Hu, X.: ZigBee based wireless sensor networks and their use in medical and health care domain. In: Seventh International Conference on Sensing Technology (ICST), pp. 756–761. IEEE Press, Wellington (2013)

3. Tan, X., Sun, Z., Akyildiz, I.F.: Wireless underground sensor networks: MI-based communication systems for underground applications. IEEE Antennas Propag. Mag. **57**, 74–87 (2015). IEEE Press, New York

4. Xiaoman, L., Xia, L.: Design of a ZigBee wireless sensor network node for aquaculture monitoring. In: 2nd IEEE International Conference in Computer and Communications (ICCC), pp. 2179–2182. IEEE Press, Ghaziabad (2016)

5. Chi, H.R., Tsang, K.F., Wu, C.K.: ZigBee based wireless sensor network in smart metering. In: 42nd Annual Conference of the IEEE Industrial Electronics Society, pp. 5663–5666. IEEE Press, Florence (2016)

6. Naruephiphat, W., Promya, R., Niruntasukrat, A.: Remote air conditioning control system base on ZigBee wireless sensor network for building. In: 2015 International Computer Science and Engineering Conference (ICSEC), pp. 1–6. IEEE Press, Chiang Mai (2015)

7. Islam, T., Rahman, H.A., Syrus, M.A.: Fire detection system with indoor localization using ZigBee based wireless sensor network. In: 2015 International Conference on Informatics, Electronics & Vision (ICIEV), pp. 1–6. IEEE Press, Fukuoka (2015)

Distributed System Model Using SysML and Event-B

Qi Zhang[(⊠)], Zhiqiu Huang, and Jian Xie

Nanjing University of Aeronautics and Astronautics,
Nanjing, People's Republic of China
zhang1993@nuaa.edu.com,
{zqhuang,xiejian_5}@nuaa.edu.cn

Abstract. Distributed system is more complicated compared with other systems due to its concurrency and distribution. Moreover, the traditional system development process is usually informal, and a large number of tests are required. On the other hand, the formal methods have been applied in many system development fields and many achievements have been made. In this paper, a method which combines SysML requirement diagrams and Event-B to model distributed system is proposed, including their mapping relations.

Keywords: Distributed system · SysML · Event-B · Requirement diagram

1 Introduction

Compared with the traditional centralized system, the distributed system is more complicated due to its concurrency and distribution. Though the distributed system has developed rapidly with kinds of specifications and standards in recent years, there still exists some shortcomings. Because these specifications and standards usually lack solid theoretical foundation, it's difficult to give a formal specification of distributed systems as well as the correctness verification. As the distributed system becomes increasingly complicated, the formal methods are needed to help overcome these shortcomings in development.

The formal methods are used to help model complex system in a mathematic way [10]. In formal development method, the text-based requirements are formalized, and with the help of formal developing tools, hazards and errors can be automatically detected. Event-B is a formal specification language for modeling and verifying system requirements [1]. The basic idea that distinguishes Event-B from other formal methods is its refinement mechanism. In Event-B refinement process, the abstract specifications can be transformed into concrete specifications gradually until all requirements in the specification contained in the model. Besides, a set of proof obligations (POs) are generated after every refinement stage, which are used to verify the consistency from its abstract model and to make sure that the functional requirements have been correctly added [9].

© ICST Institute for Computer Sciences, Social Informatics and Telecommunications Engineering 2018
X. Gu et al. (Eds.): MLICOM 2017, Part I, LNICST 226, pp. 326–336, 2018.
https://doi.org/10.1007/978-3-319-73564-1_32

Although Event-B provides a refinement mechanism to gradually model the system, one of the major problem is that there is no standard guideline to use the refinement mechanism. When modeling complex systems, it is difficult for developers to organize the refinement steps. On the other hand, the main weakness of using formal method in system modeling is the gap between text-based requirement and the initial specification. Thus, before modeling, a preliminary study of requirement analysis should be considered. There are several requirements engineering approaches used to describe requirements such as KAOs [11] and i* [13], but most of them stop at the requirements analysis stage, and do not involve later development process. Besides, SysML [2] is a modeling language for system engineering. Except for the basic diagram of UML, SysML also inherits the extensibility mechanism and provides some new diagrams, such as the requirement diagram and the parameter diagram. In [3], the author proposed to extend the SysML requirement diagram with goal model in KAOs method, and established a mapping relationships between the extended requirement diagram and the B method [12]. Considering that the B method is mainly applicable to software modeling, and the author didn't mention the consistency of the model. This paper proposes to combine SysML requirement diagram with Event-B modeling process, the paper mainly focuses on the contains relationship of SysML requirement diagram. First we use the requirement diagram to build the hierarchical relationships of requirements, then we translate these hierarchical relationships into the modeling process of Event-B, and verify the consistency of the model.

The organization of this paper is as follows, Sect. 2 gives some related knowledge of Event-B and SysML requirement diagram. Section 3 describes the methods that translates typical relationship of SysML requirement diagram into Event-B framework. Section 4 is a case study to illustrate the proposed approach. And Sect. 5 gives conclusion and future work.

2   Background

2.1   SysML

SysML [2] is a unified modeling language for complex system analysis and specification. As an extension of UML subset, some new diagrams are proposed such as requirement diagram and parametric diagram. In this paper, we focus on the requirement diagram. A requirement is represented by a specific identifier and a text-based description in requirement diagram. There are two kinds of relationships in requirement diagram, the relations *verify*, *satisfy*, and *refine* describe the relationship between requirements and other model elements [3]. The relation *contains* represents that a sub-requirement is a part of its composite requirement. The relation *derive* relate a derived requirement to its source requirement, for example a sub-system requirement may derived from a system requirement. The relation *copy* expresses that one requirement is the same version of another requirement. And these relations can be depicted as follows (Fig. 1):

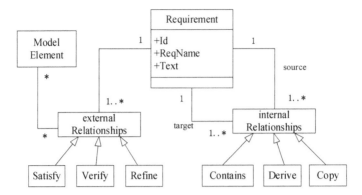

Fig. 1. Relations in SysML requirement diagram

2.2   Event-B

Event-B is a formal method for discrete system development based on first-order logic and set theory, which is evolved from the classical B method [1]. There are two main components in Event-B: context and machine. Context describes the static properties of the model. Machine describes the dynamic behavior of a model. Another important concept is the refinement mechanism in Event-B. A refinement process means more detailed properties introduced into the concrete model from the abstract model. The elements and the relationships of Event-B model can be shown as Fig. 2.

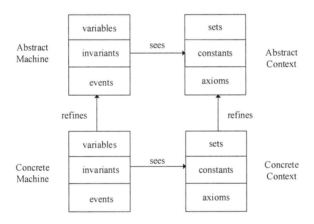

Fig. 2. Relations in Event-B model

In general, Event-B is a state-based discrete system modeling language, the mathematic model defined in machine is represented by states and its transition mechanism, i.e. the event. The state is represented by the value of the variable, and the property that states should always hold in a machine is invariant. In Event-B machines, events are used to update the state, the main elements of event are guards and actions.

Guards are conditions that the transition should satisfy, and actions are behaviors that update current states. A common form of an event is:

$$e \triangleq \text{any } x \text{ where } G(s, c, x, v) \text{ then } BA(s, c, x, v, v') \tag{1}$$

x is the parameter of the event, $G(s, c, x, v)$ is a set of conditions for triggering events, s is the carrier set and c is the constant, and v is the current value of the variable, respectively. The body of event e is $BA(s, c, x, v, v')$, where v' represents the updated value of the current state.

Through the refinement mechanism of Event-B, the abstract machine can be refined into a more specific machine. To maintain the consistency of the refinement chain in the model, a set of proof obligations (POs) should be proved, which is generated from the specification. There are two types of consistency in Event-B model, the model's self-consistency and the consistency with its abstract machine. If all POs are discharged, then the consistency of the model is confirmed.

After the model is built, it is necessary to prove that all the properties have been correctly added into the model. However, in a large project, the number of proofs may be up to thousands. Obviously, it is not possible to solve these proof manually. Rodin [4] is a development platform for Event-B, and it is based on eclipse. In rodin platform, many plug-ins are included for development, such as POs generator and prover, the first one is used to analyze the model and automatically generate corresponding proof obligations. The other is used to prove them.

3   From SysML Requirement Diagram to Event-B

Since the requirement in SysML requirement is textual and informal, it is not possible to directly translate requirement from requirement phase to formal specification phase. We propose to define rules to derive a refinement framework from the requirement diagram.

The main idea is to decompose the initial requirement into two different types, the functional requirement and the domain requirement. These two kind of requirement can be specified by contains relationship. The functional requirement is used to specify the intended behaviors that system will achieve, the domain requirement specifies the static environment factors such as the physical law the system should obey. As we have mentioned before, Context describes the static property, while machine describes the dynamic behavior of the system. Context can be extended with more properties while a domain requirement in SysML requirement diagram can be decomposed into more detailed sub-requirement [8]. The static property in domain requirement can be described by the axiom in context. In Event-B, the dynamic behavior is expressed by events and the invariants, in which the invariant is to make sure that the state converted by event is consistent with the model. The basic mapping relation from SysML requirement diagram to Event-B models is illustrated in Fig. 3.

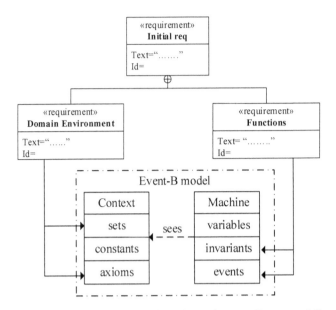

Fig. 3. Mapping relations between SysML requirement diagram and Event-B

3.1   Event-B Machine Consistency

In order to verify whether the model satisfies specified properties, Event-B defines a set of proof obligations that need to be discharged. And some POs involve the consistency and deadlock-freeness of model, such as Feasibility (FIS), invariant preservation (INV), deadlock-freeness (DLF). FIS is used to make sure that actions in events are feasible, INV is used to ensure that each event in machine maintains the property preserved in invariants, and DLF is to ensure that there are always some enabled events during the execution. The formal forms of these proof obligations are shown as follow:

$$\text{FIS: } A(s, c) \wedge I(s, c, v) \wedge G(s, c, v, x) \vdash \exists v' \cdot BA(s, c, v, x, v') \tag{2}$$

$$\text{INV: } A(s, c) \wedge I(s, c, v) \wedge G(s, c, v, x) \wedge BA(s, c, v, x, v') \vdash inv(s, c, v') \tag{3}$$

$$\text{DLF: } I(s, c, v) \vdash \bigvee_{i=1}^{n} (\exists x_i \cdot G(x_i, v)) \tag{4}$$

$A(s, c)$ is the axiom in context, $I(s, c, v)$ is invariants in machine, and $inv(s, c, v')$ are invariants that involve variables in $BA(s, c, v, x, v')$. According to the proofs in [14], the consistency property can be verified by discharging FIS and INV proof obligations. Meanwhile, with the help of plug-ins in rodin platform, these proof obligations can be automatically generated and discharged.

4   Case Study: A Leader Election Algorithm

The object of this section is to illustrate the approach through a common leader election algorithm from [1]. As we know that the leader node is a coordinator of a bunch of servers, there should be only one leader node and all servers should recognize the leader. In a word, the leader election is used to elect a leader node in a group of process.

In this paper, we consider to model a simple distributed system, the ring network. Each process in this ring network have their own id, and is able to send a message to the next process in this ring network, in addition, all processes can store the message in their buffers. In the algorithm, the process only accepts the message which is no less than its own id and rejects messages that have smaller id. The algorithm stops when a process receives its own id from other node, and this node is the leader node.

4.1   The Initial Model

At the beginning, we have an initial requirement described as "A leader node should be elected in a ring network". From this initial requirement, we can derive two sub requirements, shown as Fig. 4.

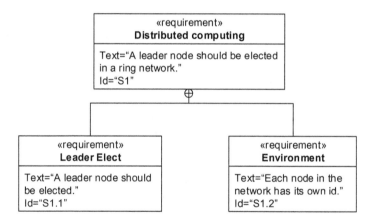

Fig. 4. Initial requirement diagram

The sub-requirement "Leader Elect" and "Environment" can be mapped into Event-B machine and context, respectively. Here, we consider to build a simple network which contains a set of nodes, and the corresponding specification in Event-B context is shown as Fig. 5.

In this context, we defined a constant *Num* to include nodes with different id. The axm4 means that there should always be a node that have the biggest id. Moreover, we don't consider about the ring structure. It will be refined into next refinement.

And the next requirement is "Leader Elect", in this event, *maxId* is a variable that can be assigned as the largest id in all nodes. The basic form can be shown as follows (Fig. 6):

constants *Num*
axioms
    @axm1 $Num \subseteq \mathbb{N}$
    @axm2 $finite(Num)$
    @axm3 $Num \neq \phi$
    @axm4 $\exists a \cdot \forall x \cdot x \in Num \Rightarrow a \geq x$

Fig. 5. Initial context in Event-B

event elect
then
    @act1 $maxId := max(Num)$
end

Fig. 6. Event elect

4.2   First Refinement

From the initial model, we have built a simple model that contains only one event and don't consider the ring structure. The requirement diagram should be extended further, as the requirement can be explained in a detailed way. In the following refinement a ring structure should be added into the context, and the requirement environment will be extended as follows (Fig. 7):

And the corresponding context in Event-B model is shown as Fig. 8.

The constant *next* is a function that maps one node to another node.

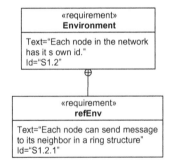

Fig. 7. Extend the Env requirement

axm1_1: $\quad next \in Num \twoheadrightarrow Num$

axm1_2: $\quad \forall S \cdot next^{-1}[S] \subseteq S \wedge S \neq \phi \Rightarrow Num \subseteq S$

Fig. 8. Extended context in Event-B

Also, the requirement *Leader Elect* will be refined into three more concrete requirements, *accept, reject* and *refElect*, which can be depicted as follows (Fig. 9):

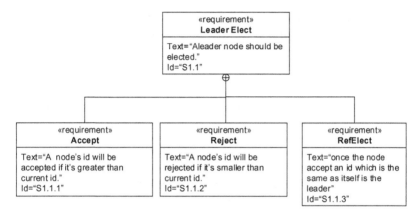

Fig. 9. Extended Leader Elect

In this requirement diagram, three refined requirements are contained in the *LeaderElect*. The requirement *Accept* means that nodes in the ring network only receive message that has bigger id. On the contrary, the requirement *Reject* rejects message that is smaller than its own id. And the requirement *RefElect* details the operation in *LeaderElect*. The corresponding events in the refined machine are described partially as follows (Figs. 10 and 11):

> event Accept
> any x
> where
>   @grd1_1 $\quad x \in dom(buffer)$
>   @grd1_2 $\quad buffer(x) < x$
> then
>   @act1_1 $\quad buffer(x) := next(buffer(x))$
> end

Fig. 10. Event Accept

> Event RefElect
> any x
> where
>   @grd1_1 $x \in dom(buffer)$
>   @grd1_2 $x = buffer(x)$
> then
>   @act1_1 $maxId := x$
> end

Fig. 11. Event RefElect

In these events, variable *buffer* is used to store the nodes that are not rejected, and the invariant is shown as follows (Fig. 12):

> Inv1_1: $buffer \in Num \nrightarrow Num$
> Inv1_2: $\forall x \cdot x \in dom(buffer) \Rightarrow x = max(i\left(x \mapsto next^{-1}(buffer(x))\right))$

Fig. 12. Invariants in refined machine

With this refinement step, a concrete model which contains more detailed information can be built. The next step would be considering the consistency of this model.

4.3   Model Verification

Although the ring network model has been built through refinement, we still have to verify the consistency and correctness of our model. In Event-B modeling, there are set of proof obligations that should be proved while the model has been build. For example, after the Accept event has been executed, we have to proof that the new value of variable a is still consistent with the corresponding invariant such as inv1_1. And the proof process can be shown as follows (Fig. 13):

> Inv1_1
> Guards of event
> Accept
> $\vdash$
> Modified invariant Inv1_1

> $buffer \in N \nrightarrow N$
> $x \in dom(buffer)$
> $buffer(x) < x$
> $\vdash$
> $(\{x\} \vartriangleleft buffer) \cup \{x \mapsto n(buffer(x))\}$
> $\in N \nrightarrow N$

Fig. 13. Event Accept INV1_1 proof obligation

If all the proof should be proved manually, it would be a long time and becomes difficult. Rodin [4] is a platform for Event-B modeling, it provides not only a development environment, but also some tools that can automatically prove POs of the model, which simplified the proof procedure [5, 6]. The ring network we have built is automatically proved by Rodin platform, which can be shown as follows (Fig. 14):

Fig. 14. All POs discharged

5 Conclusion and Future Work

As a formal specification language, Event-B is capable for complex system modeling. However, one of the major problem is that there is no standard guideline to use the refinement mechanism. On the other hand, SysML requirement diagram gives a preliminary analysis of requirements, and the hierarchical structure of requirements is built. In this paper, we propose mapping relationships between SysML requirement diagrams and Event-B refinement process. And since these relationships are partial, a more precise semantic should be added in SysML requirement relations. Here, we plan to extended SysML requirement diagram with goal model in KAOs method. Goals in goal model can be specified into LTL formula, as LTL can describe both safety property and liveness property, we will give a more precise preliminary analysis of requirements. Our future work will mainly concentrate on the translation of extended requirement diagram and Event-B model elements.

Acknowledgement. This work was supported by the National High-tech R&D Program of China (863 Program) under Grant No. 2015AA015303; Project 61272083 supported by National Natural Science Foundation of China; Supported by National key research and development program 2016YFB1000802.

References

1. Abrial, J.R.: Modeling in Event-B: System and Software Engineering. Cambridge University Press, Cambridge (2010)
2. Friedenthal, S., Moore, A., Steiner, R.: A practical guide to sysml. San Francisco Jung Inst. Lib. J. **17**(1), 41–46 (2012)

3. Laleau, R., Semmak, F., Matoussi, A., Petit, D., Hammad, A., Tatibouet, B.: A first attempt to combine sysml requirements diagrams and b. Innov. Syst. Softw. Eng. **6**(1–2), 47–54 (2010)

4. Butler, M., Hallerstede, S.: The Rodin formal modelling tool. In: The International Conference on Formal Methods in Industry, p. 2. British Computer Society (2007)

5. Le, H.A., Thi, L.D., Truong, N.T.: Modeling and verifying imprecise requirements of systems using Event-B. In: Huynh, V., Denoeux, T., Tran, D., Le, A., Pham, S. (eds.) Knowledge and Systems Engineering. Advances in Intelligent Systems and Computing, vol. 244, pp. 313–325. Springer, Cham (2014). https://doi.org/10.1007/978-3-319-02741-8_27

6. Younes, A.B., Hlaoui, Y.B., Ayed, L.J.B.: A meta-model transformation from UML activity diagrams to Event-B models. In: IEEE International Computer Software and Applications Conference Workshops, pp. 740–745. IEEE Computer Society (2014)

7. Bousse, E., Katsuragi, T.: Aligning SysML with the B method to provide V&V for systems engineering. In: The Workshop on Model-Driven Engineering, Verification and Validation, pp. 11–16. ACM (2012)

8. Mentré, D.: SysML2B: automatic tool for B Project Graphical Architecture Design Using SysML. In: Butler, M., Schewe, K.-D., Mashkoor, A., Biro, M. (eds.) ABZ 2016. LNCS, vol. 9675, pp. 308–311. Springer, Cham (2016). https://doi.org/10.1007/978-3-319-33600-8_26

9. Xu, H.: Model based system consistency checking using Event-B. Comput. Softw. (2012)

10. Krakora, J., Waszniowski, L., Pisa, P., Hanzalek, Z.: Timed automata approach to real time distributed system verification. In: IEEE International Workshop on Factory Communication Systems, Proceedings, pp. 407–410. IEEE (2004)

11. Lamsweerde, A.V.: Requirements engineering: from system goals to UML models to software specifications. Wiley Publishing, Hoboken (2009)

12. Abrial, J.R.: The B-Book - Assigning Programs to Meanings. DBLP (1996)

13. Yu, E.S.K., Mylopoulos, J.: Understanding "why" in software process modelling, analysis, and design. In: International Conference on Software Engineering, pp. 159–168. IEEE Computer Society Press (1994)

14. Traichaiyaporn, K., Aoki, T.: Preserving correctness of requirements evolution through refinement in Event-B. In: Software Engineering Conference, Vol. 1, pp. 315–322. IEEE (2014)

Intelligent Satellite Communications and Networking

A Full-Protocol-Stack Testbed for Space Network Protocol Emulation

Xiaoqin Ni, Kanglian Zhao$^{(\boxtimes)}$, and Wenfeng Li$^{(\boxtimes)}$

School of Electronic Science and Engineering, Nanjing University,
22 Hankou Rd., Nanjing 210093, Jiangsu, People's Republic of China
nixiaoqin44@163.com, zhaokanglian@nju.edu.cn, leewf_cn@hotmail.com

Abstract. With the rapid development of space networks, new space communications protocols are emerging, for which emulation is an essential step during design and test. In this paper, we propose a lab-based testbed, in which software and hardware tools are utilized together to emulate full network protocol stack. A software protocol gateway is implemented to preform protocol conversion like IP over CCSDS in Data Link Layer. A specified hardware, Cortex CRT-Q is adopted for accurate emulation of space links, which connects upper layers with Physical Layer. Thus, our testbed benefit from both the fidelity provided by hardware and flexibility brought by software.

Keywords: Lab-based testbed · Full network protocol stack
IP over CCSDS · Space link

1 Introduction

A space communications protocol is a communications protocol designed to be used over a space link, or in a network that contains one or multiple space links. According to the CCSDS blue book, the space communications protocols are defined for the following five layers of the ISO model [1]:

(a) Physical Layer;
(b) Data Link Layer;
(c) Network Layer;
(d) Transport Layer;
(e) Application Layer.

During design, implementation and utilization of space communications protocol, emulation is an essential step. Various testbeds for emulating space network have been proposed in different works. The key point of the testbed is how to

This work is supported by the National Natural Science Foundation of China (No. 61401194), the Fundamental Research Funds for the Central Universities (021014380064) and the Priority Academic Program Development of Jiangsu Higher Education Institutions.

© ICST Institute for Computer Sciences, Social Informatics and Telecommunications Engineering 2018
X. Gu et al. (Eds.): MLICOM 2017, Part I, LNICST 226, pp. 339–346, 2018.
https://doi.org/10.1007/978-3-319-73564-1_33

reproduce the space links in laboratory. A space link is a communications link between a spacecraft and its associated ground system or between two spacecraft. [1] The space communication link displays special characteristics different from those of terrestrial ones: larger link delay, higher bit error rates, bursts of errors, packet disordering, etc. To emulate a space-ground link, field testing equipment can be prohibitively expensive and deployment scheme is inflexible. [2] Another method is using software like netem to control the delay, the BER and the rate. [3] The problem of this kind of testbed is that data flows through Ethernet network, which is different from specialized transceivers running dedicated Data Link Layer protocols, like AOS [7].

Experiments with full network protocol stack is preferred for system level performance emulation. To emulate a space communications protocol, a widely used method is utilizing network simulator software like OPNET [4], which is confined to state machine in a single PC lack of fidelity. Another solution is utilizing protocol gateway based on FPGA [5] to perform IP over CCSDS, in which a certain threshold and difficulties for developing exits, with protocol configuration lack of flexibility.

In this paper, a full-protocol-stack testbed is proposed for network protocol emulation. Hardware components like Cotrex Command/Ranging/Telemetry-Quantum (hereinafter referred to as Cortex CRT-Q) [6] is applied to provide accurate space-ground link and software protocol gateway (hereinafter referred to as SPG) provides flexible configuration and emulation of full protocol stack. The remainder of this paper is organized as follows. Section 2 describes the design of our testbed including facilities and equipment. Verification experiments and relevant results are presented in Sect. 3. The conclusions and future works are drawn in Sect. 4.

2   Design for Testbed

2.1   Overview of the Architecture

The hardware architecture of the testbed is showed in Fig. 1, which consists of one Cortex CRT-Q, two SPGs and several PCs. Cortex CRT-Q provides space links, which incorporates powerful built-in simulation capabilities for functional and performance test purposes including: receiving data as simulation resource and sending out data after demodulation over the ETHERNET LAN, IF modulation (PM, FM, BPSK, QPSK, OQPSK or AQPSK) and demodulation, noise generation, etc. In this paper, Cortex CRT-Q works in the local loop-back mode to emulate a space-ground link in a lab environment. SGP functions as a border gateway, which performs protocol conversion like IP over CCSDS simultaneously. PCs act as communication nodes in space network such as ground stations, spacecraft, users, etc.

2.2   The Design of the Software Protocol Gateway

The implementation of the SPG is based on the concept of protocol layering principle. Figure 1 also shows the protocol architecture. Notice that, SPG works

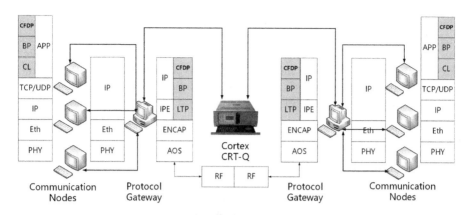

Fig. 1. Overview of the architecture

upon two protocol stacks as a border gateway, solving the protocol conversion problem. Reserving interface like socket port in different layers is convenient for debugging and monitoring with the help of wireshark or tcpdump. SPG operates in a Linux environment and program in each layer will be explained later.

In Network Layer, we write program based on libpcap and libnet, to accomplish capturing and sending IP packet. The Application Layer data extracted with IP header, needs fragmentation and reassembly sometimes when the payload length is bigger than MTU.

In Data Link Layer, Advanced Orbiting Systems (AOS) [7] protocol has been designed to meet the requirements of space missions for efficient transfer of space application data of various types and characteristics over space-to-ground, ground-to-space, or space-to-space communications links. Thus it is selected as Data Link Layer protocol in our testbed because of its maturity and universality, certainly could be replaced by others. The IP OVER CCSDS SPACE LINKS blue book [8] describes the recommended method for transferring IP PDUs over CCSDS SDLPs including AOS. IP PDUs are transferred by encapsulating them, one-for-one, within CCSDS Encapsulation Packets. The Encapsulation Packets [9] are transferred directly within one or more CCSDS SDLP Transfer Frames. This method uses the CCSDS Internet Protocol Extension (IPE) convention in conjunction with the CCSDS Encapsulation Service over CCSDS AOS. We program according to relevant books and RFCs to perform protocol conversion.

In Physical Layer, with different configuration parameters set, Cortex CRT-Q could provide different physical link. It reads data as simulated data from port 3021 or 3022. After local real-time modulation and demodulation, port 3070 is used to send telemetry data out, which is triggered by a request command. Working mode provided by Cortex CRT-Q is oriented to data stream, however, the data form involved in protocol emulation is mainly intermittent data packet. Generally, if the transmission rate of the Application Layer does not match with the bit rate of the Physical Layer, phenomenon occurs as follows: if transmission rate is higher, problems of congestion, delay and packet loss would be serious;

if bit rate is higher, in order to avoid modulation blank, given amount of data is required to wait, which resulted in unnecessary delay. The difference between data stream and data packets makes requests for link adaption. Therefore, socket programming of non-blocking mode is applied. When there is no data to send, idle data is sent to maintain channel synchronization. In brief, we program to put and get AOS frames in CRT frame format and accomplish link adaption.

2.3   Data Flow on the Testbed

Make an introduction to the data flow on the testbed. Figure 2 shows only one-direction communication process, the other direction is similar. Two subnets are representing terrestrial and space network respectively, for example, 192.168.0.0/24 (hereinafter referred to as subnet 1) and 192.168.10.0/24 (hereinafter referred to as subnet 2). SPG connects the PCs of each subnet with the Cortex CRT-Q.

PCs in subnet 1 sets the routing table, enabling all data whose destination is subnet2 are converged in SPG 1. SPG 1 receives the data from network card that would be sent to pcap program to filter out IP packets, which encapsulated into AOS frame later and sent to Cortex CRT-Q in simulated data format. Cortex CRT-Q modulation frequency is set as 70M, with different modulation parameters configured. SPG 2 keeps sending request commands to the Cortex CRT-Q. Once telemetry data is received, which would go through CRT-unpack and AOS-unpack program. Original IP packets would be sent to the PCs in subnet 2 through libnet program, after adding Ethernet frame header.

Based on Cortex CRT-Q and SPGs, data flow contains space-ground links, upon which full network protocol stack are emulated.

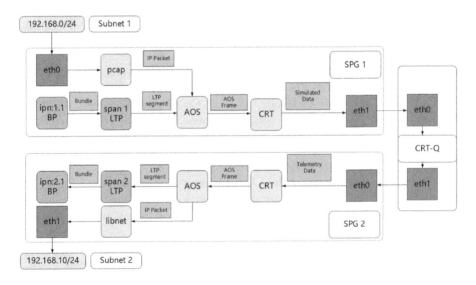

Fig. 2. Data flow

3   Test and Discussion

3.1   Fidelity of the Testbed

The fidelity of testbed mainly depends on the accuracy of bit rate and bit error rate (hereinafter referred to as BER) that Cortex CRT-Q supplies. The following two experiments is performed to verify these indicators. Because in Cortex CRT-Q, frame size is fixed after configuration. In this paper, frame size is 1024 B. Make analysis according to AOS frame format (Table 1) without noise. We could reason out:

$$Bandwidth = \frac{Payloadsize}{Framesize} BitRate \qquad (1)$$

Table 1. AOS frame format

AOS frame 1024 B						
Sync word	AOS	AOS data field				AOS
1ACFFC1D	Head	MPDU	Encap	IPE	Payload	CRC
4 B	6 B	2 B	4 B	1 B	1005 B	2 B

If payload is smaller than 100 5B, it will be filled with idle data until the total length is 1005 B. Otherwise, it will be split into several frames with length of 1005 B. At this time, the formula is revised to:

$$Bandwidth = \frac{Payloadsize}{Framesize * N} BitRate \qquad (2)$$

$$N = \lceil \frac{Payloadsize}{1005B} \rceil \qquad (3)$$

Therefore, when the payload length is set as 1005 B, actually 977 B subtract IP and UDP header, the optimal bandwidth utilization equals 95.41%. In the two subnets, two PCs are running iperf [10] server and client respectively. The bandwidth in 100 Kbps link with different payload size is tested as Fig. 3, and the best bandwidth with different bit rates is tested as Table 2. Since the measured

Table 2. Best bandwidth with different bit rate

Bit rate	Bandwidth	Channel utilization
100k	94.9k	94.90%
500k	474.0k	94.80%
1M	942.1k	94.20%

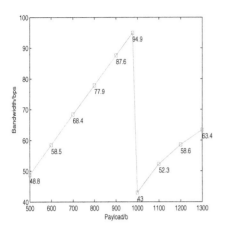 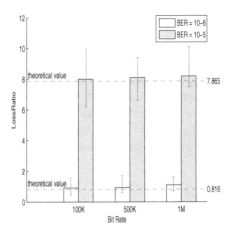

Fig. 3. Bandwidth with different Payloadsize (100 kbps)

Fig. 4. Loss ratio (different Bit rate)

results are very close to the theoretical value 95.41%, it can be concluded that the indicator of bit rate is valid and accurate.

Now, we analyze validity of configuration for BER. Essentially, software emulator like tc/netem, controls BER in Physical Layer by counting and dropping specific amount of packets in upper Layer (probably Network Layer). On the contrary, Cortex CRT-Q controls BER by setting up noise with different C/N_0 in Physical Layer, which leads to packet loss in Data Link Layer because of failing to pass checksum. The latter is more logical and credible. According to the formula:

$$P_{eBPSK} = \frac{1}{2}erfc(\sqrt{E_b/N_0}) \tag{4}$$

$$E_b/N_0 = C/N_0 - 10lgR \tag{5}$$

After C/N_0 is set to 59.5 dB (R = 100 Kbps, BSPK) in the noise modular of the Cortex CRT-Q, E_b/N_0 is showed around 9.5 dB. The BER now is 10^{-5}, according to the formula (4). As for loss ratio,

$$LossRatio = 1 - (1 - BER)^{8packetsize} \tag{6}$$

Packet size is 1024 B because each frame in Cortex CRT-Q is 1024 bytes, after conversion, the packet loss rate is 7.865%. After backing up data sent to and receive from Physical Layer (CRT), we can calculate BER by making comparisons. Analogically, after backing up data sent to and receive from Data Link Layer (AOS), we can calculate Loss Ratio. File with the size of 10 MB was sent in the configuration of BER = 10^{-5} and BER = 10^{-6} with different bit rates, the test results are as Fig. 4. The measured results are very close to the theoretical value, it can be concluded that the indicator of BER valid and accurate.

3.2   Flexibility of the Testbed

Firstly, two subnets ping each other to make analysis of delay. When bit rate is 100 Kbps without noise, average RTT is 460 ms. Considering that each ICMP packet is packed into a 1024 B CRT frame, channel delay is 82 ms and one-way program processing delay is about 148 ms.

Based on the design principle of protocol layering, we can flexibly change upper protocols to test other protocol stack for example DTN [11] (gray parts in Fig. 1). To perform testing, the Interplanetary Overlay Network (ION) version 3.5.0 open source software implementation of DTN [12] was used on Linux PCs including SPGs and communication nodes. On the basis of the IP over CCSDS, according to the relevant blue book and RFC [13–15], with ION software providing CFDP/BP/LTP application, new data flow is as follows (gray parts in Fig. 2): Gateway 1 acting as ipn:1.1, splits CFDP file into BP bundles and cuts converged bundles into LTP Blocks, then according to the link layer MTU(1005 B, optimal payload size), LTP Blocks turn into LTP segment. This is a very intuitive process of a CFDP-BP-LTP-AOS-RF protocol emulation.

We set up another testbed as a contrast (Fig. 5). A PC utilizes tc/netem acting as a link. At first, delay is configured as 222 ms and rate is 100 kbps. So that RTT of Ping is 460 ms, same as our testbed. But bandwidth measured by iperf (977 B payload size) is 96.1 Kbps, higher than 94.9 Kbps. After revising rate to make sure the result of iperf is the same as 94.9 Kbps, ION software uses different protocols, such as CFDP/BP/LTP protocol, sends the same file (200 kB), delivery time in our testbed compared with software emulator are as Fig. 6.

It is displayed that delivery time of our testbed is still a little longer than software testbed. The reason is that in software testbed, even rate and delay are the same, protocol in Data Link Layer and Physical Layer is different. Because in our testbed, LTP is directly running upon AOS (after simple Encapsulation [9]) and frame size of AOS is fixed (1024 B in our testbed) for both forward

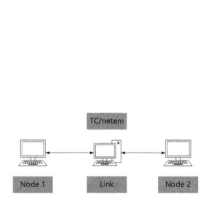

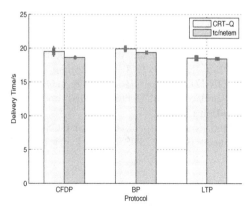

Fig. 5. TC/netem testbed   **Fig. 6.** DTN protocol testing

data packets and backward ACK packets. However, in software testbed, LTP is running upon UDP and frame size of Ethernet is not fixed. It means in software testbed, at least, ACK arrives more quickly because of small size, therefore, the total communication process is shorter. The phenomenon reflects the advantage of our testbed, full-protocol-stack-emulation, in another way.

4 Conclusion and Prospect

In this paper, software and hardware tools are utilized together to emulate full network protocol stack. Based on the accurate physical space-ground link provided by hardware components, results of the emulation is more credible. What's more important, the testbed proposed in this paper can provide the researchers and developers the feasibility to emulate or test new protocols in any layer of a reconfigurable full network protocol stack in space networks.

References

1. Green Book. Overview Of Space Communications Protocols (2007)
2. Murawski, R., Bhasin, K., Bittner, D., et al.: Hardware and software integration to support real-time space-link emulation. In: IEEE, International Workshop on Computer Aided Modeling and Design of Communication Links and Networks. IEEE (2012)
3. Lochin, E., Prennou, T., Dairaine, L.: When should I use network emulation? Ann. Telecommun. **67**, 247–255 (2012)
4. OPNET Homepage. www.opnet.com/products/modeler/home.html
5. Liu, F., Yan, H., Liu, H.: The design and implementation of configurable high-speed IP over AOS gateway. In: Computer Applications and Communications. IEEE (2014)
6. Cortex CRT-Q. http://www.zodiacaerospace.com/en/cortex-crt-q
7. Blue Book. AOS Space Data Link Protocol (2006)
8. Red Book. IP over CCSDS space links (2006)
9. Blue Book. ENcapsulation Service (2009)
10. Iperf. https://sourceforge.net/projects/iperf/?source=directory
11. Caini, C., Cruickshank, H., Farrell, S., et al.: Delay- and disruption-tolerant networking (DTN): an alternative solution for future satellite networking applications. Proc. IEEE **99**, 1980–1997 (2011)
12. ION-DTN. https://sourceforge.net/projects/ion-dtn/?source=directory
13. Standard, Draft Recommended, and Red Book. CCSDS Bundle Protocol Specification (2010)
14. Red Book. Protocol (LTP) for CCSDS (2011)
15. Sheets BBP. CCSDS File Delivery Protocol (CFDP) (2004)

Application Layer Channel Coding for Space DTN

Dongxu Hou, Kanglian Zhao$^{(\boxtimes)}$, and Wenfeng Li$^{(\boxtimes)}$

School of Electronic Science and Engineering, Nanjing University,
22 Hankou Rd, Nanjing 210093, Jiangsu, People's Republic of China
kaldon@163.com, zhaokanglian@nju.edu.cn, leewf_cn@hotmail.com

Abstract. Space communications have the characteristics of long link delays, frequent link disruptions and high error rates. With reliable Lick-lider Transmission Protocol (LTP) or Transmission Control Protocol (TCP), automatic repeat request (ARQ) is applied to enable reliable data delivery in delay/disruption tolerant networking (DTN). However, ARQ is inefficient for space communications especially in links with long round trip time (RTT). In this paper, an application layer Reed-Solomon (ALRS) channel coding scheme is proposed, which is further combined with ARQ to guarantee reliable transmission in DTN architecture. The proposed ALRS coding scheme is implemented in open source ION-DTN software and its performance is evaluated on a dedicated testbed. The results of the experiments show that this scheme in DTN can be speed up in most scenarios compared with ARQ-only scheme. With coding in application layer, the scheme is also more compatible with the overlay characteristic of DTN.

Keywords: Delay/disruption tolerant networking · Application layer Reed-Solomon channel coding

1 Introduction

Along with the development of space technology and the progress in the exploration of MARS, efficient and reliable data transmission in space is becoming more and more important. Delay/disruption tolerant networking (DTN), a new network architecture, has been proposed for deep space internetworking. To enable reliable data transmission between the sender and the receiver, ARQ is provided by Licklider Transmission Protocol (LTP) [1] or the classical Transmission Control Protocol (TCP) in space DTN. However, due to challenging link conditions in space communications, retransmissions of lost data based on ARQ is the principal reason that sharply decreases network performance.

This work is supported by the National Natural Science Foundation of China (No. 61401194), the Fundamental Research Funds for the Central Universities (021014380064) and the Priority Academic Program Development of Jiangsu Higher Education Institutions.

How can we reduce the number of retransmissions to acquire higher delivery speed in space communications? Forward error correction (FEC) with erasure codes in different layers might be a good option to the ARQ solution [2]. Some studies that incorporate erasure codes within space DTN have been proposed previously. First, erasure codes can be combined with link layer to rectify bit-level faults, which is known as the classical physical layer channel coding. However, space communications channels are characterized with long fading or even link disruptions. In such cases, typical link layer recovery fails, resulting in bursty frame-losses in the order of tens to thousands of frames. Link layer failures are reflected in the upper layers as packet losses that need to be retransmitted in reliable transmission. Hence, the network performance in this manner can be limited especially in links with long round trip time (RTT).

Second, erasure codes applied at packet level [3] is proposed to be promising to guarantee higher robustness against consistent link errors and information loss [4]. Erasure codes incorporates with Licklider Transmission Protocol is one option. When LTP is used as transport protocol, data is splitted into LTP data blocks and each block is fragmented into LTP segments. These segments are encoded by erasure codes and they can generate redundancy segments. Then the segments are encapsulated for transmission [5]. A reverse decoding process will be implemented at the receiver. As the design philosophy of DTN is an overlay network, it should work across different network domains, which might employ potocols, such as LTP, User Datagram Protocol (UDP), Transmission Control Protocol (TCP) or other new protocols in one transmission. Although erasure codes incorporating with LTP can improve network performance obviously [6], the method is LTP dedicated and can not guarantee the performance end-to-end.

In this paper, we propose an application layer channel coding scheme for DTN. Reed-Solomon code is added over Bundle Protocol (BP) [7] to provide FEC at the application layer. In this way, erasure coding is only conducted at BP, which is separated from the protocol employed in the transmission layer. Thus for variable implementation of network protocol stacks [8], this scheme inherits the good portability of the overlay DTN architecture.

The remainder of this paper is organized as follows: In Sect. 2 we briefly introduce the proposed application layer erasure coding scheme. In Sect. 3 the configuration of the experiments are given and the results of the experiments are also presented and analyzed. Finally, in Sect. 4, we conclude the paper and provide some directions for future research.

2   Application Layer Erasure Coding Scheme

We briefly describe the proposed application layer (ALRS) erasure coding scheme in this section. Erasure codes, Reed-Solomon (RS) code in this paper, is incorporated with space DTN at the application layer. Files that need to be transferred will be split into k data packets firstly, where $k = fileSize/maximumPacketSize$. Then, a set of k data packets are encoded into n packets with m redundancy packets, where $m = n - k$. The corresponding

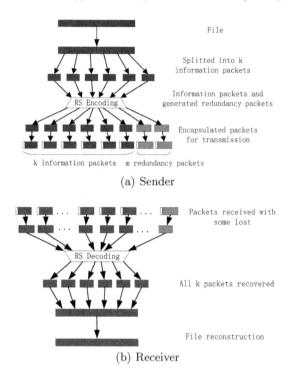

(a) Sender

(b) Receiver

Fig. 1. The hybrid ALRS encoding/decoding process for space DTN. (a) Sender, (b) Receiver.

code rate is k/n. Currently, $maximumPacketSize$ is set in accordance with the size of maximum transmission unit (MTU) in IP layer. Since RS are systematic codes, the first k encoded packets are data packets and the last m encoded packets are redundancy packets [9]. The architecture of RS encoding/decoding processes are shown in Fig. 1.

The problem of this scheme, or the problem of FEC, is that when the channel is out of the capability of the coding scheme, some errors can not be corrected and the reliable transmission can not be finished. So, we further propose a hybrid ALRS and ARQ scheme for the automatic reliable transmission in DTN. The process of this hybrid scheme is shown in Fig. 2. All the packets are first passed to BP in order. Each packet is encapsulated into a single bundle and encoded with ALRS scheme described earlier. Then the coded bundles are sent to the receiver. An additional FIN packet will be sent at the end of these encoded bundles to indicate the end of the transmission. According to the theory of RS code, random k bundles of n encoded bundles must be received at the receiver for the correct recovery of the original file. When the number of the received bundles is greater than or equal to k and the file is recovered, an END bundle will be sent to inform the sender that the file has been received successfully.

While when the number of the received bundles is less than k, the receiver will check the first four bytes of each received bundle, which indicates the sequence number of the bundle in all the n encoded bundles, to record the lost bundles. These sequence numbers will be written into a REQ bundle which will be sent to the sender and inform the sender of the lost bundles for retransmission.

As the FIN bundle, the REQ bundle and the END bundle are unique control bundles for the hybrid transmission scheme, different timers are set at the sender or the receiver for these bundles. Upon the arrival of these bundles, the timer is canceled, otherwise, upon expiration of the timer, the control bundle will be retransmitted immediately. In this way, the hybrid scheme can guarantee reliable delivery of the original file to the upper application without support of ARQ based reliable transmission protocols. Unreliable LTP (Green) convergence layer or UDP convergence layer can be adopted in this scheme.

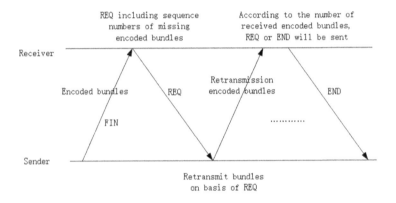

Fig. 2. Transmission of the hybrid ALRS.

3   Results and Analysis of the Experiments

3.1   Testbed Configuration

To evaluate the potential of the proposed ALRS scheme in deep-space and near-earth environments, we set up a dedicated DTN testbed, which is shown in Fig. 3. Network Emulator (Netem) is employed on a computer as a channel emulator to simulate long delays, high error rates, and link asymmetry in space communications. To realize ALRS, we modify the ION-DTN [10] software which has been installed on the computers emulating the sender and the receiver in the testbed.

For deep space communication scenario, communications between Mars orbiter and Earth is considered. For near earth communication scenario, transmission from satellites in geostationary (GEO) orbit towards Earth ground station is considered. Considering the packet loss ratio, the number of packets and

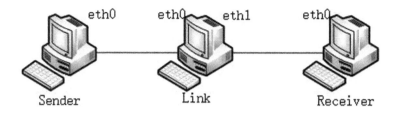

Fig. 3. Network topology for research.

Table 1. Experimental factors and values (Deep-Space)

Experimental factors	Settings/Values
Data packet size (bytes)	1460
File size (Kbytes)	250
DTN protocol layering and configuration	ALRS/BP/UDPCL/IPBP/LTPCL/IP
Downlink rate (kbps)	1500
Uplink rate (kbps)	15
One-way link delay (s)	40
PER (%)	0, 5, 10, 15, 20, 25, 30
Code rate	0.9

Table 2. Experimental factors and values (Near-Earth)

Experimental factors	Settings/Values
Data packet size (bytes)	1460
File size (Kbytes)	250
DTN protocol layering and configuration	ALRS/BP/UDPCL/IPBP/LTPCL/IP
Downlink rate (kbps)	150
Uplink rate (kbps)	1.5
One-way link delay (ms)	100
PER (%)	0, 5, 10, 15, 20, 25, 30
Code rate	0.9

the purpose of testing the transmission of the Hybrid ALRS, we set the code rate equal to 0.9. A summary of the parameters configuration is given in Tables 1 and 2.

We evaluate the performance of hybrid ALRS and ARQ scheme with various metrics. We record (1) the file transmission time, (2) total transmission data including data bundles, redundancy bundles and retransmission bundles, and (3) goodput defined as a ratio of the unique number of delivered data bytes to the total data delivery time as a measure of transmission efficiency and link utilization.

3.2   Results: Transmission Time

Figure 4(a) and (b) provides a comparison of the data transmission time between ARQ and the proposed hybrid scheme with various packet loss ratio (0%, 5%, 10%, 15%, 20%, 25%, 30%) in different communication environments. In deep space, long propagation delay time and dedicated high transmission rate are considered, the additional delivery time of redundancy bundles can be neglected. As shown in Fig. 4(a), when there is no packet loss, the transmission time of ARQ and the proposed hybrid scheme is very similar. When the packet loss ratio increases, the transmission time of ARQ increases sharply. When the packet loss ratio reaches 30%, ARQ's transmission time is nearly 6 times more than the proposed hybrid scheme.

In ARQ scheme, only when all k data bundles are received, can file be recovered at the receiver. Once there is missing data bundles, the sender simply retransmits the lost data bundles in response to a request from the receiver. Hence, the number of the transmission rounds required for successful file delivery increases greatly as the packet loss ratio increases. For the proposed hybrid scheme, as long as the receiver get k random data bundles from the all n coded bundles, the transmitted file can be reconstructed. The number of the transmission rounds for successful delivery of an entire file is decreased by applying appropriate ALRS encoding/decoding. So as shown in Fig. 4, the packet loss ratio has significant effect on ARQ, but little impact on the proposed hybrid scheme.

When near earth scenario is considered, the propagation delay time is short and the transmission rate is considered low for shared multiple access systems, the transmission time of redundancy bundles can't be neglected. Figure 4(b) shows that ARQ has a shorter transmission time than the hybrid scheme when packet loss ratio is low. As packet loss ratio increases, the transmission time of ARQ surpasses the hybrid scheme gradually.

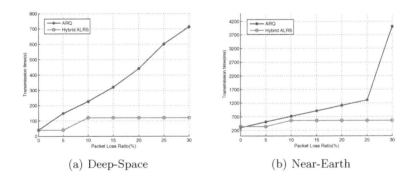

(a) Deep-Space   (b) Near-Earth

Fig. 4. Comparison of the transmission time between hybrid ALRS and ARQ.

3.3   Results: Total Transmission Data

Figure 5 gives a detailed insight about the total transmission data between ARQ and the hybrid scheme with different packet loss ratio. When packet loss ratio is no more than 10%, ARQ has a less total transmission data. With the increase of packet loss ratio, the advantage of the hybrid scheme is shown. It is obvious that the proposed hybrid scheme has a better energy efficiency in high packet loss ratio scenarios.

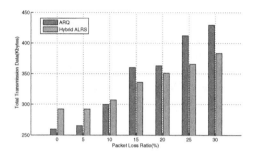

Fig. 5. Total transmission data for different packet loss ratio

3.4   Results: Goodput Performance

The comparison of goodput performance is presented in Fig. 6(a) and (b). Figure 6(a) presents the goodput in deep space, we neglect the delivery time of redundancy bundles as mentioned above. The transmission efficiency of ARQ degrades obviously with the increase of packet loss ratio. Due to the effect of ALRS encoding/decoding which decreases the number of retransmission, the proposed hybrid scheme degrades only slightly and reach a steady level when packet loss ratio equals to 10% and more.

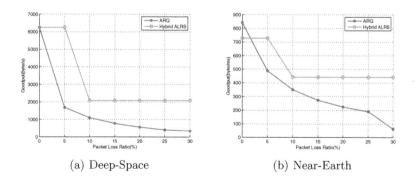

(a) Deep-Space   (b) Near-Earth

Fig. 6. Comparison of the goodput performance between hybrid ALRS and ARQ.

In near earth scenario, as shown in Fig. 6(b), the effect of the delivery time of redundancy bundles is considered for transmission efficiency. Therefore, ARQ has a better goodput when packet loss ratio is low.

4   Conclusions and Future Work

An application layer channel coding scheme that builds on top of BP in DTN is introduced in this paper. The theory behind the use of erasure codes stems from the necessity of limiting data retransmissions due to high error rate links in space. Experiment results and our analysis confirm the potential of this approach.

In the future work, on the one hand, we will investigate the performance trade-offs in multi-hop scenarios, where adaptive application layer erasure codes may be examined, in which code rate is adjusted based on the observations of the channel status at each hop. On the other hand, high code rate requires longer codec time, which may lead to lower performance. We will study the effect of different code rates.

References

1. Burleigh, S.: Delay-Tolerant Networking LTP Convergence Layer (LTPCL) Adapter (2013)
2. De Cola, T.: A protocol design for incorporating erasure codes within CCSDS: the case of DTN protocol architecture. In: Advanced Satellite Multimedia Systems Conference, pp. 68–73 (2010)
3. Paolini, E., Varrella, M., Chiani, M., Calzolari, G.P.: Recovering from packet losses in CCSDS Links. In: IEEE Advanced Satellite Mobile Systems, pp. 283–288 (2008)
4. Papastergiou, G., Bezirgiannidis, N., Tsaoussidis, V.: On the performance of erasure coding over space DTNs. In: Koucheryavy, Y., Mamatas, L., Matta, I., Tsaoussidis, V. (eds.) WWIC 2012. LNCS, vol. 7277, pp. 269–281. Springer, Heidelberg (2012). https://doi.org/10.1007/978-3-642-30630-3_23
5. De Cola, T., Marchese, M.: Joint use of custody transfer and erasure codes in DTN space networks: benefits and shortcomings. In: 2010 IEEE Global Telecommunications Conference (GLOBECOM 2010), IEEE, pp. 1–5 (2010)
6. De Cola, T., Paolini, E., Liva, G., et al.: Reliability options for data communications in the future deep-space missions. Proc. IEEE $99(11)$, 2056–2074 (2011)
7. Scott, K., Burleigh, S.: Bundle Protocol Specification. IETF RFC 5050, experimental (2007)
8. De Sanctis, M., Rossi, T., Lucente, M., Ruggirei, M.: Space system architectures for interplanetary internet. In: Aerospace Conference, pp. 1–8 (2010)
9. Reed, I.S., Solomon, G.: Polynomial codes over certain finite fields. J. Soc. Ind. Appl. Math. **8**, 300–304 (1960)
10. Interplanetary overlay network design and operation V3.2.1 (2015). http://sourceforge.net/projects/ion-dtn/files/latest/download

Routing Optimization of Small Satellite Networks Based on Multi-commodity Flow

Xiaolin Xu[1], Yu Zhang[1,2(✉)], and Jihua Lu[1]

[1] Beijing Institute of Technology, Beijing, China
{2120150826,yuzhang,lujihua}@bit.edu.cn
[2] The Science and Technology on Information Transmission and Dissemination
in Communication Networks Laboratory, The 54th Research Institute of China
Electronics Technology Group Corporation, Shijiazhuang, China

Abstract. As the scale of small satellite network is not large and the transmission cost is high, it is necessary to optimize the routing problem. We apply the traditional time-expanded graph to model the data acquisition of small satellite network so that we can formulate the data acquisition into a multi-commodity concurrent flow optimization problem (MCFP) aiming at maximizing the throughput. We use an approximation method to accelerate the solution for MCFP and make global optimization of routing between satellite network nodes. After the quantitative comparison between our MCFP algorithm and general augmented path maximum flow algorithm and exploring the detail of the algorithm, we verify the approximation algorithm's reasonable selection of routing optimization in small satellite network node communication.

Keywords: Satellite network · Multi-commodity flow · Routing optimization
Approximation algorithm · Concurrent flow

1 Introduction

Recently, more and more small satellites are launched to carry out various space missions. Small satellites receive mission data from observable objects and send these data to the data processing center via ground stations or relay satellites [1]. As the scale of small satellite network is not large and the transmission cost is high, we need to optimize the routing and allocate the resources properly.

The time-expanded graph (TEG) is a useful tool to model the topology of network [2]. To deal with the challenges caused by the impacts of satellites' movements during delivery process, Liu and Sheng apply the traditional time-expanded graph to model the data acquisition [3]. The delivery strategies and the data acquisition are formulated into an optimization problem to maximize the throughput. For the tiny topology with few satellites, the problems of routing and resources allocation have been emerged as a

Y. Zhang—Foundation Item: Science and Technology on Communication Networks Laboratory Foundation Project; Aerospace Field Pre-research Foundation Project (060501).

topic on multi-commodity problem (MCP). However, Liu and Sheng concentrate on the small satellite model using TEG instead of giving a practical algorithm to solve it.

Though finding an integer flow solution to the MCP is proved to be an NP-complete problem [4]. A polynomial time solution has been found through carrying Linear Programming by allowing fractional flows [5]. Moreover, researchers have concentrated on approximation schemes to speed up the solution. Following by Young in 1995 [7], Shahrokhi and Matula proposed a new algorithm for maximum concurrent flow problem (MCFP) in 1990 [6], whose algorithm was improved by Garg and Konemann in 1998 [8]. Garg and Konemann simplified the ideas of Young and built a framework for computing the MCFP. After that, Fleischer realized that an approximation of which commodity has the shortest path could be made in finding a shortest path between the source-sink pairs and extended the framework in 2000 [9]. She was able to describe an algorithm and its running time is independent of the number of the commodity in the MCFP problem. We will use a modified version of Fleischer's algorithm to consider the problem.

In this paper, we first extend the TEG to put up the model of a small satellite topology. Our model builds on the framework proposed by Liu and Sheng [3]. Then we apply a polynomial time multi-commodity optimization algorithm to maximize the network throughput based on this graph model. Simulation results highlight the practicality of our algorithm and explore the detail of our algorithm on parameter and running time etc.

2   System Model and Optimal Algorithm

2.1   System Setup

We consider a Graph G, which represents a small satellite network (SSN). There are nodes $SN = \{s_1, s_2, \ldots, s_n, \ldots\}$ and $TN = \{t_1, t_2, \ldots, t_n, \ldots\}$ representing the source and destination of data and a number of missions $OM = \{om_1, om_2, \ldots, om_n, \ldots\}$ to be completed over these nodes, where $om_i = [s_i, t_i, d_i]$. Mission om_i comprises source nodes which connects observable object ob_i, destination nodes which connects data processing center dc_i and its demand d_i.

First we set our demands for each mission om_i. Small satellites which revolve around the earth at a low altitude of 350–1400 km acquire mission data when they moving into the coverage of the observable objects and the ground stations get the mission data via relay satellites or the small satellites directly in SSN. Then, the mission data is transmitted from the ground stations to the data processing center (DPC). As the small satellite can send mission data to a relay satellite or ground station only when it moves close to them due to the orbiting movements, the connectivity relationships between relay satellites (or ground stations) and small satellites are time varying. On the other hand, relay satellites locate on the geosynchronous orbit. That is, the connectivity relationships between relay satellites and ground stations are fixed.

The SSN consists:

- Source of data $SN = \{s_1, s_2, \ldots, s_n, \ldots\}$.
- Observable objects $OB = \{ob_1, ob_2, \ldots, ob_n, \ldots\}$.
- Small satellites $SS = \{ss_1, ss_2, \ldots, ss_n, \ldots\}$.
- Relay satellites denoted by $RS = \{rs_1, rs_2, \ldots, rs_n, \ldots\}$.
- Ground stations $GS = \{gs_1, gs_2, \ldots, gs_n, \ldots\}$.
- A data processing center, denoted by dc.
- Destination of data $TN = \{t_1, t_2, \ldots, t_n, \ldots\}$.

During each slot, the network topology of SSN is constant. But during slot transitions it could change instantaneously. We use TEG to capture the impact of satellites' orbiting movements on data acquisition. We divide the plan horizon $[0, T)$ into K slots with duration of $\tau = T/k$.

The TEG, denoted by $G = (V, E)$, is shown in Fig. 1. Here, $G = (V, E)$, is a directed graph that corresponds to a network topology with K slots. The vertices of G represent the copy of source nodes, destination nodes, small satellites, observable objects, ground stations, relay satellites and data process centers for each slot. That is $V = V_s \cup V_{ob} \cup V_{ss} \cup V_{gs} \cup V_{rs} \cup V_{dc} \cup V_T$.

Graph G have five kinds of arcs: artificial arcs for SN and TN, data collection arcs, data storage arcs, fixed link arcs and opportunistic link arcs. We use the artificial arcs to accumulate the total transmission data and set the data rate of such links infinity, $C\left(dc_j^k, t_i\right) = \infty$, $C\left(s_i, ob_j^k\right) = \infty$. The data collection arcs represent capability of small satellites gathering mission data from observable objects, $E_{dc} = \left(ob_i^k, ss_j^k\right)$ and their capability equals the rate of mission data that small satellite ss_j can collect from observable object ob_i in the k_{th} slot,

$$C\left(ob_i^k, ss_j^k\right) = r_{dc} \tag{1}$$

where r_{dc} is the data collection rate of small satellites. The data storage arcs correspond to the capability of satellites, stations and data process centers to store data, which is defined as $E_s = \left\{\left(v_i^k, v_i^{k+1}\right) \big| v_i^k \in V_{ss} \cup V_{rs} \cup V_{gs} \cup V_{dc}, 1 \leq k \leq K - 1\right\}$. We set the capacity of data storage arc $\left(ss_i^k, ss_i^{k+1}\right)$ infinity, $C\left(ss_i^k, ss_i^{k+1}\right) = \infty$. Arcs $E_{fl} = \left\{\left(rs_i^k, gs_i^k\right) \big| 1 \leq i \leq RS, 1 \leq k \leq K.\right\} \cup \left\{\left(gs_i^k, dc^k\right) \big| 1 \leq i \leq GS, 1 \leq k \leq K\right\}$ are fixed and link arcs denoted by $E_{ol} = \left\{\left(ss_i^k, vs_j^k\right) \big| ss_i^k \in V_{ss}, vs_j^k \in V_{rs} \cup V_{gs}, 1 \leq k \leq K\right\}$ are opportunistic. Their capacity is the rate that mission data is able to be sent by the link,

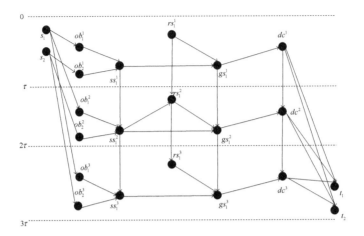

Fig. 1. An example of extending TEG to network model

$$C\left(vt_i^k, vr_j^k\right) = r\left(vt_i, vr_j\right) \tag{2}$$

where $r\left(vt_i, vr_j\right)$ is the data rate of link $\left(vt_i, vr_j\right)$. Because high speed wired links connect the data process centers and ground stations, we can assume the data transmission rate of them are enough mass, that is $CD\left(gs_i^k, dc^k\right) = \infty$.

2.2 Multi-commodity Algorithm

As according to transformation before, the impact of network dynamics on delivery process can be modeled mathematically using the extended TEG as Fig. 2. And the problem of routing optimization of small satellite network has been corresponding to a topic on a directed graph $G = (V, E)$ with k pairs of demands (s_j, t_j) $1 \le j \le k$ and the capacities of the edges are denoted by $u : E \to R$ which is equivalent to multi-commodity flow problem (MCP).

For the MCP which concludes k source-sink demand pairs (s_j, t_j), as we use the rates to present the capacity of the edges, routing optimization of small satellite networks based on TEG come to a maximum concurrent flow problem (MCFP). The MCFP is a multi-commodity flow problem and all pairs of demands concurrently flow. For MCFP, the target is to assign flow to global route so that the ratio (termed the throughput) of the flow contributed between a pair equals to all pairs of demands. This assignment must not exceed the capacities of all the edges. Each commodity corresponds to a specified demand $d_j(1 \le j \le k)$ in MCFP. Finding a flow that maximizes ratio of demands is our purpose. Letting $x(P)$ denote the quantity of the flow on path P, MCFP can be formulated as:

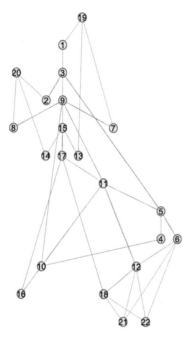

Fig. 2. Graph corresponding to the extended TEG in Fig. 1

$$\max_{s.t.} \quad \sum_{P:e\in P}^{\lambda} x(P) \le u(e) \quad \forall e$$

$$\sum_{P\in P_j} x(P) \ge \lambda d_j \quad \forall j \qquad (3)$$

$$x(P) \ge 0 \qquad \forall P$$

Polynomial solution for this problem can be found by using Linear Programming. To make the solution faster, we use a modified version of a different approximation algorithm from Fleischer [9].

Letting $l(e) = \delta/u(e)$, $z_j = \min_{P\in P_j} l(P)$, $x \equiv 0$ at first. The entire procedure is in phases and there are k iterations in each phase. The goal is routing d_j units flow from s_j to t_j in iteration j in steps. We apply the Dijkstra's shortest path algorithm with the length function and computes the shortest path P from s_j to t_j in iteration j. The minimum of the remaining demand and the bottleneck capacity of this path will be transmitted on P. Then the length $l(e)$ renews and we set z_j the current minimum length of the path from s_j to t_j. The algorithm stops until the function value $D(l)$ is upper than one, that is $\sum_e u(e)l(e) > 1$. A summary of the algorithm in Fig. 3, where we update the $l(e)$ by $1 + \varepsilon\frac{u}{u(e)}$ and set $\delta = \left(\frac{m}{1-\varepsilon}\right)^{-1/\varepsilon}$.

Input: network G,capacities $u(e)$, vertex pairs (s_j, t_j) with demands d_i,
$1 \leq i \leq k$, accuracy ε
Output: primal (infeasible) and dual solutions x and l

> Initialize $l(e) = \delta / u(e)$ $\forall e$, $x \equiv 0$.
> while $D(l) < 1$
>   for $j = 1$ to k do
> $d'_j \longleftarrow d_j$
>   while $D(l) < 1$ and $d'_j > 0$
> $P \longleftarrow$ shortest path in P_j using l
> $u \longleftarrow \min\{d'_j, \min_{e \in P} u(e)\}$
> $d'_j \longleftarrow d'_j - u$
> $x(P) \longleftarrow x(P) + u$
> $\forall e \in P$, $l(e) \longleftarrow l(e)(1 + \dfrac{\varepsilon u}{u(e)})$
>   end while
>   end while
>   Return (x, l).

Fig. 3. Algorithm for MCFP

The algorithm required no more than $2k \log m(\log k + \frac{1}{\varepsilon^2})$ iterations and the total time required by the ε-approximate solution is in $O^*(\varepsilon^{-2}m(k + m))$ time. If $D(l) > = 1$, then it will be sure that we can obtain at least $(1 - 3\varepsilon)$ times of the optimal solution by scaling the final flow by $\log_{1+\varepsilon} 1/\delta$.

3   Simulations

As the scale of small satellite network is not large, we define three scenarios of small satellites network to explore the influence of topologies and after extending TEG, there are respectively twenty-two, twenty-five and twenty-eight nodes in the graph. We assume that the capacities of all edges in the graph are twenty, except the infinity edges defined before and we set several source-sink demand pairs corresponding to specific demands. To investigate the effect of different algorithms, we choose a general method called augmented path maximum flow algorithm that is using single commodity max-flow algorithm for each source-sink demand pairs in sequence and augmenting the residual network graph every time after the single commodity max-flow is implemented. Then we will compare our MCFP algorithm with the augmented path maximum flow algorithm.

Results of the two algorithms are shown in the Figs. 4 and 5. The augmented path maximum flow algorithm is able to obtain the maximum throughput between single source-sink nodes, it cannot collaboratively optimize the maximum flow path traffic for multiple source-sink node pairs and the optimization of routing performance cannot be achieved. With different node numbers and different source-sink node pair requests, the small satellite network throughput of our method based on TEG model is obviously larger than that obtained by using the augmented path maximum flow algorithm. Furthermore,

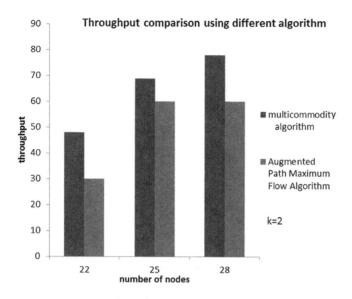

Fig. 4. Results of MCFP algorithm and augmented path maximum flow algorithm ($k = 2$)

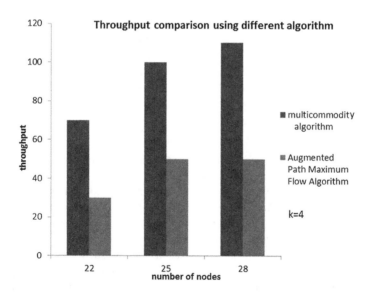

Fig. 5. Results of MCFP algorithm and augmented path maximum flow algorithm ($k = 4$)

comparing the results of two source-sink demand pairs and four source-sink demand pairs, the difference between the two algorithms is more obvious with four source-sink demands. We can see that the more complicated the topology is as well as the more demands it has, MCFP algorithm will have better effects than general solution.

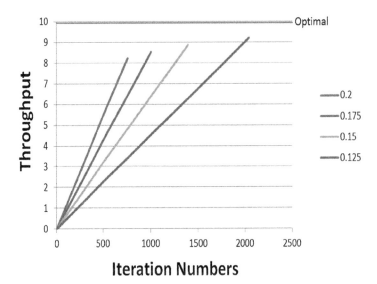

Fig. 6. Throughput vs. ε with 20 nodes ($k = 4$)

Table 1. The change of ε

ε	Iterations	Time (s)	Throughput
0.5	98	0.184	5.136
0.4	165	0.265	6.053
0.3	314	0.429	7.055
0.2	758	0.999	8.219
0.15	1395	1.672	8.861
0.1	3244	3.700	9.538

Both Fig. 6 and Table 1 show the details for the algorithm to solve the TEG graph of a satellite network with 22 vertices and 36 edges.

To explore the dependency on ε, we use the algorithm to solve a flow network of small satellite where the optimal throughout (*OPT*) is 9.9. *OPT* is marked as the gray horizontal line at the top in Fig. 6 and the closer to *OPT* ε is, the better results we get. The figure also shows the $(1 - 3\varepsilon)$ approximation guarantee of the solution. The guarantee says that the algorithm will produce a flow F such that $(1 - 3\varepsilon)OPT \leq F \leq OPT$, where F is the size of the flow. This guarantee means that the algorithm will produce a flow that its throughput is extremely close to *OPT*, in another word, is above the guarantee line, and under the *OPT* line.

The values of ε, iterations, running time and throughput can be found in Table 1. To look in detail, as the number of ε decreases, the algorithm needs more iterations and time to get the solution and the final throughput will be more optimal. From another point of view, if the network changes fast and requires making decision quickly and in time, choosing a reasonable ε to achieve the balance of the running time and the accuracy is a wise choice.

4 Conclusion

We apply the traditional time-expanded graph to model the data acquisition of small satellite network and use an approximation method to accelerate the solution for MCFP and make global optimization of routing between satellite network nodes. The quantitative comparison between our MCFP algorithm and general augmented path maximum flow algorithm proves the algorithm achieving better throughput and being closer to the optimal solution. Exploring the detail of the algorithm, we conclude that we need to make a reasonable selection of parameter in our algorithm for satellite network nodes communication to achieve the balance of the running time and the accuracy.

References

1. Jakhu, R.S., Pelton, J.N.: Small Satellites and Their Regulation. Springer, New York (2014). https://doi.org/10.1007/978-1-4614-9423-2
2. Ford, L.R., Fulkerson, D.R.: Flows in Networks. Princeton University Press, Princeton (1962)
3. Liu, R., Sheng, M., Lui, K.-S., Wang, X., Wang, Y., Zhou, D.: An analytical framework for resource-limited small satellite networks. IEEE Commun. Lett. **20**(2), 388–391 (2016)
4. Even, S., Itai, A., Shamir, A.: On the complexity of time table and multi-commodity flow problems. In: 16th Annual Symposium on Foundations of Computer Science, 1975, pp. 184–193. IEEE (1975)
5. Iri, M.: On an extension of the maximum-flow minimum-cut theorem to multicommodity flows. J. Oper. Res. Soc. Jpn **13**(3), 129–135 (1971)
6. Shahrokhi, F., Matula, D.W.: The maximum concurrent flow problem. J. ACM (JACM) **37**(2), 318–334 (1990)
7. Young, N.E.: Randomized rounding without solving the linear program. In SODA, vol. 95, pp. 170–178 (1995)
8. Garg, N., Koenemann, J.: Faster and simpler algorithms for multicommodity flow and other fractional packing problems. SIAM J. Comput. **37**(2), 630–652 (2007)
9. Fleischer, L.K.: Approximating fractional multicommodity flow independent of the number of commodities. SIAM J. Discrete Math. **13**(4), 505–520 (2000)

Modeling of Satellite-Earth Link Channel and Simulating in Space-Ground Integrated Network

Beishan Wang[(✉)] and Qi Guo

School of Information and Electronics,
Beijing Institute of Technology, Beijing, China
beishanwang@bit.edu.cn, guoqi_bit@163.com

Abstract. Space-Ground Integrated Network (SGIN) is the future network, and the satellite-earth link channel is one critical part of the SGIN. This paper simulates the satellite-earth link channel of SGIN based on the simulation environment of OMNeT++. We set up the model of space-ground network and satellite-earth link channel. The satellite-earth link channel includes two main parts, one part is the free space channel that ranges from the satellites to the aerosphere and the other part is the channel that ranges from aerosphere to the ground terminals. According to the ITU Recommendations, we simulate the satellite-earth link channel of the SGIN, from the results of the simulation. We analyze the satellite-earth link channel attenuation, obtaining the packet delay and packet arrival rate of the SGIN as well.

Keywords: Satellite-earth link channel · Space-ground integrated network
OMNeT++ network simulation · Packet delay · Packet arrival rate

1 Introduction

With the development of the STEM, especially the wireless communications. More and more information and data are propagated by satellite-communication, because there are amount of amazing advantages by using satellite to relay the signal, such as the wide coverage area, the long distance of communication and the wide frequency band. While the decreasing SNR and long-time delay since the longer distance between terminal and satellite are something we do not expect, so the research of satellite-earth link channel is worth for all satellite communication.

Multi-network fusion is one of the trends of future network, in the near future, we may build a unified network which contain the space satellite network and the ground internet. It will connect the earth with the outer space, and also is the foundation of IoT (Internet of Things). Therefore, the research of space-ground integrated network is important and worthful. In the propagation link, the satellite-earth link channel is one critical part of the SGIN [1, 2].

© ICST Institute for Computer Sciences, Social Informatics and Telecommunications Engineering 2018
X. Gu et al. (Eds.): MLICOM 2017, Part I, LNICST 226, pp. 364–372, 2018.
https://doi.org/10.1007/978-3-319-73564-1_36

2 Simulation of Satellite-Earth Link Channel

2.1 OMNeT++

There are several simulator of open source integrated development environment, such as NS2, OPNET. We choose OMNET++ software to simulate the satellite-earth channel model. OMNeT++ is the discrete event simulator which is more friendly-using and powerful to model wire communication network, wireless communication network and protocol simulation. In general, it can be used in any system simulation and modeling that can be solved by discrete event method [3, 4].

2.2 Build the Structure of the Space-Ground Network

Based on the orbit parameters of the satellites and the coordinates of the ground stations, we write the NED files and C++ and h files to set up the simulation space-ground network in the OMNeT++, the 2D view of the space-ground network is the following screenshot Fig. 1.

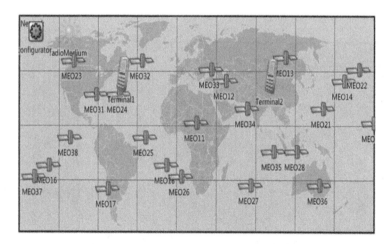

Fig. 1. 2D view of the space-ground network.

2.3 Build the Instance of the Satellite-Earth Link Channel

The satellite-earth link channel includes two main parts, one part is the free space channel that ranges from the satellites to the aerosphere and the other part is the channel that ranges from aerosphere to the ground terminals which mainly affected by three critical factors, the distance, the rainfall and the gas molecules characteristic frequency attenuation. The satellite-earth link channel attenuation is given by the following Fig. 2.

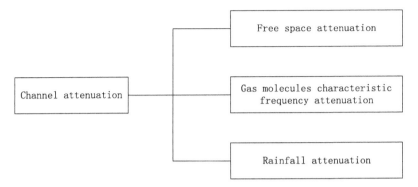

Fig. 2. The satellite-earth link channel attenuation.

According to the ITU standard of channel Recommendation ITU-R P.618-10, and Recommendation ITU-R P.676-9, we build the instance of the satellite-earth link channel. The view of the instance of the satellite-earth link channel is given by the following Fig. 3.

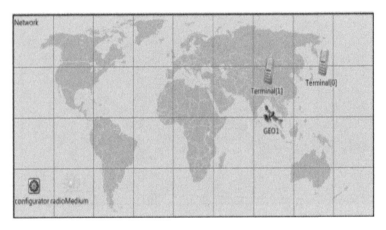

Fig. 3. The view of the instance of the satellite-earth link channel.

2.3.1 The Free Space Attenuation

The free space attenuation is easy to be derived from the equation of antenna. The attenuation F is given by the following equations:

$$F = (\lambda/D)^2/16\pi^2 L \tag{1}$$

Where:
λ: wavelength
d: distance
L: system loss

2.3.2 The Gas Molecules Characteristic Frequency Attenuation

The gas molecules characteristic frequency attenuation which is mainly determined by steam and dry air can be estimated by algorithms. The gas molecules characteristic frequency attenuation γ_o (dB/km) is given by the following equations with the different frequency interval [5].

For $f \leq 54$ GHz:

$$\gamma_o = \left[\frac{7.2r_t^{2.8}}{f^2 + 0.34r_p^2 r_t^{1.6}} + \frac{0.62\xi_3}{(54 - f)^{1.16\xi_1} + 0.83\xi_2} \right] f^2 r_p^2 \times 10^{-3}. \quad (2)$$

For 54 GHz $< f \leq 60$ GHz:

$$\gamma_o = \exp\left[\frac{\ln \gamma_{54}}{24}(f - 58)(f - 60) - \frac{\ln \gamma_{58}}{8}(f - 54)(f - 60) + \frac{\ln \gamma_{60}}{12}(f - 54)(f - 58) \right] \quad (3)$$

For 60 GHz $< f \leq 62$ GHz:

$$\gamma_o = \gamma_{60} + (\gamma_{62} - \gamma_{60})\frac{f - 60}{2}. \quad (4)$$

$$\phi(r_p, r_t, a, b, c, d) = r_p^a r_t^b \exp[c(1 - r_p) + d(1 - r_t)]. \quad (5)$$

Where:
f: requency
$r_p = p_{tot}/1013$, where p_{tot} represents total air pressure
$rt = 288/(273 + t)$
p: pressure
t: temperature.

2.3.3 The Rainfall Attenuation

The rainfall attenuation which is determined by rainfall can be estimated by the following geometry method, and there are so many correlation parameters in the calculation which we can obtain from the real physical world [6].

The diagram is presented in Fig. 4.

Step 1: Determine the rain height h_R, which can be found in P.839.
Step 2: Compute the parameter L_s

For $\theta \geq 5°$

$$L_s = \frac{(h_R - h_s)}{\sin \theta} \text{ km.} \quad (6)$$

For $\theta < 5°$

$$L_s = \frac{2(h_R - h_s)}{\left(\sin^2 \theta + \frac{2(h_R - h_s)}{R_e} \right)^{1/2} + \sin \theta} \text{ km.} \quad (7)$$

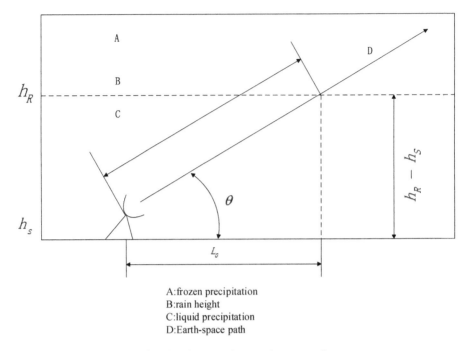

A:frozen precipitation
B:rain height
C:liquid precipitation
D:Earth-space path

Fig. 4. Diagram of an earth-space path.

If $h_R - h_s \leq 0$, the attenuation is equal to 0 and the estimation is finished.

Step 3: Compute the parameter L_G

$$L_G = L_S \cos \theta. \tag{8}$$

Step 4: If $R_{0.01} = 0$, the attenuation is equal to 0 and the estimation is finished.

Step5: Compute the parameter γ_R

$$\gamma_R = k(R_{0.01})^\alpha. \tag{9}$$

Step 6: Compute the parameter $r_{0.01}$

$$r_{0.01} = \frac{1}{1 + 0.78\sqrt{\frac{L_G \gamma_R}{f}} - 0.38(1 - e^{-2L_G})}. \tag{10}$$

Step 7:

$$\zeta = \tan^{-1}\left(\frac{h_R - h_s}{L_G r_{0.01}}\right) \text{ degrees.} \tag{11}$$

For $\zeta > \theta$

$$L_R = \frac{L_G r_{0.01}}{\cos \theta} \text{ km.} \tag{12}$$

Else,

$$L_R = \frac{(h_R - h_s)}{\sin \theta} \text{ km.} \tag{13}$$

Where:
$R_{0.01}$: average rainfall rate for 0.01% of one year
h_s: height over the average sea of station
θ: elevation angle
R_e: radius of the Earth
φ: atitude of the earth station
f: frequency.

This diagram method is one estimation of rainfall attenuation and we can obtain the specific results by the correlation parameters. This diagram method which we use is a simplification version of the ITU standard of recommendation, more specific version can be found in the Refs. [7–9].

3 Analysis of the Results

3.1 Receive Power

From the simulation of the OMNeT++, we change the parameters of the satellite-earth and debug the program to get the results of the simulation. The following table is the specific results of simulation (Table. 1).

Table 1. The parameters and results of the simulation.

	The 0.01% probability of average annual rainfall (mm/h)	Transmit power (W)	Frequency (GHz)	Angle of elevation (degree)	Relative position between the satellite and ground stations (m)	Height of ground station above the mean sea level (km)	Simulation results (Received power)
Real physical propagation model	10	100	30	60	1601932	10	2.3483491718013963e − 017 W **−136.2924 dBm**
	15	100	30	60	1601932	10	1.0210363911956929e − 017 W **−139.9096 dBm**
	30	100	30	60	1601932	10	3.1272583372063428e − 019 W **−155.0484 dBm**
Free space propagation model	N/A	100	30	N/A	1601932	N/A	2.4641907908140618e − 017 W **−136.0833 dBm**

When we set the parameter of 0.01% probability of annual rainfall 10 mm/h, the received power is **−136.2924 dBm**, as we set the parameter 15 mm/h, the received power is **−139.9096 dBm**, as we set the parameter 30 mm/h, the received power is **−155.0484 dBm**. When we use the free space propagation model channel, the received power is **−136.0833 dBm**. From the simulation results, we can see that with the increasing of rainfall, the receive power become less and less with the same transmit power. But the receive power is still acceptable for the receiver and terminals or ground stations.

We put the model of satellite-earth channel into the SGIN, so we can do more research by using this channel model.

We simulate the network packet flow as well, by changing the satellite-earth channel and the free space channel, we obtain different transmission results. As we regard the satellite-earth link as the free space channel, we can get the results of almost no error, as we add the real satellite-earth link channel into the OMNeT++, we are able to get a more specific result.

The statistical diagrams are illustrated in Figs. 5, 6, 7 and 8 below.

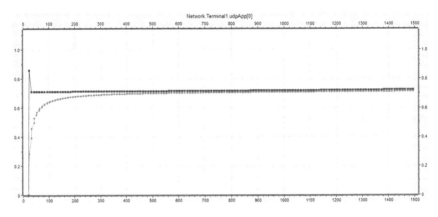

Fig. 5. Free space channel packet delay. (Color figure online)

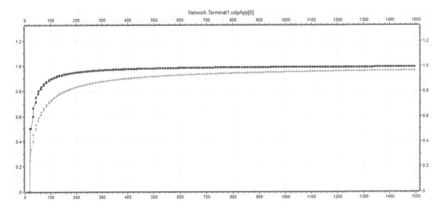

Fig. 6. Free space channel packet arrival rate. (Color figure online)

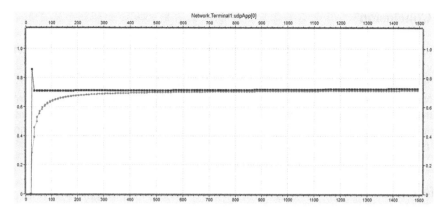

Fig. 7. Satellite-earth link channel packet delay. (Color figure online)

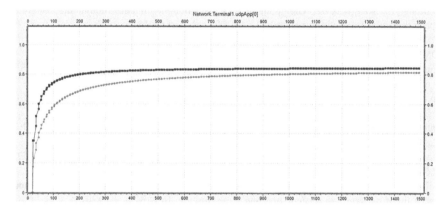

Fig. 8. Satellite-earth link channel packet arrival rate. (Color figure online)

3.2 Packet Delay and Packet Arrival Rate

From the four figures, we also get the variable results of both the packet delay and the packet arrival rate, the blue curve stands for the instant delay and packet arrival rate while the red curve stands for the mean delay and packet arrival rate. We could see that the packet delay and packet arrival rate become more and more steady as the increasing time and amount of packet. The reason is that the terminals search and get contact with the satellites in the beginning which cost some initial time. Above all, both of the results are acceptable.

From the statistical data, we not only generate the figures, but also get the characteristics of the data. The mean of packet delay of Fig. 5 which we simulate in the free space channel is typically 0.7131 s, and the variance of Fig. 5 is 0.0035. What is more, the mean of packet arrival rate is typically 96.50%, and the variance of packet arrival rate is 0.0068. In the simulation of satellite-earth link channel, the mean of packet delay is typically 0.7133 s and the variance of packet delay is 0.0035, the mean of packet arrival rate is typically 81.50%, and the variance of packet arrival rate is 0.0067.

4   Conclusion

In this paper, we build the structure of network and set up the model of satellite-earth channel link based on OMNeT++, after that, we simulate the network and satellite-earth channel to generate some data and figures that we are interested in, From the results of simulation of space-ground integrated network and satellite-earth link channel, we get the results in the channel with different parameters, and this will be a worthful reference for any communication and network scenario using satellite-earth link channel.

References

1. Fenghua, L., Lihua, Y., Wei, W., et al.: Research status and development trends of security assurance for space-ground integration information network. J. Commun. 156–168 (2016)
2. Naitong, Z., Kangjian, Z., Gongliang, L., et al.: Thought on constructing the integrated space-terrestrial information network. J. CAEIT. 223–230 (2015)
3. OMNeT++ User Guide Version5.0
4. OMNeT++ Simulation Manual Version5.0
5. International Telecommunications Union. http://www.itu.int/dms_pubrec/itu-r/rec/p/R-REC-P.676-11-201609-I.pdf
6. International Telecommunications Union. http://www.itu.int/dms_pubrec/itu-r/rec/p/R-REC-P.839-4-201309-I.pdf
7. International Telecommunications Union. http://www.itu.int/dms_pubrec/itu-r/rec/p/R-REC-P.838-3-200503-I.pdf
8. International Telecommunications Union. http://www.itu.int/dms_pubrec/itu-r/rec/p/R-REC-P.618-12-201507-I.pdf
9. Lijie, W., Hua, Z., Weitao, S., et al.: Impact of rain attenuation of relay satellite on manned space flight mission and related solutions. Telecommun. Eng. 379–384 (2015)

A Deep Learning Method Based on Convolutional Neural Network for Automatic Modulation Classification of Wireless Signals

Yu Xu[1], Dezhi Li[1], Zhenyong Wang[1,2(✉)], Gongliang Liu[1], and Haibo Lv[1]

[1] School of Electronics and Information Engineering,
Harbin Institute of Technology, Harbin, Heilongjiang, China
{xu_yu,lidezhi,ZYWang,liugl,elitelv}@hit.edu.cn
[2] Shenzhen Academy of Aerospace Technology, Shenzhen, Guangdong, China

Abstract. Automatic modulation classification (AMC) plays an important role in many fields to identify the modulation type of wireless signals. In this paper, we introduce deep learning to signal recognition. Based on architecture analysis of the convolutional neural network (CNN), we used real signal data generated by instruments as dataset, and proposed an improved CNN architecture to achieve compatible recognition accuracy of modulation classification. According to various conditions of signal noise ratio (SNR), we test the proposed CNN architecture with the real sampled signals. Experiments results show that the high-layer network is not necessary for modulation recognition with high SNR signals. The proposed CNN architecture has higher average classification accuracy than RESNET and is more compatible for modulation classification of signals with lower SNR.

Keywords: Modulation classification · Deep learning
Convolutional neural network · Wireless signal

1 Introduction

Automatic modulation classification is aiming to detect the modulation type of received signals in order to recover signals by demodulation. The dominant approach of signal modulation recognition can be categorized as likelihood-based methods and feature-based methods [1]. Most likelihood-based classifiers require parameter estimation, while feature-based methods can be free from parameter estimation and achieve high popularity in recent years. Generally, feature-based methods consist of two steps: feature extraction and classifier, which can provide classification decisions according to some particular criterion.

Although the feature-based methods have shown great advantages in classification, two problems still remain: one is the difficulty of Manually Feature Extraction, the other is Noise Covering. Most conventional feature-based methods cannot utilize full feature information when the performance of feature-based methods relies on the

© ICST Institute for Computer Sciences, Social Informatics and Telecommunications Engineering 2018
X. Gu et al. (Eds.): MLICOM 2017, Part I, LNICST 226, pp. 373–381, 2018.
https://doi.org/10.1007/978-3-319-73564-1_37

quality of the extracted features. Moreover, for modulation classification, manually feature extraction is complicated and difficult for comprehensive modulation types of wireless signals. For the Noise Covering problem, if the SNR is very low, the features we can extract are so limited that we can't get a satisfied performance for automatic modulation classification.

Deep learning is a fascinating field and has achieved a series of state-of-the-art results in different domains. However, Deep learning also has been tried for modulation classification in some related researches. In paper [2], a modulation classification method based on stacked de-noising sparse auto-encoder (SDAE) is investigated, which can extract modulation features automatically, and classify input signals based on the extracted features to get compatible results. Also based on deep learning algorithms, the stacked sparse auto-encoders to extract features from ambiguity function (AF) images of signals are proposed to discriminate digital modulated signals [3]. After that, the obtained features are fed back into a Softmax regression classifier in order to recognize 7 popular modulations including ASK, PSK, QAM, FSK, MSK, LFM and OFDM. In paper [4], deep belief network (DBN) is applied for pattern recognition and classification. Compared with those likelihood-based methods and feature-based methods, they all show great success of high recognition accuracy in various SNR conditions.

The main idea of this paper is to provide a stacked convolutional neural network of deep learning architecture for modulation classification based on extracted features of wireless signals automatically. The rest of the paper is organized as follows. In Sect. 2, principles of Convolutional Neural Network are investigated. Based on real sampled data of wireless signals, an improved CNN architecture is trained and proposed in Sect. 3. In Sect. 4, experiments are included to compare average classification accuracy with RESNET [5] under conditions of various SNR. Finally, conclusions are drawn in Sect. 5.

2 Principle of Convolutional Neural Network

The goal of a neural network is to approximate a function f^*. For a classifier, function $y = f^*(x)$ maps an input x to a category y. A neural network defines a mapping criterion $y = f(x, \theta)$ and obtains the value of the parameters θ that result in the optimal approximation function of the true mapping function.

Convolutional Neural Network is a powerful architecture of artificial neural network, which is popular because of state-of-the-art achievements in computer vision processing and natural language processing.

2.1 Architecture of Convolutional Neural Network

CNN process consists of two components: convolutional layers and pooling layers. Convolutional layers are comprised of filter kernel and feature maps. The filter kernels have weighted inputs and generate an output value like a neuron. The feature map is the output of one filter kernel applied to the previous layer. A given filter kernel is drawn across the entire previous layer and moved one point at a time, which depends on the stride. Each position results in activation of the neuron and generates an output to form the feature map, as illustrated in Fig. 1.

The pooling layer down-samples the feature map of previous layers. Pooling layers follow a sequence of convolutional layers to consolidate the learned features in the previous feature map. Therefore, pooling may be considered as a technique to compress and generalize feature representations, so as to generally reduce the model overfitting phenomena. In Fig. 2, the max pooling process is illustrated with pool width of 3 and stride of 2.

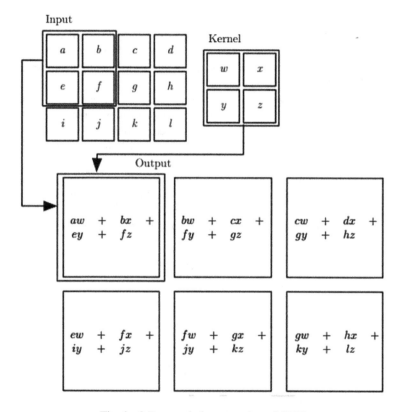

Fig. 1. 2-D convolution operation of CNN

2.2 Training Process Based on Stochastic Gradient Descent

Stochastic Gradient Descent (SGD) is typical and preferred training algorithm for neural networks. One row of data is inputted into the network at a time. The network activates neurons forward to produce an output value finally. Then the output value is compared to the expected output value to generate an error value. The error is backward propagated through the network, in which the weights of layer are updated one after another, according to the contributed amount to the error. The process is repeated for all of the examples in the training data to get a trained network of the intended goal.

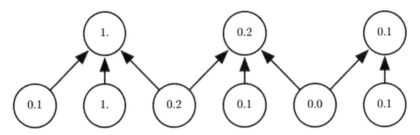

Fig. 2. Max pooling process of CNN

The weights in the network can be updated from the calculated errors for each training example, which can result in fast but also chaotic changes to the network. On the other hand, the errors can be saved up across all of the training examples and the network can be updated at the end.

For computational efficiencies, it is necessary to define the batch size of datasets. The batch size is often reduced to a small number of tens or hundreds of examples before updates. The amount that weights are updated is controlled by a configuration parameter called the learning rate, which controls the each step of network weights updating for a given error.

The cost function is important to design a deep neural network. In most cases, the parametric model defines a distribution $p(y|x; \theta)$ and the principle of maximum likelihood is used to train the model. The cost function is defined as the cross-entropy between the distribution of training data and the model predictions, as shown in Formula (1).

$$J(\theta) = -\log p_{model}(y|x) \tag{1}$$

The Softmax functions are often used as the output of a classifier, which represent the probability distribution over n different classes. The Softmax function is given by

$$soft\max(z)_i = \frac{\exp(z_i)}{\sum_j \exp(z_j)} \tag{2}$$

The exponential Softmax function works very well when the Softmax function is trained to output a target value y based on maximum log-likelihood. In this case, the Softmax function in this paper is defined in terms of exponential function:

$$\log soft\max(z)_i = z_i - \log \sum_j \exp(z_j) \tag{3}$$

When the training process maximizes the log-likelihood, the first term z_i is encouraged to be increased, while the second term is punished to be decreased. The negative log-likelihood cost function always strongly penalizes the most inactive prediction.

3   The Improved CNN for Modulation Classification

To meet the requirements of modulation classification, our network architectures are mainly inspired by ALEXNET [6], as shown in Fig. 3.

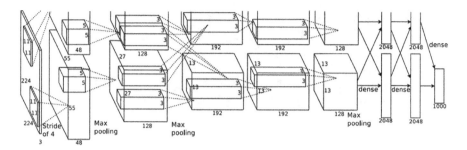

Fig. 3. The architecture of ALEXNET

3.1   Signals Data Sampled and Process

Because digital modulation has better immunity performances to interference, which is mostly discussed in the literatures for modulation classification. Here, it is assumed that there is a single carrier-transmitted signal in additive white Gaussian noise (AWGN) channel. The modulation types include 2ASK, BPSK, QPSK, 8PSK and 16QAM.

The signal data are produced by vector signal generator SMU200A. The sampling rate is 1 GHz. All the signal data of different modulation types have the same carrier frequency of 100 MHz and bandwidth of 25 MHz. Every sample has 2000 raw points and there are 25000 samples in total, 5000 samples for each modulation type. The only preprocess is to rescale the amplitude to the range of −2 V to 2 V. The spectrum map of sampled BPSK signal is shown in the Fig. 4.

For most classification and regression process, there is still possibility to get results even with small random noise added to the input. However, neural networks are proved not robust to noise [7]. One way to improve the robustness of neural networks is simply to do training process with input random noise data. So in training procedure to improve the robustness, training data of same SNR are included, which are also used to test the performance of proposed method in different SNR conditions.

When the network layers are not deep, it is not likely to encounter the problems like vanishing/exploding gradients [8, 9]. The principle of maximum likelihood is taken as the cost function, which means the cross-entropy between the training data and the prediction of the model is regarded as the cost function. The weights are initialized with Gaussian distribution initializers, which have zero means and unit variances. The SGD is involved with a mini-batch size of 256. The weight decay is 0.0001 and the momentum is 0.9. The learning rate starts from 0.1. When there are errors plateaus occur, the learning rate descends at rate of 10 times.

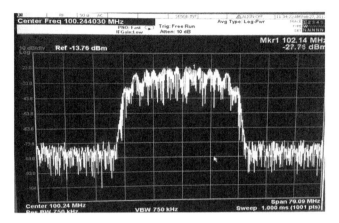

Fig. 4. The spectrum map of BPSK signal

As for the testing process, it is typically to use a simple separation of the same sampled data into training and testing datasets. In experiments, 80% data of the sampled signal is assigned to training dataset and 20% data of the sampled signal is assigned to testing dataset. Finally when the training is halt, we get the accuracy through inputting the testing datasets and statistical the accuracy.

3.2   The Improved CNN Architecture

It is found that the removal of the fully-connected layers of ALEXNET will reduce the amount of weight parameters and get little impact of the recognition accuracy performance. In this paper, the large kernel size is designed for better performances and acceptable complexity. Moreover, after investigating the deep neural network with more than 30 layers, it is found there are over-fitting problems. It is possible to apply a shallow neural network to compete modulation recognition for signals with reasonable SNR.

Based on the analysis above, the number of input neuron is set to 2000, which means every sample has 2000 raw points. The improved CNN is proposed with 3 convolutional layers, and each convolutional layer is followed by a max pooling layer. At the end of the CNN network, a 5-way fully-connected layer with Softmax is used to output the probability of 5 kinds of signal modulations classification. The convolutional layers have filter kernels with length of 40. 64 filter kernels are used in both the input layer and the second layer. For the third layer, the filter kernels are increased to length of 128. The max pooling layers perform down-sampling with stride of 2 and pool width of 3 to get overlapping pooling. We do not use the any regularization like dropout [10]. So, the improved CNN consists of 4 weighted layers, as shown in Fig. 5.

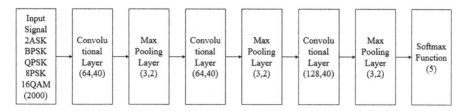

Fig. 5. The improved CNN structure

4 Experiments and Results Analysis

In order to evaluate recognition performances of deep neural networks and shallow neural networks, a 32-layers RESNET and the improve CNN with 4 layers are compared under condition of SNR = 0 dB.

Table 1. The accuracy comparison between the improved CNN and RESNET (SNR = 0 dB)

	The improved CNN	32 layers RESNET
Training accuracy	Approximate 100%	Approximate 100%
Testing accuracy	Approximate 100%	86.7%

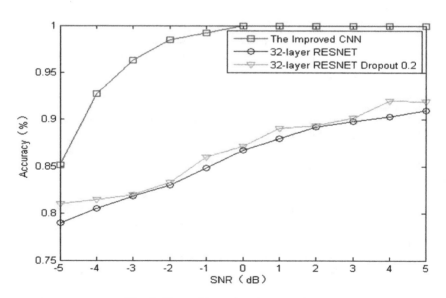

Fig. 6. Recognition accuracy comparison

As shown in Table 1, although both have similar training accuracy, the improved 4-layer CNN has better testing accuracy than the 32-layer RESNET. Because of overfitting problem, the 32-layer RESNET may be unnecessarily large for automatic modulation classification of SNR = 0 dB signals. For SNR = 0 dB signals, the modulation feature is distinct to be extracted for recognition, which can be completed by a shallow neural network. When the SNR of received signals is very weak, a deep neural network may provide stronger power to distinguish signal from noise.

As shown in Fig. 6, recognition accuracy performances of the improved CNN are compared with RESNET network in different SNR conditions. According to the results, the improved CNN has better recognition accuracy. But the descent speed in RESNET network is more stable than the improved CNN with shallow layers as the SNR drops to a low extent. The RESNET network is more powerful in extracting features when the SNR is low enough which leads to better robustness to noise. The RESNET network with dropout layer of 0.2 has little improvement, but more training time and training data are required, which is not recommend for applications of real-time signal detections.

5   Conclusions

The main purpose of this paper is to design a features extraction method based on convolutional neural network for automatic modulation classification of wireless signals. Real signal data generated by instruments are involved to train a CNN network and test recognition accuracy performances in different SNR conditions. It is found that the deep layer network architecture is not necessary for high SNR signals due to the overfitting problem, yet the shallow layer network architecture is more competent. By removing the fully-connected layer of CNN, the network topology is simplified to reduce complexity of training. According to the test results, the proposed improved CNN has better recognition accuracy than RESNET, which is attracting for real-time wireless signal detections.

Acknowledgement. This work was supported by National Natural Science Foundation of China. (No. 61601147, No. 61571316, No. 61371100) and the Fundamental Research Funds for the Central Universities (Grant No. HIT. MKSTISP. 2016013).

References

1. Hazza, A., Shoaib, M., Alshebeili, S.A., Fahad, A.: An overview of feature-based methods for digital modulation classification. In: 2013 1st International Conference on Communications, Signal Processing and Their Applications, pp. 1–6. IEEE Press, New York (2013)
2. Zhu, X., Fujii, T.: A modulation classification method in cognitive radios system using stacked denoising sparse autoencoder. In: 2017 IEEE Radio and Wireless Symposium, pp. 218–220. IEEE Press, New York (2017)
3. Dai, A., Zhang, H., Sun, H.: Automatic modulation classification using stacked sparse auto-encoders. In: 13th IEEE International Conference on Signal Processing, pp. 248–252. IEEE Press, New York (2017)
4. Mendis, G.J., Wei, J., Madanayake, A.: Deep learning-based automated modulation classification for cognitive radio. In: 2016 IEEE International Conference on Communication Systems, pp. 1–6. IEEE Press, New York (2016)

5. He, K., Zhang, X., Ren, S., Sun, J.: Deep residual learning for image recognition. In: 29th IEEE Conference on Computer Vision and Pattern Recognition, CVPR 2016, pp. 770–778. IEEE Press, New York (2016)
6. Krizhevsky A., Sutskever I., Hinton G.E.: ImageNet classification with deep convolutional neural networks. In: 26th Annual Conference on Neural Information Processing Systems, vol. 25, no. 2, pp. 1097–1105. ACM, New York (2012)
7. Tang, Y., Eliasmith, C.: Deep networks for robust visual recognition. In: 27th International Conference on Machine Learning, pp. 1055–1062. ACM, New York (2010)
8. Bengio, Y., Simard, P., Frasconi, P.: Learning long-term dependencies with gradient descent is difficult. IEEE Trans. Neural Netw. **5**, 157–166 (1994). IEEE Press, New York
9. Glorot, X., Bengio, Y.: Understanding the difficulty of training deep feedforward neural networks. In: 13th International Conference on Artificial Intelligence and Statistics, AISTATS 2010, pp. 249–256. Microtome Publishing, Brookline (2010)
10. Srivastava, N., Hinton, G., Krizhevsky, A., Sutskever, I., Salakhutdinov, R.: Dropout: a simple way to prevent neural networks from overfitting. J. Mach. Learn. Res. **15**, 1929–1958 (2014). Microtome Publishing, Brookline

Modeling and Performance Analysis of Multi-layer Satellite Networks Based on STK

Bo Li, Xiyuan Peng, Hongjuan Yang[(✉)], and Gongliang Liu

School of Information and Electrical Engineering,
Harbin Institute of Technology, Weihai 264209, People's Republic of China
{libol983,pxy,hjyang,liugl}@hit.edu.cn

Abstract. With the difference of satellite altitude, there are always some inherent defects in the traditional single-layer satellite networks. In this paper, in order to improve the performance of the single-layer networks, a multi-layer satellite network model composed of LEO/MEO/GEO and inter satellite link is proposed. In this model, the LEO and MEO layers are used as the access layer, and the data transmission is carried out to the ground. As the core layer, the GEO layer is responsible for the management of the whole network and the link assignment. Then modeling the network based on the STK satellite simulation platform and carrying out the simulation analysis of ground coverage, the performance of the inter satellite link and the link transmission. Theoretical analysis and simulation results show that the design of multi-layer satellite network is reasonable and effective, and also can be used in the construction of the integrated satellite-terrestrial networks.

Keywords: Multi-layer satellite networks · Inter satellite link
Ground coverage · Link transmission

1 Introduction

Since the concept of Multi-layer satellite networks was brought up, it has received extensive attention from various countries [1]. Up till now, most satellite systems adopt single-layer satellite network, which means that all satellites are running in the same altitude [2–5]. For instance, the famous GPS [6] satellite navigation system—Globalstar [7], applies single-layer network. However, with all satellites working on the same height, the capacity of systems will be greatly limited. The lower the satellite is, the smaller area it covers, which means it need more satellites to cover the same area. In the meanwhile, when the height of satellite declines, its speed increases, the network topology changes drastically, and the Doppler frequency increases. Comparatively, though the covered area increases when the orbit altitude of satellite augments, the transmission delay and attenuation become greater. Therefore, the single-layer satellite network is unable to satisfy our demands. If we take satellites on different altitude to constitute the system, and take advantages of each layer, it's possible to eliminate the drawbacks of single-layer network, as well as to bring some good properties.

© ICST Institute for Computer Sciences, Social Informatics and Telecommunications Engineering 2018
X. Gu et al. (Eds.): MLICOM 2017, Part I, LNICST 226, pp. 382–393, 2018.
https://doi.org/10.1007/978-3-319-73564-1_38

For most researches concerning satellite network topology, their focuses stay on the network structure design, permanent inter-satellite network and the performance of ground coverage, and very few of them model and make comprehensive estimation of the network from the perspective of ground coverage, inter-satellite network performance and network transmission features, so as to ensure the design workable and superior to others. In reference [2], the requirements for constructing permanent inter-satellite network are brought up, but it fails to give out the exact network design. In reference [3], one possible plan for designing multi-layer satellite network is brought up, but no analysis on transmission features is given out.

In this thesis, a detailed approach to how to design multi-layer satellite network and how to connect inter-satellite network is raised. Then, based on the satellite analysis toolbox—STK, analysis of ground coverage, inter-satellite network performance and transmission is carried out. Meanwhile, detailed simulation graph and data is achieved during this process. The combination of theoretical analysis and simulation proved the feasibility of the designed model of multi-layer network, and this design will give some practical suggestions on China's space-network development.

2 Multi-layer Satellite Network Modeling

2.1 Model of Multi-layer Satellite Network

The multi-layer satellite network model raised in this paper is as shown in Fig. 1. The network is divided into 3 layers, which are LEO layer, MEO layer and GEO layer. Because of the comparatively low altitude and medium coverage of LEO layer and MEO layer, they can serve as the accessing layer of the network, so as to connect to and exchange information with the ground network. GEO layer, because of its high altitude, though it has massive ground coverage, its long transmission delay and server attenuation makes it inappropriate to connect GEO layer to the ground network directly. So, it is selected as the core layer of the network, in charge of the network running and chain allocation, so as to choose the best route for data transmission among satellites [8–11].

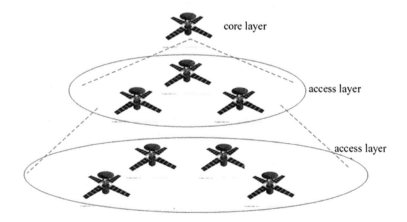

Fig. 1. Multi-layer satellite network model

2.2 Network Parameters

Quasi regression orbit is chosen in this system, which means in n2 star days, the satellite circles around the earth for n1 times, then it repeats it previous running trace. Its mathematical equation is:

$$T_s \times n_2 = T_e \times n_1 \tag{1}$$

where n_1 and n_2 are none-zero natural numbers, T_e and T_s stand for the star day length and satellite period of revolution. The exact parameters for quasi regression orbit are as shown in Fig. 2.

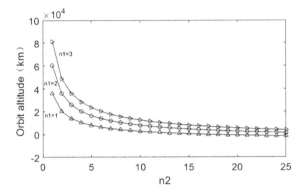

Fig. 2. Acceptable altitudes for quasi regression orbit

When the orbit altitude is h, the half geocentric-angle of covered area by satellite can be expressed as

$$\alpha = \arccos\left[\frac{R_e COSE}{h + R_e}\right] - E \tag{2}$$

where R_e is the earth radius, E is the angle of elevation from observation point to the satellite.

For the satellite network needs to realize global coverage and has to focus on China's territory, circular orbit is the best choice for this system, since satellite running on elliptic orbit can only realize steady coverage on Mid latitude region when it is at the apogee. And in terms of constellation configuration, the following drawbacks of polar orbit, which are sparse coverage on low latitude region, dense coverage on high latitude region, unbalanced coverage on different areas and high possibility of satellites crash into each other while running on the polar area, make it inappropriate for this system. Delta constellation is more appropriate for this system because of its capability of smooth coverage.

To realize globe coverage, the half geocentric angle is calculated based on the orbit height, then how many orbits are needed and how many satellites should be there on each orbit is estimated. Since Delta constellation system mainly covers the medium and low latitude areas, satellite on the LEO layer mainly cover those areas mentioned above. Then, because of the feature of massive coverage, we take advantage of satellites on the MEO layer to have supplementary coverage on the mid and low latitude area, as well as to cover the high latitude areas especially the polar area.

Finally, based on the analysis above, parameters of each orbit are calculated in combination with coverage requirements. The designed multi-layer satellite network is as show in the following Table 1:

Table 1. Parameters in the multi-layer satellite networks

Orbit	LEO	MEO	GEO
Orbit height (km)	1673	13899	35786
Orbit type	Quasi regression orbit	Quasi regression orbit	Synchronous orbit
Inclination	50°	53°	0°
Num. of orbits	4	2	1
Num. of satellite on each orbit	7	3	3
Total satellites	28	6	3

It can be seen from the table above that it takes 37 satellites in total to satisfy the coverage requirements, and the number is less than other designs of multi-layer satellite network. The declination of satellites can not only dramatically reduce the launching cost but also simplify the network management.

3   Inter-Satellite Link Design

The term inter-satellite link refers to the communication link between satellites, which are usually base on micro wave or light. Via inter-satellite link, information can be transmitted directly between satellites, which can dramatically reduce time-delay and attenuation caused by retransmission via station. Moreover, it can decrease the number of stations.

3.1   Inter-Satellite Link Design Within the Same Layer

For satellites on the same altitude, their visibility is shown in Fig. 3 (taking LEO as example).

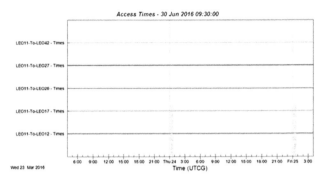

Fig. 3. Visibility within LEO layer

It can be seen from the graph that for one LEO satellite, its permanent visible to the two satellites on the same orbit with and adjacent to it. In the meanwhile, it is permanent visible to two satellites on the adjacent orbit. Therefore, each satellite on these three layers can be connected to the satellites which are permanent visible to it according to the regularity mentioned above.

3.2   Inter-Satellite Link Design Within Different Layer

Taking MEO-LEO as example, the visibility of the inter-layer link is shown in Fig. 4.

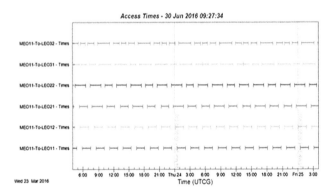

Fig. 4. Visibility within LEO layer and MEO layer

As it can be seen from the graph above, no permanent inter-satellite link can be established between satellites on different layer. However, the normal operation of inter-satellite links can be assured by the rule that satellite on the upper layer covers the satellite on the lower layer, which is to say that each satellite on the lower layer can be covered by one satellite on the upper layer. Even if in one moment that the satellite on the lower layer is not covered by the satellites on the upper layer and satellite data cannot be transmitted, the inter-satellite links can be reallocated by the system, and the data can be transmitted to a satellite covered by satellites on the upper layer, then transmitted to the upper layer.

According to this method, six MEO satellites are evenly assigned to three GEO satellites; 28 LEO satellites were assigned to six MEO satellites, where five MEO satellites are linked to five LEO Satellites, and one MEO satellite is connected to three LEO satellites. Up till now, the design of the multi-layer satellite network is accomplished, and the explicit distribution method of the inter-satellite link is shown in the following Table 2.

Table 2. Inter-satellite links allocation

Satellite orbit type	LEO	MEO	GEO
Inter-satellite link within the same layer	6	3	2
Inter-satellite within different layers	/	5 LEO and 3 LEO	2 MEO
Visibility of Inter-satellite link within the same layer	Permanent visible	Permanent visible	Permanent visible
Visibility of Inter-satellite link within different layers	/	Not permanent visible	Not permanent visible

4 Analysis and Discussion on Performance of Multi-layer Satellite Network

4.1 Coverage Analysis

For one specific area, we can make use of various satellite services only when it is covered by the satellite. And for coverage performance, we primarily care about the percentage of satellite coverage and the number of satellites can be accessed at the same time. According to introduction above, only LEO layer and MEO layer of the three layers serve as the access layer, so as to connect with the ground network. Therefore, only access layer was taken into consideration when analyze ground coverage. The percentage of covered territory of China is shown in the Fig. 5.

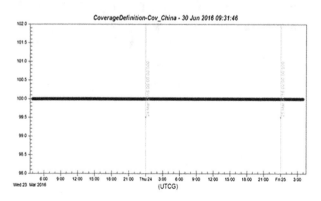

Fig. 5. Percentage of China's covered territory

It can be seen that in one cycle, satellites can reach 100% uninterrupted coverage of China. Since quasi regression orbit is adopted in this system, satellites will repeat its previous trace after one satellite circle. Therefore, the satellite network can provide coverage for China at any time, which reflects the superiority of the quasi regression orbit. Detailed information about how many satellites cover China's territory is shown in Fig. 6.

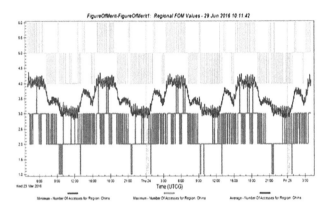

Fig. 6. No. of satellites covering China

Within one satellite cycle, the satellite network can guarantee good service for China's demands, with at most 6 satellites, at least one satellite and an average of 3.5 satellites cover China. The global coverage is as shown in Fig. 7.

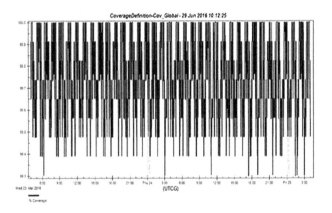

Fig. 7. Percentage of covered area on earth

In one cycle, the covered area of the globe outnumbers 99.3%, which actually promises global coverage. As for the polar area, number of satellites that covers it is as shown in Fig. 8.

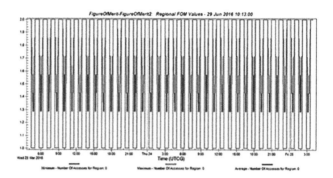

Fig. 8. No. of satellites cover the polar areas

This graph indicates that even in human population sparse polar areas that are difficult to cover, there still has 1.5 satellites in average to cover them, which satisfies the local people's daily and scientific research demands. To sum up, the designed satellite network well satisfies the designing requirements in terms ground coverage.

4.2 Performance of Inter-Satellite Link

Parameters concerning the inter-satellite link performance mainly include Azimuth Angle, Elevation Angle, and Link Range. The first two parameters determine the relative position of the satellites, as well as the complexity and direction of the satellites' antennas. The change of link range determines launching power of on-board system and its fluctuating range.

The performance of the inter-satellite links within the same layer is shown in Fig. 9.

The performance of inter-satellite links between satellites from different layer is shown in Fig. 10.

Figures 9 and 10 indicate that the performance of inter-satellite links changes in a regular way. And based on this disciplinarian, the posture of satellite in space can be predicted, which will dramatically enhance the antennas tracking and capture ability.

4.3 Performance of Link Transmission

The transmission of satellite network includes transmission from satellite to station and transmission within stars, in either way, signals, affected by the loss of free space loss, will attenuate during the process of transmission, which can be expressed as

$$L_f = 92.44 + 20 \lg d + 20 \lg f \qquad (3)$$

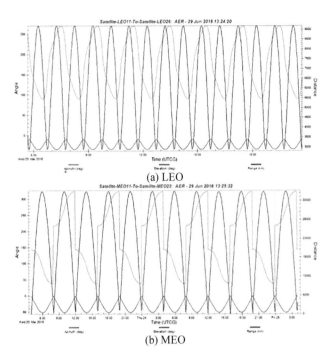

(a) LEO

(b) MEO

Fig. 9. Performance of inter-satellite links within the same layer

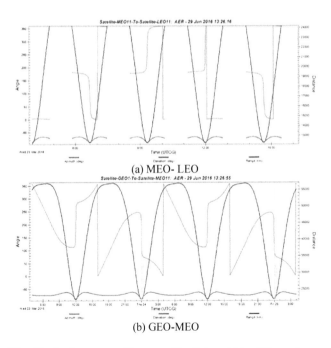

(a) MEO- LEO

(b) GEO-MEO

Fig. 10. Performance of inter-satellite links within different layers

where L_f is the free space transmission loss, d is the transmission distance, f is the frequency of microwave, c is the speed of light. The relationship between free space transmission loss and transmission distance of different frequencies is shown in the graph bellow (Fig. 11).

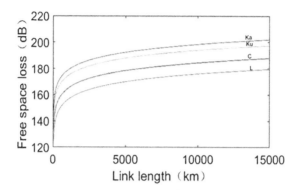

Fig. 11. The relationship between the loss of free space and the length of the link

In addition, due to the earth's unique environment, the atmospheric absorption loss and rain attenuation cannot be ignored when information is transmitted between satellites and ground station, and it should be considered in the simulation. Take Beijing station as an example, Table 3 is the simulation results which represents the transmission performance of links between Beijing station and LEO satellites.

Table 3. Transmission performance of links between Beijing station and LEO satellites

Time	Free space transmission loss	Rain attenuation	Atmospheric absorption loss	BER
23 Mar 2016 06:09:00.000	−185.8490	−6.8403	−0.1827	4.101039e−005
23 Mar 2016 06:09:20.000	−185.5830	−6.5504	−0.1706	1.135835e−005
23 Mar 2016 06:09:40.000	−185.3131	−6.2868	−0.1596	2.765264e−006
23 Mar 2016 06:10:00.000	−185.0397	−6.0466	−0.1498	5.860816e−007
23 Mar 2016 06:10:20.000	−184.7634	−5.8275	−0.1408	1.071793e−007

Atmospheric absorption loss and rain attenuation can be neglected when information is transmitted between satellites. However, the long distance between satellites usually leads to great free space transmission loss. Here, take the links between LEO satellites and MEO satellites as an example, transmission performance is simulated, which is as shown in the Table 4.

Table 4. Transmission performance of links within MEO satellites and LEO satellites

Time	Free space transmission loss	Rain attenuation	Atmospheric absorption loss	BER
23 Mar 2016 05:53:00.000	−209.4899	0	0	3.177611e−007
23 Mar 2016 05:59:40.000	−208.7834	0	0	3.293271e−008
23 Mar 2016 06:06:20.000	−207.9378	0	0	1.304739e−009
23 Mar 2016 06:13:00.000	−206.9654	0	0	1.371072e−011
23 Mar 2016 06:19:40.000	−205.9093	0	0	2.720691e−014

Simulation results show that in the process of transmission, free space loss is the main result that leads to attenuation, which can be explained that the transmission distance of space network is longer than ground network. By installing appropriate transmitters and receivers and by configuring antennas correctly, the demands of transmission can be satisfied. In the table above, parameters are fluctuating constantly due to the constant change of distance between satellites. The decrease of distance between satellites will lead to smaller transmitting loss, so as the smaller BER. And as long as the satellite is visible to each other, the BER can meet the transmitting requirements.

5 Conclusions

In this paper, a tri-layer satellite network of LEO/MEO/GEO is analyzed and established. Firstly, the type of orbit and the type of constellation are decided. Then, detailed parameters of the network including satellites' altitude, number of orbits and numbers of satellites on each orbit are selected. Eventually, a multi-layer satellites network system consisting of 28 LEO satellites, 6 MEO satellites and 3 GEO satellites is adopted.

Inter-satellite links are established in this thesis. Firstly, visibility of satellites in three circumstances, which are on the same orbit, on adjacent orbit of the same layer and orbit of different layers is analyzed. Then, permanent inter-satellite links and none-permanent inter-satellite links are established, so as to ensure that each satellite is connected to the satellite adjacent to it, as well as ensuring that satellites on the upper layer can fully cover the satellites of the lower layer.

Detailed simulation graphs and statistics from the aspects of ground coverage, performance of inter-satellite link and transmission performance are achieved based on the satellite analysis toolbox—STK. Simulation results can be expressed as follow: the approach raised in this thesis can realize full coverage around the globe, as well as continuous coverage of China; curves of inter-satellites links' performance is achieved, so as satellites' running disciplinarian, which can be used to predict satellites' relative position, as well as providing convenience for antennas on-board to track its target. Transmission performance of inter-satellite link is simulated, and the bit-error-rate can still satisfy the transmission requirements when taking free space loss and the environmental factors on earth into consideration. All these work done above Verifies the validity and superiority of the multi-layer satellite network designed in this paper.

Acknowledgments. This work is supported in part by National Natural Science Foundation of China (No. 61401118, No. 61371100 and No. 61671184), Natural Science Foundation of Shandong Province (No. ZR2014FP016), the Fundamental Research Funds for the Central Universities (No. HIT.NSRIF.2016100 and 201720) and the Scientific Research Foundation of Harbin Institute of Technology at Weihai (No. HIT(WH)201409 and No. HIT(WH)201410).

References

1. Li, D., Shen, X.: On construction of China's space information network. Geomat. Inf. Sci. Wuhan Univ. **40**(6), 711–715 (2015)
2. Wang, Z., Wang, P.: Research on permanent inter-satellite-links in satellite networks. J.-China Inst. Commun. **27**, 129–133 (2006)
3. Wang, Z.: Architecture design and analysis of multi-layer satellite networks. Doctor's thesis, Harbin Institute of Technology, Harbin, China (2007)
4. Liang, J.: Research on inter-satellite networks design of satellite communication system. Master's thesis, National University of Defense Technology, Changsha, China (2006)
5. Gao, L., Zhao, H., Jiang, T.: Modeling and simulation for dynamic topology network of SIS. J. Syst. Simu. 69–72 (2006)
6. Dogan, U., Uludag, M., Demir, D.O.: Investigation of GPS positioning accuracy during the seasonal variation. Measurement, 212–242 (2014)
7. Somov, Y.I., Butyrin, S.A., Anshakov, G.P.: Dynamics and flight support of a vehicle ikar control system at orbiting globalstar satellites. Control. Eng. Pract. **11**(5), 585–597 (2003)
8. Kimura, K., Inagaki, K., Karasawa, Y.: Double-layered inclined orbit constellation for advanced satellite communication network. IEICE Trans. Commun. **E80-B**(1), 93–102 (1997)
9. Kimura, K., Inagaki, K.: Global satellite communication network using double-layered inclined-orbit constellation with optical inter-satellite links. In: Proceedings of SPIE. 12–23 (1996)
10. Lee, K., Kang, S.: Satellite over satellite (SoS) network: a novel architecture for satellite network. In: Proceedings of 2000 IEEE Conference on Computer Communications (INFOCOMM), Tel Aviv, Israel, 26–30 March 2000, vol. 1, pp. 131–136 (2000)
11. Dasha, J.S., Durresi, A.: Routing of VoIP traffic in multi-layered satellite networks. In: Proceedings of SPIE, pp. 65–75 (2003)
12. Zhu, L., Wu, Y.: Introduction to Satellite Communication. Electronic Industry Press, Beijing (2015). pp. 35–76

Artificial-Neural-Network-Based Automatic Modulation Recognition in Satellite Communication

Yumeng Zhang[1,2(✉)], Mingchuan Yang[1], and Xiaofeng Liu[1]

[1] Communication Research Center, Harbin Institute of Technology, Harbin,
People's Republic of China
616670674@qq.com, {mcyang,liuxiaofeng}@hit.edu.cn
[2] CETC Key Laboratory of Aerospace Information Applications,
Shijiazhuang, China

Abstract. In order to improve the correct recognition rate of signals transmitted in satellite communication system, three different structures of artificial neural network (ANN), including feed forward network (FFN), cascade forward network (CFN) and competitive neural network (CNN) are investigated in this paper. Then their performance of correct recognition rate and performance of convergence rate are compared. Results of simulation indicate that typical FFN's performance dramatically deteriorates in the case of Rician fading, CFN's performance is similar to the former one while it has higher convergence rate. CNN's performance of correct recognition rate is the best among these three nets, but in the training process, its performance of convergence rate is not good.

Keywords: Modulation recognition · Artificial neural network
Satellite communication

1 Introduction

With the development of technology in satellite communication, the complexity of modulation type is growing, which makes it more complicated for receivers to recognize these modulation types correctly and effectively. Especially when considering the satellite communication scenario where the received signals are affected by noise, multipath fading and shadowing, the performance of modulation recognition will deteriorate. This paper focuses on improving the performance of modulation recognition of signals transmitted in satellite communication system.

Generally, modulation recognition is used to identify interference or choose the appropriate demodulator, and without correctly recognizing the modulation type of the received signal, further procedures such as demodulation and parameter estimation cannot be accomplished [1]. As modulation recognition plays a significant role in satellite communication applications such as spectrum management, surveillance and electronic warfare [2], it is of great importance to correctly and effectively recognize signals in satellite communication system.

© ICST Institute for Computer Sciences, Social Informatics and Telecommunications Engineering 2018
X. Gu et al. (Eds.): MLICOM 2017, Part I, LNICST 226, pp. 394–404, 2018.
https://doi.org/10.1007/978-3-319-73564-1_39

In recent years, many works have been done on automatically recognizing the modulation type of received signals using artificial neural network [3]. However, most of these signals are assumed to be received in Gaussian channel, which cannot be applied in satellite communication system. This paper investigates the situation where the ANN is used to recognize signals transmitted in the Rician fading channel, and then different structures of ANN which can improve the correct recognition rate in this situation are discussed and compared.

2   The Procedure of Automatic Modulation Recognition

In order to automatically recognize the modulation type of the received signals, the feature-based approach is usually considered as an effective method [4]. The procedure of feature-based modulation recognition is illustrated in Fig. 1.

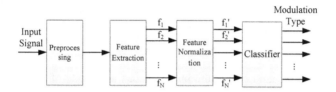

Fig. 1. Procedure of feature-based modulation recognition

The preprocessing module is used to purify the input signal because signal transmitted in satellite communication system can be affected by kinds of noise. It's worth noting that in satellite communication system, the received signal not only has line-of-sight component but also has reflecting component, which contains signal waves reflected by adjacent objects such as buildings and trees. Therefore input signals have to be denoised before feature extraction.

Then the feature of denoised signal can be extracted in the feature extraction module. The procedure of feature extraction is necessary because on the one hand, it can provide similar features of signals of one certain modulation type and that makes the recognition easier; on the other hand, this procedure can reduce the number of elements sent to the classifier, which decreases the computing amount of the classification. There are many kinds of methods with different bases to extract features from modulated signal, such as approaches based on instantaneous parameters [5], high order cumulants [6], spectral correlation [7], and wavelet transformation [8].

The feature normalization module is indispensable because features usually vary considerably in magnitude, which will decrease the convergence rate of the network in classifier. After normalization the average value of each feature will be zero and its variance will be unified, this will improve the performance of classifier [9].

Finally the normalized features will be sent to classifier, which recognizes the modulation type of the input signal. There are many methods of classifier such as decision tree [10].

3 Feature Extraction

In order to recognize different kinds of modulation types, a combination of features is used more than a single one. And the extracted features are required to be sensitive to different modulation types, while they must be insensitive to parameters of individual transmissions such as signal-to-noise ratio (SNR) and frequency.

Eight kinds of digital signals modulated by 2ASK, 4ASK, BPSK, QPSK, 8QAM, 16QAM, OQPSK and $\pi/4$-DQPSK respectively will be recognized in this article. The features extracted from the instantaneous parameters are listed as follows:

The maximum value of the spectral power density of the normalized centered instantaneous amplitude γ_{max} is defined as:

$$\gamma_{max} = \frac{\max\{FFT[a_{cn}(i)]^2\}}{N} \tag{1}$$

where N is number of samples, $a_{cn}(i)$ represents for the normalized centered instantaneous amplitude, and can be given as:

$$a_{cn}(i) = a_n(i) - 1 \tag{2}$$

where $a_n(i) = a(i)/m_a$ and $a(i)$ is the instantaneous amplitude of received signal, m_a represents for the mean value of $a(i)$, i.e. $m_a = \frac{1}{N}\sum_{i=1}^{N} a(i)$.

The standard deviation of the absolute value of the normalized centered instantaneous amplitude σ_{aa} is defined as:

$$\sigma_{aa} = \sqrt{\frac{1}{N}[\sum_{i=1}^{N} a_{cn}^2(i)] - [\frac{1}{N}\sum_{i=1}^{N} |a_{cn}(i)|]^2} \tag{3}$$

The standard deviation of the absolute value of the non-linear component of the normalized centered instantaneous phase of non-weak signal σ_{ap} is defined as:

$$\sigma_{ap} = \sqrt{\frac{1}{c}[\sum_{a_n(i) > a_t} \phi_{NL}^2(i)] - [\frac{1}{c}\sum_{a_n(i) > a_t} |\phi_{NL}(i)|]^2} \tag{4}$$

where a_t is the threshold for $a(i)$ and below which the received signal can be considered too weak and can be ignored, and c is the number of non-weak samples, $\phi_{NL}(i)$ is the value of the central non-linear component of the instantaneous phase, and when the carrier is synchronized it can be given as follows:

$$\phi_{NL}(i) = \phi(i) - \phi_0 \tag{5}$$

where $\phi_0 = \frac{1}{N}\sum_{i=1}^{N} \phi(i)$, and $\phi(i)$ is the instantaneous phase.

The standard deviation of the non-linear component of the normalized centered instantaneous phase of non-weak signal σ_{dp} is defined as:

$$\sigma_{dp} = \sqrt{\frac{1}{c}[\sum_{a_n(i) > a_t} \phi_{NL}^2(i)] - [\frac{1}{c}\sum_{a_n(i) > a_t} \phi_{NL}(i)]^2} \tag{6}$$

The standard deviation of the absolute value of the normalized centered instantaneous frequency of non-weak signal σ_{af} is defined as:

$$\sigma_{af} = \sqrt{\frac{1}{c}[\sum_{a_n(i) > a_t} f_N^2(i)] - [\frac{1}{c}\sum_{a_n(i) > a_t} f_N(i)]^2} \tag{7}$$

where $f_N(i) = \frac{f_m(i)}{R_s}$, $f_m(i) = f(i) - m_f$, $m_f = \frac{1}{N}\sum_{i=1}^{N} f(i)$, and R_s is the symbol rate of the received digital signal.

The compactness of normalized centered instantaneous amplitude is described by fourth-order moment and can be given as follows:

$$\mu_{42}^a = \frac{E[a_{cn}^4(i)]}{\{E[a_{cn}^2(i)]\}^2} \tag{8}$$

The compactness of normalized centered instantaneous frequency is also described by fourth-order moment and can be given as:

$$\mu_{42}^f = \frac{E[f_N^4(i)]}{\{E[f_N^2(i)]\}^2} \tag{9}$$

These seven features are extracted from the received signal and they provide the classifier with necessary information for modulation recognition. In this article, ANN is utilized in classifier to recognize different modulation types. It's worth mentioning that these features should be normalized before sent to ANN, otherwise some of these feature will fall into the saturation region of ANN's transfer function where the gradient of that function is almost zero, which will decrease the convergence rate of the network in training procedure.

4   Structure of Artificial Neural Network

There exist many kinds of structures of ANN such as FFN, CFN, and CNN. Their performances are different when applied in modulation recognition. Moreover, all of these ANNs must be trained before they are used as classifiers, and the error back propagation algorithm is usually used in training step.

4.1   Theory of Error Back Propagation Algorithm

ANN is composed of weights, biases and neuron nodes, which include input nodes, hidden nodes and output nodes. A typical ANN with one hidden layer can be illustrated in Fig. 2, where w_{ji}^{JI} $(j = 1, 2, \ldots, J; i = 1, 2, \ldots, I)$ is the weight between input layer and hidden layer, w_{kj}^{KJ} $(k = 1, 2, \ldots, K; j = 1, 2, \ldots, J)$ is the weight between hidden layer and output layer, b_i^J $(j = 1, 2, \ldots, J)$ is the j_{th} bias of hidden nodes, and b_k^K $(k = 1, 2, \ldots, K)$ is the k_{th} bias of output nodes.

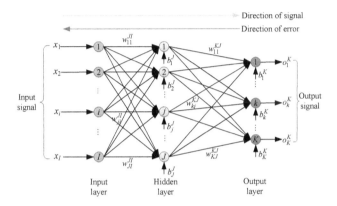

Fig. 2. Model of typical ANN with one hidden layer

Input nodes allot the input signal to hidden nodes, and each input node is connected to every hidden node. In the hidden layer, the j_{th} node sums its input data and adds a bias b_i^J to them before putting them to a certain transfer function. Then the data from hidden layer are sent to output layer where they are processed in a similar way. Usually the output signal is not the desire one, so error back propagation algorithm is used to solve this problem by correcting the weights and biases of network layer by layer.

In ANN the information of input signal is sent forward the network until the output signal is calculated. Then the error between this output signal and desire signal can be known, in order to decrease that error the weights and biases of output layer will be corrected, and after that the weights and biases of hidden layer will be corrected. This indicates that the error information propagates back from output layer to input layer. The procedure of training an ANN using error back propagation algorithm is illustrated in Fig. 3.

The essence of error back propagation algorithm is to find the proper weights and biases of network, which makes output signal to be the best estimate of desire output in minimal mean-square error sense. Moreover, the procedure of training the ANN can be regarded as a step of machine learning. We can use the features of modulated signal as the input signal and set its corresponding modulation type as desire output, after the procedure of training ANN can recognize the modulation type of a received signal according to the extracted features. However, structure of ANN can affect both the convergence rate in the procedure of training the network and the performance of modulation recognition, three different structures of ANN network are discussed and compared in this article.

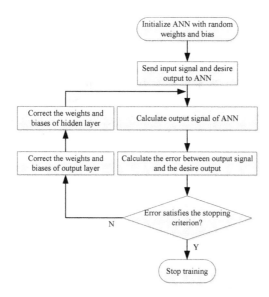

Fig. 3. Procedure of training an ANN with error back propagation algorithm

4.2 Feed Forward Network (FFN)

FFN is a typical structure of ANN, it consists of a series of layers and the first layer has a connection from the input signal. Each subsequent layer has a connection from the previous layer, and final layer produces the output signal. A FFN can be produced using the model described in Fig. 2, and its structure can be simplified in Fig. 4 for convenience's sake.

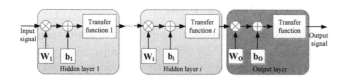

Fig. 4. Structure of feed forward network (FFN)

In Fig. 4, W_i and b_i respectively represents for the weight matrix and bias matrix of the i_{th} hidden layer, while W_O and b_O respectively represents for the weight matrix and bias matrix of the output layer. Non-linear functions such as sigmoid function, log-sigmoid function, hyperbolic tangent sigmoid transfer function etc. are usually set as transfer functions of hidden layers, while output layer usually uses linear function as transfer function. It is worth noting that every hidden layer can use different transfer function. Furthermore, the number of hidden layers, the transfer function of each hidden layer, and the number of nodes of each layer can be changed according to the complexity of problem.

4.3   Cascade Forward Network (CFN)

CFN is a variation of FFN, and they are quite similar except that CFN has a connection from the input signal to every following layer, its structure is illustrated in Fig. 5. In this network every hidden layer except the first one and output layer has two weight matrixes, one is used to weight the output data from the previous layer, and the other one is used to directly weight the input signal.

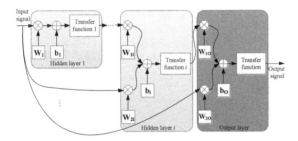

Fig. 5. Structure of cascade forward network (CFN)

This structure can provide the procedure of training with more degrees of freedom, and that will make it easier to solve some complicated problems. On the other hand, this structure can also increase the complexity of training procedure, because in error back propagation algorithm more weights and biases should be corrected. Moreover, if too many data are supplied to train this network it may lead to over fitting, which will affect the performance of modulation recognition.

4.4   Competitive Neural Network (CNN)

CNNs are proposed according to the lateral inhibition in biological neural networks, i.e. when a biological neuron is activated it will inhibit its adjacent neurons, which leads to the competition among neural networks. When the training procedure begins, every neuron has equal opportunity to respond to input signal till one neuron is activated and wins in the competition, at the same time the winner will inhibit other neurons and prevent them from being activated.

CNNs are similar to FFNs, i.e. they have similar structure shown in Fig. 3. However, the transfer functions of CNN's hidden layers are non-liner functions, but the soft max competitive function is usually used in output layer. It is worth noting that these neural networks can be trained by error back propagation algorithm and their convergence rates are different, which will be compared in the next subsection.

5   Simulation Results and Performance Analysis

In this subsection, the learning ability of each structure is compared by its convergence rate. After training these networks are utilized to recognize the modulation type according to the extracted features discussed above, and then their performance of correct recognition rate will be compared.

5.1   Simulation on Training Procedure

In order to compare the learning ability of these three structures of ANNs, they are respectively trained with the same set of rational normalized training samples. In simulation every network has only one hidden layer with 10 neuron nodes, the number of neuron nodes in input layer and output layer is equal to the number of extracted features and the number of modulation types respectively. Moreover, the transfer functions in every hidden layer are set as hyperbolic tangent sigmoid transfer function. Figure 6 illustrates the training result, and the maximum training epoch is set as 1600.

It can be known from Fig. 6 that at the beginning of training process CFN has the highest convergence rate among these three structures, while its best performance of mean squared error (MSE) is 0.0460 and this value remains the same when this net is trained over 40 epochs. On the other hand, the MSE performance of competitive neural net decreases along with the increase of epochs and can reach its minimum value 4.9717×10^{-4} at the maximum epoch. However, the convergence rate performance of competitive neural net is not good. Furthermore, the minimum MSE performance of feed forward net is 0.0541, which is the worst among these networks, but it is less complicated to train that net because of its simple structure. The results of simulation in this part show that the structure of network may affect its learning ability.

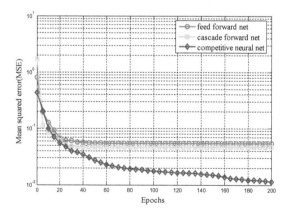

Fig. 6. Training procedure of different ANNs

5.2   Simulation on Modulation Recognition

After the training procedure, these networks can be used to recognize modulation types of received signals. The performance of each net is investigated with eight different modulation types: 2ASK, 4ASK, BPSK, QPSK, 8QAM, 16QAM, OQPSK and $\pi/4$-DQPSK. The received signals are assumed to transmit in the Rician fading channel where the Rician K-factor is set as 5 dB. The training sample contains 200 sampled signals for each modulation type, while the testing sample is composed of 1000 sampled signals for each modulation type. In simulation, every ANN is trained by the same training sample and tested by the same testing sample.

Figure 7 illustrates the correct recognition rate for each modulation type when the SNR of receiver is 6 dB. For comparison, the correct recognition rate in Gaussian channel with the same SNR is 100% for each modulation type, which can be seen in Fig. 8. The reason why the misrecognition occurs is that the difference of features between modulation types is not recognizable because of the impact from Rician fading.

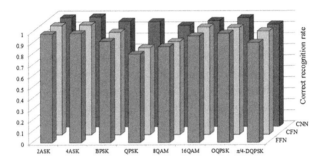

Fig. 7. Correct recognition rate for each modulation type (SNR = 6 dB)

Simulation results show that these three ANNs exhibit a satisfactory performance for the signals affected by Rician fading channel when the SNR is 6 dB. Each network's overall average correct recognition rate vs. SNR is illustrated in Fig. 8, and the corresponding performance in Gaussian channel, which is recognized by FFN, is also simulated for comparison.

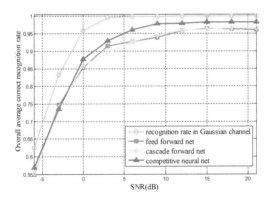

Fig. 8. Overall average correct recognition rate vs. SNR

It can be seen from Fig. 8 that the Rician fading affects the ANNs' performance of correct recognition rate and the performance of FFN deteriorates dramatically in Rician fading channel. And the overall average recognition rate of CFN is similar to that of FFN. Moreover, CNN performs better than the other two nets in the satellite communication system.

6 Conclusion

In this paper, ANNs are utilized to recognize the modulation type of signals transmitted in satellite communication system, the results of simulation show that typical FFN's performance of correct recognition rate will dramatically deteriorate because of Rician fading, but it is easier to train a FFN. In the case of Rician fading, CFN performs similarly to FFN in overall average correct recognition rate, but its convergence rate in training process is the highest among these nets. Moreover, CNN's overall average correct recognition rate is the best and it has the lowest performance of MSE in training procedure, but its convergence rate is not good.

Acknowledgment. The paper is sponsored by National Natural Science Foundation of China (No. 91538104; No. 91438205) and Open Research fund Program of CETC key laboratory of aerospace information applications (No. EX166290013).

References

1. Zeng, C.-Z., Jia, X., Zhu, W.-G.: Modulation classification of communication signals. J. Commun. Technol. **48**(3), 252–257 (2015)
2. Chen, M., Zhu, Q.: Cooperative automatic modulation recognition in cognitive radio. J. China Univ. Posts Telecommun. **17**(2), 46–52 (2010)
3. Gao, Y.-L., Zhang, Z.-Z.: Classifier of modulation recognition based on modified self-organizing feature map neural network. J. Sichuan Univ. (Eng. Sci. Edn.) **38**(5), 143–147 (2006)
4. Dobre, O.A., Abdi, A., Bar-Ness, Y., et al.: Survey of automatic modulation classification technoques: classical approches and new trends. J. IET Commun. **1**(2), 137–156 (2007)
5. Dubuc, C., Boudreau, D., Patenaude, F., et al.: An automatic modulation recognition algorithm for spectrum monitoring applications. In: IEEE International Conference on Communications, vol. 1, pp. 570–574. IEEE (1999)
6. Declouet, J.A., Naraghi-Pour, M.: Robust modulation classification techniques using cumulants and hierarchical neural networks. In: Proceedings of SPIE - The International Society for Optical Engineering, pp. 6567171 J–65671 J-11 (2007)
7. Eremenko, Y., Poleshchenko, D., Glushchenko, A.: Study on neural networks usage to analyse correlation between spectrum of vibration acceleration signal from pin of ball mill and its filling level. J. Appl. Mech. Mater. **770**, 540–546 (2015)
8. Yang, F., Zan, L.I., Luo, Z.: A new specific combination method of wireless communication modulation recognition based on clustering and neural network. Acta Scientiarum Naturalium Universitatis Sunyatseni **54**(2), 24–29 (2015)

9. Wang, K., Xie, J., Zhao, L.: Automatic modulation recognition of software radio communication signals based on neural networks. Comput. Autom. Measur. Control **12** (9), 877–878 (2014)
10. Satija, U., Ramkumar, B., Manikandan, M.S.: A novel sparse classifier for automatic modulation classification using cyclostationary features. Wirel. Pers. Commun. **96**, 1–23 (2017)

Licklider Transmission Protocol for GEO-Relayed Space Networks

Wenrui Zhang, Chenyang Fan, Kanglian Zhao$^{(\boxtimes)}$, and Wenfeng Li$^{(\boxtimes)}$

School of Electronic Science and Engineering, Nanjing University,
163 Xianlin Road, Nanjing 210023, Jiangsu, People's Republic of China
zhaokanglian@nju.edu.cn, leewf_cn@hotmail.com

Abstract. As one of the most important convergence layer (CL) protocol for delay/disruption-tolerant networking (DTN), Licklider transmission protocol (LTP) has recently been proposed for deep space communications, but it has rarely been considered for near earth applications. In this paper, LTP is adopted instead of TCP as CL with Bundle protocol (BP) for future application in GEO-relayed space networks (GRSN). Experiments are conducted on our computer based testbed in emulation of the basic scenarios during data transmission from LEO satellite to a ground station in GRSN. The results show that in transmission efficiency BP with LTPCL outperforms other protocols, such as BP with TCPCL, direct terrestrial TCP (TCP Cubic) and TCP variants (TCP Hybla) for space segments in most scenarios. It could be envisioned that DTN with LTPCL for space segment is currently the best choice for future GEO-relayed space internetworking.

Keywords: Space networking · GEO relays · DTN · LTP · TCP

1 Introduction

Space internetworking through geostationary (GEO) relaying satellites has been envisioned as a promising technology for global tracking, control and data transmission for near earth space data systems [1]. Currently, there are several GEO relaying systems which have been deployed or are under development by different authorities, such as NASA's Tracking and Data Relay Satellite System (TDRSS), China National Space Administration (CNSA)'s Tianlian system, European Data Relay Satellite (EDRS) System, and Japan Aerospace Exploration Agency (JAXA)'s Data Relay Test Satellite (DRTS).

Although the onboard computational capability has grew fast in the past 20 years, most of these GEO relaying systems are still bent-pipe relays without

This work is supported by the National Natural Science Foundation of China (No. 61401194), the Fundamental Research Funds for the Central Universities (021014380064) and the Priority Academic Program Development of Jiangsu Higher Education Institutions.

© ICST Institute for Computer Sciences, Social Informatics and Telecommunications Engineering 2018
X. Gu et al. (Eds.): MLICOM 2017, Part I, LNICST 226, pp. 405–413, 2018.
https://doi.org/10.1007/978-3-319-73564-1_40

networking functions. But GEO relayed space networks (GRSN) is getting into reality [2]. NASA's space network IP services (SNIS) has already been deployed over TDRSS to provide end-to-end IP communications between space vehicles and ground stations since around a decade ago [3]. Because of the huge success of the TCP/IP architecture in terrestrial Internet, commercial off-the-shelf (COTS) protocol stacks and networking equipments are extremely cost-attractive for space internetworking. Meanwhile, it is also well-known that the original TCP transmission control will experience severe performance degradation over satellite links which have longer round-trip times (RTTs) and higher bit error rates (BERs) compared to the terrestrial links [4]. TCP variants, such as TCP Hybla [5], have been proposed for better performance on the challenging satellite or wireless communications links.

Besides TCP/IP, a different network architecture, DTN has been adopted for communications to International Space Station (ISS) scientific payloads since May, 2010. And recently, DTN was officially announced as a communications service on board ISS by NASA. DTN is originally designed for interplanetary networking (IPN) [6]. Although DTN has been proposed as a possible network architecture instead of the terrestrial TCP/IP architecture for GEO relayed internetworking like in [7], most of the previous works have been involved in performance evaluation of DTN with TCP as convergence layer (CL) [7,8]. In the framework of DTN, Licklider transmission protocol (LTP) [9] is proposed targeted for challenging links with very long RTTs and/or interruptions characterizing deep-space communications. As one of the most important CL in the DTN architecture, LTP has been standardized with the essential bundle protocol (BP) by CCSDS. LTP is well investigated and evaluated for deep space scenarios [10,11] in the past few years. But to the best of the authors' knowledge, LTP has rarely been considered as a possible DTN CL for GRSN, in which near earth space information systems, such as low earth orbit (LEO) or mediate earth orbit (MEO) remote sensing satellites, can communicate with home ground stations through GEO relay satellites.

In this paper, we focus on the transmission efficiency of DTN with LTPCL in an emulated GRSN system characterized by various asymmetric channel rates, link delays and bit error rates. The main contributions of our work are as follows:

(1) Analytical models are built to characterize the file delivery delay in all the three basic scenarios in GRSN, which varies from 1 ms to nearly 500 ms. It is important to have a fair performance evaluation of all the possible protocols, such as BP with LTPCL, BP with TCPCL and direct TCP transmissions in all these scenarios for future applications in GRSN;
(2) Although much work has been done on performance evaluation of DTN and TCP/IP for space internetworking, the transmission efficiency of the deep-space originated LTPCL in GRSN has rarely been evaluated through network emulation.

The remainder of this paper is organized as follows, in Sect. 2, data transmissions in GRSN are categorized into three basic scenarios for fair performance comparison. And LTPCL and the DTN architecture for space internetworking are introduced as well. The setup and configuration of the testbed, the results of the emulations and the discussions are presented in Sect. 3. And finally, the conclusions and the possible future works are drawn in Sect. 4.

2   Architecture for GRSN

2.1   Transmission Scenarios in GRSN

Figure 1 presents three typical transmission scenarios classified by number of hops between the source node and the sink node. The typical end-to-end link delay in each scenario can be calculated by

$$T_{delay} = \frac{D_{linkpath}}{c} \tag{1}$$

where $D_{linkpath}$ represents the end-to-end distance between the source node and the destination node, and c is the speed of light. In different scenarios, $D_{linkpath}$ can be split into one or several hops, for example in Scenario III: $D_{linkpath} = D_{EC} + D_{CA} + D_{AF}$. D_{CA} and D_{AF} are constant values, while D_{EC} varies from D_{P1C} to D_{P3C}. As a result, the link delay varies in transmitting distance. Based on the basic geometry and the orbital information, the link delay of three scenarios can be calculated. The results are listed in Table 1. GS represents ground station in both Table 1 and Fig. 1.

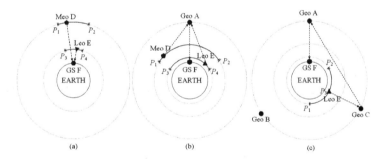

Fig. 1. Typical scenaios in GRSN. (a) Scenario I. (b) Scenario II. (c) Scenario III.

Table 1. Link delay in different scenarios

Scenarios	Hop count	Link delay	Data transfer path
I	1	1–80 ms	LEO E/MEO D → GS F
II	2	200–250 ms	LEO E/MEO D → GEO A → GS F
III	3	480–500 ms	LEO E → GEO C → GEO A → GS F

2.2   Network Architectures

TCP/IP protocol is widely used in satellite network service currently. Various enhanced versions of TCP have been proposed for performance improvement in satellite network scenarios, such as Hybla. As a matter of fact, long link delay will result in reduced performance of TCP severely. Besides, channel asymmetry is also typical in GRSN. Coverage issue at high altitude is another problem. The GRSN cannot provide global coverage. Continuous end-to-end connectivity is usually unavailable in GRSN.

DTN introduces an overlay protocol, called Bundle Protocol (BP), which interfaces either the transport layer protocols (LTP, TCP, UDP, etc.) or lower layer protocols. The essential point is that in such an overlay, delays and disruptions can be handled at each DTN node between the source and sink. Two main features of BP are the store-and-forward transmission mechanism and the custody transfer option. Nodes on the path can provide necessary storage before forwarding to the next hop.

BP has been designed as an implementation of the DTN architecture and is by far the most broadly used DTN protocol. The basic unit of data in the BP is a bundle which is a message that carries application layer protocol data units, sender/receiver names, and any additional data required for end-to-end delivery. Two reliable convergence layer (CL) protocols, TCPCL and LTPCL, are investigated in this paper. With specialized features of BP [12], DTN is particularly suited to cope with the challenges presented in satellite networks, including GRSN.

2.3   Overiew of the Licklider Transmission Protocol

LTP is designed to provide retransmission-based reliability over links characterized by extremely long RTTs and/or frequent interruptions in connectivity. LTP is intended to serve as a convergence layer protocol, underlying the BP, in deployment environment with long RTTs. Different from TCP, LTP performs selective negative acknowledgment (NAK). And LTP can provide both reliable and unreliable services. Datas are transmitted in "red" parts in a reliable service, and "green" parts in an unreliable one. We only consider the former for reliable transmission in this paper. Data encapsulation and transmission are shown as Fig. 2. Two main differences between TCP and LTP are summarized as follows:

(1) LTP data transmission is organized in sessions. A session is defined as the process of LTP segment exchanges undertaken to transmit a single data block successfully. TCP data transmission is based on connection.
(2) LTP performs selective NAKs on bytes in block, while TCP performs ACKs on bytes in windows and SACK is optional.

3   Experimental Setup and Results

To implement an emulated GRSN infrastructure for the evaluation of different protocols, we use three PCs equipped with DTN protocol stack and TCP suites

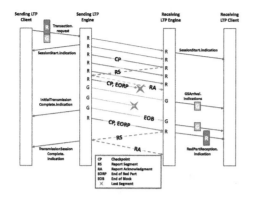

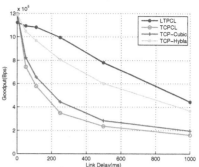

Fig. 2. Overview of LTP Interactions [13] (Color figure online)

Fig. 3. Impacts of link delays

Table 2. Experimental factors and configuration

Experimental factors	Settings/values
BP custody transfer option	Disabled
LTP red/green setting	100% red
Data bundle size	40000 bytes
LTP block size	6 bundles/block
LTP segment size	1400 bytes
Channel rate	1:1 (10 Mbps:10 Mbps)
	10:1 (10 Mbps:1 Mbps)
	50:1 (10 Mbps:200 kbps)
BER	$10^{-7}, 10^{-6}, 10^{-5}$
One-way link delay (ms)	1.5, 50, 110, 250, 500, 1000
Experimental file size	10,000,000 bytes
Sample size	16 repetitive runs

to set up a testbed, representing source node, sink node and channel emulator. As GEO relaying satellites act as bent-pipe, they only affect the link characteristics, such as delay and bit error rate (BER). Link characteristics are emulated by NetEm [14], included in Ubuntu 14.04.3 LTS kernel. The DTN BP and LTP protocol implementations used for our experiments were provided by the Interplanetary Overlay Network(ION) v3.4.1. TCP-Cubic and TCP-Hybla were supported by Ubuntu kernel. Channel ratio is defined as the ratio of data channel rate over the ACK channel rate. Parameter settings are shown in Table 2. Datas are transmitted via BP with LTPCL, BP with TCPCL (running over TCP-Cubic), direct TCP-Cubic and TCP-Hybla in our testbed. Network throughput is measured as the major performance metrics in our test.

3.1   Impacts of Link Delays

BER of 10^{-7} and CR of 10:1 is set here. The performance should not suffer degradation because of BER and CR in such a condition. Then we focus on the effect of link delays. The goodput of BP/LTPCL, BP/TCPCL, TCP-Cubic, and TCP-Hybla are measured with link delays increased from 1.5 ms to 1000 ms. This covers all the three different transmission scenarios mentioned in Sect. 2. The results are shown in Fig. 3.

From Fig. 3 we can find that performance of LTPCL, TCPCL, TCP-Cubic, and TCP-Hybla are very close when link delays are short (about 1.5 ms), which is similar to terrestrial network environments. And LTPCL shows slightly worse performance than the other three. As the link delay increases, all four protocols suffer performance degradation. LTPCL shows the best performance with increasing link delay. Among the other three, TCP-Hybla shows the best performance because of its targeted improvement in congestion mechanism under long RTTs. Perfomance of TCPCL and TCP-Cubic are very similar. Because BP caused additional overhead, performance of TCPCL is the worst.

Discarding the influence of BER and CR, a conclusion can be drawn that when link delay is short, for example, a one-hop transmission in Scenario I, TCP-Cubic, TCP-Hybla and TCPCL will be better than LTPCL in performance. But when the transmission contains more than one hop and RTT increases, as shown in Scenario II and III, LTPCL would be the best choice. As we all know, covering time of LEO only accounts for about 10 percent of entire orbital period. In other words, transmission is GRSN contains two or several hops most of the time, and LTPCL would be the best choice.

3.2   Impacts of Bit Error Rate

Channel ratio is still set as 10:1. Three BERs are investigated: $10^{-7}, 10^{-6}$ and 10^{-5}, representing low bit error rate, medium bit error rate and high bit error rate respectively. Figure 4 illustrates the goodput performance of four protocol options in three scenarios with consistent channel ratio and varying BERs.

When the BER is 10^{-7}, LTPCL and TCP-Hybla show better performance than the other two in all three scenarios. When BER increases to 10^{-6}, both TCP protocols decrease more than a half, while LTPCL decreases less than 25%. When BER further increases to 10^{-5}, which represents a high loss channel, all the four protocols show unsatisfactory performance.

As BER increases, more packets transmission will be lost, and need to be retransmitted, which is an aggravation for both the data channel and the ACK channel. When lost data being retransmitted, TCP's strategy is to retransmit all the packets before the lost packet that are unacknowledged, that causes a lot of packets which have been transmitted correctly being retransmitted again. As contrast, LTP will only retransmit segments that are not transmitted correctly, saving considerable bandwidth resources.

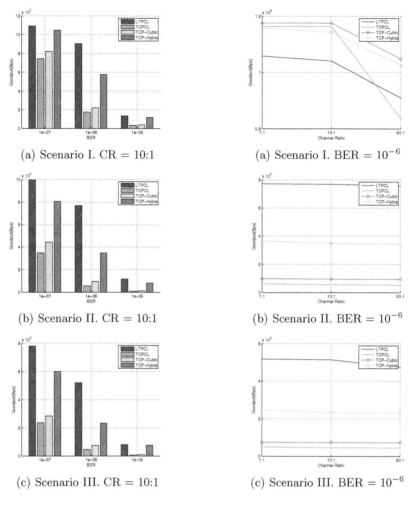

(a) Scenario I. CR = 10:1

(a) Scenario I. BER = 10^{-6}

(b) Scenario II. CR = 10:1

(b) Scenario II. BER = 10^{-6}

(c) Scenario III. CR = 10:1

(c) Scenario III. BER = 10^{-6}

Fig. 4. Impacts of BER

Fig. 5. Impacts of CA

3.3 Impacts of Channel Asymmetry

To measure impacts of channel asymmetry (CA) on the performance in different scenarios, we choose a medium BER because it won't put too much influence on results. Considering real communication environments in GRSN, we investigate three channel ratios (1:1, 10:1, 50:1). The results are shown in Fig. 5.

In scenario I, as channel ratio increases, goodput of TCPCL decrease by about 25%. And the other three suffer less performance degradation. But LTPCL outperforms the other three in both scenario II and III. And in scenario II and III, channel ratio does not show much influence on performance of four protocols. There are two reasons. One is that the channel ratio is quite small. And the other is that link delay plays a major role in the influence as we explained in Sect. 3.1.

As expected, LTPCL shows the best tolerance of channel ratio among four protocols in the scenario II and scenario III. As mentioned above in Subsect. 2, when CR increases and the ACK channel becomes narrow, large amounts of ACKs won't be transmitted to the source node in time. According to LTP's ACK strategy, a ACK will be sent corresponding with a block. Previous researches has shown that multiple BP bundles should be aggregated into a single block to resist the effect of highly asymmetric data rates in space network [11]. Benefit from this strategy, LTP only need to sent small amount of ACKs and is capable of dealing with narrow ACK channel.

4   Conclusion

In this paper, we propose to apply LTP instead of TCP as CL protocol with BP for future application in GRSN. The performance of LTPCL is compared with that of TCPCL, direct TCP-Cubic and TCP-Hybla on the emulation testbed. We also build analytical models to characterize the file delivery delay in three basic scenarios in GRSN. The theoretical analysis and results of network emulation show that LTPCL outperforms the other protocols in most cases. LTP is proved to be more promising choice for the best transmission efficiency in GRSN. Furthermore, GEO relays investigated above are still bent-pipe, and relay satellites equipped with DTN protocol suites and networking functions, served as DTN route, would be studied in further research.

References

1. Wittig M.: Data relay for Earth, Moon and Mars missions. In: International Workshop on Satellite and Space Communications. IEEE, pp. 300–304 (2009)
2. Burleigh, S., Cerf, V.G., Crowcroft, J., et al.: Space for Internet and Internet for space. J. Ad Hoc Netw. **23**(6), 80–86 (2014)
3. Israel, D.J.: Space network IP services (SNIS): an architecture for supporting low Earth orbiting IP satellite missions. In: Networking, Sensing and Control. IEEE, pp. 900–903 (2005)
4. Sun, Z.: Satellite Networking: Principles and Protocols. Wiley, Hoboken (2014)
5. Caini, C., Firrincieli, R.: TCP Hybla: a TCP enhancement for heterogeneous networks. Int. J. Satell. Commun. Netw. **22**(5), 547–566 (2004)
6. Burleigh, S., Hooke, A., Torgerson, L., et al.: Delay-tolerant networking: an approach to interplanetary Internet. IEEE Commun. Mag. **41**(6), 128–136 (2003)
7. Caini, C., Cornice, P., Firrincieli, R., et al.: A DTN approach to satellite communications. IEEE J. Sel. Areas Commun. **26**(5), 820–827 (2008)
8. Apollonio, P., Caini, C., Lülf, M.: DTN LEO satellite communications through ground stations and GEO relays. In: Dhaou, R., Beylot, A.-L., Montpetit, M.-J., Lucani, D., Mucchi, L. (eds.) PSATS 2013. LNICST, vol. 123, pp. 1–12. Springer, Cham (2013). https://doi.org/10.1007/978-3-319-02762-3_1
9. Licklider Transmission Protocol-Specification. https://tools.ietf.org/html/rfc5326
10. Yu, Q., Burleigh, S.C., Wang, R., et al.: Performance modeling of licklider transmission protocol (LTP) in deep-space communication. IEEE Trans. Aerosp. Electron. Syst. **51**(3), 1609–1620 (2015)

11. Yang, Z., Wang, R., Yu, Q., et al.: Analytical characterization of licklider transmission protocol (LTP) in cislunar communications. IEEE Trans. Aerosp. Electron. Syst. **50**(3), 2019–2031 (2014)
12. Caini, C., Cruickshank, H., Farrell, S., et al.: Delay- and disruption-tolerant networking (DTN): an alternative solution for future satellite networking applications. Proc. IEEE **99**(11), 1980–1997 (2011)
13. Consultative Committee for Space Data Systems: Licklider Transmission Protocol (LTP) for CCSDS. CCSDS 734.1-B-1 (2015)
14. Linux Fundation Wiki. https://wiki.linuxfoundation.org/networking/netem

Intelligent Remote Sensing, Visual Computing and Three-Dimensional Modeling

Design of LED Collimating Optical System

Yihao Wang, Yuncui Zhang[✉], Xufen Xie, and Yuxuan Zhang

Research Institute of Photonics, Dalian Polytechnic University, NO.
1 Qinggongyuan, Ganjingzi District, Dalian 116034, China
zhang_yc@dlpu.edu.cn

Abstract. This paper presents a design method of collimating optical system. LED has the characteristics of small size and long life. The performance of the optical system can be improved. A design of regular arrays is put forward in this paper. And this design can decrease the divergence angle through to the LED light source for the secondary light distribution. Besides the construction will be miniaturized and High-effected.

Keywords: LED · Free-form surface · Optical system

1 Introduction

Collimating optics as the foundation of optical design has wide application prospect.

The design of this optical system consults the standard specifications and investigates the current optical system structure. When making secondary optics design for LED, the light is adjusted by optimization algorithm. The 8 baseplates are arranged with equal interval. The light source meets color requirements of light source for pharos.

2 Standard of Design

According to GB12708-91-The Colours of Light Signals on Aids to Navigation, light source has white, red, green and yellow four colors. The limit equation for the chromaticity range is shown in Table 1.

Table 1. The color range

Light color	White	Red	Green	Yellow
Limit	Purple color Blue limit Green limit yellow limit	Extremely red limit White limit Red limit	Yellow limit White limit Blue limit	Red limit White limit Green limit
Boundary equation	$y = 0.047 + 0.762z$ $x = 2.85$ $y = 0.150 + 0.640x$ $x = 0.440$	$y = 0.290$ $y = 0.990$ $y = 0.320$	$y = 0.800 - x$ $y = 0660 + 1.600z$ $y = 0.5 - 0.500z$	$y = z - 0.170$ $y = 0.950 - 0.930z$ $y = z - 0.120$

© ICST Institute for Computer Sciences, Social Informatics and Telecommunications Engineering 2018
X. Gu et al. (Eds.): MLICOM 2017, Part I, LNICST 226, pp. 417–422, 2018.
https://doi.org/10.1007/978-3-319-73564-1_41

According to the Installation Specification of Pharos, it can be known that the pharos which were arranged at different heights can be seen from the every direction of object contours.The flicker frequency floats within the range of 20 times/min to 70 times/min.

3 Optical System Design

The optical system of pharos in this design is adopted by LED as the light source, the design use 8 baseplates toward 360°. Each baseplate has one yellow, green, red and white four light source respectively. Only one of four lights shining for each time on each baseplate, As shown in Fig. 1.

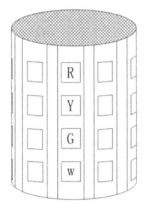

Fig. 1. Structure of pharo

The technical index of LED pharos are shown in Table 2:

Table 2. The technical index of LED pharos

Power	Light intensity	Frequency	Divergence angle	Light source	Color of light	Protection grade
20 W	4000 cd	30 times/min	10°	LED	R, G, Y, W	IP65

According to Snell and total reflection theory, the optical path graph of the lens is analyzed as shown in Fig. 2.

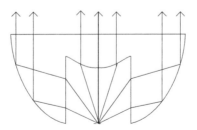

Fig. 2. Profile map

When the internal light exit in the way of collineation, the mathematical relationship between incident ray and emergent ray is shown in Fig. 3

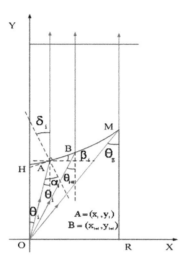

Fig. 3. Internal light rout

In Fig. 3, the light from LED chip O point via A point is refracted and then collimated exit. According to the geometric relationship and Snell theory, it can be got the following trigonometric function relationship:

$$y_{i+1} = y_i * \frac{\tan \theta_i \sin \theta_i + \cos \theta_i - n}{\tan \theta_{i+1} \sin \theta_i + \cos \theta_i - n}$$

$$x_{i+1} = \tan \theta_{i+1} * y_{i+1}$$

When the sides light exit in the way of collineation, the mathematical relationship of light is shown in Fig. 4.

In Fig. 4, the light exit from light source O is refracted through the interior concaved lens and then collimatly exit after producing total reflection on the side. According to the geometric relationship and Snell law, it can be got the following trigonometric function relationship.

$$[\tan \theta'_{i+1} - \tan(\frac{\theta'_i}{2} + \frac{\pi}{4})]x_{i+1} = [\tan \theta'_i - \tan(\frac{\theta'_i}{2} + \frac{\pi}{4})]x_i$$
$$- (\tan \theta_{i+1} - \tan'_{i+1} - \tan \theta_i + \tan \theta'_i)x_0$$

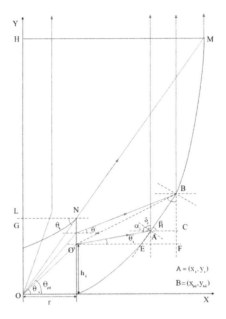

Fig. 4. Side light route

Figure 5 is a solid model:

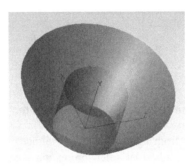

Fig. 5. Solid model of freeform lens

4 Result Analysis

The color of the identification signal plays an important role. Because signal with different colors conveys different meanings.

The optical signal color chroma range is shown as Fig. 6.

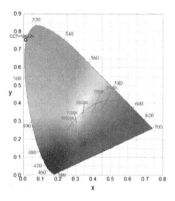

Fig. 6. Chromaticity coordinates of green

When the wave length is 510 nm, the chromaticity coordinate (0.027, 0.730) meets the specification 《GB12708-91》. Besides, the other three colors also meet the requirements.

The collimate light distribution can improve the utilization rate of light, reduce energy loss and enhance the transmission distance.

The simulation result is shown as below, The distribution angle is $10°$ and the spot diameter is 40 mm. From the light distribution curve, it can be seen that the light is collimated very well in space (Fig. 7).

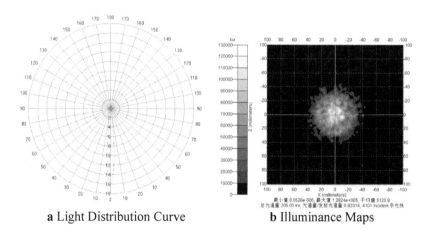

a Light Distribution Curve   **b** Illuminance Maps

Fig. 7. Light distribution curve and illuminance maps

5   Conclusion

In this paper, the optical module of LED pharos is designed in the way of optimization algorithm. Combined with the standard specifications, a method of array is put forward. The luminous flux of single LED light source is 250 lm and the luminous efficiency is

100 lm/w. A way of iterative analysis is put forword in distribution design. It can be known that the divergence angle of light distribution curve is $10°$, which achieves better simulation result.

References

1. Yuncui, Z.: Research of three color lighting-emitting diode illumination system for digital micro-mirror device. J. Lighting Eng. **21**(3), 56–58 (2010)
2. Xiaohua, D.: Application and prospects of LED in navigation mark. Mar. Traffic Eng. **12**, 89–95 (2000)
3. Chen, F., Wang, K., Qin, Z.: Design method of high-efficient LED headlamp lens. Opt. Express **18**(20), 20926–20938 (2010)
4. Zhao, S., Wang, K., Chen, F.: Lens design of LED Searchlight of high brightness and distant spot. J. Opt. Soc. Am. A **28**(5), 815–820 (2011)
5. Chen, J., Wang, T.: Freeform lens design for LED collimating illumination. Opt. Express **20**(10), 10984–10995 (2010)
6. Ries, H., Muschaweck, J.: Tailored Freeform Optical Surfaces. J. Opt. Soc. Am. A **19**(3), 590–595 (2002)

Global Depth Refinement Based on Patches

Xu Huang[1(✉)], Yanfeng Zhang[2], Gang Zhou[1], Lu Liu[1],
and Gangshan Cai[1]

[1] Wuhan Engineering Science and Technology Institute,
Jiangda Road 30, Wuhan, China
huangxu.chess@163.com
[2] School of Remote Sensing and Information Engineering,
Wuhan University, Wuhan, China

Abstract. Current stereo matching methods can be divided into 1D label algorithms and 3D label algorithms. 1D label algorithms are simple and fast, but they can't aovid fronto-parallel bias. 3D label algorithms can solve fronto-parallel bias. However, they are very time-consuming. In order to avoid fronto-parallel bias efficiently, this paper introduces a new global depth refinement based on patches. The method transforms the depth optimization problem into a quadratic function computation, which has a low time complexity. Experiments on Motorcycle imagery and Wuhan university imagery verify the correctness and the effectiveness of the proposed method.

Keywords: 1D label · 3D label · Fronto-parallel bias · Patch
Global optimization

1 Introduction

Stereo dense matching has been attracting increased attention in the photogrammetry and computer vision communities for decades [1]. According to the assignments of every pixels, stereo matching methods can be divided into 1D label methods and 3D label methods. 1D label algorithms assume fronto-parallel planes and assign one label for every pixel. 3D label algorithms assign three labels (disparity and normal direction) for every pixel [2]. The newest rank in Middlebury Benchmark show that there are no significant advantages on matching accuracies for both kinds of matching methods, as shown in Table 1. PMSC [3] and MeshStereoExt [4] belong to 3D label methods. LW-CNN [5], NTDE [6] and MC-CNN-arct [7] belong to 1D label methods.

Table 1. Rank in middlebury stereo version 3 (11/01/2017).

Matching algorithm	Rank	Running time	Weight avg.	Running environment
PMSC	1	599 s	14.8	GPU + 1 CPU @4 GHz
LW-CNN	2	314 s	14.9	GPU + 1 CPU @4 GHz
MeshStereoExt	3	161 s	15.6	GPU + 8 CPU
NTDE	4	152 s	16.2	GPU + 1 CPU @2.2 GHz
MC-CNN-arct	5	150 s	17.1	GPU + 1 CPU

© ICST Institute for Computer Sciences, Social Informatics and Telecommunications Engineering 2018
X. Gu et al. (Eds.): MLICOM 2017, Part I, LNICST 226, pp. 423–433, 2018.
https://doi.org/10.1007/978-3-319-73564-1_42

1D label algorithms are usually simple and fast, and they can acquire disparity image directly. According to the cost aggregation, 1D label algorithms can be divided into semi-global matching (SGM) [8], image-guided matching [9, 10] and global matching [11]. However, 1D label methods assume fronto-parallel planes and produces fronto-parallel bias in slanted planes, as shown in Fig. 1. Figure 1(a) shows the original reference image. The surface of the lamp is a typical slanted plane. Figure 1(b) shows the corresponding ground truth. Figure 1(c)–(g) represent the matching results of image-guided matching (IG) [10], SGM [8], Graph Cut (GC) [11], INTS [12] and NTDE [6], respectively. All of above algorithms are 1D label algorithms. The fronto-parallel bias in Fig. 1(c)–(g) influences the visualization of 3D reconstruction.

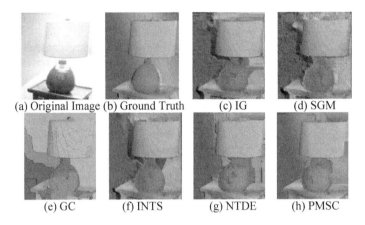

(a) Original Image (b) Ground Truth   (c) IG   (d) SGM

(e) GC   (f) INTS   (g) NTDE   (h) PMSC

Fig. 1. Results of different matching methods in slanted planes.

PMSC is a 3D label algorithm. 3D label algorithms penalize the angular difference between neighboring tangent plane normals, thus they can avoid fronto-parallel bias in slanted planes, as shown in Fig. 1(h). However, 3D label algorithms are time consuming, which is not suitable for large scale reconstruction.

This paper proposes a new global depth refinement based on patches (GDRP). It can remove fronto-parallel bias efficiently. The contributions of this paper are as follows:

(1) Traditional 3D label algorithms transform matching into a NP-hard problem, resulting in a high time complexity. The proposed GDRP transforms the depth optimization problem into a quadratic function computation, which is simple and fast.

(2) The proposed GDRP can refine not only disparity image, but also DSM/DEM products. Disparity and elevation are also called depth in this paper.

(3) The proposed GDRP can remove fronto-parallel bias and obtain continuous, smooth depths without changing the original matching accuracy.

2 Related Work

The current stereo matching algorithms consist of four steps: (1) cost computation, (2) cost aggregation, (3) disparity computation, and (4) disparity refinement [1]. 3D label algorithms mainly refine cost computation and cost aggregation.

Traditional cost computations assume regular support window with a constant disparity. In practice, the assumption is unlikely to hold in slanted planes. So far, slanted support window based cost computation can be divided into initial matching based cost computation, CNN training based cost computation and Patch Match based cost computation. Initial matching based cost computation adopts 1D label methods to achieve initial matching results quickly, and then changes the support window adaptively, according to the initial matching [13]. CNN training based cost computation [14] uses numerous examples to train a convolutional neural network (CNN). During training, affine windows are used for matching in slaned planes. Patch Match based cost computation [15, 16] adopts PatchMatch [17] method which can directly assign an approximate best 3D label by random sampling for each slanted support window.

The challenge of the cost aggregation is how to perform global optimization in the infinite three dimensional label space of each pixel. The cost aggregation of 3D label methods can be divided into initial matching based cost aggregation and direct cost aggregation. Initial matching based cost aggregation [18–23] uses window matching or 1D label algorithms to achieve initial matching results quickly. The initial matching results are approximate to the ground truth. Then, higher order smoothness constraints are used to optimize the initial matching results iteratively. The direct cost aggregations can achieve accurate matching results without initial matching [3, 4, 24–27]. They define a NP-hard global energy function and use PatchMatch [17] or fusion move [28] to reduce the huge search space in continuous infinite 3D label space. Both initial matching based cost aggregation and direct cost aggregations are iterative optimization processes which are very time consuming.

3 Proposed Method

The work flow of GDRP is shown in Fig. 2. ① The input of GDRP is a depth image. ② SLIC [29] is adopted to segment the depth image. ③, ④ A global energy function including data term and smooth term is constructed to optimize the depth image. ⑤ Feather algorithm is designed to eliminate seam lines between patches.

3.1 SLIC Segmentation

This paper assumes piecewise continuous scene and adopts SLIC [29] to segment the input depth image into a series of patches. S_i represents the i th patch. Every Patch can be described by a depth plane function:

$$d(t_i) = a_i \cdot \overline{t_{ix}} + b_i \cdot \overline{t_{iy}} + c_i; \, t_i \in S_i. \tag{1}$$

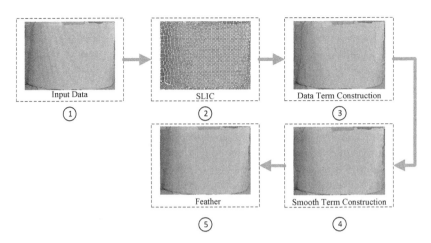

Fig. 2. Work flow of GDRP.

where, a_i, b_i, c_i represents the plane parameters of patch S_i; $t_i = (t_{ix}, t_{iy})^T$ represents a pixel in S_i; $(\overline{t_{ix}}, \overline{t_{iy}})^T$ represents centralized coordinates. The purpose of coordinate centralization is to improve the robustness of adjustment models.

Due to radiometric distortions or textureless regions, invalid depths exist in depth images inevitably. Patches in invalid regions are not considered in later optimization for two reasons: (1) Patches in invalid regions are lack of valid depths, resulting in unreliable refinement results; (2) The proposd GDRP aims at smoothing depths instead of interpolation. Number of valid depths in patches are used to judge if patches are valid or not:

$$S_i = \begin{cases} Valid & |S_i| \geq \delta \\ Invalid & |S_i| < \delta \end{cases}. \tag{2}$$

where, $|S_i|$ represents number of valid depths in S_i; δ represents threshold.

3.2 Global Energy Function Construction

D represents a depth image. $E(D)$ represents a global Energy function as follows:

$$E(D) = E_{data} + E_{smooth}. \tag{3}$$

where, E_{data} represents a data term which controls the approximation between the original depth and the refined depth; E_{smooth} represents a smooth term which controls the smoothness of depths.

3.2.1 Data Term
Data term is defined as the sum of cost of all the valid patches, as follows:

$$E_{data} = \sum_{i=1}^{q} C(S_i, \vec{n_i}). \tag{4}$$

where, q represents the number of valid patches; C represents cost of patches; $\vec{n_i} = (a_i, b_i, c_i)^{\mathrm{T}}$ represents depth plane parameters of S_i. Cost is defined as the distance between original depths and refined depths, as follows:

$$Cost(S_i, \vec{n_i}) = \sum_{t_i \in S_i} (a_i \cdot \overline{t_{ix}} + b_i \cdot \overline{t_{iy}} + c_i - d_0(t_i))^2. \tag{5}$$

where, d_0 represents original depths. t_i represents a pixel in S_i; $(\overline{t_{ix}}, \overline{t_{iy}})$ represents the centralized coordinates.

Equation (4) can be described in matrix form by defining $\tilde{x} = (\vec{n_0} \ \vec{n_1} \dots \ \vec{n_q})^{\mathrm{T}}$:

$$E_{data} = \tilde{x}^{\mathrm{T}} G_{data} \tilde{x} - 2H_{data}^{\mathrm{T}} \tilde{x} + l_{data}. \tag{6}$$

where, G_{data} represents the coefficient matrix of the quadratic term; H_{data} represents the coefficient matrix of linear term; l_{data} represents the constant term. All the terms are expressed as follows:

$$G_{data} = Diag(g_i); \ H_{data} = \left(h_0^{\mathrm{T}} \ h_1^{\mathrm{T}} \ \cdots \ h_q^{\mathrm{T}} \right)^{\mathrm{T}}; l_{data} = \sum_{i=1}^{q} l_i;$$

$$g_i = \begin{pmatrix} \sum_{t_i \in S_i} \overline{t_{ix}}^2 & \sum_{t_i \in S_i} \overline{t_{ix}} \cdot \overline{t_{iy}} & \sum_{t_i \in S_i} \overline{t_{ix}} \\ \sum_{t_i \in S_i} \overline{t_{ix}} \cdot \overline{t_{iy}} & \sum_{t_i \in S_i} \overline{t_{iy}}^2 & \sum_{t_i \in S_i} \overline{t_{iy}} \\ \sum_{t_i \in S_i} \overline{t_{ix}} & \sum_{t_i \in S_i} \overline{t_{iy}} & |S_i| \end{pmatrix};$$

$$h_i = \left(\sum_{t \in S_i} \overline{t_{ix}} \cdot d_0(t) \ \ \sum_{t \in S_i} \overline{t_{iy}} \cdot d_0(t) \ \ \sum_{t \in S_i} d_0(t) \right)^{\mathrm{T}}; \ l_i = \sum_{t \in S_i} d_0(t)^2$$

3.2.2 Smooth Term

The smooth term controls the smoothness between patches. In this paper, the smooth term uses border pixels to control the continuity between patches, and uses the center pixels to control the normal direction consistency between patches, as follows:

$$E_{smooth} = \sum_{i=1}^{q} \left(\sum_{S_j \in N(S_i)} P(i,j) \sum_{t \in E(S_i, S_j) \cup c_i} (a_i \overline{t_{ix}} + b_i \overline{t_{iy}} + c_i - a_j \overline{t_{jx}} - b_j \overline{t_{jy}} - c_j)^2 \right). \tag{7}$$

where, $N(S_i)$ represents the neighbor patch set of S_i; $E(S_i, S_j)$ represents pixels in S_i which is adjacent to S_j; $c_i = (c_{ix}, c_{iy})^{\mathrm{T}}$ represents the center pixel in S_i; $(\overline{t_{ix}}, \overline{t_{iy}})$ represents the centralized coordinates in S_i; $(\overline{t_{jx}}, \overline{t_{jy}})$ represents the centralized coordinates in S_j; $P(i,j)$ represents a penalty defined by adjacent relationship between S_i and S_j, as follows:

$$P(i,j) = P \cdot exp\left(-\left|\overline{nd_i}-\overline{nd_j}\right|/\sigma_d\right) \cdot \left(1 - exp\left(-num(i,j)/\sigma_n\right)\right). \tag{8}$$

where, $\overline{nd_i}$ and $\overline{nd_j}$ reprensets depth averages of adjacent pixels between S_i and S_j, respectively; $num(i,j)$ represents the number of adjacent pixels; σ_d and σ_n represents smooth factors; P represents the given penalty coefficient.

Equation (7) can be described in matrix form by defining $\widetilde{x} = \left(\overrightarrow{n_0} \quad \overrightarrow{n_1} \ldots \overrightarrow{n_q}\right)^{\mathrm{T}}$:

$$E_{smooth} = \widetilde{x}^T G_s \widetilde{x}. \tag{9}$$

where, G_s represents the coefficient matrix of the quadratic term, as follows:

$$G_s = \sum_{i=1}^q \left(\sum_{S_j \in N(S_i)} P(i,j) \cdot \sum_{t \in \left(E\left(S_i,S_j\right) \cup c_i\right)} g_{sr}(i,j,t)\right). \tag{10}$$

where,

$$g_{sr}(i,j,t) = \begin{pmatrix} \mathbf{0}_{3\times3} & \cdots & \mathbf{0}_{3\times3} & \cdots & \mathbf{0}_{3\times3} & \cdots & \mathbf{0}_{3\times3} \\ \vdots & \ddots & \vdots & \cdots & \vdots & \cdots & \vdots \\ \mathbf{0}_{3\times3} & \cdots & \sigma_1(i,j,t)_{i,i} & \cdots & \sigma_3(i,j,t)_{i,j} & \cdots & \mathbf{0}_{3\times3} \\ \vdots & \vdots & \vdots & \ddots & \vdots & \vdots & \vdots \\ \mathbf{0}_{3\times3} & \cdots & \sigma_3(i,j,t)_{j,i}^{\mathrm{T}} & \cdots & \sigma_2(i,j,t)_{j,j} & \cdots & \mathbf{0}_{3\times3} \\ \vdots & \vdots & \vdots & \vdots & \vdots & \ddots & \vdots \\ \mathbf{0}_{3\times3} & \cdots & \mathbf{0}_{3\times3} & \cdots & \mathbf{0}_{3\times3} & \cdots & \mathbf{0}_{3\times3} \end{pmatrix};$$

$$\sigma_1(i,j,t) = \begin{pmatrix} \overline{t_{ix}}^2 & \overline{t_{ix}} \cdot \overline{t_{iy}} & \overline{t_{ix}} \\ \overline{t_{ix}} \cdot \overline{t_{iy}} & \overline{t_{iy}}^2 & \overline{t_{iy}} \\ \overline{t_{ix}} & \overline{t_{iy}} & 1 \end{pmatrix}; \quad \sigma_2(i,j,t) = \begin{pmatrix} \overline{t_{jx}}^2 & \overline{t_{jx}} \cdot \overline{t_{jy}} & \overline{t_{jx}} \\ \overline{t_{jx}} \cdot \overline{t_{jy}} & \overline{t_{jy}}^2 & \overline{t_{jy}} \\ \overline{t_{jx}} & \overline{t_{jy}} & 1 \end{pmatrix};$$

$$\sigma_3(i,j,t) = \begin{pmatrix} -\overline{t_{ix}} \cdot \overline{t_{jx}} & -\overline{t_{ix}} \cdot \overline{t_{jy}} & -\overline{t_{ix}} \\ -\overline{t_{iy}} \cdot \overline{t_{jx}} & -\overline{t_{iy}} \cdot \overline{t_{jy}} & -\overline{t_{iy}} \\ -\overline{t_{jx}} & -\overline{t_{jy}} & -1 \end{pmatrix};$$

The global energy function can be redefined by combining Eqs. (6) and (9).

$$E(D) = \widetilde{x}^T(G_{data} + G_s)\widetilde{x} - 2H_{data}^T\widetilde{x} + l_{data}. \tag{11}$$

Computing the minimum value of Eq. (11) is equal to solving $(G_{data} + G_s)$ $\widetilde{x} = H_{data}$. Cholesky decomposition can be used to compute $\widetilde{x}$ directly.

3.3   Feather

In curved surface, obvious seam lines exist between patches. Feather algorithm is designed to smooth seam lines. Firstly, a buffer with the radius l is defined centered at seam lines between patches, as shown in Fig. 3(a). Only points in buffer are involved in feather process. p is a pixel in the buffer. The distance from p to the seam line is l'. The depth of p can be decided by the plane function of S_i, which is defined as d_i. It can also be decided by the plane function of S_j, which is defined as d_j. The depth after feather is determined by d_i and d_j in Eq. (12). The feather result is shown in Fig. 3(b).

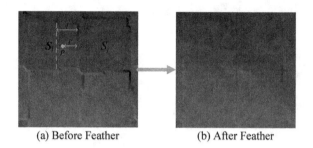

(a) Before Feather   (b) After Feather

Fig. 3.   Feather between patches.

$$d'(p) = w \cdot d_i + (1 - w) \cdot d_j. \tag{12}$$

where, d' represents the depth after feather; w represents weight, $w = 0.5 + l'/2l$.

4   Experiments

Two experiments were designed to verify the correctness and validity of GDRP. The first experiment used GDRP to refine a disparity image produced by a state-of-the-art 1D label algorithm on Motorcycle images which was provided by Middlebury Benchmark, and compared the original matching accuracy with the refined accuracy, which aimed at testing the validity of GDRP in indoor reconstruction. The second experiment used GDRP to refine a DSM generated by INTS [12] on Wuhan university images, which aimed at testing the validity of GDRP in extensive outdoor reconstruction.

4.1   Indoor Experiment

We chose the disparity image of LW-CNN which ranked the 2nd in Middlebury Benchmark for indoor experiment. The optimization result is shown in Table 2. The first column lists the original image and the ground truth, respectively. The second column lists the original disparity image of LW-CNN and the disparity image after GDRP refinement. The fourth and the fifth rows show the original matching accuracy and the refined matching accuracy, respectively. The last row lists the running time of GDRP.

Table 2. Optimization of the motorcycle disparity image.

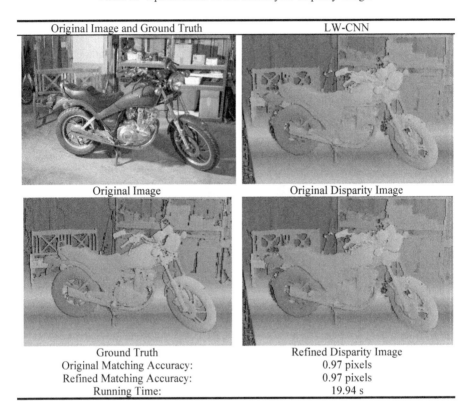

Original Image and Ground Truth	LW-CNN
Original Image	Original Disparity Image
Ground Truth	Refined Disparity Image
Original Matching Accuracy:	0.97 pixels
Refined Matching Accuracy:	0.97 pixels
Running Time:	19.94 s

Table 2 showed that obvious fronto-parallel bias existed in the original disparity image of LW-CNN. The refined disparity image was continuous and smooth, which showed that GDRP was able to remove fronto-parallel bias efficiently. The matching accuracy didn't change after refinement. It was because: (1) GDRP took original depths as the control,thus the refined accuracy after adjustment should be consistent with the accuracy of the control; (2) fronto-parallel bias was a very slight system error, which had little influence on accuracy assessment. GDRP needs no iterations. It can achieve refined results directly. In the case of single CPU @2.6 GHZ, the running time was only 19.94 s, which was much faster than current 3D label methods in Table 1. It showed that GDRP was fit for fast reconstruction.

4.2   Outdoor Experiment

INTS method [12] was used to reconstruct the DSM of Wuhan University, as shown in Fig. 4. Then, GDRP was used to refine the DSM. In order to show the refinement more clearly, local zoomed reconstruction results are shown in Table 3.

Fig. 4. DSM reconstruction of Wuhan University.

Table 3. Comparison of original DSM and refined DSM.

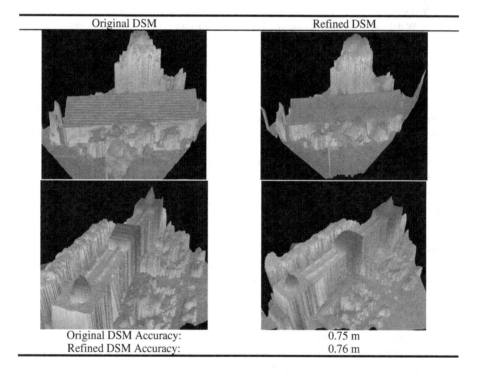

Original DSM	Refined DSM
Original DSM Accuracy:	0.75 m
Refined DSM Accuracy:	0.76 m

INTS is a 1D label algorithm. There were obvious fronto-parallel bias in slanted planes such as roofs, as shown in left column of Table 3. GDRP could smooth fronto-parallel bias effectively, as shown in right column in Table 3. No significant difference of accuracy between original and refined DSMs was detected. It suggested that GDRP only made a small change on the surface to remove the fronto-parallel bias. The DSM accuracy cannot be improved, because GDRP takes the original DSM as the control without any stereo images. The advantage of GDRP lies in the time complexity which is much lower than current 3D label. The combination of GDRP and state-of-the-art 1D label algorithms enables the efficient acquirement of continuous, smooth 3D reconstruction.

5 Conclusion

This paper proposed a new global depth refinement based on Patches. GDRP transformed the depth refinement into the minimum of a quadratic function, and achieved continuous, smooth depths without changing the original accuracy. It could remove fronto-parallel bias of 1D label algorithms efficiently. Compared with the current 3D label algorithms, GDRP was superior in low time complexity. However, GDRP cannot improve the accuracy. We will introduce stereo images into GDRP to remove fronto-parallel bias as well as improve depth accuracies in the future work.

Acknowledgements. This work was supported by the Chinese Parasol Entrepreneurial Partner Project of Wuhan Engineering Science & Technology Institute (Grant No. gkwt006).

References

1. Scharstein, D., Szeliski, R.: A taxonomy and evaluation of dense two-frame stereo correspondence algorithms. Int. J. Comput. Vision **47**(1), 7–42 (2002)
2. Olsson, C., Ulen, J., Boykov, Y.: In defense of 3D-label stereo. In: Computer Vision and Pattern Recognition, pp. 1730–1737. IEEE press, Portland (2013)
3. Li, L., Zhang, S., Yu, X., Zhang, L.: PMSC: PatchMatch-based superpixel cut for accurate stereo matching. IEEE Trans. Circ. Syst. Vid. **PP**(99), 1–14 (2016)
4. Zhang, C., Li, Z., Cheng, Y., et al.: MeshStereo: a global stereo model with mesh alignment regularization for view interpolation. In: International Conference on Computer Vision, pp. 2057–2065. Santiago (2015)
5. Park, H., Mu Lee, K.: Look wider to match image patches with convolutional neural networks. IEEE Signal Process. Lett. **PP**(99), 1–5 (2016)
6. Kim, K.R., Kim, C.S.: Adaptive smoothness constraints for efficient stereo matching using texture and edge information. In: International Conference on Image Processing, pp. 3429–3434. IEEE press, Phoenix (2016)
7. Bontar, J., Lecun, Y.: Stereo matching by training a convolutional neural network to compare image patches. J. Mach. Learn. Res. **17**(1), 2287–2318 (2016)
8. Hirschmuller, H.: Stereo processing by semiglobal matching and mutual information. IEEE Trans. Pattern Anal. **30**(2), 328–341 (2008)
9. Yang, Q.X.: Stereo matching using tree filtering. IEEE Trans. Pattern Anal. **37**(4), 834–846 (2015)
10. Pham, C.C., Jeon, J.W.: Domain transformation-based efficient cost aggregation for local stereo matching. IEEE Trans. Circ. Syst. Vid. **23**(7), 1119–1130 (2013)
11. Kolmogorov, V., Zabih, R.: Computing visual correspondence with occlusions using graph cuts. In: International Conference on Computer Vision, pp. 508–515. Vancouver (2001)
12. Huang, X., Zhang, Y., Yue, Z.: Image-guided Non-local dense matching with three-steps optimization. In: ISPRS Annals of Photogrammetry, Remote Sensing and Spatial Information Sciences, Prague, pp. 67–74 (2016)

13. Zhang, Y., Gong, M., Yang, Y.: Local stereo matching with 3D adaptive cost aggregation for slanted surface modeling and sub-pixel accuracy. In: International Conference on Pattern Recognition, pp. 1–4. Springer press, Tampa (2008)

14. Žbontar, J., LeCun, Y.: Stereo matching by training a convolutional neural network to compare image patches. J. Mach. Learn. Res. **17**, 1–32 (2016)

15. Bleyer, M., Rhemann, C., Rother, C.: PatchMatch stereo - stereo matching with slanted support windows. In: British Machine Vision Conference, Dundee, pp. 14.1–14.11 (2011)

16. Heise, P., Klose, S., Jensen, B., et al.: PM-Huber: PatchMatch with huber regularization for stereo matching. In: International Conference on Computer Vision, pp. 2360–2367. IEEE press, Sydney (2013)

17. Barnes, C., Shechtman, E., Finkelstein, A., et al.: PatchMatch: a randomized correspondence algorithm for structural image editing. ACM Trans. Graph. **28**(3), 341–352 (2009)

18. Klaus, A., Sormann, M., Karner, K.: Segment-based stereo matching using belief propagation and a self-adapting dissimilarity measure. In: International Conference on Image Processing, pp. 15–18. IEEE press, Hong Kong (2006)

19. Veldandi, M., Ukil, S., Govindarao, K.A.: Robust segment-based stereo using cost aggregation. In: British Machine Vision Conference, Nottingham, pp. 1–11 (2014)

20. Bleyer, M., Gelautz, M.: A layered stereo matching algorithm using image segmentation and global visibility constraints. ISPRS J. Photogram. **59**(3), 128–150 (2005)

21. Guney, F., Geiger, A.: Displets: resolving stereo ambiguities using object knowledge. In: Computer Vision and Pattern Recognition, pp. 4165–4175. IEEE press, Boston (2015)

22. Yamaguchi, K., McAllester, D., Urtasun, R.: Efficient joint segmentation, occlusion labeling, stereo and flow estimation. In: Fleet, D., Pajdla, T., Schiele, B., Tuytelaars, T. (eds.) ECCV 2014. LNCS, vol. 8693, pp. 756–771. Springer, Cham (2014). https://doi.org/10.1007/978-3-319-10602-1_49

23. Yamaguchi, K., Hazan, T., McAllester, D., Urtasun, R.: Continuous markov random fields for robust stereo estimation. In: Fitzgibbon, A., Lazebnik, S., Perona, P., Sato, Y., Schmid, C. (eds.) ECCV 2012. LNCS, vol. 7576, pp. 45–58. Springer, Heidelberg (2012). https://doi.org/10.1007/978-3-642-33715-4_4

24. Taniai, T., Matsushita, Y., Naemura, T.: Graph cut based continuous stereo matching using locally shared labels. In: Computer Vision and Pattern Recognition, pp. 1613–1620. IEEE press, Columbus (2014)

25. Xu, S., Zhang, F., He, X., et al.: PM-PM: PatchMatch with potts model for object segmentation and stereo matching. IEEE Trans. Image Process. **24**(7), 2182–2196 (2015)

26. Li, Y., Min, D., Brown, M. S., Do, M. N., Lu, J.: SPM-BP: sped-up PatchMatch belief propagation for continuous MRFs. In: International Conference on Computer Vision, pp. 4006–4014. IEEE press, Santiago (2015)

27. Besse, F., Rother, C., Fitzgibbon, A., Kautz, J.: PMBP: PatchMatch belief propagation for correspondence field estimation. Int. J. Comput. Vis. **110**(1), 2–13 (2014)

28. Bleyer, M., Rother, C., Kohli, P.: Surface stereo with soft segmentation. In: Computer Vision and Pattern Recognition, pp. 1570–1577. IEEE press, San Francisco (2010)

29. Lempitsky, V., Rother, C., Roth, S., Blake, A.: Fusion moves for markov random field optimization. IEEE Trans. Pattern Anal. **32**(8), 1392–1405 (2009)

3D Surface Features Scanning System with UAV-Carried Line Laser

Yilang Sun, Shuqiao Sun, Zihao Cui, Yanchao Zhang,
and Zhaoshuo Tian[✉]

School of Information and Electrical Engineering,
Harbin Institute of Technology (Weihai), Weihai, China
sun_yilang@163.com, Shuqiao_sun@yahoo.com,
cui_zh@hit.edu.cn, zhangyanchao66@sina.com,
tianzhaoshuo@126.com

Abstract. As one of the newest spatial information gathering methods, three-dimensional laser scanning technique is widely adopted in various fields due to its attributes of high accuracy and non-contact. However, currently, most systems of this kind are costly and with complex data post-processing requirements, which makes them not welcome enough for public usages. To deal with this, a novel terrain scanning system using line laser based on trigonometric survey is proposed. The system is capable of terrain data collection, data pre-processing, and 3D display. The data collection circuit is designed under Labview and PCL is applied for interface design. Collected data will be imported to the interface after pre-processing, thus providing the measured 3D terrain information. The experiment results show that the proposed system is capable of large area terrain scanning and display at a high speed and with low cost, and is more portable comparing to existing systems.

Keywords: 3D laser scanning · Trigonometric survey · Data collection
Point cloud · 3D display

1 Introduction

Recently, geospatial data is playing a more and more important role in social and economic development. As one of the newest spatial information gathering methods, 3D laser scanning is capable of obtaining 3D model of terrain and complex objects with attributes such as high accuracy, high initiative, high speed, and non-contact, which greatly reduce time and money costs [1, 2]. Most importantly, it achieves the digitization of real objects, thus allowing a transformation from analogue quantity to digital quantity and solving many digital information collections problems [3].

Currently, multiple companies has developed commercialized 3D laser scanning system, including Cyra, Leica, Riegl and I-SITE [4, 5], etc. As for airborne laser scanning systems, TopScan and Optech [6] are much stronger. Products from these companies are widely adopted for business usages. However, they are not only costly for the device and data post-process, but also heavy and complex to operate. In order to overcome these drawbacks, a novel airborne 3D line laser scanning system based on triangulation is proposed.

© ICST Institute for Computer Sciences, Social Informatics and Telecommunications Engineering 2018
X. Gu et al. (Eds.): MLICOM 2017, Part I, LNICST 226, pp. 434–443, 2018.
https://doi.org/10.1007/978-3-319-73564-1_43

The proposed system can be divided into three parts: point cloud collection, data pre-processing and 3D display interface designing. Images with laser projections are captured by CCD and transmitted to the ground base station through wireless image transmission. The signal will be processed by capture card and transformed into computers as digital signals. After using Labview and VS2015 to collect the data and display, the 3D model of object is then obtained.

One of the main contributions of the proposed system is to reduce the scanning cost and make the system more portable. Meanwhile, three-dimensional display interface is integrated to the system so that no extra processing software is required for observation. With the rapid development of unmanned aerial vehicle, the system provides an easier operated and cheaper system for 3D object modeling by combining the scanning system to the UAV.

2 UAV-Carried Scanning System

2.1 System Design

Considering that line laser scanning is faster than point scanning in imaging while reaching a further distance comparing to surface scanning, the proposed system applies trigonometric survey and line laser to obtain the depth image of a target object [7]. Figure 1 is the schematic diagram.

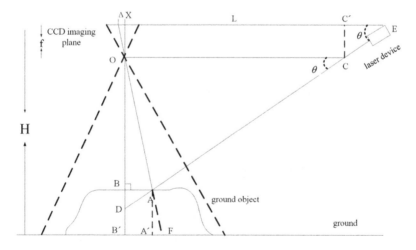

Fig. 1. Schematic diagram of trigonometric survey applied in the system.

Line ED is the light transmitted from the laser device. It is reflected by the surface of object A and imaging on the CCD imaging plane through the lens center O. Distance between point A on the image plane and the midcourt line of the image plane is Δx, level inclination of the laser device is θ, distance between the laser device and the midcourt line of the image plane is L, focal length of CCD lens is f, and height of the image plane from the ground is H. According to similar triangles, we have

$$\begin{cases} \frac{\Delta x}{BA} = \frac{f}{OB} \\ \frac{L}{BA} = \frac{L \tan \theta}{BD} \\ OB = L \tan \theta - BD \end{cases} \tag{1}$$

$$AA' = BB' = H - f - OB = H - f - \frac{f L \tan \theta}{f + \Delta x \tan \theta} \tag{2}$$

where AA' is the required object surface height. Using this method, the whole 3D model of the scanned object can be easily obtained.

Figure 2 is the structure diagram of the entire scanning system, which consists of data collection circuit, data pre-processing circuit, and 3D display interface. The first part is designed on Labview and achieved using hardware part, while the later two parts are mainly designed on Labview and Visual Studio respectively. Figure 3 is the flow chart of the hardware part of the entire system and Fig. 4 is that of the software design.

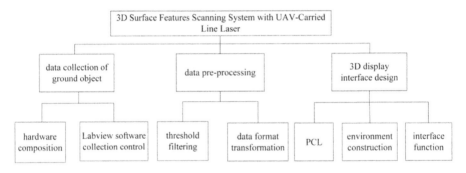

Fig. 2. Structure diagram of the entire 3D scanning system.

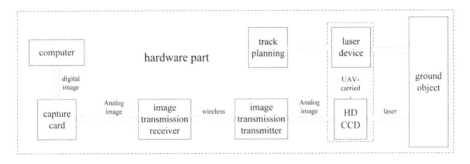

Fig. 3. Hardware part diagram.

CCD is installed on the UAV according to trigonometric survey and then is connected to the transmitter. The receiver is connected to the capture card and the computer. When the UAV is scanning according to the designed track, all pictures with laser lines captured by the CCD are live transmitted to the computer.

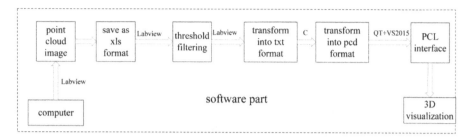

Fig. 4. Software part diagram.

After receiving the imported images, the system starts to move forward to the software parts which includes three parts: (a) Transform images into xls format point cloud based on Labview; (b) point cloud data pre-processing; (c) Display interface design using PCL. The whole processing part achieves the system function of 3D display of the scanned object.

2.2 Data Collection

The first part of the data collection procedure is the hardware of the scanning system, which is divided into two groups: onboard ones and on-the-ground ones. The former part includes UAV, one-wavelength laser, HD mini camera, optical filter, image transmission system (transmitter), and several 12 V lithium batteries. The later part contains image transmission system (receiver), capture card, and computer. Figure 5 is the system hardware part sketch map.

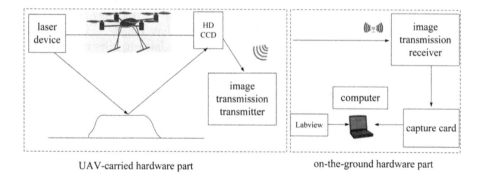

Fig. 5. System hardware part sketch map.

Data collection also involves software control which is reached by upper computer programming on Labview in the proposed system. Figure 6 is the flow chart of the whole procedure of image collection, processing and point cloud storage.

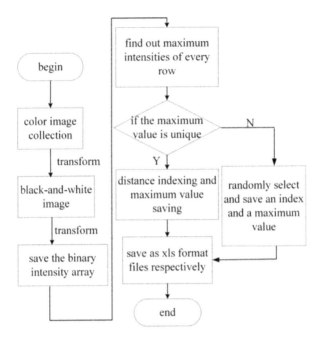

Fig. 6. Flow chart of image collection, processing, and point cloud storage.

For image capture part, color frames captured by CCD will be transformed into black-and-white images, and then be stored into queues as two-dimensional arrays. Object surface parts that are lightened by laser lines ought to have stronger intensity values comparing to the surroundings. As a result, pixels with maximum intensity values of each row are found frame by frame. If the maximum intensity of a row corresponds to more than one pixel, then one of them will be randomly selected and stored. This can be handled in the threshold filtering procedure. Finally, newly obtained arrays are stored in the format of xls as distance files and intensity files respectively.

Reasons for choosing the xls format are as follows: (a) Labview contains functions to specially process xls files, which makes the designed 3D scanning program much simpler and easier to achieve; (b) Data size of xls files are smaller than txt files of a same quantity of stored information which benefits online data storage, thus saving all experiment data without deadlocks caused by capture program; (c) xls format files can be transformed into txt files and help saving the point cloud in a format of (x, y, z), which is more convenient for further processing.

2.3   Data Pre-processing

Collected data contains information of all scanned surfaces and threshold filtering can be used to eliminate extra ones while saving the interested data. Size of the interested part can be altered by changing the threshold. Figure 7 is the Labview program for this part.

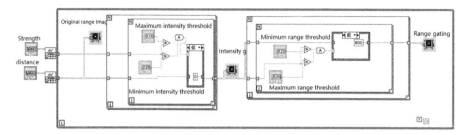

Fig. 7. Threshold filtering program diagram.

Threshold filtering contains intensity filtering and distance filtering. The intensity filtering do comparing between stored intensity values and the threshold. If the intensity value is greater than the threshold, the same position information as the original array will be saved; otherwise, the corresponding position will be set to a distance of zero. After gating the new distance array, the required object image is successfully obtained. Figure 8 is the scanned object, and Fig. 9 is the corresponding filtering result.

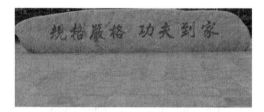

Fig. 8. Original image of the scanned object.

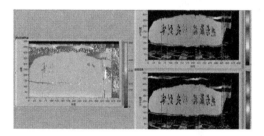

Fig. 9. Filtering results.

The left image is the original distance image; the upper right one is the intensity gating result and the bottom right one is the distance gating result after intensity gating. It is clear that filtering results are better than the original image.

The designed software requires pcd format inputs. As a result, the collected and filtered xls format data need to be transformed before using the interface. First, xls format data is transformed into txt format. Figure 10 is the transformation Labview program. Each case in xls refers to a distance value z. If the rows and columns are stored as x and y, then all data will be restored into a format of txt as (x, y, z). The new txt file is two times larger than the original xls file. Secondly, the txt file is transformed into a final pcd file using PCL functions based on VS2015 [8].

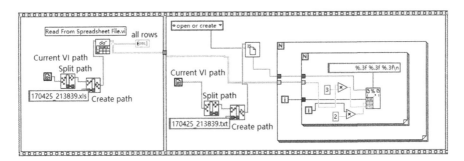

Fig. 10. Transform program from xls format to txt format.

2.4 Display Interface

Point Cloud Library, along with VS, QT, and VTK, is used for display interface design. VTK is applied for point cloud 3D display, PCL for core algorithms and data input/output, and QT for interface layout design. The programming language is VC++ under VS2015. The combination of those greatly improves the performance of the designed interface. It can read point cloud, do filtering, achieve curve planar reconstruction and human-machine interaction. The interface frame is shown in Figs. 11 and 12 is the display result of the mentioned object.

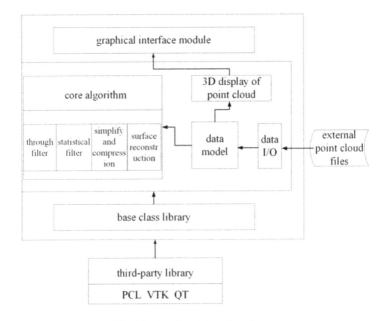

Fig. 11. Designed interface frame.

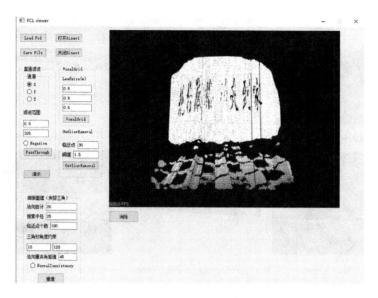

Fig. 12. Display result.

3   Experiment

The laser device used in experiments is 200 mw 532 nm green line laser. Lens focus of the HD mini CCD is 6 mm. Other hardwares are 5.8G image transmission transceiver and drive-free capture card. The experiment is carried out at night in a school parking and the scanned object is the parked vehicles. There was a south wind of force 2 to 3. Designed air lines are two parallel lines at a height of 11 m. Figure 13 shows the scanning results.

It is clear that point cloud collected by the proposed system is capable of revealing the outlines of the scanned vehicles, especially for details like the rearview mirrors and the car windows. This indicates that the proposed system performs desirably in high-quality data collecting. As for the point cloud display, comparing to Geomagic, the proposed PCL interface describes the object features more clearly and intuitively, and its displayed images are more similar to the original appearance of the scanned objects. As a result, the proposed PCL interface is betterin collected data display.

Above experimental results shows that the proposed UAV-carried 3D line laser scanning system is capable of wide range ground object information collection and 3D display of the collected data. The experiment results verified the correctness and rationality of the proposed system.

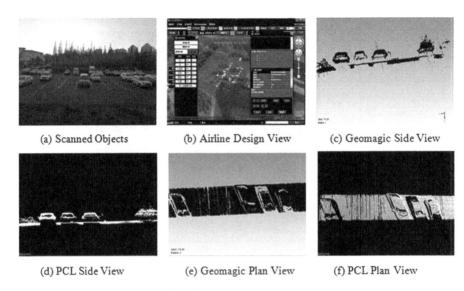

| (a) Scanned Objects | (b) Airline Design View | (c) Geomagic Side View |
| (d) PCL Side View | (e) Geomagic Plan View | (f) PCL Plan View |

Fig. 13. Experiment results.

4   Conclusion

As a modern non-contact high accuracy sensor technology, airborne 3D laser scanning technology can directly obtain the 3D information of various real objects and surroundings, thus having more advantages that cannot be achieved by traditional surveying instruments. In this paper, a novel triangulation-based UAV-carried 3D laser scanning system for ground objects is proposed, which can achieve both data collection and display. Comparing to existing methods, the proposed system is capable of wide range scanning and is smaller, lighter, simpler, cheaper and easier for post-process. The experiment results indicate that the system can also be enhanced by applying CCD with higher resolution ratio and wireless image transmission. These improvements will be done in the future.

References

1. Zuxun, Z., Jianqing, Z.: Methods and key technologies in urban modeling. World Sci. Technol. R&D **03**, 23–29 (2003)
2. Jizhou, W., Chengming, L., Zongjian, L.: Discussion on 3D urban data collection and development. Sci. Surv. Mapp. **29**(4), 71–74 (2004)
3. Lewen, Y., Da, Z., Bin, Y.: Survey on miner-used 3D laser scanning system. Metal Mine **41** (10), 101–103 (2012)
4. Haiying, F., Lun, Y., Zhihui, X.: Applied research on Cyra 3D laser scanning system. Mining Survey (3), 16–18 (2004)
5. Ke, Z.: Study on Reigl-based 3D laser scanning device. J. CNU **28**(1), 77–81 (2007)

6. Hu, Y.: Automated Extraction of Digital Terrain Models Roads and BuildingsUsing Airborne Lidar Data. University of Calgary, Calgary (2003)
7. Jianhui, L., Qin, W.: 3D laser scanning system for sliding mass visualization. Bull. Surv. Mapp. (10), 51–54 (2010)
8. Zengtao, W.: 3D point cloud processing platform design. Dalian University of Technology (2014)

Contourlet Based Image Denoising Method Combined Recursive Cycle-Spinning Algorithm

Hongda Fan, Xufen Xie$^{(\boxtimes)}$, Yuncui Zhang, and Nianyu Zou

Research Institute of Photonics, Dalian Polytechnic University,
No. 1 Qinggongyuan, Ganjingzi District, Dalian 116034, China
xiexf@dlpu.edu.cn

Abstract. Contourlet transform lacks shift invariance, and threshold processing on the coefficients may produce pseudo Gibbs phenomena. For recursive cycle spinning algorithm can reduce the pseudo Gibbs phenomena. This paper studies the image denoising method combined with Contourlet transform and recursive cycles pinning algorithm, The analysis show that the factor need to be adjusted. When the adjustment factor takes best value, the corresponding image objective index PSNR (Peak Signal to Noise Ratio) is the largest, and images visual effects are optimal. The experimental results show that: compared with original algorithm, changing adjustment factor, the PSNR of denoised image can be improved 0.6–1.2.

Keywords: Contourlet transform · Recursive cycle-spinning · Image denoising

1 Introduction

Image acquisition, transmission and storage process is limited by environmental conditions and physical limitations of imaging equipment. Different levels blur and noise will happened in those images, quality. i.e. images degradation. Image restoration technology obtained clear and high quality images from degraded images; it has been widely used in satellite image, industry and medical image processing.

Recent years, wavelet transform performs very well on image processing. However, a separable two-dimensional orthogonal wavelet transform has limited directionality and cannot effectively represent the direction information in image. Therefore it cannot effectively capture the contour and texture information. Wavelet transform can optimally represent piecewise smooth signals in one dimension, and capture point singularity of 1-D signal. Two-dimensional separable wavelet composed by tensor product can effectively capture single edge points in 2-D images. It is cannot optimally represent line singularities in 2-D images, such as the outline of object or a certain direction in image.

In 2002, Do and Vetterli proposed a two-dimensional representation of images [1]. Contourlet transform is a two-dimensional image sparse representation. It is more effectively capture high dimensional singularity. Compared with wavelet transform, the contourlet transform can expression small directional contours and line segments with

© ICST Institute for Computer Sciences, Social Informatics and Telecommunications Engineering 2018
X. Gu et al. (Eds.): MLICOM 2017, Part I, LNICST 226, pp. 444–450, 2018.
https://doi.org/10.1007/978-3-319-73564-1_44

fewer coefficients. Contourlet transform not only inherits the multi-resolution, localization and strict sampling characteristics of wavelet, but also has the characteristics of directionality and anisotropy. The contourlet transform can capture the edge details of images from different scales, different directions, and different frequencies. In image compression, denoising, feature extraction etc., can provide superior information. It has been widely used in image denoising, image fusion, digital watermarking etc., However, like wavelet transform, lacks translational invariance, the coefficients threshold processing in Contourlet transform also produce pseudo Gibbs phenomena. This phenomenon results in image distortion, and affects image visual effect. In 1995, the Cycle Spinning algorithms proposed by Coifman and Donoho [2], and the recursive cycle spinning proposed by Fletcher et al. [3, 4]. This algorithm can suppress pseudo Gibbs phenomenon and made threshold denoising more effectively. [5–7] have carried on correlation research.

This paper studied a Contourlet-Recursive cycle Spinning denoise method. It can obtained better visual image and higher PSNR by changing the adjusting factor.

2 Contourlet Transform

The base support interval of contourlet transform is 'Rectangle' structure. This rectangle is directional and anisotropic, and vary with aspect ratio.

The contourlet transform utilizes Laplace pyramid (LP) and directional filter bank (DFB) achieve multi-resolution, localization, multi direction decomposition.

Laplace pyramid (LP) decomposition was used to complete multi-scale decomposition. The LP decomposition at each level generates a down sampled lowpass version of the original and the difference between the original and the prediction, resulting in a bandpass image. Figure 1 depicts this decomposition process, where H and G are called (lowpass) analysis and synthesis filters. The outputs are a coarse approximation a and a difference b between the original signal and the prediction.

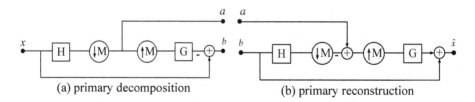

(a) primary decomposition   (b) primary reconstruction

Fig. 1. Laplace pyramid decomposition and reconstruction

The wedge-shaped division of the directional filter banks is achieved by the directional frequency decomposition and resampling of the quincunx filter banks. The quincunx fan filter bank QFB is shown in Fig. 2. The signal is decomposed into basic vertical and basic horizontal subbands using H_0, H_1, G_0, G_1 quincunx filter banks. When they satisfy orthogonal or biorthogonal, complete reconstruction can be achieved.

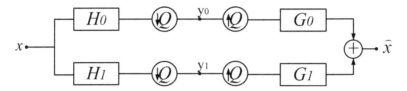

Fig. 2. Quincunx filter banks

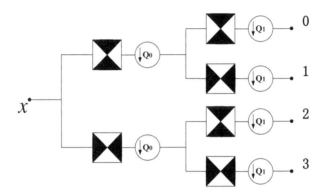

Fig. 3. The two layers of the DFB decomposition structure

The DFB is efficiently implemented via an l-level binary tree decomposition that leads to 2^L subbands with wedge-shaped frequency partitioning as shown in Fig. 3.

3   Recursive Cycle Spinning Algorithm

3.1   Recursive Cycle Spinning

The shift of the contourlet transform causes the pseudo Gibbs phenomenon in discontinuities signal, spurious Gibbs phenomenon means image distorted. To suppress the spurious Gibbs phenomenon in process of threshold denoising, inverse shift of denoised signal can make pseudo Gibbs phenomenon appear in different places, such as Eq. (1). Linear averaging of all the denoising results can inhibiting the pseudo Gibbs phenomenon, this is described as Eq. (2).

$$\hat{s}_{i,j} = C_{-i,-j}\left(F^{-1}\left(\theta\left(F\left(C_{i,j}(I(x, y))\right)\right)\right)\right) \tag{1}$$

$$\hat{s} = \frac{1}{N_1 N_2} \sum_{i=1,j=1}^{N_1 N_2} \hat{s}_{i,j} \tag{2}$$

Where, $I(x, y)$ is the gray value of noise image, N_1, N_2 is the maximum translation in row and column direction, C is the Cycle spinning operator, i, j is shift in row and column direction, F is a transform operator, F^{-1} is an inverse transformation operator, θ is threshold operator.

Usually, the average is not optimized, literature [3] proposes an recursive cycle spinning algorithm. The algorithm assumes that $\hat{s}_l$ represents an estimation sequence, the initial value is original noise signal, $\hat{s}_0[n] = I[n]$, iterate through Eq. (3).

$$\hat{s}_{l+1} = D_i(\hat{s}_l), \, i = l \bmod N \tag{3}$$

Where, $D_i(\bullet)$ is denoising operator, N is max displacement. In this algorithm, the sequence is shifted, transformed, threshold processed, inverse transformed, and the output sequence as input of next iteration operation. For all i, the fixed point $\hat{s}_\infty$ satisfy $\hat{s}_\infty = D_i(\hat{s}_\infty)$.

3.2 Denoising Algorithm

For image, the high frequency information is concentrated on the edges, contours, and normals of certain textures, represents the details of image changes. Therefore, the detail coefficients in directional subbands described high frequency information at each layer decomposition.

Stochastic characteristics of noise, leading it often appeared in high frequency information, and they are described by some detail coefficients. Those coefficients are quite small in general. After decompose at an appropriate scale, signal and noise often can be separated effectively. Contourlet threshold denoising achieved denoise by modifying the detail component coefficients of different scales.

The general steps of contourlet threshold denoising are described below:

(1) Multi-scale contourlet decomposition of image;
(2) According to the different characteristics of image and noise in Contourlet domain, the detailed component coefficients of each dimension are modified by setting threshold.
(3) Reconstruction image with the modified coefficients;

The modification of the detail component coefficients is key steps in image denoising processing, and it is affecting the final quality.

The hard threshold denoising mathematical expressions, such as Eq. (4):

$$T_{hard} = \begin{cases} W, \, |W| \geq T \\ 0, \, |W| < T \end{cases} \tag{4}$$

Where, W is contourlet coefficients of noise image, T is threshold.

In contourlet transform threshold denoise processing, the coefficients φ_{ct} should be determined. It can be expressed as Eq. (5):

$$\varphi_{ct} = \frac{4}{3} \lambda \delta \sqrt{\varphi_{yt}} \tag{5}$$

Where, φ_{ct} is sub-band adjusted coefficient, and φ_{yt} is the noise image each sub-band coefficients, λ is regulatory factor.

By changing λ, the sub-band coefficients φ_{ct} can be adjusted. λ affects the final denoising quality. λ is set by experience, and average is 3.

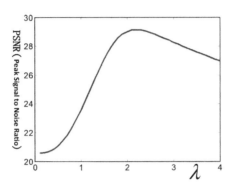

Fig. 4. The curves of PSNR

In this paper, the experimental results of Fig. 4 are obtained by adjusting the λ values. It can be seen that with the change of λ value, the PSNR value curve shows rise first and then decrease. When λ is 2.2, the maximum PSNR value is 29.2.

4 The Results of Simulation

In simulation experiment, when cycle times equal 10, the image distortion is well suppressed. This paper, the number of iterations is 10. The experimental image is 'lena.bmp (512 * 512)', The gaussian white noise $\sigma = 10$ are added to the standard image as noise image. The quality evaluation standard is PSNR. Contourlet transform choose '9–7' and 'pkva' filter.

The results are as follows:

Figure 5(c) is based on Contourlet transform denoising results, we can see that the denoised image has very serious pseudo Gibbs phenomena; Fig. 5(d), (e) and (f) are denoised image of this article algorithm, which pseudo Gibbs phenomena in those image has been reduced and the PSNR value of denoised image is improved. The values of λ in Fig. 5(d), (e), and (f) are 1.8, 2.2, 2.6, respectively. The PSNR of Fig. 5(e) is the largest, and it is visual effects are better. The larger λ value causes some blocky blur in recovery image, as shown in Fig. 5(f). It is concluded that the λ value should be set smaller. Otherwise, the denoised image may produce blocky blur, which is due to improper threshold selection. This affects the visual effect of denoised image. According to experimental results, it can be seen that the image denoising algorithm studied in this paper can improve the PSNR value, about 0.6–1.2.

(a) Lena raw image

(b) Noise image

(c) Lena recovery image，PSNR=28.0

(d) Lena recovery image, PSNR=28.6

(e) Lena recovery image, PSNR=29.2

(f) Lena recovery image, PSNR=28.8

Fig. 5. The results of simulation

5 Conclusion

In this paper we studied a image denoising method, which based on contourlet transform and recursive cycle spinning algorithm. Analyzed the influence of adjustment factor on denoising. From experimental results, when the adjustment factor equal 2.2, PSNR of denoised image is 29.2; the adjustment factor equal 1.8, PSNR is 28.6, and those images have better visual effects. Compared with the original algorithm, changing adjustment factor, the PSNR of denoised image can be improved 0.6–1.2.

References

1. Do, M.N., Vetterli, M.: An efficient directional multiresolution image representation. J. IEEE Trans. Image Process. **14**(12), 2091–2106 (2005)
2. Coifman, R.R., Donoho, D.L.: Translation-invariant de-noising. J. Wavelets Stat. **103**, 125–150 (1995)
3. Fletcher, A.K., Ramchandran, K., Goyal, V.K.: Wavelet denoising by recursive cycle spinning. In: 2002 Proceedings of the International Conference on Image Processing, Rochester, NY, vol. 2, pp. 873–876. IEEE (2002)
4. Fletcher, A.K., Ramchandran, K., Goyal, V.K.: Iterative projective wavelet methods for denoising. In: Proceedings Wavelets: Application in Signal & Image Processing X, Part of SPIE International Symposium on Optical Science & Technology, vol. 5207, no. 1, pp. 9–15 (2003)
5. Deng, C., Hou, M.Y., Liu, Z.Q.: Infrared image enhancement algorithm using wavelet-contourlet transform with recursive cycle spinning. J. Laser Infrared **43**(9), 1068–1071 (2013)
6. Cheng, Y.: Cycle-spinning based contourlet denoising for multiple image. In: International Conference on Consumer Electronics, Communications and Networks, pp. 209–212. IEEE (2014)
7. Kumar, K.K., Pavani, M.: A new PCA based hybrid color image watermarking using cycle spinning - sharp frequency localized contourlet transform for copyright protection. In: Unal, A., Nayak, M., Mishra, D.K., Singh, D., Joshi, A. (eds.) SmartCom 2016. CCIS, vol. 628, pp. 355–364. Springer, Singapore (2016). https://doi.org/10.1007/978-981-10-3433-6_43

Green Communication and Intelligent Networking

RETRACTED CHAPTER: A Resource Allocation Algorithm Based on Game Theory in UDN

Changjun Chen[1(✉)], Jianxin Dai[2], Chonghu Cheng[1], and Zhiliang Huang[3]

[1] College of Telecommunications and Information Engineering,
Nanjing University of Posts and Telecommunications, Nanjing 210003, China
1807822499@qq.com, chengch@njupt.edu.cn
[2] School of Science, Nanjing University of Posts and Telecommunications,
Nanjing 210023, China
daijx@njupt.edu.cn
[3] College of Mathematics, Physics and Information Engineering,
Zhejiang Normal University, Jinhua 321004, China
zlhuang@zjnu.cn

Abstract. In ultra-dense networks (UDNs), large-scale deployment of femtocells base stations is an important technique in improving the network throughput and quality of service (QoS). However, traditional resource allocation algorithms are concerned with the improvement of the overall performance of the network. In this paper, a new resource allocation algorithm based on game theory is proposed to manage the resource allocation in UDNs. The quality of service (QoS) and energy consumption of each femtocell are considered. Firstly, a modified clustering algorithm is performed. Then we transform this resource allocation problem to a Stackelberg game. In sub-channel resource allocation, we aim to maximize the throughput of the whole system by cluster heads (CHs). The power allocation takes account of the balance between QoS requirement and transmit power consumption. Simulation results show that this method has some advantages in improving the overall system throughput, while obtaining a performance improvement compared with other algorithms.

Keywords: UDN · Femtocells · Clustering · Stackelberg game

1 Introduction

With the rapid growth of Internet applications, for the users, mobile phone traffic doubled and redoubled, bringing large volume to satisfy the needs the future development of radio telecommunications. A new generation of mobile networks 5G in 2020 maybe large-deployed in ultra-dense networks to meet this challenge [1]. The UDN can improve the overall throughput and increase the coverage of the network, UDN is a prospecting network technology now. However, achieving UDN will face two challenges [2]. First, geographically randomness, compactness, and unplanned micro and macro base stations make efficient resource allocation algorithm and the design of a

---

The original version of this chapter was revised: The plagiarized chapter has been retracted. The retraction to this chapter is available at https://doi.org/10.1007/978-3-319-73564-1_73

© ICST Institute for Computer Sciences, Social Informatics and Telecommunications Engineering 2018
X. Gu et al. (Eds.): MLICOM 2017, Part I, LNICST 226, pp. 453–462, 2018.
https://doi.org/10.1007/978-3-319-73564-1_45

low complexity become a problem. The existence of severe system interference directly affects the whole performance of the network [3]. Second, due to the large number of users and the high rate of data transmission speed demands, the operators must enhance the maintenance costs and network operation [4]. To decrease the energy consumption and reduce the interference of the system is also an important problem.

Through appropriate collaborative resource allocation algorithms, interference in networks can be reduced. Clustering algorithm is an efficiently algorithm for dealing with interference problems and has been extensively discussed. In the UDN, there are two methods can be used to cluster. One is between the femtocell base stations based on the different characteristics, using different sub-channels at different base stations reduce the same level of interference. And the other between femtocells is based on similar characteristics, while the entire sub-channels is classified. Abdelnasser et al. used previous algorithm to cluster, and two femtocells with good channel gain were allocated in the same cluster [5]. Tong et al. used latter clustering algorithm, mutual distraction between the femtocells in clustering standard and the smaller mutual distraction between the femtocell base stations is placed in a cluster [6]. Peromchelakis et al. using previous clustering algorithm, The weight of edge determines mutual interference between the apexes in an interfering map [7]. Lin and Tian used the latter different sub-channels are given to them [8]. However, the latter this clustering schemes are not suitable for use in ultra-dense networks on account of limited amount of clusters and spectrum effectiveness doesn't increase with amount of femtocells [6–8]. Thus, this paper proposes an improved clustering method by using the former scheme.

Some work has been done on the problem of resource allocation in Ultra dense networks. Kang et al. proposed a game theory [9]. In the performance assessment, the quality of service can be used to assess customer satisfaction. Guruacharya et al. proposed networks which aim at maximizing the overall system throughput and satisfying the demand for quality of the macro cell [10]. In order to meet the requirements of femtocell quality, [11] proposed a downlink resource allocation algorithm, in which the macro base station and the micro base station are cut into two classes to maximize the utilization rate.

This paper presents a method of resource allocation based on game theory. In this paper, we propose a dynamic multi-dimensional resource joint optimization model to solve the cross-level and same-level interference of dense networks. Multi-dimensional resources have transmission point association, user channel and power allocation. The simulation results show that the algorithm has certain advantages in suppressing the interference, improving the total system throughput and the total transmit power, and the home base station guarantees the QoS of the user. In addition, as the density of the femtocell base station increases, the system throughput increases. Today, due to the rising of energy costs at a high rate of speed and contributions to global climate issue, EE is becoming an important design standard in green wireless communications [12].

2 System Model and Optimization Problem

2.1 Social Network Model

This paper focuses on the downlink transmission system in ultra-dense networks. The system structure is a two-tier heterogeneous network. A macro cell and some highly dense deployed femtocells. The number of femtocells ranges from 40 to 200. The cluster head is connected to the macrocells via a super-speed link. We put the C as a cluster, for example, $C = \{C_1, C_2, \ldots, C_k\}$, k is the number of clusters. There is n_k femtocell in the cluster C_k. Femtocells and macrocells are allocated in different spectra. Orthogonal sub channels in each cluster is assigned to the femtocell, $N = \max\{n_k\}$. Transmission losses include penetration loss. We can define u_f the propagation gain as a user who is serviced by fly honeycomb f and $G_{u_f,j}^n$ as cellular f and N sub-channels u_f the spread between the gain.

(1) Femtocell and its transmission gain between users

$$G_{u_f,f}^n = K_f d_{u_f,f}^{-\chi} g_f^n,$$ (1)

K_f defined as corrected path loss, χ is the interior exponential path loss, d_{u_f} and g_f^n represent the transmission distance of the femtocell f and its user, and the Rayleigh fading.

(2) Femtocell and another user interference between the gain

$$G_{u_f,j}^n = K_f WL^{-2} d_{u_f,j}^{-\chi} g_j^n,$$ (2)

K_f and χ have the same meaning in (1). WL is called the strike loss. d_{u_f} and g_j^n are transport distances between the femtocell i and another femtocell f for u_f, respectively. The SINR can be defined as follows:

$$\gamma_{u_f,f}^n = \frac{P_{u_f,f}^n G_{u_f,f}^n}{\sum_{j \neq f, j \in F} P_{u_f,j}^n G_{u_f,j}^n + N_0} = \frac{P_{u_f,f}^n G_{u_f,f}^n}{I_{u_f,f}^n}$$ (3)

$P_{u_i,i}^n$ is the transmission power allocated to the user u_i at the base station i. For more predigest, The interference of the user u_f is $I_{u_f,f}^n$, then we define $I_{u_f,f}^n = \sum_{j \neq f, j \in F} P_{u_f,f}^n G_{u_f,f}^n + N_0$.

2.2 Problem Optimization

Our aim is each femtocell supports different services and has itself service needs. However, the increase in transmission power has a greater influence for other femtocells, while affecting the network's overall performance. Therefore, it is not enough to satisfy only maximizing total performance. We also need to consider the allocation of network resources in the process of service quality requirements and transmission power balance. We use game theory to handle the balance between service requirements and network performance. At the same time, within a specific spectrum of resources, all competing femtocells want to make their benefits maximum. When the network resources are allocated to the femtocell, it will lead to a reduction in the utilization of other femtocells. So the use of game is appropriate. Therefore, the use of multi-follower multi-leadership game framework to solve our problem of resource allocation.

In this framework, Leaders taking different measures will lead to different options for followers. Make the radio resource allocated to the cluster head change.

For the cluster head, they make their throughput maximum, and strive to sub-bandwidth in the limited conditions to acquire the best network benefits. Cluster heads compete with each other and control the allocation of radio resources within each cluster. So there is a weight between their throughput gains. Leadership strategy is a comprehensive set $\{B_{ij}\} = \{N_i, P_j\}$, N_i is sub-channel distribution vectors P_j power distribution vectors. The use of the i cluster head is

$$U_i(\Gamma,\ P_{-i},\ P_j) = \sum_{f \in C_k} \sum_{n=1}^{N} \Gamma_{u_f,f}^n \Delta B \log_2(1 + \gamma_{u_f,f}^n) \tag{4}$$

P_{-i} represents the transmission power allocated to each cluster head that does not contain cluster head i, P_j and Γ represent the transmission power and all of the femtocells that assigned to cluster k. $\Gamma_{u_f,f}^n$ is the sub-channel assignment index when assign the sub-channel n to the user u_f and the femtocell f, $\Gamma_{u_f,f}^n = 1$, otherwise $\Gamma_{u_f,f}^n = 0$.

Then, the optimization problem for cluster head can be summarized as follows:

$$\max \sum_{f \in C_k} \sum_{n=1}^{N} \Gamma_{u_f,f}^n \Delta B \log_2(1 + \gamma_{u_f,f}^n) \tag{5}$$

$$s.t. \begin{cases} \sum_n \Gamma_{u_f,f}^n = 1,\ \forall f \\ \Gamma_{u_f,f}^n \in \{0,1\},\ \forall n,\ f, \\ 0 \le P_{u_f,f}^n \le P_{max} \end{cases}$$

However, the femtocells need to meet the needs of their users' quality of service. Besides, they need think about power issues to lessen distraction with other femtocells. The tactics of the follower set is a set $\{P_j\} = \{p_j : 0 \le p_j \le P_{max}\}$. Thus, the utilization function of the femtocell f is:

$$U_{u_f,f}^n\left(P_{u_f,f}^n,\ P_{u_f,-f}^n,\ \Gamma\right) = \alpha(\gamma_{u_f,f}^{tar} - \gamma_{u_f,f}^n)^2 + \beta P_{u_f,f}^n \tag{6}$$

$P_{u_f,-f}^n$ represents the transmission power of all the femtocells allocated to the cluster i that does not include the femtocell f, P_{max} is the total transmission power budget, $\gamma_{u_f,f}^{tar}$ is SINR of the user u_f who is served by femtocell f, α and β is the non-negative adjustment factor.

Then, the optimization problem can be defined simply:

$$\min \alpha(\gamma_{u_f f}^{tar} - \gamma_{u_f f}^n)^2 + \beta P_{u_f f}^n \tag{7}$$

$$s.t. \begin{cases} \gamma_{u_f f}^n \geq \gamma_{u_f f}^{tar}, \ \forall f \\ 0 \leq P_{u_f f}^n \leq P_{\max} \end{cases}$$

2.3 Game Balance

In this part, For a given game, Our goal is that the model reaches the equilibrium point [13].
The follower level game is $P_j^* = \{P_{K_f f}^{n^*} : f \in c_i\}$,

$$P_{k_f f}^{n^*} = \arg \min U_{u_f f}^n(P_{u_f f}^n, \ P_{u_f,-f}^{n*}, \ \Gamma), f \in c_i \tag{8}$$

The Nash Balance of the leadership game is

$$B_{ij}^* = \{\Gamma^* \times P_j^* : \Gamma^* \in N_i\}, i \in \Phi, j \in \Psi,$$

$$b_{ij}^* = u_{ij}(\Gamma^*, P_i, P_j^*) \tag{9}$$

Based on (8) and (9), for the hierarchical game, we can define the Starkerberg equilibrium bellow:

Definition 1: The result of the (9) is defined as B_{ij}^* and the result of the (8) is defined as P_j^*. The fixed point $\left(B_{ij}^*, P_j^*\right)$ is the hierarchy game of the Starkerberg equilibrium point.

In order to obtain the Starkerberg equilibrium point, we find the optimal solution game. Typically, the leader gets the response of the follower, and gets the strategy based on their use of the strategy. This paper calculates the process of the Starkerberg equilibrium as follows: First given Γ^0 and P_j^0 solved the problem of the follower level game; then get the cluster i's P_j^* of femtocell. Then we solve the cluster head of the leadership level game problem.

In order to solve this problem, we must get the cluster results first. The problem of resource allocation is segmented into cluster problem and resource allocation problem.

3 Clustering Algorithm

In this section, The clustering arithmetic is based upon not the same femtocells using distinct sub-channels to cut down the different characteristics of the interference femtocells. First, a definition of the degree of interference is expressed as follows:

$$\omega_{ab} = \frac{I_{a,b}}{avg.I} \tag{10}$$

Which ω_{ab} is the degree of interference between the femtocell a and b, $I_{a,b}$ represent the interference gain between the femtocell a and b. When I is large, there is more interference with transmission among the two femtocells on both sides of the edge. Thus, two femtocells should be divided into clusters in order to maximize the degree of inter-cluster interference.

4   Resource Allocation

4.1   Sub-channel Allocation

After completing the cluster of femtocell, the head of cluster dispatched configuration message to the femtocells which gathers around the cluster head in each cluster. The head of cluster in each cluster controls resource allocation, for example, the allocation of sub-carrier and allocation of power. Below initialized power conditions, the allocation of channel constraints and the maximum constraints of power, every cluster wants to make throughput maximum. Then, the problem of optimization can be solved as below:

$$\max_{f, u_f} \sum_{f \in C_k} \sum_{n=1}^{N} \Gamma_{u_f f}^{n} \Delta B \log_2(1 + \gamma_{u_f f}^{n}) \tag{11}$$

$$s.t. \begin{cases} \sum_n \Gamma_{u_f f}^{n} \leq 1, \forall f \\ \Gamma_{u_f f}^{n} \in \{0, 1\}, \forall n, f \\ \leq P_{u_f f}^{n} \leq P_{max} \end{cases}$$

If we further set the value of $\Gamma_{u_f f}^{n}$ to [0, 1], we have a convex non-linear scheme on $\Gamma_{u_f f}^{n}$ [14]. By using the KKT condition, the solution of (11) can be derived as:

$$\Gamma_{u_f f}^{n} = [\frac{(1 + \lambda_1)\Delta B}{\lambda_2 \ln 2} - \frac{1}{\gamma_{u_f f}^{n}}]^+ \tag{12}$$

Here λ_1, λ_2 is the Lagrange factor allocation restrictions and the transmission power restrictions. Maximizing SINR value aim to make user u_f obtain a performance gain.

4.2   Power Distribution

Each femtocell transmit power to get more to meet its service quality requirements [15]. Therefore, for making system throughput maximum, we should consider the adverse effects of increased transmission power.

Then, focus on conditions [17]. The problem of power allocation can be represented as:

$$U_{u_f,f}^{n^*} = \min\{\alpha(\gamma_{u_f,f}^{tar} - \gamma_{u_f,f}^{n})^2 + \beta P_{u_f,f}^{n}\} \qquad (13)$$

$$s.t. \begin{cases} \gamma_{u_f,f}^{n} \geq \gamma_{u_f,f}^{tar}, \ \forall f \\ 0 \leq P_{u_f,f}^{n} \leq P_{\max} \end{cases}$$

Distinguish $U_{u_f,f}^{n}$, and set the derivative equal to 0, we can get

$$\frac{\partial U_{u_f,f}^{n}}{\partial P_{u_f,f}^{n}} = -2\alpha \times (\gamma_{u_f,f}^{tar} - \gamma_{u_f,f}^{n}) \times \frac{\partial \gamma_{u_f,f}^{n}}{\partial P_{u_f,f}^{n}} + \beta, \qquad (14)$$

$$-2\alpha \times \left(\gamma_{u_f,f}^{tar} - \gamma_{u_f,f}^{n}\right) \times \frac{g_{u_f,f}^{n}}{I_{u_f,f}^{n}(P_{-u_f,f}^{n})} + \beta = 0 \qquad (15)$$

Reorder (15), we have

$$\gamma_{u_f,f}^{n} = \gamma_{u_f,f}^{tar} - \frac{\beta}{2\alpha} \times \left(\frac{I_{u_f,f}^{n}(P_{-u_f}^{n})}{g_{u_f}}\right) \qquad (16)$$

The expression of $\gamma_{u_f,f}^{n}$ will be used in formula (16), we can get

$$P_{u_f,f}^{n} = \gamma_{u_f,f}^{tar} \times \frac{I_{u_f,f}^{n}(P_{-u_f,f}^{n})}{g_{u_f,f}^{n}} - \frac{\beta}{2\alpha} \times \left(\frac{I_{u_f,f}^{n}(P_{-u_f,f}^{n})}{g_{u_f,f}^{n}}\right)^2. \qquad (17)$$

Through the usage can be obtained

$$(P_{u_f,f}^{n})^{l+1} = \gamma_{u_f,f}^{tar} \times \frac{(P_{u_f,f}^{n})^l}{\gamma_{u_f,f}^{n}} - \frac{\beta}{2\alpha} \times \left(\frac{(P_{u_f,f}^{n})^l}{\gamma_{u_f,f}^{n}}\right)^2 \qquad (18)$$

The number of iterations is l.
The final results of the algorithm iteration until convergence.

5 Performance Evaluation

5.1 Parameters

Our simulation area is an area with a length equals width. A high-density deployment of a macro cell and a series of femtocells. The amount of femtocells ranges from 80 to 240. Our system, macrocells and femtocells use different spectra to avoid inter-layer interference. The value of $\gamma_{u_f,f}^{tar}$ obey uniform distribution of [5, 10] dB [11] (Table 1).

Table 1. Parameters and its Values

Symbol	Description	Value
F	Number of femtocells	[40:80:240]
Pmax	Maximum transmit power	200 mW
△B	Sub-channel bandwidth	180 kHz
N0	Noise power density	−174 dBm/Hz
Rf	Femtocell radius	10 m
WL	Wall loss	10 dB
Kf	Fix path loss	103.7

5.2   Simulation Results

We will allocate the heuristic FFI algorithm for the two-stage Starkerberg game resource management scheme and the sub-channel based on clustering (HFMS) and the clustering greedy sub-channel allocation algorithm (CBGS) [17].

In Fig. 1, we can see that our program's system throughput smaller than the CBGS scheme. When the number of femtocell is 160, the maximum acceptable reduction is 6.32%. One of the most challenging issues identified is how to decrease the SINR formerly because of the influence of the Quality of service and sum rate of the network straightforward [16]. The throughput decreased and the overall system throughput is constant.

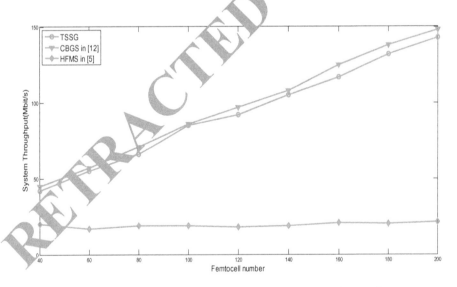

Fig. 1. System throughput diagram for the number of femtocells

Figure 2 shows that our system of system energy efficiency compared to CBGS achieve a more substantial increase. The total system power is reduced. System throughput is increasing, the system energy efficiency compared to CBGS achieves a substantial increase.

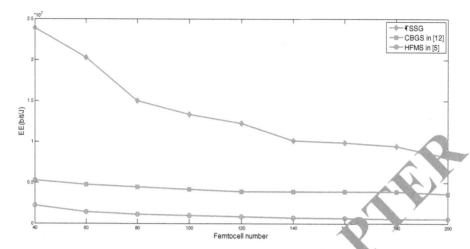

Fig. 2. Energy efficiency diagram for the number of femtocells

6 Conclusion

In this thesis, because of clustering, we proposed a special resource allocation scheme. We introduced a two-stage novelty resource allocation schema. The cluster head controls the distribution of neutron channel in each and every cluster to achieve maximum total system performance. The power splitting considers for the trade-off between user quality requirement and consumed transmission power. Simulation results show that the presented arithmetic has a significant improvement in system efficiency. Future work will be considered by a femtocell service for several users as well as deploying a femtocell on a high building. We certainly have to consider the ultra-dense network in the user's mobility and service base station switching problems.

Acknowledgments. The research was supported in part by Postdoctoral Research Funding Plan in Jiangsu Province (Grant No. 1501073B), Natural Science Foundation of Nanjing University of Posts and Telecommunications (Grant No. NY214108), Natural Science Foundation of China (NSFC) (Grant No. 61401399), and the Open Research Fund of National Mobile Communications Research Laboratory, Southeast University (Grant No. 2016D05).

References

1. Xie, H., Gao, F., Zhang, S., Jin, S.: A unified transmission strategy for TDD/FDD massive MIMO systems with spatial basis expansion model. IEEE Trans. Veh. Technol. **66**(4), 3170–3184 (2017)
2. Xie, H., Gao, F., Jin, S.: An overview of low-rank channel estimation for massive MIMO systems. IEEE Access **4**, 7313–7321 (2016)
3. Xie, H., Wang, B., Gao, F., Jin, S.: A full-space spectrum-sharing strategy for massive MIMO cognitive radio. IEEE J. Select. Areas Commun. **34**(10), 2537–2549 (2016)

4. Wang, Y., Zhang, Y., Chen, Y., et al.: Energy-efficient design of two-tier femtocell networks. EURASIP J. Wirel. Commun. Netw. **2015**(1), 40 (2015)

5. Abdelnasser, A., Hossain, E., Dong, I.K.: Clustering and resource allocation for dense femtocells in a two-tier cellular OFDMA network. IEEE Trans. Wirel. Commun. **13**(3), 1628–1641 (2014)

6. Tang, H., Hong, P., Xue, K., et al.: Cluster-based resource allocation for interference mitigation in LTE heterogeneous networks. In: Vehicular Technology Conference, pp. 1–5. IEEE (2012)

7. Pateromichelakis, E., Shariat, M., Quddus, A., et al.: Dynamic clustering framework for multi-cell scheduling in dense small cell networks. IEEE Commun. Lett. **17**(9), 1802–1805 (2013)

8. Lin, S., Tian, H.: Clustering based interference management for QoS guarantees in OFDMA femtocell. In: Wireless Communications and Networking Conference, pp. 649–654. IEEE (2013)

9. Kang, X., Liang, Y.C., Garg, H.K.: Distributed power control for spectrum sharing femtocell networks using stackelberg game. In: IEEE International Conference on Communications, pp. 1–5. IEEE (2011)

10. Guruacharya, S., Niyato, D., Dong, I.K., et al.: Hierarchical competition for downlink power allocation in OFDMA femtocell networks. IEEE Trans. Wirel. Commun. **12**(4), 1543–1553 (2013)

11. Han, Q., Bo, Y., Chen, C., et al.: Multi-leader multi-follower game based power control for downlink Heterogeneous networks. In: Control Conference, pp. 5486–5491. IEEE (2014)

12. Zhao, N., Yu, F.R., Sun, H.: Adaptive energy efficient power allocation in green interference-alignment-based wireless networks. IEEE Trans. Veh. Technol. **64**(9), 4268–4281 (2015)

13. Xin, K., Rui, Z., Motani, M.: Price-based resource allocation for spectrum-sharing femtocell networks: a stackelberg game approach. In: Global Communications Conference, GLOBECOM 2011, 5–9 December 2011, Houston, Texas, USA, pp. 1–5. DBLP (2011)

14. Boyd, S., Vandenberghe, L., Faybusovich, L.: Convex optimization. IEEE Trans. Autom. Control **51**(11), 1859 (2006). 1859

15. Gajic, Z.R., Koskie, S.: Newton iteration acceleration of the Nash game algorithm for power control in 3G wireless CDMA networks. Proc. SPIE - Int. Soc. Opt. Eng. **5244**, 115–121 (2003)

16. Zhao, N., Yu, F.R., Sun, H.: Adaptive power allocation schemes for spectrum sharing in interference-alignment-based cognitive radio networks. IEEE Trans. Veh. Technol. **65**(5), 3700–3714 (2016)

17. Wei, R., Wang, Y., Zhang, Y.: A two-stage cluster-based resource management scheme in ultra-dense networks. In: IEEE/CIC International Conference on Communications in China, pp. 738–742. IEEE (2015)

Optimal Relay Selection Algorithm for Combining Distance and Social Information in D2D Cooperative Communication Networks

Kaijian Li[1(✉)], Jianxin Dai[2], Chonghu Cheng[1], and Zhiliang Huang[3]

[1] College of Telecommunications and Information Engineering,
Nanjing University of Posts and Telecommunications, Nanjing 210023, China
15651036692@163.com, chengch@njupt.edu.cn
[2] School of Science, Nanjing University of Posts and Telecommunications,
Nanjing 210023, China
daijx@njupt.edu.cn
[3] College of Mathematics, Physics and Information Engineering,
Zhejiang Normal University, Jinhua 321004, China
zlhuang@zjnu.cn

Abstract. With the rapid growth of mobile data traffic demand, D2D relay technology is becoming an essential technology for the next generation mobile network. In order to select the optimal node in a shorter time, a cooperative D2D relay model considering the physical distance and social information is proposed. And then a threshold based on distance and social information is introduced, which is used to filter out the nodes with poor performance to get a relatively small candidate relay set. According to the optimal stopping theory, this paper presents a D2D relay optimal selection algorithm in order to weigh the consumption of exploration and system performance. The simulation results show that the algorithm proposed is superior to the traditional algorithm in system performance and algorithm complexity.

Keywords: Device-to-Device (D2D) communications · Relay selection
Social information · Optimal stopping theory · Cooperative communication

1 Introduction

The demand for mobile data is growing over the next decade, so it poses a huge challenge to mobile networks. In general, there are three main ways to improve the capacity of wireless networks: increasing the spectrum resources, improving the spectrum utilization and improving the spatial multiplex ratio [1–7]. However, due to the lack of spectrum resources, the capacity of the wireless communication system improved by increasing the spectrum is limited, and the price of spectrum is very expensive. In recent years, with the continuous development of mobile communications, spectrum utilization continues to increase and has gradually close to the Shannon limit, so just by improving the spectrum utilization is difficult to meet the huge business needs. On this basis, the increase in spectral space reuse rate will be the inevitable choice to improve the capacity of wireless network. D2D (Device-to-Device)

© ICST Institute for Computer Sciences, Social Informatics and Telecommunications Engineering 2018
X. Gu et al. (Eds.): MLICOM 2017, Part I, LNICST 226, pp. 463–474, 2018.
https://doi.org/10.1007/978-3-319-73564-1_46

technology, refers to allowing cell users to directly perform end-to-end communication under the control of the base station, so it has great potential to solve the problem. D2D communication can improve the spectral efficiency of the cellular communication system, reduce battery energy consumption of the mobile device. In contrast, Bluetooth, WiFi and other traditional end-to-end communication has many drawbacks. First, their communication distances are short in many cases they can't meet the needs of users. Second, Bluetooth needs to manually set the terminal pairing, and WiFi access point requires user-defined settings. In addition, both work in the non-authorized band, which will lead to unstable communications and poor communication quality. In contrast, the D2D communication technology assisted by the cellular network has a wider application prospect, and the related research has very important theoretical significance and application value. D2D relay technology is a key implementation of D2D communication. When the channel quality between D2D users is not ideal, a suitable relay user can be found to establish a connection, which enables users to communicate and greatly improve the capacity of the base station.

In addition, because the energy and storage space of the mobile terminal are limited, the design of the relay algorithm must be simple enough. Although the base station can obtain the channel information of all potential relay users, it will not only increase the burden of the base station, but also take many time slots to complete the process of finding the relay. Therefore, in the D2D relay network, the choice of optimal relay and encouraging relay nodes to forward data are worth studying.

Because the carriers and users of mobile devices are people, it forms a mobile social network. A series of parameters in social networks, such as social relationships, centrality, and communities, can reflect relationships among mobile users. Using the behavior of people in social networks can help solve the problem of relay selection in D2D communications. Because, for a mobile user, there are usually family members, neighbors, friends, or colleagues nearby. Therefore, most of the potential relay nodes of the user have a social relationship with him, so that they can choose the trusted node to forward data for themselves, thus improving the information security, and because of social relations, these relay nodes are more willing to forward data.

There are already many options for D2D relay schemes. In [8], a random selection scheme is proposed, which does not filter the potential nodes, and then randomly takes a node as a relay. In [9], a terminal device with energy acquisition function is proposed as relay, and an optimal relay selection is proposed to minimize the probability of interruption. In [10], a scheme is proposed to select the relay scheme for D2D users to maximize the signal-to-noise ratio. In [11], an optimal stopping scheme is proposed based on the SNR threshold structure. Similarly, the document [12] combines social information with an optimal stop scheme to stimulate relay users to relay information through intrinsic factors. However, these schemes have a common drawback that they must obtain information about each potential relay node, which requires not only a large amount of signaling overhead, but also a lot of energy consumption.

The rest of this paper is arranged as follows. D2D relay system model will be proposed in Sect. 2. In Sect. 3, we introduce the algorithm proposed in this paper. Section 4 presents the simulation results, we give conclusions in Sect. 4.

2 System Model

In the section, a social networking model to quantify the social relationships between the users firstly is built. Besides, a D2D relay system model on social relations network is proposed.

2.1 Social Network Model

Today's social network architecture has subverted the original network structure, the architecture of the social layer network has been added to the original network architecture, which is based on social relationships. As shown in Fig. 1, the scenario considered in this article is data transmission within a single cell D2D mode in a cellular network. The model is a two-tier model that includes a social layer and a physical layer, where the physical layer includes multiple D2D users and cellular users. D2D users reuse uplink resources of cellular users. Sometimes, even in the same cell, the distance between the two D2D users is far away, and the connection cannot be established directly, so communication must be achieved by relay, for example, DUE1 and DUE2 in Fig. 1.

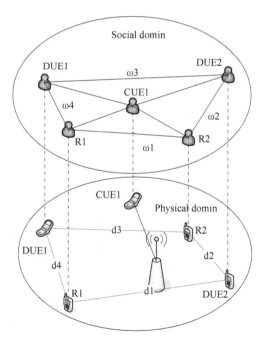

Fig. 1. Two-tier model

There may be multiple idle relays between DUE1 and DUE2, which can be used as potential relays, and we need to select the best nodes as the relay. Suppose there are n D2D user devices (DUE) in the diagram, which can be represented as a set

$D = \{D_1, D_2, \ldots D_n\}$, and assuming that there are m adjacent users near D_i, the adjacent user set can be expressed as $R_i = \{R_{i,1}, R_{i,2}, \ldots, R_{i,m}\}$. We exploit an indirect weighted graph $G^p = \{V, E^p\}$ to model the physical relation between DUE D_i and its each neighbor user. In graph G^p, we build the vertex set V, and the set of edges $E^p = \{(D_i, R_{i,j}) : e_{D_i,R_{i,j}} = 1, R_{i,j} \in R_i\}$, where $e_{D_i,R_{i,j}} = 1$ if $R_{i,j}$ can communication directly with D_i. Moreover, in the social layer, social relationships are quantified with $\omega_{D_i,R_{i,j}} (\omega_{D_i,R_{i,j}} \in [0, 1))$ between users, and the greater the $\omega_{D_i,R_{i,j}}$, the stronger the social relationship between the two users, it also means that they are more willing to forward data to each other. But in fact, we can't directly measure the social relationships between two users, so we have to quantify social relationships. Typically, there are two factors that directly affect social relationships, namely, time factors and interaction factors. This paper uses the average length of time $T_{D_i,R_{i,j}}$ between two users to express the time factor, which can visually reflect the frequency of contact between two users:

$$E(T_{D_i,R_{i,j}}) = \frac{\int_0^\phi \delta_{D_i,R_{i,j}}(t)dt}{S_{D_i,R_{i,j}}} \tag{1}$$

where ϕ denotes the observation time, $S_{D_i,R_{i,j}}$ is the number of communications between two users during $\phi.\delta_{D_i,R_{i,j}}(t) = 1$ if D_i and $R_{i,j}$ communicate within the observation, otherwise $\delta_{D_i,R_{i,j}}(t) = 0$.

According to [13], we get the time factor as follows:

$$F_{D_i,R_{i,j}} = \exp(-\frac{E(T_{D_i,R_{i,j}})^2}{2\sigma^2}) \tag{2}$$

where σ denotes the length of the previous communication. The second interactive factor is the number of common friends between two users. The more friends there are between two users, the more intimate their social relationships are. According to [14], a common friend index is proposed to represent interaction factors:

$$K_{D_i,R_{i,j}} = \frac{|k_{D_i} \cap k_{R_{i,j}}|}{|k_{D_i} \cup k_{R_{i,j}}|} \tag{3}$$

where $|.|$ is the cardinality of set, k_{D_i} and $k_{R_{i,j}}$ indicate the friends set of D_i and $R_{i,j}$.

Use the combination of two factors, we can indicate social relationships with $\omega_{D_i,R_{i,j}}$ as:

$$\omega_{D_i,R_{i,j}} = \alpha F_{D_i,R_{i,j}} + (1 - \alpha)K_{D_i,R_{i,j}} \tag{4}$$

where $\alpha(\alpha \in [0, 1])$ is used to adjust the impact of two factors on social relationships. In different scenarios, the two factors may have different effects on social relationships, so α may be different.

In physical layer, the distance between users will affect the quality of communication. It is obvious that the quality of communication is inversely proportional to the distance between users, and in the relay selection process, users prefer to select nodes closer to their own.

2.2   Social Network Analysis in Specific Scenarios

As mentioned above, distance and social factor are the two major factors that affect the choice of relay, so we are talking about it in social networks. As shown in Fig. 2, we consider a single cell model for mixed communication of CUE and DUE. CUE is represented later with C, while D2D users can be divided into sender and receiver, represented with DT and DR respectively. Suppose there are N candidate relay nodes between DT and DR, which can be represented as sets $N = \{n_1, n_2, \ldots, n_N\}$. These candidate relay nodes are the intersection of adjacent nodes of DT and DR, represented by the shadow part in Fig. 2. Because D2D users reuse the downlink resources with cellular users, D2D communications will inevitably interfere with cellular users. The channel gain between the node i and the node j can be represented by $|h_{i,j}|^2$, which follows the exponential distribution of the parameter $\lambda_{i,j}$. To ensure that the transmission power P_{DT} does not exceed the maximum interference threshold I_{th} of CUE, while ensuring that the DT can achieve the optimum QoS, we define transmission power as $P_{DT} = \frac{I_{th}}{|h_{C,DT}|^2}$. As mentioned earlier, the stronger the social relationship between the two nodes, they are more willing to help each other. So the SNR received by the relay node $n_i(n_i \in N)$ from the DT is proportional to the social relationships weight coefficient between them, which can be expressed as:

$$S_{n_i} = \omega_{DT,n_i} \frac{I_{th}|h_{DT,n_i}|^2}{\sigma^2 |h_{C,DT}|^2} \tag{5}$$

where ω_{DT,n_i} stands for the intensity of social relationships between DT and node n_i, and σ^2 represents Gaussian noise variance. According to [12], $|h_{DT,n_i}|^2 = \frac{1}{d_{DT,n_i}}$,

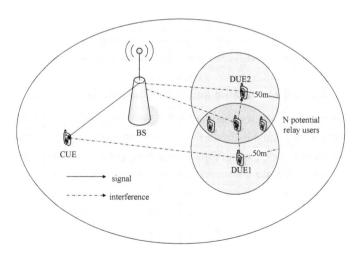

Fig. 2. D2D relay network

where d_{DT,n_i} is the distance between the DT and the relay node n_i, so that it can be obtained:

$$S_{n_i} = \omega_{DT,n_i} \frac{I_{th}}{d_{DT,n_i} \sigma^2 |h_{C,DT}|^2} \tag{6}$$

Thus, sequence $\{S_{n_i}\}$ is a sequence of i.i.d random variables. Assuming $G = \frac{\lambda_{C,DT} I_{th}}{\sigma^2}$. The probability density function of S_{n_i} can be calculated based on [15], that is:

$$f(S_{n_i}) = \omega_{DT,n_i} \frac{\lambda_{DT,n_i} G}{(\lambda_{DT,n_i} S_{n_i} + G)^2} \tag{7}$$

Based on the Shannon formula, the channel capacity of S_{n_i} can be obtained as:

$$C(S_{n_i}) = W \log_2(1 + S_{n_i}) \tag{8}$$

where W is the channel bandwidth.

In Fig. 2, the quality of the channel between DT and DR is poor and the relay node must be sought to forward the data, so it is important to find a suitable relay. In order to find the optimal relay, DT must explore all candidate relays, which is not only inefficient, but also high energy consumption. Therefore, in order to balance performance and consumption, we propose a D2D relay optimal selection algorithm based on distance and social information to solve this problem.

3   The Proposed OSRS Algorithm

First, a threshold based on distance and social information is introduced, which is used to filter out the nodes with poor performance to get a relatively small candidate relay set, then the optimal relay node is found by the optimal stopping theory.

3.1   Threshold Based on Distance and Social Information

From the formula (6) we can see that the SNR S_{n_i} of the relay n_i is proportional to the ratio of the social factor and the distance $\frac{\omega_{DT,n_i}}{d_{DT,n_i}}$. So we can first screen the ratio of social factors and distances, which can not only reduce the number of searches, but also save energy consumption. We use φ to represent the binding threshold:

$$\varphi = \frac{\rho \sum_{i=1}^{N} \frac{\omega_{DT,n_i}}{d_{DT,n_i}}}{N} \tag{9}$$

where ρ ($\rho \in (0, 1)$) is a percentage value used to adjust the size of φ. ω_{DT,n_i} in the DT communication list can be obtained, and d_{DT,n_i} through the base station to obtain.

Therefore, when the base station gets the relevant information, it does not immediately traverse all the relays, but instead filters out the nodes with poor performance through this information. Through φ, DT filters the nodes based on the following principles:

- Abandon node n_i if $\frac{\omega_{DT,n_i}}{d_{DT,n_i}} < \varphi$,
- Reserve node n_i if $\frac{\omega_{DT,n_i}}{d_{DT,n_i}} \geq \varphi$

Thus, a relatively small candidate relay set can be obtained from the above filter, which can be represented as $M = \{m_1, m_2, \ldots, m_M\}$, but then we still need to select the best relay nodes. Because we have to weigh the consumption and system performance, based on the optimal stopping theory, we propose a solution to select optimal node as relay.

3.2   Relay Selection Algorithm

As can be seen from Fig. 3, Assumed that the total length of a slot is T, and this time can be divided into two parts: the exploration time and the transmission time. Where the exploration time $i\tau$ is used to find the optimal relay time, i on behalf of the number of exploration, each time slot τ is a time to explore, and the total transmission time for the $T - i\tau$. So we define the immediate reword r_{m_i} that the DT can achieve from node m_i:

$$r_{m_i} = \mu_i C(S_{m_i}) \tag{10}$$

where $\mu_i(\mu_i \in (0, 1))$ is a discount factor that decreases as the number of explorations increases and can be expressed as:

$$\mu_i = 1 - \frac{i\tau}{T} \tag{11}$$

The larger the instantaneous reward, the better the performance of the node. In the process of probing, we are not sure whether the node is the best node. So a reward

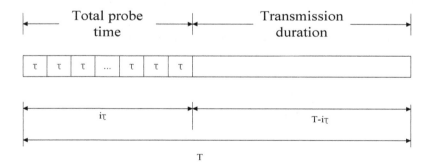

Fig. 3. A slot of the relay

threshold expressed as $\theta_{m_i}^* = E\{R_{m_{i+1}}\}$ in each probing stage is set. Here $E\{R_{m_{i+1}}\}$ is reward expected while DT is probing next node. Based on (10), when the user relay node is explored, the maximum reward that DT can obtain can be expressed as:

$$R_{m_i} = \max\{r_{m_i}, \theta_{m_i}^*\} \tag{12}$$

It is clear that when R_{m_i} equals to r_{m_i}, we can get the best node m_i, and stop probing, otherwise DT will explore the next potential node m_{i+1}.

When the i-th exploratory phase, DT must make the following choices:

- If $r_{m_i} < \theta_{m_i}^*$, ignore the node and explore next node
- If $r_{m_i} \geq \theta_{m_i}^*$, stop exploring and selecting the node as relay to forward data

And the reward threshold $\{\theta_{m_i}^*\}_{i=1}^M$ is defined as follows:

$$\theta_{m_M}^* = -\infty \tag{13}$$

$$\theta_{m_i}^* = \theta_{m_{i+1}}^* \int_0^{\frac{\theta_{m_{i+1}}^*}{\mu_{i+1}}} f(S_{m_i})dS_{m_i} + \mu_{i+1} \int_{\frac{\theta_{m_{i+1}}^*}{\mu_{i+1}}}^\infty W \log_2(1 + S_{m_i})f(S_{m_i})dS_{m_i} \tag{14}$$

Proof: We can use reverse derivation to prove this problem. In the last step of the exploration, DT does not have the remaining nodes to explore, but can only choose the last node as a relay, so $\theta_{m_M}^* = -\infty$. Then we can obtain:

$$\begin{aligned}
\theta_{m_i}^* &= E\{R_{m_{i+1}}(C(S_{m_{i+1}}))\} \\
&= E\{\max\{r(S_{m_i}), \theta_{m_{i+1}}^*\}\} \\
&= \theta_{m_{i+1}}^* \int_0^{\frac{\theta_{m_{i+1}}^*}{\mu_{i+1}}} f(S_{m_i})dS_{m_i} + \mu_{i+1} \int_{\frac{\theta_{m_{i+1}}^*}{\mu_{i+1}}}^\infty W \log_2(1 + S_{m_i})f(S_{m_i})dS_{m_i}
\end{aligned} \tag{15}$$

For the above proved sequence $\{\theta_{m_i}^*\}_{i=1}^M$, we can also prove that it is monotonically decreasing. Combine (13) and (14) we can know $\theta_{m_M}^* \geq \theta_{m_{M-1}}^*$. According to Sect. 2, we have the sequence of $\{S_{n_i}\}_{i=1}^M$ is i.i.d. sequence. So the following can be deduced as:

$$\begin{aligned}
\theta_{m_{M-2}}^* &= E\{\max\{r_{m_{M-1}}, \theta_{m_{M-1}}^*\}\} \\
&= E\{\max\{\mu_{M-1} W \log_2(1 + S_{m_{M-1}}), \theta_{m_{M-1}}^*\}\} \\
&\geq E\{\max\{\mu_M W \log_2(1 + S_{m_{M-1}}), \theta_{m_{M-1}}^*\}\} \\
&= E\{\max\{\mu_M W \log_2(1 + S_{m_M}), \theta_{m_{M-1}}^*\}\} \\
&\geq E\{\max\{\mu_M W \log_2(1 + S_{m_M}), \theta_{m_M}^*\}\} \\
&= E\{\max\{r_{m_M}, \theta_{m_M}^*\}\} \\
&= \theta_{m_{M-1}}^*
\end{aligned} \tag{16}$$

Then we can deduce $\theta^*_{m_1} \geq \theta^*_{m_2} \geq \ldots \geq \theta^*_{m_M}$. So the sequence $\{\theta^*_{m_i}\}^M_{i=1}$ is monotonically decreasing. According to these analysis, a relay selection algorithm based on threshold which combine distance and social information is proposed, as shown in Algorithm 1.

Algorithm 1.   Relay selection algorithm based on threshold which combines distance and social information

1.Initialize the D2D transmission system, including DT and DR

2.Obtain their neighbor set K_{D_T}, K_{D_R}

3.Obtain the intersection N of the DT and DR neighbor sets, and obtain their social coefficients ω_{DT, n_i} with DT, and obtain their distance d_{DT,n_i} from the DT through the base

station

4.Calculate φ by (9)

5.In the set N, select the M nodes that satisfy $\dfrac{\omega_{DT, n_i}}{d_{DT,n_i}} \geq \varphi$

6. $\theta^*_{m_M} = -\infty$

7.for $j = M - 1$ to 1

Calculate $\theta^*_{m_j}$ according to (14)

end for

8.for $j = 1$ to M

　　Calculate r_{m_j} according to (10)

　if $r_{m_j} \geq \theta^*_{m_j}$ then

　　Stop the exploration process, the optimal node j is obtained

　end if

　end for

---

4   Simulation

The relay selection algorithm over this section will be analyzed. This section considers the distribution of D2D users and cellular users in a single cell scenario. We first consider the reward of the relay and compare it with the traditional algorithm. Besides, we simulate the number of the whole relay exploration. This algorithm is mainly compared with the social relation based optimal stop algorithm (SARS) proposed by [12]. The main simulation parameters are given in Table 1.

In Fig. 4, we can see clearly that the reward value provided by D2D increases as the number of candidate relays increases. Because as the number of candidate relays increases, the probability of obtaining a better relay increases. In addition, we can find that the algorithm proposed in this paper is superior to the traditional algorithm in terms

Table 1. Simulation parameters

Parameter	Value
τ	0.01 s
T	1 s
N	10
λ	1
G	5

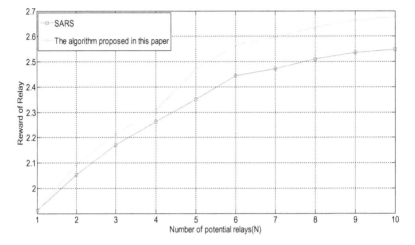

Fig. 4. Returns of different numbers of potential relays

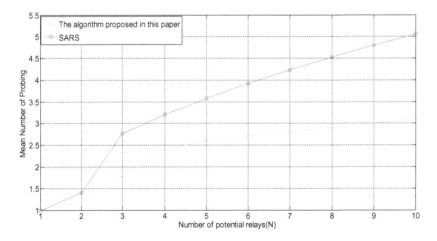

Fig. 5. The probing numbers with different number of potential relays

of relay reward, because the algorithm of this paper has screened some poorly performing nodes according to the social coefficient and distance before the relay exploration began.

In Fig. 5, we can see that as the number of candidate relay increases, the average number of explorations increases, and the average number of explorations proposed in this paper is significantly less than that of traditional algorithms. This is because we have filtered the poorly performing candidate nodes through thresholds before exploring the iterations so that we can find the optimal relay nodes faster.

5 Conclusion

In this paper, a threshold is obtained by combining the social coefficients and distances between D2D users, and an optimal relay selection algorithm is proposed based on the optimal stopping theory. And the simulation results show that the algorithm is superior to the traditional algorithm. However, there are some areas that are not fully considered. For example, only a single cell scene is considered, but not in a multi cell scenario. This is the future research direction.

Acknowledgments. The research was supported in part by Postdoctoral Research Funding Plan in Jiangsu Province (Grant No. 1501073B), Natural Science Foundation of Nanjing University of Posts and Telecommunications (Grant No. NY214108), Natural Science Foundation of China (NSFC) (Grant No. 61401399), and the Open Research Fund of National Mobile Communications Research Laboratory, Southeast University (Grant No. 2016D05).

References

1. Shanmugam, K., Golrezaei, N., Dimakis, A.G., Molisch, A.F., Caire, G.: Femtocaching: wireless content delivery through distributed caching helpers. J. IEEE Trans. Inf. Theory **59**(12), 8402–8413 (2013)
2. Xie, H., Gao, F., Zhang, S., Jin, S.: A unified transmission strategy for TDD/FDD massive MIMO systems with spatial basis expansion model. IEEE Trans. Veh. Technol (2016). Earlier access available online
3. Xie, H., Gao, F., Zhang, S., Jin, S.: An overview of low-rank channel estimation for massive MIMO systems. IEEE Access **4**, 7313–7321 (2016)
4. Xie, H., Gao, F., Zhang, S., Jin, S.: A full-space spectrum-sharing strategy for massive MIMO cognitive radio. IEEE J. Sel. Areas Commun. **34**(10), 2537–2549 (2016)
5. Ma, J.P., Li, H.Y., Zhang, S., Zhao, N., Arumugam, N.: Pattern division for massive MIMO networks with two-stage precoding. IEEE Commun. Lett. **21**(7), 1665–1668 (2017)
6. Zhao, N., Yu, F.R., Leung, V.C.M.: Opportunistic communications in interference alignment networks with wireless power transfer. 2015 IEEE Commun. Soc. **22**, 88–95 (2015). MWC 2015
7. Li, X.H., Zhao, N., Sun, Y., Yu, F.R.: Interference alignment based on antenna selection with imperfect channel state information in cognitive radio networks. IEEE Trans. Veh. Technol. **65**, 5497–5511 (2016)
8. Pan, P., Zheng, B.: Outage probability analysis of a cooperative diversity method based on random relay selection. Acta Electron. Sin. **38**(1), 79–82 (2010)

9. Yang, H.H., Lee, J., Quek, T.Q.S.: Heterogeneous cellular network with energy harvesting-based D2D communication. IEEE Trans. Wirel. Commun. **15**(2), 1406–1419 (2016)
10. Ryu, H.S., Lee, J.S., Kang, C.G.: Relay selection scheme for orthogonal amplify-and-forward relay-enhanced cellular system in a multi-cell environment. In: 71st 2010 IEEE Vehicular Technology Conference (VTC 2010-Spring), pp. 1–5. IEEE (2010)
11. Zheng, D., Ge, W., Zhang, J.: Distributed opportunistic scheduling for ad-hoc communications: an optimal stopping approach. In: Proceedings of the 8th ACM International Symposium on Mobile Ad Hoc Networking and Computing, pp. 1–10. ACM (2007)
12. Zhang, M., Chen, X., Zhang, J.: Social-aware relay selection for cooperative networking: an optimal stopping approach. In: 2014 IEEE International Conference on Communications (ICC), pp. 2257–2262. IEEE (2014)
13. Cai, Y., Wu, D., Yang, W.: Social-aware content downloading mode selection for D2D communications. In: 2015 IEEE International Conference on Communications (ICC), pp. 2931–2936. IEEE (2015)
14. Von, L.U.: A tutorial on spectral clustering. Stat. Comput. **17**(4), 395–416 (2007)
15. Berggren, F., Jantti, R.: Multiuser scheduling over rayleigh fading channels. In: Global Telecommunications Conference (GLOBECOM 2003), vol. 1, pp. 158–162. IEEE (2003)

Linear Massive MIMO Precoding Based on Nonlinear High-Power Amplifier

Xudong Yin[1(✉)], Jianxin Dai[2], Chonghu Cheng[1],
and Zhiliang Huang[3]

[1] College of Telecommunications and Information Engineering,
Nanjing University of Posts and Telecommunications, Nanjing 210003, China
2697718806@qq.com, 1275418944@qq.com
[2] School of Science, Nanjing University of Posts and Telecommunications,
Nanjing 210023, China
daijx@njupt.edu.cn
[3] College of Mathematics, Physics and Information Engineering,
Zhejiang Normal University, Jinhua 321004, China
zlhuang@zjnu.cn

Abstract. Large-scale multiple-input multiple-output (MIMO) system has the advantages of high energy efficiency and spectrum utilization. But using some cheap hardware may cause some problems, such as nonlinearity of the high power amplifier (HPA). When HPA works in the nonlinear region, it will affect the received signal and greatly reduce the performance of the system. In this paper, we first study the impact caused by nonlinear HPA, and then we optimize the traditional precoding algorithm to design an improved precoding algorithm which can reduce the impact. The simulation results show that the proposed algorithms perform better in bit error ratio and system capacity compared to the block of diagonalization (BD) precoding algorithm and forced zero (ZF) precoding algorithm, especially in the condition of high signal to noise ratio (SNR). So we can draw the conclusion that the algorithms proposed in this paper are able to reduce the impact caused by nonlinear HPA to the system.

Keywords: Massive MIMO · High-power amplifier (HPA)
Precoding algorithm · Bit error ratio

1 Introduction

HPA plays an important role in wireless communication system. In general, in order to simplify the performance analysis and system design, we usually assume that HPA works in the linear region. However, in fact, this case is not always founded. HPA will also work in the nonlinear region in some cases. When it works in the nonlinear region, nonlinear distortion will be introduced to the received signal including amplitude distortion and phase distortion.

There are two kinds of nonlinear HPA model: memoryless models and memory models [1]. Between them, depending on their type, memoryless HPA have their own amplitude-to-amplitude (AM/AM) and amplitude-to-phase (AM/PM) conversion

© ICST Institute for Computer Sciences, Social Informatics and Telecommunications Engineering 2018
X. Gu et al. (Eds.): MLICOM 2017, Part I, LNICST 226, pp. 475–483, 2018.
https://doi.org/10.1007/978-3-319-73564-1_47

formulas. [2] mainly introduces three memoryless models: the TWTA model [3], SSPA model [4] and SEL model [5]. The memory HPA models include Volterra, Wiener, Hammerstein and memory polynomial models.

In recent years, [5] have studied the impact to the symbol error probability (SEP) caused by nonlinear HPA. [6] study the influence of nonlinear HPA on the system capacity and the average SEP of MIMO system, in which the signal is encoded by STBC. To deal with the problem caused by nonlinear HPA, the receiver or transmitter will be demanded to compensate to eliminate or reduce the impact of the nonlinear HPA. In terms of compensation scheme, they can be divided into two kinds: compensate in the transmitter or receiver respectively. Power back-off, peak to average power ratio (PAPR) reduction techniques methods [1–10] belong to the processing at the transmitter. The other kind contains the methods of post-distortion and iterative detection [1].

To resolve the problem, we first analyze the impact caused by nonlinear HPA on the transmission signal in the base station. Then we improve the traditional precoding algorithms, such as BD, ZF [11, 12], to present the improved precoding algorithms which can reduce the impact according to the impact caused by the nonlinear HPA. The simulation results show that the improved algorithms make up for the impact caused by nonlinear HPA. When HPA works in the linear region, the performance of traditional algorithms and improved algorithms are similiar. When HPA works in the nonlinear region, the performance of it is better than that of the traditional algorithms.

The structure of this paper is discribed below: the system model is introduced in the second section, which includes the impact of nonlinear HPA on the signal. The third section mainly analyzes the impact of the nonlinear HPA in details and puts forward the improvement scheme. The fourth section shows the numerical simulation results. When the HPA works in the nonlinear region, we compare the proposed precoding algorithm with BD and ZF precoding algorithms in term of bit error ratio and system capacity. The fifth section is the summary of the full paper.

The symbols used in this article are as follows: $(A)^T$, $(A)^H$ represent the matrix transpose and conjugate transpose; $tr\{A\}$, $\|A\|_F = \sqrt{tr\{A^H A\}}$ represent matrix trace and the Frobenius norm respectively. $E\{\bullet\}$ denotes expectation.

2   System Model

This paper mainly studies on the single cell scenario, where the central base station services k users and the k-th user has M_k antennas. Therefore, the antennas of all users are $M = \sum_{k=1}^{K} M_k$. The base station has $N(N \geq 100)$ antennas. Under the Assumption that channel state information (CSI) is known to the base station and the power allocation of all the users are the same, the system model is shown in Fig. 1.

In Fig. 1, $W \in \mathbb{C}^{N \times M}$ is the precoding matrix of all users. $H_k \in \mathbb{C}^{M_k \times N}$ is the channel matrix of k-th user, each element of which is a Gauss random variable whose mean is zero and variance is one. $s_k \in \mathbb{C}^{M_k}$ is the k-th user's original signal vector.

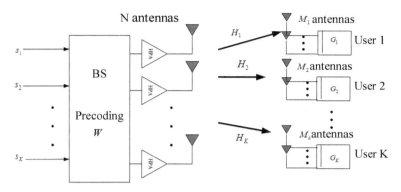

Fig. 1. System model

Thus, when the HPA is working in the linear region, we can obtain that the received signal of all users $y = [y_1, y_2, \cdots, y_k]^T$ is given by

$$y = HWs + n = HX + n \tag{1}$$

where $H = [H_1^T, H_2^H, \cdots, H_k^T]^T$ is the channel matrix of all users. And $X \in \mathbb{C}^N$ is the signal matrix after precoding. $n \in \mathbb{C}^M$ is the user's noise vector, each element of which is a Gauss random variable whose mean is zero and variance is σ^2.

When HPA works in the nonlinear region, in order to simplify the expression, modulated signal can be rewritten into polar form

$$s_{in} = re^{j\theta} \tag{2}$$

Passing through nonlinear HPA, the signal can be expressed as:

$$s_{out} = f_A(r)e^{jf_P(r)}e^{j\theta} \tag{3}$$

where $f_A(\cdot)$ and $f_P(\cdot)$ are AM/AM and AM/PM conversion formulas. Next, we will list some types of memoryless HPA model. And we mainly analyze the first one.

The first is SSPA, whose conversion formulas are

$$f_A(r) = \frac{r}{\left[1 + \left(\frac{r}{A_{os}}\right)^{2\beta}\right]^{1/2\beta}}, \quad f_P(r) = 0 \tag{4}$$

where A_{os} is the output voltage, and β is the conversion factor.

The second is TWTA, whose conversion formulas are

$$f_A(r) = A_{is}^2 \frac{r}{r^2 + A_{is}^2}, \quad f_P(r) = \frac{\pi}{3} \frac{r^2}{r^2 + A_{is}^2} \tag{5}$$

where A_{is} is the input voltage.

The third is SEL, whose conversion formulas are

$$f_A(r) = \begin{cases} r & r \leq A_{is} \\ A_{is} & r > A_{is} \end{cases}, \quad f_P(r) = 0 \tag{6}$$

When the HPA is operating in the nonlinear region, passing through the channel, we can get the received signal $y = [y_1, y_2, \cdots, y_k]^T$

$$y = Hu + n \tag{7}$$

where $u \in \mathbb{C}^N$ is the output signal which has been effected by nonlinear HPA. According to (3), we can get $u_i(i = 1, 2, \cdots, N)$

$$u_i = f_A(|x_i|)\exp[j(\theta_i + f_P(|x_i|))] \tag{8}$$

It can be seen from (8) that the nonlinear HPA has some impact on the transmitted signal. In the next section, we will analyze the impact of nonlinear HPA and according to the impact, we can propose an improved precoding algorithms.

3   Precoding Design

By (8), we can rewrite the received signal as a product of transmitting signal and the factor

$$u_{ij} = f_A(|x_{ij}|)\exp[j(\theta_{ij} + f_P(|x_{ij}|))] = \frac{f_A(|x_{ij}|)}{|x_{ij}|} x_{ij} \tag{9}$$

As can be seen from the above that, passing through the nonlinear HPA, the emission signal will multiply a factor $d_{ij} = \frac{f_A(|x_{ij}|)}{|x_{ij}|}$, which represents the level of the impact. And we can see from the factor that the level of the impact only relies on the signal' s amplitude.

Hence, we can construct a function by (4) and (9)

$$\tilde{y} = \frac{f_A(\frac{1}{\tilde{x}})}{\frac{1}{\tilde{x}}}\exp(f_P(\frac{1}{\tilde{x}})) = \frac{1}{\left[1 + \left(\frac{1}{A_{os}\tilde{x}}\right)^{2\beta}\right]^{1/2\beta}} \tag{10}$$

where $\tilde{x} > 0$. For the convenience of analysis, we assume $t = 1/\tilde{x}$ and $A_{os} = 1$. $\beta \in [2, 3]$. So

$$\lim_{\tilde{x} \to \infty} 1/\tilde{x} = \lim_{t \to 0} t = 0$$

$$\lim_{\tilde{x} \to \infty} \tilde{y} = \lim_{t \to 0} \frac{1}{(1 + t^{2\beta})^{1/2\beta}} \tag{11}$$

Let $t^{2\beta} = m$, we can get

$$\lim_{\tilde{x} \to \infty} \tilde{y} = \lim_{m \to 0} \left(\frac{1}{1+m} \right)^{1/2\beta} = 1 \tag{12}$$

Because $t > 0, 1 + t^{2\beta} > 1$, that is $\frac{1}{(1+t^{2\beta})^{1/2\beta}} < 1$, The simulation is shown in Fig. 2.

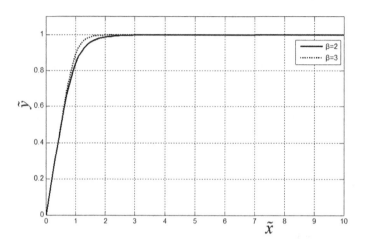

Fig. 2. The curve of relationship between A and B

We can see from Fig. 2 that $\tilde{y}$ increases with $\tilde{x}$ and gradually tends to be plat. When $\tilde{x} > 3$, $\tilde{y}$ gradually tends to be 1 and now the impact of nonlinear will be very small.

From the analysis above, we know that when $\tilde{x}$ is large enough, the impact of nonlinear will be very small. Hence, we can design a new precoding algorithm by dividing a factor α from the traditional precoding algorithm to eliminate the influence of nonlinear HPA. But if α is too large, it will reduce the power of emission signal, and if it is too small, we cannot eliminate the impact. So, in order to get proper α, we structure the following inequality

$$|1 - \tilde{y}| \le 10^{\theta} \tag{13}$$

where $\theta < 0$ is the precision factor, $\tilde{y}$ is mentioned above. Take (10) into (13)

$$|1 - \tilde{y}| \le 10^{\theta}$$

$$\left| 1 - \frac{1}{\left[1 + \left(\frac{1}{\tilde{x} A_{os}} \right)^{2\beta} \right]^{1/2\beta}} \right| \le 10^{\theta}$$

$$\tilde{x} \geq \frac{1}{A_{os}\left[\left(\frac{1}{1-10^{\theta}}\right)^{2\beta} - 1\right]^{1/2\beta}} \tag{14}$$

From above, we can get that when $\alpha = \tilde{x} \geq \frac{1}{A_{os}\left[\left(\frac{1}{1-10^{\theta}}\right)^{2\beta} - 1\right]^{1/2\beta}}$, $\tilde{y}$ meet the need of the precision factor θ. The simulation is shown in Fig. 3

We can see clearly in Fig. 3 that factor α decreases with the increase of precision factor θ and the speed became faster and faster. But, we can see that when the precision is bigger enough and the precision reaches 10^{-4}, the factor α is still around 5. So it meets the need of α.

So, when we use the new precoding matrixes, the received signal can be expressed as

$$u_i = f_A([ws]_i)\exp[j(\theta_i + f_P([ws]_i))] = \frac{f_A([ws]_i)}{[ws]_i}\exp(f_P([ws]_i))[ws]_i = [ws]_i \tag{15}$$

Hence, we can deduce the improved precoding matrix $W_{LNBD} = W_{BD}/\alpha$, $W_{LNZF} = W_{ZF}/\alpha$ (LN represents linear normalization) which can remove the impact of nonlinearity from traditional precoding matrices.

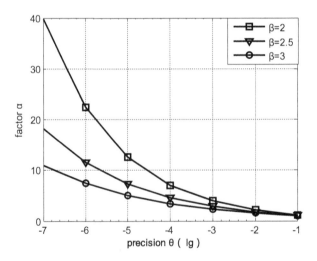

Fig. 3. The factor α under different θ

4 Numerical Results

In order to verify it's performance, we will compare the performance of improved algorithms with the BD and ZF precoding algorithms by simulation. The simulation parameters are as follows: the number of users per cell $k = 50$, the number of antennas

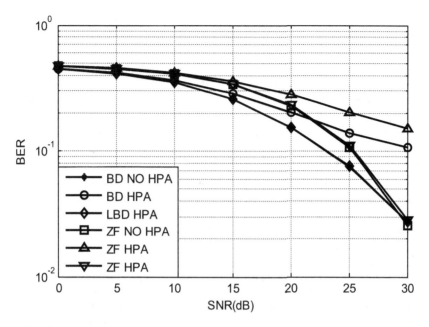

Fig. 4. BER comparison of different precoding algorithms under nonlinear HPA

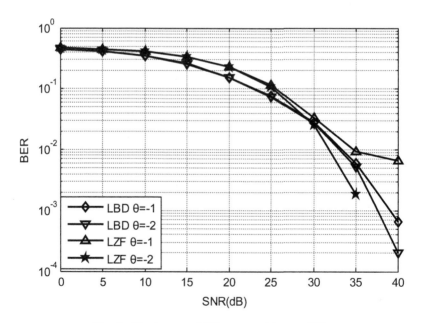

Fig. 5. The impact of different precision on BER

per user $M_k = 2$, noise variance $\sigma_n^2 = 1$. Signal-noise-ratio (SNR) is defined as $P_k/M_k\sigma_n^2$. Bit error ratio (BER) is calculated based on quadrate phase shift keying (QPSK) modulation.

Figure 4 shows the difference between traditional algorithms (BD, ZF) and the proposed algorithms on bit error ratio when HPA works in the nonlinear region and the precision is 0.1. In the low SNR region, these two kinds of algorithms make no difference. With the increase of SNR, the difference between them becomes larger and larger. BER of the proposed algorithms is clearly lower than BD and ZF precoding algorithms. We also can see from it that the BER of the proposed algorithms is similar to that of the condition where there is no influence of nonlinear HPA and it uses the traditional algorithm. So the proposed algorithms remedy the influence of nonlinear HPA on BER.

Figure 5 shows the impact of different precision on BER. As shown in the figure that in the low SNR region, it makes no difference. In high SNR region, the BER decreases as the precision increasing. Under the same θ, the performance of LBD is better than LZF, and as the SNR increases, the difference is getting greater and greater.

Figure 6 shows the difference between traditional algorithms (BD, ZF) and the proposed algorithms on system capacity when HPA works in the nonlinear region and the precision is 0.1. In the low SNR region, these two kinds of algorithms make no difference. With the increase of SNR, the difference between them becomes larger and larger. The capacity of the proposed algorithms is clearly larger than BD and ZF precoding algorithms. So the proposed algorithms remedy the influence of nonlinear HPA on capacity.

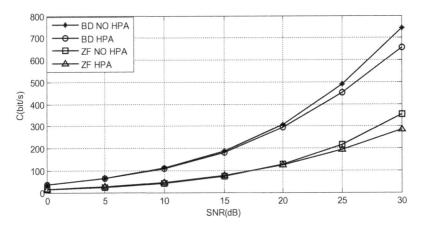

Fig. 6. Capacity comparison of different precoding algorithms under nonlinear HPA

5   Conclusion

Aiming at the problem of nonlinear HPA in large-scale MIMO system, this paper analyzes its impact on the system at first, and then we propose the improved precoding algorithms according to the impact. We can see clearly from the simulation results that the improved algorithms can effectively compensate for the influence of nonlinear HPA caused on the system. In addition to the research mentioned in this paper, it is necessary to further study the situations where there are some other hardware problems accompany with incomplete channel information.

Acknowledgments. The research was supported in part by Postdoctoral Research Funding Plan in Jiangsu Province (Grant No. 1501073B), Natural Science Foundation of Nanjing University of Posts and Telecommunications (Grant No. NY214108), Natural Science Foundation of China (NSFC) (Grant No. 61401399), and the Open Research Fund of National Mobile Communications Research Laboratory, Southeast University (Grant No. 2016D05).

References

1. Gregorio, F.H.: Analysis and compensation of nonlinear power amplifier effects in multi-antenna OFDM systems. J. Helsinki Univ. Technol. **22**(6), 75–84 (2007)
2. Zhao, N., Yu, F.R., Leung, V.C.M.: Opportunistic communications in interference alignment networks with wireless power transfer. J. IEEE Wirel. Commun. **22**, 88–95 (2015)
3. Saleh, A.A.M.: Frequency independent and frequency dependent nonlinear model of TWT amplifier. J. IEEE Trans. Commun. **29**(11), 1715–1720 (1981)
4. Rapp, C.: Effects of HPA-nonlinearity on a 4-DPSK/OFDM-signal for a digital sound broadcasting system. In: European Conference on Satellite Communications, pp. 179–184 (1991)
5. Rowe, H.E.: Memoryless nonlinearities with Gaussian inputs: elementary results. J. Bell Syst. Tech. J. **61**(7), 1519–1526 (1982)
6. Sulyman, A.I., Ibnkahla, M.: Performance of space time codes over nonlinear MIMO channels. IEEE Signal Process. Appl. **1**, 407–410 (2005)
7. Qi, J., Aissa, S.: Impact of HPA nonlinearity on MIMO systems with quantized equal gain transmission. In: IEEE International Symposium on Personal, Indoor and Mobile Radio Communications, pp. 2891–2895 (2009)
8. Xie, H., Gao, F., Zhang, S., Jin, S.: A unified transmission strategy for TDD/FDD massive MIMO systems with spatial basis expansion model. J. IEEE Trans. Veh. Technol. **66**, 3170–3184 (2016)
9. Xie, H., Gao, F., Jin, S.: An overview of low-rank channel estimation for massive MIMO systems. J. IEEE Access **4**, 7313–7321 (2016)
10. Xie, H., Wang, B., Gao, F., Jin, S.: A full-space spectrum-sharing strategy for massive MIMO cognitive radio. J. IEEE J. Sel. Areas Commun. **34**(10), 2537–2549 (2016)
11. Peel, C.B., Hochwald, B.M., Swindlehurst, A.L.: A vector-perturbation technique for near-capacity multiantenna multiuser communication-part I: channel inversion and regularization. J. Commun. IEEE Trans. **53**(1), 195–202 (2005)
12. Spencer, Q.H., Swindlehurst, A.L., Haardt, M.: Zero-forcing methods for downlink spatial multiplexing in multiuser MIMO channels. J. IEEE Trans. Signal Process. **52**(2), 461–471 (2004)

Linear Precoding for Massive MIMO Systems with IQ Imbalance

Juan Liu[1(⊠)], Jianxin Dai[2], Chonghu Cheng[1], and Zhiliang Huang[3]

[1] College of Telecommunications and Information Engineering,
Nanjing University of Posts and Telecommunications, Nanjing 210003, China
15705102101@163.com, 1275418944@qq.com
[2] School of Science, Nanjing University of Posts and Telecommunications,
Nanjing 210023, China
daijx@njupt.edu.cn
[3] College of Mathematics, Physics and Information Engineering,
Zhejiang Normal University, Jinhua 321004, China
zlhuang@zjnu.cn

Abstract. The massive multiple-input multiple-output (MIMO) system is one of the most promising techniques, which extends degrees of freedom, increases the throughput of systems, supports more data streams and decreases transmit power. However, using cheap hardware in massive MIMO system can affect the overall performance of the system and deteriorate the user experience. The IQ imbalance caused by using cheap hardware is one of the important factors affecting system performance. To solve this problem, this paper proposes the design of precoding matrix based on the minimum mean square error (MMSE) criterion to suppress the influence of IQ imbalance on system performance. The numerical simulation results validate the effectiveness of the proposed algorithm, and show that the bit error rate (BER) performance of the proposed algorithm has obvious better than that of ZF, BD and WL-BD precoding.

Keywords: Massive MIMO · IQ imbalance · Minimum mean square error
Linear precoding · Bit error rate

1 Introduction

Massive multiple-input multiple-output (MIMO) extends degrees of freedom, increases the throughput of systems, supports more data streams and decreases transmit power by deploying excessive number of antennas at the base station (BS). Based on the above advantages, massive MIMO will become one of the key technologies of 5G wireless communication in the future [1–10].

However, due to the employment of an excessive number of transmit and receive antennas, the circuit power and cost of radio frequency (RF) chains in large-scale MIMO systems is much higher than that of conventional MIMO systems, which is one of its drawbacks. Fortunately, this problem can be solved by using cheap hardware. Because large-scale MIMO can limit performance degradation by providing sufficient degree of freedom in case of individual antenna units fail. Therefore, large-scale MIMO systems can relax the hardware accuracy requirements [8]. Unfortunately, the use of

© ICST Institute for Computer Sciences, Social Informatics and Telecommunications Engineering 2018
X. Gu et al. (Eds.): MLICOM 2017, Part I, LNICST 226, pp. 484–493, 2018.
https://doi.org/10.1007/978-3-319-73564-1_48

inexpensive hardware has a greater possibility of deteriorating system performance, such as in-phase and quadrature-phase (IQ) imbalance. IQ imbalance (IQI) refers to the mismatches between the real and imaginary parts of the complex signal. This paper focuses on the impact of IQI on system performance. In addition, the use of limited precision analog hardware will also produce IQ imbalance [10–12].

IQ imbalance degrades the overall performance of the system, therefore, deteriorates user experience. One of the ways to overcome IQ imbalance is measuring and compensating IQ imbalance parameters in each antenna [10, 12]. Reference [19] proposed a compensation algorithm for overcoming IQ imbalance in single-input single-output (SISO) system. However, due to large-scale MIMO systems are equipped with excessive antennas, the calculation of the compensation algorithm is too complicated, and the cost is too expensive in real implementations [10]. Therefore, some researchers have proposed to solve IQ imbalance by widely linear signal processing. Reference [14] proposed widely-linear block diagonal (WL-BD) precoding scheme. The numerical simulation results show that the WL-BD precoding scheme is superior to block diagonal (BD) precoding algorithm when the antennas of the BS occur IQ imbalance. Though reference [15] designs the precoding scheme based on the minimum mean square error (MMSE) criterion, its results are only for single user MIMO systems without IQI. Reference [12] proposed widely-linear regularized zero-forcing (WL-RZF) precoding scheme, which results indicate that when base station antennas are more than total user antennas, the proposed precoding scheme can eliminate the effect of IQ imbalance and the system sum rate close to the systems without IQ imbalance. In order to reduce the complexity of computing inverse of high-dimensional matrix, reference [18] proposed the reduced-rank widely linear precoding algorithm based on Krylov Subspace (KS), which greatly reduce the calculate complexity of widely linear precoding.

Based on the above analysis, this paper proposes a precoding algorithm based on MMSE in a single-cell downlink massive MIMO system to overcome IQ imbalance. Numerical simulation results illustrate that with the number of users increasing, the bit error rate (BER) performance is better than that of ZF, BD and WL-BD precoding algorithm. The structure of this article is described as below. The system model is introduced in Sect. 2. In Sect. 3, we can obtain the closed-form solution of the precoding matrix based on the MMSE criterion when the BS has IQ imbalances in large-scale MIMO systems. In Sect. 4, the simulation analysis of the proposed precoding algorithm and ZF, BD, WL-BD precoding algorithm at bit error ratio do the comparison. We also analysis bit error ratio of the four precoding schemes under different the number of base station antennas and users. Conclusions are drawn in Sect. 5.

The symbols used in this article are as follows: $(A)^T$, $(A)^H$ represent the matrix transpose and conjugate transpose; $tr\{A\}$, $\|A\|_F = \sqrt{tr\{A^H A\}}$ represent matrix trace and the Frobenius norm respectively. $E\{\bullet\}$ denotes expectation.

2   System Model

The research in this paper is carried out in downlink of a single cell with a base station (BS) and K users. The BS deploys N antennas and the k-th user has M_k antennas.

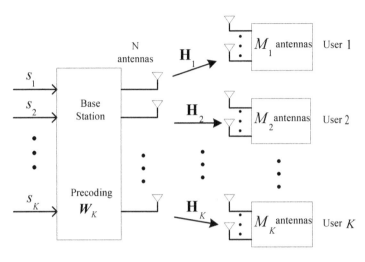

Fig. 1. System model

The number of users' antennas is $M = \sum_{k=1}^{K} M_k$. Assuming that BS has perfect channel state information (CSI), and users are distributed with the same power. The system model is shown in Fig. 1.

The MIMO channel of user k is denoted as $\boldsymbol{H}_k \in \mathbb{C}^{M_k \times N}$. The precoding matrix $\boldsymbol{W} \in \mathbb{C}^{N \times M}$ is defined for all users. The transmit signal and the precoding vector of k-th user are denoted respectively as $\boldsymbol{s}_k \in \mathbb{C}^{M_k \times L_k}$ and $\boldsymbol{W}_k \in \mathbb{C}^{N \times M_k}$, where L_k is the length of signal vector $\boldsymbol{s}_k$. Then, the combined precoding matrix and signal matrix are given by $\boldsymbol{W} = [\boldsymbol{W}_1, \cdots, \boldsymbol{W}_K]$, $\boldsymbol{s} = [\boldsymbol{s}_1^T, \cdots, \boldsymbol{s}_K^T]^T$. We assume the signal before precoding of users are independent, i.e.,$\forall k \neq j$, $E\{\boldsymbol{s}_k \boldsymbol{s}_j^H\} = 0$, $E\{\boldsymbol{s}_k \boldsymbol{s}_k^H\} = \boldsymbol{I}_{L_k}$.The precoded signal vector is $\boldsymbol{x} = \boldsymbol{W}\boldsymbol{s}$. The BS transmits the precoded signal $\boldsymbol{x}$ to the users, and then passes through the channel to the user terminal. Assume that there is IQ imbalance at the BS in a large-scale MIMO system. Then the precoded signal $\boldsymbol{x}_n$ transmit by the n-th antenna will become $a_{n1}\boldsymbol{x}_n + a_{n2}\boldsymbol{x}_n^*$, where a_{n1} and a_{n2} are imbalance parameters. We can obtain their values by applying the formula (1) [9]:

$$
\begin{aligned}
a_{n1} &= \cos(\theta_n/2) + jg_n \sin(\theta_n/2) \\
a_{n2} &= g_n \cos(\theta_2/2) - j \sin(\theta_n/2)
\end{aligned}
\tag{1}
$$

where θ_n and g_n are relative phase error and gain error of I and Q, respectively. Generally, their values are 2°, 0.25 [9]. When θ_n and g_n are zero, the massive MIMO system without the presence of IQ imbalance at the BS.

When the BS has IQ imbalance, we can get the k-th received signal $\boldsymbol{y}_k \in \mathbb{C}^{M_k \times L_k}$:

$$
\boldsymbol{y}_k = \beta \boldsymbol{H}_k \boldsymbol{A}_1 \boldsymbol{x} + \beta \boldsymbol{H}_k \boldsymbol{A}_2 \boldsymbol{x}^* + \boldsymbol{n}_k
\tag{2}
$$

From Eq. (2), we know that the k-th received signal is disturbed by its conjugate signal, so that the error of the received signal becomes larger, which is the adverse effect of IQ imbalance on massive MIMO system. The IQI parameters of all antennas at the BS side can be expressed as diagonal matrices $A_1 = diag\{a_{11}, \cdots, a_{N1}\}$, $A_2 = diag\{a_{12}, \cdots, a_{N2}\}$; The k-th additive white Gaussian noise vector can be denoted as $n_k \sim CN(0, I_{M_k})$, the entries of which are independent distributed variables with zero mean and variance 1.

3 Precoding Design

A transformation of a matrix or vector that transforms the complex matrix or vector into the real and imaginary parts is introduced in this section. Then we use this transformation to design the precoding matrix based on the MMSE criterion.

3.1 T Transformation

T transformation can separate the complex matrix or vector into the real and imaginary parts to form a new matrix or vector. It is defined as [20]:

$$T(x) = \begin{bmatrix} \mathrm{Re}(x) \\ \mathrm{Im}(x) \end{bmatrix},$$

$$T(X) = \begin{bmatrix} \mathrm{Re}(X) & -\mathrm{Im}(X) \\ \mathrm{Im}(X) & \mathrm{Re}(X) \end{bmatrix} \tag{3}$$

where $\mathrm{Re}(\bullet)$ represents the real parts and $\mathrm{Im}(\bullet)$ represents imaginary parts of a vector or matrix. From reference [20], we can get some properties of this transformation:

$$\begin{aligned}
&T(AB) = T(A)T(B), \ T(A^{-1}) = [T(A)]^{-1}, \\
&T(x + y) = T(x) + T(y), \ T(Ax) = T(A)T(x), \\
&T(A + B) = T(A) + T(B), \ T(A^H) = [T(A)]^H, \\
&\det(T(A)) = [\det(A)]^2 = \det(AA^H)
\end{aligned} \tag{4}$$

Then we apply T transformation to rewrite the Eq. (2), and get $\tilde{y}_k$:

$$\begin{aligned}
\tilde{y}_k &= T(y_k) \\
&= T(\beta H_k A_1 x + \beta H_k A_2 x^* + n_k) \\
&= T(\beta H_k)T(A_1 x + A_2 x^*) + T(n_k) \\
&= \beta T(H_k)[T(A_1) + T(A_2)E_N]T(x) + T(n_k)
\end{aligned} \tag{5}$$

For simplicity, we define $\widetilde{H}_k = T(H_k)$, $\widetilde{A} = [T(A_1) + T(A_2)E_N]$, $\tilde{x} = T(x)$, $\widetilde{n}_k = T(n_k)$, where $E_N = diag\{I_N, -I_N\}$. Equation (5) can be equivalent:

$$\widetilde{\boldsymbol{y}}_k = \beta \widetilde{\boldsymbol{H}}_k \widetilde{\boldsymbol{A}} \widetilde{\boldsymbol{x}} + \widetilde{\boldsymbol{n}}_k \tag{6}$$

From above analysis, we know that the precoded signal is $\boldsymbol{x} = \boldsymbol{Ws}$. Applying T transformation to $\boldsymbol{x}$ gives $\widetilde{\boldsymbol{x}} = T(\boldsymbol{Ws}) = T(\boldsymbol{W})T(\boldsymbol{s}) = \widetilde{\boldsymbol{W}}\widetilde{\boldsymbol{s}}$, where $\widetilde{\boldsymbol{W}} = [\widetilde{\boldsymbol{W}}_1, \cdots, \widetilde{\boldsymbol{W}}_K]$, $\widetilde{\boldsymbol{s}} = [\boldsymbol{s}_1^T, \cdots, \boldsymbol{s}_K^T]^T$, β is power limiting factor which satisfied $E\left\{\|\beta\widetilde{\boldsymbol{x}}\|^2\right\} = E\left\{\|\beta\widetilde{\boldsymbol{W}}\widetilde{\boldsymbol{s}}\|^2\right\} = P$, that is, $E\left\{\|\beta\widetilde{\boldsymbol{W}}\|^2\right\} = P$, P is the total user's transmit power. We can rewrite (6):

$$\widetilde{\boldsymbol{y}}_k = \beta \widetilde{\boldsymbol{H}}_k \widetilde{\boldsymbol{A}} \widetilde{\boldsymbol{W}} \widetilde{\boldsymbol{s}} + \widetilde{\boldsymbol{n}}_k \tag{7}$$

We denote $\widetilde{\boldsymbol{y}} = [\widetilde{\boldsymbol{y}}_1^T, \cdots, \widetilde{\boldsymbol{y}}_K^T]^T$, $\widetilde{\boldsymbol{H}} = [\widetilde{\boldsymbol{H}}_1^T, \cdots, \widetilde{\boldsymbol{H}}_K^T]^T$, $\widetilde{\boldsymbol{n}} = [\widetilde{\boldsymbol{n}}_1^T, \cdots, \widetilde{\boldsymbol{n}}_K^T]^T$, then the received signal of all users is:

$$\widetilde{\boldsymbol{y}} = \beta \widetilde{\boldsymbol{H}} \widetilde{\boldsymbol{A}} \widetilde{\boldsymbol{W}} \widetilde{\boldsymbol{s}} + \widetilde{\boldsymbol{n}} \tag{8}$$

3.2   Precoding Algorithm

Based on MMSE criterion, the problem of precoding matrix can be formulated as:

$$\min_{\widetilde{\boldsymbol{W}}} E\left\{\|\beta^{-1}\widetilde{\boldsymbol{y}} - \widetilde{\boldsymbol{s}}\|^2\right\}$$
$$s.t \quad \beta^2\|\widetilde{\boldsymbol{A}}\widetilde{\boldsymbol{W}}\|^2 = P \tag{9}$$

The solution of the (9) is the optimal solution of the proposed precoding algorithm. From (8), we can get:

$$E\left\{\|\beta^{-1}\widetilde{\boldsymbol{y}} - \widetilde{\boldsymbol{s}}\|^2\right\} = E\left\{\|\widetilde{\boldsymbol{H}}\widetilde{\boldsymbol{A}}\widetilde{\boldsymbol{W}}\widetilde{\boldsymbol{s}} + \beta^{-1}\widetilde{\boldsymbol{n}} - \widetilde{\boldsymbol{s}}\|^2\right\}$$
$$= E\left\{\|\widetilde{\boldsymbol{H}}\widetilde{\boldsymbol{A}}\widetilde{\boldsymbol{W}}\widetilde{\boldsymbol{s}} - \widetilde{\boldsymbol{s}}\|^2 + \beta^{-2}\|\boldsymbol{n}\|^2\right\} \tag{10}$$

From (9), we can obtain $\beta^2 = P \Big/ \|\widetilde{\boldsymbol{A}}\widetilde{\boldsymbol{W}}\|^2$. Then, (11) is given by:

$$E\{\|\beta^{-1}\widetilde{\boldsymbol{y}} - \widetilde{\boldsymbol{s}}\|^2\} = E\{\|\widetilde{\boldsymbol{H}}\widetilde{\boldsymbol{A}}\widetilde{\boldsymbol{W}}\widetilde{\boldsymbol{s}} - \widetilde{\boldsymbol{s}}\|^2\} + \frac{\|\widetilde{\boldsymbol{A}}\widetilde{\boldsymbol{W}}\|^2}{P}M\sigma_n^2$$

$$= E\{tr(\widetilde{\boldsymbol{H}}\widetilde{\boldsymbol{A}}\widetilde{\boldsymbol{W}}\widetilde{\boldsymbol{s}} - \widetilde{\boldsymbol{s}})(\widetilde{\boldsymbol{H}}\widetilde{\boldsymbol{A}}\widetilde{\boldsymbol{W}}\widetilde{\boldsymbol{s}} - \widetilde{\boldsymbol{s}})^H\} + \frac{\|\widetilde{\boldsymbol{A}}\widetilde{\boldsymbol{W}}\|^2}{P}M\sigma_n^2$$

$$= tr(\widetilde{\boldsymbol{W}}^H\widetilde{\boldsymbol{A}}^H\widetilde{\boldsymbol{H}}^H\widetilde{\boldsymbol{H}}\widetilde{\boldsymbol{A}}\widetilde{\boldsymbol{W}} - \widetilde{\boldsymbol{H}}\widetilde{\boldsymbol{A}}\widetilde{\boldsymbol{W}} - \widetilde{\boldsymbol{W}}^H\widetilde{\boldsymbol{A}}^H\widetilde{\boldsymbol{H}}^H + \boldsymbol{I}_M + \frac{\widetilde{\boldsymbol{W}}^H\widetilde{\boldsymbol{A}}^H\widetilde{\boldsymbol{H}}\widetilde{\boldsymbol{A}}\widetilde{\boldsymbol{W}}}{P}M\sigma_n^2) \tag{11}$$

We define:

$$f(\widetilde{W}) = \widetilde{W}^H \widetilde{A}^H \widetilde{H}^H \widetilde{H} \widetilde{A} \widetilde{W} - \widetilde{H} \widetilde{A} \widetilde{W} - \widetilde{W}^H \widetilde{A}^H \widetilde{H}^H + I_M + \frac{\widetilde{W}^H \widetilde{A}^H \widetilde{A} \widetilde{W}}{P} M\sigma_n^2 \quad (12)$$

In order to get $\widetilde{W}$, we assume that $\widetilde{W}$ is dependent on $\widetilde{W}^H$. Then, the first order derivatives of (12) on $\widetilde{W}$ is given by:

$$\frac{\partial f(\widetilde{W})}{\partial \widetilde{W}} = \widetilde{W}^H \widetilde{A}^H \widetilde{H}^H \widetilde{H} \widetilde{A} - \widetilde{H} \widetilde{A} + \frac{\widetilde{W}^H \widetilde{A}^H \widetilde{A}}{P} M\sigma_n^2 \quad (13)$$

Letting the above formula be equal to zero, we can obtain the solution of the $\widetilde{W}$:

$$\widetilde{W}^H \widetilde{A}^H \widetilde{H}^H \widetilde{H} \widetilde{A} - \widetilde{H} \widetilde{A} + \frac{\widetilde{W}^H \widetilde{A}^H \widetilde{A}}{P} M\sigma_n^2 = 0$$

$$\widetilde{W}^H \left(\widetilde{A}^H \widetilde{H}^H \widetilde{H} \widetilde{A} + \frac{\widetilde{A}^H \widetilde{A}}{P} M\sigma_n^2 \right) = \widetilde{H} \widetilde{A}$$

$$\widetilde{W}^H = \widetilde{H} \widetilde{A} \left(\widetilde{A}^H \widetilde{H}^H \widetilde{H} \widetilde{A} + \frac{\widetilde{A} \widetilde{A}^H}{P} M\sigma_n^2 \right)^{-1} \qquad (14)$$

$$\widetilde{W} = \left(\widetilde{A}^H \widetilde{H}^H \widetilde{H} \widetilde{A} + \frac{\widetilde{A} \widetilde{A}^H}{P} M\sigma_n^2 \right)^{-1} \widetilde{A}^H \widetilde{H}^H$$

4 Numerical Results

This section analyzes the proposed algorithm in the previous section by numerical simulating in the downlink of a single-cell with IQ imbalance. The BER of the proposed precoding algorithm is comparable to that of ZF, BD, WL-BD algorithms in this section. It is assumed that the total number of antennas at the BS is $N = 100$, the total number of users is $K = 50$, and each user has $M_k = 2$ antennas. According to reference [9], we know the general value of IQ imbalance parameters g_n and θ_n are 0.25, 2°, respectively. The definition of signal to noise ratio (SNR) is $P_k / M_k \sigma_n^2$. Based on the modulation of quadrate phase shift keying (QPSK), we can calculate the bit error ratio (BER).

Figure 2 shows the BER comparison of the proposed precoding scheme, ZF, BD, and WL-BD in the single-cell multi-user scenarios under the presence of IQ imbalance at the BS. We can clearly see that the BER of the proposed precoding scheme and ZF, BD and WL-BD are decreasing with the increase of SNR from Fig. 2. When the SNR is less than 8 dB, the gap between the proposed algorithm and other algorithms is gradually widening; When the SNR is greater than 8 dB and less than 10 dB, the gap between the proposed algorithm and WL-BD algorithms is narrow. Although the BER of the proposed algorithm is inferior to the algorithm when the value of signal to noise ratio is more than 10 dB, the BER of the proposed precoding scheme is superior to ZF, BD and the calculate complexity of WL-BD is too high.

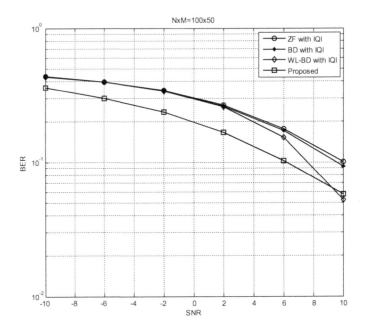

Fig. 2. Comparison of BER for different precoding algorithms on SNR

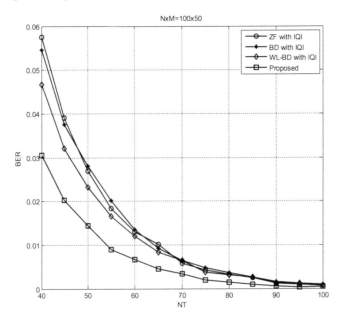

Fig. 3. Comparison of BER for different precoding algorithms on antennas of BS

Figure 3 shows the BER of the four precoding schemes when the number of the BS antennas is different. It is assumed that SNR is 2 dB, the number of users is 50, and every user has 2 antennas. Figure 3 clearly shows that the BER of the proposed precoding scheme and ZF, BD and WL-BD algorithms are decreasing when the number of antennas is increasing. The proposed algorithm has been superior to ZF, BD and WL-BD algorithms when the number of antennas at the BS increased from 40 to 100.

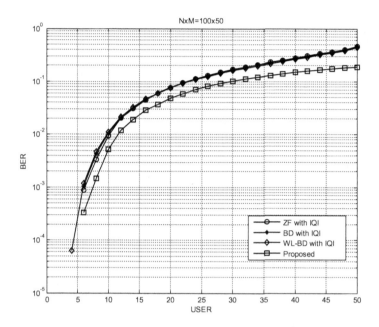

Fig. 4. Comparison of BER for different precoding algorithms on the numbers of users

Figure 4 shows the BER of the four precoding schemes for different the number of users, when the single-cell multi-user scenarios under the base station has IQ imbalance. Assuming that the value of SNR is 2 dB; the number of the BS antennas is 100. As can be seen from Fig. 4, with the number of users increasing, the BER of the four precoding scheme is increasing, the performance of system is declining, the emergence of this situation is reasonable. Though the number of users is increasing, the proposed algorithm has obvious advantages. The reason is the BER of other algorithms has been increasing, and the BER of this algorithm increased tend to be slow. This shows that this algorithm is suitable for application in massive MIMO scenarios.

5 Conclusions

Aiming at the problem of IQ imbalance in the large-scale MIMO system, this paper obtains a solution to the precoding matrix based on MMSE criterion to eliminate IQ imbalance. The numerical simulation results show that compared with ZF, BD and WL-BD precoding scheme, the BER of the proposed scheme has obvious advantages. In this paper, the algorithm offsets the effect of IQ imbalance on system performance, reduces the interference among users, and improves the overall performance of the system. However, there are still some deficiencies in this paper. For example, we do not consider the the scenario of total number of the BS receiving antennas is more than transmiting antennas and multi-cell scenarios, which will be the direction for further research in the future.

Acknowledgments. The research was supported in part by Postdoctoral Research Funding Plan in Jiangsu Province (Grant No. 1501073B), Natural Science Foundation of Nanjing University of Posts and Telecommunications (Grant No. NY214108), Natural Science Foundation of China (NSFC) (Grant No. 61401399), and the Open Research Fund of National Mobile Communications Research Laboratory, Southeast University (Grant No. 2016D05).

References

1. Lu, L., Li, G.Y., Swindlehurst, A.L.: An overview of massive MIMO: benefits and challenges. IEEE J. Sel. Top. Sig. Process. **8**, 742–758 (2014)
2. Wang, C.X., Haider, F., Gao, X.: Cellular architecture and key technologies for 5G wireless communication networks. J. IEEE Commun. Mag. **52**, 122–130 (2014)
3. Larsson, E.G., Edfors, O., Tufvesson, F., Marzetta, T.L.: Massive MIMO for next generation wireless systems. J. IEEE Commun. Mag. **52**, 186–195 (2014)
4. Lamarey, R.C.D.: Massive MIMO systems: signal processing challenges and future trends. URSI Radio Sci. Bull. **2013**, 8–20 (2013)
5. Xie, H., Gao, F., Zhang, S., Jin, S.: A unified transmission strategy for TDD/FDD massive MIMO systems with spatial basis expansion model. IEEE Trans. Veh. Technol. **66**, 3170–3184 (2016). Earlier access available online
6. Xie, H., Gao, F., Zhang, S., Jin, S.: An overview of low-rank channel estimation for massive MIMO systems. IEEE Access **4**, 7313–7321 (2016)
7. Xie, H., Gao, F., Zhang, S., Jin, S.: A full-space spectrum-sharing strategy for massive MIMO cognitive radio. IEEE J. Sel. Areas Commun. **34**(10), 2537–2549 (2016)
8. Björnson, E., Hoydis, J., Kountouris, M., Debbah, M.: Massive MIMO Systems with non-ideal hardware: energy efficiency, estimation, and capacity limits. J. IEEE Inf. Theory Soc. **60**, 7112–7139 (2014)
9. Hakkarainen, A., Werner, J., Dandekar, K.R., Valkama, M.: Widely-linear beam-forming and RF impairment suppression in massive antenna array. J. Commun. Netw. **15**, 383–397 (2013)
10. Zarei, S., Gerstacker, W.H., Aulin, J., Schober, R.: I/Q Imbalance aware widely-linear receiver for uplink multi-cell massive MIMO systems: design and sum rate analysis. J. IEEE Trans. Wireless Commun. **15**, 3393–3408 (2016)
11. Ma, J., Zhang, S., Li, H., Zhao, N., Nallanathan, A.: Pattern division for massive MIMO networks with two-stage precoding. IEEE Commun. Lett. (2017), (to appear)
12. Zarei, S., Gerstacker, W.H., Schober, R.: I/Q imbalance aware widely-linear pre-coding for downlink massive MIMO systems. In: 2014 IEEE Globecom Workshops, GC Wkshps 2014, pp. 301–307. IEEE Press, Austin (2014)
13. Hakkarainen, A., Werner, J., Dandekar, K.R.: Precoded massive MU-MIMO uplink transmission under transceiver I/Q imbalance. In: 2014 IEEE Globecom Workshops, GC Wkshps 2014, pp. 320–326. IEEE Press, Austin (2014)
14. Zhang, W., Lamarey, R.C.D., Pan, C.: Widely linear block-diagonalization type pre-coding in massive MIMO systems with IQ imbalance. In: 2015 IEEE International Conference on Communications, ICC 2015, pp. 1789–1794. IEEE Press, London (2015)

15. Sterle, F.: Widely linear MMSE transceivers for MIMO channels. J. IEEE Trans. Sig. Process. **55**, 4258–4270 (2007)

16. Ma, J., Zhang, S., Li, H., Zhao, N., Nallanathan, A.: Pattern division for massive MIMO networks with two-stage precoding. In: 2017 IEEE Communications Society LCOMM. 2017, p. 1. IEEE Press (2017)

17. Zhao, N., Yu, F.R., Leung, V.C.M.: Opportunistic communications in interference alignment networks with wireless power transfer. J. IEEE Commun. Soc. **22**, 88–95 (2015)

18. Zhang, W., Lamarey, R.C.D., Chen, M.: Reduced-rank widely linear precoding in massive MIMO systems with I/Q imbalance. In: 2014 European Signal Processing Conference, pp. 331–335. IEEE Press, Lisbon (2014)

19. Tarighat, A., Bagheri, R., Sayed, A.H.: Compensation schemes and performance analysis of IQ imbalances in OFDM receivers. J. IEEE Trans. Sig. Process. **53**, 3257–3268 (2005)

20. Telatar, E.: Capacity of multi-antenna Gaussian channels. J. Eur. Trans. Telecommun. **10**, 585–595 (1999)

Research on Insurance Data Analysis Platform Based on the Hadoop Framework

Mingze Xia[(✉)]

Heilongjiang University (HLJU), Harbin, China
hlju_xia@yeah.net

Abstract. With the development of IT technology, the traditional information technology cannot meet magnitude data analysis in GB level, let alone in TB level. So it is a perfect time for APACHE company to launch a new product, Hadoop framework, which is a JAVA based basic framework of distributed system, and the versions are now already designated as 2.X series, which means this Hadoop framework is one of the mainstream framework of massive data storage, data procession and analytical in this present.

Keywords: Hadoop framework · Insurance · HDFS · MapReduce · HBase

1 Introduction of Hadoop Framework

With the rapid development of economy of our country, we can see that people's living standard, especially the income, has been rising greatly, people begin to pay more and more attention to their health, property, pension, medical aspects and so on. In recent years, all kinds of natural disasters and the unnatural factors which caused lots of accidents, has brought immensely material and spiritual loss to the people. Just one car accident can perish more than two families. So the property insurance, life insurance and the reinsurance has quickly developed recently, and the insurance companies launched kinds of insurance products depend on different situation. According to the relevant data which announced by the CIRC (The China Insurance Regulatory Commission), the original premium in life insurance business had achieved about 174.42 billion yuan, with year-on-year growth of 31.72% in 2016. and the original premium in property insurance had achieved about 87.245 billion yuan, with year-on-year growth of 9.12%. In this internet+ age, with the information construction upgrades, the insurance industry develops rapidly. According to their own situation, every insurance company use different information platforms, which respectively designed for customers, salespeople, managers and senior leaders, for integrating, screening, excluding, combining and analyzing the insurance data to provide precise guidance, exact sale, and accurate management services.

Hadoop framework [1], which is configured under Linux platform with lower hardware environment, can provide storage and analytics capabilities for massive data. With the development of applications of big data, Hadoop framework can be applied in daily operation system, such as agriculture, finance, medical system and traffic system.

© ICST Institute for Computer Sciences, Social Informatics and Telecommunications Engineering 2018
X. Gu et al. (Eds.): MLICOM 2017, Part I, LNICST 226, pp. 494–504, 2018.
https://doi.org/10.1007/978-3-319-73564-1_49

Developers and users are widely recognized this product because of its compatibility, dependability, low cost and high efficiency.Hadoop framework as shown in Fig. 1.

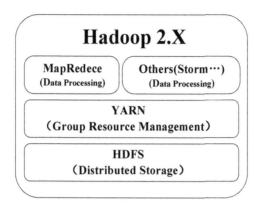

Fig. 1. Hadoop framework

1.1   Introduction of HDFS

Abbreviation in HDFS, Hadoop Distributed File System is one of the main technique in Hadoop framework, which can classify files into blocks, by default, each block set the memory limit to 64 MB, which also can be 128 MB [2]. In this way, it provides convenience for storing subsystem and backing up data. HDFS accessed though block by data stream, which fitted the design principle of HDFS well and improved the inquiry efficiency greatly [3].

HDFS includes two types of nodes, name node and data node respectively. Name node, which called manager node, is responsible for maintaining the whole file system directory, and receiving clients' requirement. At the same time, Name node can retain all information of data note, but not persistent. When the Hadoop starts, the data node will be rebuilt. So does the information.

Data note is the work node, it performs creating, replication and deletion. And it also sent the heartbeat information to name node for proving survival. Data note and name node has made TCP/TP protocol as their communication protocol. By storing data, data note can classify files into blocks, and have a backup copy of blocks in other racks. If the file got loss or damage, the system will invoke alternate block, and repair the damaged one. We can configure backup volumes in HDFS-SITE.SH, when built the Hadoop environment.

Each name node in the HDFS system is one or more corresponding date node. But when the name node got invalid, the system will be crashed. So we use standby name node in Hadoop 2.X series, when the running name node got invalid, the standby name node will take over the system in one minute for maintaining the normal operation of the system. HDFS framework as shown in Fig. 2.

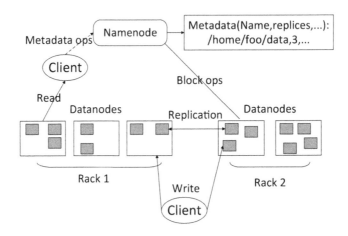

Fig. 2. HDFS framework

1.2　MapReduce

MapReduce is a distributing computing programming model with the program designing idea of "image" and "reduction" [4].

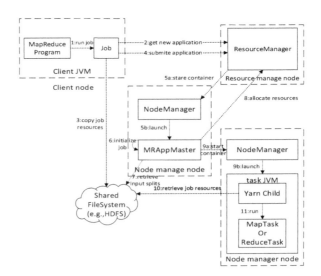

Fig. 3. MapReduce framework

There are two levels in Map Reduce task processes, map level and reduce level [5]. In map level, the system read data in data block at the first time, then map() breakdown data to result output for key-value pairs in Reduce level. Reduce begin to work after the Map finish its task. It can copy and output the received key-value pairs. Reduce has many threads, so the copy process is concurrent, and output the last result to HDFS [6].

After 2.0 version launched, Hadoop framework introduces a new mechanism named YARN, which also can be called Map Reduce2. YARN sets off Jobtrack's functions for avoiding some bottleneck questions, like development insufficient. MapReduce framework as shown in Fig. 3.

1.3 HBase Database

Hadoop Database is a distributed, column-oriented, open-source database which is JAVA language-based. HBase uses Hadoop HDFS as its file storage system, uses Hadoop Map Reduce to process the huge data in HBase, it also can use Zookeeper as collaborative service [7]. Like HDFS, Hbase use one master node to manage one or more region-server dependent computer. At this stage, HBase got widely apply because of its high-reliability, high-performance, colimn-oriented store and scalability. framework as shown in Fig. 4.

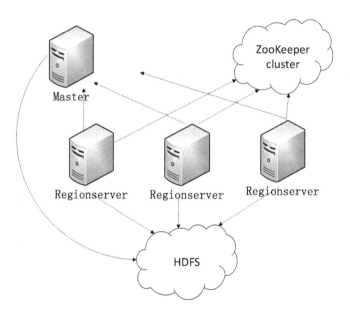

Fig. 4. HBase framework

2   Application of Hadoop Framework in Insurance Industry

At the present stage, most insurance companies, even financial enterprises use Oracle database, which is a distributed-memory relational database developed by Oracle Corporation. It is a classical row store database, but the row store database has the disadvantages.

Oracle database divides the overall data into pieces, as it implements row store, each row of data huddle together. When users access database and want to extract one row, database will put the overall data in the memory and read each row of data. Then, the database separates data for users want to get. Thus, I/O is enhanced greatly.

In insurance industry, the related data is not merely insurance policy information that we see. According to industrial standard JR/T 0048-2015 "Basic Data Model of Insurance", we can see the normal insurance data includes the following several aspects: subject of participants, contract subject, claim settlement subject, asset subject, risk evaluation subject, financial activity subject and insurance product subject. The data is very large. However, manager and decider just concern few about them, even one or several row of these data. For example, when the leader of one provincial branch makes decision, he may ask for IT personnel to acquire the overall premium and completion progress of the administrative city in a certain period, while risk control personnel only concerns if there is large sum of insurance cancellation existed among consumers. The paper, according to Hadoop frame, carries out data enquiry, index analysis, etc.

2.1   Overall Platform Achitecture

The platform mainly consists of three-layer structure, data source layer, data processing layer and data presentation layer. The Overall platform architecture is shown in Fig. 5.

1. Data source layer. It is the storage platform of data source, according to the fact of our country's insurance, it is also the Oracle database platform.
2. Data processing layer. It stores, backs up, calculates and queries the data which imported from the data source layer.
   Data importation. Data importation used open-source tools, like Sqoop, import the data from Oracle into HBase.
   (1) Data storage. Data storage import the data into HBase by Sqoop, and the HBase operated by HDFS.
   (2) Data backup. The backup of the data relies on the redundancy backup function of HDFS framework, which the number of copies is three by default.
   (3) Data calculations and inquiry. We can use the Mepraduce model of Hadoop framework when we want to query the data. And we can use Hive, the data warehouse tool, which can transform SQL into Map Reduce, to set analysis norm.

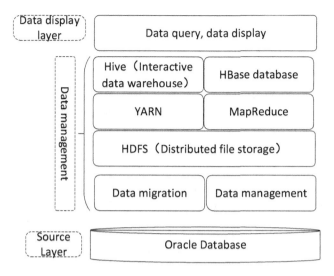

Fig. 5. Overall platform architecture

3. Data presentation layer. It can provide intuitive data for insurance industry managers and policymakers, and it also can quickly provide data querying and data index.

2.2 Related Optimization Adopted in the Implementation of Platform

1. The storage platform of data source is Oracle. During data migration, Sqoop+JDBC technology is usually adopted. According to the literatures, the system adopts open-sourcing OraOOp. In property, compared with traditional Sqoop+JDBC, OraOOp doesn't read data from the same Oracle data block, which reduces I/O. Moreover, OraOOp allocates the loading evenly according to the resource of downloading platform so as to maximize the network bandwidth and I/O.
2. HBase is non-relational database stored based on row. It has great difference with Oracle database. Owing to the difference, when importing data, it should consider the list structure of HBase. Therefore, before importing data, it associates the related lists by using internal connection method so as to form new list. At last, it imports the new list to HBase. Thus, it reduces data redundancy.
3. In job scheduling mechanism, Hadoop2.0 version above pushes two schedulers, including fair scheduler and capacity scheduler. Capacity scheduler corresponds to first in first out principle of old version, while fair scheduler supports the seizing principle. Developer makes choice according to different demands, which avoids the awkwardness that there is only one job scheduling mechanism.
4. In coding, it adopts UTF-8 coding method. Thus, it avoids messy code in the data import process.

3 Analysis and Subsequent Progress of Platform Characteristic

3.1 Characteristic Analysis

Compared with traditional relational database, data computation mode, development mode and equipment resource, the insurance data enquiry platform based on Hadoop frame has the following characteristic (Table 1):

Table 1. The characteristic of the insurance data enquiry platform

Special category	Traditional mode	Mode based on Hadoop frame
Equipment resource	High-end database, server	Common PC
Function	Single	Be expanded as per the demand
Property	Low efficient	High safety and efficiency
Capacity	Be expanded but limited	Be increased as per the demand

To sup up, the insurance data platform based on Hadoop frame has unique advantages of the storage, enquiry and analysis of mass insurance data.

1. Equipment resource is cheap. Compared with expensive advanced computer (database, server), the platform can be mounted on the cheap PC with less expense.
2. High expansibility. Owing to high expansibility of Hadoop, it is superior to traditional mode in data storage and data computation.
3. Safe and reliable. The redundant backup of HDFS enhances the data safety and motor, which avoids the economic loss caused by data loss.
4. High efficiency. The distributed storage of HDFS and parallel computation of MapReduce provide fundamental guarantee for efficient storage and computation of mass insurance data.

3.2 Data Analysis Example

For customers at the age of 22–35 and marriage bond existed between the policy holder and the insured, according to experiences, it is known such couple are not married for a long time. Such customers are potential customers of children insurance. Data mining analysis using Apriori algorithm of MapReduce can screen the potential customers. Database is implemented and computed using MapReduce model of such algorithm. The MapReduce model is described as below:

Map: (Row_ID, Transaction) list(Itemset, $V_1 = 1$)
Reduce: (Itemset, List (V_1)) (Itemset Sum(V_1))

Apriori algorithm is originality algorithm of frequent item set mined according to Boole association rules. The main thought is to find frequent k item set (fail to continue finding k + 1 item set) using iterative method of layer-by-layer searching. According to frequent k item set, produce strong association rule and compute confidence coefficient (confidence coefficient: certainty of rule occurrence). The algorithm is as below:

Algorithm Apriori

Input: Transaction DataBase D. Minimum support threshold min_sup .
Output: Frequent pattern L
1: L_1=search_frequent_1_itemsets(D);
2: **for**($k = 2; L_{k-1} \neq \varnothing; k++$) {
3:   $C_k = aproiri\_gen(L_{k-1})$;
4: **for each** transactions $t \in D$ {
5:     $C_t = subset(C_k, t)$;
5: **for each** candidates $c \in C_t$
6:       $c.count++$;
7: }
8:   $L_k = \{c\,C_k \mid c.count \geq \min\_sup\}$
9: }
9: **Return** $L = \bigcup_k L_k$;

Procedure apriori_gen(sssss L_{k-1} : $frequent(k-1)$ itemset)
1:   **for each** itemset $l_1 \in L_k$ $_{SSS}$
2:   **for each** itemset $l_2 \in L_k$
3:     **if** $(l_1[1] = l_2[1]) \wedge \ldots \wedge (l_1[k-2] = l_2[k-2]) \wedge (l_1[k-1] < l_2[k-2])$
     then {
4:       $c = l_1 l_2$;
5:     **if has_infrequent_subset**(c, L_{k-1}) **then**
6:         **delete** c ;
7:     **else add** c **to** C_k ;
8: }
9:   **return** C_k ;

Procedure has_infrequent_subset(c , candidate k itemset ; L_{k-1} : frequent(k-1) itemset)
1:   **for each** $(k-1)$subset s of c
2:   **if** $s \notin L_{k-1}$ **then**
3:     **return TURE**;
4: **return FALSE** ;

Combining Apriori algorithm with actual situation, the author summarizes the purchase phenomenon of customers at the age of 20–35 on Branch A. The mining result of association rule is shown in the following figure:

According to the data, it is known customers at the age of 20–35 pay more attention to accidental injury. Meanwhile, whatever the customer effect the insurance for spouse or himself, more than 50% of them buy children insurance for his children. It indicates that young customer has strong insurance sense and is capable of purchasing insurance for children (Table 2).

Table 2. The result of the association rule mining

No.	Rule description	Confidence coefficient %
1	Relation = spouse, type of insurance = accidental injury => type of insurance = children insurance	60.1
2	Relation = oneself, type of insurance = accidental injury => type of insurance = children insurance	49.7
3	Relation = spouse, type of insurance = critical illness => type of insurance = children insurance	59.4
4	Relation = oneself, type of insurance = critical illness => type of insurance = children insurance	50.5
5	Relation = oneself => type of insurance = critical illness	40.9
6	Relation = oneself => type of insurance = accidental injury	59.1
7	Relation = spouse => type of insurance = critical illness	43.3
8	Relation = spouse => type of insurance = accidental injury	56.7

Similarly, for group insurance system, according to the age structure, sex ratio and recruitment practice of the insurance application unit and loss situation at present, loss phenomenon in the future 5 years can be calculated. Thus, insurance company can forecast capital budget and human input, which provides powerful guarantee for decision in the future.

3.3   System Performance Test

When the data size is different, the author returns 30,000 items of specific data and compared time used by Oracle database and distributed cluster. In this way, the difference between distributed system performance and traditional database system performance was compared. The test result was shown in the following Fig. 6:

3.4   Subsequent Promotion of Platform

Insurance data platform based on Hadoop frame provides mass data enquiry and index analysis, which provides convenience for manager and decider of insurance industry. With social development, it is not enough for insurance data platform only providing

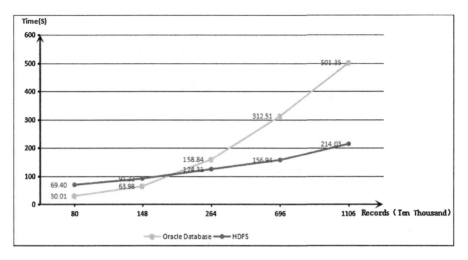

Fig. 6. The test result

data enquiry function. thus, it is necessary to carry out more research according to the characteristic of Hadoop frame.

According to the function difference of user, more data research and exploration should be done through the platform. Combined with lecturer in marketing department and the market experience of salesperson, product development is carried out through data analysis so as to push product according to the demand of different groups. Through combining with external data of medical insurance, the platform can market accurately, as well as avoiding customer loss. Model library establishment can help insurance company and supervisory agency to find illegal behavior earlier, such as money laundering so as to avoid the occurrence of delinquency.

4   Conclusion

With economic development of increasing enhancement of living level, people pay more attention to health and property safety. Meanwhile, according to the online and surrounding cases, more people purchase insurance to guarantee the health and property safety so as to reduce loss.

Based on characteristic of Hadoop frame, the paper analyzes its application in insurance industry. With the development of Internet, intelligence analysis appears very important. Finding "relation" in the mass data and making rational use of it provide great help for insurance company. Future is unpredictable, while the platform based on big data and Hadoop frame can provide relatively accurate prediction analysis for insurance company so that the insurance company can master the market quotation earlier and create more profit and benefit.

References

1. Apache: Hadoop: Open Source Implementation of MapReduce. http://hadoop.apache.org/
2. Yuanqi, C., Yi, Z., Shubbhi, T., Xiao, Q., Jianzhong, H.: aHDFS: an erasure-coded data archival system for Hadoop clusters. IEEE Trans. Parallel Distrib. Syst. **PP**(99), 1 (2017)
3. Yanfei, G., Jia, R., Dazhao, C., Xiaobo, Z.: iShuffle: improving Hadoop performance with shuffle-on-write. IEEE Trans. Parallel Distrib. Syst. **28**(6), 1649–1662 (2017)
4. Akash, H., Kiran, B.: A MapReduce based approach for classification. In: 2016 Online International Conference on Green Engineering and Technologies (IC-GET), pp. 1–5. IEEE Press, Coimbatore (2016)
5. Jeffrey, D., Sanjay, G.: MapReduce: simplified data processing on large clusters. In: Proceedings of the 6th Conference on Symposium on Operating Systems Design and Implementation, p. 10 (2004)
6. Manjunath, R., Tejus, Channabasava, R.K., Balaji, S.: A big data MapReduce Hadoop distribution architecture for processing input splits to solve the small data problem. In: 2016 2nd International Conference on Applied and Theoretical Computing and Communication Technology (iCATccT), Bangalore, pp. 480–487 (2016)
7. Frank, P., Johannes, G., David, B.: Pick your choice in HBase: security or performance. In: 2016 IEEE International Conference on Big Data (Big Data), Washington, D.C., pp. 548–554 (2016)

SNR Analysis of the Millimeter Wave MIMO with Lens Antenna Array

Min Zhang[1(✉)], Jianxin Dai[2], Chonghu Cheng[1], and Zhiliang Huang[3]

[1] College of Telecommunications & Information Engineering,
Nanjing University of Posts and Telecommunications, Nanjing 210003, China
2810729610@qq.com, chengch@njupt.edu.cn
[2] School of Science, Nanjing University of Posts and Telecommunications,
Nanjing 210023, China
daijx@njupt.edu.cn
[3] College of Mathematics, Physics and Information Engineering,
Zhejiang Normal University, Jinhua 321004, China
zlhuang@zjnu.cn

Abstract. The lens antenna array is typically composed of an electromagnetic (EM) lens and has elements in the focal area of the lens in order to achieve its large antenna gain. In this paper, we first analyze the response model of the lens antenna array, and conclude that the model follows the "sinc" function. The lens array is then applied to a MIMO system that allows millimeter-wave input and the use of new path-division multiplexing. On this basis, we model the channel of the system to derive the channel impulse response, which follows the "sinc sinc" function. Finally, the beamforming process is performed at the receiving end to obtain the received signal, and the signal-to-noise ratio expression is analyzed and optimized to obtain the maximum signal-to-noise ratio (SNR) of the system and the system performance is simulated.

Keywords: Millimeter wave · Lens antenna array · Signal-to-noise ratio
Path-division multiplexing · AoA/AoD

1 Introduction

According to the development law of mobile communication, 5G will be better than 4G mobile communication in terms of transmission rate and resource utilization. Nowadays, 5G has become a research hotspot in the field of mobile communication at home and abroad.

(1) On May 29, 2015, Coolpad first mentioned 5G new concept: terminal base station.
(2) On June 24, 2015, the International Telecommunication Union (ITU) announced a timetable for the 5G technical standardization. The official name of the 5G technology is IMT-2020 and the 5G standard will be finalized by 2020.
(3) On January 7, 2016, the Ministry of Industry held a meeting announcing the "5G technology research and development test".

© ICST Institute for Computer Sciences, Social Informatics and Telecommunications Engineering 2018
X. Gu et al. (Eds.): MLICOM 2017, Part I, LNICST 226, pp. 505–515, 2018.
https://doi.org/10.1007/978-3-319-73564-1_50

(4) On February 9, 2017, the international communications standards organization 3GPP announced the "5G" official Logo.

However, the low frequency of the radio spectrum has become saturated because of the rapid development of communication industry, so the future development needs can not be met, which leads people to seek higher spectrum. Millimeter wave has the characteristics of short wavelength and wide frequency band, having the ability to solve many problems faced by future development of communication. Also it has a wide range of applications in short distance communication. For traditional communication systems, Multiple Input Multiple Output (MIMO) technology can increase the spectrum utilization to a great extent, making the system transmit higher-speed data services in a limited wireless band. With the development of technology, the future of 5G communication broadband or wireless access integration system has become a popular research topic, and MIMO system is one of the more people to study the direction [1–5]. The MmWave signal typically suffers from more path losses than frequencies that are much lower at a given distance at an existing cellular system. So efficient MIMO technology can be used to compensate for severe path losses, which achieves highly directional communication [6–9]. The general MIMO processing is usually digitally realized at the baseband, so a special radio frequency (RF) chain is set for communication. However, in the mmWave system, we generally do not take this approach because a large number of RF chain hardware costs are relatively large. In order to realize spatial reuse, hybrid analog/digital precoding has been proposed, in which precoding is implemented in two phases. Due to the need of many phase shifters in the case of hybrid precoding, it is also proposed to select the subset of antennas by using the switch instead of the phase shifter. However, because of the limited array gain, antenna selection can lead to significant performance degradation [10–14]. In our study, the mmWave MIMO communications is analyzed, where a lens antenna array is applied in the transmitter and receiver. Because of the energy focusing characteristics of AoA/AoD, the signal power in the mmWave lens MIMO with a limited number of multipath is usually concentrated only on the small set of the receiver/transmitter antenna elements.

The following structure of the article is described below: the system model is introduced in the second section. The third section mainly analyzes the SNR ratio. The fourth section shows the numerical simulation results. The fifth section is the summary of the full paper.

2 System Model

2.1 Analysis of Lens Antenna Array

In optics, the spherical wave radiated by a point light source placed on the focal point of a lens is refracted into a plane wave by refraction of a lens. The lens antenna is made by this principle. Figure 1 shows the configuration of the lens antenna array. It is easy to see that the array element happens to be located in the focal region of the lens. In generally, EM lens can be realized through some techniques,such as a conventional planar lens composed of transmit and receive antenna arrays with variable length transmission lines. No matter what the actual realization, the fundamental of the EM lens is to offer a variable phase shift to the EM rays of the lens, with the aim of achieving the energy focusing properties depending on the angle. In particular, the receiving lens antenna array can be used to focus the incident signal to a plurality of receiving antenna subsets with sufficient separation angle of arrival (AoA). Similarly, the emission lens array can be used to manipulate the deviation signal from a subset of different transmit antennas with a sufficient separation of the angle of departure (AoD) [15].

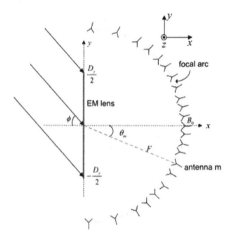

Fig. 1. An example of a lens receiving a plane wave incident.

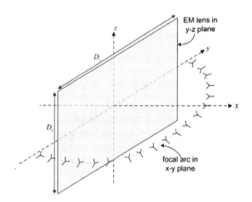

Fig. 2. A stereogram of a lens antenna array.

In this paper, we placed a plane EM lens on the yz plane, making it centered on the origin. Its size is Dy × Dz, which can be neglected, as exhibited in Fig. 2. Only taking the azimuth angles AoA and AoD into consideration, in Fig. 1, it is assumed that the array element is set on a semicircle around the center of a lens in a plane. The semicircle has a radius of F, which is called the focal length of the lens. Thus, the antenna position of the lens antenna array can be mathematically expressed as B_m $(x_m = F \cos \theta_m, y_m = -F \sin \theta_m, z_m = 0)$, where $\theta_m \in [-\pi/2, \pi/2]$ is the m-th antenna element's angle with respect to the x-axis, $m \in M$, and M represents the total number of antennas using in the lens antenna array. For convenience, we assume that M is odd. In addition, we assume that the antenna has a critical antenna spacing, for example, the antenna element is deployed on the coke arc, making $\{\tilde{\theta}_m \triangleq \sin \theta_m\}$ in the interval $[-1,1]$ equally spaced, i.e. $\tilde{\theta}_m = \frac{m}{\tilde{D}}, m \in M$, where $\tilde{D} = \frac{D_y}{\lambda}$ is the size of the lens in antenna array and normalized by the carrier wavelength λ. Besides, M and $\tilde{D}$ are satisfied $M = 1 + \lfloor 2\tilde{D} \rfloor$, i.e., for larger lens sizes $\tilde{D}$, more antennas should be deployed. Naturally, with the specified deployment of the antenna array, the number of antennas at the two edges of the array is less than that in the center.

First of all, let us assume that the lens antenna array is irradiated with a uniform plane wave with AoA ϕ to study the reception array response, as shown in Fig. 1. $x_o(\phi)$ represents an incident signal whose point of incidence is located on the reference point on the lens (for example, the center of the lens), and $r_m(\phi)$ represents the receiving signal by the m-th element [15], $m \in M$. In addition, the response vector of the array is $a(\phi) \in C^{M \times 1}$, whose element $a_m(\phi) = \frac{r_m(\phi)}{x_o(\phi)}$ can be shown as

$$a_m(\phi) \approx e^{-j\phi_o} \sqrt{A} \sin c(m - \tilde{D}\tilde{\phi}), m \in M \tag{1}$$

where ϕ is the angle of arrival (AoA), $A \triangleq D_y D_z / \lambda^2$ is the normalized aperture, i.e., the physical area of the EM lens normalized by wavelength squares, ϕ_0 is the common phase shift from the lens aperture to the array [15], and $\tilde{\phi} \triangleq \sin \phi \in [-1, 1]$ is called the spatial frequency corresponding to AoA ϕ.

Without loss of generality, for an integer n in the remainder of the text, we have $\phi_o = 2n\pi$, making it possible to ignore the phase term in (1), thus the expression (1) becomes

$$a_m(\phi) = \sqrt{A} \sin c(m - \tilde{D}\tilde{\phi}), m \in M \tag{2}$$

As we all know, the incident and outgoing signals passing through the EM lens remain interchangeable because the EM lenses are passive devices. Therefore, the transmission response vector that turns the signal to AoD ϕ can be obtained in the same way. The details are omitted for simplicity.

2.2   Analysis of Channel Model

In this section, a special MIMO transceiver that based on Path Division Multiplexing (PDM) is designed, which is suitable for narrowband and broadband mmWave communication. Using PDM, L independent data streams are typically transmitted via transmit beamforming/precoding, each of which passes through one of the

L multi-paths. In particular, the discrete time equivalent of the transmitted signal $x_{Qs}[t]$ may be expressed as

$$x_{Qs}[n] = \sum_{l=1}^{L} \sqrt{\frac{p_l}{A_T}} a_{T,Qs}(\phi_{T,l}) s_l[n] \tag{3}$$

where n represents the symbol index, $s_l[n] \sim CN(0, 1)$ (circle symmetric complex Gaussian) represents the independent CSCG distributed information bearing symbol with the transmit power p_l for the data stream; and $a_{T,Qs}(\phi_{T,l})/A_T$ represents the unit norm of the AoD $\phi_{T,l}$ towards path l per path MRT beamforming vector. Note that we use $\left\| a_{T,Qs}(\phi_{T,l}) \right\|^2 \approx \left\| a_T(\phi_{T,l}) \right\|^2 = A_T, \forall l$. At the receiving end, we apply a low complexity detection to the receive signal, where the beamforming vector $v_l \in C^{M_S \times 1}$ is received and $\|v_l\| = 1$.

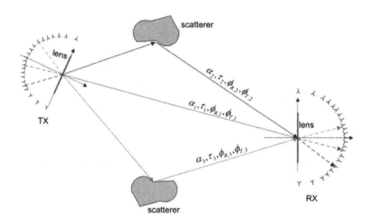

Fig. 3. The schematic diagram of multi-path environment.

As shown in the Fig. 3, at the transmitter and receiver, we set Q and M antenna elements. In a typical MIMO system, the channel impulse response can be represented as

$$H(t) = \sum_{l=1}^{L} \alpha_l a_R(\phi_{R,l}) a_T^H(\phi_{T,l}) \delta(t - \tau_l) \tag{4}$$

The signal at the receiving end is

$$r(t) = H(t) * x(t) + z(t) \tag{5}$$

$$r(t) = \sum_{l=1}^{L} \alpha_l a_R(\phi_{R,l}) a_T^H(\phi_{T,l}) x(t - \tau_l) + z(t) \tag{6}$$

However, because there is multipath sparsity in mmWave communication, the discrete received signal at the receiving end in this system is expressed as

$$r_{Ms}[n] = \sum_{k=1}^{L} \alpha_k a_{R,k} a_{T,k}^H x_{Qs}[n - n_k] + z_{Ms}[n] \tag{7}$$

where each component is a subset of the components in the expression (6).

We decompose the received signal in the expression (7) into the desired signal passing through the l-th path, which has the symbol delay nl; the ISI from the other $L - 1$ paths, which have different delays; and the other $L - 1$ data streams interference from the L signal paths, which are as the expression (8) [15].

$$r_{Ms}[n] = \sqrt{p_l A_T} \alpha_l a_{R,l} s_l[n - n_l] + \sum_{k \neq l}^{L} \sqrt{\frac{p_l}{A_T}} \alpha_k a_{R,k} a_{T,k}^H a_{T,l} s_l[n - n_k]$$
$$+ \sum_{l' \neq l}^{L} \sum_{k=1}^{L} \sqrt{\frac{p_{l'}}{A_T}} \alpha_k a_{R,k} a_{T,k}^H a_{T,l'} s_{l'}[n - n_k] + z_{Ms}[n] \tag{8}$$

The receiver beamforming is applied in the above equation [20, 21], besides, ISI together with inter-stream interference are treated as interference [16–18]. Thus the effective SNR of the l-th data stream at the receiver is shown as

$$\gamma_l = \frac{p_l A_T |\alpha_l|^2 |v_l^H a_{R,l}|^2}{\sum_{k \neq l}^{L} \frac{p_l}{A_T} |\alpha_k|^2 |v_l^H a_{R,k}|^2 |a_{T,k}^H a_{T,l}|^2 + \sum_{l' \neq l}^{L} \sum_{k=1}^{L} \frac{p_{l'}}{A_T} |\alpha_k|^2 |v_l^H a_{R,k}|^2 |a_{T,k}^H a_{T,l'}|^2 + v_l^H \sigma^2 v_l} \tag{9}$$

3 Analysis and Optimization

SNR is a measure of communication system communication quality reliability of a major technical indicator. The SNR is generally the ratio of the channel output, that is, the average power of the carrier signal at the receiver input to that of the noise in the channel. It can also be called a carrier to noise ratio. Increasing or improving signal-to-noise ratio is a major task in improving communication quality. In the following, we will optimize the SNR expression in (9) to obtain the maximum signal-to-noise ratio of the millimeter wave MIMO system.

The part of the beamforming vector is split into

$$\gamma_l = \frac{p_l A_T |\alpha_l|^2 v_l^H a_{R,l} a_{R,l}^H v_l}{\sum_{k \neq l}^{L} \frac{p_l}{A_T} |\alpha_k|^2 v_l^H a_{R,k} a_{R,k}^H v_l |a_{T,k}^H a_{T,l}|^2 + \sum_{l' \neq l}^{L} \sum_{k=1}^{L} \frac{p_{l'}}{A_T} |\alpha_k|^2 v_l^H a_{R,k} a_{R,k}^H v_l |a_{T,k}^H a_{T,l'}|^2 + v_l^H \sigma^2 v_l} \tag{10}$$

Extracting the beamforming vector, then we get

$$\gamma_l = \frac{v_l^H p_l A_T |\alpha_l|^2 a_{R,l} a_{R,l}^H v_l}{v_l^H \left(\sum_{k \neq l}^{L} \frac{p_l}{A_T} |\alpha_k|^2 a_{R,k} a_{R,k}^H \left| a_{T,k}^H a_{T,l} \right|^2 + \sum_{l' \neq l}^{L} \sum_{k=1}^{L} \frac{p_{l'}}{A_T} |\alpha_k|^2 a_{R,k} a_{R,k}^H \left| a_{T,k}^H a_{T,l'} \right|^2 + \sigma^2 I \right) v_l} \tag{11}$$

Let $A = p_l A_T |\alpha_l|^2 a_{R,l} a_{R,l}^H$, which is a $Ms \times Ms$ order matrix; $B = \sum_{k \neq l}^{L} \frac{p_l}{A_T} |\alpha_k|^2 a_{R,k} a_{R,k}^H \left| a_{T,k}^H a_{T,l} \right|^2 + \sum_{l' \neq l}^{L} \sum_{k=1}^{L} \frac{p_{l'}}{A_T} |\alpha_k|^2 a_{R,k} a_{R,k}^H \left| a_{T,k}^H a_{T,l'} \right|^2 + \sigma^2 I$, which is a $Ms \times Ms$ order matrix.

Then,

$$\gamma_l = \frac{v_l^H A v_l}{v_l^H B v_l} \tag{12}$$

Derive the expression (12)

$$\gamma_l' = \frac{A v_l v_l^H B v_l - B v_l v_l^H A v_l}{\left(v_l^H B v_l \right)^2} \tag{13}$$

Let the expression (13) be equal to 0,

$$A v_l v_l^H B v_l = B v_l v_l^H A v_l \tag{14}$$

Rearranging the equation, we get

$$A v_l = \frac{v_l^H A v_l}{v_l^H B v_l} B v_l \tag{15}$$

Therefore,

$$A v_l = \gamma_l B v_l \tag{16}$$

$$B^{-1} A v_l = \gamma_l v_l \tag{17}$$

Hence, the maximum value of the SNR ratio γ_l is the maximum eigenvalue of $B^{-1}A$, and the beamforming vector at this time is the eigenvector corresponding to the largest eigenvalue of $B^{-1}A$ [19–21].

4 Simulation and Results

In this section, MATLAB is utilized to simulate the performance of a MIMO system which uses the proposed lens antenna array and allows millimeter-wave input. It is assumed that the lens apertures are AT = 100 and AR = 50 respectively at the transmitter and receiver. The input mmWave frequency is 73 GHz. And also azimuthal lens sizes at the transmitter and receiver are $\tilde{D}_T = 20$ and $\tilde{D}_R = 10$ respectively. For simplicity, here we assume all path power pl ($l = 1, \ldots L$) is evenly distributed.

The maximum signal-to-noise ratio of the system has been given in the paper. Here we give different system configurations. And the performance of the system is simulated and compared based on these configurations. The comparison of system performance under these different configurations will help us to further study the millimeter-wave MIMO communication.

Figure 4 shows the variation of the maximum SNR ratio versus the multipath number in different number of antenna configurations at the receiving and transmitting ends. Here are three cases where the number of antennas at the transmitting and receiving ends is 31 and 51, 21 and 41 respectively, and both are 41. Obviously, with the increase of the number of multipaths, the maximum SNR ratio at the receiver decreases, that is, the performance of the system decreases and the trend slows down. In the case of a certain number of multipaths, when the number of antennas at the transmitting end is larger than that of antennas on the receiving side, the system performance is the best. As can be seen from the Fig. 4, when the number of transmit antennas and antennas on the receiving side are 41 and 21, the maximum SNR ratio is greater than the other two configurations. While the system performance is the worst when the number of transmit antennas is less than that of antennas on the receiving side. The maximum SNR ratio is smaller when the number of antennas on the receiving side are 31 and 51, as is shown in Fig. 4.

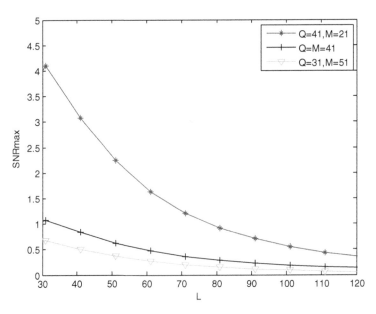

Fig. 4. The maximum signal-to-noise ratio versus the number of multipath under different numbers of antennas at the receiver and transmitter.

Figure 5 depicts curve of the maximum SNR versus the number of multipath at different spatial frequencies. When the multipath number is the same, the larger the spatial frequency interval of the antenna, the better the performance of the system. It can be seen that the curve of the maximum signal-to-noise ratio is more and more upward when the spatial interval changes from [−0.25, 0.25], [−0.5, 0.5] to [−0.7, 0.7]. And the maximum SNR ratio of the system with the spatial interval [−0.7, 0.7] is the largest when the multipath number L is fixed.

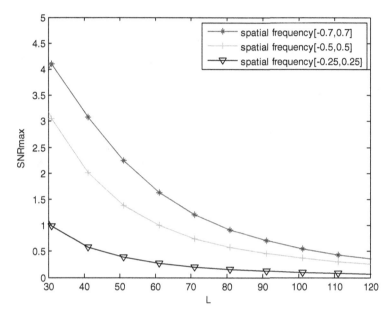

Fig. 5. The maximum signal-to-noise ratio versus the number of multipath at different spatial frequencies.

5 Conclusion

As the key technology of 5G, millimeter wave has become one of the hotspots of current research. In this paper, a millimeter-wave MIMO system model based on lens array is established, and a new path segmentation technique is used to analyze the SNR of the system. In communication systems, the signal power often needs to be increased as much as possible while suppressing noise and various disturbances within the system. The maximum SNR expression of millimeter-wave MIMO system is deduced theoretically in this paper. Based on the maximum SNR expression, the performance of a lens MIMO system with mmWave input is evaluated by simulation and we can easily find with the increase in the number of multipath, the maximum SNR is gradually reduced. Besides, the maximum SNR is important for us to study the performance of millimeter-wave MIMO systems and to lay the foundation for further research.

Acknowledgments. The research was supported in part by Postdoctoral Research Funding Plan in Jiangsu Province (Grant No. 1501073B), Natural Science Foundation of Nanjing University of Posts and Telecommunications (Grant No. NY214108), Natural Science Foundation of China (NSFC) (Grant No. 61401399), and the Open Research Fund of National Mobile Communications Research Laboratory, Southeast University (Grant No. 2016D05).

References

1. Ma, J., Li, H., Zhang, S., Zhao, N., Nallanathan, A.: Pattern division for massive MIMO networks with two-stage precoding. IEEE Commun. Lett. **21**(7), 1665–1668 (2017)
2. Xie, H., Gao, F., Zhang, S., Jin, S.: A unified transmission strategy for TDD/FDD massive MIMO systems with spatial basis expansion model. IEEE Trans. Veh. Technol. **66**(4), 3170–3184 (2017)
3. Xie, H., Gao, F., Jin, S.: An overview of low-rank channel estimation for massive MIMO systems. IEEE Access **4**, 7313–7321 (2016)
4. Xie, H., Wang, B., Gao, F., Jin, S.: A full-space spectrum-sharing strategy for massive MIMO cognitive radio. IEEE J. Sel. Areas Commun. **34**(10), 2537–2549 (2016)
5. Wang, J.-B., Chen, M., Wan, X., Wei, J.: Ant-colony-optimization-based scheduling algorithm for uplink CDMA nonreal-time data. IEEE Trans. Veh. Technol. **58**(1), 231–241 (2009)
6. Agrawal, S.K., Sharma, K.: 5G millimeter wave (mmWave) communications. In: 2016 3rd International Conference on Computing for Sustainable Global Development (INDIACom), New Delhi, pp. 3630–3634 (2016)
7. Zhang, J., Ge, X., Li, Q., Guizani, M., Zhang, Y.: 5G millimeter-wave antenna array: design and challenges. IEEE Wirel. Commun. **PP**(99), 2–8
8. Luo, F.-L., Zhang, C.: 5G millimeter-wave communication channel and technology overview. In: Signal Processing for 5G: Algorithms and Implementations, vol. 1, p. 616. Wiley-IEEE Press (2016)
9. Rangan, S., Rappaport, T.S., Erkip, E.: Millimeter-wave cellular wireless networks: potentials and challenges. Proc. IEEE **102**(3), 366–385 (2014)
10. Jing, J., Xiaoxue, C., Yongbin, X.: Energy-efficiency based downlink multi-user hybrid beamforming for millimeter wave massive MIMO system. J. China Univ. Posts Telecommun. **23**(4), 53–62 (2016)
11. Wang, J.-B., Qing-Song, H., Wang, J., Chen, M., Wang, J.-Y.: Tight bounds on channel capacity for dimmable visible light communications. IEEE/OSA J. Lightwave Technol. **31**(23), 3771–3779 (2013)
12. Wang, J.-Y., Wang, J.-B., Chen, M., Tang, Y., Zhang, Y.: Outage analysis for relay-aided free-space optical communications over turbulence channels with nonzero boresight pointing errors. IEEE Photonics J. **6**(4), 1–15 (2014)
13. Samimi, M.K., Sun, S., Rappaport, T.S.: MIMO channel modeling and capacity analysis for 5G millimeter-wave wireless systems. In: 2016 10th European Conference on Antennas and Propagation (EuCAP), Davos, pp. 1–5 (2016)
14. Rappaport, T.S., MacCartney, G.R., Samimi, M.K., Sun, S.: Wideband millimeter-wave propagation measurements and channel models for future wireless communication system design. IEEE Trans. Commun. **63**(9), 3029–3056 (2015)
15. Zeng, Y., Zhang, R.: Millimeter wave MIMO with lens antenna array: a new path division multiplexing paradigm. IEEE Trans. Commun. **64**(4), 1557–1571 (2016)

16. Liu, L., Matolak, D.W., Tao, C., Li, Y., Ai, B., Chen, H.: Channel capacity investigation of a linear massive MIMO system using spherical wave model in LOS scenarios. Sci. China Inf. Sci. **59**(2), 45–59 (2016)
17. Jin-Yuan, W., Jun-Bo, W., Nuo, H., Ming, C.: Capacity analysis for pulse amplitude modulated visible light communications with dimming control. J. Opt. Soc. Am. A **31**(3), 561–568 (2014)
18. Ali, S., Aslam, M.I., Ahmed, I.: MIMO channel modeling and capacity analysis using 3-D spatial statistical channel model for millimeter wave outdoor communication. In: 2017 14th International Bhurban Conference on Applied Sciences and Technology (IBCAST), Islamabad, pp. 735–740 (2017)
19. Samimi, M.K., Sun, S., Rappaport, T.S.: MIMO channel modeling and capacity analysis for 5G millimeter-wave wireless systems. In: 2016 10th European Conference on Antennas and Propagation (EuCAP), Davos, pp. 1–5 (2016)
20. Kamga, G.N., Xia, M., Aissa, S.: Channel modeling and capacity analysis of large MIMO in real propagation environments. In: 2015 IEEE International Conference on Communications (ICC), London, pp. 1447–1452 (2015)
21. Wang, J.-B., Su, Q., Wang, J., Feng, M., Chen, M., Jiang, B., Wang, J.-Y.: Imperfect CSI based joint resource allocation in multirelay OFDMA networks. IEEE Trans. Veh. Technol. **63**(8), 3806–3817 (2014)
22. Zhao, N., Yu, F.R., Leung, V.C.M.: Opportunistic communications in interference alignment networks with wireless power transfer. IEEE Wirel. Commun. **22**(1), 88–95 (2015)

Cross-Entropy Optimization Oriented Antenna Selection for Clustering Management in Multiuser MIMO Networks

Xinyu Zhang, Jing Guo, Qiuyi Cao, and Nan Zhao[✉]

School of Information and Communication Engineering,
Dalian University of Technology, Dalian 116024, China
{xinyuzhang,guojing94}@mail.dlut.edu.cn, cccqiu_yi@163.com,
zhaonan@dlut.edu.cn

Abstract. In this paper, antenna selection (AS) is considered for clustering management (CM) to improve the spectrum efficiency of asymmetric interference networks. Through the proposed CM scheme, the whole network can be divided into several clusters, which will lead to a relative redundance of antenna resource for each interference alignment (IA) pair in the IA cluster. Therefore, the AS technique is adopted to improve the performance through selecting the optimal antenna combination for IA pairs. Considering the high computational complexity of the exhaustive search (ES) AS method, the cross-entropy optimization (CEO) algorithm is used to perform the IA technique, which can achieve relatively high performance with low computational complexity. From the simulation results, we can find that the proposed AS method in clustering management can further enhance the performance of the IA-based network.

Keywords: Antenna selection · Cross-entropy optimization
Clustering management · Interference alignment

1 Introduction

As a novel interference management method, interference alignment (IA) has been proposed by Jafar in 2008 [1,2]. For the IA technique, the interference from different transmitters is constrained into a low dimensional vector-space at each receiver, and then the desired signal can be retrieved according to the remaining interference-free vector space. Recently, there is a great increase of research interest in IA, and it has been applied to all kinds of multiuser networks [3–7].

In most of existing IA-based researches, the network topology is assumed to be symmetric, which is difficult to be satisfied in practical wireless networks. Therefore, the asymmetric model of interference network is introduced into IA research recently [8–10]. In [9], authors expanded the idea of clustered IA proposed in [8] into the IA network. According to the distance information between

© ICST Institute for Computer Sciences, Social Informatics and Telecommunications Engineering 2018
X. Gu et al. (Eds.): MLICOM 2017, Part I, LNICST 226, pp. 516–523, 2018.
https://doi.org/10.1007/978-3-319-73564-1_51

pairs, the proposed topology management scheme in [9] can divide the whole network into one IA subnetwork and several spatial multiplexing (SM) subnetworks to improve the performance in the low and moderate signal-to-noise ratio (SNR) range. In [10], the resource management of [9] was further researched.

After performing topology management in the asymmetric interference network, antenna resource will be relatively redundant in the IA subnetwork [9]. Hence, the antenna selection (AS) technique can be applied in the IA subnetwork to select the optimal antenna combination to further improve the performance under the IA feasibility condition, which is a kind of methods based on opportunistic communications [11]. As known, the AS technique can provide selection gain and improve received SNR with simple and cheap hardware architecture, which has been successfully applied in several multi-input and multi-output (MIMO) systems [12–15]. In [12], Sanayei et al. presented an overview of the application of antenna selection in MIMO systems. Through two types of antenna selection, i.e., transmit and receive antenna selection, the received SNR and system capacity can be effectively improved. In [13], the AS technique was introduced into IA-based wireless networks. The performance of interference wireless networks was evaluated under several antenna selection criteria. Three suboptimal selection algorithms were proposed to achieve an acceptable performance with low computational complexity. In [14], Li et al. investigated the antenna selection problem in the IA-based cognitive radio network. The proposed antenna selection IA algorithm based on discrete stochastic optimization can achieve high performance with low computational complexity. In [15], the antenna switching based on reconfigurable antennas was utilized for IA networks.

Although the optimal antenna combination can be easily selected through the ES-based AS method, the high computational complexity makes it unpractical. Therefore, the cross-entropy optimization (CEO) method [16], which is an increasingly popular method to solving difficult combinatorial optimization problems, has been adopted to optimize the AS problem in MIMO systems [17,18]. In [17], a novel receive AS algorithm based on cross-entropy optimization was proposed to improve the capacity of MIMO systems over spatially correlated channel. Simulation results show that the proposed algorithm can achieve the optimal or near-optimal capacity with low computational complexity. In [18], Ali et al. introduced the CEO method into the IA-based network based on maximizing the minimum signal-to-interference plus noise ratio (SINR) metric. The proposed algorithm can effectively improve the bit-error-rate (BER) of the system.

In the paper, the CEO method is used to perform the AS technique to further improve the spectrum efficiency for the clustering management (CM) scheme of multiuser interference network. The rest of the paper is organized as follows. In Sect. 2, clustering management scheme is presented. Then, the cross-entropy optimization method in the CM scheme is introduced in Sect. 3. Section 4 discusses the simulation result. In Sect. 5, we conclude this paper.

2   Clustering Management Scheme

In this section, we consider the asymmetric interference network with K users as shown in Fig. 1, where $M^{[k]}$ and $N^{[k]}$ antennas are equipped at the k-th transmitter and its corresponding receiver, respectively. The received signal at the k-th Rx can be denoted as

$$\mathbf{y}^{[k]} = \sqrt{\rho^{[kk]}}\mathbf{U}^{[k]\dagger}\mathbf{H}^{[kk]}\mathbf{V}^{[k]}\mathbf{x}^{[k]} + \sum_{j=1,j\neq k}^{K}\sqrt{\rho^{[kj]}}\mathbf{U}^{[k]\dagger}\mathbf{H}^{[kj]}\mathbf{V}^{j}\mathbf{x}^{[j]} + \mathbf{U}^{[k]\dagger}\mathbf{z}^{[k]}. \quad (1)$$

where $\mathbf{H}^{[kj]} \in \mathbb{C}^{N^{[k]}\times M^{[j]}}$ is the small-scale fading gain matrix from the j-th Tx to the k-th Rx, whose entity is i.i.d. with the complex Gaussian distribution $\mathcal{CN}(0,1)$. The matrix $\mathbf{V}^{[j]} \in \mathbb{C}^{M^j \times d^{[j]}}$ is the precoding matrix of the k-th Tx, and the matrix $\mathbf{U}^{[k]} \in \mathbb{C}^{N^k \times d^{[k]}}$ is the decoding matrix of the k-th Tx. The transmitted signal $\mathbf{x}^{[k]}$ from the k-th Tx to k-th Rx satisfies a equal power constraint P_t, i.e., $\mathbf{E}\left[||\mathbf{x}^{[k]}||^2\right] = P_t^{[k]} = P_t$. $\mathbf{z}^{[k]} \in \mathbb{C}^{N^k \times 1}$ denotes the additive Gaussian noise with distribution $\mathcal{CN}(0,\sigma\mathbf{I}_{N^k})$. The lager-scale fading gain from the j-th Tx to the k-th Rx $\rho^{[kj]}$ can be given as

$$\rho^{[ji]} = \left(r^{[kj]}\right)^{-\alpha}. \quad (2)$$

where $r^{[kj]}$ expresses the distance between the j-th Tx and the k-th Rx, and α is the path-loss exponent, which is determined by different wireless environment.

In a feasible IA-based network satisfying the condition, i.e., $M + N = d(K + 1)$, after performing the proposed CM scheme in [9], the whole network will be divided into several cluster as shown in Fig. 1, including one IA cluster and several SM clusters. Those pairs close to each other jointly comprise one IA cluster (the set $\mathcal{A}$), where the strong inner-interference among IA pairs is eliminated through linear IA and the weak inter-cluster interference is treated as noise. On the other hand, those pair far away others will act as some SM clusters independently (belonging to the set $\mathcal{S}$), in which the SM scheme is adopted and the weak inter-subnetwork interference is also treated as noise.

For the convenience of analysis, we assume that each pair has the same antenna configuration, i.e., $M^{[k]} = M, N^{[k]} = N, \forall k \in \{1, 2, \ldots, K\}$. Besides, the number of the transmitted data stream of each IA pair is set to $d^{[k]} = d, k \in \mathcal{A}$, and the number of the transmitted data stream of each SM pair is set to $d^{[k]} = \hat{d}, k \in \mathcal{S}$.

3   Cross-Entropy Optimization Method

In this section, we will first present the AS problem in the CM scheme. Then, antenna selection based on cross entropy optimization method will be presented to improve the performance.

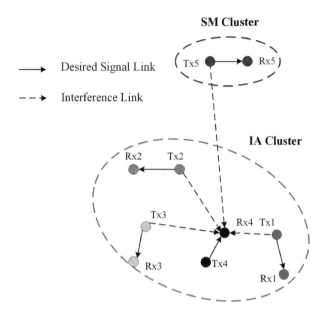

Fig. 1. A K-pair asymmetric IA-based interference network using clustering management scheme.

3.1   Antenna Selection in Cluster Management Scheme

After performing the CM scheme in the network, the number of IA pairs K_{IA} in the IA cluster will be generally smaller than K, i.e., $K_{IA} < K$. Hence, antenna resource in the IA cluster will be relatively abundant, which can be utilized to perform the AS technique. In this paper, the AS technique is just performed at the Rx side of each IA pair to reduce the CSI feedback overhead.

Taking the network with the configuration $(M, N, K, d) = (3, 3, 5, 1)$ as an example to analyze the implementation of the AS technique in the IA cluster. Assuming that there exist one IA cluster and one SM cluster after performing the TM scheme. The number of the optional antenna combinations for the k-th pair is summarized in Table 1. There will be $z = (3+1)^4 = 256$ optional antenna combinations in the IA cluster, and the set of all the optional combinations is denoted as $\boldsymbol{\Phi} = \{\Omega_1, \Omega_2, \ldots, \Omega_z\}$.

Table 1. Number of optional antenna combinations for the j-th IA Pair

Configuration	Number of antenna combinations
$M_{IA}^{[j]} = 3, N_{IA}^{[j]} = 2, d = 1$	3
$M_{IA}^{[j]} = 3, N_{IA}^{[j]} = 3, d = 1$	1

We can select the optimal antenna combinations from the set $\boldsymbol{\Phi}$ to improve the spectrum efficiency of the IA cluster, and the problem can be expressed as

$$\Omega^* = \arg\max_{\Omega \in \Phi} \left\{ \sum_{k=1}^{K} R_{\text{IA}}^{[k]}(\Omega) \right\}. \tag{3}$$

The combinatorial optimization problem (3) can be easily solved through the ES-based AS method. However, when the size of the set $\boldsymbol{\Phi}$ is large, the computational complexity will become extremely high. To overcome the shortcoming, the cross entropy optimization method is applied to implement the AS technique, which can achieve the optimal or near-optimal performance with low computational complexity.

3.2 Cross-Entropy Optimization Method

The main idea of CEO for antenna selection is to iteratively update the probability vector $\mathbf{p}$, which can be defined as

$$\mathbf{p} = \left\{ p^{(1,1)}, \ldots, p^{(1,M)}, \ldots, p^{(k,j)}, \ldots, p^{(K,1)}, \ldots, p^{(K,M)} \right\}. \tag{4}$$

where $p^{(k,j)}$ represents the probability of the j-th antenna of the k-th Rx to be selected. To effectively update the probability vector $\mathbf{p}$, there are two iterative phrases which should be carefully designed as follows.

1. The random mechanism to generate a sample of random data. In this paper, Bernoulli probability mass functions $f(\Omega_q; \mathbf{p})$ is used to generate Q samples

$$f(\Omega_q; \mathbf{p}) = \prod_{k=1}^{K} \prod_{i=1}^{M} \left[p^{(k,i)} \right]^{\Omega_q^{(k,i)}}, q = 1, \ldots, Q. \tag{5}$$

2. The way to update the parameters of the random mechanism. The probability vector $\mathbf{p}$ is updated according to the following equation

$$\mathbf{p}^{iter} = \frac{\sum_{q=1}^{Q} I_{\left\{ S(\Omega_q^{iter}) >= \gamma^{iter} \right\}} \Omega_q^{iter}}{\sum_{q=1}^{Q} I_{\left\{ S(\Omega_q^{iter}) >= \gamma^{iter} \right\}}}. \tag{6}$$

where $I_{\{x\}}$ is an indicator function. When the condition x is satisfied, $I_{\{x\}} = 1$, $I_{\{x\}} = 0$, otherwise. Ω_q^{iter} is the selected antenna vector for sample q at the $iter$-th iteration. $S\left(\Omega_q^{iter}\right)$ represents the minimum stream SINR of sample q at the $iter$-th iteration. $\gamma^{iter} = S^{(\lceil(1-\eta)Q\rceil)}$ is the $(1-\eta)$-th quantile in the sequence $S^{(1)} >= S^{(2)} >= \cdots >= S^{(Q)}$, $\lceil \cdot \rceil$ is the ceiling operation, and $\eta \in (0,1)$. To smooth out the values of $\mathbf{p}$ and prevent some component $p^{(k,j)}$ of $\mathbf{p}$ from being zero or one in first few iteration, the smooth parameter $\lambda \in (0.7, 1]$ is introduced as follows

$$\mathbf{p}^{iter} = \lambda \mathbf{p}^{iter} + (1 - \lambda) \mathbf{p}^{iter-1}. \tag{7}$$

Hence, the implementation of the AS technique based on the CEO algorithm in the TM scheme can be summarized as follows

Algorithm 1. Antenna selection based on the CEO algorithm

1: Determine the set of the optional antenna combinations $\boldsymbol{\Phi}$ according to the feasibility conditions of IA in the IA subnetwork, i.e., the number of the selected antenna N_{IA} at the Rx side of each IA pair.

2: Set $iter = 0$ and initialize the probability vector $\mathbf{p}^0 = \frac{N_{\text{IA}}}{N}\mathbf{1}$.

3: **repeat**

4:     Generate Q samples according to the random mechanism Bernoulli probability mass function (5).

5:     For each sample, calculate the precoding and decoding matrices based on the MinIL algorithm, and the minimum stream SINR.

6:     Sort the minimum SINRs in descending order.

7:     Update the probability vector $\mathbf{p}^{iter}$ by (4), and smoothen it by (7).

8:     $iter = iter + 1$.

9: **until** The stopping criterion is satisfied.

4 Simulation Results

In this section, the asymmetric interference network with the configuration $(M, N, K, d) = (3, 3, 5, 1)$ is considered. Assuming that the path-loss exponent α is set to 3. All the pairs are randomly and uniformly scattered in a $1\,\text{km} \times 1\,\text{km}$ square area, and the distance between the transmitter and its corresponding receiver is set to $100\,\text{m}$.

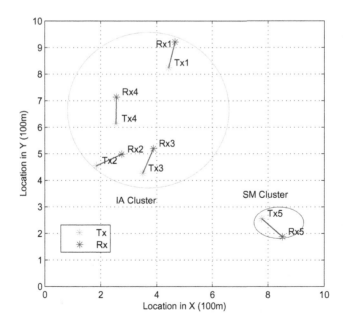

Fig. 2. The network topology after performing the clustering management scheme when the transmitted SNR is $12\,\text{dB}$.

A network shown in Fig. 2 is taken as an example to analyze the performance of the CEO-based AS method in the clustering management scheme. After performing the clustering management scheme in the network when the transmitted SNR is 12 dB, the whole network is divided into one IA cluster and one SM cluster. From the figure, we can observe that the four pairs, i.e., the 1-st, 2-nd, 3-rd and 4-th pair, jointly comprise the IA cluster, and the 5-th pair acts as the SM cluster independently.

According to the result of clustering, the spectrum efficiency of different schemes under various transmit SNRs is compared in Fig. 3. From the simulation results, we can find that the CEO-based AS method can effectively improve the performance of the IA cluster compared to the original clustering management scheme. However, compared to the ES-based AS method, there exist a little performance gap. Considering the high computational complexity of the ES-based AS method, the CEO-based AS method can achieve a balance between the spectrum efficiency and the computational complexity.

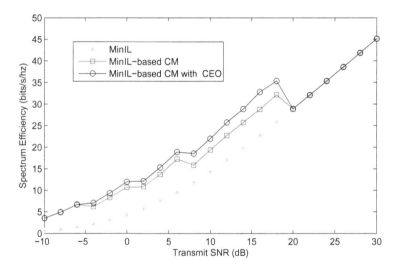

Fig. 3. The spectrum efficiency versus the transmit SNR under different schemes.

5   Conclusions

In this paper, the implementation of antenna selection in the clustering management scheme was analyzed. The redundant antenna resource was used to perform the AS technique. However, the ES-based AS method was unfriendly for performing in practical wireless networks due to the high computational complexity. The another effective combinatorial optimization method, i.e., cross-entropy optimization (CEO) algorithm, was selected as the substituted method. Finally, the simulation results were presented to show the effectiveness of the proposed CEO-based AS method in the clustering management scheme.

References

1. Cadambe, V.R., Jafar, S.A.: Interference alignment and degrees of freedom of the K-user interference channel. IEEE Trans. Inf. Theory **54**, 3425–3441 (2008)
2. Gomadam, K., Cadambe, V.R., Jafar, S.A.: A distributed numerical approach to interference alignment and applications to wireless interference networks. IEEE Trans. Inf. Theory **57**, 3309–3322 (2011)
3. Zhao, N., Yu, F.R., Jin, M., Yan, Q., Leung, V.C.M.: Interference alignment and its applications: a survey, research issues and challenges. IEEE Commun. Surv. Tutor. **18**, 1779–1803 (2016)
4. Zhao, N., Yu, F.R., Li, M., Yan, Q., Leung, V.C.M.: Physical layer security issues in interference-alignment-based wireless networks. IEEE Commun. Mag. **54**, 162–168 (2016)
5. Zhao, N., Yu, F.R., Sun, H., Li, M.: Adaptive power allocation schemes for spectrum sharing in interference-alignment-based cognitive radio networks. IEEE Trans. Veh. Technol. **65**, 3700–3714 (2016)
6. Zhao, N., Yu, F.R., Leung, V.C.M.: Wireless energy harvesting in interference alignment networks. IEEE Commun. Mag. **53**, 72–78 (2015)
7. Zhao, N., Yu, F.R., Sun, H.: Adaptive energy-efficient power allocation in green interference-alignment-based wireless networks. IEEE Trans. Veh. Technol. **64**, 4268–4281 (2015)
8. Chen, S., Cheng, R.S.: Clustering for interference alignment in multiuser interference network. IEEE Trans. Veh. Technol. **63**, 2613–2624 (2014)
9. Zhao, N., Zhang, X., Yu, F.R., Leung, V.C.M.: To align or not to align: topology management in asymmetric interference networks. IEEE Trans. Veh. Technol.
10. Zhang, X., Zhao, N., Yu, F.R., Jin, M., Leung, V.C.M.: Resource allocation in topology management of asymmetric interference networks. IEEE Syst. J.
11. Zhao, N., Yu, F.R., Leung, V.C.M.: Opportunistic communications in interference alignment networks with wireless power transfer. IEEE Wirel. Commun. **22**, 88–95 (2015)
12. Sanayei, S., Nosratinia, A.: Antenna selection in MIMO systems. IEEE Commun. Mag. **42**, 68–73 (2004)
13. Koltz, J.G., Sezgin, A.: Antenna selection criteria for interference alignment. In: Proceedings of the IEEE PIMRC 2010, pp. 527–531. IEEE Press, Instanbul (2010)
14. Li, X., Zhao, N., Sun, Y., Yu, F.R.: Interference alignment based on antenna selection with imperfect channel state information in cognitive radio networks. IEEE Trans. Veh. Technol. **65**, 5497–5511 (2016)
15. Zhao, N., Yu, F.R., Sun, H., Nallanathan, A., Yin, H.: A novel interference alignment scheme based on sequential antenna switching in wireless networks. IEEE Trans. Wirel. Commun. **12**, 5008–5021 (2013)
16. Rubinstein, R.Y., Kroese, D.P.: The Cross-Entropy Method: A Unified Approach to Combinatorial Optimization, Monte-Carlo Simulation and Machine Learning. Springer, New York (2004). https://doi.org/10.1007/978-1-4757-4321-0
17. Zhang, Y., Ji, C., Malik, W.Q., O'Brien, D.C., Edwards, D.J.: Receive antenna selection for MIMO systems over correlated fading channels. IEEE Trans. Wirel. Commun. **8**, 4393–4399 (2009)
18. Ali, A.O.D., Yetis, C.M., Torlak, M.: Receive antenna selection for MIMO systems over correlated fading channels. In: 2014 IEEE 25th Annual International Symposium on Personal, Indoor, and Mobile Radio Communication (PIMRC), pp. 402–406. IEEE Press, Washington (2014)

Subcarrier Allocation-Based Simultaneous Wireless Information and Power Transfer for Multiuser OFDM Systems

Xin Liu[1(✉)], Xiaotong Li[2], Zhenyu Na[2], and Qiuyi Cao[1]

[1] School of Information and Communication Engineering,
Dalian University of Technology, Dalian 116024, China
liuxinstar1984@dlut.edu.cn, cccqiu_yi@163.com
[2] School of Information Science and Technology,
Dalian Maritime University, Dalian 116026, China
565856998@qq.com, nazhenyu@dlmu.edu.cn

Abstract. Most of existing works on simultaneous wireless information and power transfer (SWIPT) for OFDM systems are studied based on power splitting or time splitting, which may lead to the time delay and the decreasing of subcarrier utilization. In this paper, a multiuser orthogonal frequency division multiplexing (OFDM) system is proposed, which divides the sub-carriers into two parts, one for information decoding and the other one for energy harvesting. We investigate the optimization problem for maximizing the sum rate of users under the constraint of energy harvesting through optimizing the channel allocation and power allocation. By using the iterative algorithm, the optimal solution to the optimization problem can be achieved. The simulation results show that the proposed algorithm converges fast and outperforms the conventional algorithm.

Keywords: SWIPT · OFDM · Subcarrier allocation · Power allocation

1 Introduction

Orthogonal frequency division multiplexing (OFDM) is a viable air interface for providing ubiquitous communication services and high spectral efficiency, due to its ability to combat frequency selective multipath fading and flexibility in resource allocation. However, power-hungry circuitries and the limited energy supply in portable devices remain the bottlenecks in prolonging the lifetime of networks and guaranteeing quality of service (QoS). As a result, energy-efficient mobile communication has attracted considerable interest from both industry and academia [1–4]. Traditionally, energy has been harvested from natural renewable energy sources such as solar, wind, and geothermal heat, thereby reducing substantially the reliance on the energy supply from conventional energy sources. As a result, simultaneous wireless information and power transfer (SWIPT) is emerged. In [5], the concept of SWIPT is first put forward and the capacity-energy function is defined. Two classical models are put forward in paper [6, 7], including time switching (TS) model and power switching (PS) model. In TS model, the receiver switches into energy harvesting mode or

© ICST Institute for Computer Sciences, Social Informatics and Telecommunications Engineering 2018
X. Gu et al. (Eds.): MLICOM 2017, Part I, LNICST 226, pp. 524–531, 2018.
https://doi.org/10.1007/978-3-319-73564-1_52

information mode within one transmission time. In PS model, the receiver splits the power into two parts with some ratio, one for information decoding and the other one for energy harvesting. SWIPT is combined with multiple-input-single-output (MISO) in [8], where a transmitter with multi-antenna transmits the same information to several banks of single antenna simultaneously. In [9], the optimization algorithm of power splitting based on down-link OFDMA is proposed by the iterative algorithm. A tradeoff between TS and PS is proposed in [10].

Different from the PS and TS models, we study a sub-carrier allocation-based SWIPT for multiuser OFDM systems without a splitter at the receiver. The sub-carriers of each user are separated into information decoding part and energy harvesting part. We address the problem of maximizing the sum rate of users while keeping enough harvested energy. The non-convex problem is solved by an iterative algorithm.

2   System Model

Consider a wireless OFDM down-link system consisting of one cognitive base station (CBS) and K users. Each user is only equipped with one antenna. Let K denote the sets of k users for $k = \{1, 2, \cdots K\}$. The OFDM bandwidth is assumed to be divided into $N (N \geq K)$ channels equally. The sub-carriers set is denoted with N for $N = \{1,...,n\}$. Each sub-carrier must be allocated to only one user. Parts of sub-carriers are used for energy harvesting, and the others are utilized for information decoding simultaneously. We suppose that the channel power gain on each sub-carrier is always constant in one transmission period time, which is given at the base station. Let $h_{k,n}$ represent the gain of the k-th user on the n-th sub-carrier. Then the noise power of each sub-carrier can be corrupted by n_k, which is modeled as an additive white Gaussian noise (AWGN) random variable with zero mean and variance σ^2. The total transmission power is limited to power budget P. Therefore, the power allocated on the n-th sub-carrier is denoted as P_n. Let S^P represent the sub-carriers used for energy harvesting to power transfer. Accordingly, the other sub-carriers used for information decoding is denoted by S^I. Hence, S_K^I represents the sub-carriers used for information transfer on K-th user. One sub-carrier cannot be used for energy harvesting and transfer information simultaneously, so we have $S^I \cap S^P = \emptyset$ and $S^I \cup S^P = N$ (Fig. 1).

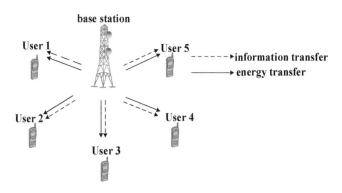

Fig. 1. System model.

3   Problem Formulation

Our aim is to maximize the sum rate of OFDM down-link under a restricted condition of the minimum harvested energy for each user. Let B_k represent to the minimum harvested energy of k-th user. Since one sub-carrier can only be allocated to one user, let $\alpha_{n,k}$ be a binary channel allocation index. In other words, $\alpha_{n,k} = 1$ means that the sub-carrier n is only allocated to the user k and $\alpha_{n,k} = 0$ is determined on other terms. So it is written as

$$\sum_{k=1}^{K} \alpha_{k,n} = 1, \forall n \in N \tag{1}$$

The sum rate of system can be formulated as

$$\sum_{k=1}^{K} \sum_{n \in S^I} \alpha_{k,n} \log\left(1 + \frac{h_{k,n} P_n}{\sigma^2}\right) \tag{2}$$

where $n \in S^I$. With energy harvesting efficiency ε, the harvested energy during one transmission block for user k is determined by

$$\sum_{n \in S^P} \left(\varepsilon h_{k,n} P_n + \sigma^2\right) \tag{3}$$

For $\forall k \in K$. Therefore, optimization model of maximum sum rate can be written as follows

$$\begin{aligned}
&\max_{\alpha_{n,k}, S^I, P_n} \sum_{k=1}^{K} \sum_{n \in S^I} \alpha_{k,n} \log\left(1 + \frac{h_{k,n} P_n}{\sigma^2}\right) \\
&\text{s.t.} \sum_{n \in N} P_n \leq P \\
&S^P \cup S^I = N \\
&S^P \cap S^I = \emptyset \\
&\sum_{k=1}^{K} \alpha_{k,n} = 1, \forall n \in N \\
&\alpha_{k,n} \in \{0, 1\}, \forall k \in K, n \in N \\
&P_n \geq 0, \forall n \in N
\end{aligned} \tag{4}$$

4   Optimal Solution

Due to the non-convex problem, it is impossible to obtain the optimal solution directly. In this section a sub-optimal algorithm is proposed for solving this problem.

We firstly optimize $\alpha_{k,n}$ with given P_n and $S^I(S^P)$, then optimize P_n with given $\alpha_{k,n}$ and $S^I(S^P)$, and optimize $S^I(S^P)$ with given $\alpha_{k,n}$ and P_n at last. As mentioned above, P_n and $S^I(S^P)$ are determined, so $\alpha_{k,n}$ is optimized as follows

$$\begin{aligned}
&\max_{\alpha_{n,k}} \sum_{k=1}^{K} \alpha_{k,n} \log\left(1 + \frac{h_{k,n}P_n}{\sigma^2}\right), n \in S^l \\
&\text{s.t.} \sum_{k=1}^{K} \alpha_{k,n} = 1, \forall n \in N \\
&\alpha_{k,n} \in \{0, 1\}, \forall k \in K, n \in N
\end{aligned} \tag{5}$$

The problem above is regarded as allocating the sub-carrier n to the assigned user for obtaining the maximum sum rate. In other words, the sub-carrier n ($n \in S^l$) is allocated to the user k which can get the maximum $h_{k,n}P_n$, i.e., $\alpha_{k^*,n} = 1$, $k^* = arg\max_{k \in K} h_{k,n}P_n$ and $\alpha_{k^*,n} = 0, \forall k \neq k^*, k \in K$.

Secondly, P_n is optimized by $\alpha_{k,n}$ and $S^l(S^P)$. In this proposition, the problem can be rewritten as

$$\begin{aligned}
&\max_{P_n} \sum_{n \in S_k^l} \log\left(1 + \frac{h_{k^*,n}P_n}{\sigma^2}\right) \\
&\text{s.t.} \sum_{n \in S^P} \left(\varepsilon h_{k^*,n}P_n + \sigma^2\right) \geq B_k \\
&\sum_{n \in N} P_n \leq P \\
&P_n \geq 0, \forall n \in N
\end{aligned} \tag{6}$$

Note that $\alpha_{k^*,n} = 1, \alpha_{k,n} = 0, \forall k \neq k^*, k \in K$. The converted problem is satisfied with convex model. Thus, the Lagrange dual decomposition is employed for solving this problem. The Lagrange dual function is given as follows:

$$g(\beta_1, \beta_2) = \max_{\{P_n\}} L(P_n) \tag{7}$$

where β_1, β_2 are the Lagrange multipliers and they are determined by the sub-gradient method. Meanwhile, $L(P_n)$ is expressed as:

$$L(P_n) = \sum_{n \in S_k^l} \log\left(1 + \frac{h_{k^*,n}P_n}{\sigma^2}\right) + \beta_1\left\{\sum_{n \in S^P} \left(\varepsilon h_{k^*,n}P_n + \sigma^2\right) - B_k\right\} + \beta_2\left(P - \sum_{n \in N} P_n\right) \tag{8}$$

Then the dual problem can be simplified as follows:

$$\begin{aligned}
&\min_{\beta_1, \beta_2} g(\beta_1, \beta_2) \\
&\text{s.t} \quad \beta_1, \beta_2 \geq 0
\end{aligned} \tag{9}$$

Because the dual problem is differentiable, it can be solved with the sub-gradient method. The sub-gradient is shown as follow:

$$\Delta\beta_1 = \sum_{n \in S^P} \varepsilon h_{k^*,n}P_n + \sigma^2 - B_k \tag{10}$$

$$\Delta\beta_2 = P - \sum_{n \in N} P_n \tag{11}$$

For given β_1, β_2, the optimal power P_n ($n \in S^l$) is obtained by KKT conditions by using mathematical manipulation, as follows

$$P_n = \left(\frac{1}{\beta_2} - \frac{\sigma^2}{h_k}\right)^+ \tag{12}$$

where $(.)^+$ denotes max$(.,0)$. Similarly, the allocated power P_n used for information transfering is determined as:

$$P_n = \begin{cases} P_{max} & h_{k,n}\varepsilon > \beta_2 \\ P_{min} & h_{k,n}\varepsilon \leq \beta_2 \end{cases} \tag{13}$$

where P_{max} and P_{min} represent the maximum and minimum power constraints on information decode respectively. According to P_n and $\alpha_{n,k}$, $S^I(S^P)$ can be obtained by substituting (11) and (12) into (8). Consequently, Lagrange dual function can be rewritten as

$$
\begin{aligned}
L(S^P) &= \sum_{k=1}^{K} \sum_{n\in N} \alpha_{n,k} \log\left(1 + \frac{h_{k,n}P_n}{\sigma^2}\right) - \sum_{k=1}^{K} \sum_{n\in S^P} \alpha_{n,k} \log\left(1 + \frac{h_{k,n}P_n}{\sigma^2}\right) \\
&\quad + \beta_1 \sum_{n\in S^P} \left(\varepsilon h_{k,n}P_n + \sigma^2\right) - \beta_1 B_k + \beta_2 P - \beta_2 \sum_{n\in N} P_n \\
&= \sum_{n\in S^P} \left\{ \beta_1 \left(\varepsilon h_{k,n}P_n + \sigma^2\right) - \sum_{k=1}^{K} \alpha_{n,k} \log\left(1 + \frac{h_{k,n}P_n}{\sigma^2}\right) \right\} \\
&\quad + \sum_{n\in N} \left\{ \sum_{k=1}^{K} \alpha_{n,k} \log\left(1 + \frac{h_{k,n}P_n}{\sigma^2}\right) - \beta_2 P_n \right\} - \beta_1 B_k + \beta_2 P \\
&= \sum_{n\in S^P} F_n + \sum_{n\in N} \left\{ \sum_{k=1}^{K} \alpha_{n,k} \log\left(1 + \frac{h_{k,n}P_n}{\sigma^2}\right) - \beta_2 P_n \right\} \\
&\quad - \beta_1 B_k + \beta_2 P
\end{aligned}
\tag{14}
$$

where

$$F_n = \beta_1\left(\varepsilon h_{k,n}P_n + \sigma^2\right) - \sum_{k=1}^{K} \alpha_{n,k} \log\left(1 + \frac{h_{k,n}P_n}{\sigma^2}\right) \tag{15}$$

Analyzing the formulate (13), only the first item on the right side is about to S^P. Thus, the optimal S^P can be achieved by maximum the item F_n, as follows

$$S^{P*} = \arg \max_{S^P} \sum_{n\in S^P} F_n^* \tag{16}$$

S^{P*} can be easily gotten by substituting all the n into F_n to find the ones which are make F_n positive, then the rest of the set N are belongs to S^{I*}. The proposed algorithm to solve the optimal problem is listed as the Algorithm 1.

Algorithm 1. Proposed Algorithm for the Joint Optimization Problem

1. Initialize $P_n(0)$, $\alpha_{n,k^*}(0)$ and the error tolerance ε;
2. Given $P_n(0)$ and $\alpha_{n,k^*}(0)$, obtain $S^I(0)$ from (15);
3. $R_k(0) = \sum_{k=1}^{K} \alpha_{n,k}(0) \log\left(1 + \frac{h_{k,n}P_n(0)}{\sigma^2}\right)$, $n \in S^I$;
4. Given $P_n(t)$ and $S^I(t)$, set $\alpha_{n,k^*}(t) = 1, k^* = arg\max_{k\in K} h_{k,n}P_n$ and $\alpha_{n,k^*}(t) = 0, \forall k \neq k^*, k \in K$;
5. Given $\alpha_{n,k^*}(t+1)$ and $S^I(t)$, obtain $P_n(t+1)$, $n \in N$ from (11) and (12);
6. Given $\alpha_{n,k^*}(t+1)$ and $P_n(t+1)$, obtain $S^I(t+1)$;
7. $R_k(t+1) = \sum_{k=1}^{K} \alpha_{n,k}(t+1) \log\left(1 + \frac{h_{k,n}P_n(t+1)}{\sigma^2}\right)$, $n \in S^I$;
8. $t=t+1$;
9. Repeat (4) to (8) Until $|R_k(t+1) - R_k(t)| \leq \varepsilon$.
10. Output optimal parameters.

5 Simulation Results

In this section, the performance of the proposed algorithm based on multi-users SWIPT is demonstrated by simulation results.

We denote all the channels involved are following Rayleigh fading with unit mean. For simplicity, we assume that the minimum harvested energy limits for all the users are the same, i.e., $B_k = B$. In addition, we set N = 16, K = 5, $\sigma^2 = 1$, $P_{max} = P/N$, $P_{min} = 0$, and $\varepsilon = 1$.

Figure 2 shows the convergence behavior of the proposed algorithm. It is seen that the proposed algorithm converges fast, which indicates that the proposed algorithm can be implemented practically. Figure 3 shows that the comparison between the proposed optimization algorithm and the conventional algorithm. It can be seen that the proposed algorithm performance better compared with conventional algorithm. The conventional allocated N sub-carriers to K users. By contrast, all the sub-carriers are used for information decoding and the consumed energy comes from the system. In the conventional algorithm, the water-filling approach is used for power allocation, this will cause some power waste. Moreover, all the sub-carriers are allocated to information decoding which results the energy consumption and less power can be used for information decoding. Figure 3 also shows that the sum rate of users increases as the sum transmit power P increases. This is because with the same target harvested energy, when the sum transmission power increases there will be more power allocated for information decoding.

Figure 4 shows that the total transmission power used for information decoding of user k. It can be seen that the user 5 is allocated the most power and user 2 is the least. That is because in our emulation, the user 5 has the best channel condition which can achieve higher sum rate.

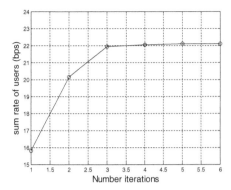

Fig. 2. Convergence behavior of the proposed algorithm.

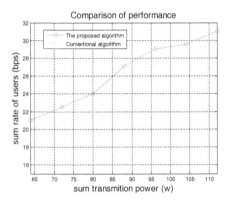

Fig. 3. The sum transmit power vs sum rate of users

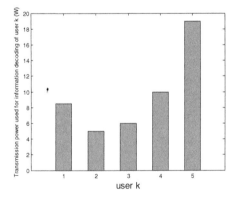

Fig. 4. The power used for information decoding of user k

6 Conclusion

In this paper, we propose a joint optimization algorithm for SWIPT-based multi-user OFDM systems. Specifically, the OFDM sub-carriers of each user are divided into two parts, one for information decoding and the other one for energy harvesting. Therefore, we can obtain enough information rate without using time or power splitter at the receiver, on the premise of harvesting enough energy. The simulation results show that the proposed algorithm converges fast and outperforms the conventional algorithm.

Acknowledgments. This work was supported by the National Natural Science Foundations of China under Grant No. 61601221, the Natural Science Foundations of Jiangsu Province under Grant No. BK20140828, the China Postdoctoral Science Foundations under Grant No. 2015M580425 and the Fundamental Research Funds for the Central Universities under Grant No. DUT16RC(3)045.

References

1. Chen, T., Yang, Y., Zhang, H., Kim, H., Horneman, K.: Network energy saving technologies for green wireless access networks. IEEE Wirel. Commun. **18**, 30–38 (2011)
2. Arnold, O., Richter, F., Fettweis, G., Blume, O.: Power consumption modeling of different base station types in heterogeneous cellular networks. In: Proceedings of Future Network and Mobile Summit, pp. 1–8 (2010)
3. Yang, J., Ulukus, S.: Optimal packet scheduling in an energy harvesting communication system. IEEE Trans. Commun. **60**, 220–230 (2012)
4. Ng, D.W.K., Lo, E., Schober, R.: Energy-efficient resource allocation in OFDMA systems with large numbers of base station antennas. IEEE Trans. Wirel. Commun. **11**, 3292–3304 (2012)
5. Varshney, L.R.: Transporting information and energy simultaneously. In: International Symposium on IEEE Information Theory, ISIT 2008, pp. 1612–1616. IEEE (2008)
6. Liu, L., Zhang, R., Ho, C.K.: Wireless information transfer with opportunistic energy harvesting. IEEE Trans. Wirel. Commun. **12**(1), 288–300 (2013)
7. Liu, L., Zhang, R., Ho, C.K.: Wireless information and power transfer: a dynamic power splitting approach. IEEE Trans. Wirel. Commun. **61**(9), 3990–4001 (2013)
8. Ng, D.W.K., Schober, R.: Spectral efficient optimization in OFDM systems with wireless information and power transfer. In: 21st European Signal Processing Conference (EUSIPCO 2013), Marrakech, pp. 1–5 (2013)
9. Zhou, X., Zhang, R., Ho, C.K.: Wireless information and power transfer in multiuser OFDM systems. In: 2013 IEEE Global Communications Conference (GLOBECOM), Atlanta, GA, pp. 4092–4097 (2013)
10. Ng, D.W.K., Lo, E.S., Schober, R.: Wireless information and power transfer: energy efficiency optimization in OFDMA systems. IEEE Trans. Wirel. Commun. **12**(12), 6352–6370 (2013)

Intelligent Ad-Hoc and Sensor Networks

A 100 MHz SRAM Design in 180 nm Process

Zhuangguang Chen and Bei Cao[✉]

Electronic Engineering School, Heilongjiang University, Harbin 150080, China
caobei@hlju.edu.cn

Abstract. With the development of integrated circuit, SoC systems are more and more used in products. Memory is an important part of SoC, SRAM design is a key research area. In this paper, based on ASIC design methodology, 2 K-bits SRAM is designed. A 6T-SRAM memory cell is designed and simulated with circuit level to improve reliability. The memory cell is used to construct the storage array, which are the word line 32 bits and the bit line 8 bits. Then, the SRAM peripheral circuit is designed and simulated by using SMIC 0.18 μm process, including the data input/output buffer circuit, clock circuit, address decoding circuit, data read/write circuit and sense amplifier. The structure, function and performance of latch type sense amplifier are analyzed emphatically. The simulation results demonstrate that the function of SRAM is verified correctly. The clock frequency of the SRAM can reach 100 MHz.

Keywords: Static random access memory · Memory array · Peripheral circuits

1 Introduction

With the rapid development of digitalization process, the information industry is going into the era of large data. SoC chip has become the key of information and data processing. The data storage in SoC is an important part. In order to solve the storage problems of SoC data storage, improve the working performance of SoC processor, and reduce the speed gap between processor and external memory, memory hierarchical technology is adopted in this paper. Static random access memory (SRAM) with high speed and low capacity is used as the key technology to solve the above problems. In this paper, with the analysis of the internal working mechanism about SRAM, the design methodology based on ASIC is adopted, in order to achieve 256 × 8 bytes.

A variety of design implementation and improvement schemes are proposed for SRAM. A novel power gated 9T SRAM cell is proposed, which uses read decoupling access buffers and power gated transistors to perform reliable read and write operations [1]. A bit line equivalent scheme is proposed to eliminate the leakage dependence of the data pattern. Thus, the read bit line sensing and its stability to the process, voltage and temperature variations are improved [2]. A 6T SRAM operating down to near threshold regime is presented [3]. A dual-port spin-orbit torque magnetic RAM for on-chip caching applications with reduced power consumption is proposed to reduce the impact of write delay on performance [4].

© ICST Institute for Computer Sciences, Social Informatics and Telecommunications Engineering 2018
X. Gu et al. (Eds.): MLICOM 2017, Part I, LNICST 226, pp. 535–544, 2018.
https://doi.org/10.1007/978-3-319-73564-1_53

2 SRAM Cell Structure

SRAM refers to a memory capable of accessing any unit in the memory array, which can perform data writing or data reading operations within an applicable range of address for multiple of cycles. The SRAM structure mainly includes the storage array, decoding circuit, clock circuit and data read/write control circuit, and so on. A storage array is a key part, which is electrically interconnected by the memory cell in accordance with certain rules. The decoding circuit is used to process the address information to select the particular cell. The clock circuit provides a series of working clock pulses for the operation of the peripheral circuit. Sense amplifier circuit is used to increase the speed of reading the stored data from SRAM array.

The basic memory cell of SRAM is shown in Fig. 1. It is composed of a pair of inverters and the pass transistors, which are connected in a cross-coupled manner. The output of an inverter becomes the input of the other inverter, and vice versa.

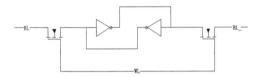

Fig. 1. Static memory cell based on 6T.

The simulation circuit for the 6T static memory cell is shown in Fig. 2. The data reading/writing and data holding for the 6T static memory cell are controlled by the BL_CTR_W, BL_CTR_R switches signal on the control bit line and the word line switch signal WL respectively. When the word line signal is valid, BL_CTR_W signal responds. If BL_CTR_R signal is invalid, the DC voltage source and bit line cascade are controlled by BL_CTR_W signal. By simulating the charging and discharging for the storage node on the bit line capacitor, the data is in the write state.

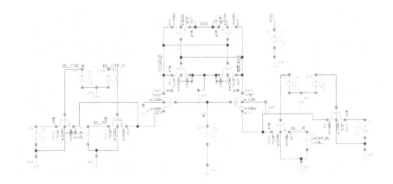

Fig. 2. The simulation circuit for the 6T static memory cell.

The simulation result for the 6T static memory cell is shown in Fig. 3.

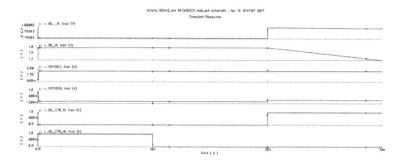

Fig. 3. The simulation result for the 6T Static memory cell.

Data can be read through the STORE0 and STORE1 signals to verify that the data has been written successfully. When the word line signal is invalid, the switch controlled by the BL_CTR_W and BL_CTR_B signals is disconnected from the memory node, which is the data holding state at this time. The data signal on the memory node can be latched properly if the STORE0 and STORE1 signals can be read out.

When the word line signal is valid, BL_CTR_W signal is invalid and BL_CTR_R signal is valid. At this point, the BL_CTR_R signal controls the pre-charged capacitor and the memory node for cascade connection. It is the data reading process through the BL_R and BL_R signals. The correct voltage difference is generated successfully on the two bit line capacitors, and the data is successfully read out.

3 Memory Array

The static memory cells are arranged and joined together to construct a memory array, as shown in Fig. 4. Each row of memory cells shares a word line WL. The static memory cells on each column share a pair of the bit lines BL and BL_. The selection signal of the word line and bit line is generated by the decoding circuit according to the address.

In the intersection selection of rows and columns, the position of intersection points can be obtained. It is the memory cell corresponding to the address information. By combining the memory array with the decoding circuit, the memory cell can be positioned quickly according to the address information. The corresponding operation of the memory cell is performed according to the data changes on the bit lines.

The address information used to locate the memory cells in the storage array is transmitted by code, which could reduce the number of inter-chip or on-chip interactive connections. Because binary code has area validity and easy implementation within the circuit, most of the code which adopted in CMOS memory is using the binary form. In a memory array, address information used to locate the memory cell is transmitted through code for reducing the number of interconnects for between chips or internal chip. Most of the code used in CMOS memory is binary encoding, because binary code can optimize chip area and easy to implement inside the integrated circuit.

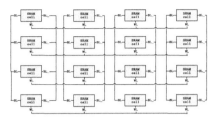

Fig. 4. Storage array diagram of 4 × 4.

The input signal used in the experimental simulation is shown in Fig. 5. The input patterns are 00–11 four bit signals for the address input ports ADD0 and ADD1 in the 2–4 decoder circuit. A signal is input at each interval of 5 ns. ADD0 and ADD1 are the lowest and highest addresses, respectively.

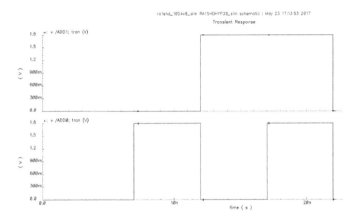

Fig. 5. The input signal excitation for 2–4 decoder transient simulation.

The output signals in simulation experiment are shown in Fig. 6. OUT0–OUT3 is the fore decoding ports of the 2–4 decoder. Since the address input signals are increased gradually from 0 to 3, with a step of 1 and an interval of 5 ns, the OUT0–OUT3 output ports will be high voltage at every 5 ns. These indicate that the address lines are selected.

When the SRAM is in normal mode, the write enable or read enable signal is valid. The corresponding memory cell will write or read data accordingly in each clock cycle. The bit line pairs are controlled, and the bit line data is given by the bit line control circuit in the above process. A bit line control circuit is shown as Fig. 7.

The CS is the selection signal of the bit line, and the GTP is the on-chip clock signal. When the clock is on the rising edge, the GTP rises to the highest voltage, and the bit lines BL and BL_ are pre-charged to the maximum voltage VDD. When the write data enable signal and the bit line signal CS are valid, the bit line BL_ and the BL are controlled by the DW and the DW_ respectively. These determine whether the bit

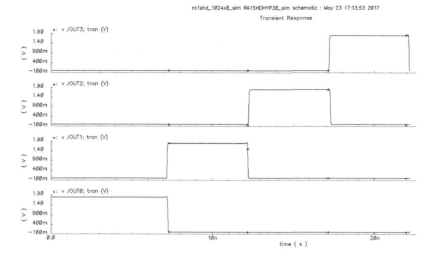

Fig. 6. The simulation output results of 2–4 decoder.

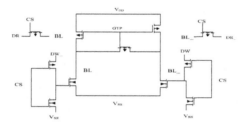

Fig. 7. Bit line control circuit.

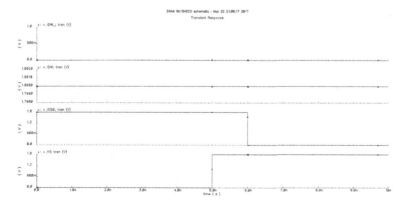

Fig. 8. The transient simulation excitation for bit line control circuit.

lines are pulled down to the low voltage. A voltage difference (VDD-Vss) is formed on a pair of bit lines, i.e., BL and BL_. Data are written successfully into the corresponding memory cell. When the read data enable signal he bit line selection signal CS are valid, the DR and the DR_ are accessed in the bit line BL and the BL_ respectively. The voltage difference signals on the bit line pairs are thus read out.

The input signals used in the simulation are shown in Fig. 8, and the simulation results are shown in Fig. 9.

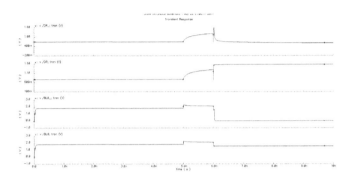

Fig. 9. The simulation results of bit line control circuit.

The bit line charges both the BL0 and the BL0_ to the high voltage because the on-chip clock signal is in a low voltage state at first. The bit line selection signal is so high that the pull-down tubes used to control the bit line pairs are turned off simultaneously. The internal bit line pairs are all at high voltage in the 0–5 ns time periods. The on-chip clock signal is converted to the high voltage in the 5–6 ns time periods. And the bit line selection signal is maintained at a high level. At this time, pull-up transistors and pull-down transistors are turned off, so the pairs of bit lines are in the high impedance. When the on-chip clock signal is maintained at the high voltage, the bit line select signal is converted to the low voltage after 6 ns. At this point, the BL0 and BL0_ signals are controlled by the DW_ and DW for bit lines, respectively. The DW_ signal is the low voltage, and the DW signal is the high voltage. Therefore, the BL0 signal is maintained at a high voltage and the BL0_ signal is pulled down to a low voltage. The data read ports DR and DR_ for bit line are connected to the BL0 and the BL0_ respectively because the bit line selection signal is in the low level. Voltage difference on bit line pair are read out.

When the reading data is simulated for the memory cell, the voltage on the bit line after the pre-charge will change with the voltage on the corresponding storage node. Voltage difference is generated. A sense amplifier is used in the SRAM circuit in order to increase the speed of data reading. When the voltage difference on the bit line reaches a certain value for reading data, the difference is amplified into full voltage through the sense amplifier, so as to improve the speed of data reading. The goal of improving the speed for data reading is achieved. The transient simulation results of a sensitive amplifier are shown in Fig. 10.

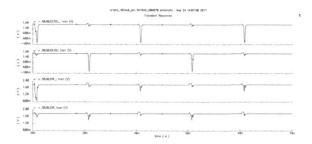

Fig. 10. The simulation results of sensitive amplifiers.

In the simulation results, SD and SD_ are two inverting output ports of the sense amplifier. The DR and DR_ ports correspond to bit lines, BL and BL_ respectively, which signals are read from the memory cell. When the sense amplifier is not in normal operation, the output ports SD and SD_ are pre-charged at the highest voltage. When the voltage difference is generated on the bit line pair, the sense amplifier is excited. At this time, the DR and DR_ ports carry information of bit line pair, thus creating a voltage difference of $V_{DR}-V_{DR\_}$. The voltage difference is detected by the sense amplifier so that the SD or SD_ signal level is pulled down to output the result. The higher the resolution of the sense amplifier, the smaller the voltage difference required for the bit line pair, and the faster the data read in the memory cell, the smaller the power dissipation caused by the bit line voltage swing.

4   The Data Read/Write and Hold Process

In the whole circuit, all of them are effective for low voltage, such as, CEN used as the select signal on chip, OEN as a data read enable signal, WEN as a data write enable signal. The enable signals WEN and OEN are valid in a specified period to control read/write operations by holding CEN on low voltage during the simulation.

In this transient simulation, the funciton of read/write data and hold data are verified by changing the address signal and data signal periodically. The address signals will change periodically over the 00000000-00000001, while the data signal will change over the period of 10101010 and 01010101 during the simulation. The address signals are shown in Fig. 11. The input data signals are shown in Fig. 12.

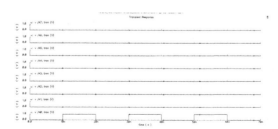

Fig. 11. Address signal.

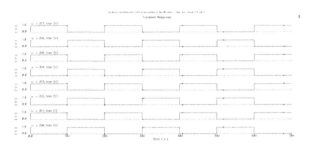

Fig. 12. Data signal.

The period changes of the address signal and the data signal are varied. The control enable signals WEN and OEN are valid within a given time period. The SRAM can be observed to write the two memory cells once respectively. Behavioral level simulation for two data reads are also shown as Fig. 13. Informations can be obtained from the simulation, as follows:

1. The data can be written normally and read correctly for the first time;
2. It can be proved that the read failure is not caused during the first reading process by reading the data correctly second times. The data information can be normally kept in the memory cell under the condition of constant power supply.

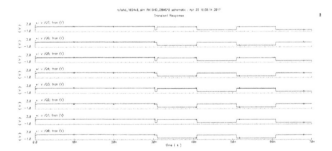

Fig. 13. Simulation for read data.

5   The Randomness for SRAM Circuit

To verify whether SRAM circuit can write or read operations at the same rate for any address cell, eight addresses are selected respectively from 0–255 addresses. As an example, the number information is stored in these addresses and read out. The selected addresses are arranged in order of 0, 5, 80, 90, 120, 50, 180, 250, respectively. The addresses used in the transient simulation are shown in Fig. 14.

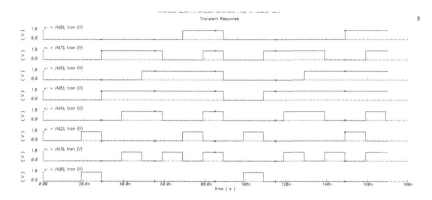

Fig. 14. Address information excitation chart.

The address data will be repeated after 90 ns because the data written needs to be read to verify data consistency. The stored data are shown in Fig. 15.

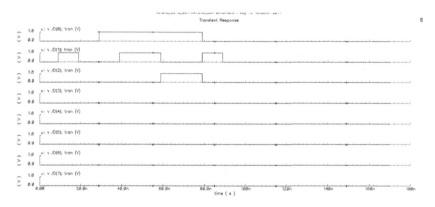

Fig. 15. The stored data signal.

The data is written before 90 ns. The data read operation is performed after the 90 ns according to enable signals. The random write/read function is verified in SRAM.

The transient simulation about 170 ns is completed by applying the address and data information, an external clock signal, and read/write select enable signal, and so on. The read data is consistent with the write data in the simulation results. The data at high 5 bits are kept to zero because each stored data is less than 8. We can only observe low 3 bits data. The comparison results between the write data and read data are shown in Fig. 16.

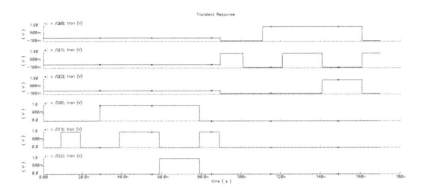

Fig. 16. Compare input data with read data.

D[0]–D [2] is the write data, and Q[0]–Q [2] is the output data in Fig. 16. The output signal remains in the high impedance because the data are written before 90 ns. The signals in output ports are serially output if the data read enable signal is valid. The consistency and randomness of write data and read date can be verified.

The calculation and analysis are carried out respectively in transient simulation, including the data writing process, data reading process and data hold process. The power consumption of writing is 48.33 mw. The power dissipation of reading is 47.83 mw. The power consumes 46.85 mw in the hold process. The operating frequency is 100 MHz.

6   Conclusion

The array based on 6T SRAM memory cell is completed in this paper. The functions of read/write operations and data hold can be achieved in memory array. The peripheral circuits of SRAM are designed and realized, which is decoder circuit, clock circuit and sense amplifier circuit, and so on. The peripheral circuit function can be verified successfully in transient simulation. SRAM function and its read/write randomness can also be implemented correctly.

References

1. Woo-oh, T., Jeong, H., Kang, K.: Power-Gated 9T SRAM cell for low-energy operation. IEEE Trans. Very Large Scale Integr. VLSI Syst. **7**, 1–5 (2016)
2. Wang, B., Li, Q., Kim, T.T.: Read bitline sensing and fast local write-back techniques in hierarchical bitline architecture for ultralow-voltage SRAMs. IEEE Trans. Very Large Scale Integr. Syst. **4**, 2156–2173 (2016)
3. Wu, S.L., Li, K.Y., Huang, P.T.: A 0.5 V 28 nm 256-kb Mini-array based 6T SRAM with Vtrip-Tracking write-assist. IEEE Trans. Circ. Syst.-I:Regul. Pap. **64**, 1791–1793 (2017)
4. Seo, Y., Kwon, K.W., Fong, X.: High performance and energy-efficient on-chip cache using dual port (1R /1 W) spin-orbit torque MRAM 181–184. IEEE J. Emerg. Sel. Top. Circ. Syst. **3**, 293–298 (2016)

A Modified AODV Protocol Based on Nodes Velocity

Tong Liu[(⊠)], Zhimou Xia, Shuo Shi, and Xuemai Gu

Harbin Institute of Technology, Harbin 150080, China
89376016@qq.com, 826744903@qq.com,
{crcss,guxuemai}@hit.edu.cn

Abstract. MANET has been widely used in many fields with the development of wireless communication technology. The AODV routing protocol which is known as a well-designed protocol of MANET has received widespread attention. However, high node velocity and frequent changes of network topology pose a challenge to the classic AODV protocol. Considering the stability of link, this paper proposes an algorithm to quantify the change frequency of network topology at first. Then a modified AODV protocol based on node velocity which is named RAODV is introduced in detail for high dynamic network topology. RAODV can build a more stable link according to the node velocity and reduce the normalized overhead of routing and average end-to-end delay by prolonging routing's survival time.

Keywords: Ad hoc network · High dynamic network topology
Node velocity · AODV · NS2

1 Introduction

When the network topology changes frequently, it is very important to establish a stable routing to guarantee the QoS of communication. Because that a stable route can effectively reduce the number of rerouting, thus the overall network latency and normalized routing overhead decrease. In the mobile ad hoc network, however, the traditional routing protocol lacks an effective mechanism to ensure the stability of the route.

In recent years, there are four methods for establishing the stable routing, they are the stable routing protocol based on the survival time of routing, the stable routing protocol on the speed of the node, the stable routing protocol on the strength of the signal and the stable routing protocol on the location of the node, respectively. In paper [6], a stable routing protocol based on link survival time is proposed. In this paper the motion model of random nodes is analyzed by a simulation experiment. Through the experiment the probability distribution of the survival time of the link corresponding to the motion mode which can be used to calculate the stability factor of the link is got. But this approach requires a large amount of experimental data and it is also very sensitive to the network topology boundary conditions. That is what we don't expect. Article [9] proposing a stable routing algorithm based on the velocity of the node. As the algorithm describes, the velocity variance of the two nodes is used as the link

© ICST Institute for Computer Sciences, Social Informatics and Telecommunications Engineering 2018
X. Gu et al. (Eds.): MLICOM 2017, Part I, LNICST 226, pp. 545–554, 2018.
https://doi.org/10.1007/978-3-319-73564-1_54

stability coefficient between the two nodes and the routing whose overall link stability coefficient is the smallest is the first choice when choosing the routing path. This method has a good performance in term of routing overhead and routing delay when the network topology changes frequently. However, when the network topology tends to be stable, the growing number of hops will result in a significant increase in the end-to-end latency time. Because of that, this algorithm can't adapt to adjust the routing strategy and then makes the route overhead increased. In the literature [12], the signal power of the two nodes is used to judge the change of the relative position of the node. Whether the two nodes are in the stable state is decided by the threshold of the ratio of the power. If the two neighbor nodes are in the stable state, these two nodes are the prior choice for the establishment of stable routing. In this paper, we first introduce the concept of the neighbor node changing ratio, that means in a period of time how often the neighbor node changes. The neighbor node changing ratio reflects the network topology changes fast or slowly. The link stability coefficient between the two nodes is defined as the sum of square of the difference between the velocity on the vertical direction and the horizontal direction. The routing with the smallest number of hops or the minimum link stability coefficient is selected adaptively according to the change rate of the neighbor node. As a result, the problem that the routing established by the stable path algorithm will greatly increase the network latency and routing overhead when the network topology tends to be stable is solved.

2   Algorithm Quantifying High Dynamic Network Topology

It's hard to judge the simulation results of traditional AODV protocol and its modified versions in the same standard assessment because of the diversity of applications. There is no uniform standard for quantifying network topology changes and most research introduced the node velocity to solve this problem.

Even if the node velocity is same, whether the node is docked and the duration of node docking will both affect the network topology changes because of their different trajectories. That is the reason for simulation results varying widely when using NS2 to generate SCENE FILE even under the same node velocity. In this paper, network topology's change is measured by neighbor nodes' rate of change, then the relationship of the degree of topology change, the node velocity and node docking time is analyzed by NS2. Simulation parameters are set as Table 1 shows:

Using NS2"setdest" toolkit to generate SCENE FILE:

./setdest −v 2 −n 50 −s 1 −m 30 −M 30 −t 500 −P 1 −p 0 −x 1000 −y 300 >scen-50n-30 s-p0

The command generates the following SCENE FILE: The node randomly selects its destination in the set simulation area (1000 m * 300 m), moving at a constant speed of 30 m/s to the destination. After reaching the specified coordinates, the node stays for the specified time (0 s) and then repeats the above-mentioned movement.

Figure 1 shows the neighbor node changing ratio of a random node when the velocities varies based on above scene. As we can see from the figure, on the same node, the velocity and neighbor node changing ratio. when the velocity is less than 5 m/s, the neighbor node changing ratio increases with increasing velocity, when the

Table 1. Simulation parameters

Simulation parameters	Parameter values
Network range	1000 m * 300 m
Number of nodes	50
Network service	CBR
MAC protocol	IEEE 802.11b
Signal transmission range	250 m
Maximum carrier sense rang	550 m
Simulation time	300 s
Radio model	Two_Ray
Maximum queue	50
Packet size	512bits

velocity is greater than 15 m/s, the neighbor node changing ratio is random. Figure 2 shows the neighbor node changing ratio after enlargement of a certain period of time.

Figures 1 and 2 are the relationship between the neighbor node changing ratio and node velocity, to further verify the relationships, the normalization of neighbor node changing ratio on total network topology as shown in Fig. 3.

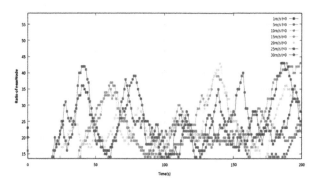

Fig. 1. Neighbor node changing ratio, when nodes velocities varies

We can see from the Fig. 3 when the node velocity is less than 15 m/s, neighbor node changing ratio increases with increasing node velocity, when the speed is greater than 15 m/s, there was no positive relationship between the neighbor changing rate and node velocity, in order to reduce the error due to the random network topology, decreases the velocity step simulation, we can get the results shown in Fig. 4, which proved the above conclusion further.

From the above analysis simulation, using the node velocity to measure the network topology changing rate is not exactly right. On the basis of this research, using node residence time to measure topology changing rate, we can get the following simulation results.

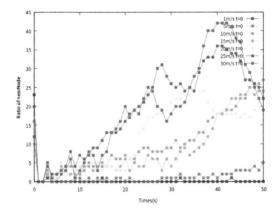

Fig. 2. Neighbor nodes changing ratio with velocities variation after enlargement

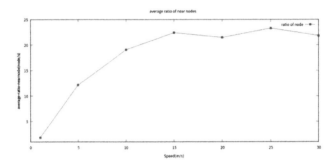

Fig. 3. Neighbor nodes changing ratio with velocities variation

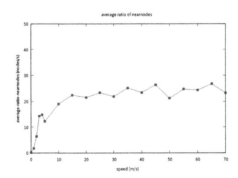

Fig. 4. Neighbor nodes changing ratio with velocities variation

Figure 5 is the relationship between the neighbor node changing ratio of some random nodes and the node residence time. It shows that There is no strict linear relationship between the neighbor node changing ratio of the single node and the node residence time. After normalization analysis, we can get Fig. 6. The figure shows that when the node velocity is constant, with the increase of residence, neighbor node changing ratio is gradually reduced. When node residence time is more than 20 s, the average neighbor node changing ratio decreases slowly, with the maximum residence time continue to increase, the average neighbor node changing ratio will gradually approach 0, namely when the network node keeping static, the neighbor node changing ratio is 0.

The simulation results show that using the residence time as a measure of the degree of network topology's changing is more convincing. In this paper, the rest simulation will use the node residence time to measure the frequency of network topology changes.

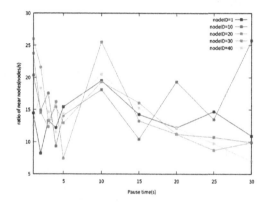

Fig. 5. Neighbor node changing ratio of some random nodes with node residence time varies

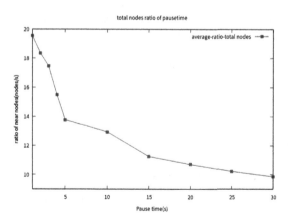

Fig. 6. Neighbor node changing ratio of total network topology, when node residence time varies

3 Link Stability Calculation and Routing Strategy

In high dynamic networks, the relative speed between nodes is the main factor that affects the life cycle of the link. When the velocity of two nodes are relatively large, the distance between nodes will increase rapidly, which leads to the interruption of the link. A new parameter is introduced here "σ_{ij}", It is defined as:

$$\sigma_{ij} = \left(v_{xi} - v_{xj}\right)^2 + \left(v_{yi} - v_{yj}\right)^2 \tag{1}$$

σ_{ij}:   Stability coefficient between node i and node j
v_{xi}:   Node i in horizontal velocity
v_{yi}:   Node i in vertical velocity
v_{xj}:   Node j in horizontal velocity
v_{yj}:   Node j in vertical velocity

The sum of the stability coefficients of each adjacent two nodes on the link is defined as the link stability factor, defined as "σ_{sum}".

On this basis, Modify the AODV routing protocol RREQ and RREP, Add $v_x, v_y, \sigma_{sum}, \theta_{node}$ three data fields. v_x, v_y are used to store the node level and vertical direction velocity, σ_{sum} is used to store the link stability coefficient, θ_{node} is used to store the neighbor node changing ratio.

In the routing request phase, firstly, the source node obtains the velocity of itself and the neighbor node changing ratio which will be stored separately in v_x, v_y, θ_{node}, and then sets the link stability coefficient σ_{sum} to "0". Secondly, broadcasting the route request message to their neighbor nodes, when a neighbor node received this route request message, it will calculate the stability coefficient between the last hop node and itself according to Eq. (1), then update σ_{sum} in the routing request message. Also, the received routing request message's v_x, v_y were updated to its own velocity. Forwarding this RREQ until the destination node received it. The destination node will select the route request message through the neighbor node changing ratio θ_{node} or the stable coefficient of link σ_{sum} to reply before it created a routing. If θ_{node} is greater than 10, the destination node select the routing which has a smaller σ_{sum}, otherwise, the routing which has minimum hop will be selected.

4 Performance Simulation

4.1 Calculation of Performance Index

In this paper, packet loss rate, end-to-end delay, routing initiation frequency, normalized routing overhead are simulated.

The main performance evaluation criteria for the stable path algorithm is the normalized routing control overhead, and the other auxiliary evaluation criteria are routing initiation frequency, end-to-end delay and packet loss rate.

(a) Routing initiation frequency, the ability to maintain the stability of the routing protocol. The formula is as follows:

$$Request\_rate = \frac{count(route\_request)}{time_{stop}} \tag{2}$$

(b) Normalized routing control overhead, the number of routing control packets required to send a packet to the destination node. The smaller the normalized routing control overhead is, the lower the cost of routing protocol is, the better the protocol performance is. The formula is as follows:

$$Load_{Normalization} = \frac{count(control\_packet)}{max(packet\_id)} \tag{3}$$

(c) The packet loss rate, investigate routing protocol packet delivery ability of the source node to destination node, the packet loss rate is the number of packets lost accounted for the ratio of the number of total package, packet loss rate is small, the agreement will show that packet delivery success more ability to better the performance of the agreement. The formula is as follows:

$$Rate_{loss} = \frac{count(send\_packet) - count(receive\_packet)}{count(send\_packet)} \tag{4}$$

(d) Average end to end delay, the average value of the packet passing from the source node to the destination node, which reflects the speed of the packet passing through the routing protocol. The formula is as follows:

$$average\_delay = \frac{sum(T_{end\_time}(i) - T_{start\_time}(i))}{count(T_{end\_time}(i))} \tag{5}$$

Among them, T is the effective time, that is, at this time the packet can be received by the destination node. Taking NS2 as the simulation platform, the improved algorithm is simulated and compared with the traditional AODV routing protocol. The feasibility and correctness of the algorithm are verified by the parameter analysis model.

4.2   Analysis of Performance

Figure 7 shows Packet loss rate when the node residence time varies, compared with traditional AODV protocol, it has great advantages in packet loss rate when the residence time less than 20 s. With the increase in the residence time, the dynamic of network topology is reduced, the difference between these two routing protocol decreases, RAODV protocol may have a bit greater loss ratio than the traditional AODV protocol.

Figures 8 and 9 shows the routing average end to end delay according to the variation of residence time. We can see from the figure that the difference between

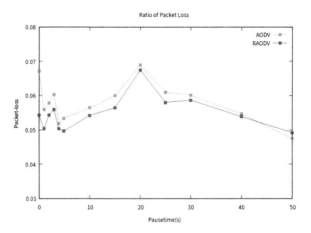

Fig. 7. AODV and RAODV Packet loss rate performance simulation

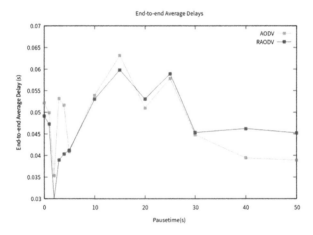

Fig. 8. Average end to end delay performance simulation

RAODV protocol and AODV protocol is small, with the increase in node residence time, the delay of AODV protocol reduces gradually, when the residence time is greater than 30 s, the delay performance of AODV protocol is better than RAODV protocol, the reason is nodes hop, although the outage probability of stable routing is small, the routing repair process decreases can make delay decreases, but due to the choice of the stable routing is not minimum hop routing, packet transmission delay caused by the increase in the residence time is very small, when the network topology changes frequently, the advantages of stable RAODV protocol is apparent, the overall delay is slightly better than that of the AODV protocol, with the increase of time to stop the network topology changes frequently decreased, then AODV protocol routing outage probability decreases, at this time the AODV protocol to establish the minimum

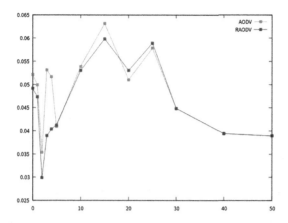

Fig. 9. Average end to end delay performance simulation

number of hops routing strategy is reflected in the overall delay will be lower than the
RAODV protocol. When we take into consideration, as the neighbor node changing
ratio less than 10, we may select the minimum hop routing instead which will decrease
the end to end delay.

5   Conclusion

In this paper a modified AODV protocol based on the node velocity is introduced.
When the network topology changes frequently, this improved protocol enables to
reduce the overhead of route discovery process. Also, end to end delay is reduced as a
result of considering self-adaption routing discovery. Simulation results shows that the
proposed protocol has better end to end delay compared with traditional AODV
protocol.

References

1. Yawan, N., Keeratiwintakorn, P.: AODV improvement for vehicular networks with cross
   layer technique and mobility prediction. In: 2011 International Symposium on IEEE
   Intelligent Signal Processing and Communications Systems (ISPACS), pp. 1–6 (2011)
2. Panichpapiboon, S., Ferrari, G., Tonguz, O.K.: Connectivity of ad hoc wireless networks: an
   alternative to graph-theoretic approaches. Wirel. Netw. **16**, 793–811 (2010)
3. Sarma, N., Nandi, S.: Route stability based QoS routing in mobile ad hoc networks. Wirel.
   Pers. Commun. **54**, 203–224 (2010)
4. Li, B., Liu, Y., Chu, G.: Improved AODV routing protocol for vehicular ad hoc networks
   advanced computer theory and engineering. In: 2010 3rd International Conference on
   V4-337-V4-340 (2010)
5. Lee, S.J., Gerla, M.: AODV-BR: backup routing in ad hoc networks. In: Wireless
   Communications and Networking Conference, vol. 3. pp. 1311–1316. IEEE Press (2000)

6. Park, G.W., Lee, S.H.: A routing protocol for extend network lifetime through the residual battery and link stability in MANET. In: Proceedings of the WSEAS International Conference on Applied Computing Conference World Scientific and Engineering Academy and Society, pp. 199–204 (2010)

7. Chiang, C.-C., Wu, H.-K., Liu, W., Gerla, M.: Routing in clustered multihop mobile wireless networks with fading channel. In: IEEE SICON 1997, Kent Ridge, Singapore, pp. 197–211 (1999)

8. Feng, J., Zhou, H.: A self-repair algorithm for ad hoc on-demand distance vector routing. In: International Conference on Personal Communication (2006)

9. Lee, S.J., Gerla, M.: AODV-BR: backup routing in ad hoc networks. In: Proceedings of IEEE WCNC 2000, Chicago, vol. 9, pp. 156–162. IEEE Press (2000)

10. Hajlaoui, R., Guyennet, H., Moulahi, T.: A survey on heuristic-based routing methods in vehicular ad-hoc network: technical challenges and future trends. IEEE Sens. J. **16**, 6782–6792 (2012)

11. Lu, J., Ma, M.: Cross-layer QoS support framework and holistic opportunistic scheduling for QoS in single carrier WiMAX system. J. Netw. Comput. Appl. **34**, 76–773 (2011)

12. Nabil, M., Hajami, A., Haqiq, A.: Improvement of location aided routing protocol in vehicular ad hoc networks on highway. In: 2015 5th World Congress on Information and Communication Technologies, pp. 53–58. IEEE Press (2015)

RSA Encryption Algorithm Design and Verification Based on Verilog HDL

Bei Cao[1(✉)], Tianliang Xu[1,2], and Pengfei Wu[1]

[1] Electronic Engineering School, Heilongjiang University,
Harbin 150080, China
caobei@hlju.edu.cn
[2] Microelectronic Center, Harbin Institute of Technology (Wei Hai),
Harbin 150000, China

Abstract. Prime number generation and the large number operations directly affect the efficiency of RSA encryption algorithm. In order to reduce the number of the calculation process about modular operation and to reduce the difficulty of division in the calculation process, the Montgomery optimization algorithm is used to carry out the modular multiplication of RSA encryption algorithm, so that the efficiency of the algorithm is improved. Based on the application and research of hardware implementation to information encryption, the Verilog hardware description language is used to design the RSA encryption algorithm in 1024 bits. The simulation results of encryption and decryption experiment show that Montgomery modular multiplication algorithm and RSA encryption algorithm are verified to be correct and effective.

Keywords: RSA encryption algorithm · Verilog HDL
Modular multiplication · Montgomery optimization algorithm

1 Introduction

The public key cryptography, which plays an important role in the modern encryption system, has high information security. RSA encryption algorithm is the first to meet the requirements of the public key cryptography [1]. The inverse of the modular exponentiation operation is calculated so that the decomposition of large integer is difficult. In this way, we can ensure the security of information [2]. It is a perfect password system which is in theoretical research and application.

At present, the security of RSA encryption system is also threatened. In 1999, the 512-bit RSA encryption algorithm was worked out after five months. In recent years, the RSA encryption algorithm with 768-bit length of secret key has been cracked, and the crack time is thousands of times as long as 512-bit encryption's crack time. Obviously, the key length is closely related to the encryption reliability. The security of RSA algorithm with 1024-bit secret key length can be guaranteed. A lot of research has been done for the 1024-bit RSA at home and abroad. Montgomery optimization algorithm based on the pipeline technology and the hard algorithm of the hardwire multiplier are proposed to improve the computational speed [3]. The modular multiplication circuit architecture is used to 4-radix multiplication RSA algorithm [4].

© ICST Institute for Computer Sciences, Social Informatics and Telecommunications Engineering 2018
X. Gu et al. (Eds.): MLICOM 2017, Part I, LNICST 226, pp. 555–563, 2018.
https://doi.org/10.1007/978-3-319-73564-1_55

CMOS technology is used to design and implement Montgomery encryption algorithm [5]. RSA encryption algorithm has received extensive attention in the field of research and application.

RSA encryption algorithm can be used software and hardware to achieve. In order to ensure information security, tedious data calculations are needed. For the hardware implementation, the encrypted data are applied to the hardware device to obtain the encrypted information code. In this paper, RSA encryption algorithm and optimization technology will be studied and design. Based on hardware information encryption technology, Verilog hardware description language (HDL) is used to implement the algorithm, and the RSA system is verified by simulation tool.

2　RSA Encryption Algorithm Basis

The public-key cryptography belongs to asymmetric cryptosystem whose encryption and decryption process use different keys. They are called public key and private key respectively. Double secret keys make it possible for both parties to communicate securely, even on insecure information channels.

2.1　Cryptosystem

In the encryption and decryption process, first, pair of encryption key "e" and decrypt key "d" are generated in the receiving terminal. Encryption key can be disclosed to other parties. The sender encrypt the information of the plaintext M which will be conveyed, and generate incomprehensible symbol or information as a ciphertext C. Then, it is sent to the receiving terminal. The encryption process:

$$C = E_e(M) \tag{1}$$

The receiving terminal obtains the ciphertext C. It can decrypt the ciphertext C by using the decryption algorithm D and the decryption key "d". The plaintext M is restored. The decryption process:

$$M = D_d(C) \tag{2}$$

RSA encryption algorithm has high strength and security. Key management is simple and clear. The two sides of the communication use different keys so that the encryption key can be spread. In this way, it is difficult to crack from the encryption key to get the decryption key. So it can reduce the burden of key management. The algorithm is difficult and slow to operate. The process of generating keys is complex for the mathematical theory, and these also are the advantages to protect the information security.

2.2　RSA Encryption Algorithm Principle and Large Number Processing

The working of the algorithm consists of three processes: key generation, encryption and decryption. The important technology is mainly large prime generation, large number of processing, solving equations and fast modular exponentiation for the hardware implementation. The encryption algorithm requires the prime number detection before the key is generated. The modular exponentiation operation will be used. And the modular exponent operation use the Euclidean algorithm, which is the process of the decrypt key "d" generating. RSA encryption algorithm as a system is interrelated, and it is not independent of each other.

Key generation is achieved through the key generation algorithm. The specific steps of the algorithm are as follows.

[1] Generate two different large prime p, q;
[2] Calculate $n = p \cdot q$ and $\Phi(n) = (p - 1)(q - 1)$, where $\Phi(n)$ is the Euler function of n;
[3] Select random integer e to make $gcd(e, \Phi(n)) = 1$, and satisfy $1 < e < \Phi(n)$, that is, e and $\Phi(n)$ are coprime;
[4] Seeking private key d to make $ed \equiv 1(\bmod \Phi(n))$, and d is the modulo anti-element, also called multiplication inverse d; satisfying $1 < d < \Phi(n)$;
[5] (e, n) is the public key, (d, n) is the private key, then p, q, $\Phi(n)$ are destroyed.

Encryption and decryption process is also the key to the design of the algorithm. If Party B sends an encrypted message M to the Party A, it would need to use the public key (e, n) to encrypt the plaintext M to obtain ciphertext C. In this paper, when encrypting, the plaintext is first grouped. And the value of each group is less than the integer N. The binary width of the packet is less than the value of $\log 2^N$ [6]. Then, plaintext grouping for the integer m, and the string can be obtained ASCII value to conduct encryption. Such as function (3), note that m must be less than n.

$$C = E_e(M) = M^e(\bmod N) \tag{3}$$

Party A receives the information code from Party B, and it is necessary to decrypt the ciphertext packet, such as in function (4).

$$M = D_d(C) = C^d(\bmod N) \tag{4}$$

3 RSA Encryption Algorithm and System Design

3.1 Large Prime Generation and Computing Processing

An important question of RSA encryption algorithm is how to generate large prime numbers quickly. In this paper, the binomial probability detection method is used to generate random numbers, and then we can judge the number of prime numbers by the designed test algorithm. The steps are as follows.

[1] Calculate the odd number M so that $N = (2^r) * M + 1$;
[2] Select the random number $A < N$;
[3] for $i < r$, $A^{((2^i)*M)} \bmod N = N - 1$, then N through the random number A test;
[4] or, if $A^M \bmod N = 1$, then N passes the test of random number A;
[5] Through the value of A is different to give N five tests. If the results are passed, then N is prime.

As the number of tests N increases, N satisfies that the probability is not prime, that is, the probability that N is prime can reach $1 - (1/4^t)$. For example, when $t = 5$, the probability that N is prime is more than 99.99%. Most compilers support 64-bit. In order to avoid the problem of low efficiency in establishment of large number of arithmetic and decimal number and a large number of storage space. In this paper, the 1024-bit large number is expressed as 0x1_0000_0000 hexadecimal. For example, 0x0000_0000 $\sim$ 0xffff_ffff, that is, with 32-bit * 32-bit interval, 1024-bit large number conversion into 32 elements of the interval array, for the interval array is only more 32 Sub-cycle operation than before. In terms of computers, the binary is similar to the 0x1_0000_0000 system and it is easy to convert.

3.2   Modular Multiplication

The modular exponential operation complicates the data through the power exponential operation to make the operation process complicated and achieve the effect of information security. Therefore, the modular exponentiation is transformed into multiple modular multiplication operations, that is, $C = A * B \bmod N$, where A, B and N are integers that satisfy the relation of $0 \leq A, B \leq N$. Considering the security, the 1024-bit modulo operation requires a higher hardware design. And the multiplication rule will produce 2048 bits of the process. And avoiding the direct calculation of $A * B$ is the primary problem to be solved by the modular multiplication. Montgomery algorithm is used to modular multiplication. It is defined as follows.

Definition 1.   Assuming that the two integers of x and y are satisfied with $0 < a, b < N$, select a radix r, and then select a number R with respect to N and satisfy $R = r^n$, then $X = x * R (\bmod N), Y = y * R (\bmod N)$. Represent the mapping of a, b in N residual.

$$Z = X * Y * R^{-1} (\bmod N) \tag{5}$$

Where R^{-1} is the inverse of the R-mode N and satisfy $R^{-1}R = 1 (\bmod N)$, which is called the Montgomery multiplication.

Montgomery multiplication can avoid the use of division. On the contrary, it can use shift operation to achieve modular operation. Under the K power of 2, division only needs to perform the left shift operation. In this way, we can simplify the complexity of the operation and reduce the number of modes. Table 1 shows the Montgomery modular expression, N represents the modulus, and T is the reduced number $R = 2^n$, in the binary conditions, n is the number of bits width. $T + qN$ is the actual number of the remaining classes in which T is actually represented.

It can be seen that $Mon \bmod N = T * R^{-1} \bmod N$, the value of $Mon \bmod N$ can be used to calculate the value of $T * R^{-1} \bmod N$. If q is found to be a multiple of R, the divisor would be an integer. If

$$N[0] * N[0]'\%r = 1, q = (C'[0] + A * B[0]) * (r - N[0]')\%r \tag{6}$$

Table 1. Expressions about Montgomery modular multiplication.

Character	Expression
Montgomery reduction	$Mon = (T + qN)/R = (T + qN) * 1/R$
Operation of residue class	$M(T) * M(1) = M(T) * M(R) * M(R - 1)$

Then,

$$(C'[0] + A * B[0] + q * N[0]\%r = (C'[0] + A * B[0] - ((C'[0] + A * B[0]) * N[0]' \\ * N[0])\%r)\%r = 0) \tag{7}$$

Where C'[0] represents the initial state. If $r = 0x1\_0000\_0000$ is used, division and modulo operation will become simple. For example, the result is $q[63:0]$, $\%r = q[31:0]$, $/r = q[63:32]$. There is no more than 32 times the number of cycles k for the key length in 1024-bit. Only the intermediate variables of $C' = C' + A * B + q * N$ will appear multiple times so that the efficiency of the algorithm will be improved. The only thing that needs to be calculated is the $N[0]'$ value, which makes $N[0] * N[0]'\%r = 1$. Since N is a fixed value, it is only necessary to perform a calculation on $N[0]'$ without affecting the efficiency of the operation.

3.3 RSA Encryption System Design

RSA encryption hardware application requirements are analyzed. RSA encryption algorithm top-level module is described based on Verilog HDL and named RSA_1024. The system module and external pin definition are shown in Fig. 2. The parallel data input is used in this system, and the maximum can support 1024-bit data operations. In order to optimize the structure, reduce the port cost, the input data will be taken 32-bit as a group and 32 consecutive units of input in cycles (Fig. 1).

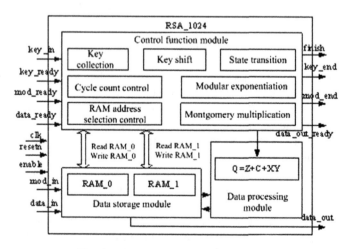

Fig. 1. 1024-bit RSA encryption system.

When data_ready signal of encryption key *e*, mod *n* and whisper data are pulled high, the data are entered. After the encryption operation is completed, the data_out_ready signal is pulled high and the outputted encrypted data is valid. Then, the system mainly includes the control function realization module, the data processing module and the data storage module.

3.4   RSA Control Module Design

The RSA control function module performs packet acquisition on the encryption key e and d input. We can select RAM_0, RAM_1 for the module of store data by judging the data by the key shift, executes the data Montgomery modular multiplication, and controling the two sub-modules through the RAM address selection control and the cyclic count control to store the data The module selects RAM_0, RAM_1, and stores the data values in the middle of the operation. In addition, the control state transfer switch plays a role of connecting each module in the process of RSA algorithm implementation. Finally, the signal processing of the plaintext ciphertext, plus the key, the modulo input are done by the relevant module data storage and encryption operation. The realization process can be represented by the state Fig. 2.

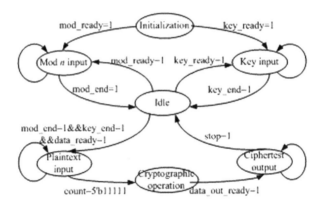

Fig. 2. State diagram about implementation module of RSA control function

The data input and output sections are analyzed according to the actual situation of the state transition and the parallel input data shown in Fig. 2. Starting from the data initialization, when the input key data signal is 1, the key e is input until 32 groups 32 Bit data input is completed, and the key data input end signal is 1 and jumps to the idle state. When the input modulo data signal is 1, the input data N is started. When 32 sets of 32-bit data input are completed. The modulo data input end signal is 1 and jumps to the idle state. In addition, when the key e and the modulo data N input are completed and the input plaintext data signal is ready to be 1, the plaintext data is input until 32 sets of 32-bit data input completion with countering from 0 to 31, before entering the encryption operation state; when the encryption operation is over, then ready to output ciphertext data signal is 1, and all the data output to stop the entire operation process, then jump back to the end of the idle state.

Considering the problem of large data storage capacity, the data storage module uses memory RAM_0 and RAM_1, which are 128×32 and used as input group of plaintext or ciphertext data input and module n input. Finally, it will store the middle of the calculation process, Remainder and modulo and other data values.

4   RSA Encryption Algorithm Simulation

In order to verify the function of Verilog HDL based RSA encryption algorithm, the simulation tool ModelSim is used to simulate the algorithm and we will analyse whether the sub-module achieves the expected function. The security key is set to p = 47, q = 59, e = 101, d = 317, n = 2773, i.e. the public key is (101, 2773) and the private key is (317, 2773). When 32 sets of plaintext data are M = 1088, 32 sets of ciphertext data are C = 1992, and this data is taken as an example to verify the function of the corresponding module.

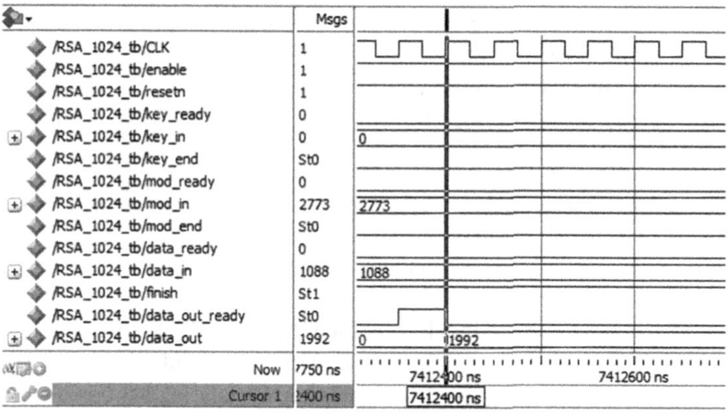

Fig. 3. Encryption process simulation results

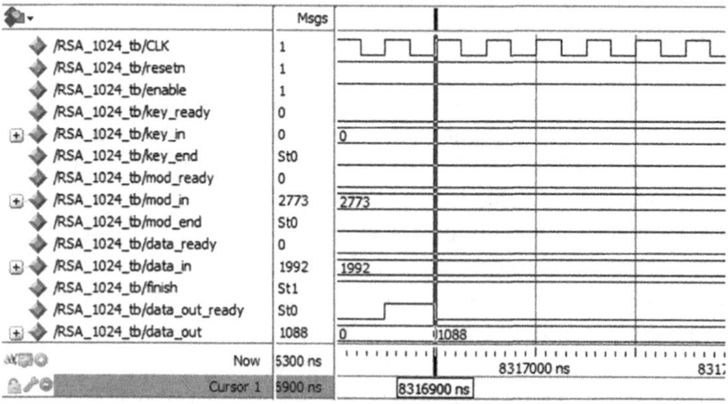

Fig. 4. Decryption process simulation results

When the 32 groups of input text are $M = 1088$, encryption key $e = 101$, 32 group mode are $N = 2773$, Fig. 3 shows the encryption operation of 32 sets of ciphertext data are $C = 1992$; when the input ciphertext $C = 1992$, decryption key $d = 317$, modulo $N = 2773$, Fig. 4 shows the decryption operation of plaintext M is 1088. After the encryption and decryption of the data can be found in each other, the function is correct, that is, algorithm can be achieved. It should be noted that the plaintext, modulo, ciphertext are 1024 bits of data, except that each of the 32 groups is the same, and the encryption key is 32 bits and only have one group. Finally, the remaining 31 groups are 0.

As shown in Fig. 5, the modular multiplication algorithm realize the function of the algorithm by outputting the 12_bit command through the output terminal. These commands control the data path and the data storage of the four registers to realize the core algorithm calculation, that is, $Q = Z + C + XY$.

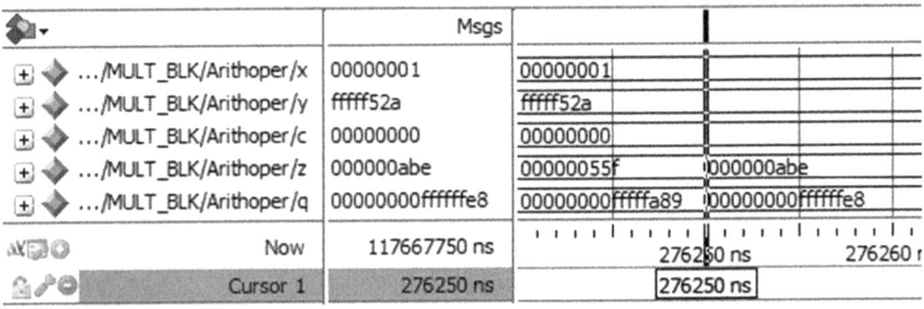

Fig. 5. Modular multiplication simulation results

We can check when the error is obtained by $x = 32'h0000\_0001$ and $y = 32'hffff\_f52a$, $c = 32'H0000\_0000$, $z = 32'h0000\_055f$, the simulation result is the same as the calculated result. In this paper, the latter set of data is also consistent with the simulation results. So we can verify the correctness of the Montgomery modular multiplication.

5 Conclusion

There are six security parameters in the RSA encryption algorithm, which are named p, q, n, $\Phi(n)$, e, d. There is the public key (e, n) only on the encryption. And the decryption side have the private key (d, n) and the parameter p, q. In this paper, the design of Verilog HDL is achieved by 1024-bit key length algorithm. And it used Rabin Miller primality probability detection method to generate the binomial number. And the large number is processed, stored and computed by the N array and the Montgomery modular multiplication algorithm. In this way, we can solve the huge amount of data problems. In order to solve the input and output data time between the numbers of pins of mutual restriction. And a large number of input and output are used a parallel way. The simulation results show that this paper can realize the information encryption and decryption function requirements.

References

1. Adleman, L., Rivest, R.: The use of public key cryptography in communication system design. Commun. Soc. Mag. **16**, 20–23 (1978)
2. Yan, G.X.: Information security under encryption technology. Netw. Secur. Technol. Appl. **393**, 100–104 (2013). (in Chinese)
3. Hentabli, W., Merazka, F.: An extension of RSA_512 to RSA_1024 core under hardware platform based on Montgomery powering. In: International Conference for Internet Technology and Secured Transactions, pp. 448–453 (2013)
4. Tamura, S., Yamada, C., Ichikawa, S.: Implementation and evaluation of modular multiplication based on coarsely integrated operand scanning. In: Networking and Computing, pp. 334–335 (2012)
5. Tenca, A.F., Ruggiero, W.V.: CRT RSA decryption: modular exponentiation based solely on Montgomery multiplication. In: Asilomar Conference on Signals, Systems and Computers, pp. 431–436 (2015)
6. Liu, Z., Jing, J., Xia, L.: An optimized architecture to speed up the Montgomery modular. In: International Conference on Computers, Communications, Control and Automation, pp. 58–62 (2011)

A Novel High Efficiency Distributed UEP Rateless Coding Scheme for Satellite Network Data Transmission

Shuang Wu[1], Zhenyong Wang[1,2(✉)], Dezhi Li[1], Qing Guo[1], and Gongliang Liu[1]

[1] School of Electronics and Information Engineering,
Harbin Institute of Technology, Harbin 150001, China
wooshuang@126.com, {zywang,lidezhi,qguo,liugl}@hit.edu.cn
[2] Shenzhen Academy of Aerospace Technology, Shenzhen 518057, China

Abstract. As the satellite networks can provide Internet access services, there are more and more kinds of data are transmitted on it. To ensure all kinds of data can be transmitted satisfied their own reliable requirements and obtain high transmission efficiency, a novel UEP transmission scheme based on distributed LT codes was proposed in this paper. In which scheme, the sub-codes on each node in the satellite network are performed with EEP property. By assigned different output degree distributions for the sub-codes, different kinds of data transmitted under the proposed scheme can be recovered by different reliable levels with nearly optimal transmission efficiency. On other hand, compared with the traditional distributed LT codes based transmission schemes, the relay nodes in proposed scheme do not have to know the reliable level of each source node, hence the security of the data can be guaranteed. We also make the asymptotic and finite-length analysis of proposed coding scheme, and the numerical results shows that the proposed scheme can provide UEP property between different kinds of data with low overhead performance, which can ensure the efficiency of data transmission.

Keywords: Satellite networks · LT codes · Unequal error protection
Low overhead · Asymptotic analysis · Finite length evaluation

1 Introduction

Satellite networks providing a global coverage area, which can provide ubiquitous Internet access services [1]. As a growing number of users expect access these services in different areas, this wide coverage requirement could be achieved by using the satellite networks [2]. To satisfy the various requirements of the users, there are many kinds of data have to be transmitted on the satellite networks, it is worth to note various kinds of data always lead to various reliability requirements. Satellite systems always with long transmission distances, especially for geosynchronous orbits (GEO), and the lossy and possible disruption channels [3].

© ICST Institute for Computer Sciences, Social Informatics and Telecommunications Engineering 2018
X. Gu et al. (Eds.): MLICOM 2017, Part I, LNICST 226, pp. 564–573, 2018.
https://doi.org/10.1007/978-3-319-73564-1_56

To transmit multi-kinds of data on such complex channel and dynamic network structure conditions, make sure all kinds of data can be recovered with their own reliability requirements and ensure the overall transmission efficiency, many previous work have been proposed in the past decade.

Rateless codes were proposed for efficient data transmission over multi users with different channel conditions. As the decoder of rateless codes can recover original message packets (i.e., input symbols) by collecting a little larger number of encoded message packets (i.e., output symbols), which codes can provide capacity-achieving property on channels with various conditions, it worth noting that in most scenarios the encoder of rateless codes continuously generate output symbols until received a feedback message. LT codes were developed by Luby [4] as the first practical realization of rateless codes, although LT codes is capacity-achieving, but which is designed for scenarios with single source node. To ensure the data transmission efficiency in network scenarios with multi-source nodes, the distributed LT codes is invented in [5,6], by encoded the input symbols on different source and relay nodes, the capacity-achieving property can be obtained in the network systems.

To transmit multi kinds of data with different reliability requirements, a class of rateless codes with unequal error protection (UEP) property are first proposed by Rahnavard et al. [7–9]. In which codes, the input symbols are divided into different sets, as the encoder assigned different selection probabilities of these sets, the input symbols in different sets can be recovered with different error probabilities. To face for the network scenarios in which there are multi kinds of data with different reliability requirements have to be transmitted, the distributed UEP LT codes also been proposed [10]. Different with the distributed LT codes, the input symbols of distributed UEP LT codes are only encoded on source nodes, the relay nodes only forward the output symbols to destination node with two rules. The first rule is forward a part of output symbols and forward to destination node directly, the other one is forward the XOR of two incoming output symbols to destination. It is clear that the feedback messages of distributed UEP LT codes would passed by both the destination-relay and relay-source channels. By using the distributed UEP LT codes to transmit multi kinds of data on satellite networks, the long transmission distances would lead to large delay times and extremely influence the data transmission efficiency. To overcome the influences, we proposed a novel distributed UEP rateless coding scheme to transmit multi kinds of data on satellite networks. In the proposed distributed UEP rateless coding schemes, both the source and relay nodes would perform LT codes, the feedback message of each encoder would sent from the next node, hence the influence of delay times can be reduced and thus improve the transmission efficiency.

This paper is organized as follows. Section 2 illustrate the related works. The proposed codes are proposed in Sect. 3, and then we derive the asymptotic analysis of proposed codes. In Sect. 4, we give the finite length analysis of proposed codes and then the criteria of output degree distributions and overheads for subcodes are also given. The numerical results are given in Sect. 5, which shown that the proposed codes can provide better overhead property than traditional distributed UEP rateless codes. Finally, we summarized conclusions in Sect. 6.

2   System Model

To propose the distributed UEP rateless codes, a system model of satellite networks is proposed in this section.

For simplicity, consider a multi-source and single-relay satellite network, in which network the source nodes are low earth orbits (LEO) satellite and the relay node is a geosynchronous orbit (GEO) satellite. The data (input symbols) on different LEO satellites with the different reliability requirements. By using the error control codes on the physical layer, the channels in this system can be considered as erasure channels.

The satellite network is shown as Fig. 1, where the data are transmit from J LEO satellites (source nodes) S_1, S_2, ..., S_J to ground station (destination) D through the GEO satellite (relay node) R. Where the channels between LEOs and GEO are named *source channel*, which between GEO and ground station is called *relay channel*. The erasure rates of the source channel between S_i and R is e_i, and for relay channel is e_R.

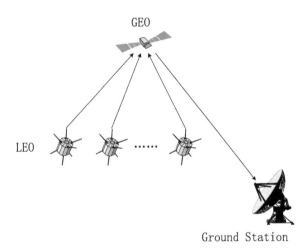

Fig. 1. The structure of multi source and single relay satellite network.

3   Proposed Coding Scheme

In this section, we proposed the coding scheme for satellite network data transmission, which scheme is based on the distributed LT codes, by assign the different coding parameters of sub-codes on each nodes, the proposed scheme can provide UEP property between the data from different source nodes.

3.1   The Encoding Process of Proposed Coding Scheme

The encoding process of proposed scheme is shown in Fig. 2. Where the encoding process is divided into 2 steps: In the first step, the encoders on source nodes generate intermediate symbols and then these symbols are transmitted to the relay node. In the second step, the encoder on GEO select intermediate symbols to generate output symbols and transmit to ground station D.

In the first step, each node S_i generate intermediate symbols by selected input symbols and using the output degree distribution $\Omega^{(i)}(x) = \sum_d \Omega^{(i)} x^d$. Assuming the number of input symbols on S_i is k_i, and encoding overhead of this sub-code is γ_i, which means there are $\frac{\gamma_i k_i}{1-e_i}$ intermediate symbols are generated on the node S_i. In the second step, there are $\sum_{i=1}^{J} \gamma_i k_i$ intermediate symbols are collected by the relay node R, and the encoder on R generate output symbols by selected intermediate symbols using output degree distribution $\Omega^{(R)}(x)$. In the both two steps, the encoders all process as the classical LT encoder [4]. Define the total number of input symbols is k, where $k_i = \alpha_i k$, then we have $k = \sum_i k_i = \sum_i \alpha_i k$.

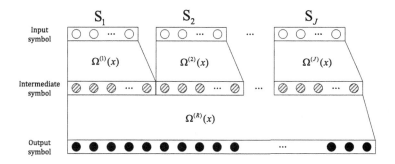

Fig. 2. The encoding structure of proposed codes.

3.2   The Decoding Process of Proposed Coding Scheme

There are only one decoder on the destination in proposed coding scheme, which decoder implement belief propagation (BP) decoding algorithm to recover the input symbols. Although the input symbols came from different source nodes, these input symbols and the collected output symbols can be considered as a independent LT code in the destination, the bipartite graph of the decoding process is shown in Fig. 3.

To analysis the decoding process of proposed coding scheme, the overall output degree distributions $\Omega(x)$ are needed. Let $\Phi(x)$ represent the degree distribution of intermediate symbols, which distribution can be given by the following Lemma.

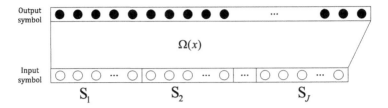

Fig. 3. The decoding structure of proposed codes.

Lemma 1. *The degree distribution of intermediate symbols $\Phi(x)$ can be calculated by*

$$\Phi(x) = \sum_{i=1}^{J} \frac{\gamma_i k_i \Omega^{(i)}(x)}{\sum_{j=1}^{J} \gamma_j k_j}. \tag{1}$$

Proof. The number of intermediate symbols is $\sum_{j=1}^{J} \gamma_j k_j$ and the intermediate symbols with degree d is $\sum_{i=1}^{J} \gamma_i k_i \Omega_d^{(i)}$, then we have $\Phi_d = \frac{\sum_{i=1}^{J} \gamma_i k_i \Omega_d^{(i)}}{\sum_{j=1}^{J} \gamma_j k_j}$. Hence Eq. (1) is obtained.

As the $\Phi(x)$ and $\Omega^{(R)}(x)$ are known, the overall output degree distribution $\Omega(x)$ can be obtained.

Theorem 1. *The overall output degree distribution $\Omega(x)$ of the proposed coding scheme is given by*

$$\Omega(x) = \Omega^{(R)}(\Phi(x)). \tag{2}$$

Proof. For the intermediate symbols, the number is $\sum_{i=1}^{J} \gamma_i k_i$ and degree distribution is $\Phi(x)$. When the GEO R generate output symbols with degree 1, which means these output symbols are generated by select only one intermediate symbol, then the output degree distribution of these output symbols are $\Phi(x)$. When R generate output symbols with degree d ($d > 1$), which means the output symbols are generated by XORed d intermediate symbols, then the output degree distribution of these output symbols are $(\Phi(x))^d$. As the generate degree distribution of relay node R is $\Omega^{(R)}(x)$, then the output degree distribution $\Omega(x)$ can be calculated as

$$\Omega(x) = \Omega_1^{(R)}(\Phi(x)) + \Omega_2^{(R)}(\Phi(x))^2 + \cdots + \Omega_d^{(R)}(\Phi(x))^d + \cdots.$$

Consider an intermediate symbol with degree d, the probability this symbol generated by the source node S_i is

$$q_{d,i} = \frac{\gamma_i k_i \Omega_d^{(i)}}{\sum_{l=1}^{J} \gamma_l k_l \Omega_d^{(l)}}. \tag{3}$$

As the encoder on relay node perform EEP LT encoding process, the probability that an input neighbor of each output symbol came from source node S_i is

$$
q_i = \frac{\sum_d d\Phi_d \frac{\gamma_i k_i \Omega_d^{(i)}}{\sum_{l=1}^J \gamma_l k_l \Omega_d^{(l)}}}{\Phi'(1)} = \frac{\sum_d d\gamma_i k_i \Omega_d^{(i)}}{\gamma k \Phi'(1)}. \tag{4}
$$

To quantify the UEP properties of source nodes, define K_i is the *priority disparity* of the source S_i, and $K_i = \frac{q_i}{\alpha_i}$.

3.3   Asymptotic Analysis of Proposed Codes

In this section, we use And-Or tree technique to analyze the asymptotic performance of proposed codes.

The encoding process of proposed code are divided in 2 steps, the one is on the source node, the other is on the relay nodes. When first step is finished, the input degree distribution of input symbols on S_i is denoted by $\Lambda^{(i)}(x)$, where

$$
\Lambda_d^{(i)} = \binom{k_i(\Omega^{(i)}(1))'}{d}\left(\frac{1}{k_i}\right)^d \left(\frac{k_i-1}{k_i}\right)^{k_i(\Omega^{(i)}(1))'-d}. \tag{5}
$$

In asymptotic conditions, which means $k_i \to \infty$, we have

$$
\Lambda^{(i)}(x) = \exp\left\{(\Omega^{(i)}(1))'\gamma_i(x-1)\right\}. \tag{6}
$$

Let $\lambda^{(i)}(x)$ is the input edge distribution of input symbols on S_i, then we have

$$
\begin{aligned}
\lambda^{(i)}(x) &= \frac{(\lambda^{(i)}(x))'}{(\lambda^{(i)}(1))'} \\
&= \frac{(\Omega^{(i)}(1))'\gamma_i e^{(\Omega^{(i)}(1))'\gamma_i(x-1)}}{(\Omega^{(i)}(1))'\gamma_i e^{(\Omega^{(i)}(1))'\gamma_i(x-1)}\big|_{x=1}} \\
&= \exp\left\{(\Omega^{(i)}(1))'\gamma_i(x-1)\right\}.
\end{aligned} \tag{7}
$$

Then consider the second step of encoding process, as the probability an intermediated symbol is generated by S_i is q_i, then for an output symbol, the probability its neighbors belong to S_i is also q_i. As the compute complexity of second step is $(\Omega^{(R)}(1))'\gamma_R$, hence the average degree of input symbols on S_i of the overall LT code is $(\Omega^{(i)}(1))'\gamma_i(\Omega^{(R)}(1))'\gamma_R$, and the input edge distribution is $\lambda_{i,\text{overall}}(x) = \exp\{(\Omega^{(i)}(1))'\gamma_i(x-1)(\Omega^{(R)}(1))'\gamma_R\}$.

Following with paper [9], denote the error rate of input symbols in S_i is $y_{i,l}$, then we have

$$
y_{i,l} = \lambda_{i,\text{overall}}\left(1 - \omega\left(1 - \sum_{i=1}^J q_i(y_{i,l-1})\right)\right), \quad l > 1 \tag{8}
$$

in which $\omega(x) = \frac{\Omega'(x)}{\Omega'(1)}$.

4   Design of Proposed Coding Scheme

The UEP performance of UEP LT codes are mainly determined by the selection probabilities. It is can be seen from Eq. (4), for the proposed distributed UEP LT coding scheme, the selection probability of each source node S_i is mainly determined by the variables γ_i and $\Omega^{(i)}(x)$. As overheads γ_i represent the transmission efficiency of proposed codes, we will mainly focus on the output degree distributions of proposed coding scheme.

4.1   The Output Degree Distributions of Sub-codes

As the advisable overheads of sub-codes are obtained, the UEP properties of the proposed coding scheme should be determined by the output degree distributions of sub-codes.

Consider each source node S_i, to obtain priority disparity K_i, the output degree distribution $\Omega^{(i)}(x)$ should satisfies

$$\left(\Omega^{(i)}(1)\right)'\gamma_i = K_i\gamma\Phi'(1), \tag{9}$$

where γ is the overall overhead, and the left part of Eq. (9) is the average degree of the input symbols on source node S_i after the first encoding step.

After the second step of the encoding process, the average degree of input symbols on each source node S_i are increased by times $(\Omega^{(R)}(1))'$, but for each in put symbol, the number of its identity neighbors has not been increased. In other word, although the average degrees of input symbols increased after the second step of encoding process, but all the output neighbors of each input symbol are also been the neighbors of the intermediate symbols which are connected with this input symbol. For this reason, the LT encoder on relay node was not implemented to improve the error performance but to overcome the erasure probability of the relay channel. For this reason, and consider the overall compute complexity, the LT encoder on relay node should be assigned output degree distribution $\Omega^{(R)}(x)$ with low average degree.

As the Robust degree distributions of LT codes can provide nearly optimal decoding performances, and the Robust degree distribution is determined by the variables k, δ and c, where δ is the allowable decoding failure probability and c is a constant, then by assign different value to δ and c, one can obtain different Robust degree distribution. Hence, for the source nodes, the degree distributions should satisfy Eq. (9), and for the relay node.

5   Simulation Results

In this section, we first take the asymptotic and finite length evaluation of proposed codes, then the comparisons between proposed codes and conventional distributed UEP codes are also given.

Consider a proposed code with two LEOs and single GEO, where the number of input symbols and overhead of sub-codes on LEOs are the same, and output degree distributions for sub-codes on LEOs are $\Omega^{(1)}(x) = 0.007969x^1 + 0.493570x^2 + 0.166220x^3 + 0.072646x^4 + 0.082558x^5 + 0.056058x^8 + 0.037229x^9 + 0.055590x^{19} + 0.025023x^{64} + 0.003137x^{66}$ and $\Omega^{(2)}(x) = 0.0782x + 0.4577x^2 + 0.1706x^3 + 0.0750x^4 + 0.0853x^5 + 0.0376x^8 + 0.0380x^9 + 0.0576x^{19}$, respectively. The output degree distribution for sub-code on GEO is $\Omega^{(R)}(x) = 0.057x + 0.4589x^2 + 0.17x^3 + 0.1156x^4 + 0.0754x^5 + 0.0575x^6 + 0.0382x^7 + 0.0274x^8$, and the overhead on GEO is 1.05. The asymptotic error performance of the proposed code is shown in Fig. 4, where the input symbols on LEO S_1 can provide better error performance than which on S_2, which means the proposed code can provide UEP property between input symbols on different LEOs. Figure 5 shows the finite length error performances of proposed codes with $k_1 = k_2 = 10000$ and $k_1 = k_2 = 1000$, it is easy to say the overhead and error performances of proposed codes would as better as larger number of input symbols on source nodes.

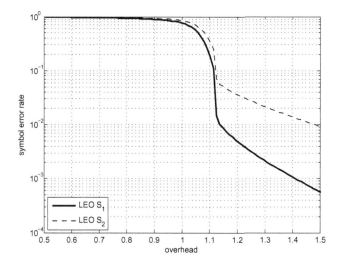

Fig. 4. Asymptotic error performance of proposed code with 2 source nodes and single relay node.

Then we make the comparison between proposed codes and conventional distributed UEP codes. Assume the sub-codes on LEOs of conventional code with the same output degree distribution, which is same as $\Omega^{(1)}(x)$, and the sub-code on GEO also share the same output degree distribution as the proposed code. Different with the proposed codes, the UEP property of conventional codes are mainly determined by the sub-code on relay nodes, then we assume the overhead of both sub-codes on source nodes are 1.05. To compare fairly, the conventional code has been assigned priority disparity $K_M = 1.7$, then the proposed code

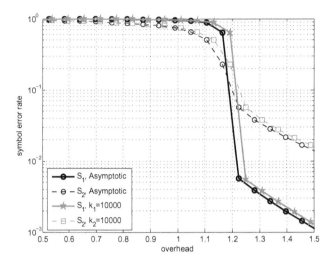

Fig. 5. Finite length error performance of proposed code with two source nodes and single relay node.

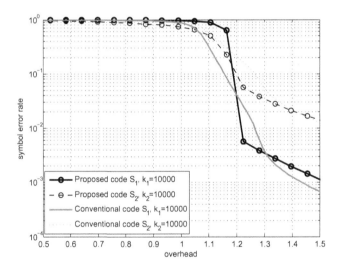

Fig. 6. Finite length error performance of proposed code and conventional distributed UEP rateless code.

and conventional codes would provide the same UEP properties at the finite length condition where the input symbols on both source nodes are $k_1 = k_2 = 10000$, its can be found in Fig. 6, the proposed code can provide better overhead performance than conventional codes, which because of the drawback of the LT-based UEP codes.

6 Conclusion

In this paper, we propose a new class of distributed UEP rateless codes which can be using transmit multi kinds of data with different reliable requirements on satellite networks. All the sub-codes of proposed UEP rateless codes are EEP LT codes, hence the proposed code can provide better overhead property than the conventional distributed UEP rateless codes. As the relay node (GEO) in proposed code provide EEP property, which means the relay node not have to know the reliable requirements of input symbols on different source nodes, hence the security of input symbols can be ensured. We also derive the asymptotic and finite-length analysis of proposed codes. And the numerical results shown the proposed can provide the same UEP property as conventional distributed UEP rateless codes with low overhead performance.

Acknowledgment. This work was supported by National Natural Science Foundation of China. (No. 61601147, No. 61571316, No. 61371100) and "the Fundamental Research Funds for the Central Universities" (Grant No. HIT. MKSTISP. 2016013).

References

1. Nishiyama, H., Kudoh, D., Kato, N., Kadowaki, N.: Load balancing and QoS provisioning based on congestion prediction for GEO/LEO hybrid satellite networks. Proc. IEEE **99**(11), 1998–2007 (2011)
2. Araniti, G., Bisio, I., Sanctis, M.D., Orsino, A.: Multimedia content delivery for emerging 5G-satellite networks. IEEE Trans. Broadcast. **62**(1), 10–23 (2016)
3. Caini, C.: Delay- and disruption-tolerant networking (DTN): an alternative solution for future satellite networking applications. Proc. IEEE **99**, 1980–1997 (2011)
4. Luby, M.: LT codes. In: Proceedings of 43rd Annual IEEE Symposium on Foundations of Computer Science, pp. 271–280 (2002)
5. Puducheri, S., Kliewer, J., Fuja, T.E.: Distributed LT codes. In: Proceedings of IEEE International Symposium on Information Theory, Seattle, USA, pp. 987–991 (2006)
6. Puducheri, S., Kliewer, J., Fuja, T.E.: The design and performance of distributed LT codes. IEEE Trans. Inf. Theory **53**(10), 3740–3754 (2007)
7. Rahnavard, N., Fekri, F.: Finite-length unequal error protection rateless codes: design and analysis. In: Proceedings of IEEE Global Telecommunications Conference, St. Louis, Missouri, USA, vol. 3, pp. 1353–1357 (2005)
8. Rahnavard, N., Fekri, F.: Generalization of rateless codes for unequal error protection and recovery time: asymptotic analysis. In: Proceedings of IEEE International Symposium on Information Theory, pp. 523–527 (2006)
9. Rahnavard, N., Vellambi, B., Fekri, F.: Rateless codes with unequal error protection property. IEEE Trans. Inf. Theory **53**(4), 1521–1532 (2007)
10. Talari, A., Rahnavard, N.: Distributed unequal error protection rateless codes over erasure channels: a two-source scenario. IEEE Trans. Commun. **60**(8), 2084–2090 (2012)

A New Class of Unequal Error Protection Rateless Codes with Equal Recovery Time Property

Shuang Wu[1], Zhenyong Wang[1,2(✉)], Dezhi Li[1], Gongliang Liu[1], and Qing Guo[1]

[1] School of Electronics and Information Engineering,
Harbin Institute of Technology, Harbin 150001, China
wooshuang@126.com, {zywang,lidezhi,liugl,qguo}@hit.edu.cn
[2] Shenzhen Academy of Aerospace Technology, Shenzhen 518057, China

Abstract. A new class of rateless codes which are able to provide unequal error protection (UEP) and equal recovery time (ERT) properties is proposed in this paper. Existing UEP-based LT codes have an important property termed unequal recovery time (URT), which means the data with different reliability requirements can be recovered with different overhead, and it is worth noting that the most important bits (MIB) also have better recovery time performance. The proposed codes can recover data with the same overhead and different error performance. We analyze the asymptotic and experimental error performance of the proposed codes, and give the comparison between the proposed and traditional codes, our results show that the new class of UEP rateless codes are useful for scenarios in which the data have different reliability and same timeliness requirements.

Keywords: Unequal error protection · Asymptotic analysis
Finite-length analysis · Equal recovery time · Rateless codes

1 Introduction

LT codes, the first practical codes of the family named rateless codes, were invented by Luby [1]. The code rate of rateless codes are not fixed, in other words, the output symbols can be generated as many as needed.

Rateless codes could also provide an important property which named unequal error protection (UEP). The UEP rateless codes proposed by Rahnavard in [2,3] by distribute different selection probabilities to input symbols in different blocks in the encoding process, Sejdinovic etc. construct the UEP rateless codes by dividing the data into a series windows, and different window have different encoding times [4]. The mentioned schemes are all based on single source, Talari and Rahnavard also proposed a coding scheme by using distributed rateless codes to fit for two source one relay scenario and provide UEP property [5,6]. The UEP rateless codes also be used to solve some practical scenarios where the different data have different reliability requirements.

© ICST Institute for Computer Sciences, Social Informatics and Telecommunications Engineering 2018
X. Gu et al. (Eds.): MLICOM 2017, Part I, LNICST 226, pp. 574–583, 2018.
https://doi.org/10.1007/978-3-319-73564-1_57

All the above mentioned UEP rateless codes have the same property which named unequal recovery time (URT). As for UEP rateless codes, the data which have better error performance, they always can be recovered faster, and the others are slower. In the ground transmission systems, as each entire encoding and decoding process only need a very short time slot duration, the URT property is negligible. Therefore, the URT property always be considered as by product, but for some scenarios where the duration time of each entire encoding and decoding process must be concerned, (for example, the deep space data transmission systems), the URT property may influence the user experience. Aiming to solve this problem, we proposed a new class of rateless codes which can provide UEP property and the recovery time of each block is nearly same. The proposed codes could provide UEP property, but as the data in different parts have different error protection level, these data could be recovered nearly at the same time, in other words, this cods could provide equal recovery time (ERT) property. For the proposed LT codes in this paper, the MIB and LIB parts would be recovered nearly at the same time, then the overall timeliness property would be better than the mentioned UEP/URT LT codes.

The paper is organized as follows. In Sect. 2, We review the related works, including the And-Or Tree analysis and the UEP cods [3]. The codes we proposed which could provide UEP and ERT properties are introduced in Sect. 3, a simple example and its asymptotic performance analysis are also given. Section 4 shows the comparison between the proposed UEP/ERT LT codes and the comparative UEP/URT LT codes by asymptotic and experimental results. And the conclusion of this paper is drawn in Sect. 5.

2   Related Works

In this section, we review the coding scheme proposed in [3] and analyze the UEP and URT properties of these codes.

For the UEP property, which means different parts of input symbols would be decoded with different error rates as there are same parts of output symbols are received. The URT property means that different parts of input symbols can be decoded with the same error rate as there are different parts of output symbols are received.

In [3], the authors interpret the URT as the UEP. As the encoding scheme which proposed in this paper, the input symbols in different blocks have different chosen probabilities when encoding an output symbol, the chosen probabilities for input symbols in each block are different, where the MIB symbols have higher chance to be selected to generate an output symbol than in LIB.

Consider a given LT code with parameters $\Omega(x)$, k, γ, where the k input symbols can be divided into a series of blocks $b_1, b_2, \ldots, b_i, \ldots$, and the number of input symbols in each block b_i is $\alpha_i k$, where $\sum_i \alpha_i = 1$. As the encoding scheme proposed in [3], input symbols in each block have their own selected probability when generating an output symbol, for the ith block, the selected probability is q_i, then the input degree distribution of block i which denotes by $\Lambda_i(x) = \sum_d \Lambda_{i,d} x^d$ can be calculated as

$$\Lambda_{i,d} = (\bar{d}_i^d e^{-\bar{d}_i})/d!, \tag{1}$$

where $\bar{d}_i = \frac{\gamma q_i \sum_d d\Omega_d}{\alpha_i}$. The input degree distribution of block i can be rewritten as

$$\Lambda_i(x) = e^{\bar{d}_i \gamma(x-1)}, \tag{2}$$

and the input edge distribution can be given as

$$\lambda_i(x) = e^{\bar{d}_i \gamma(x-1)} = e^{\frac{\gamma^2 q_i \sum_d d\Omega_d}{\alpha_i}(x-1)}. \tag{3}$$

For this encoding scheme, the output degree distributions of each block are all $\Omega(x)$. Therefore, we have the edge distribution $\omega(x) = \sum_d \omega_d x^d$, where $\omega_d = d\Omega_d$. The error rate of input symbols in each block can be calculated by

$$y_{l,i} = \lambda_i \left(1 - \sum_d \omega_d \left(\sum_i q_i (1 - y_{l-1,i})\right)^{d-1}\right). \tag{4}$$

As the output edge distributions are uniform, the error rate of input symbols in each block depends on their input edge distributions. As x in (3) is the probability of the output symbols which could transmit "1" to their neighbors, we have $0 \le x \le 1$. All the parameters except q_i are constant, so the value of $\lambda_i(x)$ monotonically decreases as q_i increases. Thus for the ith block, the error rate of input symbols is lower as q_i is larger, whatever the value of overhead γ. In other words, for a given error rate requirement, the input symbols in this block can be recovered with a lower overhead than the others. Therefore, in these codes, the UEP property can be interpret as URT.

3   Equal Recovery Time UEP Rateless Codes

In this section, we describe the proposed UEP rateless codes which provides the equal recovery time property.

The cause of UEP property can be shown by And-Or Tree analysis. For a given LT code is encoded uniformly at random, when the decoding process is finished, the probability of output symbols which could transmit "1" to its neighbor is p_l. Then for an input symbol with degree d, as there are d output neighbors, the error rate of this input symbol can be calculated as $e_d = (1 - p_l)^d$.

It is not hard to find that, as $0 < p_l < 1$, e_d is monotonically decreases as d increases. Hence, the input symbols with higher average degree have better error performance than the others.

Then we consider the recovery time of each input symbol for the given LT code, as the definition of the BP decoding process for LT codes. Each input symbol can be recovered only if it is a neighbor of an output symbol with degree 1. Consider a moment in which the error rate of the input symbols is e_l, then for an output symbol with degree d, the probability this output symbol could recover one of its neighbors is $(1 - e_l)^d$, as this probability is monotonically decreases as d increases, we could give the following hypothesis: The input symbol connected with output symbols with lower degrees have a higher chance to be recovered earlier.

3.1   Proposed Encoding Scheme

Consider a given LT code with parameters $\Omega(x)$, k, γ, where k input symbols can be divided into a series blocks $b_1, b_2, \ldots, b_i, \ldots$. The number of input symbols in each block b_i is $\alpha_i k$, where $\sum_i \alpha_i = 1$. To obtain UEP property, all the prior schemes use different selection probabilities or distribute degree distribution for input symbols in different block, these methods make the input symbols in different block have different input degree distribution and different average degree, so that the input symbols can perform different error rate. In these methods, the input symbols with higher average degrees have higher chance to be connected with output symbols with lower degree, and also provide URT property.

Aiming to obtain UEP LT codes without URT property, let $Q = (q_{i,d})$ be a probability matrix with size $I \times D$, where element $q_{i,d}$ denotes the probability that the input neighbor belongs to the ith block of an output symbol with degree d, and $\sum_i q_{i,d} = 1$.

Consider the ith block, the total number of the edges connected with it E_i can be calculated as $E_i = \sum_d \gamma k d \Omega_d q_{i,d}$.

Then the input degree distribution $\Lambda_i(x)$ of the block i can be calculated as

$$\Lambda_{i,d} = \binom{E_i}{d}\left(\frac{1}{\alpha_i k}\right)^d \left(\frac{\alpha_i k - 1}{\alpha_i k}\right)^{(E_i - d)}, \tag{5}$$

if exist $\alpha_i k \rightarrow \infty$, and the average degree of input symbols is denoted by $\bar{d}_i$, where $\bar{d}_i = E_i/\alpha_i k$, Eq. (5) can be also rewritten as shows in (1) and the input edge distribution of this block can be calculated as

$$\lambda_i(x) = e^{\bar{d}_i \gamma (x-1)} = e^{\frac{\gamma^2 \sum_d d \Omega_d q_{i,d}}{\alpha_i}(x-1)}. \tag{6}$$

The expression of the output edge distribution of the ith block $\omega_i(x) = \sum_d \omega_{i,d} x^d$ as $\omega_{i,d} = (d\Omega_d q_{i,d})/(\sum_d d\Omega_d q_{i,d})$, as $\lambda_i(x)$ and $\omega_i(x)$ are obtained, then we make the And-Or tree analysis for the given LT code. Following with the and or tree theorem which proposed in [9], for block i, the error rate of input symbols in this block can be calculated by $y_{l,i}$, and

$$y_{l,i} = \lambda_i\left(1 - \sum_d \omega_{i,d}\left(\sum_i q_{i,d}(1 - y_{l-1,i})\right)^{d-1}\right) \tag{7}$$

$$= e^{-\frac{\gamma^2 \sum_d d\Omega_d q_{i,d}}{\alpha_i}(\sum_d \omega_{i,d}(\sum_i q_{i,d}(1-y_{l-1,i}))^{d-1})}.$$

Considering the ith block and assuming the input symbol in this block have higher level reliable requirement, we should make the average degree of the input symbols in this block larger than others, which means $\bar{d}_i = \max\{\bar{d}_1, \bar{d}_2, \ldots, \bar{d}_I\}$, as the input symbols also need to be recovered at the same time with the others, then the series $q_{i,d}$ should satisfy the following conditions: for a certain degree value $\hat{d}$, where $\hat{d}$ is not too small, if $d < \hat{d}$, $q_{i,d} = \alpha_i$, and if $d \geq \hat{d}$, $q_{i,d} > \alpha_i$, thus the average degree of the input symbols in the block i is larger than the others and for the lower degree output symbols, the probability of them choosing an input symbol in the ith block is equal to the others. Hence, the input symbols in the block i have better error performance than the others and the recovery time diversity is negligible.

3.2   A Special Case with 2 Blocks

For simplicity, consider a simple example with only 2 blocks, $\alpha_1 = 0.1$ and $\alpha_2 = 0.9$. The output degree distribution is $\Omega(x) = 0.007969x^1 + 0.493570x^2 + 0.166220x^3 + 0.072646x^4 + 0.082558x^5 + 0.056058x^8 + 0.037229x^9 + 0.055590x^{19} + 0.025023x^{64} + 0.003137x^{66}$, which is proposed in [15]. The input symbols in the first block are more important than which in the second block.

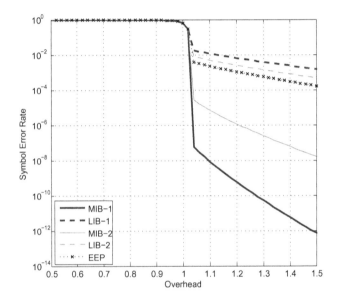

Fig. 1. Asymptotic UEP performance of the given LT code with 2 blocks.

As the And-Or tree iterative expression is given by (7), we can show the asymptotic performance of an given LT code to provide UEP and ERT property. For $1 \leq d \leq 66$, there exist $q_{i,d} = \alpha_i$, then the error rate of the symbols in each block are equal. The performance of this condition is shown as the curve "EEP" in Fig. 1. Then make $q_{1,64} = 0.5$ and $q_{1,66} = 1$, the asymptotic performance of the given code can be shown as the curves "MIB-1" and "LIB-1", the input symbols in block 1 are most important bits (MIB), and the others are less important bits (LIB), as the MIB have been distributed with higher average input degrees, then the error floor have better performance than the LIB, and the beginning of error floor for both MIB and LIB are nearly with the same overhead. Therefore the input symbols in blocks 1 and 2 with the UEP and the equal recovery time (ERT) properties. As the block with higher average degree have better error performance than the lower, then let $q_{1,64} = 0.4$ and $q_{1,66} = 0.8$, and the asymptotic performance of this case is shown as the curves "MIB-2" and "LIB-2", it is easy to find the difference between the error floor region of case 1 is larger than case 2. Then we can give the following lemma.

Lemma 1. *The difference of the error performance between MIB and LIB would increase as the difference of the average input degree between MIB and LIB.*

3.3   Asymptotic Performance Analysis

Here we should analyze the relationship between the error rate and recovery time of the proposed coding scheme. Consider the given LT code, as there are $n = \gamma k$ output symbols that are received, then for an output symbol with degree d, assume the And-Or Tree iterative process could convergence at the Lth round, then the probability this output symbol could recovered an input symbol is $(\sum_i q_{i,d}(1 - y_{L,i}))^{d-1}$, as $\sum_i q_{i,d} = 1$ and $1 - y_{L,i} < 1$, then $\sum_i q_{i,d}(1 - y_{L,i}) < 1$, for this reason, this probability monotonically decreases as d increases.

Then consider the error rate of the ith block $y_{L,i}$, as this probability is monotonically decreases as the overhead γ increases and exist $0 \leq y_{L,i} < 1$, assume there exists an overhead Γ, which is the beginning of the error floor, if $\gamma < \Gamma$, $1 - y_{L,i} \ll 1$ and cannot be ignored. Therefore for an output with degree d, if d is very high, the probability this output symbol could recover an input symbol $(\sum_i q_{i,d}(1 - y_{L,i}))^{d-1}$ is infinitesimal of higher order of probabilities for output symbols with lower degree. As a result, this probability could be ignored. In other words, nearly all the input symbols which have been recovered are recovered by output symbols with lower degree. As for each block, the probabilities input symbols covered by output symbols with lower degrees are the same. Thus if $\gamma < \Gamma$, we have the following $y_{L+1,1} \approx y_{L+1,2}$, which means as the overhead is less than Γ, the input symbols in both 2 blocks have the same error rate.

If $\gamma \geq \Gamma$, exist $1 - y_{L,i} \to 1$, then for the output symbols with high degree d, $(\sum_i q_{i,d}(1 - y_{L,i}))^{d-1}$ is not very less and cannot be ignored, then as $q_{1,d} > q_{2,d}$, we have the following inequality $y_{L+1,1} < y_{L+1,2}$, which means that if the overhead is larger than Γ, the input symbols in first block have better error rate performance than the others in the second block.

4   Experimental Results

In this section, we will compare the performances of the comparative UEP LT codes [3] and the proposed codes.

For simplicity, we choose the number of input symbols to be $k = 1000$, then the mentioned degree distribution proposed in [15] and design for the codes with $k = 65536$ is not suitable. For this reason, we design a robust degree distribution for LT codes with $k = 1000$ and make some adjustments as following $\Omega(x) = 0.0782x + 0.4577x^2 + 0.1706x^3 + 0.0750x^4 + 0.0853x^5 + 0.0376x^8 + 0.0380x^9 + 0.0576x^{19}$.

For the comparative UEP LT codes, $q_1 = 0.2189$ and $q_2 = 0.7811$, for the proposed UEP LT codes, the select probability is shown in Table 1.

Table 1. Selection probabilities for 2 blocks when generate an output symbol with different degree

Degree	1	2	3	4	5	6	7	8
Block 1	0.1	0.1	0.1	0.1	0.1	0.1	0.2	0.5
Block 2	0.9	0.9	0.9	0.9	0.9	0.9	0.8	0.5

Figures 2 and 3 show the asymptotic error rate performance of the comparative UEP LT codes and the proposed codes. For the comparative codes, the MIB symbols have better recovery time performance than the MIB symbols of the proposed codes, and the LIB symbols with worse recovery time performance than the LIB symbols of proposed codes. For the scenarios in which only MIB symbols have the requirement to be recovered, then the comparative codes have better recovery time performance than the proposed. But if all the symbols have to be recovered, then the proposed code have better recovery time performance than the comparative codes.

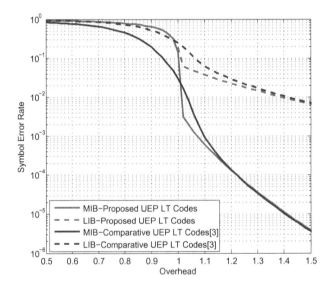

Fig. 2. Asymptotic UEP performance comparison of the given LT codes in log scale.

Figures 4 and 5 show the experimental error rate performance comparison between the comparative UEP LT codes and proposed UEP LT codes. As mentioned before, the number of input symbols is $k = 1000$ and the simulation

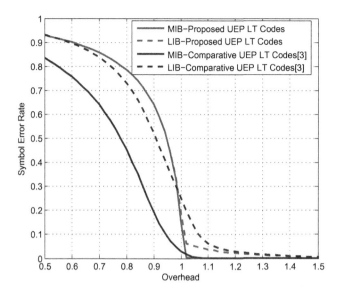

Fig. 3. Asymptotic UEP performance comparison of the given LT codes in linear scale.

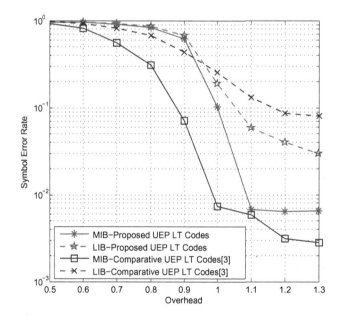

Fig. 4. Experimental UEP performance comparison of finite-length LT codes in log scale.

times is 1000. These two figures show the error performance of the comparative and proposed UEP LT codes in both the log and linear scales. The finite-length experimental results show the same as the asymptotic results, which means for

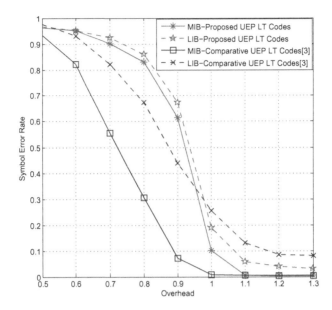

Fig. 5. Experimental UEP performance comparison of finite-length LT codes in linear scale.

the proposed codes the recovery time of both two blocks are nearly the same. But it is worth noting that there exists a difference between the asymptotic and finite-length experimental results, which is although the asymptotic results shows the error performance of comparative and proposed codes. The experimental error performance of these codes are not the same both for MIBs and LIBs. This is because the number of the input symbols is finite, although the overhead γ is large enough, the error rate cannot be considered as infinitesimal, and the probability that an output symbol with higher degree could recover one of its neighbor also cannot tend to 1. And the source of the errors between the asymptotic and finite-length experimental results is the calculated error of the And-Or Tree analysis.

5   Conclusion

In this paper, we proposed a new class of UEP LT codes which provide the ERT property. We derive the asymptotic error performance of the proposed codes, and we also analyzed the error performance by using experimental results. The results shows that we can use these codes to make the data with different reliability requirements to be recovered with the same overhead. In other words, these symbols could be recovered at the same time. For applications where the duration of each encoding and decoding process must be concerned, if all the data have timeliness requirements, the overall timeliness property of the proposed codes would better than the comparative ones. This means that the overall decoding overhead of the proposed codes would less than the comparative codes.

Acknowledgment. This work was supported by National Natural Science Foundation of China. (No. 61601147, No. 61571316, No. 61371100) and "the Fundamental Research Funds for the Central Universities" (Grant No. HIT. MKSTISP. 2016013).

References

1. Luby, M.: LT codes. In: Proceedings of the 43rd Symposium on Foundations of Computer Science, pp. 271–280 (2002)
2. Rahnavard, N., Fekri, F.: Finite-length unequal error protection rateless codes: design and analysis. In: Proceedings IEEE Global Telecommunication Conference, vol. 3, p. 5 (2005)
3. Rahnavard, N., Vellambi, B., Fekri, F.: Rateless codes with unequal error protection property. IEEE Trans. Inf. Theory **53**, 1521–1532 (2007)
4. Sejdinovic, D., Vukobratovic, D., Doufexi, A., Senk, V., Piechocki, R.J.: Expanding window fountain codes for unequal error protection. IEEE Trans. Commun. **57**, 2510–2516 (2009)
5. Talari, A., Rahnavard, N.: Distributed rateless codes with UEP property. In: Proceedings of the IEEE International Symposium on Information Theory, pp. 2453–2457 (2010)
6. Talari, A., Rahnavard, N.: Distributed unequal error protection rateless codes over erasure channels: a two-source scenario. IEEE Trans. Commun. **60**, 2084–2090 (2012)
7. Stefanovic, C., Vukobratovic, D., Chiti, F., Niccolai, L., Crnojevic, V., Fantacci, R.: Urban infrastructure-to-vehicle traffic data dissemination using UEP rateless codes. IEEE J. Sel. Areas Commun. **29**, 94–102 (2011)
8. Talari, A., Rahnavard, N.: A low-latency and error-resilient video-on-demand broadcasting protocol using UEP-rateless codes. In: Forty-Sixth Annual Allerton Conference, pp. 991–995, September 2008
9. Luby, M.G., Mitzenmacher, M., Shokrallahi, A.: Analysis of random processes via And-Or tree evaluation. In: Proceedings of the 9th Annual ACM-SIAM Symposium on Discrete Algorithms, pp. 364–373 (1998)
10. Yuan, X., Ping, L.: Quasi-systematic doped LT codes. IEEE J. Sel. Areas Commun. **27**, 866–875 (2009)
11. Yuan, X., Sun, R., Ping, L.: Simple capacity-achieving ensembles of rateless erasure-correcting codes. IEEE Trans. Commun. **58**, 110–117 (2010)
12. Kozat, U.C., Ramprashad, S.A.: Unequal error protection rateless codes for scalable information delivery in mobile networks. In: Proceedings of the IEEE INFOCOM, pp. 2316–2320 (2007)
13. Karp, R., Luby, M., Shokrollahi, A.: Finite length analysis of LT codes. In: Proceedings of International Symposium on Information Theory, p. 37 (2004)
14. Maatouk, G., Shokrollahi, A.: Analysis of the second moment of the LT decoder. IEEE Trans. Inf. Theory **58**(5), 2558–2569 (2012)
15. Shokrollahi, A.: Raptor codes. IEEE Trans. Inf. Theory **52**, 2551–2567 (2006)

Stochastic Geometry Analysis of Ultra Dense Network and TRSC Green Communication Strategy

Guoqiang Wang[(⊠)] and Bai Sun

Key Lab of Electronic and Communication Engineering,
Heilongjiang University, Harbin, People's Republic of China
13936697869@163.com, 444967247@qq.com

Abstract. In recent years, with the rapid development of wireless communication, the traditional cellular with isomorphic and regular structure has been unable to meet the increasing number of users and business needs involving data of big volume. The trend is evolving into Ultra Dense Network (UDN) architecture which is covered by cellular of irregular complex structure. In UDN, the spatial distribution of the base station plays an important role in the interference and performance evaluation of the whole cellular network, and the concept of green communication has also been put on agenda. In this paper, stochastic geometry theory is used to model UDN and to analyze the key performance of interference and wireless network. Moreover, a green communication strategy called TRSC is proposed, which is aimed at save energy and reduce the signal interference among cells to some extent.

Keywords: UDN · Stochastic geometry · Relay · Modeling analysis TRSC

1 Introduction

Mobile communication networks have evolved from the original first generation analog cellular systems to 4G currently. The cell radius is constantly shrinking and the density is increasing. In the future, there will be more and more hotspots of high speed data access getting denser. The existing heterogeneous networks will gradually develop into high speed ultra-dense cells, namely Ultra Dense network (UDN), consisting of regular macro cells and high density irregular small cells.

The statistical characteristics of Inter-cell interference (ICI) are different because UDN is completely different from the traditional cellular network topology, and there are different requirements on interference control. UDN's dynamic irregular network topology needs to be simulated by Poisson's process based on stochastic geometry theory. Under this model, the ICI concentration effect is reduced, and the power distribution curve becomes flat, the trailing effect is remarkable as well. It is necessary to reform the interference control method technology according to the interference characteristics of UDN.

Earlier, Baccelli et al. introduced the uniform Poisson point process into base station modeling, but they did not use metrics such as coverage to measure the

© ICST Institute for Computer Sciences, Social Informatics and Telecommunications Engineering 2018
X. Gu et al. (Eds.): MLICOM 2017, Part I, LNICST 226, pp. 584–591, 2018.
https://doi.org/10.1007/978-3-319-73564-1_58

advantages of modeling [1, 2]. In recent years, Andrews et al. assumed that the base stations were independent of each other and took the uniform Poisson point process as a model. The rate and coverage of the downlink (only related to SINR) were analyzed [3, 4]. They derived a universal expression for coverage of interference fading shadows in a wireless communication network that follows any distribution. In particular, the distribution of received power was calculated. The experimental results showed that the coverage rate of the Poisson point process provides the lower bound of the coverage rate of the measured base station distribution, while the hexagonal lattice cell model provides the upper bound of its coverage. Document [5] uses stochastic geometry theory to analyze the performance of multilayer dense homogeneous networks composed of different types of wireless access points. Each layer has different base station transmit power, data rate and deployment density. Compared with the actual LTE network performance, the validity of the stochastic geometry theory in multi-layer heterogeneous network performance analysis was verified. Tsinghua University professor Niu team used stochastic geometry theory to analyze the energy efficient base station distribution density [6] in heterogeneous cellular networks.

2   Spatial Poisson Point Process Theory

The spatial point process is different from the usual one dimensional point process. It is a higher dimensional point process that does not have the characteristics of temporal ordering of one-dimensional processes. In the spatial point process, although each point has the characteristics of sequential arrival, the spatial point process can be defined by the number of points falling into the unit region rather than by counting process. Human settlements, tourist attractions and macro base stations show the characteristic of entity in space. Spatial point model is based on the spatial location of these points, and researchers are trying to find the potential law of these points.

2.1   Spatial Homogeneous Poisson Point Process

If two conditions of a spatial point process X are satisfied, we called X as spatial homogeneous Poisson point process.

(1) For any bounded region $B \subseteq R^2$, N(B) subjects to Poisson distribution whose mean is $\lambda v_d(B)(\lambda > 0)$, $P(N(B) = m) = (\lambda v_d(B))^m \cdot exp \frac{-(\lambda v_d(B))}{m!}$

(2) If the bounded regions $B_1, B_2 \ldots B_n$ do not intersect with each other, then $N(B_1), N(B_2) \ldots N(B_n)$ are independent of each other. Thus, N(B) is the number of points in region B, and the density λ is a constant, which represents the number of the average points in unit area, and $v_d(B)$ represents the area of the bounded region.

According to the above definition, we can conclude that spatial homogeneous Poisson point process has following characteristics: (1) The spatial distribution of points is completely random; (2) The expectation μ_B of the number of points on the unit area is a constant, without changing with the change of space.

2.2 Applications in Wireless Networks

In spatial stochastic geometry model, it is assumed that the location of the base station is not fixed but random, so usually we suppose that the position of the base station obeys spatial homogeneous Poisson point process. In fact, the distribution of base station is not completely independent, but relevant researches discovered that using spatial stochastic geometry model to calculate the performance of system was close to actual testing, high reliability was provided as well. And after using stochastic geometry model, it is convenient to obtain system parameters such as outrage probability and capacity of multi-cell system model. They will help the designers optimize and adjust the parameters of the system easily.

Relevant simulations and comparisons [3] indicated that the performance index calculated by using system model structured through spatial homogeneous Poisson point process have an accuracy extremely close to the data measured in real network, and more precisely than using the hexagonal or square network model. Therefore, the method of stochastic geometry modeling can simulate the cellular network more accurately, and the computational complexity of this method is low, the system performance index can be easily obtained as well.

3 Modeling and Analysis of Relays in UDN

Cooperative relaying is an effective way to expand network coverage and improve network capacity. Compared with macro base station, relay has smaller coverage and lower transmission power. Therefore, the majority of users are able to obtain a higher value of Signal to Interference plus Noise Ratio (SINR). As the relay does not require wired backbone connections, its deployment costs will be greatly reduced. So the cooperative relay technology in UDN can be used with less energy consumption and the cost of deployment to improve network capacity and expand the network coverage, but also do not need to make any changes for existing cellular network architectures. This chapter models for double-layer heterogeneous relays in UDN based on spatial homogeneous Poisson point process, and derives the SINR distribution and the average achievable rate of the cooperative users and non-cooperative users. Meanwhile, the theoretical derivations are verified through system simulation.

3.1 Network Model

Consider a downlink double layer heterogeneous relay cellular network, as shown in Fig. 1. There are two kinds of access points in the network: macro base station and relay, respectively modeling by the density of λ_b homogeneous Poisson point process with θ_b and density of λ_r homogeneous Poisson point process with θ_r. The coverage area of each relay is a circle with a radius of R_r, and the cooperative coding strategy of adaptive source retransmission check bits is adopted in cooperative transmission. Especially, for a provided Poisson point process, the quantity of points in a closed region is a random variable subjected to Poisson distribution. Figure 2 shows the implementation of a two-layer heterogeneous relay cellular network model consisting of a macro base station and a relay consisting of Poisson distribution, characterized by a grid diagram. The small areas divided into grids are called cells, namely the coverage area of the macro base station. The area is a random variable, expressed as its probability distribution function which is approximated as follow:

$$F(S) = \lambda_b \sqrt{\frac{1830}{\pi}} (S\lambda_b)^{\frac{5}{2}} \exp\left(-\frac{7}{2} S\lambda_b\right) \tag{1}$$

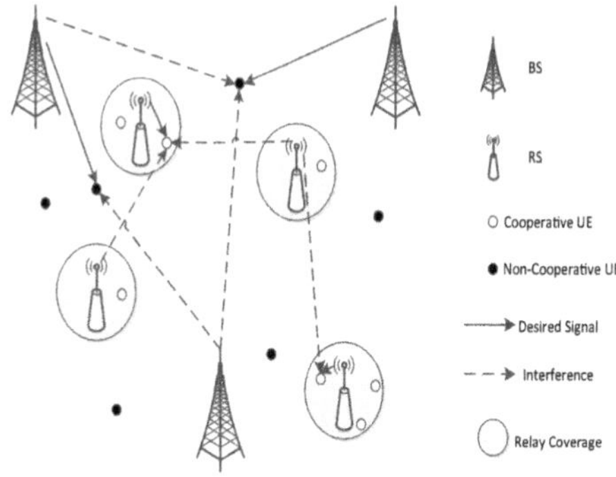

Fig. 1. Downlink double layered heterogeneous UDN model

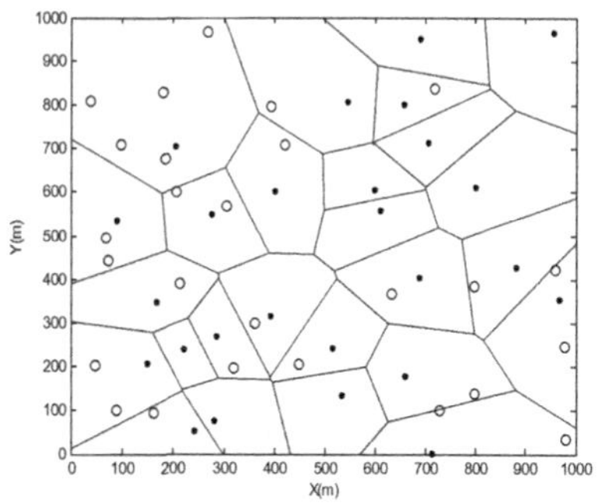

Fig. 2. Voronoi network topology

Considering two types of users, one is homogeneous Poisson point process θ_{nc} with the density of λ_{nc} distributed on the whole network plane, communicating directly with the macro base station, and accessed with the nearest macro base station, called non-cooperative users. Its distance distribution from the service station is: $f(r) = 2\pi\lambda_b r e^{-\lambda_b \pi r^2}$. The other is homogeneous Poisson point process θ_c with the density of λ_c distributed within the round area covered by each relay. It works through the relay and macro base station, called cooperative users, whose distance distribution from the relay in services is: $f_R(r) = 2r/R_r^2$. All these Poisson point processes $(\theta_b, \theta_r, \theta_{nc}, \theta_c)$ used for modeling are independent of each other.

Based on the fact that the coverage area of the relay is far less than the coverage area of macro base station, we propose a two level approximation model for the analysis of subsequent performance. It contains two angles: macroscopic and microscopic. The macroscopic angle refers to the observation in the relay coverage area of the entire network. At this time all the relay coverage area will shrink to a point, and the number of cooperative users is marked. Micro perspective refers to the observed network within the covered area of relay network. At this time the cooperative users in the round coverage of relay are observed. This approximation will avoid the problems of site selection while user accessing with relay and relay accessing with macro base station.

3.2   Users Distribution

Take V_c as the number of cooperative users covered by a relay, then $V_c \sim$ Poisson $(\lambda_c \pi R_r^2)$. Take V_{nc} as the number of non-cooperative users covered by a macro base station.

$$G_{V_{nc}}(z) = \int_0^\infty \exp(\lambda_{nc}(y-1)S)F(S)dS = \frac{341}{8}\sqrt{\frac{7}{2}\left(\frac{7}{2} - \frac{\lambda_{nc}}{\lambda_b}(y-1)\right)^{\frac{7}{2}}} \quad (2)$$

The relation between the discrete probability distribution and its corresponding probability generating function can be obtained. The distribution of the quantity of non-cooperative users V_{nc} is as follow:

$$P\{V_{nc} = i\} = \frac{G_{V_{nc}}^i(0)}{i!}, i = 0, 1, \dots \quad (3)$$

3.3   Performance Analysis

Assume a macro base station that the user access distance is r, occupying a sub channel, whose power is $P_b = P_B/M_b$, g is the interference channel gain, and R is the distance from user to the interference source. Then the received SINR of the user is:

$$\gamma = \frac{P_b h r^{-\alpha}}{I_b + \sigma^2} \quad (4)$$

The cumulative probability distribution function of γ is:

$$Pr(\gamma \leq T) = 1 - \int_0^\infty \exp\left(-\frac{\mu T r^\alpha \sigma^2}{P_b}\right)\mathcal{L}\left(\frac{\mu T r^\alpha}{P_b}\right)f(r)dr \quad (5)$$

$$f(r) = 2\pi\lambda_b r e^{-\lambda_b \pi r^2} \quad (6)$$

Average achievable speed of non-cooperative users is:

$$\bar{\tau}_{nc} = \frac{\sum_{i=1}^{M_{b1}} P\{V_{nc} = i\} + \sum_{i=M_{b1}+1}^{\infty} P\{V_{nc} = i\}\frac{M_{b1}}{i}}{1 - P\{V_{nc} = 0\}}\tau_{nc} \quad (7)$$

Likely, average achievable speed of cooperative users is:

$$\bar{\tau}_c = \frac{\sum_{i=1}^{M_r} P\{V_c = i\} + \sum_{i=M_r+1}^{\infty} P\{V_c = i\}\frac{M_r}{i}}{1 - P\{V_c = 0\}}\tau_c \quad (8)$$

3.4 Simulation Analysis

This section gives the simulation results of the performance of the relay cellular network in terms of SINR and single user rate (Table 1).

Table 1. This is the simulation configuration of network model.

Symbol	Interpretation	Value
λ_b	Density of BS	10^{-5} BS/m^2
λ_r	Density of RS	9×10^{-5} RS/m^2
P_b/P_r	Max trans power of BS div by RS	43 dBm/36 dBm
M	Quantity of sub channels	320 (M_b = 295, M_r = 16)
R	Coverage radius of RS	25 m
μ	Rayleigh fading parameter	1
α	Path loss parameter	4
σ^2	Noise power	−90 dBm
β	Cooperative parameter	0.7
R_{ts}	Target speed of RS	0.5 bits/Hz

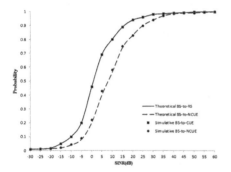

Fig. 3. CDF of SINR for CUEs and NCUES

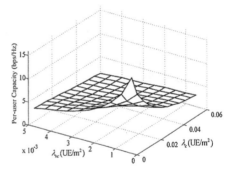

Fig. 4. The relationship between single user rate and the density of CUEs and NCUEs

Figure 3 shows the SINR distribution of both collaborative and non-cooperative users. The outline of non-cooperative users shows that the results are in good agreement with the theoretical results, so the correctness of the theoretical analysis is proved. For cooperative users, the theoretical outline shows the SINR distributing of the B-to-R link, indicating that the distribution of SINR of B-to-U link could approximately be B-to-R link, according to the research.

Figure 4 shows the relation that single user rate varies with the density of CUEs and NCUEs. The result indicates that the single user rate reached the highest point when the density of two types of users hit the bottom. With the growth of their density, single user rate decreased rapidly, reaching the lowest point when the density of two kinds of users reached the peak. This phenomenon exists out of two reasons: One is that the density of users increased, and the number of users was greater than sub channels, on which users got less resources so that the single user rate decreased; The other is that increasing user density augmented the probability of BS or RS occupied a channel, so the effective interference source link strengthen, which would reduce the user's SINR and decrease the rate of single user.

4   TRSC Green Communication Strategy

Nowadays, heterogeneity and irregularity of UDN architecture become more and more obvious. Based on the key performance analysis of last chapter, we find that the control of interference and energy efficiency for UDN is one of the most crucial problems that constrain green communication developing. Therefore, this chapter presents a green communication strategy called TRSC (Time slot and Region Stratified Control).

TRSC is the short form of Time slot and Region Stratified Control. This strategy needs some human intervention, but the core idea is using inter communication of cells to build an adaptive control mechanism to optimize the network energy efficiency and interference control. Figure 5 shows the working mechanism of TRSC, which can be divided into two phases.

The first is constructing phase: firstly, TRSC needs people to investigate relays' working state in intensive, general and sparse scenarios based on region, and record relays' working power in rush hour, flat peak and idle time based on time slot. Then configure different work modes according to the statistical values. Next, the relays start to communicate and coordinate whether the power needs further adjustment (up, down or remain). If the adjustment is necessary, relays take regular increments, step by step, in order to achieve the dynamic balance of the energy efficiency of relays. After then, the data of the mean value of the dynamic balance state will be fed back providing reference for human.

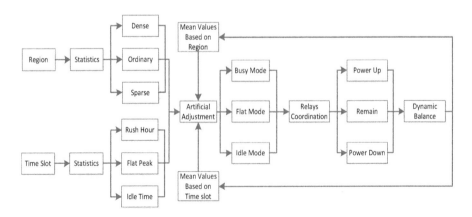

Fig. 5. The working mechanism of TRSC

Second is adjusting phase: In fact, according to the feedback data to configure relays' work mode, and then the workload of relays coordination will be greatly reduced comparing to the first stage. Because the space needs to be adjusted is very small, the overhead of relay work will be greatly reduced as well. Once a dynamic balance is reached, a virtuous circle will be formed, and a nice working mechanism will also be formed with little human intervention.

TRSC strategy is based on real time and scenario, so the best working state of relays will be reached under less human intervention: Relays can provide working power values to meet users' communication needs, and won't produce lack of flow or overflow conditions. In other words, TRSC is able to meet the user's demand, meanwhile, energy saving can also reduce the signal interference among relays to some extent. Therefore, TRSC is a green communication strategy.

5 Conclusions

In this paper, we modeled and analyzed UDN by using spatial homogeneous Poisson point process of stochastic geometry theory, and derived SINR distribution and average rate of cooperative users and non-cooperative users. Through system simulation, the theoretical derivations are verified. This research indicates that lower user density, weak interference and sufficient resources would lead to the highest rate of single user. On the contrary, a great number of users would be blocked or the single user rate would decrease rapidly. Therefore, this paper proposed a green communication strategy called TRSC, which is able to not only save energy to some extent on the basis of meeting the user's needs, buy also reduce parts of the signal interference among cells.

References

1. Baccelli, F., Klein, M., Lebourges, M., Zuyew, S.: Stochastic geometry and architecture of communication networks. J. Telecommun. Syst. 7(1), 209–227 (1997)
2. Baccelli, F., Zuyev, S.: Stochastic geometry models of mobile communication networks. In: Frontiers in Queueing, pp. 227–243. CRC Press (1997)
3. Andrews, J.G., Baccelli, F., Ganti, R.K.: A tractable approach to coverage and rate in cellular networks. J. IEEE Trans. Commun. 59(11), 3112–3134 (2011)
4. Andrews, J.G., Ganti, R.K., Haenggi, M., Jindal, N., Weber, S.: A primer on spatial modeling and analysis in wireless networks. J. IEEE Commun. Mag. 48(11), 156–163 (2011)
5. Dhillon, H.S., Ganti, R.K., Baccelli, F.: Modeling and analysis of K-tier downlink heterogeneous cellular networks. IEEE J. Sel. Areas Commun. 30(3), 550–560 (2012)
6. Cao, D., Zhou, S., Niu, Z.: Optimal base station density for energy efficient heterogeneous cellular networks. In: IEEE International Conference on Communications (ICC), vol. 11, no. 18, pp. 4379–4383. Ottawa, Canada (2012)

Reputation-Based Framework for Internet of Things

Juan Chen[1]([✉]), Zhengkui Lin[1], Xin Liu[2], Zhian Deng[1], and Xianzhi Wang[3]

[1] School of Information Science and Technology,
Dalian Maritime University, Dalian 116026, China
juanchencs@gmail.com
[2] School of Information and Communication Engineering,
Dalian University of Technology, Dalian 116024, China
[3] School of Computer Science and Engineering,
University of New South Wales, Sydney, NSW 2052, Australia

Abstract. Internet of Things (IoT) is going to create a world where physical objects are integrated into traditional networks in order to provide intelligent services for human-beings. Trust plays an important role in communications and interactions of objects in IoT. Two vital tasks of trust management are trust model design and reputation evaluation. However, current literature cannot be simply and directly applied to the IoT due to smart node hardware constraints, very limited computing and energy resources. Therefore a general and flexible model is needed to meet the special requirements for IoT. In this paper, we firstly design LTrust, a layered trust model for IoT. Then, a Reputation Evaluation Scheme for the Node (RES-N) has been presented. The proposed trust model and reputation evaluation scheme provide a general framework for the study of trust management for IoT. The efficiency of RES-N is validated by the simulation results.

Keywords: Internet of Things · Reputation evaluation scheme
Trust management

1 Introduction

Internet of Things (IoT) is going to create a world where wireless devices are integrated into networks in order to provide intelligent services for human beings. The increasingly popularity of IoT greatly helps people to control and enjoy their lives. Generally, a tag which is attached to an object can only communicate with a nearby reader. A large number of readers are deployed by different organizations to provide service for commercial or military use. Thus, readers of different organizations need to work together for object information tracking and retriving. For instance, each organization manages many application servers, through which parents would like to trace the information of their child wearing tag-attached hand chain. Firstly, they will send the request to one of an application

© ICST Institute for Computer Sciences, Social Informatics and Telecommunications Engineering 2018
X. Gu et al. (Eds.): MLICOM 2017, Part I, LNICST 226, pp. 592–597, 2018.
https://doi.org/10.1007/978-3-319-73564-1_59

servers managed by an organization. Then, the request will be sent to the IoT. Once a reader finds the target child, it tries to return the requested message to the application server.

Though there are lots of trust protocols for traditional wired and wireless networks such as P2P [1, 2] and ad hoc sensor networks, little research has been done on trust management for IoT [3]. Previous work about trust in IoT are designed for some specific applications and therefore cannot be applied to other applications [4]. In addition, new nodes join in and existing nodes leave from IoT frequently. Trust management must address this issue to allow newly joining nodes to build up trust quickly with a reasonable degree of accuracy [5–7].

In order to overcome the above issues in previous work, we propose a reputation-based framework for IoT in this paper. Firstly, we propose LTrust, a four-layered trust model. The layered model can be applied to various applications. Furthermore, a reputation evaluation schemes for the node has been proposed respectively. The proposed trust model and reputation evaluation scheme provide a general framework for the study of trust management for IoT.

The rest paper is organized as follows. In Sect. 2 the four-layered trust model is proposed. In Sect. 3 our reputation evaluation scheme for the node is explored in detail. Finally, we conclude the paper in Sect. 5.

2   Layered Trust Model

We present LTrust, a layered trust model for IoT according to different functions of entities. LTrust provides new insights for research on trust-based interaction in IoT.

We classify the entities in IoT into four typies including tag-attached objects or tags, nodes, organizations and the RMC (Reputation Management Center). Then LTrust is designed as a four-layered model including the object layer, the node layer, the organization layer and the reputation management layer. The bottom object layer which is responsible for real-data collection consisting of a large number of moving tag-attached objects. Before joining the IoT, each tag has to register at an organization. The node layer, consisting of nodes such as readers, sensors and so on, lies above the object layer. This layer manages data retrieval and then routs data from the object to an organization. Specifically, nodes retrieve data from tags nearby and then return required results to the organization. Above the node layer is the organization layer which composed of different commercial or government organizations. Each organization deploys a certain number of nodes to perform operations on tags such as data update or retrieval. Since nodes from one organization can not cover the large area in IoT, it is necessary for different organizations and nodes to work together. However, a malicious node or an organization among good ones can launch attacks on the tag, thereby cause severely damage to the network. Thus, reputation is used to identify malicious nodes from good ones. Based on LTrust, we then evaluate the reputation of each node by the reputation evaluation schemes which will be introduced in Sect. 3 by RMC. According to the node's reputation, the tag's organization will decide whether grant the authorization to the node which requests to access to the tag.

3 Reputation Evaluation

For safety consideration, we have to prevent attacked nodes from accessing to the target tag. Different from good nodes, attacked nodes usually perform malicious behavior. So, we identy an attacked node according to its behavior. Specifically, we propose a Reputation Evaluation Scheme for the Node in the following Subsect. 3.1.

3.1 Reputation Evaluation Scheme for the Node

The node's reputation is evaluted based on the node's state which will be obtained by the node's behavior in RES-N. The tag T will record the node's behavior as evidence ED. Then, T will include ED as part of the response message when interacting with the next node R_n. After that, the message will be sent to O_T by the node R_n. Once receiving the response message, O_T determines and then submits R's behavior to RMC. Finally, RMC updates R's reputation by R's state which is determined by R's behavior. In all, the node reputation evalutation process includes the following three steps.

- **Node's Behavior Determination**
  In order to perform operations on tag T, the node R must be authorized by the tag's organization O_T. Therefore, R requests authorization from O_T by sending a request message $AUTH\_R$ to O_T. Once being authorized, R can access to the tag. When the interaction between T and R is completed, T will generate an evidence ED to record the operation of the node. Specifically, $ED = <ID_R, OP, rand, seq>$ where ID_R is the identity of R. 'OP' stands for the performed operation such as data reading, writing or updating. 'seq' is a sequence number which is initialized to 1 and will be increased by one after each operation. 'rand' is a random number generated by the tag. When the tag is requested by the next node R_n, ED will be included in $AUTH\_R = <ID_T, ID_{R_n}, OP_n, ED, \varpi>$ and sent to the tag's organization O_T by R_n. Specifically, $\varpi = E_k(Hash(ED))$ which is obtained by first hashing ED as $Hash(ED)$ and then encrypting $Hash(ED)$ by key k, where k is the symmetric key shared by T and O_T. Once receiving $AUTH\_R$, O_T firstly verifies ϖ. If the received $AUTH\_R$ pass the verification, O_T will then obtain R's operation from ED and determine R's behavior as follows. Obviously, R's behavior, either normal or malicious, can be observed accurately since each operation of R will be sent to O_T.
  (a) *normal* behaivor is detected, if node R only performs operation permitted by O_T.
  (b) *fault* behaivor is detected, if node R performs unpermitted operation occasionally probably due to its random breakdown. This kind of *fault* behaivor such as data dropping or injection may not be allowed by O_T but won't do harm to T.

(c) *malicious* behaivor is detected, if node R performs operation strictly prohibited by O_T such as compeletly wipe data.

- **Node's State Determination**
After obtaining R' behaviors from different organiztions, RMC can determine
node R's state according to R's 'Major Behavior'. The 'Major Behavior' is
the behavior which occurs most frequently. For example, if the *malicious*,
fault and *normal* behavior occurs 6, 4 and 2 times during 10 min, the 'Major
Behavior' is *malicious*. According to Table 1, we then find that the status of
R is *Attacked* .

Table 1. Node state based on its major behavior

Behavior	Status
Normal	*Good*
Fault	*Temporary breakdown*
Malicious	*Attacked*

- **Node's Reputation Evaluation**
Once obtaining the state of R, RMC can compute R's reputation p_R. If the
state of R is good, p_R will be updated to the maximum reputation value p_0,
where p_0 denotes the initialization reputation value of a node. Or else, if R
is in temporary breakdown or even attacked states, p_R will be reduced to
$\zeta * p_0$ or even 0. Specifically, ζ is an impact factor affecting the reputation of
a breakdown node, where $0 < \zeta \leq 1$.

4   Simulation

In this section, we implement RES-N in a network covering over 1000*800 square
meters. There are one RMC, 3 organizations, 30 tags and a large number of
nodes. The moving speed of each node is 3 m/s. The available communication
distance between a node and a tag is less than 30 m. The maximum communication distance between two nodes is 150 m. Both the reputation of a node and
an organization are initialized to 1.

Figure 1 shows how the moving speed of tags affects the number of attacked
nodes being detected for RES-N. We set that 30% of the nodes has been attacked.
Each organization deploys 100 readers and 5 tags. We can observe from Fig. 1
that the number of attacked nodes being detected grows over time. This is
because tags can encounter more readers and then capture the readers' behavior
over time with a high possibility.

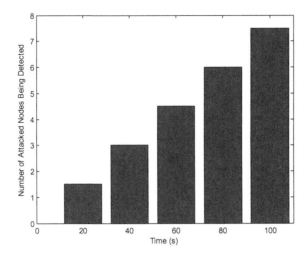

Fig. 1. Number of attacked nodes being detected over time

5 Conclusion

In this paper, we studied the trust issues in the IoT. In order to provide a general framework for trust management in IoT, we firstly design LTrust, a layered trust model for IoT. Then, a Reputation Evaluation Scheme for the Node (RES-N) and an a Reputation Evaluation Scheme for the Organization (RES-O) have been presented. The efficiency of RES-N and ORES is valided by the simulation results.

Acknowledgement. This research is supported in part by the Natural Science Foundation of China under grants No. 61300188 and 61601221; by the Fundamental Research Funds for the Central Universities No. 3132016024 and No. 3132017129; by Scientific Research Staring Foundation for the Ph.D in Liaoning Province No. 201601081; by Scientific Research Projects from Education Department in Liaoning Province No. L2015056.

References

1. Chen, R., Bao, F., Chang, M.J., et al.: Dynamic trust management for delay tolerant networks and its application to secure routing. IEEE Trans. Parallel Distrib. Syst. **25**, 1200–1210 (2014)
2. Cho, J.H., Swami, A., Chen, R.: Modeling and analysis of trust management with trust chain optimization in mobile ad hoc networks. J. Netw. Comput. Appl. **35**, 1001–1012 (2012)
3. Sicari, S., Rizzardi, A., et al.: Security, privacy and trust in Internet of Things: the road ahead. Comput. Netw. **76**, 146–164 (2015)
4. Nitti, M., Girau, R., Atzori, L.: Trustworthiness management in the social Internet of Things. IEEE Trans. Knowl. Data Eng. **26**, 1253–1266 (2014)

5. Ganeriwal, S., Balzano, et al.: Reputation-based framework for high integrity sensor networks. ACM Trans. Sens. Netw. (TOSN) **4** (2008)
6. Hellaoui, H., Bouabdallah, A., et al.: TAS-IoT: trust-based adaptive security in the IoT. In: IEEE 41st Conference on Local Computer Networks, pp. 599–602 (2016)
7. Bernabe, J.B.: Ramos, et al.: TACIoT: multidimensional trust-aware access control system for the Internet of Things. Soft Comput. **20**, 1763–1779 (2016)

Gain-Phase Error Calculation in DOA Estimation for Mixed Wideband Signals

Jiaqi Zhen[(⊠)], Yong Liu, and Yanchao Li

College of Electronic Engineering, Heilongjiang University,
Harbin 150080, China
zhenjiaqi2011@163.com

Abstract. Gain-phase error is inevitable in direction of arrival (DOA) estimation, it will lead to the mismatch between actual and ideal array manifold. Therefore, a novel gain-phase error calculation approach in DOA estimation for mixed wideband signals is provided in this paper. First, the signals are transformed on the focusing frequency. Then peak searching is employed for determining the far-field sources. Finally, gain-phase error can be calculated according to the orthogonality of far-field signal subspace and noise subspace, simulation results manifest the effectiveness of the proposed approach.

Keywords: DOA estimation · Gain-phase error · Far-field signals
Near-field signals · Wideband signals

1 Introduction

With the development of array signal processing, more and more DOA estimation methods are springing up [1–8]. Such as multiple signal classification (MUSIC) [9], ESPRIT [10], maximum likelihood [11] and so on, all of them can achieve a high precision and resolution capability under ideal condition. But as a matter of fact, due to the processing technology and some disturbance, gain-phase error often exists in hardware, which leads to the deviation between actual and ideal array manifold, then most DOA estimation methods have deteriorated, so how to calculate this kind of error is very important.

In recent years, gain-phase error calculation has attracted many scholars: Friedlander [12] analyzed its effect to MUSIC algorithm, then approximate expression of the estimation variance is given; Weiss and Friedlander [13] discussed the first and second order statistical properties of the spatial spectrum, then deduced the resolution threshold; Su et al. [14] inferred the expression of spatial spectrum, the relation

J. Zhen—This work was supported by the National Natural Science Foundation of China under Grant No. 61501176 and 61505050, University Nursing Program for Young Scholars with Creative Talents in Heilongjiang Province (UNPYSCT-2016017), China Postdoctoral Science Foundation (2014M561381), Heilongjiang Province Postdoctoral Foundation (LBH-Z14178), Heilongjiang Province Natural Science Foundation (F2015015), Outstanding Young Scientist Foundation of Heilongjiang University (JCL201504) and Special Research Funds for the Universities of Heilongjiang Province (HDRCCX-2016Z10).

© ICST Institute for Computer Sciences, Social Informatics and Telecommunications Engineering 2018
X. Gu et al. (Eds.): MLICOM 2017, Part I, LNICST 226, pp. 598–605, 2018.
https://doi.org/10.1007/978-3-319-73564-1_60

between gain-phase and resolution capacity; Wang et al. [15] concluded the quadric equation in one unknown of average signal to noise ratio (SNR) resolution threshold for MUSIC algorithm. All the research have shown the effect of the gain-phase error to the DOA estimation, they also greatly promoted the practical application of corresponding techniques, but there are rare published literatures in DOA estimation for mixed signals.

A novel gain-phase error calculation approach in DOA estimation for mixed far-field and near-field wideband signals (abbreviate as FS and NS) is provided in this paper. First, the signals are transformed on the focusing frequency. Then peak searching is employed for determining the far-field sources. Finally, Gain-phase error can be calculated according to the orthogonality of far-field signal subspace and noise subspace.

2   Array Signal Model

Define the wavelength of the signal is λ, D is the array aperture, l is the distance between the signal and the reference. Generally speaking, if $l > > 2D^2/\lambda$, it will be in the far-field; if $l \in (\lambda/2\pi, 2D^2/\lambda)$, it will be in the near-field. As is shown in Fig. 1, assume that N_1 wideband far-field and N_2 near-field sources impinge onto a $2M+1$-element uniform linear array from directions of $\theta = [\theta_1, \cdots, \theta_{N_1}, \theta_{N_1+1}, \cdots, \theta_N]$, the middle sensor is treated as the reference, where $N = N_1 + N_2$, $0 < \theta < \pi$, the space of sensors d equals half of the wavelength of the center frequency, and N_1, N_2 is assumed to be known in advance, then array output is

$$X(f_i) = A(f_i, \theta)S(f_i) + E(f_i) \quad (i = 1, 2, \cdots, J) \tag{1}$$

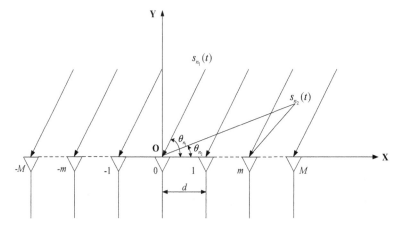

Fig. 1. Signal model

where J is number of divided narrowband frequency bins, $A(f_i, \theta)$ is the array manifold

$$
\begin{aligned}
A(f_i, \theta) &= [a_{FS}(f_i, \theta_1), \cdots, a_{FS}(f_i, \theta_{n_1}), \cdots, a_{FS}(f_i, \theta_{N_1}), a_{NS}(f_i, \theta_{N_1+1}), \cdots, a_{NS}(f_i, \theta_{n_2}), \cdots, a_{NS}(f_i, \theta_N)] \\
&= [A_{FS}(f_i), A_{NS}(f_i)]
\end{aligned}
\tag{2}
$$

where $A_{FS}(f_i) = [a_{FS}(f_i, \theta_1), \cdots, a_{FS}(f_i, \theta_{n_1}), \cdots, a_{FS}(f_i, \theta_{N_1})]$ is the array manifold of FS, and $a_{FS}(f_i, \theta_{n_1})$ is the steering vector of $s_{n_1}(t)$; $A_{NS}(f_i) = [a_{NS}(f_i, \theta_{N_1+1}), \cdots, a_{NS}(f_i, \theta_{n_2}), \cdots, a_{NS}(f_i, \theta_N)]$ is the array manifold of NS, and $a_{NS}(f_i, \theta_{n_2})$ is the steering vector of $s_{n_2}(t)$, here

$$
\begin{aligned}
a_{FS}(f_i, \theta_{n_1}) = [&\exp(-j2\pi f_i \tau_{-M}(\theta_{n_1})), \cdots, \exp(-j2\pi f_i \tau_{-m}(\theta_{n_1})), \cdots, 1, \\
&\cdots, \exp(-j2\pi f_i \tau_m(\theta_{n_1})), \cdots, \exp(-j2\pi f_i \tau_M(\theta_{n_1}))]^{\mathrm{T}}
\end{aligned}
\tag{3}
$$

and

$$
\tau_m(\theta_{n_1}) = m\frac{d}{c}\cos\theta_{n_1} \quad (m = -M, \cdots, -m, \cdots, 0, \cdots, m, \cdots, M; \\
n_1 = 1, 2, \cdots, N_1)
\tag{4}
$$

is the delay for $s_{n_1}(t)$ arriving at the mth sensor with respect to the origin, on the other hand

$$
\begin{aligned}
a_{NS}(f_i, \theta_{n_2}) = [&\exp(-j2\pi f_i \tau_{-M}(\theta_{n_2})) \cdots, \exp(-j2\pi f_i \tau_{-m}(\theta_{n_2})), \cdots, 1, \\
&\cdots, \exp(-j2\pi f_i \tau_m(\theta_{n_2})), \cdots, \exp(-j2\pi f_i \tau_M(\theta_{n_2}))]^{\mathrm{T}}
\end{aligned}
\tag{5}
$$

according to the geometrical relationship, we can deduce the $\tau_m(\theta_{n_2})$ from Fig. 1

$$
\tau_m(\theta_{n_2}) = \frac{l_{n_2} - \sqrt{l_{n_2}^2 + (md)^2 - 2l_{n_2}md\cos\theta_{n_2}}}{c}
\tag{6}
$$

reference Taylor series, Eq. (6) can be transformed into [16]

$$
\tau_m(\theta_{n_2}) = \frac{m^2 d^2}{4l_{n_2}c}\cos 2\theta_{n_2} + \frac{1}{c}md\cos\theta_{n_2} - \frac{m^2 d^2}{4l_{n_2}c}
\tag{7}
$$

and

$$
\begin{aligned}
S(f_i) &= [S_{FS}(f_i), S_{NS}(f_i)]^{\mathrm{T}} \\
&= [S_1(f_i), \cdots, S_{n_1}(f_i), \cdots, S_{N_1}(f_i), S_{N_1+1}(f_i), \cdots, S_{n_2}(f_i), \cdots, S_N(f_i)]^{\mathrm{T}}
\end{aligned}
\tag{8}
$$

here $S_{FS}(f_i) = [S_1(f_i), \cdots, S_{n_1}(f_i), \cdots, S_{N_1}(f_i)]^{\mathrm{T}}$ is signal vector of FS, $S_{NS}(f_i) = [S_{N_1+1}(f_i), \cdots, S_{n_2}(f_i), \cdots, S_N(f_i)]^{\mathrm{T}}$ is that of NS. $E(f_i)$ is the Gaussian white noise matrix with mean 0 and variance σ^2, then corresponding covariance matrix is

$$\begin{aligned}
\boldsymbol{R}(f_i) &= \frac{1}{Z}\boldsymbol{X}(f_i)\boldsymbol{X}^{\mathrm{H}}(f_i) \\
&= \frac{1}{Z}\boldsymbol{A}(f_i,\ \theta)\boldsymbol{S}(f_i)\boldsymbol{S}^{\mathrm{H}}(f_i)\boldsymbol{A}^{\mathrm{H}}(f_i,\ \theta) + \sigma^2(f_i)\boldsymbol{I} \\
&= \boldsymbol{R}_{FS}(f_i) + \boldsymbol{R}_{NS}(f_i) + \sigma^2(f_i)\boldsymbol{I}
\end{aligned} \tag{9}$$

the covariance matrix of FS is $\boldsymbol{R}_{FS}(f_i) = \frac{1}{Z}\boldsymbol{A}_{FS}(f_i)\boldsymbol{S}_{FS}(f_i)\boldsymbol{S}_{FS}^{\mathrm{H}}(f_i)\boldsymbol{A}_{FS}^{\mathrm{H}}(f_i)$, that of NS is $\boldsymbol{R}_{NS}(f_i) = \frac{1}{Z}\boldsymbol{A}_{NS}(f_i)\boldsymbol{S}_{NS}(f_i)\boldsymbol{S}_{NS}^{\mathrm{H}}(f_i)\boldsymbol{A}_{NS}^{\mathrm{H}}(f_i)$.

We can also model the gain-phase error as

$$\boldsymbol{W}(f_i) = \mathrm{diag}\left([W_{-M}(f_i),\cdots,\ W_{-m}(f_i),\cdots,\ 1,\cdots,\ W_m(f_i),\cdots,\ W_M(f_i)]^{\mathrm{T}}\right) \tag{10}$$

where

$$W_m(f_i) = \rho_m(f_i)e^{j\varphi_m(f_i)},\ m = -M,\cdots,\ -m,\cdots,\ 0,\cdots,\ m,\cdots,\ M, \tag{11}$$

is the gain-phase error of the sensor m, $\rho_m(f_i)$, $\varphi_m(f_i)$ are the corresponding gain and phase errors, and they are independent with each other, so the array output with gain-phase error is

$$\boldsymbol{X}'(f_i) = \boldsymbol{A}'(f_i,\ \theta)\boldsymbol{S}(f_i) + \boldsymbol{E}(f_i) = \boldsymbol{W}(f_i)\boldsymbol{A}(f_i,\ \theta)\boldsymbol{S}(f_i) + \boldsymbol{E}(f_i) \tag{12}$$

3   Estimation Theory

First, we need to estimate the covariance matrix with gain-phase error

$$\begin{aligned}
\boldsymbol{R}'(f_i) &= \frac{1}{Z}\boldsymbol{X}'(f_i)(\boldsymbol{X}'(f_i))^{\mathrm{H}} \\
&= \frac{1}{Z}\boldsymbol{A}'(f_i,\ \theta)\boldsymbol{S}(f_i)\boldsymbol{S}^{\mathrm{H}}(f_i)(\boldsymbol{A}'(f_i,\ \theta))^{\mathrm{H}} + \sigma^2(f_i)\boldsymbol{I} \\
&= \frac{1}{Z}\boldsymbol{W}(f_i)\boldsymbol{A}(f_i,\ \theta)\boldsymbol{S}(f_i)\boldsymbol{S}^{\mathrm{H}}(f_i)\boldsymbol{A}^{\mathrm{H}}(f_i,\ \theta)\boldsymbol{W}^{\mathrm{H}}(f_i) + \sigma^2(f_i)\boldsymbol{I} \\
&= \boldsymbol{R}'_{FS}(f_i) + \boldsymbol{R}'_{NS}(f_i) + \sigma^2(f_i)\boldsymbol{I}
\end{aligned} \tag{13}$$

where the covariance matrix of the FS is $\boldsymbol{R}'_{FS}(f_i) = \frac{1}{Z}\boldsymbol{W}(f_i)\boldsymbol{A}_{FS}(f_i)\boldsymbol{S}_{FS}(f_i)\boldsymbol{S}_{FS}^{\mathrm{H}}(f_i) \times \boldsymbol{A}_{FS}^{\mathrm{H}}(f_i)\boldsymbol{W}^{\mathrm{H}}(f_i)$, that of the NS is $\boldsymbol{R}'_{NS}(f_i) = \frac{1}{Z}\boldsymbol{W}(f_i)\boldsymbol{A}_{NS}(f_i)\boldsymbol{S}_{NS}(f_i)\boldsymbol{S}_{NS}^{\mathrm{H}}(f_i) \times \boldsymbol{A}_{NS}^{\mathrm{H}}(f_i)\boldsymbol{W}^{\mathrm{H}}(f_i)$. We can employ some coherent signal subspace methods to transform the received data on the focusing frequency

$$\boldsymbol{R}''(f_0) = \frac{1}{J}\sum_{i=1}^{J}\boldsymbol{T}(f_i)\boldsymbol{R}'(f_i)\boldsymbol{T}^{\mathrm{H}}(f_i) \tag{14}$$

here $T(f_i) = U'_S(f_0)\left(U'_S(f_i)\right)^H$ is the focusing matrix, $U'_S(f_0)$ is the signal subspace of $R'(f_i), f_0$ is the focusing frequency, then we can found the MUSIC spatial spectrum of FS

$$
\begin{aligned}
P_{MU-F}(\theta) &= \frac{1}{\left(a'_{FS}(f_0,\ \theta)\right)^H U_E(f_0) U_E^H(f_0) a'_{FS}(f_0,\ \theta)} \\
&= \frac{1}{a_{FS}^H(f_0,\ \theta) W^H(f_0) U_E(f_0) U_E^H(f_0) W(f_0) a_{FS}(f_0,\ \theta)} \\
&= \frac{1}{Y}
\end{aligned}
\tag{15}
$$

where $U_E(f_0)$ is the noise subspace of $R''(f_0)$, in order to be convenient to the derivation, we express the gain-phase error with another form

$$
w(f_i) = [\rho_{-M}(f_i)e^{j\varphi_{-M}(f_i)}, \cdots, \rho_{-m}(f_i)e^{j\varphi_{-m}(f_i)}, \cdots, 1, \cdots, \rho_m(f_i)e^{j\varphi_m(f_i)}, \cdots, \rho_M(f_i)e^{j\varphi_M(f_i)}]^T
\tag{16}
$$

then we can simplify the denominator of the function above

$$
\begin{aligned}
Y &= a_{FS}^H(f_0,\ \theta) W^H(f_0) U_E(f_0) U_E^H(f_0) W(f_0) a_{FS}(f_0,\ \theta) \\
&= \sum_{n_1=1}^{N_1} a_{FS}^H(f_0,\ \theta_{n_1}) W^H(f_0) U_E(f_0) U_E^H(f_0) W(f_0) a_{FS}(f_0,\ \theta_{n_1}) \\
&= \sum_{n_1=1}^{N_1} w^H(f_0)\left\{ (\mathrm{diag}(a_{FS}(f_0,\ \theta_{n_1})))^H U_E(f_0) U_E^H(f_0)\mathrm{diag}(a_{FS}(f_0,\ \theta_{n_1})) \right\} w(f_0) \\
&= w^H(f_0) D(f_0,\ \theta) w(f_0)
\end{aligned}
\tag{17}
$$

where $D(f_0,\ \theta) = \sum_{n_1=1}^{N_1}\left\{ (\mathrm{diag}(a_{FS}(f_0,\ \theta_{n_1})))^H U_E(f_0) U_E^H(f_0)\mathrm{diag}(a_{FS}(f_0,\ \theta_{n_1})) \right\}$, the DOA of FS can be solved by minimizing (17). $w(f_0)$ is not null matrix, so $w^H(f_0) D(f_i,\ \theta) w(f_0) = 0$ holds only if $D(f_0,\ \theta)$ is singular, then $\theta_1, \cdots \theta_{N_1}$ can be estimated by searching N_1 peaks of $D(f_0, \theta)$.

Next, the orthogonality of signal subspace of FS and noise subspace can be utilized

$$
\left(a'_{FS}(\theta_{n_1})\right)^H U'_E = a_{FS}^H(\theta_{n_1}) W^H U'_E = \mathbf{0}_{1\times(2M+1-N)}
\tag{18}
$$

it can be transformed into

$$
a_{FS}^H(\theta_{n_1}) W^H U'_E = w^H\{ \mathrm{diag}(a_{FS}(\theta_{n_1})) \}^H U'_E = w^H Q(\theta_{n_1})
\tag{19}
$$

here $Q(\theta_{n_1}) = \{ \operatorname{diag}(a_{FS}(\theta_{n_1})) \}^H U'_E$, define D as the middle row of U'_E, as the middle row of $a_{FS}(\theta_{n_1})$ equals 1, the middle element of $Q(\theta_{n_1})$ is D too. Combining all FS, and let $Q(\theta) = [Q(\theta_1), \cdots, Q(\theta_{n_1}), \cdots, Q(\theta_{N_1})]$, therefore

$$
w^H Q(\theta) = w^H \begin{bmatrix} Q_1(\theta) \\ D \cdots D \\ Q_2(\theta) \end{bmatrix} = [w_1^H, \ 1, \ w_2^H] \begin{bmatrix} Q_1(\theta) \\ D \cdots D \\ Q_2(\theta) \end{bmatrix} = [0, \cdots, 0]_{1 \times (2M+1-N)N_1}
$$

(20)

where w_1 is the first M rows of w, w_2 is the latter M rows of w, $Q_1(\theta)$ is the first M rows of $Q(\theta)$, $Q_2(\theta)$ is the latter M rows of $Q(\theta)$, define $G = [D \cdots D]_{1 \times (2M+1-N)N_1}$, w_1 and w_2 will be acquired according to (20), that is

$$
\hat{w}_1 = -\left(G(Q_1(\theta))^\# \right)^H
$$

(21)

$$
\hat{w}_2 = -\left(G(Q_2(\theta))^\# \right)^H
$$

(22)

$\hat{w}_1$ and $\hat{w}_2$ is the estimation of w_1 and w_2, $()^\#$ means solving pseudo-inverse, then we have

$$
\hat{w} = [\hat{w}_1^T, \ 1, \ \hat{w}_2^T]^T
$$

(23)

Thus, estimation of gain-phase error can be calculated, and the number of sensors and the signals must satisfy $2M + 1 > N_1 + N_2$, the method is suitable for gain-phase error calculation in DOA estimation for mixed wideband signals, so we call it GPW for short.

4 Simulations

The structure of the array is illustrated as Fig. 1, consider two FS and two NS impinge on a uniform linear array with 7 omnidirectional sensors from $(73°, 85°)$ and $(40°, 65°)$ simultaneously, the frequency of the signals limited in 0.9 GHz–1.1 GHz. The band is divided into 9 frequency bins, here the gain and phase errors are generated in [0, 0.5] and [−20°, 20°] randomly respectively, 500 Monte-Carlo trials are repeated. SNR is 6 dB, number of snapshots is 30, Figs. 2 and 3 have shown gain and phase error estimation of different sensors at every frequency bin, where ith s-A means actual value of ith sensor, and ith s-E means the corresponding estimation, we can see from Figs. 2 and 3, GPW can estimate the gain and phase error of the array, especially when the frequency is near to the center point. As the center frequency corresponds to half of the wavelength, so it is more precise than the others.

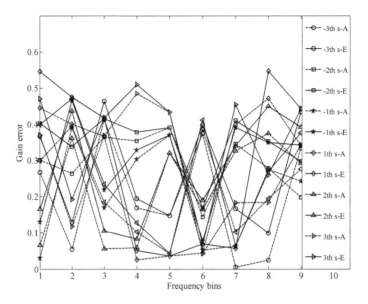

Fig. 2. Gain error estimation

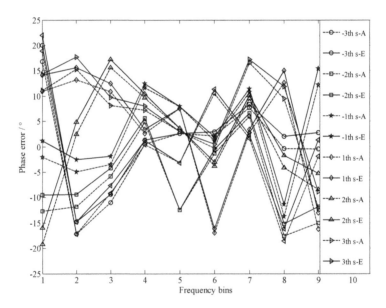

Fig. 3. Phase error estimation

5 Conclusion

A novel gain-phase error calculation approach in DOA estimation for mixed wideband signals is provided in this paper. First, the signals are transformed on the focusing frequency. Then peak searching is employed for determining the far-field sources.

Finally, Gain-phase error can be calculated according to the orthogonality of far-field signal subspace and noise subspace. However, it just applies to uniform linear array, we will be committed to study the technique for planar array in future.

References

1. Luis, S., Luis, M., Jose, A.G.: SmartSantander: IoT experimentation over a smart city testbed. Comput. Netw. **61**, 217–238 (2014)
2. Li, J., Zhao, Y.J., Li, D.H.: Accurate single-observer passive coherent location estimation based on TDOA and DOA. Chin. J. Aeronaut. **27**, 913–923 (2014)
3. Giuseppe, F., Andrew, H.: A multipath-driven approach to HF geolocation. Signal Process. **93**, 3487–3503 (2013)
4. He, Z.Q., Shi, Z.P., Huang, L.: Underdetermined DOA estimation for wideband signals using robust sparse covariance fitting. IEEE Signal Process. Lett. **22**, 435–439 (2015)
5. Tan, Z., Yang, P., Nehorai, A.: Joint-sparse recovery method for compressed sensing with structure dictionary mismatches. IEEE Trans. Signal Process. **62**, 4997–5008 (2014)
6. Azais, J.M., Castro, Y.D., Gamboa, F.: Spike detection from inaccurate samplings. Appl. Comput. Harmon. Anal. **38**, 177–195 (2015)
7. Jagannath, R., Hari, K.V.S.: Block sparse estimator for grid matching in single snapshot DoA estimation. IEEE Signal Process. Lett. **20**, 1038–1041 (2013)
8. Amin, M.G., Wang, X.R., Zhang, Y.D.: Sparse arrays and sampling for interference mitigation and DOA estimation in GNSS. Proc. IEEE **104**, 1302–1317 (2016)
9. Schmidt, R.O.: Multiple emitter location and signal parameter estimation. IEEE Trans. Antennas Propag. **34**, 276–280 (1986)
10. Roy, R., Kailath, T.: ESPRIT-estimation of signal parameters via rotational invariance techniques. IEEE Trans. Acoust. Speech Signal Process. **37**, 984–995 (1989)
11. Ziskind, I., Wax, M.: Maximum likelihood localization of multiple sources by alternating projection. IEEE Trans. Acoust. Speech Signal Process. **36**, 1553–1560 (1988)
12. Friedlander, B.: A sensitivity analysis of the MUSIC algorithms. IEEE Trans. Acoust. Speech Signal Process. **38**, 1740–1751 (1990)
13. Weiss, A.J., Friedlander, B.: Effects of modeling errors on the resolution threshold of the MUSIC algorithm. IEEE Trans. Signal Process. **42**, 1519–1526 (1994)
14. Su, W.M., Gu, H., Ni, J.L.: A statistical performance analysis of the MUSIC algorithm in the presence of amplitude and phase perturbation. Acta Electron. Sin. **28**, 105–107 (2000)
15. Wang, D., Wang, C., Wu, Y.: Analysis of the effects of the amplitude-phase errors on spatial spectrum and resolving performance of the MUSIC algorithm. J. Commun. **31**, 55–63 (2010)
16. Lee, J., Chen, Y., Yeh, A.: A covariance approximation method for near-field direction-finding using a uniform linear array. IEEE Trans. Signal Process. **43**, 1293–1298 (1995)

Mutual Coupling Estimation in DOA Estimation for Mixed Wideband Signals

Jiaqi Zhen$^{(\boxtimes)}$, Yong Liu, and Yanchao Li

College of Electronic Engineering,
Heilongjiang University, Harbin 150080, China
zhenjiaqi2011@163.com

Abstract. With the electromagnetic frequency getting higher and higher, the distance between the sensors is becoming smaller and smaller, so the mutual coupling is increasingly obvious, it will lead to the mismatch between actual and ideal array manifold. Therefore, a novel mutual coupling error calculation approach in direction of arrival (DOA) estimation for mixed wideband signals is provided in this paper. First, the signals are transformed on the focusing frequency. Then root finding is employed for determining the far-field signals. Finally, mutual coupling error can be calculated according to the orthogonality of far-field signal subspace and noise subspace.

Keywords: DOA estimation · Mutual coupling · Far-field signals
Near-field signals · Wideband signals

1 Introduction

Direction of arrival (DOA) estimation has developed very rapidly in recent years [1–5], and many excellent algorithms has been proposed, such as multiple signal classification (MUSIC) [6], ESPRIT [7], maximum likelihood [8] and so on, all of them can achieve a high precision and resolution capability under ideal condition, but they are always not in common use due to the complex circumstance. One of the reasons is the mutual coupling effect in the array, it is the interference among sensors. Due to the unambiguous demand for the array in direction of arrival (DOA) estimation, the interval of the adjacent sensor is often not allowed larger than half of the wavelength, which leads to the serious mutual coupling, then estimation result will deviate the actual direction, so we need to fundamentally resolve this kind of problem.

In recent years, mutual coupling error calculation has attracted many scholars. Generally speaking, they can be classified into active calibration and passive

J. Zhen—This work was supported by the National Natural Science Foundation of China under Grant No. 61501176 and 61505050, University Nursing Program for Young Scholars with Creative Talents in Heilongjiang Province (UNPYSCT-2016017), China Postdoctoral Science Foundation (2014M561381), Heilongjiang Province Postdoctoral Foundation (LBH-Z14178), Heilongjiang Province Natural Science Foundation (F2015015), Outstanding Young Scientist Foundation of Heilongjiang University (JCL201504) and Special Research Funds for the Universities of Heilongjiang Province (HDRCCX-2016Z10).

© ICST Institute for Computer Sciences, Social Informatics and Telecommunications Engineering 2018
X. Gu et al. (Eds.): MLICOM 2017, Part I, LNICST 226, pp. 606–613, 2018.
https://doi.org/10.1007/978-3-319-73564-1_61

calibration, the former needs a known source in advance: Zhang and Zhu [9] proposed two kinds of compensation algorithms, but they both need to set a standard source; Ng and See [10] presented a maximum algorithm to compensate the no calibration damage, and it has very obvious improvement. The latter omits the hardware, but increase the computation: Friedlander and Weiss [11] opened the door to the passive calibration; then Sellone and Serra [12] provided a method through minimum mean square iteration; In [13], researchers studied the calibration methods for the special array structure, comparing with the active calibration, this kind of method has more computation. All the researchers above have shown the effect of the mutual coupling to the DOA estimation, they also greatly promoted the practical application of corresponding techniques, but there are rare published literatures in DOA estimation for mixed signals.

A novel mutual coupling calculation method in DOA estimation for mixed far-field and near-field wideband signals (abbreviate as FS and NS) is provided in this paper. First, the signals are transformed on the focusing frequency. Then root finding is employed for determining the far-field sources. Finally, mutual coupling error can be calculated according to the orthogonality of far-field signal subspace and noise subspace.

2 Array Signal Model

Define the wavelength of the signal is λ, D is the array aperture, l is the distance between the signal and the reference. Generally speaking, if $l >> 2D^2/\lambda$, it will be in the far-field; if $l \in (\lambda/2\pi, 2D^2/\lambda)$, it will be in the near-field. As is shown in Fig. 1, assume that N_1 far-field and N_2 near-field wideband signals impinge onto a uniform linear array with $2M+1$ sensors from directions of $\theta = [\theta_1, \cdots, \theta_{N_1}, \theta_{N_1+1}, \cdots, \theta_N]$, the middle sensor is deemed to be the origin, and $N = N_1 + N_2$, $0 < \theta < \pi$, the space of sensors d is half of the wavelength of the center frequency,

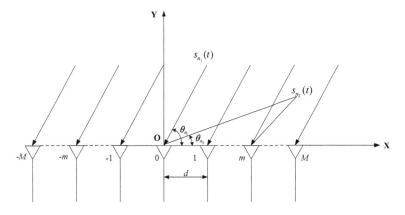

Fig. 1. Signal model

and N_1, N_2 is assumed to be known beforehand, we divide output of array into J parts, that is

$$X(f_i) = A(f_i, \theta)S(f_i) + E(f_i) \quad (i = 1, 2, \cdots, J) \tag{1}$$

where $A(f_i, \theta)$ is the array manifold

$$\begin{aligned} A(f_i, \theta) &= [a_{FS}(f_i, \theta_1), \cdots, a_{FS}(f_i, \theta_{N_1}), a_{NS}(f_i, \theta_{N_1+1}), \cdots, a_{NS}(f_i, \theta_N)] \\ &= [A_{FS}(f_i), A_{NS}(f_i)] \end{aligned} \tag{2}$$

where $A_{FS}(f_i) = [a_{FS}(f_i, \theta_1), \cdots, a_{FS}(f_i, \theta_{N_1})]$ is the array manifold of FS; $A_{NS}(f_i) = [a_{NS}(f_i, \theta_{N_1+1}), \cdots, a_{NS}(f_i, \theta_N)]$ is the array manifold of NS, here

$$a_{FS}(f_i, \theta_{n_1}) = [\exp(-j2\pi f_i \tau_{-M}(\theta_{n_1})), \cdots, \exp(-j2\pi f_i \tau_M(\theta_{n_1}))]^T \tag{3}$$

and

$$\tau_m(\theta_{n_1}) = m\frac{d}{c}\cos\theta_{n_1} \ (m = -M, \cdots, -m, \cdots, 0, \cdots, m, \cdots, M;$$
$$n_1 = 1, 2, \cdots, N_1) \tag{4}$$

is the delay for $s_{n_1}(t)$ arriving at the mth sensor with respect to the origin, meanwhile

$$a_{NS}(f_i, \theta_{n_2}) = [\exp(-j2\pi f_i \tau_{-M}(\theta_{n_2})) \cdots, \exp(-j2\pi f_i \tau_M(\theta_{n_2}))]^T \tag{5}$$

according to the geometrical relationship, we can deduce the $\tau_m(\theta_{n_2})$ from Fig. 1.

$$\tau_m(\theta_{n_2}) = \frac{l_{n_2} - \sqrt{l_{n_2}^2 + (md)^2 - 2l_{n_2}md\cos\theta_{n_2}}}{c} \tag{6}$$

reference Taylor series [14], Eq. (6) can be transformed into

$$\tau_m(\theta_{n_2}) = \frac{m^2 d^2}{4l_{n_2}c}\cos2\theta_{n_2} + \frac{1}{c}md\cos\theta_{n_2} - \frac{m^2 d^2}{4l_{n_2}c} \tag{7}$$

and

$$S(f_i) = [S_{FS}(f_i), S_{NS}(f_i)]^T = [S_1(f_i), \cdots, S_{N_1}(f_i), S_{N_1+1}(f_i), \cdots, S_N(f_i)]^T \tag{8}$$

here $S_{FS}(f_i) = [S_1(f_i), \cdots, S_{N_1}(f_i)]^T$ is signal vector of FS, $S_{NS}(f_i) = [S_{N_1+1}(f_i), \cdots, S_N(f_i)]^T$ is that of NS. $E(f_i)$ is the Gaussian white noise matrix with mean 0 and variance σ^2, then corresponding covariance matrix is

$$\begin{aligned}
\boldsymbol{R}(f_i) &= \frac{1}{Z}\boldsymbol{X}(f_i)\boldsymbol{X}^{\mathrm{H}}(f_i) \\
&= \frac{1}{Z}\boldsymbol{A}(f_i,\ \theta)\boldsymbol{S}(f_i)\boldsymbol{S}^{\mathrm{H}}(f_i)\boldsymbol{A}^{\mathrm{H}}(f_i,\ \theta) + \sigma^2(f_i)\boldsymbol{I} \\
&= \boldsymbol{R}_{FS}(f_i) + \boldsymbol{R}_{NS}(f_i) + \sigma^2(f_i)\boldsymbol{I}
\end{aligned} \tag{9}$$

the covariance matrix of FS is $\boldsymbol{R}_{FS}(f_i) = \frac{1}{Z}\boldsymbol{A}_{FS}(f_i)\boldsymbol{S}_{FS}(f_i)\boldsymbol{S}_{FS}^{\mathrm{H}}(f_i)\boldsymbol{A}_{FS}^{\mathrm{H}}(f_i)$, that of NS is $\boldsymbol{R}_{NS}(f_i) = \frac{1}{Z}\boldsymbol{A}_{NS}(f_i)\boldsymbol{S}_{NS}(f_i)\boldsymbol{S}_{NS}^{\mathrm{H}}(f_i)\boldsymbol{A}_{NS}^{\mathrm{H}}(f_i)$, Z is the sampling times at f_i.

The degree of mutual coupling is closely related to signal frequency, when there is mutual coupling among sensors, perturbation matrix can be expressed by $\boldsymbol{W}(f_i)$, we itemize Q corresponding the freedom degree of the array, according to the property of uniform linear array, the mutual coupling among sensors is independent with one another, then we know $\boldsymbol{W}(f_i)$ can be expressed as

$$\boldsymbol{W}(f_i) = \begin{bmatrix}
1 & c_1(f_i) & \cdots & c_Q(f_i) & & \\
c_1(f_i) & 1 & c_1(f_i) & & \ddots & \\
 & c_1(f_i) & & & & c_Q(f_i) \\
\vdots & & \ddots & & \ddots & \ddots \\
c_Q(f_i) & & & \ddots & & \\
 & \ddots & & & 1 & c_1(f_i) \\
 & & c_Q(f_i) & & c_1(f_i) & 1
\end{bmatrix} \tag{10}$$

where $c_q(f_i)$ $(q = 1, 2, \cdots, Q)$ is the mutual coupling coefficient, when the distance between two sensor is q, signal frequency is f_i, the steering vector of the array can be revised to

$$\boldsymbol{a}'(f_i, \theta_n) = \boldsymbol{W}(f_i)\boldsymbol{a}(f_i, \theta_n) \quad (n = 1, 2, \cdots, N) \tag{11}$$

corresponding array manifold is

$$\boldsymbol{A}'(f_i, \theta) = [\boldsymbol{a}'(f_i, \theta_1), \cdots, \boldsymbol{a}'(f_i, \theta_N)] = \boldsymbol{W}(f_i)\boldsymbol{A}(f_i, \theta) \tag{12}$$

so the array output is

$$\boldsymbol{X}'(f_i) = \boldsymbol{A}'(f_i, \theta)\boldsymbol{S}(f_i) + \boldsymbol{E}(f_i) = \boldsymbol{W}(f_i)\boldsymbol{A}(f_i, \theta)\boldsymbol{S}(f_i) + \boldsymbol{E}(f_i) \tag{13}$$

3   Proposed Method

The covariance matrix at the present time is

$$
\begin{aligned}
\mathbf{R}'(f_i) &= \frac{1}{Z}\mathbf{X}'(f_i)(\mathbf{X}'(f_i))^{\mathrm{H}} \\
&= \frac{1}{Z}\mathbf{A}'(f_i, \theta)\mathbf{S}(f_i)\mathbf{S}^{\mathrm{H}}(f_i)(\mathbf{A}'(f_i, \theta))^{\mathrm{H}} + \sigma^2(f_i)\mathbf{I} \\
&= \frac{1}{Z}\mathbf{W}(f_i)\mathbf{A}(f_i, \theta)\mathbf{S}(f_i)\mathbf{S}^{\mathrm{H}}(f_i)\mathbf{A}^{\mathrm{H}}(f_i, \theta)\mathbf{W}^{\mathrm{H}}(f_i) + \sigma^2(f_i)\mathbf{I} \\
&= \mathbf{R}'_{FS}(f_i) + \mathbf{R}'_{NS}(f_i) + \sigma^2(f_i)\mathbf{I}
\end{aligned}
\tag{14}
$$

then we can employ coherent signal method (CSM) [15] to transform the information on the focusing frequency

$$
\mathbf{R}''(f_0) = \frac{1}{J}\sum_{i=1}^{J} \mathbf{T}(f_i)\mathbf{R}'(f_i)\mathbf{T}^{\mathrm{H}}(f_i)
\tag{15}
$$

here $\mathbf{T}(f_i) = \mathbf{U}'_S(f_0)\left(\mathbf{U}'_S(f_i)\right)^{\mathrm{H}}$ is the transforming matrix, $\mathbf{U}'_S(f_i)$ is the signal eigenvector of $\mathbf{R}'(f_i)$, f_0 is the center frequency, then we can deduce the MUSIC spatial spectrum of FS

$$
\begin{aligned}
P_{MU-F}(\theta) &= \frac{1}{\left(\mathbf{a}'_{FS}(f_0, \theta)\right)^{\mathrm{H}}\mathbf{U}_E(f_0)\mathbf{U}_E^{\mathrm{H}}(f_0)\mathbf{a}'_{FS}(f_0, \theta)} \\
&= \frac{1}{\mathbf{a}_{FS}^{\mathrm{H}}(f_0, \theta)\mathbf{W}^{\mathrm{H}}(f_0)\mathbf{U}_E(f_0)\mathbf{U}_E^{\mathrm{H}}(f_0)\mathbf{W}(f_0)\mathbf{a}_{FS}(f_0, \theta)} \\
&= \frac{1}{Y}
\end{aligned}
\tag{16}
$$

where $\mathbf{U}_E(f_0)$ is the noise subspace of $\mathbf{R}''(f_0)$, for the sake of analyzing the equation easily, we express the mutual coupling error with another shape

$$
\mathbf{w}(f_i) = [1, c_1(f_i), \cdots, c_Q(f_i)]^{\mathrm{T}} = [1, \mathbf{w}_1^{\mathrm{T}}(f_i)]^{\mathrm{T}}
\tag{17}
$$

combining [11], $\mathbf{W}(f_0)\mathbf{a}_{FS}(f_0, \theta)$ can be written as another form

$$
\mathbf{W}(f_0)\mathbf{a}_{FS}(f_0, \theta) = \mathbf{G}(f_0, \theta)\mathbf{w}(f_0)
\tag{18}
$$

where $\mathbf{G}(f_0, \theta) = \mathbf{G}_1(f_0) + \mathbf{G}_2(f_0)$, and

$$
[\mathbf{G}_1(f_0)]_{\alpha,\beta} = \begin{cases} [\mathbf{a}(f_0, \theta)]_{\alpha+\beta-1}, & \alpha + \beta \le 2M \\ 0, & \text{otherwise} \end{cases}
\tag{19}
$$

$$[G_2(f_0)]_{\alpha,\beta} = \begin{cases} [a(f_0, \theta)]_{\alpha-\beta+1}, & \alpha \geq \beta \geq 2 \\ 0, & \text{otherwise} \end{cases} \tag{20}$$

then we can abbreviate Y as

$$\begin{aligned} Y &= a_{FS}^H(f_0, \theta)W^H(f_0)U_E(f_0)U_E^H(f_0)W(f_0)a_{FS}(f_0, \theta) \\ &= w^H(f_0)G^H(f_0, \theta)U_E(f_0)U_E^H(f_0)G(f_0, \theta)w(f_0) \\ &= w^H(f_0)D(f_0, \theta)w(f_0) \end{aligned} \tag{21}$$

where $D(f_0, \theta) = G^H(f_0, \theta)U_E(f_0)U_E^H(f_0)G(f_0, \theta)$, the DOA of FS can be solved by minimizing (21). $w(f_0)$ is not null matrix, so $w^H(f_0)D(f_i, \theta)w(f_0) = 0$ sets up only if $D(f_0, \theta)$ is singular, then $\theta_1, \cdots \theta_{N_1}$ can be estimated by solving N_1 roots of the determinant of $D(f_0, \theta)$ below

$$\det[D(f_0, \theta)] = 0 \tag{22}$$

Then we can use the orthogonality between noise and signal space of FS, that is

$$\left(U_E'(f_i)\right)^H a_{FS}'(f_i, \theta_{n_1}) = \left(U_E'(f_i)\right)^H W(f_i)a_{FS}(f_i, \theta_{n_1}) = 0_{(2M+1-N)\times 1} \tag{23}$$

combining the information of $\theta_1, \cdots, \theta_{N_1}$, we have

$$\begin{bmatrix} \left(U_E'(f_i)\right)^H a_{FS}'(f_i, \theta_1) \\ \vdots \\ \left(U_E'(f_i)\right)^H a_{FS}'(f_i, \theta_{N_1}) \end{bmatrix} = \begin{bmatrix} \left(U_E'(f_i)\right)^H G(f_i, \theta_1) \\ \vdots \\ \left(U_E'(f_i)\right)^H G(f_i, \theta_{N_1}) \end{bmatrix} w(f_i) \tag{24}$$

$$= \Theta(f_i)w(f_i) = \begin{bmatrix} B_1(f_i) \vdots B_2(f_i) \end{bmatrix} \begin{bmatrix} 1 \\ w_1(f_i) \end{bmatrix} = 0_{N_1(2M+1-N), 1}$$

where $B_1(f_i)$ is the first column of $\Theta(f_i)$, and $B_2(f_i)$ is the other parts of $\Theta(f_i)$, then we can estimate the mutual coupling error as

$$\hat{w}_1(f_i) = -\text{pin}(B_2(f_i))B_1(f_i) \tag{25}$$

here pin() means solving the pseudo-inverse, then $W(f_i)$ can also be obtained according to (10), and the number of sensors and the signals must satisfy $2M + 1 > N_1 + N_2$, the method we proposed is suitable for mutual coupling error calculation in DOA estimation for mixed wideband signals, so we call it MCW for short.

4 Simulations

The structure of the array is illustrated as Fig. 1, consider two FS and two NS impinge on a uniform linear array with 8 sensors from $(50°, 60°)$ and $(70°, 80°)$, the frequency of the signals limited in 0.8 GHz–1.0 GHz. The band is divided into 9 frequency bins, suppose that the freedom degree among sensors $Q = 2$, mutual coupling perturbation vector $\mathbf{w}_{(1)}(f_i) = [c_1(f_i), c_2(f_i)]^T = [a_1(f_i) + b_1(f_i)\mathrm{j}, a_2(f_i) + b_2(f_i)\mathrm{j}]^T$, $a_1(f_i)$ and $b_1(f_i)$ is selected between $(-0.5\text{--}0.5)$ randomly, $a_2(f_i)$ and $b_2(f_i)$ is selected between $(-0.25\text{--}0.25)$ randomly; SNR is 12 dB, the sampling times at every frequency is 30, 300 Monte-Carlo simulations are repeated, their average values are deemed as the final results, Figs. 2 and 3 have shown the mutual couple estimation of $c_1(f_i)$ and $c_2(f_i)$ at every frequency, where $fi - A$ means actual value at the ith ($i = 1, \cdots, 9$) frequency bin, and $fi - E$ is the corresponding estimation.

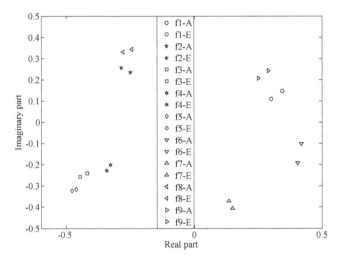

Fig. 2. Mutual couple error estimation of $c1$

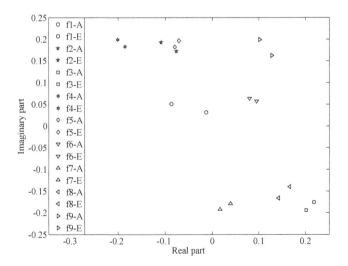

Fig. 3. Mutual couple error estimation of $c2$

It can be seen from Figs. 2 and 3, the MCW method can effectively estimate the mutual couple perturbations, especially when the frequency is near to the center frequency. As the center frequency corresponds to half of the wavelength, so it is more precise than the other parts. Then we can use these results to calibrate the array and acquire the actual DOA of the wideband signals.

5 Conclusion

A novel mutual couple error calculation approach in DOA estimation for mixed wideband signals is provided in this paper. First, the signals are transformed on the focusing frequency. Then root finding is employed for determining the far-field sources. Finally, mutual couple error can be calculated according to the orthogonality of far-field signal subspace and noise subspace. However, it just applies to uniform linear array, we will be committed to study the technique for planar array in future.

References

1. Tan, Z., Yang, P., Nehorai, A.: Joint-sparse recovery method for compressed sensing with structure dictionary mismatches. IEEE Trans. Sig. Process. **62**, 4997–5008 (2014)
2. Li, J., Zhao, Y.J., Li, D.H.: Accurate single-observer passive coherent location estimation based on TDOA and DOA. Chin. J. Aeronaut. **27**, 913–923 (2014)
3. He, Z.Q., Shi, Z.P., Huang, L.: Underdetermined DOA estimation for wideband signals using robust sparse covariance fitting. IEEE Sig. Process. Lett. **22**, 435–439 (2015)
4. Azais, J.M., Castro, Y.D., Gamboa, F.: Spike detection from inaccurate samplings. Appl. Comput. Harmon. Anal. **38**, 177–195 (2015)
5. Amin, M.G., Wang, X.R., Zhang, Y.D.: Sparse arrays and sampling for interference mitigation and DOA estimation in GNSS. Proc. IEEE **104**, 1302–1317 (2016)
6. Schmidt, R.O.: Multiple emitter location and signal parameter estimation. IEEE Trans. Antennas Propag. **34**, 276–280 (1986)
7. Roy, R., Kailath, T.: ESPRIT-estimation of signal parameters via rotational invariance techniques. IEEE Trans. Acoust. Speech Sig. Process. **37**, 984–995 (1989)
8. Ziskind, I., Wax, M.: Maximum likelihood localization of multiple sources by alternating projection. IEEE Trans. Acoust. Speech Sig. Process. **36**, 1553–1560 (1988)
9. Zhang, M., Zhu, Z.: Compensation for unknown mutual coupling in bearing estimation. Int. J. Electron. **75**, 965–971 (1993)
10. Ng, B.C., See, C.M.S.: Sensor-array calibration using a maximum-likelihood approach. IEEE Trans. Antennas Propag. **44**, 827–835 (1996)
11. Friedlander, B., Weiss, A.J.: Direction finding in the presence of mutual coupling. IEEE Trans. Antennas Propag. **39**, 273–284 (1991)
12. Sellone, F., Serra, A.: A novel online mutual coupling compensation algorithm for uniform and linear arrays. IEEE Trans. Sig. Process. **55**, 560–573 (2007)
13. Lin, M., Yang, L.: Blind calibration and DOA estimation with uniform circular arrays in the presence of mutual coupling. IEEE Antennas Wirel. Propag. Lett. **5**, 315–318 (2006)
14. Su, W.M., Gu, H., Ni, J.L.: A statistical performance analysis of the MUSIC algorithm in the presence of amplitude and phase perturbation. Acta Electron. Sin. **28**, 105–107 (2000)
15. Wang, H., Kaveh, M.: Coherent signal-subspace processing for the detection and estimation of angles of arrival of multiple wideband sources. IEEE Trans. Acoust. Speech Sig. Process. **33**, 823–831 (1985)

Efficient Data Gathering with Compressed Sensing Multiuser Detection in Underwater Wireless Sensor Networks

Rui Du, Wenjing Kang, Bo Li, and Gongliang Liu[✉]

School of Information and Electrical Engineering,
Harbin Institute of Technology, No. 2 West Wenhua Road,
Weihai 264209, China
337150406@qq.com, {kwjqq,libol983,liugl}@hit.edu.cn

Abstract. Bandwidth and energy constraints of underwater wireless sensors networks necessitate an intelligent data transmission between sensor nodes and the fusion center. This paper considers a data gathering underwater networks for monitoring oceanic environmental elements (e.g. temperature, salinity) and only a portion of measurements from sensors allows for oceanic information map reconstruction under compressed sensing (CS) theory. By utilizing the spatial sparsity of active sensors' data, we introduce an activity and data detection based on CS at the receiver side, which results in an efficient data communication by avoiding the necessity of conveying identity information. For an interleave division multiple access (IDMA) sporadic transmission, CS-CBC detection that combines the benefits from chip-by-chip (CBC) multi-user detection and CS detection is proposed. Further, by successively exploring the sparsity of sensor data in spatial and frequency domain, we propose a novel efficient data gathering scheme named Dual-domain compressed sensing (DCS). Simulation results validate the effectiveness of the proposed scheme and an optimal sensing probability problem related to minimum reconstruction error is explored.

Keywords: Compressed sensing · Data gathering · Multiuser detection
Underwater wireless sensor networks

1 Introduction

Underwater wireless sensor networks (UWSN) [1] are widely applied in various advanced applications including environmental monitoring, marine fuel exploration, basic marine sciences and so on. Two main constraints of UWSN enabled by acoustic communications are the limited available bandwidth and the difficulty of frequently recharging the batteries of sensors with regard to economic efficiency and technical consumption. UWSN is believed to be a typical energy-limited and bandwidth-limited system, and hence a robust and efficient network data aggregation scheme is an essential foundation for reliable high-performance in large-scale ocean environmental monitoring networks.

Due to the observation that sensory data are mainly oceanic nature signal which are sparse or compressible in an appropriate basis, compressive sensing (CS) [2, 3] can be

© ICST Institute for Computer Sciences, Social Informatics and Telecommunications Engineering 2018
X. Gu et al. (Eds.): MLICOM 2017, Part I, LNICST 226, pp. 614–625, 2018.
https://doi.org/10.1007/978-3-319-73564-1_62

applied to provide an efficient data gathering scheme, which allows the aggregation node reconstruct the information map with relatively small amount of measurements rather than the raw data from the whole wireless networks [4]. To the best of our knowledge, authors in [5] are the first attempt to introduce the application of compressed sensing in network data processing. The appealing reduction in signal processing and resource requirement has spawned a range of advanced data gathering schemes in wireless sensor networks. For example, Fazel et al. have develop a networking scheme, namely Random Access Compressing Sensing (RACS), that combines compressed sensing and the concepts of random channel access aiming at achieving energy and bandwidth efficiency by only randomly activating a small part of sensor nodes [6]; Xue et al. propose a CS-based medium access control scheme for efficient data transmission in data gathering networks and in-depth analyze the effect of SNR on the accuracy of transmission symbol recovery [7]. Such been investigated data gathering networks either require complicated control overhead including identity information of active sensor nodes or no in-depth eliminate the effect of multiple access interference on data transmission, and hence there are still imperfections to be improved on.

Recently, a novel PHY layer approach for multi-user detection has been investigated, namely multi-user detection based on compressed sensing [8], that allows for jointly reliable user activity and data detection for direct random access in a sporadic communication scenario, where only a small portion of transmitters are active at a given time instant. For such sporadic transmission, the coordination of node access enabled by access reservation protocol would consume a significant amount of additional control overhead. From the view of whole networks' physical topology, the location distribution of active sensors can be viewed as one kind of sparse in spatial domain, and hence compressed sensing can be applied to jointly detect the activity and data information of active sensors, while at the same time a highly resource-efficient transmission can be expected. These advantages greatly innovates the development of multi-user detection based on compressed sensing. In [9], in order to perform a reliable MUD in the case of different sparsity, the author adopted a switching MUD schemes from linear minimum mean square error (LMMSE) to Orthogonal matching pursuit (OMP), which is the most famous of CS reconstruction algorithms. Bringing CS to MUD attracts many researchers to develop MUD schemes based on CS. So far, the multi-user detection based on CS has been applied to many wireless systems, see [10, 11] and references therein.

In this work, we concentrate on data gathering underwater sensor network that collects information of interest for applications such as geographical and environmental monitoring. We consider that only a portion of active sensors are selected during the monitoring cycle and simultaneously communicate their sensory data in uplink transmission, i.e., direct random access. This partial sensor selection method makes the sensory measurements of physical phenomenon which is sparse in frequency domain, are sparse in the spatial domain. In this paper, we innovatively introduce multi-user detection based on compressed sensing into data gathering networks, and propose a dual-dimensional compressed sensing (DCS) for underwater wireless data gathering networks by successively utilizing sparsity of frequency and spatial domain. The proposed scheme guarantees high-performance data measurements collection and allows for the most energy-efficient data gathering networks at the same time.

2 Preliminaries and Problem Formulation

2.1 Compressed Sensing Theory

Originated as a method for acquiring sparse solutions even for under-determined linear systems, compressed sensing provides a new paradigm for signal processing and data acquisition, with which the network data or signals can be efficiently sampled and accurately reconstructed from much fewer measurements than Nyquist sampling theory.

Consider an original signal $x = (x_1, x_2, \ldots, x_n)^T$, which is an n-dimensional vector. Supposing that x is sparse itself or can be represented over a certain appropriate basis $\Psi = \{\varphi_i\}_{i=1}^n$, where $\varphi_i \in \mathbb{R}^n$. As shown in (1), x can be sparse expressed as the linear combination of a subset of basis vector:

$$x = \sum_{i=1}^n \theta_i \varphi_i \quad \text{or} \quad \theta = \Psi^T x, \tag{1}$$

where θ_i is an $n \times 1$ vector which denotes the weights vector, $\theta_i = <x, \varphi_i>$ and Ψ is the basis matrix. Ψ is an identity matrix when x is sparse vector. We say that vector θ is perfectly s-sparse if it has at most $s(s \ll n)$ non-zero elements. In addition, vector θ is approximately s-sparse means that it has at most s large coefficients while the remaining coefficients are small. For simplicity and without of generality, s-sparse signal vector include perfect sparse and approximately sparse in this paper.

According to CS theory, the original vector x can be reduced-dimensional measured by taking a smaller number (m) of samples by using a linear/convex programming operator Φ; hence the reduced-dimensional measurement vector y can be written as

$$y = \Phi x = \Phi \Psi \theta = A\theta, \tag{2}$$

where $\Phi = \{\varphi_1, \varphi_2, \ldots, \varphi_m\}^T$, $A = \Phi \Psi$, $s \leq m \leq n$, and the original vector x is compressed into an $m \times 1$ vector y. Several imposing conditions on measurement matrix Φ guarantee the uniqueness of the solution, such as restricted isometry property (RIP), incoherence and so on [12].

The problem of recovering original vector x from the compressed m-length measurement vector y is equivalent to finding sparsest solution of (2), which can be expressed as an optimization problem:

$$\min_{\theta} \|\theta\|_p \quad \text{s.t.} \quad y = \Phi \Psi \theta, \tag{3}$$

where $\|\bullet\|_p = (\sum_{i=1}^n |\bullet|)^{1/p}$ denotes the l_p-norm. $l_p(0 < p \leq 1)$ guarantees the RIP condition, and hence original vector x can be accurately reconstructed in highly probability.

2.2 Problem Formulation

Consider a typical UWSN architecture for oceanic data gathering with N sensor nodes deployed in a two-dimensional plane and a fusion center (FC) as shown in Fig. 1. Specifically, the sensor nodes are uniformly distributed to collect some kinds of ocean monitoring elements (e.g. temperature, salinity, and ocean current) and report data to the FC via uplink multiple access channel by one hop. Generally speaking, all sensors transmit collected information with low cost and low-energy consumption, whereas the FC can support more complex computational consumption, such as advanced signal processing. Typically the readings of sensor nodes have spatial correlation due to the closeness of sensors, and hence the reconstruction of network data can be accomplished by collecting a portion of sensory data at the FC according to CS theory. The resource-constraint underwater network necessitates an efficient data transmission between SNs and FC. Channelization access schemes (e.g. time division multiple access, code division multiple access) for selected sensors' communication would produce a significant coordination overhead and increase the time latency. In view of the facts, this paper aims to find an efficient data gathering approach for the large-scale ocean monitoring underwater sensor networks as shown in Fig. 1.

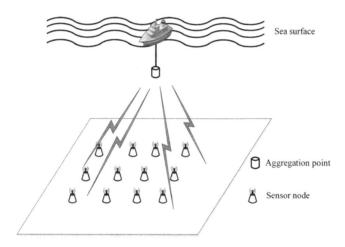

Fig. 1. Two-dimension underwater wireless sensor network for ocean monitoring

3 Dual-Domain Compressed Sensing

In this section, the dual-domain compressed sensing for data gathering scheme is proposed and illustrated for the large-scale ocean monitoring underwater sensor networks. The framework of the proposed scheme is simple and clear. The proposed scheme consists of four components: (1) random sensing with probability p_a. (2) multiple access over noisy channels. (3) activity and data detection based on CS (4) network data recovery based on CS, as shown in As shown in Fig. 2.

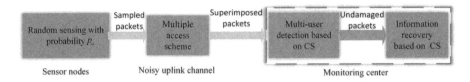

Fig. 2. Framework of data gathering based on dual-domain compressed sensing.

3.1   Random Sensing at Sensor Nodes

Due to the fact that most natural phenomenon has a compressible/sparse representation in an appropriate basis, random sensing is considered in this paper to conserve power of the sensor nodes, in which case only a portion of sensors participates in sensing. To model sensor node activity, we adopt a statistical approach, where each sensor node equips with a simple Bernoulli random generator with a probability p_a denoted as *sensing probability*. Those sensors who are engaged in data transmission are referred to as being *active*, while the other sensors are kept silent and overhearing state to conserve power energy. This activity probability, that determines the total number of active sensors N_{act} in a statistical sense, is assumed to be identical for all deployed sensor nodes. Since not all sensors signaling in a given time, that is, only a few sensors are only active on occasion and we call this *sporadic transmission* [13].

At the beginning of the monitoring cycle, each sensor node performs one independent Bernoulli trial to determine which sensors participating sensing. It is noteworthy that active sensors report data in a time frame which is assumed to be less than the coherence time of nature phenomenon. According to CS theory, a simple and efficient measurement matrix, random extractive matrix Φ, is considered in this paper to reflect the process of random sensing. Φ is easily formed by randomly selecting N_{act} rows from the $N \times N$ identity matrix. The elements in the random extractive matrix have the following property:

$$
\begin{aligned}
\sum_{i=1}^{N_{act}} \phi_{ij} &\leq 1, j = 1, 2, \ldots, N \\
\sum_{j=1}^{N} \phi_{ij} &= 1, i = 1, 2, \ldots, N_{act}
\end{aligned}
\tag{4}
$$

3.2   Multiple Access Over Noisy Channel

IDMA is a relatively novel multiple access method, which can be considered as a special case of CDMA due to use low rate code as spreading and separating users from specific interleavers [14]. Such a multiple access inherits many distinguished features of the well-studied CDMA, and further improvement in terms of performance and spectrum efficiency in UWSN. Therefore, IDMA is attractive for underwater wireless communication.

All sensors are equipped with IDMA transmitter. In prior to access channel, multiple access techniques are adopted in processing the symbol frame to implement multi-user transmission. Neither access reservation protocols for node coordination or signing the activity of sensor nodes are assumed in order to avoiding significant additional transmission. Further, we assume slotted random access for data transmission and one frame of data are transmitted per slot.

After that, all transmitted symbols are superimposed in the receiver, and the receiver signal y is modeled as

$$\mathbf{y} = \sum_{k=1}^{K} \mathbf{H}_k \mathbf{\Pi}_k \mathbf{S} \mathbf{d}_k + \mathbf{n}$$
$$= \mathbf{A}\mathbf{d} + \mathbf{n}.$$
(5)

For the kth sensor, $\mathbf{d}_k \in \mathcal{A}_0^M$ is the vector including the transmitted symbols, Each column of $\mathbf{S} \in \mathbb{R}^{F \times M}$ contains the spreading sequence $\mathbf{s}_k$, $\mathbf{\Pi}_k \in \mathbb{R}^{F \times F}$ describes the matrix form of user specific interleaver φ_k, and $\mathbf{H}_k \in \mathbb{R}^{F' \times F}$ is channel matrix for the node-specific block-fading channel $\mathbf{h}_k$. Then, the total influence of transmission can be represented as $\mathbf{A} \in \mathbb{R}^{F' \times M}$, and vector $\mathbf{d} \in \mathcal{A}_0^L$ is the stacked vector of all $\mathbf{d}_k$, where $L = KM$. Further, the noise vector $\mathbf{n} \in \mathbb{R}^{F'}$ is i.i.d. zero-mean Gaussian distributed, i.e., $\mathbf{n} \sim \mathcal{N}(0, \sigma_\mathbf{n}^2 \mathbf{I})$. Herein, the symbols of $\mathbf{d}$ are taken from the discrete augmented alphabet $\mathcal{A}_0$.

Synchronous reception and perfect channel state information are assumed in system model (5).

3.3 Activity and Data Detection Based on CS by Utilizing Sparsity of Spatial Domain

IDMA allows a low-cost chip-by-chip (CBC) iterative multi-user detection strategy to implement multi-user detection. However, it assumes that active sensors are exactly known at the receiver, which is challenging in practice.

Due to the fact that each sensor is activated to transmitting measurements with a sensing probability p_a in one time frame, the number of active SNs at one time instance, K_{act}, is small, resulting in a sparse signal $\mathbf{d}$ in the process of multiple access. Furthermore, as to sporadic wireless communication, the connected nodes transmit signals continuously on a frame basis by a low probability. Since sensors are active or inactive for a whole frame, the non-zeros symbols of the sparse vector $\mathbf{d}$ appear in groups or blocks form in a fixed length. Therefore, this feature is also known as *block sparsity* or *group sparsity* [15]. For the sake of uniform expression in this paper, we choose *block sparsity* in the following. The multi-user detection problem can be treated as a block sparse signal recovery inherently, which naturally incorporate the powerful tool CS into the joint sensor activity and data detection problem. Therefore, the greedy group orthogonal matching pursuit (GOMP) [16] is a good choice for CS detection.

In order to enhance the robustness of uplink sporadic IDMA transmission, we propose a CS-CBC multi-user detector that can accurately detect the sensor activity and efficiently implement data detection. It should be noted, while classical CS could provide jointly recovery the activity and data detection, CS-CBC only need CS detection to accurately detect positions of nonzero elements of sparse signal $\mathbf{d}$, rather than the values of non-zero elements.

After the user activity information obtained above, the received signal $\mathbf{y}$, which compose of the active sensor transmitted symbols modulated by the interleaved spreading sequences, can be expressed as

$$
\begin{aligned}
\mathbf{y} &= \sum_{n=1}^{N_{act}} \mathbf{H}_n \mathbf{\Pi}_n \mathbf{S} \mathbf{d}_n + \mathbf{n} \\
&= \mathbf{A}_2 \mathbf{d}_{active} + \mathbf{n},
\end{aligned}
\tag{6}
$$

where $\mathbf{d}_{active}$ only contains the transmitted symbols of active sensors, $\mathbf{A}_2$ has the same form as $\mathbf{A}$ in system model (5) except that it only includes interleaved spreading sequences and channel influence for active sensors. Then, CBC algorithm can be implemented to realize active data detection.

Differing from the typical application of CS, the goal of detection based on CS is capable of determining the activity of sensors and recovering the symbol data packets of active sensors. Activity information of all SNs enables the construction of measurement matrix $\mathbf{\Phi}$, while symbol data packets of active SNs contain the successfully collected packets utilized for network recovery. Therefore, implementing multi-user detection based on CS at the FC simultaneously provide two prerequisite information for network data recovery.

3.4   Network Data Recovery Based on CS by Utilizing Sparsity of Frequency Domain

In view of the fact the network data acquired from the monitored underwater characteristics are usually are compressible or sparse representation in the frequency domain (such as sea currents, temperature and salinity), CS theory further enables the possibility of reconstruction a high-resolution information map of the monitoring network by utilizing sparsity of frequency domain.

Supposed by the end of monitoring, the data measurement vector from the active sensor nodes $\mathbf{d}_\Gamma$ has been successfully acquired via MUD, which is given by

$$
\mathbf{d}_\Gamma = \mathbf{\Phi} \mathbf{f} = \mathbf{\Phi} \mathbf{\Psi} \boldsymbol{\theta},
\tag{7}
$$

where $\mathbf{\Phi}$ is the random extractive matrix that can be received from the recovered sparse vector $\mathbf{d}$, $\boldsymbol{\theta}$ is the sparse representation of original network data $\mathbf{f}$. Therefore, the network data recovery can be solved by the following optimization problem

$$
\min_{\mathbf{d}} \|\boldsymbol{\theta}\|_1 \text{ s.t. } \mathbf{d}_\Gamma = \mathbf{\Phi} \mathbf{\Psi} \boldsymbol{\theta}.
\tag{8}
$$

CS theory indicates that if the number of measurements exceeds a certain threshold r_s, the original network data $\mathbf{f}$ can be reconstructed in high probability by solving the problem of (8).

4   Simulation Results

4.1   Performance of the Proposed CS-CBC

We will discuss simulation results for the reliability of the detection in terms of Symbol Error Rate (SER), define as

$$SER = p(\hat{\mathbf{d}} \neq \mathbf{d}). \tag{9}$$

Here, the SER is given by the probability that the symbol frames of all sensors are detected incorrectly at the FC and therefore it summarizes both activity and data detection errors.

We consider an overloaded IDMA system, which result in under-determined equation system for CS detection. The main simulation parameters are set as follows. The total number of sensor nodes is $N = 100$ and the frame length M is set to 50 symbols. In order to separate users, random interleavers are adopted. All sensor nodes use the same spreading sequence, which is generated based on repetition coding multiplied by a mask sequence with alternant signs, i.e., [+1, −1, +1, −1, ...]. The spreading length N_s is 64. Therefore, the overloading factor is 156%. BPSK signaling is always considered.

Figure 3 compare the SER performance of the following four detectors: Conventional CBC, CS detection, CS-CBC and Genie-knowledge CBC assuming the perfect knowledge of active sensors, where the active probabilities is $p_a = 0.2$. Herein, the Genie-knowledge CBC algorithm plays a lower bound of the algorithm for sensor activity detection and data recovery. CS-CBC is superior to CS detection and CBC-AD and their gaps become larger with higher E_b/N_0. Furthermore, it can achieve the performance of Genie-knowledge CBC under high E_b/N_0. This means that CS-CBC

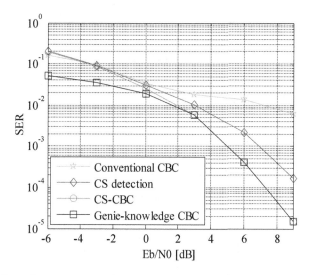

Fig. 3. SER performance comparison against SNR, where active probability $p_a = 0.2$.

has perfect knowledge of active sensors due to the reliable performance of CS detection to positioning non-zeros items and CS-CBC do better data recovery than CS detection.

4.2 Performance of Data Gathering Based on DCS

We consider a UWSN consisting of N sensor nodes in a simple single-path multiple access underwater channel model with ideal power control. Real ocean meridional current data of Monterey Bay is experiment subject, which is obtained by the Regional Ocean Modeling System (ROMS) at 3GMT 05/13/2012. The monitored region is 100 m below the sea surface and ranged over $[-122.8°E, -122.6°E]$ in longitude and $[36.6°N, 36.8°N]$ in latitude. Considering that the number of active sensors is usually large in the ocean monitoring sensor networks, the uplink frame will be split into several subframes and IDMA scheme is operated in each subframe. The main procedure is as following: Firstly, downlink control information included subframe index and interleaver is broadcasted to all sensor nodes. Secondly, the selected nodes transmit subframes separated by a guard time to FC. Finally, the FC implement CS-CBC and OMP algorithm to recovery the network data. The main simulation parameters are summarized in Table 1.

Table 1. Simulation parameters

Parameters	Value
Data packet length	50 bit
Spreading length	64
Noise power spectral density	−100 dBm
Underwater depth	100 m
Carrier frequency	10 kHz

Ideal power control for each sensor node is adopted and the required power of each sensor at the FC is P_0, the distance between the sensor node and the FC is d (km), and the carrier frequency is f (kHz). In order to achieve the required BER, the transmitted power should be $P_0 \cdot A(d,f)$, where

$$A(d,f) = d^c \cdot a(f)^d. \tag{10}$$

The constant c is usually set as 1.5, and

$$a(f) = 10^{\alpha(f)/10}, \tag{11}$$

where $\alpha(f)$ is the absorption coefficient, with an experiential formula as follows:

$$a(f) = \frac{0.11f^2}{1+f^2} + \frac{44f^2}{4100+f^2} + \frac{2.75f^2}{10^4} + 0.003. \tag{12}$$

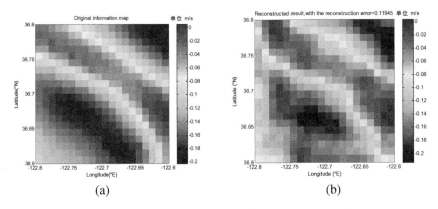

Fig. 4. Information map about ocean meridional current of the given area. (a) Original information map. (b) Reconstructed information map.

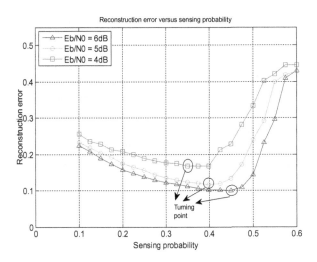

Fig. 5. Reconstruction error versus sensing probability.

The reconstruction error P_e is defined as $\|\hat{\mathbf{f}} - \mathbf{f}\|_2 / \|\mathbf{f}\|_2$ to evaluate the quality of network data recovery.

To visually illustrate the DCS scheme for data gathering network, the simulations for real data are shown in Fig. 4. E_b/N_0 is 6 dB at the FC and the sensing probability p_a is 0.3. The simulation result of PER is 0.0913 and hence about of 110 of the 120 random measurements are successfully collected for the network data recovery, leading to a reconstruction error $P_e = 0.11945$.

The relationship between reconstruction error P_e and the sensing probability p_a is illustrated in Fig. 5. An interesting phenomenon that the relationship curve presents downward bending and an optimal sensing probability exists in the turning point is

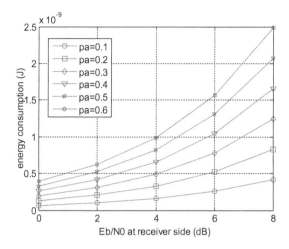

Fig. 6. Average energy consumption per sensor vs E_b/N_0 at receiver side.

observed. Further, the turning point varies with different channel conditions and appears latter with the increasing E_b/N_0. As mentioned above, the sensing probability p_a is negatively correlated with p_{suc}, and positively correlated with N_{act}. Consequently, the optimal sensing probability reaches a balance between two influence factor related to reconstruction error P_e in a given channel condition. The increasing E_b/N_0 improves the p_{suc}, which breaks the original balance and push sensing probability to increase in order to build a new balance. In addition, the reconstruction evidently deteriorates with the increase of E_b/N_0 because of the high PER. However, higher E_b/N_0 consume more energy, and the average energy consumption per sensor versus E_b/N_0 at FC is shown in Fig. 6. The performance tradeoff between resource requirement and quality of reconstruction should be taken into consideration in system design.

5   Conclusion

In this paper, we have elaborated the role of activity and data detection based on CS in data gathering networks in terms of symbol data recovery. The DCS scheme for data gathering that exploits the spatial sparsity of active sensors' data and the frequency sparsity that exists in most natural signals is proposed. The proposed CS-CBC that combines the benefits of CBC and conventional CS detection guarantees an efficient data transmission in DCS. Moreover, the influence of the activity and data detection on network recovery has been illustrated and the performance of proposed DCS scheme has been simulated in terms of reconstruction error and energy consumption. The optimal sensing probability problem related to minimum reconstruction error is illustrated and should be considered in system design.

Acknowledgments. This work was supported by the National Natural Science Foundation of China (No. 61371100, No. 61501139, No. 61401118).

References

1. Heidemann, J., Zorzi, M.: Underwater sensor networks: applications, advances and challenges. Philos. Trans. **370**, 158–175 (2012)
2. Donoho, D.L.: Compressed sensing. IEEE Trans. Inf. Theory **52**, 1289–1306 (2006)
3. Candès, E.J., Romberg, J., Tao, T.: Robust uncertainty principles: exact signal reconstruction from highly incomplete frequency information. IEEE Trans. Inf. Theory **52**, 489–509 (2006)
4. Han, Z., Li, H., Yin, W.: Compressive Sensing for Wireless Networks. Cambridge University Press, Cambridge (2013)
5. Haupt, J., Bajwa, W.U., Rabbat, M., Nowak, R.: Compressed sensing for networked data: a different approach to decentralized compression. IEEE Signal Process. Mag. **25**, 92–101 (2008)
6. Fazel, F., Fazel, M., Stojanovic, M.: Random access compressed sensing for energy-efficient underwater sensor networks. IEEE J. Sel. Areas Commun. **29**, 1660–1670 (2011)
7. Xue, T., Dong, X., Shi, Y.: Multiple access and data reconstruction in wireless sensor networks based on compressed sensing. IEEE Trans. Wirel. Commun. **12**, 3399–3411 (2013)
8. Schepker, H.F., Dekorsy, A.: Sparse multi-user detection for CDMA transmission using greedy algorithms. In: 8th ISWCS, Aachen, pp. 291–295 (2011)
9. Shim, B., Song, B.: Multiuser detection via compressive sensing. IEEE Commun. Lett. **16**, 972–974 (2012)
10. Monsees, F., Woltering, M., Bockelmann, C., Dekorsy, A.: Compressive sensing multi-user detection for multicarrier systems in sporadic machine type communication. In: IEEE Vehicular Technology Conference (VTC Spring), pp. 1–5. IEEE Press, Glasgow (2015)
11. Wang, B., et al.: Dynamic compressive sensing-based multi-user detection for uplink grant-free NOMA. IEEE Commun. Lett. **16**, 972–974 (2012)
12. Baraniuk, R., Davenport, M., DeVore, R., Wakin, M.: A simple proof of the restricted isometry property for random matrices. Constr. Approx. **28**, 253–263 (2008)
13. Bockelmann, C., Schepker, H., Dekorsy, A.: Compressive sensing based multi-user detection for machine-to-machine communication. Trans. Emerg. Telecommun. Technol. **24**, 389–400 (2013). Special Issue on Machine-to-Machine: An Emerging Communication Paradigm
14. Ping, L., Liu, L., Wu, K., Leung, W.K.: Interleave division multiple access. IEEE Trans. Wirel. Commun. **5**, 938–947 (2006)
15. Eldar, Y.C., Kuppinger, P., Bölcskei, H.: Block-sparse signals: uncertainty relations and efficient recovery. IEEE Trans. Signal Process. **58**, 3042–3054 (2010)
16. Majumdar, A., Ward, R.K.: Fast group sparse classification. Can. J. Electr. Comput. Eng. **34**, 136–144 (2009)

An Efficient Data Collection and Load Balance Algorithm in Wireless Sensor Networks

Danyang Qin[✉], Ping Ji, Songxiang Yang, and Qun Ding

Key Lab of Electronic and Communication Engineering,
Heilongjiang University, No. 74 Xuefu Road, Harbin,
People's Republic of China
qindanyang@hlju.edu.cn

Abstract. The fact of multi-hop data transmission in wireless sensor network will lead serious load unbalance. Considering the limited energy supply, the load distribution will cause great restraints in relative applications. Existing algorithm mostly perform the load balance inside each cluster without considering about the entire network consumption. A cluster-based Balanced Energy Consumption Algorithm (BECA) is proposed by collecting the data more efficiently to avoid heavy traffic nodes so as to achieve global load balance. Simulating results show that BECA can obtain better balance properties and prolong the network lifetime greatly.

Keywords: Wireless sensor network · Load balance · Cluster algorithm
Lifetime

1 Introduction

In recent years, wireless sensor network technology has developed rapidly. It has extensive potential application, including environmental monitoring and forecasting, health care, smart home, etc., so as to require the sensor nodes to become low-consumption, low-energy, multi-functional [1–3]. Due to the reason that the energy of the sensor nodes is provided by the battery, the energy supply is very limited. Then how to maximize the lifetime of network is one of most important problems in relative researches. Existing studies have shown [4] that the lifetime of the sensor nodes can be extended by increasing the capacity of the battery or reducing the energy consumption of each node. It is found that, however, the battery capacity can not be significantly improved due to weight and size limitations. Therefore, a method is proposed to reduce the loss of the energy effectively by data collecting and load balancing.

D. Qin—This work was supported in part by the National Natural Science Foundation China under Grant 61302074, in part by the Natural Science Foundation of Heilongjiang Province under Grant QC2013C061, in part by the Modern Sensor Technology Research and Innovation Team Foundation of Heilongjiang Province under Grant 2012TD007, in part by the Postdoctoral Research Foundation of Heilongjiang Province under Grant LBH-Q15121.

© ICST Institute for Computer Sciences, Social Informatics and Telecommunications Engineering 2018
X. Gu et al. (Eds.): MLICOM 2017, Part I, LNICST 226, pp. 626–634, 2018.
https://doi.org/10.1007/978-3-319-73564-1_63

Data collection is of great importance to wireless sensor network. Some of the existing energy efficiency protocols [5] suggest that sensor nodes data can be delivered to the BS through a path. Most of them apply a cluster-based approach [6], which select some sensor nodes as cluster-heads which collect data from their neighbor nodes, and then they deliver the data to an adjacent cluster-head so that the cluster members consume less energy. Therefore, this method of sending data can greatly reduced energy consumption. In addition, studies have shown that the application of cluster-based algorithm network, its lifetime increased by 8 times than the average network [7].

The existing cluster-based approach allows a small range of energy consumption to balance, but the entire network load is still unbalanced. Currently sent data from the cluster head to the BS, there are two main methods are direct connection and shortest path routing. The direct connection is shown in Fig. 1(b), the node near the BS consumes less energy than those away from the BS. The shortest path routing is shown in Fig. 1(c), a hot spot could transmit sensor data just like a hub, which is usually located near the base station. The above two methods will lead to a part of the network failure prematurely. So the better load balancing could extend the lifetime of the entire network.

In this paper, a cluster-based data gathering algorithm is proposed to solve the problem of unbalanced energy consumption in the network. The Balanced Energy Consumption Algorithm (BECA) is shown in Fig. 1(d), cluster heads are organized into multiple parallel links.

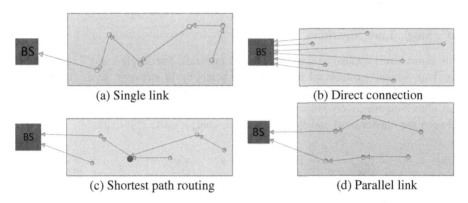

(a) Single link   (b) Direct connection

(c) Shortest path routing   (d) Parallel link

Fig. 1. Inter-cluster routing scheme

2   LEACH and HEED

At present, cluster-based data collection methods are LEACH, HEED and their conversion. There are two parts in these methods. One part is to select a cluster head and recovery system to effectively collect data, another part is an internal cluster system that passes these collected data to the BS. About the communication range, each node in the network is either in a DS [8] or near a DS node. In order to let different cluster-based data collection algorithms compare fairly, DS is applied to all of my algorithmic studies.

2.1   The Direct Connection of LEACH

As shown in Fig. 1(b), each cluster head sends sensor data directly to the BS. The algorithm is applied to the LEACH protocol and it cannot balance the loss of energy. The farther away from the base station, the transmission distance is longer, so the cluster head nodes far from the base station to send data will consume more energy. In WSN, inconsistency can lead to premature failure of the node at the far end of the sensing area, which will become a blind spot.

2.2   The Shortest Path Tree of HEED

As shown in Fig. 1(c), the shortest path tree (SPT) is formed by these shortest paths, all cluster heads in HEED deliver data to the BS through the shortest path. Although this method minimizes the loss of energy, the entire network of energy load is still not balanced the loss of energy is still unbalanced. It is worth noticing that the number of data packets which are sent depends on the location of each node in the SPT. The neighbor node of the BS is responsible for restoring all data packets to the BS, and the node near to the root has a heavier traffic load. A hot spot is a very crowded small area for data transmission, which is usually distributed near the BS and its energy consumption is the fastest compared to the rest of the network. When the energy of the area is exhausted, these nodes will become blind spots because they will not be able to transfer data to other nodes.

2.3   Single Link Algorithm

This algorithm is applied to the cluster-based protocol. The single link [7] is shown in Fig. 1(a), which is connected by the cluster heads in the network. Each cluster head communicates only with its neighbor nodes, which sequentially send data to the BS. This algorithm effectively reduces the energy consumption, but because of the distance between the cluster head and the base station, energy waste still exists.

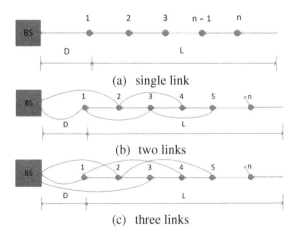

(a) single link

(b) two links

(c) three links

Fig. 2. Link structure in one-dimensional networks

3   BECA

In order to achieve energy efficient and balanced inter-cluster routing we propose BECA algorithm. As shown in Fig. 1(d), cluster heads are organized into multiple parallel links. Although the total energy consumption of the SPT is slightly lower than the BECA network, the maximum energy consumption of a single node is reduced in BECA, so that the network lifetime is extended.

3.1   Intra-link Scheduling Algorithm in One-Dimensional Networks

In the one-dimensional network model, the sensing area is a line of length L. As shown in Fig. 2(a), the base station is located in the leftmost area, n cluster heads are placed from the left to the right on this line. The distance between any two adjacent cluster heads is L/n and the distance from the base station to the node 1 is D, so the distance from the base station to the node n is $D + (n - 1)L/n$. In order to form m links, we set nodes $i, m + i, 2m + i, \ldots$ for each link $i(1 \leq i \leq m)$.

We use a single link solution to explain our inter-link scheduling algorithm. In the first loop, as shown in Fig. 3(a), cluster head 1 transmits one packet to the BS, and cluster head 2 transmits the remaining packets to the BS. In the second loop, as shown in Fig. 3(b), cluster head 1 transmits two packets of the cluster head 2 to the BS, while cluster head 3transmits the remaining packets to the base station. In the r loops, as shown in Fig. 3(c), cluster head 1 transmits r packets to the BS, and like this the cluster head $r + 1$ transmits $n - r$ packet to the BS. In the last loop, as shown in Fig. 3(d), there is no separate link and cluster head 1 transmits all n packets to the BS. After the n loops, it repeats from the first loop.

Using a single link, each packet is delivered by a node on average. For any L and D, when n exceeds a certain limit the cost of the relay may exceed the plan. The number of optimal links will be discussed.

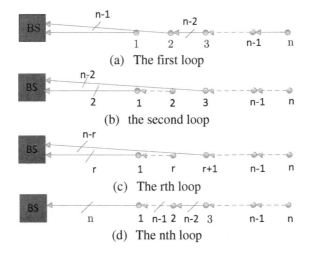

Fig. 3. Intra-chain scheduling

3.2   BECA Performance Analysis

In this part, we will compare the performance of BECA, LEACH and HEED through a one-dimensional network model. The focus of this paper is how to achieve the maximum balance of energy consumption in a single node.

In order to send l bit packet through the length of the distance d, so the transmission and receiving power are:

$$E_{tx}(d) = E_{elec}l + E_{amp}ld^2 \tag{1}$$

$$E_{tx} = E_{elec}l \tag{2}$$

where $E_{elec} = 50$ nJ/bit is the total energy consumed by the radio to run the transmitter or receiver circuit and the transmit amplifier consumes the total energy is $E_{amp} = 100$ pJ/(bit.m^2).

In LEACH, the energy consumption of delivering a packet at node k is:

$$E^{dc}(k) = E_{tx}(D + \frac{k-1}{n}L) \tag{3}$$

And the maximum loss of energy is:

$$E^{dc}_{Max} = E^{dc}(n) = E_{tx}(D + \frac{n-1}{n}L) \tag{4}$$

In HEED, the nodes far from the base station are called the upstream node, and the upstream node delivers $n - k$ packets for each node k. The nodes closer to the base station are called downstream nodes, and the downstream node collects $n - k + 1$ packets from each node k. The energy consumed by node k is:

$$E^{spt}(k) = \begin{cases} (n-1)E_{rx} + nE_{tx}(D), & k = 1 \\ (n-1)E_{rx} + (n-k+1)E_{tx}(\frac{L}{n}), & k > 1 \end{cases} \tag{5}$$

Suppose $D > 1/nL$. The maximum energy consumption is:

$$E^{spt}_{Max} = E^{spt}(1) = (n-1)E_{rx} + nE_{tx}(D) \tag{6}$$

Now we assume that BECA uses single link. The average consumption per loop of the node k:

$$E^{eedp}(k) = \frac{1}{n}\sum_{r=1}^{n}\left[N^{k,r}_{rx}E_{rx} + N^{k,r}_{tx}E_{tx}\left(\frac{1}{n}L\right) + N^{k,r}_{tx'}E_{tx}\left(D + \frac{k-1}{n}L\right)\right] \tag{7}$$

Where $N^{k,r}_{rx}$ is the number of packets that received by node k in loop r; $N^{k,r}_{tx}$ is the number of packets that are sent to the next sensor and $N^{k,r}_{tx'}$ is the number of packets sent to BS.

$$N_{rx}^{k,r} = \begin{cases} n - k, & r \le k \\ r - k + 1, & r > k \end{cases} \tag{8}$$

$$N_{tx}^{k,r} = \begin{cases} 0, & k = 1 \vee k = r \\ N_{rx}^{k,r} + 1, & \text{otherwise} \end{cases} \tag{9}$$

$$N_{tx'}^{k,r} = \begin{cases} 0, & k \ne 1 \wedge k \ne r \\ N_{rx}^{k,r} + 1, & \text{otherwise} \end{cases} \tag{10}$$

Combined with (10):

$$E^{eedp}(k) = \begin{cases} \frac{(n-1)}{2}E_{rx} + \frac{n+1}{2}E_{tx}(D), & k = 1 \\ \frac{(n-k)(n+k-1)}{2n}E_{rx} + \frac{(n-k+1)(n+k-2)}{2n}E_{tx}\left(\frac{1}{n}L\right) + \frac{n-k+1}{n}E_{tx}\left(D + \frac{k-1}{n}L\right), & k > 1 \end{cases} \tag{11}$$

$$E_{Max}^{eedp} = \max_{1 \le k \le n} E^{eedp}(k) \tag{12}$$

Now let $n = 4$, $L = 200$, $D = 100$, $l = 2000$ in one dimension network. As shown in Fig. 4, comparing the maximum and minimum values of the energy consumption of the three algorithms, it can be seen that the BECA is better than the other two algorithms in terms of balancing the energy consumption of nodes.

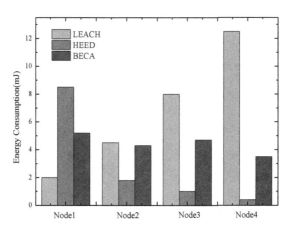

Fig. 4. Distribution of energy consumption of four cluster heads in one-dimensional networks

Let's consider using m links in BECA. We assume $n = n'm$. The link i contains nodes $i, m + i, \ldots, (n' - 1)m + i$. The energy consumption of each node $k = k'm + i$ is:

$$E^{eedp}(m, k) = \frac{1}{n'} \sum_{r=1}^{n'} [N_{rx}^{k',r} E_{rx} + N_{tx}^{k',r} E_{tx}(\frac{1}{n'}L) + N_{tx'}^{k',r} E_{tx}(D + \frac{k-1}{n}L)] \qquad (13)$$

$N_{rx}^{k',r}$, $N_{tx}^{k',r}$ And $N_{tx'}^{k',r}$ can be obtained from Eqs. (8–10). So,

$$E^{eedp}(m, k) = \begin{cases} \frac{(n'-1)}{2} E_{rx} + \frac{n'+1}{2} E_{tx}(D), & k = 1 \\ \frac{(n'-k')(n'+k'-1)}{2n'} E_{rx} + \frac{(n'-k'+1)(n'+k'-2)}{2n'} E_{tx}(\frac{L}{n'}) + \frac{n'-k'+1}{n'} E_{tx}(D + \frac{k-1}{n}L), & k > 1 \end{cases}$$
$$(14)$$

$$E_{Max}^{eedp}(m) = \max_{1 \le k \le n} E^{eedp}(m, k) \qquad (15)$$

LEACH, HEED and BECA in the one-dimensional network performance with change of L, D and n. We calculate the maximum energy consumption of single nodes in three algorithms respectively to compare the load balancing of different algorithms.

The $L = 200$, $D = 100$, $l = 2000$, the number of cluster heads n decreases from 2 to 32. Each n corresponds to an optimal number of links m, such as BECA (with m links) superior to LEACH and HEED. The value of n is greater, the number of links m is more, as shown in Fig. 5, the energy consumption is smaller. As shown in Fig. 6, as D increases, the value of m is greater, the energy saving effect is better. When $n = 8$, BECA-8 and LEACH the same. Figure 7 shows that the value of L is greater, the number of links is greater, so the energy consumption is more.

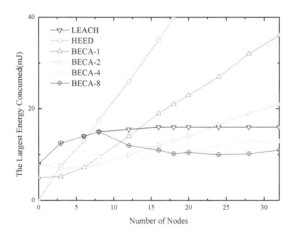

Fig. 5. The largest energy consumption of single-node in one-dimensional networks ($L = 200$, $D = 100$, $l = 2000$)

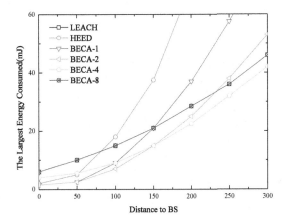

Fig. 6. The largest energy consumption of single-node in one-dimensional networks ($L = 200$, $n = 8$, $l = 2000$)

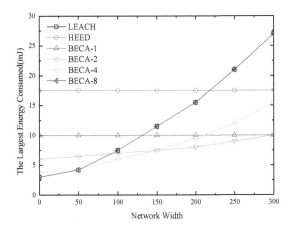

Fig. 7. The largest energy consumption of single-node in one-dimensional networks ($D = 100$, $n = 8$, $l = 2000$)

4 Conclusion

In this paper, the BECA algorithm can effectively utilize the energy and reduce the energy loss and prolong the network lifetime. In contrast, the cluster head in the LEACH algorithm away from the BS bear a higher energy loss, resulting in some nodes premature failure, reducing the WSN network life. In the HEED algorithm, the BS will form a hot spot around it, and WSN will fail due to the existence of hot spots. The BECA algorithm not only solves the hot issues, but also reduces the problem that single node-constrained and premature failure due to unbalanced energy consumption in WSN.

References

1. Hergenroeder, A., Wilke, J., Meier, D.C.: Distributed energy measurements in WSN testbeds with a sensor node management device. Schloer, Hannover (2010)
2. Zhang, Y., Yang, J., Li, W.J.: An authentication scheme for locating compromised sensor nodes in WSNs. J. Netw. Comput. Appl. 33, 50–62 (2010)
3. Wu, K., Dreef, D., Sun, B.: Secure data aggregation without persistent cryptographic operations in wireless sensor networks. Ad Hoc Netw. 5, 100–111 (2007)
4. Wang, C., Xing, L., Vokkarane, V.M.: Reliability and lifetime modeling of wireless sensor nodes. Microelectron. Reliab. 54, 160–166 (2014)
5. Ran, G., Zhang, H., Gong, S.: Improving on LEACH protocol of wireless sensor networks using fuzzy logic. JICS 7, 213–218 (2010)
6. Li, J., Shi, X.: Improved HEED routing protocol in wireless sensor networks. Comput. Eng. Appl. 43, 165–167 (2007)
7. Hu, J.H., Liu, X.C., Tan, Z.F.: Improved scheme based on PEGASIS algorithm. Microelectron. Comput. 11, 36–40 (2014)
8. Zhang, J., Xu, L., Zhou, S.M.: Constructing connected dominating set based on crossed cube in WSN. In: International Conference on Intelligent Networking and Collaborative Systems, pp. 443–447. IEEE, Xi'an (2013)

RFID Based Electronic Toll Collection System Design and Implementation

Yang Li and Peidong Zhuang[✉]

College of Electronics Engineering, Heilongjiang University, Harbin 150080,
People's Republic of China
2960320140@qq.com, zhuangpeidong@163.com

Abstract. Electronic toll collection system (ETC) is usually used in Open road tolling (ORT) or free-flow tolling. In this project, ETC system is designed both in software and hareware. Radio frequency identification (RFID) technology is used to further improve performance of this system. This ETC system can be installed without tearing up the road, also this system can collect the data from the passing vehicles, identify the license plate and vehicle model and RFID electronic tag, retrieve the related registration informatiom from database, match registration information with the data ETC system collected, prevent switching license plates, collect the tolls automatically without having vehicles to slow down to pay.

Keywords: ETC · Vehicle recognition · License plate · RFID

1 Introduction

People's living standards continue to increase, the number of private cars is also increasing, the vehicles through the toll station will be substantially increased, which need to wait in line, the automobile exhaust in parking in a line brings much more damage than running on the road. And starting the car again makes the fuel consumption to increase. So it is urgent to develop completely open road tolling system suitable for toll road.

RFID is the technology of radio frequency identification, it uses the road test reader to identify the electronic tags on the vehicles. The cost of electronic tag is now relatively high, so the use of identification is limited to only on the license plate. If the electronic tag could be cheap enough that many most drivers would like to equip their cars with it, RFID may get the full use to provide more accurate informaiton and show more benefitail features. RFID technology is applied to a number of fields, without direct contact with the identified objects, or even completely blocked objects can also be identified, it uses electromagnetic waves to transmit data, fast, accurate and very useful.

P. Zhuang—Project Fund: National Undergraduate Training Program for Innovation Entrepreneurship (2016102127251)

2 Identification Technology

(1) Vehicle Identification

The main steps to achieve vehicle identification are shown in Fig. 1.:

Fig. 1. Vehicle identification

The photos taken by the camera are preprocessed, the quality of the pretreatment affects the extraction and matching. So, pretreatment is important. Color photos use a large storage space black and white photos use less storage space, the general pretreatment is to take the color photos in gray scale. Use the preprocessed images to extract information, the identified vehicles' side view is processed to extract the features, calculated the following data by the calculation: the length of the roof and body; the roof length and height of the vehicle; the ratio of the two parts to the length, the body is divided by the vertical line into two parts. Using these features to distinguish. The eigenvalue of the standard model (car, bus, train) is calculated and then the features are brought together to do matching work, and then output the vehicle results.

Install the camera above the lane, the background is the lane, set the gray scale of the background as $b(x, y)$, set the gray scale of identified vehicle and the background as $f(x, y)$, set the gray scale of the identified vehicle as $d(x, y)$:

$$d(x, y) = f(x, y) - b(x, y) \qquad (1)$$

The vehicle movement is calculated by comparing the difference between the gray image of the camera and the background image, the pixel of the moving vehicle is calculated, and the resulting video is framed, the background of each frame is constant, segmenting the identified vehicle, filter out the interference and noise in the image, to get a higher quality image, the image is scanned through the calculation, get three feature ratio.

(2) License Plate Recognition

Fig. 2. License plate recognition

The main steps to achieve license plate recognition are shown in Fig. 2.:

The image acquired by the camera is pre-processed, and the image quality acquired by the camera may be affected by the factors of is greatly reduced by the influence of the environment such as fog, rain, etc., the efficiency of license plate recognition is reduced. Since the license plate is a regular rectangle, the aspect ratio of the inner contour is about 4.5:1, the subgraph calculates the gray scale approximation of the pixels in the image. The lateral convolution factor is:

$$\begin{bmatrix} -1 & 0 & 1 \\ -2 & 0 & 2 \\ -1 & 0 & 1 \end{bmatrix} \tag{2}$$

The vertical convolution factor is:

$$\begin{bmatrix} 1 & 2 & 1 \\ 0 & 0 & 0 \\ -1 & -2 & -1 \end{bmatrix} \tag{3}$$

$$G = \sqrt{G_x^2 + G_y^2} \tag{4}$$

$$\begin{aligned}
G_x &= (-1) * f(x-1, y-1) + 0 * f(x, y-1) + 1 \\
&\quad * f(x+1, y-1) + (-2) * f(x-1, y) + 0 * f(x, y) + 2 \\
&\quad * f(x+1, y) + (-1) * f(x-1, y+1) + 1 * f(x+1, y+1) \\
&= [f(x+1, y-1) + 2 * f(x+1, y) + f(x+1, y+1)] \\
&\quad - [f(x-1, y-1) + 2 * f(x-1, y) + f(x-1, y+1)]
\end{aligned} \tag{5}$$

$$\begin{aligned}
G_y &= 1 * f(x-1, y-1) + 2 * f(x, y-1) + 1 * f(x+1, y-1) \\
&\quad + 0 * f(x-1, y) + 0 * f(x, y) + 0 * f(x+1, y) + (-1) \\
&\quad * f(x-1, y+1) + (-2) * f(x, y+1) + (-1) * f(x+1, y+1) \\
&= [f(x-1, y-1) + 2 * f(x, y-1) + f(x+1, y-1)] \\
&\quad - [f(x-1, y+1) + 2 * f(x, y+1) + f(x+1, y+1)]
\end{aligned} \tag{6}$$

$f(a, b)$ indicates the gray scale of the image point (a, b), the gray scale of a pixel is made by formula $G = \sqrt{G_x^2 + G_y^2}$.

Find and scan the approximate location of the license plate, extract the license plate information quickly. Cut each character on the license plate, then wait for the computer to identify the characters.

License plate number can be used to retrieve the owner's and vehicle's information. After the gray scale processing, the license plate change into black and white two colors, the pixel is 0 or 1, the degree of the brightness on character projection is different, according to the darkness to write the bit, separate each character, the computer identifies characters' feature. Just like before the Spring Festival the Ailpay had an activity called scan the "Bless", the similar characters can be identified. For example, when we use the Alipay to scan "Blass" can also be identified as correct, that is the proof of the bug in Ailpay. The system designed here already considered this problem of all similarities, such as: "8" "B" and other words, so that error won't happen in this system.

3 RFID Technology

(1) RFID Hardware Design

It consists electronic radio frequency tag design, reader module design, power module and serial port design, antenna design.

Radio frequency identification can provide high accuracy data by identify the objects in long distance, so the electronic tags should use active electronic tag design to get the full benefit of RFID, passive electronic tag can only be recognized within near distance, also the accuracy is relatively low. The reader module mainly identify the electronic tags information, the electronic tags can be input the information about license plate and vehicle. The reader can read the information in the tag and write information to the tag to collect toll. The power module mainly provide the RF voltage, use bridge rectifier, use large capacitance for voltage regulation. Serial port do send and receive, and the antenna should be chosen according to the application, to achieve the best performances.

(2) The Overall Framework Design

When the RFID system is working, the vehicle with the electronic tag come into the area with a specific frequency of the RF signal launched by the reader. The electronic tag will produce the induced current and activate itself, send the data to the reader through the network, and the reader transmit the information to the computer, after computer's operation to achieve the identify on the vehicle's information, and then the computer send the command to the reader, complete the task of tolling.

When vehicles are passing the reader, if there are two or more tags appear at the same time, they will interfere each other, cause that electronic tags can not be accurately read, so the use of the electronic tag anti-collision method is important. The reader selects one of the tag groups, then inquire the tag one by one. If there is no tag, the counter is 0, only one tag counter shows 1, there is no collision, if there are multiple tags, the counter shows greater than or equal to 2, then there are many tags collide, at the moment the reader come into next round to send the inquire adjustment command, all the tags in the magnetic field are receiving this command, identify the tags one by one, to avoid missing any tag that should be identified.

The information identified through RFID and the images acquired in camera are send to the database server and image recognition server through the network and then return the electronic tag to collect the toll through the network. Identify the system flow chart as shown in Fig. 3.

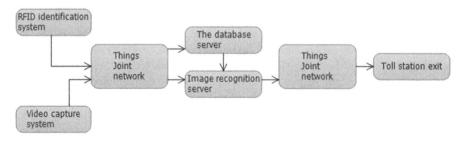

Fig. 3. Identify the system flow chart

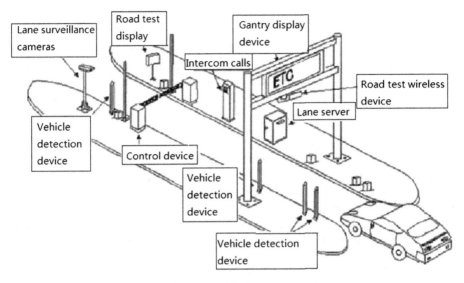

Fig. 4. Identify the diagram

The camera shoot on the vehicles to identify the vehicle models, license plates and other information is compared with the RFID tag (Tag), the same is normal, different is abnormal, when the comparison shows normal, it can finish toll collecting through the RFID reader (Reader) and the antenna on the electronic tag (Fig. 4).

4 Tolling System Software

Tolling system software functions consist a few sub-system: user login interface, login interface, sub-management login, owner login. Management personnel can carry out user management, toll station intersection query, vehicle traffic query, vehicle violation view, a single owner information, the owner can do the basic information query, violation of detailed inquiries, consumer information query and other functions. As shown in Fig. 5.

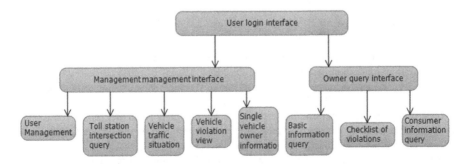

Fig. 5. system function flow chart

5 Conclusion

With the rapid development of China's economy and the continuous increase in car ownership, the highway brings people convenient travel, at the same time is also facing enormous problems. The electronic toll collection system is an automatic tolling system for roads, bridges and tunnels that are being developed and promoted internationally. This technology prevents some speculators to change large vehicle license plates to small car license plates secretly, and it prevents a lot of payment loopholes. Electronic toll collection system is a huge system, the popularity of electronic tags is a problem yet to be solved, vehicle license plates recognition technology also need to be improved by use higher technology. Now Alipay and other software launched a credit live, consume first and then pay for it, prepaid is a good trend, sesame credit deposit, these all have brought great convenience, so this technology needs to be developed in this area.

ETC technology has the obvious characteristics and advantages of eliminating cash transactions, eliminating the need for slowing down, effectively improving the road capacity, greatly enhance the service level, simplify the process of tolling and reduce environmental pollution. Without vehicles' slowing down to pay and manully process tolling, this system can autoamticaly collect toll, especially through network environment, help to improve the road network of integrated transport capacity and service levels.

Electronic toll collecting system (ETC) use radio frequency identification technology (RFID), road test reader and camera to identify the electronic tag, take photos of vehicle license plate, do the corresponding match, if the matching is correct, the tolling system will be able to access the reader, the reader write information of tolling into electronic tags to finish process of tolling.

The cost of RFID tags are high now. The current software like WPS, CAJViewer 7.2 can convert image into characters then into text files, we can also develop such software, read the characters in the image and write to text by using file functions in C language., collect toll of vehicles that are not equipped with electronic tag by using Visual Studio 2012, this is practible and achievable, the quality of acquired data will be affected by the factors of enviroments like fog or other extrem weather.

Radio frequency identification (RFID) is a non-contact, long distance technology, it can identify the tag that is even being blocked, coupled with the image to match, it would be more efficient electronic toll collection system (ETC) with electronic tags being widely used in the future.

References

1. He, P., Shi, W.C., Chen, H.: RFID technology in electronic charging system path identification application design. Electron. Des. Eng. **17**, 15–17 (2015)
2. Zhong, W.: Based on image recognition technology vehicle identification system research. Huazhong Univ. Sci. Technol. **1**, 15–20 (2016)
3. Tong, J.J.: Vehicle identification research. Inst. Autom. Chin. Acad. Sci. **1**, 23–103 (2005)
4. Xue, C.F., Liu, H.Y.: Design of expressway ietc system based on multi-layer C/S structure. Comput. Eng. **18**, 283–285 (2017)
5. Wang, Y.N., Li, S.T., Mao, J.X.: Computer image processing and recognition technology. Higher Education Press, pp. 131–145 (2016)

Design and Implementation of Survey Vehicle Based on VR

Weiguang Zhao and Peidong Zhuang[✉]

College of Electronics Engineering, Heilongjiang University, Harbin 150080,
People's Republic of China
827332093@qq.com, zhuangpeidong@163.com

Abstract. This project is aiming to design a kind of survey robot that has the combined functions of the large-scale disaster search and rescue equipment and industrial surveillance camera, use virtual reality (VR) technology to improve human-robot interface, to provide more simpler way to present the true images of the survey environment. The whole design solution consists of three parts: survey vehicle, VR (virtual reality) display system, Hand grip remote control. Remote control can control survey vehicle mode conversion, robot movement, and high beam brightness adjustment. Data collected by survey vehicle are used to construct the image by VR imaging method, coupled with the VR on the camera point of the somatosensory remote control. This can enhance the sense of environmental immersion.

Keywords: VR · Manipulator · Multi-machine communication
Survey robot

1 Introduction

The development of archaeology nowadays has played an important role in the process of peoples' learning of ancient culture. However, there may be several conditions when the archaeologists are not so familiar with the surroundings that they could not take on archaeological investigation immediately. Thus, it will be beneficial for the members to be able to use the survey robot with the aim at reducing the destruction of the surroundings when they know little about it. In addition, some high risk industrial plants are still using corner camera to monitor, which is not good enough to satisfy the needs of data collection when some emergency like nuclear leakage occurs. With the growth of robot technology, many research are being carried out with the aim at applying various robots to related specific environment, trying to improve peoples' operation ways and efficiency in different environments [1]. In our research, a kind of survey robot that not only has the combined functions of large survey facility and traditional industrial surveillance camera. But also provides the real images of the environment in a simpler user friendly way, with the help of manipulator it can also satisfy the need of investigation and material transfer.

P. Zhuang—Project Fund: National Undergraduate Training Program for Innovation and Entrepreneurship (2016102127251).

2 Scheme of the Design

2.1 The Design of Overall System

The works designed in this project consists three subsystems, respectively, using different data transmission means to communicate with (shown in Fig. 1). The data transmission between the survey vehicle and the grip remote control is required to be achieved through very long distance and with better wall penetration, so enhanced WIFI transmission circuit is used. This circuit use the MSP430 as the core, with enhanced nRF24l01 as a data receiver and transmitter. The data transmission distance of the open area can reach up to 2 km; VR display system and grip remote control is used by an operator, so the requirement is not very strict, in the aspect of transmission distance. But the packet loss rate and bit error rate are strictly required to maintain in a very low range, therefore these two systems can use Bluetooth for data transmission, and set the algorithm filter at the receiving end to achieve the purpose of data stability.

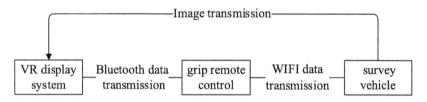

Fig. 1. Subsystem data transfer chart

2.2 The Design of Hardware Structure

All of the three sub-systems: the survey vehicle, VR display system, and hand grip remote control are based on microprocessor MSP430 made by TI, which is an ultra low power consumption with 16-bites mixed signal processing, it has several characteristics including lower voltage range, several operation modes with low power consumption, high-speed operational capability, and abundant functional models. It is playing an increasingly important role in embedded system, low-end areas especially in instrument, supervision, medical equipment, and automobile [2].

Survey vehicle's hardware structure is complicated, it consists of several parts (Fig. 2), including: caterpillar-belt body frame, manipulator of three degrees of freedom, 10 W high beam adjustment circuit, camera rotation positioning circuit, WIFI wireless data receiving circuit, image transmission circuit, and power supply circuit.

VR display system uses original left-right display modes, with two convex lens, it creates the sense of environmental immersion for the operator [3]. The hardware structure of this system includes blue-tooth data transmission circuit, image receiving circuit, and somatosensory measurement circuit.

Hand grip remote control has four function keys and a rocking bar, with those working together it can realize modes transfer of survey vehicles and other functions. Circuits of this part is as follows (Fig. 3): blue-tooth data receiving circuit, WIFI wireless data transmitting circuit, AD collection circuit, and power-supply circuit. Besides, the remote control also has somatosensory measurement circuit to make manual change of camera angle in mode 1.

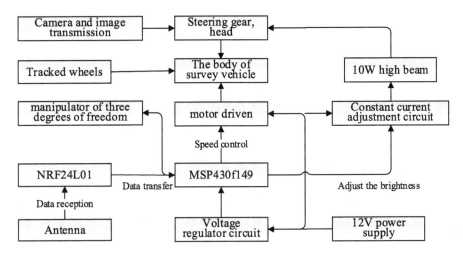

Fig. 2. Block diagram of the survey vehicle structure

2.3   Data Processing and Improvements in Algorithm

2.3.1   Improvements in Continuously Variable Algorithm

Continuously variable is in general realized by pulse width modulation technique (PWM), if the duty ratio can be continuously adjusted, then continuously variable of direct current machine can be developed [4]. Because there are only 8 comparable timers of MCU, if four timers are used to regulate the speed, the regulation of degrees of freedom in manipulator must be realized by externally connecting PWM output model, so the improvement in algorithm is needed [5]. The function of speed regulation is achieved by the electrical level changing of two PWMs and two TLLs. When the electrical level of two TLLs is low, the bigger of the duty ratio of PWM, the higher its speed, then the vehicle body would have a tendency of advance; when the electrical level of two TLLs is high, the smaller of the duty ratio of PWM, the higher its speed, then the vehicle body would have a tendency of retreat; the value of two PWMs is depended on the value of two ADs of the rocking bar, Omni direction of the vehicle body can be approximately obtained by the Omni direction of the rocking bar.

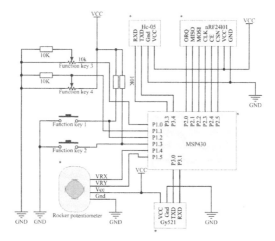

Fig. 3. Handle remote control circuit diagram

2.3.2   Improvements in Mean Filtering Algorithm

Filtering calculation using traditional method is to select a certain amount of continuous array elements and calculate the average value as the final numerical value, then eliminate the first value and the left will shift left as a whole to meet the next one, and so on [6, 7]. Whole left shift algorithm costs too much time, if it is still used to filter waves, vision delay of VR will excess the range of persistence of vision, reaction ability of the vehicle body will be decreased dramatically. Therefore, the improvement in algorithm is needed. Improved algorithm eliminates the part of whole left shift, and uses received value and data replacement: recording the average value of the last group of data as "result", then the average value of the next group of data is the sum of the last one minus the contribution value (data value "f1"/total data "atn") of the original data and the contribution value of the last data (fn/atn): result = result + (f1 − fn)/atn, after that, replacing the first one with the last, the second with the next, and so on. Key process is listed as below:

```
void init_filter()
{
  for(int i=0;i<40;i++)    filter[i]=2000;
}
int filter_LV(int fn,int num)
{
result=result+(fn-filter[num])/40;
 filter[num]=fn;
 return result;
}
```

2.3.3 Data Receiving and Examination

According to the difference between transmit media and transmit protocol, data receiving of this work consists two parts: data receiving of grip remote control with blue-tooth and data receiving of survey vehicle body with WIFI. In fact, the package loss rate and bit error rate of blue-tooth transmission are of seriousness. When there is a bit error or data disorder, the receiver with no ability to identify would face data chaos, as a result, it will cause the collapse of the whole system. Especially when the somatosensory information is transmitted disorderly in the head, the camera would shake dramatically, even make the wearer of VR feel dizzy [8]. Because of the uncertainty of the loss of data and the change, it is only possible to filter data in the receiving end [9].

Filtering process is composed of the following two steps: examination of data identity and examination of rationality (Fig. 4). Examination of data identity aims to identify data transmitted belongs to which category, like information of head pitching movement and information of head horizontal movement. Flags can be set in this part, every category of information has its own flag, only when all flags are matched can data be used. Although the problem of package loss and bit error can't be solved completely by this method, it improves the anastomosis rate of data processed to a reasonable range. Examination of data rationality aims at eliminating few error points. For example, when the numerical value is possible within the range of 0–180, but the data received is 2000, this can be eliminated with if statement.

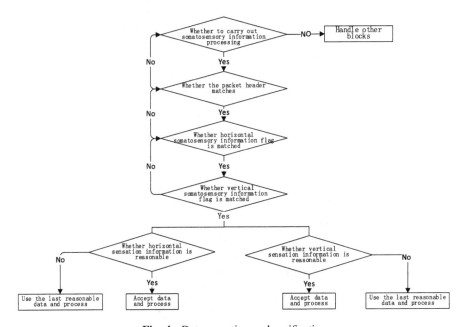

Fig. 4. Data reception and verification

3 Functional Analysis and Product Samples

3.1 Main Specifications

(1) The data packet loss rate after filtering is ≤ 0.001 and the bit error rate is ≈ 0.
(2) VR visual effects delay is ≈ 0.1 s within the scope of persistence of vision.
(3) Control distance and VR video transmission distance ≤ 2 km.
(4) Camera monitoring horizontal angle has adjustable range from 0 to 360°, and vertical angle is range from 0 to 180°.
(5) The controllable angles of the three-degree-of-freedom manipulator are 90°, 180°, 180°, respectively, and the torque force is 13 kg/cm.
(6) The power of high beam has adjustable range from 0 to 10 W.
(7) Length, width and height of the vehicle:35 cm × 15 cm × 20 cm.

3.2 Sample Pictures

See Figs. 5 and 6.

Fig. 5. The sample of vehicle

Fig. 6. The sample of VR display system and grip remote

4 Conclusion

There are several survey vehicles in the current market, but all of them have problems of monotonous function and complicated operation. The PackBot robots designed by a US company called iRoBot have three types: situational awareness robot, reconnaissance robot, and explosive ordnance disposal robot, they are suitable for different situations [10]. In this report, the work is a combination of situational awareness robot and explosive ordnance disposal robot, which can be switched between these two models randomly and conveniently, and it can be applied in areas like engineering construction, medical rescue, and accident handling. What is more, operational steps and processes can be simplified greatly and the ability to control can be improved greatly by using VR technique, which can effectively reduce labor cost and increase working efficiency. Therefore, compared to most products in the current market, this design is of great superiority and great prospect.

References

1. Sun, Q., Wang, W.T.: Design of omni-directional mobile robot based on somatosensory remote control. Appl. Electron. **41**, 157–160 (2015)
2. Wang, X.Z., Shu, G.H.A., Zhang, S.W.: Experimental example of MSP430 single chip microcomputer experiment based on computer simulation technology. Lab. Res. Explor. **32**(9), 94–97 (2013)
3. Zhang, J., Li, M.Q., Li, Z.J.: Research on application of VR technology to real-combat teaching. Comput. Knowl. Technol. **2**, 34–38 (2016)
4. Yue, D.H., Yan, P.: Design of PWM stepless speed control system for DC motor. Value Eng. **29**(2), 135–136 (2010)
5. Li, C., Yin, W.Q., Feng, X.B.: Study on stepless speed regulating system of brushless DC motor based on fuzzy adaptive PI control. Electr. Eng. **29**(1), 49–52 (2012)
6. Hong, X.Y., Xu, B.G.: Study on denoising effect of mean filter and its improved algorithm. J. Shangqiu Teachers Coll. **32**(6), 21–25 (2016)
7. Lin, X.F.: Comparison of several filtering algorithms. Fujian Comput. **33**(2), 107–108 (2017)
8. Volpicelli, G.: Why do more women than men feel sick in VR. N. Sci. **232**, 3104–3106 (2016)
9. Li, F.M., Han, P., Luo, T.: Adaptive region positioning algorithm based on packet loss rate and RSSI in wireless sensor networks. J. Commun. **30**(9), 15–23 (2009)
10. Wang, Y.C., Shen, Y.L.: US service robot industry innovation - experience and revelation from iRobot. Glob. Technol. Econ. Outlook **29**(4), 61–66 (2014)

Development of the Embedded Multi Media Card Platform Based on FPGA

Songyan Liu[✉], Ting Chen, Shangru Wu, and Cheng Zhang

Electronic Engineering College, Heilongjiang University,
Xuefu Road 74, Harbin 150080, China
liusongyan@hlju.edu.cn,
{2151302,2141258,2161419}@s.hlju.edu.cn

Abstract. For the validation of eMMC device performance problems involving the effectiveness of testing and non-real time on parameters controlling, it may not be possible to obtain the performance data flexibly and efficiently, requiring consideration of the multi-channel parallel processing and real-time controlling. This paper presents a development platform for eMMC 5.0 device based on Zynq-7000. By combining hardware and software design, this platform is able to support eight eMMC devices working in parallel and get testing information in real time. Meanwhile, the device driver aims at achieving high performance data transfer by using DMA.

Keywords: eMMC · Zynq · Parallelism · DMA

1 Introduction

As the storage device widely used in mobile devices, this requires the device having the characteristics of small volume, big storage capacity, high data rate and short development cycle. Embedded Multi-Media Card (eMMC) consisted of the NAND Flash and a controller is perfect for these immediate needs. One of the major advantages of eMMC is that it provides the standardized interfaces to the external devices, which make it easier for developers to develop without dealing with the compatibility of NAND Flash. Facing with the fast-growing eMMC market, it is necessary to design an eMMC development platform, which is used to validate the stability, reliability, and veracity of the product during the development and testing stage.

In recent years, many domestic and foreign researchers have been proposed some development and testing solutions for flash memory. Kim et al. designed a development platform for flash memory solid state disks, which adopt a Xilinx Virtex-4 FPGA as the main processor [1]. The platform has four NAND Flash memory modules and supports different SSD architectures. Wei et al. presented a platform for NAND Flash based Zynq [2]. They combined the programmable logic with a processing system within Zynq to achieve sequence control, bad block management and error correction. Fu et al. proposed a test system for eMMC 5.0 devices based on FPGA [3]. They used Verilog hardware description language to implement the control of eMMC device. However, the system can only control an eMMC device to send commands at one time.

© ICST Institute for Computer Sciences, Social Informatics and Telecommunications Engineering 2018
X. Gu et al. (Eds.): MLICOM 2017, Part I, LNICST 226, pp. 648–656, 2018.
https://doi.org/10.1007/978-3-319-73564-1_66

Furthermore, there are some researches on the storage performance of eMMC device. Deng suggested two methods of automatic data transmission synchronization, with emphasis on eMMC busy/ready controlling and device status returning [4]. Amato et al. putted forward four eMMC key performance indicators: sequential read, sequential write, random read, and random write by analyzing the model of controller [5]. To address the random write performance issue, Byungjo Kim et al. introduced a way of the background command [6]. Compared with the conventional power-off way, the random writing capability has gone up by 173% in this method. The studies above are using different approaches to improve the efficiency of data reading/writing.

In order to validate the eMMC devices' operation and data reading/writing performance, this paper aims to design an eMMC platform based on the eMMC 5.0 protocol. The remainder of this paper is organized into five sections. Section 2 introduces the related background about eMMC. Section 3 describes the overall architecture of this platform. Section 4 details the design of software, and the result of the experiment is given in Sect. 5. The Final section concludes the paper.

2 Background

EMMC, a storage card oriented to smart phone and table computer, is made up of NAND Flash memory and a storage controller. The first version of embedded memory standard specification was released by the Joint Electron Device Engineering Council (JEDEC) in 2007. Today, it has already been updated to the eMMC 5.1 version. EMMC 5.0 supports three data transfer modes: 1-bit, 4-bit and 8-bit. Its maximum data transfer rate, 400 MB/s in HS400 mode, is the same with eMMC 5.1. So it is with good graces by manufacturers of mobile device.

All manipulation of eMMC device is based on the protocol. The eMMC system has five operation modes: boot mode, device identification mode, interrupt mode, data transfer mode and inactive mode. After power up, if the device received the CMD0 with argument of 0xF0F0F0F0, it would be set in the boot mode. Otherwise, it would go into device identification mode.

To realize eMMC bus data transmission, the host needs to some special signals, including command, response, and data. All the commands and responses are transferred on the CMD line. Each of them begins with a start bit and terminates with an end bit. The second bit indicated the transmission direction. If the bit is 1, it means this is a host command, otherwise card response. A 7-bit CRC checksum is used to guarantee the correctness of transmission.

Furthermore, if a data read-write command is sent, the host sends the data block on the DAT lines subsequently. If there are no data in these lines, the lines will hold a high level until data block is arrived. It is important to determine whether the mode is single block or multiple blocks before executing read and write command. Figure 1 shows read and write operations. The multiple block transmission can be terminated by the use of CMD12. A busy signal on the DAT0 line is used to indicate that the device is writing now. During the standby state, eMMC device could be switched into a sleep state to save the power consumption.

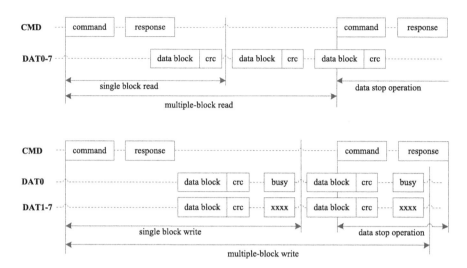

Fig. 1. The read and write operation.

3 System Design

The eMMC platform consists of three parts: PC client, server application and eMMC control module. The specific design of this platform is shown in Fig. 2.

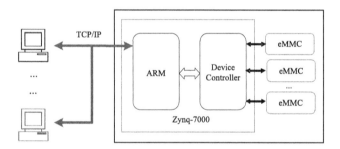

Fig. 2. The overview of eMMC development platform.

The hardware is composed of a Zynq-7000, eMMC chips, power module, network interface, USB 3.0 port and serial port. The Zynq-7000 chip is mainly composed of dual-core ARM9 processor and FPGA material. For this structure, not only the difficulty in data interaction between processor with FPGA can be solved, but also it reduces the system's power consumption and enhances productivity. It needs to accomplish the following work: (1) receive commands from the client; (2) control eMMC chips to complete operation task; (3) calculate the data performance; (4) send back the response to the client. The response will be returned after the command is executed. In order to improve the data processing efficiency, this system is designed to support eight eMMCs working in parallel.

The client helps users to send commands, acquire response information and check the error status. If a fatal error occurs, the current processing will stop. This application is visual and concise so that it is very convenient to be used.

The server takes charge of establishing the connection with the clients. It runs on the PetaLinux operating system, which runs on the ARM9 processor. The PetaLinux, oriented for the MicroBlaze microprocessor soft cores, has a set of software development kit for Xilinx FPGAs. Not only does it provide the BSP's builder, but it also provides a lot of program templates to design the device driver and application. In this way, it can simplify the processing of system transplant and shorten the development cycle.

4 Implementation of Software

This section describes the software implementation of this platform in detail. Software architecture involves client program, server program and block driver. The device driver plays a key role in the overall system. Figure 3 depicts the software block diagram.

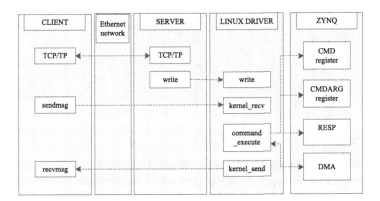

Fig. 3. The software block diagram.

4.1 PC Client

The main goals of this work are to packet the data exactly, establish reliable network connection and provide access to error checking. This design provides a user interface to input commands and arguments flexible. A lookup table is used to set clock frequency and determine the level of error. All of the error message will be printed to the user. If there is a fatal error, the current task would be interrupted, which achieves the efficiency of the system. This approach is quite convenient and accurately for a great number of commands.

Command Parsing. Since each client instruction contains some configuration parameters, including command index, command argument, data and block size, it is necessary to packet the instruction data at a specified format. Package data into entries is the main task of this module, which can be executed when the user inputs a series of parameters. Depending upon its parameter types, the order is parsed into various forms. If the command is a read and write command, this module should create the data buffer, which is used to hold the data file. The parsed commands are merged in a structure and then transferred to the device.

Message Scheduling. This module is responsible for the communication with the hardware devices to obtain the response information. Thus, it provides two main functions: (1) send and receive data; (2) check the returned message so that it can be monitored implementation of the commands and see whether any error occurred.

To make sure that all the data can be processed in real-time, this design applies a method: it communicates with the kernel layer directly. Considering the efficiency of this system, the command entries are transferred in a batch way. In other words, one or more commands can be transmitted to the device.

4.2   Interface of Application

As the kernel layer cannot establish a network connection over the TCP/IP protocol easily, it is required to set up the connection at the application level. Following this design, the server also has a feature that it could establish network connections with multi-user. As the number of clients request increases, the server's response rate may be slow commonly. To solve this problem, this design adopts the I/O multiplexing technology [7], which could be reduced the consumption of system resources. The idea of this mechanism is that it monitors the state of all socket descriptors. If there are any changes, the read event will be triggered [8].

4.3   Device Driver

In order to realize data transmission between ARM and eMMC devices, this research develops a device driver for the eMMC controller. The software flow diagram of the device driver is shown in Fig. 4. And the driver performs the following steps.

- Device initialization, requesting an interrupt for the eMMC device interrupt event, initializing the controller.
- Receiving commands from users.
- Once the command data have been successfully received, the command will be sent to eMMCs.
- If it read/write command, DMA operation would be started. Then creating send/write descriptors, loading descriptors, and initiating a DMA transfer.
- Returning the response to the users.

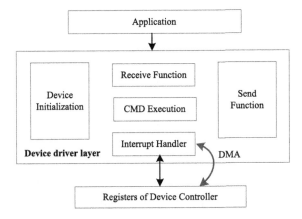

Fig. 4. The device driver software model.

Command Execution. The driver invokes the `emmct_send_serial_command()` function to complete the controlling of eMMC devices. Because the device contains specific information in different states, the implementation of eMMC command depends on the current device state. Given this fact, the state checking module was designed, which verifies that the next command operation conforms to the current state. On successful validation of the device status, the command is allowed to send to the device. The command execution has been elaborated in the following aspects:

- Disable interrupt before sending the command on the CMD line.
- Set the correct clock frequency according to current command.
- Initiate the command sending.
- Enable the interrupt.
- Check the error status, and then a command execution has completed.

Interrupt Handler. After the command or data has been sent to the eMMC device, the device generates an interrupt to the controller. Since the interrupt types are various, the driver should judge what interrupt is raised based on the value of mask interrupt status. To illustrate the interrupt has done, this interruption mechanism should make an interruption finished sign at appropriate times. Otherwise, it is considered as a timeout.

This interrupt will read the response from the response registers, and read pending data from the FIFO. Five types of eMMC response might be resulted, depending on the type of command. In addition to the R2, the length of other responses all is 48 bits. If a response error happens, this module might check the specific error message by reading the interrupt mask register. Figure 5 depicts the architecture of interrupt handler.

Data Read and Write. To transmit data on the DAT lines, two modes of data transfer can be chosen, single block data and multiple block data transfer. While, there are two types of multi-block transaction, open-ended multiple block read/write and multiple block read/write with pre-defined block count. It can change the block numbers by using CMD23 before the actual read/write command.

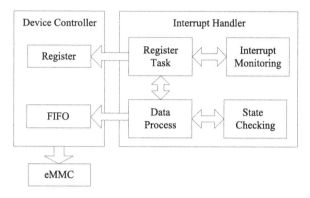

Fig. 5. Architecture of interrupt handler.

In order to improve the efficiency of this system, the DMA based on ring mode structure is used [9]. In this mode, each descriptor points to two different data buffers. The buffer1 holds a pointer to the data buffer, and buffer2 is not used in this driver. When the system needs to read/write data, the only thing it required is sending the command to eMMCs on each channel. The DMA engine then takes care of the operations of reading and writing without the processor's intervention. However, there are some undesired data stored in the DMA cache sometimes. If the DMA operation is initiated at this time, a data reading/writing error might be occurred. To address this issue, this design invokes the dma_sync_single_for_device() and dma_sync_single_for_cpu() functions to make the cached entry invalid and ensures the security of the buffer access.

5   Experiment and Result

To verify the feasibility and efficiency, we have been implemented a suite of functional tests for this system. The application connects to this platform via a network interface. And we choose eight eMMC 5.0 devices (8 GB) made by Skymedi as test objects. Five test routines are completed: initialization, bus test, single/multiple block write, single/multiple block read and erase. Table 1 shows the specific procedure of this experiment.

Table 1. The items of eMMC commands

Test item	Command sequence
Initialization	CMD0 -> CMD1 -> CMD2 -> CMD3 -> CMD9
Bus test	CMD19 -> CMD14
Single/multiple block write	CMD13 -> CMD7 -> CMD16 -> CMD13 -> CMD24/CMD25
Single/multiple block read	CMD13 -> CMD7 -> CMD16 -> CMD13 -> CMD17/CMD18
Erase	CMD13 -> CMD7 -> CMD35 -> CMD36 -> CMD38

For the data transfer performance, we can obtain the data transfer rate by calling `emmc_dev_data_perform()` function. The total amount of data written in is 1024 MB. After finishing writing, we read the data back again in this experiment. Table 2 shows the write and read performance of the eMMCs respectively by high speed SDR mode and HS200 mode.

Table 2. The data rate for writing and reading

Mode	Write	Read
High speed	46.45 MB/s	48.02 MB/s
HS200	91.39 MB/s	97.11 MB/s

On the performance side, the eMMC 5.0 device can support the maximum clock frequency (200 MHz) in the HS400 mode. However, the maximum clock frequency of this platform can only reach 100 MHz. When the clock frequency is set to 100 MHz, there is a phenomenon of high frequency harmonic. Within this problem we are still finding a solution.

6 Conclusion

This paper described a development platform for testing eMMC 5.0 devices efficiently and timely. Using the client/server architecture, this design is allowed to control and obtain the command information in real time. The approach of multi-channel parallel processing is applied that improves the system performance. The system only needs to send read/write command to eMMCs on each channel, DMA controller then takes charge of the operations of reading and writing. From the experiment, the feasibility of the design has been proven and it features the average write speed of 91.39 MB/s and read speed of 97.11 MB/s in the HS200 mode. However, the issue of clock frequency, which has the limits of data transfer rate, is needed to improve in the future work.

References

1. Kim, H., Nam, E.H., Choi, K.S., Seong, Y.J., Choi, J.Y., Min, S.L.: Development platforms for flash memory solid state disks. In: 2008 11th IEEE International Symposium on Object Oriented Real-Time Distributed Computing (ISORC), pp. 527–528. IEEE (2008)
2. Wei, D., Gong, Y., Qiao, L., Deng, L.: A hardware-software co-design experiments platform for NAND flash based on Zynq. In: 2014 IEEE 20th International Conference on Embedded and Real-Time Computing Systems and Applications (RTCSA), pp. 1–7. IEEE (2014)
3. Fu, N., Li, Y., Liu, B., Xu, H., Zhang, Y.: Realization of controlling eMMC 5.0 device based on FPGA for automatic test system. In: 2015 IEEE AUTOTESTCON, pp. 251–255. IEEE (2015)
4. Deng, S.: A new data transfer scheme for eMMC connected subsystems (2014)
5. Amato, P., Caraccio, D., Confalonieri, E., Sforzin, M.: An analytical model of eMMC key performance indicators. In: 2015 IEEE International Memory Workshop (IMW), pp. 1–4. IEEE (2015)

6. Reddy, A.K., Paramasivam, P., Vemula, P.B.: Mobile secure data protection using eMMC RPMB partition. In: 2015 International Conference on Computing and Network Communications (CoCoNet), pp. 946–950. IEEE (2015)
7. Kim, C., Lee, C.: Design of eMMC controller with multiple channels. In: 2016 International SoC Design Conference (ISOCC), pp. 317–318. IEEE (2016)
8. Ribeiro, I.L.B., Kimura, B.Y.L.: Enabling efficient communications with session multi-pathing. In: 2014 Brazilian Symposium on Computer Networks and Distributed Systems (SBRC), pp. 231–238. IEEE (2014)
9. Kavianipour, H., Muschter, S., Bohm, C.: High performance FPGA-based DMA interface for PCIe. IEEE Trans. Nucl. Sci. **61**, 745–749 (2014)

An Implementation of Special Purpose SSD Device

Songyan Liu[⊠], Shangru Wu, Ting Chen, and Cheng Zhang

Electronic Engineering College, Heilongjiang University,
Xuefu Road 74, Harbin 150080, China
liusongyan@hlju.edu.cn,
{2141258,2151302,2161419}@s.hlju.edu.cn

Abstract. Under the background that SSD is more and more popular, this paper shows an efficient implementation of an SSD device designed for special function and interface on Xilinx SoC platform. The Device uses MLC NAND Flash as storage chips and uses Xilinx's Zynq-7000 series SoC as the processor. The device adopts the method of multi-channel parallel data transmission and pipeline operation to achieve high performance. Enhanced ECC checking ability is provided to against the flash internal errors. The storage system also uses the RAID5 architecture to improve reliability significantly. Finally, the test results show that the designed SSD storage device reaches the expected performance and reliability.

Keywords: SSD · DMA · Linux · FPGA

1 Introduction

Data storage plays an important role in today's information society. With advantages in performance, low-power and reliability, SSD (Solid-State Disk) is more and more popular in data storage domain. As the price drops, the storage scheme based on NAND Flash is becoming increasingly attractive relative to traditional mechanical disk scheme in vast application area. Under this background, more and more needs of customization of various application and interface happen.

Authors in reference 1 propose a RAID0 array storage scheme to improve the transmission performance of the solid-state drives at the interface of SATA II [1]. Authors in reference 2 and 3 combines SSD with the PCI Express bus, PCI Express basics and different PCI Express SSD architectures are reviewed. Finally, they present an overview on the standardization effort around PCI Express [2, 3]. Authors in reference 4 put the SSD device together with the AHB bus and an 8 channels transmission mechanism was put forward to improve the transmission speed [4].

This paper shows an SSD device which is optimized for volume, power consumption and none general purpose computer dependency, with an additional board to extend various interfaces like Ethernet, USB and Rocket IO. Linux DMA driver implementation is emphatically discussed.

The rest of this paper is organized as follows. Section 2 gives the hardware design of SSD device and the software design for the device in Sect. 3. Tests and results of the device are showed in Sect. 4. Finally, conclusion is in Sect. 5.

© ICST Institute for Computer Sciences, Social Informatics and Telecommunications Engineering 2018
X. Gu et al. (Eds.): MLICOM 2017, Part I, LNICST 226, pp. 657–665, 2018.
https://doi.org/10.1007/978-3-319-73564-1_67

2 Hardware and Architecture Design

The hardware contains two boards: an SSD board and a download board. The SSD board focusses on optimized volume and power consumption for embedding into the special purpose device. The download board is designed to download data from SSD and forward it to various bus interfaces like network and USB. Download board is also a test platform for testing the SSD. Two boards connect through the FMC (FPGA Mezzanine Card) interface. The overall architecture of the system is shown in the Fig. 1.

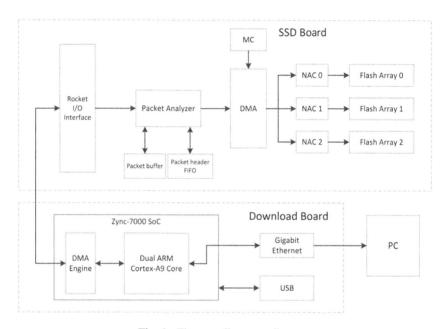

Fig. 1. The overall system diagram.

2.1 Module Partition of SSD Board

The SSD hardware can be divided into following modules:

Packet Analyzer. The data are transmitted in the form of packet. Packet analyzer is responsible to deal with the packet, extract packet header information and store it in packet header FIFO for subsequent processing of software. Packet buffer is a true dual-port SRAM, which makes it easy to move data between each end in parallel.

DMA Controller. The main task of DMA controller is data transmission, but it also handles transparent RAID function. Data that reach SSD disk is first deposited in the packet buffer. Data is transmitted from the packet buffer to the page buffer which controlled by NAC via DMA, and then wrote into the Flash arrays.

MC (Master Controller). It is responsible for the NAND Flash management works such as bad block management and wear-leveling. It also handles packets sent by the upper machine and forwarding to flash array with help of Packet analyzer and DMA. Data pipeline and parallel stream of every logical channel are organized in MC.

NAC (NAND Array Controller). The number of NACs depends on tradeoffs of capacity, performance and cost. Each NAC controls 8 Flash chips as a logical channel, so that it can store data in the Flash arrays in parallel efficiently [5].

2.2 Hardware Design of Download Board

The processor of download board is Zynq-7000 series SoC which produced by the Xilinx company. Zynq-7000 products incorporate a dual core ARM Cortex-A9 based Processing System (PS) and Xilinx Programmable Logic in a single device [6]. It contains a Xilinx IP AXI Direct Memory Access (AXI DMA) core, which provides high-bandwidth direct memory access between memory and AXI4-Stream target peripherals [7]. Its optional scatter/gather capabilities also offload data movement tasks from the CPU. Besides, this system has a serial port and a network port to debug and test procedures. There is a FMC port to connect with the SSD board.

2.3 Hardware Overview of AXI DMA

To achieve enough performance, this paper uses scatter/gather mode of AXI DMA to transmit data. Scatter/gather mode can put the discrete memory together as one descriptor used for transmission [8]. AXI DMA can be divided into MM2S (memory-mapped to stream) used to send data and S2MM (stream to memory-mapped)

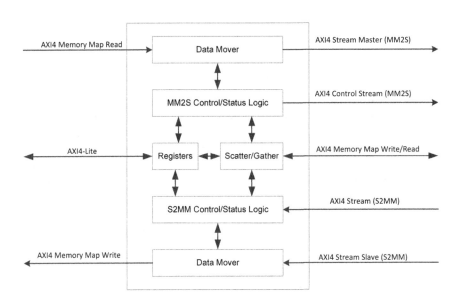

Fig. 2. The AXI DMA hardware block diagram.

used to receive data. To send data as an example, put the first section of memory physical address in MM2S_CURDESC register, and the last section of memory address in MM2S_TAILDESC register, then give '1' to the lowest position of MM2S_DMACR register to start DMA, data can be transmitted from download board to SSD board. Receiving data is similar. The block diagram of AXI DMA is shown in Fig. 2.

3   Software Design of Download Board

3.1   Linux Kernel DMA Framework

The primary components of the Linux kernel DMA framework include the DMA device control together with memory allocation and cache control.

Memory Allocation. Memory allocation is needed to provide data buffer for DMA, but also limited by some condition of continuity and consistency. There are various methods to allocate contiguous memory in Linux. The `kmalloc()` function allocates cached memory which is physically contiguous. It is limited in the size of a single allocation. The `dma_alloc_coherent()` function allocates non-cached physically contiguous memory. It uses a new feature of Linux kernel called Contiguous Memory Allocator (CMA) since version 3.5, and allows very large amounts of physically contiguous memory to be allocated. We adopt `kmalloc()` function to allocate memory, so the cache control should be considered that is described below.

DMA Cache Control. What modern CPU direct access is cache, but DMA direct accesses memory, this causes the cache consistency problem. So the data buffer that DMA used should be non-cached, or, cache must be flushed and invalidated at the right time to assure the validity of data. Linux provides DMA functions for cache control of DMA buffers. Function `dma_map_single()` is provided to transfer ownership of a buffer from the CPU to the DMA hardware. It can cause a cache flush for the buffer in memory to device direction. Function `dma_unmap_single()` is provided to transfer ownership of a buffer from the DMA hardware back to the CPU. It can cause a cache invalidate for the buffer in the device to memory direction.

DMA Device Control. The DMA driver is designed to be a multithreaded and asynchronous program to improve performance [9]. Sending thread uses the completion mechanism to know if a DMA transfer task is done. The tasklet mechanism is used to send the completion signal when DMA transmission complete interruption comes, which replaces older bottom half mechanisms for drivers. Some DMA slave API use a piece of opaque data called cookie to exchange communicating information. For example, a DMA cookie is returned from `dmaengine_submit()` and is passed to `dma_async_is_tx_complete()` to check for completion of a specific DMA transaction.

3.2   Linux DMA Engine Slave API

The integral flow of DMA operation using Linux DMA engine slave API is shown in Fig. 3:

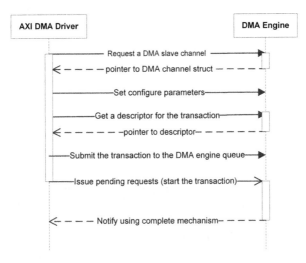

Fig. 3. The operational flow of DMA engine slave API.

1. Use `dma_request_channel()` to request a DMA channel, for AXI DMA, the 1st channel is the transmit channel and the 2nd channel is the receive channel.
2. Set slave and controller specific parameters, include DMA direction, DMA addresses, bus widths, DMA burst lengths etc.
3. `dmaengine_prep_slave_single()` function gets a descriptor for a DMA transaction, which is the key data structure of a DMA transfer.
4. The `dmaengine_submit()` function submits the descriptor to the DMA engine to be put into the pending queue.
5. The `dma_async_issue_pending()` function is used to start the DMA transaction that was previously put in the pending queue.
6. Program waits for the DMA transfer done on a completion.

3.3   Data Stream in DMA Driver

Read Data. When the user reads the data, it will first send a packet include read command to SSD. When the SSD receives the command, host controller of SSD parses the command, read the NAND Flash chip on specific addresses, and sent it to the download board via DMA. After receiving the data, the data will be sent to the computer through the network port. The specific process as showed in Fig. 4.

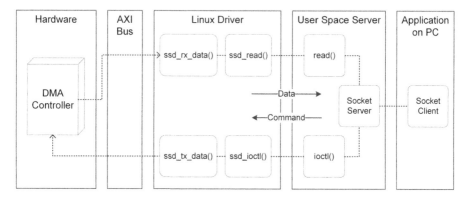

Fig. 4. The flow chart of read data.

1. Application on PC send the read command via Ethernet. The user space server calls the standard ioctl interface to send command and the read interface to read data.
2. DMA driver use `ssd_ioctl()` and `ssd_read()` functions to implement the read and ioctl interface, which invoke `ssd_tx_data()` function to send the command packet, and `ssd_rx_data()` function to receive data.
3. Start receiving DMA and then send a packet includes read command.
4. Command arrives at the SSD. SSD parses the command, reads data from Flash chips and send them via DMA.

Write Data. Compared to the read operation, write data operation is more simple. When the application calls the write function, the Download Board will prepare the data and send it to the SSD. SSD receives the data and puts it into Flash chips.

1. The application send write the command. Server use write interface to call the underlying `ssd_write()` function.
2. SSD_write function calls the `ssd_tx_data()` function.
3. Start DMA to send the prepared data to the SSD.
4. SSD receives the data and stores it into Flash chips.

3.4   Interrupt Handling

This function is so important because the processing will impact the performance of the system directly. The interruption of this driver can be divided into three types: the transmission complete interruption, transmission error interruption and transmission delay interruption. The device can only generate one interruption at a time. The 13, 14, 15 bits of transmission status register are the flag bits of these interrupts. When an interrupt generates, the driver determines if an interrupt is triggered by reading the status register and calls the corresponding function. Whether to send data or receive data, when a descriptor transmission is complete, a transmission complete interrupt will be triggered. When the complete interrupt happens, the driver executes interrupt handlers to judge whether there is a descriptor needs to transfer, if it does, the driver continues the transmission, if not, it ends the transmission. When hardware generates a transmission error interrupt, which indicates transmission error, the program will release resources and print warning information. Transmission delay interruption will happen within a certain time interrupt is merged into an interrupt notifies the user. The specific process is shown as Fig. 5.

1. The system generates an interrupt, read the value of the status register.
2. Use a spin-lock to mask other interruptions.
3. Determine the type of interrupt by reading the state of the register values.
4. Executes interrupt handler function [10].
5. Release resources and open spin-lock.

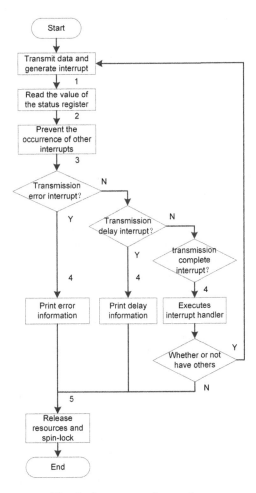

Fig. 5. Interrupt service routine.

4 Tests and Results

The AXI bus connectivity, data communication and DMA functionality have been tested using Xilinx ChipScope Pro Analyzer. The software test can be divided into two aspects: correctness test and performance test. For correctness test, a large file contains random data can be prepared in advance. The file is written to SSD and read out again, and a byte-for-byte comparison of two times file will find any data corruption. For the performance test, operating any prepared data on SD card or network is too slow to test. And data transfer between user space and kernel space is also intolerable overhead. So, a test mode is implemented in DMA driver directly. Small amount of data/buffer is prepared in memory, and sent/receive to/from SSD in a cycle. Getting system time at the beginning and end of test, and performance is obtained by total data that sent/received divide total time. For configuration of two and three channel write, measured throughput between SSD and download board reach 227 MB/s and 357 MB/s. For configuration of two and three channel read, measured results reach 240 MB/s and 374 MB/s.

5 Conclusion

The needs for high speed storage become more and more extensive, SSDs designed for general purpose do not apply to any domain. This paper proposed a software and hardware co-design architecture of special purpose SSD device based on SoC. It's two board design is verified that can balance the customized requirements and extendability efficiently. We focus on the exposition of a DMA driver that controls a DMA engine implemented by Xilinx AXI DMA IP. The results of tests show an ideal performance is achieved. Since the architecture of this design is flexible, we will focus on performance improvement, more interfaces and more application scenarios in further works.

References

1. Eshghi, K., Micheloni, R.: SSD architecture and PCI express interface. In: Micheloni, R., Marelli, A., Eshghi, K. (eds.) Inside Solid State Drives (SSDs), pp. 145–148. Springer, Netherlands (2013). https://doi.org/10.1007/978-94-007-5146-0_2
2. Hung, J.J., Bu, K., Sun, Z.L., Diao, J.T., Liu, J.B.: PCI express-based NVMe solid state disk. J. Appl. Mech. Mater. **464**, 365–368 (2013)
3. Yu, Z.L., Hua, J., Feng, L.: The design and implement of SSD chip with multi-bus and 8 channels. J. Appl. Mech. Mater. **58–60**, 2592–2596 (2011)
4. Zhang, P., Wang, X.: SSD performance analysis and RAID 0 scheme design. J. Microcomput. Appl. (2016)
5. Zertal, S.: Exploiting the fine grain SSD internal parallelism for OLTP and scientific workloads. In: 2014 IEEE International Conference on High Performance Computing and Communications, 2014 IEEE International Symposium on Cyberspace Safety and Security, 2014 IEEE International Conference on Embedded Software and System, pp. 990–997. IEEE (2014)

6. Crockett, L.H., Elliot, R.A., Enderwitz, M.A., Stewart, R.W.: The Zynq book: embedded processing with the ARM Cortex-A9 on the Xilinx Zynq-7000 all programmable Soc. Strathclyde Academic Media, Glasgow (2014)
7. Na, S., Yang, S., Kyung, C.: Low-power bus architecture composition for AMBA AXI. J. Semicond. Technol. Sci. **9**, 75–79 (2009)
8. Cutting, D.R., Karger, D.R., Pedersen, J.O.: Scatter/gather: a cluster-based approach to browsing large document collections. In: International ACM SIGIR Conference on Research & Development in Information Retrieval, pp. 318–329. ACM (1996)
9. Lian, P.P.: Multi-thread chain DMA data transfer method for SuperSpeed bus video transmissions. J. Adv. Mater. Res. **1046**, 277–280 (2014)
10. Lee, J., Park, K.H.: Interrupt handler migration and direct interrupt scheduling for rapid scheduling of interrupt-driven tasks. J. ACM Trans. Embed. Comput. Syst. (TECS) **9**, 1–34 (2010)

Performance Evaluation of DTN Routing Protocols in Vehicular Network Environment

Yongliang Sun[1,2(✉)], Yinhua Liao[1], Kanglian Zhao[2], and Chenguang He[3]

[1] School of Computer Science and Technology,
Nanjing Tech University, Nanjing, China
syl_peter@163.com
[2] School of Electronic Science and Engineering, Nanjing University, Nanjing, China
[3] Communication Research Center, Harbin Institute of Technology, Harbin, China

Abstract. Compared with the traditional Internet architecture, Delay/Disruption Tolerant Networking (DTN) has a bundle layer between the application layer and transport layer and is able to tolerate delays and disruptions. In this paper, we simulate typical DTN routing protocols and configure a vehicular network environment to evaluate the protocol performance. We compare the performance evaluation indicators that include delivery ratio, overhead ratio, average delay, and average buffer time with different node numbers and buffer sizes. We finish the simulation using Opportunistic Network Environment (ONE) simulator and the DTN routing protocols are evaluated according to the simulation results.

Keywords: DTN · Routing protocol · Vehicular network
Performance evaluation · ONE simulator

1 Introduction

Currently, vehicular communication technology has been a research hot-spot of automotive industry. In vehicular environment, vehicles are usually equipped with short-range wireless equipments in order to communicate with other vehicles or roadside infrastructures, so the communications of vehicular network can be used for different applications and services. With the development of Vehicular Ad-Hoc Network (VANET) [1], it is necessary for vehicles to transmit collected information at any time. Although traditional Internet protocol is very mature and many routing protocols have been proposed, VANET is different from traditional network. Vehicles may move at a fast speed on the road and road topologies are various that may lead network delays, disruptions and other problems. Because of the facts mentioned above, a better solution is needed and therefore the emergence of Delay/Disruption Tolerant Networking (DTN) has attracted intensive attention [2].

DTN is a new emerging network architecture in recent years. It is used to solve the problem that is frequent network disruptions due to node movement

© ICST Institute for Computer Sciences, Social Informatics and Telecommunications Engineering 2018
X. Gu et al. (Eds.): MLICOM 2017, Part I, LNICST 226, pp. 666–674, 2018.
https://doi.org/10.1007/978-3-319-73564-1_68

and sparsity distribution [3,4]. Thus, DTN has been applied to VANET. Messages can be stored, forwarded and then delivered to the destination node finally. In order to transmit messages effectively, nodes may follow some routing protocols so that they can cooperate with each other and achieve a better Quality of Service (QoS).

In this paper, we evaluate six typical DTN routing protocols in a vehicular network environment and draw some valuable conclusions. The simulation platform is Opportunistic Network Environment (ONE) simulator [5], which is designed for DTN environment simulation. It integrates movement models, DTN routing protocols and visual graphical interfaces, so ONE is a powerful simulation tool. We select a specific map through the OpenStreetMap [6] and configure the simulation scenario to make it approximate to a real scenario. Then we evaluate the performance of the six typical DTN routing protocols with different node numbers and buffer sizes.

The remainder of this paper is organized as follows: Sect. 2 introduces the related works including traditional routing protocols and DTN routing protocols. The performance evaluation indicators that include delivery radio, overhead ratio, average delay, and average buffer time are described in Sect. 3. Section 4 gives the details of simulator parameter configuration and evaluates the performance of typical DTN routing protocols. Finally, Sect. 5 concludes this paper.

2 Related Works

Recently, researchers make great efforts to deal with collaboration communications between mobile nodes, so many routing protocols have been proposed. For example, Geographic Source Routing (GSR) protocol is one of them [7]. It abstracts map topology data and uses the road intersections as anchor nodes. Then it calculates the shortest path from the source node to the destination node with Dijkstra algorithm. Messages are forwarded along the selected anchor nodes. Improved Greedy Traffic Aware Routing (GyTAR) protocol [8] dynamically selects anchor nodes for forwarding messages according to real-time node density. Through considering neighbor node velocity, the neighbor node is exploited to carry and forward messages at the next moment. Another protocol is called Adaptive Connectivity Aware Routing (ACAR) protocol [9]. ACAR selects the optimal path for forwarding messages based on Global Positioning System (GPS), electronic map and so on. However, these routing protocols have their limitations. Thus, considering the advantages of DTN, researchers apply several DTN routing protocols to VANET as follows:

A. *Epidemic*
   Epidemic routing protocol is based on flooding strategy [10]. When two nodes meet each other, they exchange messages. After exchanging the messages multiple times, each non-isolated node will receive all the messages.
B. *Spray and Wait*
   Spray and Wait routing protocol is also based on flooding strategy [11]. The routing protocol has two phases: spray phase and wait phase. In the spray

phase, messages of the source node are spread to neighbor nodes. In the wait phase, if the destination node is not found in the spray phase, then the messages will be passed to the destination node by Direct Delivery algorithm.

C. *First Contact*

First Contact routing protocol is based on forwarding strategy [12]. In the transmission process, only one message copy of each message is transmitted in the network. In the First Contact routing protocol, source node will send the message to the node that it first meets.

D. *Direct Delivery*

Direct Delivery routing protocol is also based on forwarding strategy [5]. Different from First Contact routing protocol, the source node will keep the message until it meets the destination node and then the message is transmitted.

E. *Prophet*

Prophet routing protocol is based on probability strategy [12]. The protocol defines a transmission prediction value to describe the probability of successful transmission between nodes. When two nodes meet, the two nodes update the transmission prediction values and then decide whether to forward the messages or not.

F. *MaxProp*

MaxProp routing protocol is based on scheduling strategy [12]. This protocol sets priorities for messages. When two nodes meet, messages are transmitted according to the priorities. The messages with low priority are less likely to be transmitted, which makes the protocol more effective.

3   Performance Evaluation Indicators

We simulate these routing protocols under a vehicular network scenario, through which these routing protocols are compared and analyzed. There are many factors that can be used for evaluating routing protocol performance. In this paper, the routing protocol performance is evaluated through comparing the following four indicators:

A. *Delivery Ratio*

Delivery ratio is the success rate of transmitting messages, which indicates the ratio of the total number of messages arrive at the destination node to the total number of messages transmitted by the source node in a certain time period. This indicator describes the ability of the routing protocol to forward messages correctly to the destination node.

B. *Overhead Ratio*

Overhead ratio refers to the ratio of difference between the messages that arrive at the destination node and forwarded messages to number of the messages that arrive at the destination node in a certain period of time. High overhead ratio means that a large number of messages are forwarded, which will increase the collision probability and energy consumption.

C. *Average Delay*

Average delay is the average time that the messages arrive at the destination node from source node. Small average delay means strong transmission capability, high transmission efficiency and low network resource occupation.

D. *Average Buffer Time*

Average buffer time is the average time that messages are stored in the node buffers. It is generally measured for performance evaluation.

4   Performance Evaluation of Typical DTN Routing Protocols

The map of downtown area in Nanjing City is selected in this paper, which is shown in Fig. 1. The DTN routing protocol simulation is performed using ONE simulator and the simulation interface of ONE simulator is shown in Fig. 2. With different node numbers and buffer sizes, the performance evaluation indicators that are delivery ratio, overhead ratio, average delay, and average buffer time of the six DTN routing protocols are obtained and compared.

Fig. 1. Road topology map of Nanjing downtown area.

4.1   Node Number

We compare the performance of six typical DTN routing protocols with different node numbers. In order to make the simulation approximate to a real scenario, we mainly set four node types that are bus, taxi, car, and people with a ratio of 1:4:10:25. The simulator parameters are shown in Table 1.

The number of nodes varies from 80 to 280 and the simulation results are shown from Figs. 3, 4, 5 and 6. From these simulation results, we can see that the number of nodes has a great impact on the four indicators of these routing protocols. Figure 3 shows that, with the growth of node number, the delivery ratio increases and the impacts on MaxProp and Spray and Wait are significant.

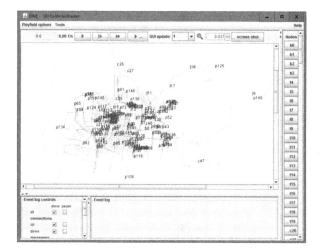

Fig. 2. Simulation interface.

Table 1. ONE simulator parameter configuration with different node numbers

Parameters	Bus	Taxi	Car	People
Number of nodes	2–7	8–28	20–70	50–175
Moving speed (m/s)	2.7–11.1	2.7–22.2	2.7–13.9	1.0–3.0
Buffer size (Mbytes)	8			
Transmission range (m)	10			
Transmission speed (Kbps)	250			
Message size (Kbytes)	500–1000			
Message creation interval (sec)	25–35			
Map size (m)	Width: 35000, Height: 30000			
Movement model	Shortest path map based movement			
Message time to live (hr)	5			
Simulation time (sec)	14400			

In Fig. 4, the network overhead ratios of Direct Delivery and Spray and Wait are independent of the node number while the overhead ratios of the other four protocols raise when the node number increases. Figure 5 shows that the number of nodes has different effects on the average delay. The average delay generally decreases when the node number increases. As shown in Fig. 6, with the growth of node number, the average buffer time of Spray and Wait protocol increases slowly. Regarding Direct Delivery, the upward trend is not obvious. At the same time, the average buffer times of the other protocols slowly decrease.

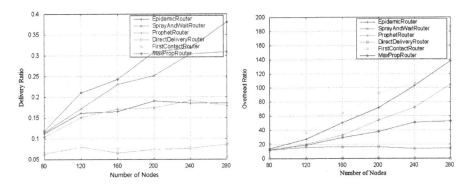

Fig. 3. Delivery ratio vs number of nodes.

Fig. 4. Overhead ratio vs number of nodes.

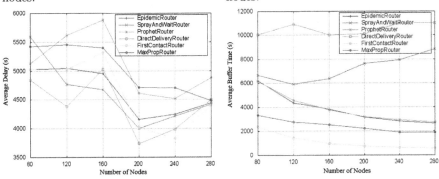

Fig. 5. Average delay vs number of nodes.

Fig. 6. Average buffer time vs number of nodes.

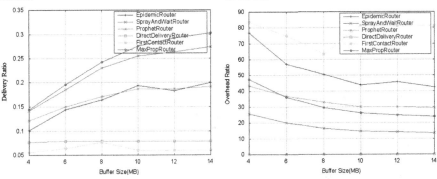

Fig. 7. Delivery ratio vs buffer size.

Fig. 8. Overhead ratio vs buffer size.

4.2   Buffer Size

We compare the performance of six typical DTN routing protocols with different buffer sizes. The simulator parameters are shown in Table 2.

Table 2. ONE simulator parameter configuration with different buffer sizes

Parameters	Bus	Taxi	Car	People
Number of nodes	4	16	40	100
Moving speed (m/s)	2.7–11.1	2.7–22.2	2.7–13.9	1.0–3.0
Buffer size (Mbytes)	4-14			
Transmission range (m)	10			
Transmission speed (Kbps)	250			
Message size (Kbytes)	500–1000			
Message creation interval (sec)	25–35			
Map size (m)	Width: 35000, Height: 30000			
Movement model	Shortest path map based movement			
Message time to live (hr)	5			
Simulation time (sec)	14400			

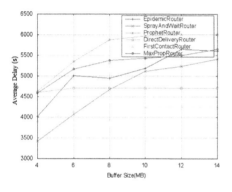

Fig. 9. Average delay vs buffer size.

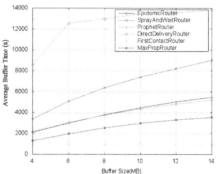

Fig. 10. Average buffer time vs buffer size.

The buffer sizes of the nodes vary from 4M to 14M and the simulation results are shown from Figs. 7, 8, 9 and 10. From these simulation results, we can see that the buffer size also has an effect on the performance of each routing protocol. Figure 7 shows that buffer size has no effect on the delivery ratios of Direct Delivery and First Contact. But regarding the other protocols, the larger node buffer size is set, the higher delivery ratio can be obtained. In Fig. 8, when the buffer size increases, the overhead ratio of Direct Delivery basically has not been influenced and the overhead ratios of other routing protocols have a small downward trend. As shown in Fig. 9, the impacts of the buffer size on the average delays of Direct Delivery and First Contact are not obvious, but a certain degree of transmission delays of the other protocols are caused when the buffer size increases. Figure 10 shows that, with the growth of buffer size, there is no influence on First Contact, the average buffer times of the other protocols increase a little.

5   Conclusion and Future Work

In this paper, through evaluating the performance of DTN routing protocols in a vehicular network environment, some valuable conclusions are draw as follows: (1) the node number and buffer size both have significant effects on the performance of each routing protocol. (2) Epidemic has a poor performance in the simulation. Its delivery ratio is low and transmission delay has no obvious advantages. (3) Spray and Wait has the high delivery ratio and low overhead ratio, so it outperforms the other routing protocols in the simulation. (4) Regarding First Contact, it has low delivery ratio and high overhead ratio, so its performance is generally worse than the other protocols. (5) The overhead ratio of Direct Delivery is closed to 0 with different node numbers and buffer sizes, which make it the best routing protocol among the six protocols in a low energy node scenario. (6) Prophet does not have an outstanding performance in the simulation and MaxProp has a high delivery ratio with different node numbers and buffer sizes.

In the future, we will try more road topologies and analyze the influences of road topologies on the routing protocol performance. Additionally, according to previous research and analysis, we expect to improve an existing DTN routing protocol to achieve a better performance.

Acknowledgment. The authors gratefully thank the referees for the constructive and insightful comments. This work was supported by the Scientific Research Startup Foundation of Nanjing Tech University under Grant No. 39809106.

References

1. Bi, Y., Shan, H., Shen, S.M., Wang, N., Zhao, H.: A multi-hop broadcast protocol for emergency message dissemination in urban vehicular ad hoc networks. IEEE Trans. Intell. Transp. Syst. **17**(3), 736–750 (2016)
2. Tornell, S.M., Calafate, C.T., Cano, J.C., Manzoni, P.: DTN protocols for vehicular networks: an application oriented overview. IEEE Commun. Surv. Tutorials **17**(2), 868–887 (2015)
3. Laoutaris, N., Smaragdakis, G., Rodriguez, P., Sundaram, R.: Delay tolerant bulk data transfers on the internet. IEEE/ACM Trans. Networking **21**(6), 1852–1865 (2013)
4. Wang, R.H., Qiu, M.J., Zhao, K.L., Qian, Y.: Optimal RTO timer for best transmission efficiency of DTN protocol in deep-space vehicle communications. IEEE Trans. Veh. Technol. **66**(3), 2536–2550 (2017)
5. Oda, T., Elmazi, D., Spaho, E., Kolici, V., Barolli, L.: A simulation system based on one and sumo simulators: performance evaluation of direct delivery, epidemic and energy aware epidemic DTN protocols. In: 2015 18th International Conference on Network-Based Information Systems, pp. 418–423 (2015)
6. OpenStreetMap homepage. http://www.openstreetmap.org
7. Zaimi, I., Houssaini, Z.S., Abdelali, B., Oumsis, M.: An improved GPSR protocol to enhance the video quality transmission over vehicular ad hoc networks. In: 2016 International Conference on Wireless Networks and Mobile Communications, pp. 146–153 (2016)

8. Jerbi, M., Meraihi, R., Senouci, S.M., et al.: GyTAR: improved greedy traffic aware routing protocol for vehicular ad hoc networks in city environments. In: ACM International Workshop on Vehicular Ad Hoc Networks, pp. 88–89 (2006)
9. Yang, Q., Lim, A., Li, S., Fang, J.: ACAR: adaptive connectivity aware routing protocol for vehicular ad hoc networks. In: IEEE International Conference on Computer Communications and Networks, pp. 1–6 (2008)
10. Sun, H.F., Song, L.L.: Performance analysis of epidemic routing in 1-D linear sparse VANETs. IEEE Commun. Lett. **20**(10), 2087–2090 (2016)
11. Cao, Y., Sun, Z.L., Wang, N., Riaz, M., Cruickshank, H., Liu, X.L.: Geographic-based spray-and-relay (GSaR): an efficient routing scheme for DTNs. IEEE Trans. Veh. Technol. **64**(4), 1546–1564 (2015)
12. Abdelkader, T., Naik, K., Nayak, A., Goel, N., Srivastava, V.: A performance comparison of delay-tolerant network routing protocols. IEEE Netw. **30**(2), 46–53 (2016)

Benefits of Compressed Sensing Multi-user Detection for Spread Spectrum Code Design

Yan Wu, Wenjing Kang, Bo Li, and Gongliang Liu[✉]

School of Information and Electrical Engineering,
Harbin Institute of Technology, Weihai 264209, China
liugl@hit.edu.cn

Abstract. In sporadic machine-to-machine (M2M) communication, for the Code Division Multiple Access (CDMA) system with random access, applying compressed sensing (CS) algorithms to communication processes is a solution of multi-user detection (MUD). Many papers have shown that compressed sensing multi-user detection (CS-MUD) brings the benefits of jointly detecting activity and data. This paper focuses on the benefits of CS-MUD to the design of spread spectrum code in CDMA systems. Simulations show that CS-MUD brings two advantages in the spread spectrum code design: (1) There exist code sets with short code length can accommodate more users. (2) Code sets design is not limited to the design requirements of pseudo-random sequences, and the CS measurement matrix can be used as the code set. That is, CS-MUD provides a new idea for design and selection of spread spectrum code sets.

Keywords: Compressed sensing · Multi-user detection
Spread spectrum code design

1 Introduction

Effective machine-to-machine (M2M) communication for performing specific tasks is an important part in future communication. So communication processing design which is compatible with communication requirements and characteristics for physical layer in M2M communication has been the research direction of concern.

1.1 CS-MUD for M2M Communication

In a sensor network where large numbers of users can be accessed, the data transmission rate is low and only a portion of the total users implement access operations at some moment. Therefore, in order to improve data transmission efficiency, transmission of control information, such as resource allocation information, should be avoided. This requires the data fusion node to perform user activity detection and data detection. According to the communication requirements and characteristics described above, facilitated by the sparse feature of user activity, the technology that applies compressed sensing (CS) to a multi-user detection (MUD) process is called compressed sensing multi-user detection (CS-MUD).

© ICST Institute for Computer Sciences, Social Informatics and Telecommunications Engineering 2018
X. Gu et al. (Eds.): MLICOM 2017, Part I, LNICST 226, pp. 675–681, 2018.
https://doi.org/10.1007/978-3-319-73564-1_69

In sporadic transmission, only a portion of the total users are active at a given time. Here, if view the non-active users send zeros, then the vector stacked by all users' data is a sparse vector. So MUD can be performed by using the sparse signal reconstruction characteristic of CS algorithm. With the sparsity of user activity, many achievements have been made in the combination of CS technology and MUD technology. Most of them are based on direct sequence spread spectrum (DSSS) communication mode and received data at chip rate. The CS problem is constructed on the basis of the data received at the chip rate, and joint detection of user activity and data is carried out. Based on the assumption of different communication system architectures or the use of multiple information, there have been many improvement schemes for user activity detection, data detection and user capacity expansion. Such as, to consider multi-path channel [1] or asynchronous transmission [2], and to establish received signal model in the corresponding case. For improving the accuracy of activity detection and data detection, the temporal correlation feature of activity can be used to improve the activity detection accuracy [1]. Bayesian algorithm, information based on finite modulation symbol set and tree search algorithm are adopted to improve detection performance [3]. Combined with channel coding and decoding, soft method is used in detection [4, 5]. Channel estimation is introduced into the detection process to detect activity, data and channel state simultaneously [6].

1.2   Paper Focus and Contribution

Bockelmann points out that "With respect to communications, two properties of CS are especially interesting in M2M scenarios: both data and activity can be reconstructed at the same time and reconstruction is possible for underdetermined equation systems [1]." As mentioned above, many papers have shown that CS-MUD can provide good joint detection of activity and data for the Code Division Multiple Access (CDMA) system. The detection performances of different active probabilities and different overload conditions have been studied [7]. Some papers also consider the influences on the detection performance that exerted by different codes or the designs of spread spectrum code under the considered system model [8]. However, according to the existing knowledge, there is no discussion about the benefits of CS-MUD for spread spectrum code design in sporadic communication. In this paper, for overloaded CDMA system, the CS-MUD performances based on group orthogonal matching pursuit (GOMP) algorithm are simulated under different spread spectrum code sets and different active probabilities of users. And the results are compared with the performances of the minimum mean-square-error (MMSE) algorithm when using m-sequences as spread spectrum codes in fully loaded system. Simulations show that, for the considered active probability and overload condition, on the premise that the total number of users is the same and the detection performance is similar, compared to typical spread spectrum codes, code sets with shorter code length which are based on CS measurement matrices can be found. Although compared with the typical spread spectrum code sets, such as m-sequences, the code set based on the CS measurement matrix has poorer auto-correlation and cross-correlation performance, using the measurement matrix as the code set and supplemented by appropriate CS detection algorithm can achieve better detection performance. That is, the MUD process based on appropriate CS detection algorithm does not harshly require the code set has very good auto-correlation and cross-correlation performance. From this and the fact that CS detection allows overload condition, it can be seen that, for sporadic communication in CDMA systems, CS-MUD brings two advantages in the spread spectrum code design: (1) There exist code sets with short code length can accommodate more users. (2) Code sets design is not limited to the design requirements of pseudo-random sequences, and the CS measurement matrices can be used as the code sets. That is, CS-MUD provides a new idea for the design and selection of spread spectrum code sets.

1.3   Organization and Notation

The rest of the paper is organized as follows. Section 2 illustrates the system model considered in this paper. Section 3 contains the simulation conditions, results and discussions based on the system model. Finally, the conclusion is given in Sect. 4.

The notation employed in this paper is as follows. I is a set of indices that indicate active users and I^c is the complementary set. $A^{L \times N}$ denotes that matrix A has L rows and N columns. For matrix A, $A_{i,j}$ represents the element in row i, column j.

2   System Model

Considering a sensor network with star topology, there are some ordinary sensors that have specific tasks and a data fusion node which allows complex signal processing in the network. When an ordinary sensor has a demand to communicate with the data fusion node, it sends the data to the data fusion node according to the established transmission mode. That is, random access mode is implemented. The received data is processed by the data fusion node and MUD is carried out, including activity detection and data detection. Of course, sporadic communication is considered. At a given time, only a portion of the total users send data to the data fusion node.

Adopt CDMA communication mode. Suppose the total number of users is represented by N. Each user is assigned a specific spread spectrum code of length L. The code set which consists of all users' spread spectrum codes is represented by matrix $A^{L \times N}$. A column of the matrix represents a spread spectrum code, $s_n(t)\ 1 \leq n \leq N$, used by a specific user. Active users adopt Binary Phase Shift Keying (BPSK) modulation mode and modulate their symbols to spread spectrum code waveforms. The symbol sent by an active user is represented as $b_n \in \{1, -1\}$ for $n \in I$, where I contains indices of active users. Non-active users can be considered as sending zeros. That is, $b_n = 0$ for $n \in I^c$. The data of a user is transmitted in frame structure, and when a user is active, an entire frame of data is sent, i.e., the user activity is unchanged in one frame time. The frame length is represented by M. A frame contains M symbols. This paper assumes that all users' active probabilities are independent and identical. It is represented by $pa\ (0 < pa < P)$. The upper limit of active probability, P, here ensures the sparsity of communication. Of course, the active probability of each user can be different, or the active probabilities of different users are related, which has concern with the specific communication scene and is not considered in this paper.

To consider the frames are received synchronously. MUD input is the result of multi-path compensation, attenuation compensation and other front-End processing. It is a superposition signal of the active users' baseband signals that pass through the equivalent Additive White Gaussian Noise (AWGN) channel.

$$y = \sum_{n=1}^{N} b_n s_n(t) + w(t) \; t \in [0, T].$$ (1)

$w(t)$ is Gaussian noise with zero mean and variance σ^2, T is the symbol duration time.

3 Simulation and Discussion

Based on the above system model, the performances of CS-MUD with GOMP algorithm are simulated under different spread spectrum code sets and different active probabilities for an overload condition. In the simulations, the total number of users is $N = 127$. The spread spectrum code length of each user is $L = 80$, so overload degree is $\frac{L}{N} \approx 0.63$. The frame length of active users is $M = 100$. The active probabilities considered in this paper are 0.3 and 0.4. Because the activity of each user is in frame form, the sparse form of the sparse vector obtained by all users' symbols is structured. Therefore the sparse structure of the sparse vector can be used to conduct CS-MUD with GOMP algorithm. The details of GOMP algorithm can refer to [1].

Of course, in order to compare with the traditional method, the traditional pseudo-random sequence, m-sequence, is used as the spread spectrum code set under the corresponding active probabilities, and the performances of MUD based on MMSE algorithm are simulated. In the experiments, the simulations of traditional detection method take fully loaded condition into account. That is, for traditional detection method, there is $L = N = 127$.

3.1 CS Measurement Matrices Considered in Simulations

Simulations show the performances of CS-MUD when three CS measurement matrices are used as spread spectrum code sets with active probabilities of 0.3 and 0.4 respectively. The three CS matrices are two Toeplitz matrices based on two different generation element sets and a Bernoulli matrix.

Restricted Isometry Property (RIP) [9] is a well-known condition that should be satisfied by CS measurement matrix. Bernoulli matrix and Toeplitz matrix can satisfy the RIP condition with high probability. They are constructed as follows.

(1) Bernoulli matrix: Construct a matrix $A^{L \times N}$. Each element in the matrix obeys the Bernoulli distribution independently.

$$A_{i,j} = \begin{cases} +\dfrac{1}{\sqrt{L}} & p = \dfrac{1}{2} \\ -\dfrac{1}{\sqrt{L}} & p = \dfrac{1}{2} \end{cases}.$$ (2)

(2) Toeplitz matrix: If $r = N + L - 1$, to construct Toeplitz matrix $A^{L \times N}$. Its basic structure is as follows.

$$
A = \begin{bmatrix} a_N & a_{N-1} & \cdots & a_1 \\ a_{N+1} & a_N & \cdots & a_2 \\ \vdots & \vdots & \ddots & \vdots \\ a_{N+L-1} & a_{N+L-2} & \cdots & a_L \end{bmatrix}.
\tag{3}
$$

It can be seen that the Toeplitz matrix is constructed by r generation elements. In this paper, two Toeplitz matrices based on two different generation element sets are constructed. The generation elements of Toeplitz matrix 1 obey the Bernoulli distribution independently. The generation elements of Toeplitz matrix 2 come from a pseudo-random sequence.

3.2 Discussion

From Figs. 1 and 2, it can be seen that, for the considered active probability and overload condition, compared with the MUD scheme based on traditional long m-sequences and MMSE algorithm, A MUD scheme with appropriate CS algorithm and short spread spectrum codes that come from CS measurement matrix can achieve the same or even better detection performance while supporting the same number of total users. This shows that in the consideration of communication scenario, performance requirements, communication processing and system model, a code set with short codes based on CS measurement matrix can be chosen as spread spectrum code set.

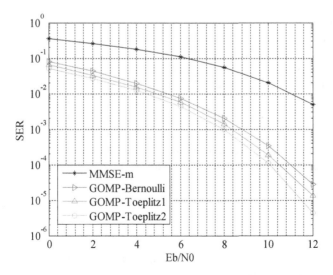

Fig. 1. SER simulation results for $L = 80$, $N = 127$, $pa = 0.3$.

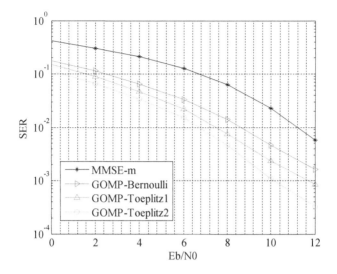

Fig. 2. SER simulation results for $L = 80$, $N = 127$, $pa = 0.4$.

It is a fact that different CS measurement matrices have different impacts on the performance of CS algorithms. This also can be seen in the two figures. If a CS algorithm is to be applied to the process of communication, it must be compatible with the whole communication process. Therefore, on the basis of the above discussions, we can consider the characteristics of communication signals and the characteristics of processing in communication, then design and select the spread spectrum code sets for communication systems that combine with the CS algorithms.

The good performances of CS-MUD based on GOMP algorithm are related to system model. The assumption that the signal before entering the detector has experienced attenuation compensation and multi-path compensation makes the equivalent channel model an AWGN channel. So that GOMP algorithm has such a good performance. In other system models, the performances of the GOMP algorithm might not be so good. The purpose of the experiments is to indicate that, under the considered active probability, front-End processing method of receiver and CS algorithm, on the premise that the detection performance is not bad and the number of users is the same, compared with the traditional MUD based on pseudo-random codes and MMSE algorithm, we can find the spread spectrum code sets that come from CS measurement matrices and of shorter lengths and various forms. That is, CS-MUD provides a new idea for the design and selection of spread spectrum code sets.

4   Conclusion

In this paper, we focus on the benefits of CS-MUD for spread spectrum code design in CDMA systems when sporadic communication is considered. Simulation results show that, for the considered active probability and the same total number of users, compared with traditional MUD, CS-MUD can achieve better detection performance based on appropriate system structure, front-End processing of receiver, measurement matrix and CS algorithm. And because the CS algorithm can deal with overload condition, the code length can be shortened. That is, CS-MUD provides a new idea for the design and selection of spread spectrum code sets.

Many papers assume that the detector has known the channel state information of each user, but the way and process of channel state acquisition as well as its conjunction with the detection process have great influence on the detection performance. Moreover, the design and selection of spread spectrum code set and its adaptability to synchronization and channel estimation also have an impact on the system performance. The design of receiver's each part that is compatible with the performance of the selected spread spectrum code set needs to be considered. This remains to be done for further studies.

Acknowledgments. This work was supported by the National Natural Science Foundation of China (No. 61371100, No. 61501139, No. 61401118).

References

1. Bockelmann, C., Schepker, H.F., Dekorsy, A.: Compressive sensing based multi-user detection for machine-to-machine communication. Trans. Emerg. Telecommun. Technol. **24**, 389–400 (2013)
2. Schepker, H.F., Bockelmann, C., Dekorsy, A.: Coping with CDMA asynchronicity in compressive sensing multi-user detection. In: 2013 IEEE 77th Vehicular Technology Conference (VTC Spring), pp. 1–5. IEEE Press (2013)
3. Monsees, F., Bockelmann, C., Wubben, D., Dekorsy, A.: Compressed sensing Bayes risk minimization for under-determined systems via sphere detection. In: 2013 IEEE 77th Vehicular Technology Conference (VTC Spring), pp. 1–5. IEEE Press (2013)
4. Schepker, H.F., Bockelmann, C., Dekorsy, A.: Efficient detectors for joint compressed sensing detection and channel decoding. IEEE Trans. Commun. **63**, 2249–2260 (2015)
5. Bockelmann, C.: Iterative soft interference cancellation for sparse BPSK signals. IEEE Commun. Lett. **19**, 855–858 (2015)
6. Schepker, H.F., Bockelmann, C., Dekorsy, A.: Exploiting sparsity in channel and data estimation for sporadic multi-user communication. In: The Tenth International Symposium on Wireless Communication Systems, pp. 1–5. VDE Press (2013)
7. Schepker, H.F., Dekorsy, A.: Sparse multi-user detection for CDMA transmission using greedy algorithms. In: 2011 8th International Symposium on Wireless Communication Systems, pp. 291–295. IEEE Press, Aachen (2011)
8. Abebe, A.T., Kang, C.G.: Compressive sensing-based random access with multiple-sequence spreading for MTC. In: 2015 IEEE Globecom Workshops (GC Workshops), pp. 1–6. IEEE Press (2015)
9. Candes, E.J., Tao, T.: Decoding by linear programming. IEEE Trans. Inf. Theory **51**, 4203–4215 (2005)

Application of Time-Varying Filter
in Time-Frequency Resource Allocation

Zhongchao Ma[1,2], Liang Ye[1], and Xuejun Sha[1(✉)]

[1] School of Electronics and Information Engineering,
Harbin Institute of Technology, Harbin 150001, China
2279779526@qq.com, coldwound@163.com,
shaxuejun@hit.edu.cn
[2] Science and Technology on Information Transmission and Dissemination
in Communication Networks Laboratory, Shijiazhuang, China

Abstract. With the rapid development of wireless communication industry, the problem of spectrum resource scarcity is becoming more and more serious. To improve the spectral efficiency by compressing the adjacent carrier frequency intervals will increase the inter carrier interference. At this point, the performance of time-invariant filter is poor. If the communication system can make full use of the low energy slots in the time-frequency domain, the spectral efficiency could be improved. This paper proposes a time-frequency resource allocation method in which there is a delay of half a symbol between adjacent carriers. Accordingly, a time-varying filter is proposed. The simulation results show that the proposed time-varying filter performs better than the time-invariant filter.

Keywords: Time-frequency transform · Time-varying filter
Root raised cosine signal

1 Introduction

In recent years, the mobile communication industry has developed rapidly, and various communication services have greatly facilitated production and life. However, as the number of terminals increases, the problem of spectrum resource scarcity is increasingly serious. It is an effective approach to alleviate this problem by improving spectral efficiency. Conventional resource allocation method is allocating the resources only in frequency domain and applying the time-invariant filter to suppress the adjacent channel interference. But this solution performs poor if the adjacent carrier frequency interval is compressed. An efficient allocation scheme is to sense the low energy slots in the time-frequency domain, and allocate the time-frequency resources according to the time-frequency distributions of adjacent signals. In this case, the time-varying filter is used to mitigate the interference. In addition, time-varying filter can also be applied to cellular systems, such as D2D communication by using guard bands, non-orthogonal multiple access in 5G, and frequency reuse in adjacent cellular cells.

Fourier transform can only be used to analyze stationary signals because it can only tell what frequency components the signal contains, but can not tell the time when the components appear. Short-time Fourier transform [1] is based on Fourier transform,

X. Gu et al. (Eds.): MLICOM 2017, Part I, LNICST 226, pp. 682–691, 2018.
https://doi.org/10.1007/978-3-319-73564-1_70

and the signal is processed by adding analysis window. When the window is short, short-time Fourier transform can show the time-varying spectrum of the signal. In 1996, Stockwell proposed the famous S transform [2]. S transform can be seen as an evolution of short-time Fourier transform. Unlike STFT whose length of time window is fixed, S transform uses the Gaussian window, and the length of the time window is inversely proportional to the frequency. In addition to the linear time-frequency distribution, there are also nonlinear time-frequency distributions [3]. WVD is a typical nonlinear distribution. It has good characteristics in time-frequency concentration, but WVD has serious cross-term problems. In recent years, there have been many studies on weighted-type fractional Fourier transform [4, 5].

In order to improve the efficiency of time-frequency resource utilization, some new technologies have emerged in recent years, such as MIMO and context awareness [6, 7]. The allocation of time-frequency resources is determined by perceiving the user's behavior, such as the type of application, whether the user is interacting with the program, and so on. This method not only improves the spectral efficiency, but also improves the quality of service. In paper [8], a context aware time-frequency resource scheduling algorithm is proposed, which has lower computational complexity. However, this algorithm uses the channel resources fully, but does not change the energy distribution of the signal when transmitting data, and does not use the low energy characteristics in time-frequency domain. When all channels are transmitting data, this method has no ability to further improve resource utilization.

In recent years, researches on time-varying filter have been in full swing. Although there have been some researches on the time-invariant filter [9, 10], this paper forgoes an introduction. In paper [11], a fast algorithm of inverse S transform is proposed. Based on this, a time-varying filter for synthetic aperture radar is designed. Since the root raised cosine signal does not have a relatively fixed time-frequency spectrum under S transform, this filtering method is not applicable to a communication system which employs root raised cosine signal. The time-varying filter based on S transform proposed in [12] has similar problems. Paper [13] studies the interferences of adjacent cell in SC-FDMA system. A time-varying filter is designed based on Choi-Williams distribution. The signal which includes a desired signal and two interfering signals is used in simulation, and the channel is an additive white Gauss noise channel. The time-frequency filtering pass region (Mask) used by the receiver is generated by the received signal in real time. The method of generating Mask is as follows: (1) transform the received signal to time-frequency domain; (2) set the region to Mask whose energy exceeds the threshold value. Since the Mask is determined by the received signal, the characteristics of the received signal can significantly affect the performance of filter. The simulation results show that the time-varying filter has advantages when the signal to noise ratio is in a suitable range. However, when the power of noise and interference is large, this method can't provide the effective pass region, and can't be used to suppress the noise and interference.

In view of these shortcomings and based on the low energy slots of root raised cosine signal in time-frequency domain, a new method of time-frequency resource allocation is proposed in this paper. On this foundation, a time-varying filter is used to eliminate interference and noise. Simulation results show that this method performs better than the time-invariant filter.

2   Time-Frequency Resource Allocation and Filter Design

2.1   Fundamentals of STFT Analysis

It is very important to learn the signal's energy distribution characteristics at different time for a non-stationary signal. Fourier transform maps the signal to a one-dimensional spectral distribution, so it only shows what frequencies it contains. When the time-frequency analysis method is used, the signal can be mapped to a time-frequency plane. This plane shows the spectral characteristics of non-stationary signals at different times. Short time Fourier transform (STFT) is a common time-frequency analysis method. It is widely used in various fields. The main principle of STFT is to add a window which slides with time. The window intercepts the original signal and considers the signal to be stationary within the window. Then Fourier transform is applied to the signal within the window, and the time-frequency distribution of the signal is formed. For discrete sequence $x(n)$, its instantaneous data at the moment n is defined as

$$x_n(m) = x(m)w(n - m) \tag{1}$$

Where $w(n)$ is a window function whose length is N.
DFT of (1) can be expressed as

$$STFT(n, \omega) = \sum_{m=-\infty}^{+\infty} x(m)w(n - m)e^{-jm\omega} = \sum_{m=-\infty}^{+\infty} x_n(m)e^{-jm\omega} \tag{2}$$

This is the discrete STFT formula of the signal $x(n)$.

2.2   Time-Frequency Distribution of Root Raised Cosine Signal and Resource Allocation

The root raised cosine signal is expressed as

$$h(t) = \frac{(4\alpha t/T)\cos[\pi(1 + \alpha)t/T] + \sin[\pi(1 - \alpha)t/T]}{(\pi t/T)[1 - (4\alpha t/T)^2]} \tag{3}$$

A system which uses root raised cosine signal as the transmit pulse and the receive filter is an optimum receiver without inter-symbol interference. Assume that the symbol transmit rate $R_b = 3.84$ Mbps, sampling rate $f_s = 1.61 \times 10^8$ Hz, and the raised cosine coefficient $\alpha = 0.22$. The time-frequency spectrum of the signal with different window lengths is shown in Fig. 1 where T represents the length of the time window and $T_0 = 1/R_b$.

Figure 1 shows that when the window length is longer than the length of symbol, the energy concentration regions and the low energy slots emerge randomly which is determined by the transmit symbol. In other words, the energy concentration region will become low energy slot at the next simulation because of different transmitting symbols. This adds obstacles to time-frequency resource allocation and filtering. With the shortening of time window, the randomness of energy concentration region and low energy slots decrease gradually. Low energy slots are usually present at the junction of

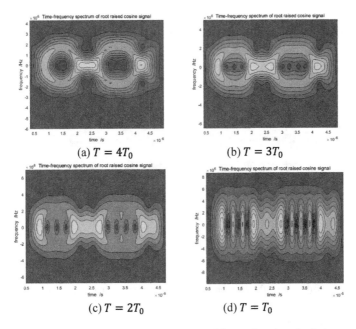

(a) $T = 4T_0$ (b) $T = 3T_0$

(c) $T = 2T_0$ (d) $T = T_0$

Fig. 1. The time-frequency spectrum at different lengths of window

two symbols. It is possible to determine the time-frequency domain occupied by the signal when $T = T_0$. The analysis window length used in this paper is $T = T_0/2$. The STFT spectrum of root raised cosine signal is shown in Fig. 2.

Figure 2 shows that there are low energy slots in the time-frequency spectrum of

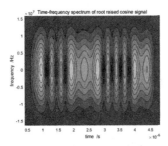

Fig. 2. Time-frequency distribution when $T = T_0/2$

the signals, and the positions of these low energy slots are relatively fixed. When the transmit sequence produces a positive and negative conversion, a low energy slots is generated at the junction of the two symbols. When two consecutive 1 (or -1) occurs, an energy concentration region is generated at the junction of the two symbols. If the communication system allocate the frequency of each channel and adjust the time delay of the transmitting symbols properly, these low energy slots can be fully utilized, and then the utilization ratio of the resource will be improved. The time-frequency resource allocation is shown in the Fig. 3.

Figure 3 shows that there is a delay of half a symbol between two adjacent signals,

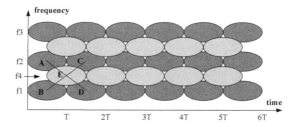

Fig. 3. Time-frequency resource allocation

which can make full use of the low energy slots in the spectrum and enhance the spectral efficiency. However, it will add interference to the original signal. Time-invariant filter can not distinguish two signals overlapped in frequency spectrum very well. So time-varying filter based on time-frequency transform has some advantages.

2.3   The Proposed Time-Varying Filter

There are two ways to design time-varying filters: explicit design method and implicit design method. Explicit design method is based on time-frequency weighting function $M(t,f)$ to calculate the impulse response $h(t,t')$. Finally we will get filtering result $y(t)$ by calculating the convolution of $x(t')$ and $h(t,t')$.

$$y(t) = \int_{-\infty}^{+\infty} h(t,t')x(t')dt' \tag{4}$$

Implicit design method is implemented in three steps: analysis, emphasis and synthesis. First, get the time-frequency distribution $X(t,f)$ of signal $x(t)$ by the method of WVD or STFT, and then use the time frequency weighting function $M(t,f)$ to handle with $X(t,f)$ where we will get $X'(t,f)$. Finally, do inverse transform to convert $X'(t,f)$ into time domain.

The performance of filter designed by explicit design method and implicit design method is similarly. Therefore, the filter involved in this paper is designed by implicit design method.

In this paper, STFT transform is used to analyze time-frequency spectrum. Four types of time-frequency weighting functions are designed.

When the spectrum of a signal is relatively fixed, the filtering pass region of the signal can be selected according to the time frequency distribution of the signal with a selection threshold constraint. Moreover, the filtering pass region can seriously affect the performance of filter. In time-frequency spectrum, the energy region is selected from high to low. When the total energy reaches the threshold, a filter pass region ($mask_1$) can be obtained. The threshold ξ can be expressed as

$$\xi = \frac{P_{sum}}{P_{total}} \tag{5}$$

where P_{sum} is the energy of the region selected, and P_{total} is the energy of the signal. The filter domain is shown in Fig. 4.

Figure 4 shows that the filtering pass region shrinks as the energy threshold

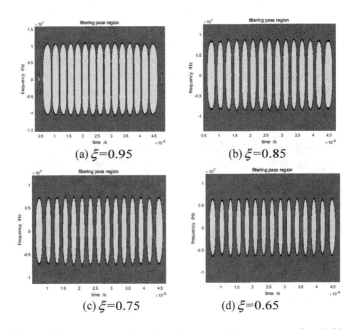

(a) ξ=0.95

(b) ξ=0.85

(c) ξ=0.75

(d) ξ=0.65

Fig. 4. Filtering pass region ($mask_1$) under different energy thresholds

decreases. In general the larger the power of noise and interference, the smaller the optimal threshold. Small energy threshold may filter out some of the useful signal, but it also means filtering out more noise and interference. Using this filtering pass region, the energy between the two energy concentration regions is discarded. But the desired signal has some energy here, so the filtering pass region can be improved. When the energy concentration region is connected to each other, another filtering pass region ($mask_2$) is generated which is show in Fig. 5.

Figure 5 shows that the width of the energy concentration region changes with different energy threshold, and the width of the added area change in proportion. Two filtering pass regions above are generated by alternately sending positive and negative signals. The signal transmitted by actual communication system are random, so the filtering pass region generated by the statistical probability may have some advantages.

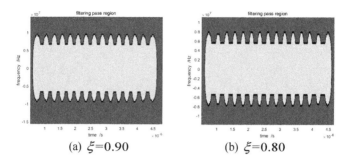

(a) ξ=0.90   (b) ξ=0.80

Fig. 5. The filtering pass region ($mask_2$) under different energy thresholds

The process is to send random symbols and generate some filtering pass regions according to the energy threshold ξ. The filter pass region ($mask_3$) which is shows in Fig. 6 can be generated by superimposing all the filtering pass regions.

Figure 6 shows that the width of filtering pass region shrinks as the energy

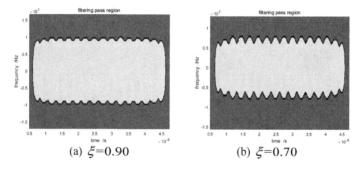

(a) ξ=0.90   (b) ξ=0.70

Fig. 6. The filtering pass region ($mask_3$) under different energy thresholds

threshold decreases, and the energy concentration region is connected. It is worth noting that the widest position of $mask_3$ exactly corresponds to the narrowest position of $mask_1$ and $mask_2$. The filtering pass region is generated by the method of super-position, thus it shows the energy distribution under various transmit sequences. The problem is that there is energy of desired signal at some time-frequency area in $mask_3$, but the probability is very small. This region will introduce interference at most time, without much benefit to the desired signal. Then, another filtering pass region is proposed to remove the time-frequency regions with small occurrence probability of the desired signal from $mask_3$. The regions are preserved where the occurrence probability is above the threshold p. Figure 7 shows the filtering pass region ($mask_4$).

Figure 7 shows that the widest part of the region narrows gradually as the probability threshold p increases. That leads to the filtering pass region becoming isolated.

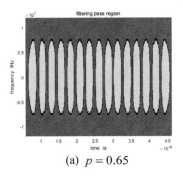 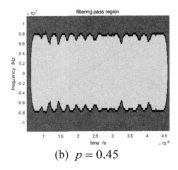

(a) $p = 0.65$ (b) $p = 0.45$

Fig. 7. The filtering pass region (*mask₄*) under different probability thresholds

3   Simulation Results

The signal used in this paper includes a desired signal and two interference signals. There is a delay of half a symbol between desired signal and interference signals. The signal transmitted can be expressed as

$$
\begin{aligned}
f(t) &= f_1(t) + f_2(t) + f_3(t) \\
&= \sum_{n=-\infty}^{+\infty} a_n g\left(t - \frac{T_0}{2}\right) \cos(2\pi ft) * \delta(t - nT_0) \\
&+ \sum_{n=-\infty}^{+\infty} b_n g(t) \cos[2\pi(f + \Delta f)t] * \delta(t - nT_0) \\
&+ \sum_{n=-\infty}^{+\infty} c_n g(t) \cos[2\pi(f - \Delta f)t] * \delta(t - nT_0)
\end{aligned}
\tag{6}
$$

where a_n, b_n, c_n is the sequences transmitted. $1/T_0 = R_b = 3.84$ Mbps is the symbol transmission rate. $g(t)$ is the root raised cosine signal, $f = 10$ MHz is the carrier frequency of the desired signal, $f + \Delta f, f - \Delta f$ are the carrier frequencies of the interference signals, and $\alpha = 0.22$ is raised cosine roll off coefficient.

In this paper, a time-invariant filter is used before time-varying filter. Figure 8 shows the simulation results.

Figure 8(a) shows that several filtering methods perform similarly when $\Delta f = 5$ MHz. The reason is that the bandwidth of the desired signal is 5 MHz in simulation. The interference is basically mitigated after a low pass filter, so the time-varying filter doesn't provide any advantages. In the case of $\Delta f = 3.5$ MHz and $\Delta f = 2.5$ MHz, the time-varying filter with *mask₂* performs better. In the case of $\Delta f = 1.5$ MHz, the time-varying filter with *mask₁* performs better. The smaller the adjacent carrier frequency interval, the worse the interference. At this point, although desired signal is attenuated by using smaller filtering pass region, we can also benefits by suppressing more interferences. So it's better to use the time-varying filter with *mask₁* when $\Delta f = 1.5$ MHz.

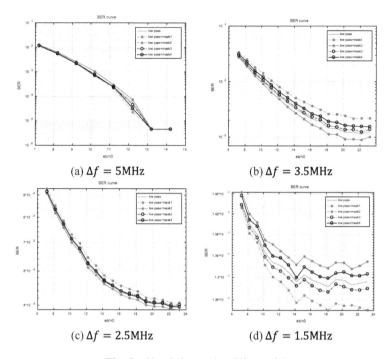

Fig. 8. Simulation under different Δf

4   Conclusion

In this paper, a method of resource allocation in the time-frequency domain is proposed. On the basis of that, the time-varying filter based on STFT transform is used to suppress the interference. The simulation results show that the method of time-varying filter performs better than the time-invariant filter. Moreover, when the carrier frequency intervals between interference signals and desired signal are small, it is better to use $mask_1$ in the time-varying filter. When the intervals are big, it is better to use $mask_2$.

Acknowledgment. This paper was supported by the National Natural Science Foundation Program of China (No. 61671179) and the Science and Technology on Information Transmission and Dissemination in Communication Networks Laboratory project (EX156410046).

References

1. Gabor, D.: Theory of communication. J. Inst. Electr. Eng. Part I: Gen. **94**(73), 58–59 (1947)
2. Stockwell, R.G., Mansinha, L., Lowe, R.P.: Localization of the complex spectrum: the S transform. IEEE Trans. Signal Process. **44**(4), 998–1001 (1996)
3. Cohen, L.: Time-frequency distribution-a review. Proc. IEEE **77**(7), 941–981 (1989)
4. Mei, L., Zhang, Q., Sha, X.: WFRFT precoding for narrowband interference suppression in DFT-based block transmission systems. IEEE Commun. Lett. **17**(10), 1916–1919 (2013)

5. Wang, K., Sha, X., Mei, L.: On interference suppression in doubly-dispersive channels with hybrid single-multi carrier modulation and an MMSE iterative equalizer. IEEE Wirel. Commun. Lett. **1**(5), 504–507 (2012)
6. Bangerter, B., Talwar, S., Arefi, R.: Networks and devices for the 5G era. IEEE Commun. Mag. **52**(2), 90–96 (2014)
7. Wang, C.X., Haider, F., Gao, X.: Cellular architecture and key technologies for 5G wireless communication networks. IEEE Commun. Mag. **52**(2), 122–130 (2014)
8. Shan, H., Zhang, Y., Zhuang, W.: User behavior-aware scheduling based on time-frequency resource conversion. IEEE Trans. Veh. Technol. **99**, 1 (2017)
9. Wu, Y., Nan, L., Jiao, L.: Dual-band coupled-line bandpass filter with independently tunable bandwidths. China Commun. **13**(9), 60–64 (2016)
10. Wen, J., Hua, J., Li, S.: Interference-driven designs of nonlinear-phase FIR filter with application in FBMC system. China Commun. **13**(12), 15–24 (2017)
11. Dong, H., Wang, Z., Ding, D.: Event-based filtering for discrete time-varying systems. In: International Conference on Automation and Computing, pp. 116–121. IEEE (2014)
12. Yin, B., He, Y., Li, B.: An adaptive SVD method for solving the pass-region problem in S-transform time-frequency filters. Chin. J. Electron. **24**(1), 115–123 (2015)
13. Li, Y., Sha, X., Ye, L.: An SC-FDMA inter-cell interference suppression method based on a time-varying filter. In: IEEE INFOCOM 2016 - IEEE Conference on Computer Communications Workshops, pp. 909–914. IEEE (2016)

Secure Communication Mechanism Based on Key Management and Suspect Node Detection in Wireless Sensor Networks

Danyang Qin$^{(\boxtimes)}$, Songxiang Yang, Ping Ji, and Qun Ding

Key Lab of Electronic and Communication Engineering,
Heilongjiang University, Harbin, People's Republic of China
qindanyang@hlju.edu.cn

Abstract. The limitation of bandwidth, environment and multipath fading in wireless sensor network (WSN) cannot satisfy the need of users. Cooperative multiple-input-multiple-output (C-MIMO) technology is introduced to improve the communication performance, which brings in security problem as the same time. The key management technology may ensure the confidentiality with fewer keys but is unable to resist the compromised node attack. A new detection algorithm is proposed to sign the compromised node and recover the information during the transmission. Combining the key management and compromised node detection, a secure communication mechanism for WSN is proposed to resist the external and internal attack. Simulation results verify the advantages of security and performance by the proposed communication mechanism.

Keywords: WSN · Security · Routing protocol · Key management

1 Introduction

WSNs have been widely used in many fields with the rapid development of electronic information and wireless communication [1]. However, the WSN can hardly satisfy the need of users with the limitation of bandwidth, environment and multipath fading. So, researchers invent the MIMO communication system to break through the bottlenecks of wireless channel capacity, which can against multipath fading and improve channel capacity. MIMO technology can hardly be applied to the mobile terminal with the limited size and power. So C-MIMO communication is proposed, which can make use of mutual collaboration among the single antennas to form virtual multi-antenna matrix. Comparing with the single-input-single-output system, the C-MIMO system can enhance the transmission quality and the lifetime of the network without increasing the hardware complexity [2, 3]. However, the credibility of all nodes is a basis for cooperation mode, which provides an opportunity for attacker to destroy the network.

D. Qin—This work was supported in the part by the National Natural Science Foundation of China under Grant 61771186, University Nursing Program for Young Scholars with Creative Talents in Heilongjiang Province under Grant UNPYSCT-2017125, and Postdoctoral Research Foundation of Heilongjiang Province under Grant LBH-Q15121.

X. Gu et al. (Eds.): MLICOM 2017, Part I, LNICST 226, pp. 692–700, 2018.
https://doi.org/10.1007/978-3-319-73564-1_71

Generally, the attack in WSN can be divided into external attack and internal attack. The encryption technique can defense external attack but unable to resist the internal attack caused by the injured nodes, since they can encrypt and decrypt the information. Thus, suspect nodes may affect network security seriously [4, 5].

A detection model is designed for WSN to identify the suspect nodes by a few keys, based on which a cross-layer security communication mechanism is proposed to overcome the external attack and the internal attack caused by suspect nodes in the C-MIMO communication. Comparing with the similar schemes [6], the proposed mechanism can against the attack of the suspect nodes without increasing the system complexity. In addition, the user can achieve the balance among the power, the efficiency and the reliability of received data by adjusting the security level. It's a small probability event for intruder to break through the security authentication and infect the nodes in network, so this paper uses deterministic parameters as the model parameters of WSN nodes.

2 WSN Security Architecture Based on C-MIMO

2.1 Network System Model

Figure 1 shows a multi-hop cooperative WSN model which is composed of many single antenna sensor nodes, namely host nodes. These host nodes form clusters called MIMO nodes by a distributed clustering algorithm. The rest of the system is shown in the figure.

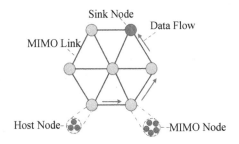

Fig. 1. System model

The most common collaborative communication strategies are Amplify-and-Forward (AF) and Decode-and-Forward (DF). AF amplifies and forwards the useful signal and the noise at the same time, which will directly affect the information transmission in network. DF can eliminate the noise and improve the reliability of system. Moreover, system needs to decode the data that aggregates in cluster head, so this paper adopts DF strategy.

Assuming that there are n_T and n_R nodes in the transmitting cluster and receiving cluster, respectively. The relationship between received signal y and sending signal x can be expressed as:

$$y = Hx + w \tag{1}$$

$y = [y_1, y_2, \ldots, y_{n_R}]^T, x = [s_1, s_2, \ldots, s_{n_T}]^T$. H is $n_R \times n_T$ matrix of channel coefficients. $w = [w_1, w_2, \ldots, w_{n_R}]^T$ represents Gaussian noise.

The channel matrix H is known to the receiving cluster instead of the transmitting cluster, which can enhance the security of MIMO network. H could be calculated by the known transmitting bit sequence and the corresponding received signal.

The proposed cross-layer secure communication mechanism for C-MIMO WSN is as follows: Each host node determines whether the suspect node needs to be identified. Normal cooperative data transmitting or forwarding will be performed if the detection is not required. Otherwise, suspect node detection will be performed. Normal data transmitting or forwarding will continue, if there is not any suspect node in the testing result. Otherwise, messy code will be eliminated by symbol filter. Then, the sink node will receive the test report, and the key management system will update key and re-build network.

2.2 C-MIMO Network Architecture

N denotes a network with many sensor nodes. d-cluster represents a disjoint part of N. There are two clusters with n_T and n_R nodes, namely A and B. This paper defines single-antenna wireless nodes as the host nodes, and calls d-cluster and C-MIMO transmission link as MIMO nodes and MIMO link, respectively. A C-MIMO network with given N and d can be formed by the following steps:

Step 1: The host nodes in N construct a C-MIMO network N_{CMIMO} through the distributed clustering algorithm.
Step 2: MIMO nodes form a multi-hop backbone tree in N_{CMIMO}.
Step 3: The backbone tree provides the routing which is used for data dissemination and data receiving.

After the C-MIMO network was formed, each cluster will obtain a ID. And each host node will contain the cluster's ID, all host nodes' IDs, the IDs and the size of neighbor clusters.

2.3 Secure Key Management Mechanism

Considering the limitation of energy and the correlated behaviors between MIMO nodes, this paper proposes a key management system, which requires a few preloading keys. This section establishes the key management system through the topology knowledge rather than the location knowledge which is more complex. Figure 2 shows two kinds of keys adopted in C-MIMO system, namely $C\_key(A)$ (for local communication) and $L\_key(A, B)$ (for long-haul communication between two clusters). The nodes in A encrypt transmitted signal by $L\_key(A, B)$, and the nodes in B decrypt the received signal by the same key. Main components of the key management system are as follows:

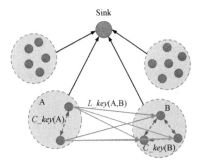

Fig. 2. Keys used in the proposed secured communication system

(1) Key pre-distribution: A shared secret key pre_key(b, m) is pre-distributed for b and m in WSN.

(2) Key establishment algorithm:

Step 1: A host node m sends the plaintext message (IDs of m and b) and the encrypted message (ID of m and b, clusters list, neighbors of m) encrypted by pre_key(b, m) to b.

Step 2: b decrypts the information by pre_key(b, m) after receiving a key request from m. And b would obtain the topology information of the whole C-MIMO network after receiving the key request from all nodes. Then, b generates C_key(A) and L_key(A, B) for A and link AB respectively, and responses to each x in A, which consists the plaintext message (IDs of b and x) and the encrypted message (IDs of b and x, C_key(A), L_key(A, B)) encrypted by pre_key(b, x).

Step 3: x uses pre_key(b, x) to decode the message and then to obtain C_key and L_key, after receiving a key response.

(3) Secure communication link establishment:

The communication in A is encrypted by C_key(A), and the communication in link AB is encrypted by L_key(A, B). Only one pre-distributed key is required for each host node m in the proposed key management mechanism. Each host node m has one C_key and i L_keys, where i is the number of neighbor nodes of m in the backbone tree. The sum of C_keys and L_keys in the whole network is n (the number of clusters) and $n - 1$ (the number of links in the backbone tree), respectively.

3 Suspect Node Detection with Information and Network Recovery

Suspect nodes represent the physical or logical unsafe nodes which bring security issues that cannot be solved by encryption techniques. Moreover, the cooperative nature of C-MIMO makes the effect of suspect nodes on network security more serious.

So, this section proposes the suspect node detection algorithm, and insulates the suspect nodes by updating the key, which can eliminate the influence of suspect nodes on data transmission. Finally, network will be reconfigured to reduce the transmission delay caused by the isolation of key nodes.

3.1 Suspect Node Detection

Figure 3 shows a model of suspect node detection, where *A* is the transmitting cluster and *D* is the detecting cluster.

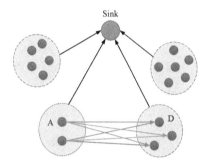

Fig. 3. Model for suspect nodes detection

Security enforcement is a challenging task in cooperative communication with multiple nodes and complex forwarding rules. To solve this problem, this paper proposes an identification method in physical layer, which can detect suspect nodes without increasing the transmission overhead.

Algorithm 1 is proposed to determine whether each cluster needs to detect the suspect node.

Algorithm 1.

---

1. generate s ($s \in [0,1]$) at node k randomly

2. compare s with l

3. **if** $s > l$ **then**

4. sends the detection signal to the other nodes

5. detect the suspect node before transmitting data

6. **else**

7. transmit the data

8. **end if**

The cluster will perform the detection, if there are suspect nodes. In the proposed mechanism, the detecting clusters cannot detect the transmitting cluster, since they are always the receiving side. The suspect nodes can be ignored which always send the correct message, because they do not influence the stability of the network.

In the proposed algorithm, all the transmitting nodes in cluster A transmit the same data stream to get the diversity gain. The host nodes in cluster A transmit the data flow $I_1 = I_2 = \cdots = I_{n_T}$ to the host node in D for detection. Every host node in D can obtain the complete data sequence R and detect the suspect node in cluster A by obtaining the received symbols form all other nodes. The suspect node detection algorithm at each host node in D is as follows.

Step 1: After receiving the complete data sequence R, each host node in D estimates the transmitted symbol I by the reverse channel detection, i.e. $\hat{I} = W^H R$, where W is $|D| \times n_T$ weighting matrix, $|D|$ is the number of nodes in D, and $(\cdot)^H$ represents the conjugate transpose. Assume that the channel coefficients matrix H is known for the detecting cluster. W can be determined as:

$$W = \begin{cases} H^{-1} & n_T = |D| \\ (H^H H)^{-1} H^H, & |D| > n_T \end{cases} \tag{2}$$

Step 2: The detecting node can identify the suspect nodes x_i and record their IDs by checking the symbols, since the data flow sent by the normal nodes are identical. The nodes which send the same symbols are divided into one group to simplify the detection. The group with the most nodes is credible, and others may contain the suspect nodes.

Step 3: When the host node m detects the suspect node x, the cryptographic detection report with the plaintext message (ID of m and b) and the encrypted message (ID of m, b and x) which is encrypted by pre_key(m, b) will be transmitted to b by each detecting host node. The nodes are classified as a suspect node, if more than half of the host nodes in the cluster claim that node x is suspected.

Figure 4 shows a data forwarding path to describe the selection of detecting clusters and the upper limit of identifiable suspect nodes, where the Pre_A forwards data to A, and then A forwards the data to the $Post\_A$. Let $|A|$, $|Pre\_A|$ and $|Post\_A|$ denote the number of nodes in A, Pre_A and $Post\_A$, respectively. If $|A| \le |Post\_A|$, the suspect node in A will be detected by the $Post\_A$, and the upper limit of identifiable suspect nodes is $|A|/2 - 1$. If $|A| > |Post\_A|$ and $|A| \le |Pre\_A|$, the suspect node in A will be detected by Pre_A, and the upper limit of identifiable suspect nodes is $|A|/2 - 1$. If $|A| > |Post\_A|$ and $|A| > |Pre\_A|$, the suspect node in A will be detected by a larger cluster between Pre_A and $Post\_A$. The upper limit of detectable suspect nodes in A and the n_T can be determined by the following equation:

$$\begin{aligned} N_{\max} + n_T &= |D| \\ N_{\max} &= \tfrac{n_T}{2} - 1 \end{aligned} \tag{3}$$

N_{max} is the upper limit of suspect nodes in A, and $|D|$ represents the nodes in the detecting cluster. By solving (3), we can get

$$N_{\mathrm{max}} = (|D|+1) \cdot \tfrac{1}{3} - 1$$
$$n_T = (|D|+1) \cdot \tfrac{2}{3} \tag{4}$$

N_{max} and n_T will be rounded to the nearest integer if they are not integers.

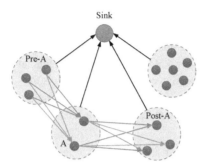

Fig. 4. Selection of cluster for detection

3.2   Key Update and Network Recovery

The sink node will update the key and recover the network if there is a suspect node in cluster A. This method could prevent the suspect nodes from obtaining information or sending false reports. Sink node b takes the following approach to update the key and recover the network:

Step 1: b sends a key update message including the plaintext message (IDs of b and u) and the encrypted message (IDs of b and u, new $C\_key(A)$, and the ID list of suspect node) which is encrypted by pre_key(b, u) to all nodes u in cluster A except for x.

Step 2: b sends a key update message that includes the plaintext message (IDs of b and u) and the encrypted message (IDs of b and u, new $L\_key(A, B)$) which is encrypted by pre_key(b, u) to each node u in every neighbor cluster B of A except x.

Step 3: After receiving the key update information from the above steps, u decrypts the message by pre_key(b, u) and obtains the new C_key and L_key. The suspect node x cannot obtain information from the network, since it does not have a new key.

The report will be sent to the sink node b layer by layer, if the suspect node in A is detected by its parent node. b may send a key revocation packet to A and its neighbor nodes via the reverse path of the transmission report, if each node maintains the record of the transmission path.

The suspect nodes are often deployed on the important transmission link in actual network. Screening out these nodes may affect the quality of the network transmission, and even lead to an island effect. So, network need to be rebuilt after the above work.

4   Implementation and Performance Analysis

4.1   Simulation Settings

The performance of the proposed algorithm and system is evaluated by MATLAB. The sink node sends a random signal on the premise of connected domain assurance. The fast Rayleigh fading channel is selected to imitate a multipath fading environment. The number of receiving symbol is 100, the modulation scheme is BPSK. This section evaluates the proposed detection algorithm by comparing with distributed compromised node detection algorithm.

4.2   Simulation Results

Figure 5 shows the accuracy of two detection algorithms with one suspect node in the transmitting cluster.

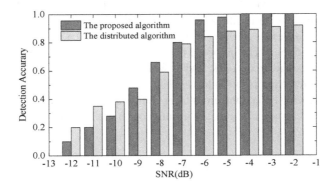

Fig. 5. Accuracy of two detection algorithms with one suspect node

There are four nodes in the transmitting cluster and five nodes in the detecting cluster in the simulation, since all the cases satisfy $|D| > n_T$. Figure 5 shows that the accuracy of distributed algorithm is higher than that of the proposed algorithm, when SNR is less than -9 dB. And the result is just the reverse when SNR is higher than -9 dB, which is the actual wireless channel environment. Moreover, the identification accuracy of proposed algorithm is close to 100% when SNR is greater than -4 dB. The simulation results suggest that the proposed algorithm has higher identification accuracy in the actual wireless channel environment.

Figure 6 shows the bit error rate of the proposed system and the traditional system, respectively. The case without any suspect node is simulated as a reference. Obviously, the proposed system can significantly improve the reliability of the communication when the SNR is higher than −8 dB. It is clear that the proposed mechanism cannot only improve the suspect node detection accuracy and the performance of network security, but also ameliorate the quality of network information transmission.

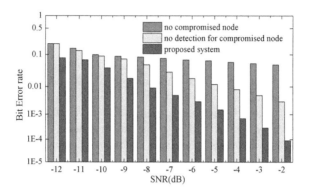

Fig. 6. Bit error rate of three systems

5   Conclusions

This paper proposes a cross-layer communication mechanism for C-MIMO communication to solve the security threat and improve the performance of the WSN. The mechanism contains a low cost key management system and a high-accuracy suspect node detection algorithm. The proposed mechanism may allow the network to transmit the data between authorized nodes, and it will update keys and recovery network if necessary. The simulation result indicates that the detection algorithm can identify the suspect nodes effectively, and the cross-layer communication mechanism may improve the stability and accuracy of the data transmission in the network.

References

1. Chang, F.C., Huang, H.C.: A survey on intelligent sensor network and its applications. J. Netw. Intell. **1**, 1–5 (2016)
2. Gao, Q., Zuo, Y., Zhang, J., Peng, X.H.: Improving energy efficiency in a wireless sensor network by combining cooperative MIMO with data aggregation. IEEE Trans. Veh. Technol. **59**, 3956–3965 (2010)
3. Islam, M.R., Kim, J.: On the cooperative MIMO communication for energy-efficient cluster-to-cluster transmission at wireless sensor network. Ann. Telecommun. **65**, 325–340 (2010)
4. Karlof, C., Wagner, D.: Secure routing in wireless sensor networks: attacks and countermeasures. Ad Hoc Netw. **1**, 293–315 (2003)
5. Choudhury, P.P., Bagchi, P., Sengupta, S., Ghosh, A.: On effect of compromised nodes on security of wireless sensor network. Ad. Hoc Sens. Wirel. Netw. **9**, 255–273 (2010)
6. Chen, X., Makki, K., Kang, Y., Pissinou, N.: Sensor network security: a survey. J. IEEE. Commun. Surv. Tutor. **11**, 52–73 (2009)

Research on the Pre-coding Technology of Broadcast Stage in Multi-user MIMO System

Guoqiang Wang[✉] and Shangfu Li

Key Lab of Electronic and Communication Engineering,
Heilongjiang University, Harbin, People's Republic of China
13936697869@163.com, 949435879@qq.com

Abstract. For the poor transmission reliability of data, this paper focuses on the precoding techniques of the multi-user MIMO system in the broadcast phase in, and the single-user MIMO and multi-user MIMO precoding techniques have been studied. In the multi-user MIMO system, BD-MMSE-VP coding algorithm is proposed to improve the BER performance of the system by using the MMSE criterion to optimize the perturbation vector, and the system uses QR technique to decompose BD channel matrix. Simulation results verify the effective of the proposed precoding algorithm.

Keywords: Multi-user · MIMO system · Precoding · Block diagonalization

1 Introduction

With advent of the era of "Internet +", the mobile Internet has been seen everywhere and played an important role in the development of human society. People enjoy the convenience of mobile communications at the same time, but also put forward higher requirements on the mobile communication technology, which promoted the rapid development of mobile communications [1]. It has developed from the first generation mobile communication (1st-generation, 1G) based on analog cellular technology to the fourth generation mobile communication (4th-generation, 4G) mainly based on MIMO systems through 30 years' development. 1G only provided high quality speech services, but now mobile communication has to meet all aspects of the demand, including work, leisure and entertainment. Mobile communication brings people endless convenience and well-being [2]. However, 4G cannot meet the current requirements of achieving interconnectedness of all things. Therefore, the next generation of communication technology - the fifth generation mobile communication (5th-generation, 5G) has also started to be studied.

In this paper, we focus on the preprogramming in the multi-user MIMO system broadcast phase. The inter-user interference can be eliminated by precoding the signals sent to the multiuser at the base station.

© ICST Institute for Computer Sciences, Social Informatics and Telecommunications Engineering 2018
X. Gu et al. (Eds.): MLICOM 2017, Part I, LNICST 226, pp. 701–709, 2018.
https://doi.org/10.1007/978-3-319-73564-1_72

2   The Precoding Technique of Multi-user MIMO System

2.1   Traditional Precoding Technology

Multi-user MIMO system can achieve the communication between base station and multiple users in the same frequency domain or time domain, increasing the spectrum efficiency and the reliability of communication system [3]. Multi-user MIMO as the 5G core technology has attracted many researchers' attention. In the broadcast link, the base station needs to send multiple data streams to multiple users. The signals obtained by each user contain not only the signals sent by the base station to them, but also the interference signals of other users. In addition, the users cannot cooperate among each other. The multi-user interference (MUI) occurs. Therefore, it is necessary to encode the transmitted signal before the signal is transmitted or to performing the detection operation at the receiving end, in order to eliminate the interference between the users and separate the information required by each user.

The precoding in Multi-user MIMO system is classified into linear and non-linear precoding. The linear precoding mainly includes channel inversion (CI) and block diagonalization (BD). The nonlinear precoding includes Dirty Paper Coding (DPC) and Tomlinson-Harashima Precoding (THP) [4].

CI precoding can be divided into the following two types: channel inversion precoding (ZF-CI) based on zero forcing and channel inversion precoding (MMSE-CI) based on minimum mean square error. Similar to the linear precoding of single-user MIMO, CI preprogramming is simple, with low computational complexity and thus easy to be implemented in communication systems, but weak at the anti-jamming. Block diagonalization precoding uses singular value decomposition of the channel matrix and is more suitable for the case of multi-antenna users. The computational complexity of Block diagonalization precoding is much smaller than other precoding algorithms, but it increases significantly as the number of users and receiving antennas increases. Therefore, it is important to find a new precoding algorithm that can reduce the block diagonalization precoding complexity and improve the system performance.

For non-linear dirty paper coding, the key idea is to treat other user signals as interference in addition to the effective user. Dirty paper coding can achieve close to the total channel capacity of multiple users, but is too complicated in computation to be applied to real communication system. Nonlinear THP precoding is formed on the basis of dirty paper coding. Although it does a compromise in terms of computational complexity and performance, it is still necessary to perform multiple iterations to eliminate user interference. THP is not suitable to the real communication system due its computational complexity. Therefore, in this section, we go into more detail on BD precoding and propose an optimization scheme.

2.2   An Optimal Coding Scheme Based on Block Diagonalization

The traditional block diagonalization coding (BD) uses the singular value decomposition (SVD) to decompose the channel matrix and obtains the zero matrix of the unitary matrix as the coding matrix. However, computational complexity of the singular value decomposition increases sharply as the number of transmitting and receiving antennas increases [5]. The study on precoding with low complexity and ideal performance is very important. In this paper, a block diagonalization scheme based on Perturbation Vector (VP) is proposed. The optimization of the perturbation vector is based on the MMSE criterion. Therefore, we name the proposed code scheme as BD-MMSE-VP.

In this paper, we use the multiuser MIMO system as a model to study the BD pre-coding optimization scheme. The base station transmits the perturbation signal vector, and for the optimization of the perturbation vector, the MMSE is used as the criterion. The client needs to carry out simple modulo operation on the received signal to restore the signal. Unlike traditional BD precoding, BD-MMSE-VP encoding uses QR decomposition channel matrix, while traditional BD precoding uses SVD.

H is the channel matrix between the base station and all users, $H = \left[H_1^T H_2^T \cdots H_K^T \right]^T$, $\hat{H}$ is H's pseudo inverse matrix, $\hat{H} = H^H \left(H H^H \right)^{-1}$, and $\hat{H} = \left[\hat{H}_1 \hat{H}_2 \cdots \hat{H}_K \right]$, so

$$
\begin{aligned}
H \hat{H}_1 &= \begin{bmatrix} H_1 \\ \vdots \\ H_K \end{bmatrix} \begin{bmatrix} \hat{H}_1 & \cdots & \hat{H}_K \end{bmatrix} = \begin{bmatrix} H_1 \hat{H}_1 & \cdots & H_1 \hat{H}_K \\ \vdots & \ddots & \vdots \\ H_K \hat{H}_1 & \cdots & H_K \hat{H}_K \end{bmatrix} \\
&= \begin{bmatrix} I_{N_{R,1}} & & \\ & \ddots & \\ & & I_{N_{R,K}} \end{bmatrix} = I_{N_R}
\end{aligned}
\tag{1}
$$

From the above can be seen when $j \neq k$, $H_j \hat{H}_k = 0$. The channel matrix of all other users except the user j is constructed as follows:

$$
\tilde{H}_j = \left[H_1^T \cdots H_{j-1}^T H_{j+1}^T \cdots H_K^T \right]^T
\tag{2}
$$

If you want to avoid other users on the user j caused by user interference, then the user j pseudo inverse matrix must fall in the matrix of zero space, so

$$
\tilde{H}_j \hat{H}_j = 0, \quad j = 1, 2 \ldots, K
\tag{3}
$$

Now, QR decomposition of the pseudo inverse matrix of user j is performed

$$
\hat{H}_j = \hat{Q}_j \hat{R}_j \quad j = 1, \ldots, K
\tag{4}
$$

According to QR decomposition properties, $\hat{R}_j$ is the upper triangular matrix, and $\hat{Q}_j$ column vector can form the standard orthogonal basis of the matrix $\hat{H}_j$. In order to eliminate inter-user interference, $\tilde{H}_j \hat{H}_j = \tilde{H}_j \hat{Q}_j \hat{R}_j = 0$, because $\hat{R}_j$ is reversible matrix, so $\tilde{H}_j \hat{Q}_j = 0$. $\hat{Q}_j$ is removing the orthogonal base forming the zero space.

Let $W_j = \hat{Q}_j$, construct a valid matrix $H_{eff,j} = W_j H$, BD-MMSE-VP coding principle is shown in Fig. 1:

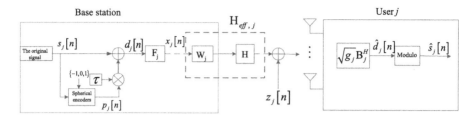

Fig. 1. BD-MMSE-VP precoding diagram

The optimal perturbation vector and power constraint factor are found by using MMSE criterion, $d_j[n]$ is the user j wants to get the signal, $\hat{d}_j[n]$ is the user j actually receives the signal, The minimum homogeneous error of the two signals is expressed by the formula (4), while B_j^H is the user receives the detection matrix, if it is unit array, then the system optimization problem is transformed into the base station transmitter optimization problem, and we know $H_{eff\,j}$, $d_j[n]$, $tr(R_n)$. So the problem to be solved is when $p_j[n]$, $x_j[n]$, g_j are what values, the $d_j[n]$ and $\hat{d}_j[n]$ mean square error is minimal, and power constraint is $\sum_{n=1}^{N_B} x_j^H[n]x_j[n] = P$, P is the base station total transmit power.

$$
\begin{aligned}
\varepsilon\big(p_j[n], x_j[n], g_j\big) &= \sum_{n=1}^{N_B} E\Big(\big\|\hat{d}_j[n] - d_j[n]\big\|^2\Big) \\
&= \sum_{n=1}^{N_B} E\Big(\big\|g_j B_j^H \big(H_{eff\,j}x_j[n] + z_j[n]\big) - d_j[n]\big\|^2\Big) \\
&= \sum_{n=1}^{N_B} E\Big(\big(g_j B_j^H \big(H_{eff\,j}x_j[n] + z_j[n]\big) - d_j[n]\big)^H \\
&\quad \times \big(g_j B_j^H \big(H_{eff\,j}x_j[n] + z_j[n]\big) - d_j[n]\big)\Big) \\
&= \sum_{n=1}^{N_B} E\left(
\begin{array}{l}
g_j^2 x_j^H[n]H_{eff\,j}^H H_{eff\,j}x_j[n] - g_j d_j^H[n]B_j^H H_{eff\,j}x_j[n] \\
+ g_j^2 tr(R_n) - g_j x_j^H[n]H_{eff\,j}^H B_j d_j[n] + d_j^H[n]d_j[n]
\end{array}
\right)
\end{aligned}
\tag{5}
$$

Firstly, the Lagrangian function is constructed by using the Lagrangian algorithm:

$$
f\big(p_j[n], x_j[n], g_j, \lambda\big) = \varepsilon\big(p_j[n], x_j[n], g_j\big) + \lambda\left(\sum_{n=1}^{N_B} x_j^H[n]x_j[n] - P\right)
\tag{6}
$$

And then $p_j[n]$, $x_j[n]$, λ were partial guide:

$$
\frac{\partial f(\cdot)}{\partial x_j[n]} = g_j^2 x_j^H[n]H_{eff\,j}^H H_{eff\,j} - g_j d_j^H[n]B_j^H H_{eff\,j} + \lambda x_j^H[n] = 0
\tag{7}
$$

$$\frac{\partial f(\cdot)}{\partial g_j} = \sum_{n=1}^{N_B} 2g_j x_j^H[n] H_{eff,j}^H H_{eff,j} x_j[n] - d_j^H[n] B_j^H H_{eff,j} x_j[n]$$
$$+ 2g_j tr(R_n) - x_j^H[n] H_{eff,j}^H B_j d_j[n] = 0 \tag{8}$$

$$\frac{\partial f(\cdot)}{\partial \lambda} = \sum_{n=1}^{N_B} x_j^H[n] x_j[n] - P = 0 \tag{9}$$

Let $\xi = \frac{N_B tr(R_n)}{P}$, finally we can obtain

$$x_j[n] = F_j d_j[n] = \frac{1}{g_j} H_{eff,j}^H \left(H_{eff,j} H_{eff,j}^H + \xi I \right)^{-1} B_j d_j[n] \tag{10}$$

$$g_j = \sqrt{\frac{1}{P} \sum_{n=1}^{N_B} d_j^H[n] B_j^H H_{eff,j} \left(H_{eff,j} H_{eff,j}^H + \xi I \right)^{-2} H_{eff,j}^H B_j d_j[n]} \tag{11}$$

Relative to the perturbation vector signal $d_j[n]$ coding matrix is $F_j = \frac{1}{g_j} H_{eff,j}^H \left(H_{eff,j} H_{eff,j}^H + \xi I \right)^{-1} B_j$, and the perturbation vector $p_j[n]$ can be formed by a spherical encoder.

$$p_j[n] = \arg\min \left\| B_j \left(s_j[n] + \tau p_j'[n] \right) \right\| \tag{12}$$

The user j receive signal can be expressed as

$$y_j[n] = H_{eff,j} x_j[n] + z_j[n]$$
$$= \frac{1}{g_j} H_{eff,j} H_{eff,j}^H \left(H_{eff,j} H_{eff,j}^H + \xi I \right)^{-1} B_j \left(s_j[n] + \tau p_j[n] \right) + z_j[n]$$
$$\approx \frac{1}{g_j} B_j \left(s_j[n] + \tau p_j[n] \right) + z_j'[n] \tag{13}$$

The equation $z_j'[n]$ contains the Gaussian redundant interference noise, which is multiplied by the power of the user j to remove the power scaling, and the user j knows the value of the spherical encoder τ, so the receiver can eliminate $\tau p_j[n]$ influence by modulo operation.

3   Implementation and Performance Analysis

In this section, the performance of the proposed algorithm and system will be evaluated and analyzed in terms of the optimized coding sum rate and complexity of optimized coding.

3.1   Optimized Coding Sum Rate Analysis

The sum of the rates of the multiuser MIMO systems is the sum of all single user rates. Through the use of BD-MMSE-VP precoding in multi-user MIMO systems, $H_{eff,j}$ is the equivalent matrix of base station and user j, transmit a signal is $x_j[n] = \frac{1}{g_j} H_{eff,j}^H$ $\left(H_{eff,j} H_{eff,j}^H + \xi I \right)^{-1} B_j d_j[n]$, the receiving signal where in the user is $y_j[n] = H_{eff,j}$ $x_j[n] + z_j[n]$. According to feature decomposition, we can easily obtain $H_{eff,j} H_{eff,j}^H = Q \Lambda Q^H$, $H_{eff,j} x_j[n]$ is decomposed:

$$H_{eff,j} x_j[n] = \frac{1}{\sqrt{g_j}} Q \Phi Q B_j d_j[n] \tag{14}$$

While Q is the unit matrix, Φ is the diagonal matrix, and the value on the diagonal is $\frac{\lambda_j}{\lambda_j + \xi}$, λ_j is Λ matrix's diagonal elements. According to (14), and it can be seen that the user j input signal can be expressed as:

$$
\begin{aligned}
\left[H_{eff,j} x_j[n] \right]_k = \frac{1}{\sqrt{g_j}} & \left[q_{k,1} \frac{\lambda_1}{\lambda_1 + \xi} \cdots q_{k,N_{R,j}} \frac{\lambda_{N_{R,j}}}{\lambda_{N_{R,j}} + \xi} \right] \\
\times & \begin{bmatrix} q_{1,1}^H & \cdots & q_{N_{R,j},1}^H \\ \vdots & \ddots & \vdots \\ q_{1,N_{R,j}}^H & \cdots & q_{N_{R,j},N_{R,j}}^H \end{bmatrix} \begin{bmatrix} c_{j,1}[n] \\ \vdots \\ c_{j,N_{R,j}}[n] \end{bmatrix}
\end{aligned} \tag{15}
$$

So the user j's k-th received signal is represented by the following equation:

$$y_{j,k}[n] = \frac{1}{\sqrt{g_j}} \left(\sum_{l=1}^{N_{R,j}} \frac{\lambda_l}{\lambda_l + \xi} |q_{k,l}|^2 \right) c_{j,k}[n] + z_{j,k}''[n] \tag{16}$$

While $z_{j,k}''[n] = \frac{1}{\sqrt{g_j}} \sum_{m=1,m \neq k}^{N_{R,j}} \left(\sum_{l=1}^{N_{R,j}} \frac{\lambda_l}{\lambda_l + \xi} q_{k,l} q_{m,l}^H \right) c_{j,k}[n] + z_{j,k}[n]$, including internal data stream interference and signal noise $z_{j,k}[n]$, so the user j SINR is:

$$SINR_{j,k} = \sum_{n=1}^{N_B} \frac{\|s c_{j,k}[n]\|^2}{\|t c_{j,m}[n]\|^2 + \|z_{j,k}[n]\|^2} \tag{17}$$

While $s = \frac{1}{\sqrt{g_j}} \left(\sum_{l=1}^{N_{R,j}} \frac{\lambda_l}{\lambda_l + \xi} |q_{k,l}|^2 \right)$, $t = \frac{1}{\sqrt{g_j}} \sum_{m=1,m \neq k}^{N_{R,j}} \left(\sum_{l=1}^{N_{R,j}} \frac{\lambda_l}{\lambda_l + \xi} q_{k,l} q_{m,l}^H \right)$, so the BD-MMSE-VP coding sum rate is:

$$R_{BD-MMSE-VP} = \sum_{j=1}^{K} \sum_{k=1}^{N_{R,j}} \log_2 \left(1 + SINR_{j,k} \right) \tag{18}$$

3.2   Complexity Analysis of Optimized Coding

For multiuser MIMO precoding complexity analysis, this section considers only the complexity of the base station precoding algorithm and measures the computational complexity using floating-point arithmetic. Traditional BD precoding uses the SVD decomposition, its complexity:

$$C_{SVD} = K \times \left(4N_B^2 N_R + 13 \left(N_R - N_{R,j} \right)^3 \right) \tag{19}$$

The BD-MMSE-VP coding uses QR decomposition and perturbation vector optimization, QR decomposition complexity is

$$C_{QR} = \frac{11}{3} N_B^3 + \frac{5}{3} N_B^2 + K N_{R,j}^2 \times \left(N_B - \frac{1}{3} N_{R,j} \right) \tag{20}$$

It can be seen that the QR operation is much smaller than the SVD by comparing the SVD and QR operations, because the QR is decomposed $N_B \times N_{R,j}$, and the matrix of the traditional BD precoding SVD is $\left(N_R - N_{R,j} \right) \times N_B$.

3.3   Simulation Results

In this paper, BD-MMSE-VP precoding and traditional BD precoding algorithm is simulated by Matlab. In the multi-user MIMO system broadcast stage, QPSK is used for modulation and demodulation. The number of base stations is 8, and each user adopts two receiving antennas, the number of users is 4. The simulation compares the system and the rate and BER performance, the specific simulation parameters are shown in Table 1 below:

Table 1. Multi-user MIMO precoding simulation parameter

Parameter	Set values
System	Multiple-MIMO
Antenna configuration/User number	8 * 2/K = 4
Channel condition	Zero mean complex Gaussian random channel
Noise	White Gaussian Noise
Modulation mode	QPSK
Precoding algorithm	Traditional BD/BD-MMSE-VP algorithm

It can be seen from Figs. 2 and 3 that the BD-MMSE-VP precoding proposed in this paper has a great advantage over traditional BD precoding, both BER performance and system sum rate performance, and the signal-to-noise ratio In the case of no more than 10 dB, BD-MMSE-VP pre-coding performance advantage is more obvious. When the signal-to-noise ratio is 5 dB, the BD-MMSE-VP precoding is improved by 5 bps/Hz compared with the traditional BD precoding algorithm. When the SNR is

15 dB, the BD-MMSE-VP precoding is better than the traditional BD precoding The algorithm improves the rate of 2 bps/Hz. This is because the BD-MMSE-VP uses the Lagrangian algorithm to allocate the transmit power, allocates more transmit power for subchannels with good channel states, and the channel subcarriers are allocated less or do not allocate transmit power. Noise ratio is maximized, but with the increase of the signal-to-noise ratio, the BD-MMSE-VP precoding is almost evenly distributed to all subchannels, so its rate performance is high Noise ratio is similar to the traditional BD precoding. BD-MMSE-VP precoding BER performance is better than traditional BD precoding. At BER = 10^{-2}, BD-MMSE-VP precoding obtains a gain of 2.7 dB relative to traditional BD algorithm.

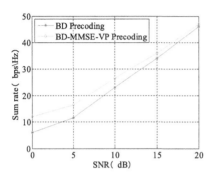

Fig. 2. The contrast of Multi-user MIMO precoding sum rate

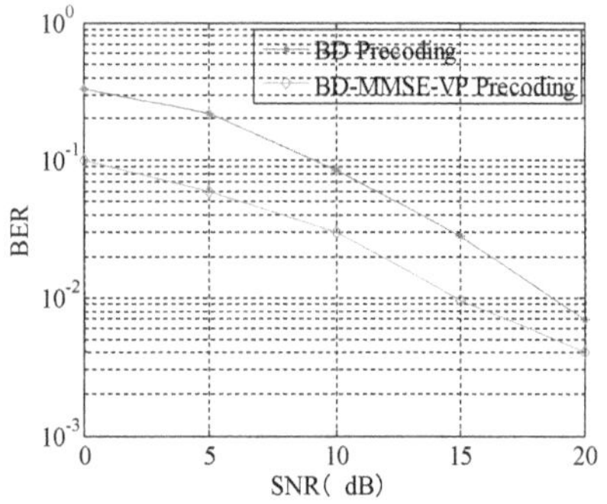

Fig. 3. The contrast of Multi-user MIMO precoding BER performance

4 Conclusions

In the multiuser MIMO system, two kinds of linear precoding of CI and BD are preliminarily studied, and two kinds of nonlinear codes such as DPC and THP coding are difficult to be applied because of the high complexity of non-linear coding DPC and THP coding. The performance of BD pre-coding is better than that of the CI pre-coding, and the BD-MMSE-VP precoding is proposed at the same time, which is combined with the BD algorithm of QR decomposition, and the MMSE criterion is used to optimize the perturbation vector. Simulation results show that the performance of sum rate and BER has been greatly improved by comparison.

References

1. Zheng, K., Zhao, L., Mei, J., Shao, B., Xiang, W., Hanzo, L.: Survey of large-scale MIMO systems. IEEE Commun. Surv. Tutorials **17**(3), 1738–1760 (2015)
2. Gao, X., Dai, L., Ma, Y., et al.: Low-complexity near-optimal signal detection for uplink large-scale MIMO systems. Electron. Lett. **50**(18), 1326–1328 (2015)

3. Lu, L., Li, G., Swindlehurst, A., Ashikhmin, A., Zhang, R.: An overview of massive MIMO: benefits and challenges. IEEE J. Sel. Top. Sig. Process **8**(5), 742–758 (2014)
4. Feng, W., Wang, Y.M., Ge, N., Lu, J.H., Zhang, J.S.: Virtual MIMO in multi cell distributed antenna systems: coordinated transmissions with large-scale CSIT. IEEE J. Sel. Areas Commun. **31**(10), 2067–2081 (2013)
5. Stankovic, V., Haardt, M.: Generalized design of multi-user MIMO precoding matrices. IEEE Trans. Wireless Commun. **7**(3), 953–961 (2008)

Retraction Note to: A Resource Allocation Algorithm Based on Game Theory in UDN

Changjun Chen, Jianxin Dai, Chonghu Cheng, and Zhiliang Huang

Retraction Note to:
Chapter "A Resource Allocation Algorithm Based on Game Theory in UDN" in: X. Gu et al. (Eds.): *Machine Learning and Intelligent Communications*, LNICST 226, https://doi.org/10.1007/978-3-319-73564-1_45

The authors have retracted this conference chapter [1] because it shows significant overlap with a previously published chapter [2]. All authors agree to the retraction.

[1] Chen C., Dai J., Cheng C., Huang Z. (2018) A Resource Allocation Algorithm Based on Game Theory in UDN. In: Gu X., Liu G., Li B. (eds) Machine Learning and Intelligent Communications. MLICOM 2017. Lecture Notes of the Institute for Computer Sciences, Social Informatics and Telecommunications Engineering, vol 226. Springer, Cham

[2] Y. Liu, Y. Wang, Y. Zhang, R. Sun and L. Jiang, "Game-theoretic hierarchical resource allocation in ultra-dense networks," 2016 IEEE 27th Annual International Symposium on Personal, Indoor, and Mobile Radio Communications (PIMRC), Valencia, 2016, pp. 1–6. https://doi.org/10.1109/PIMRC.2016.7794819

The retracted version of this chapter can be found at
https://doi.org/10.1007/978-3-319-73564-1_45

© ICST Institute for Computer Sciences, Social Informatics and Telecommunications Engineering 2019
X. Gu et al. (Eds.): MLICOM 2017, Part I, LNICST 226, p. C1, 2019.
https://doi.org/10.1007/978-3-319-73564-1_73

Author Index

Aijun, Liu II-233
An, Fei I-231

Bao, Dongxing II-326, II-333
Bi, Zongjie II-263
Bu, Xiangyuan II-79

Cai, Gangshan I-423
Cai, Shuhao II-558
Cao, Bei I-535, I-555, II-285
Cao, Lin II-391
Cao, Qiuyi I-516, I-524
Changjun, Yu II-233
Chen, Bing I-271
Chen, Changjun I-453
Chen, Dawei II-43
Chen, Fangni I-103, II-243
Chen, Hao II-437
Chen, Jiamei I-3
Chen, Jiaxin II-546
Chen, Juan I-97, I-592
Chen, Lu I-212
Chen, Qi I-145
Chen, Ruirui II-343
Chen, Ting I-648, I-657
Chen, Xiaolong II-225
Chen, Xifeng I-30
Chen, Xing II-23
Chen, Xinwu II-428, II-612
Chen, Yanping I-239
Chen, Yi-jun II-132, II-169, II-198
Chen, Zhuangguang I-535
Cheng, Chonghu I-453, I-463, I-475, I-484,
    I-505
Cheng, Fangfang II-634
Cheng, Lele II-8, II-15
Chi, Yonggang I-212
Chong, Kun I-158, I-168
Cong, Haifeng I-133
Cong, Ligang II-498
Cui, Luyao II-206
Cui, Yuwei II-316
Cui, Zihao I-434

Dai, Fusheng I-212, I-231
Dai, Fu-sheng II-254
Dai, Jianxin I-453, I-463, I-475, I-484, I-505
Deng, Yiqiu II-577
Deng, Zhian I-592
Di, Xiaoqiang II-498
Ding, Guoru I-247
Ding, Qun I-626, I-692
Dong, Hang I-22, II-402
Du, Rui I-614
Duan, Shiqi II-569

Fan, Chenyang I-405
Fan, Hongda I-444
Fang, Yuan II-658
Feng, Naizhang I-49, II-569
Feng, Yuan II-254
Fu, Fangfa II-333
Fu, Shiyou II-263
Fu, Ying I-49

Gai, Yingying II-391
Gai, Zhigang II-391, II-482
Gao, Chao I-3
Gao, Xiaozheng II-79
Gao, Yulong I-239
Gao, Yunxue I-205
Gong, Yi-shuai II-198
Gu, Fu-fei II-160
Gu, Xuemai I-545, II-43
Guan, Jian II-225
Guo, Jing I-516
Guo, Qi I-364
Guo, Qing I-564, I-574
Guo, Xiaojuan II-361
Guo, Xiaomin I-300
Guo, Yanqing I-168
Guo, Ying II-53
Guo, Yongan I-300

Han, Mo II-577
Hao, Ganlin II-585
He, Can I-57

He, Chenguang   I-666, II-316
He, Dongxuan   II-71
He, Qi-fang   II-132
He, Xiaoyuan   II-142
He, You   II-225
Hou, Dongxu   I-347
Hou, Yunfei   I-12
Hu, Xiaofeng   II-142
Hua, Jingyu   I-103, II-96, II-243
Hua, Siyang   II-23
Huang, Fangjun   I-145
Huang, Linlin   II-215
Huang, Minling   II-215
Huang, Xu   I-423
Huang, Zhiliang   I-453, I-463, I-475, I-484, I-505
Huang, Zhiqiu   I-326, II-294

Ji, Ping   I-626, I-692
Jiang, Teng   II-569
Jin, Guiyue   II-634
Jin, Jiyu   II-634
Jin, Xiaoxiao   I-133

Kang, Hui   I-258
Kang, Le   II-160
Kang, Wenjing   I-40, I-614, I-675
Khudadad, Mirza   II-294

Li, Bo   I-382, I-614, I-675
Li, Chenming   II-23
Li, Dezhi   I-373, I-564, I-574, II-371
Li, Dongqing   II-455
Li, Feng   I-103, II-8, II-15
Li, Haowei   II-490
Li, Heng   II-391
Li, Hong-guang   II-53
Li, Hui   II-391
Li, Jiamin   I-103, II-96
Li, Jin   II-326
Li, Jingming   I-247
Li, Kaijian   I-463
Li, Kaiming   II-142
Li, Kai-ming   II-198
Li, Lei   II-53
Li, Peng   II-634, II-647
Li, Ruide   II-603
Li, Runxuan   II-518
Li, Ruya   I-122

Li, Shangfu   I-701
Li, Sunan   I-103
Li, Wenfeng   I-339, I-347, I-405, II-658
Li, Xiangkun   II-3
Li, Xiaoming   II-326, II-333
Li, Xiaotong   I-524
Li, Xinyou   I-40
Li, Xuan   I-3
Li, Xuebin   II-418
Li, Xujie   II-23
Li, Yabin   I-158, I-168
Li, Yanchao   I-598, I-606
Li, Yang   I-635
Li, Yangyang   II-603
Li, Yong   I-112
Li, Zhe   I-195
Li, Zhen   II-622
Li, Zhonghua   I-145
Lian, Yinghui   I-112
Liang, Guang   II-61
Liang, Xian-jiao   II-150
Liao, Yinhua   I-666
Lin, Weiyi   I-271
Lin, Zhengkui   I-592
Linwei, Wang   II-233
Liu, Aijun   II-206
Liu, AiJun   II-509
Liu, Cheng   II-333
Liu, Chungang   I-181, II-33
Liu, Enxiao   II-391, II-482
Liu, Fugang   I-258
Liu, Fuqiang   II-463
Liu, Ge   I-145
Liu, Gongliang   I-40, I-373, I-382, I-564, I-574, I-614, I-675, II-371, II-418
Liu, Juan   I-484
Liu, Lu   I-423
Liu, Mengmeng   II-668
Liu, Peipei   II-106
Liu, Rongkuan   I-85
Liu, Shousheng   II-391
Liu, Songyan   I-648, I-657
Liu, Ting   I-49
Liu, Tong   I-300, I-545
Liu, Wanjun   II-437
Liu, Xiaofeng   I-394
Liu, Xin   I-97, I-524, I-592, II-8, II-15
Liu, Xiyu   II-361
Liu, Yong   I-598, I-606, II-410
Liu, Zhiyong   II-87

Long, Keping   II-418
Lu, Jiang   I-12
Lu, Jihua   I-355
Lu, Weidang   II-96, II-243, II-273
Lu, Xiaoyi   II-472
Luo, Chunfeng   II-647
Luo, Jian   II-188
Luo, Junxin   II-455
Luo, Xiao   II-463
Luo, Ying   II-117
Lv, Haibo   I-373, II-371
Lv, Shengmiao   I-122

Ma, Liyong   II-558
Ma, Yongkui   I-239
Ma, Zhongchao   I-682
Man, Le   II-304
Meng, Di   II-169
Mou, Jun   II-634, II-647

Na, Zhenyu   I-97, I-524
Ni, Jia-cheng   II-150
Ni, Xiaoqin   I-339
Nie, Yulei   II-71, II-106

Pan, Jie   II-179
Pei, Ximing   II-3
Peng, Hong   II-273
Peng, Xiyuan   I-382

Qi, Feng   II-668
Qian, Daxing   II-3
Qiao, Haiyan   I-12
Qin, Danyang   I-626, I-692, II-428
Qin, Jitao   II-437
Qu, Haicheng   II-437
Quan, Taifan   II-206

Ren, Haoliang   I-133
Ren, Xiangshi   II-333

Sha, Xuejun   I-682
Shao, Shuai   II-351
Shen, Di   II-15
Shi, Jianfei   II-8
Shi, Jun   II-577
Shi, Pushuai   II-263
Shi, Shuo   I-545, II-43
Shi, Yahui   I-49
Song, Dongyu   I-315

Song, Weibin   II-577
Song, Yuanyuan   II-188
Song, Zhaohui   II-381
Su, Changran   II-273
Sui, Ping   II-53
Sun, Bai   I-584
Sun, Li   II-150
Sun, Mingjian   I-49, I-122, II-569
Sun, Qingquan   I-12, I-291, II-518
Sun, Shuqiao   I-434
Sun, Siyue   II-61
Sun, Wenjing   II-603
Sun, Yejun   II-528
Sun, Yilang   I-434
Sun, Ying   II-23
Sun, Yongliang   I-666, II-528
Sun, Yu   I-12, I-291, II-518
Sun, Yuxue   II-117

Tang, Lidan   II-558
Tian, Lu   II-79
Tian, Xuanxuan   II-381
Tian, Zengshan   I-112, I-133
Tian, Zhaoshuo   I-434, II-263

Van, Nguyen Ngoc   II-463

Wang, Baobao   II-418
Wang, Beishan   I-364
Wang, Bo   I-158, I-168
Wang, Chen   I-181
Wang, Chenxu   II-304
Wang, Erfu   II-428, II-612
Wang, Gang   I-30, I-76, I-85, I-205, II-490,
    II-622
Wang, Guoqiang   I-584, I-701
Wang, Hang   I-291
Wang, Hongyuan   I-282
Wang, Hui   I-97
Wang, Jianlun   I-57
Wang, Jing   II-304
Wang, Kun   II-61
Wang, Lei   II-472
Wang, Li   II-15
Wang, LinWei   II-509
Wang, MingFeng   II-509
Wang, Ping   II-463
Wang, Xianzhi   I-97, I-592
Wang, Xinhong   II-463

Wang, Xinsheng   II-304
Wang, Yanghui   II-498
Wang, Yao   I-3
Wang, Yi   II-79
Wang, Yihao   I-417
Wang, Yinghua   II-87
Wang, Yinyin   II-87
Wang, Yongsheng   II-285, II-537
Wang, Zhenyong   I-373, I-564, I-574, II-371
Wang, Zhisen   II-647
Wang, Zhongpeng   II-243
Wang, Ziya   II-23
Wei, Shouming   II-316
Wen, Jiangang   II-96
Wu, Lili   I-195
Wu, Pengfei   I-555
Wu, Qihui   I-247, II-546
Wu, Shangru   I-648, I-657
Wu, Shaohua   II-455
Wu, Shuang   I-564, I-574
Wu, Yan   I-675
Wu, Yue   I-76, I-205, II-490

Xia, Hongyang   I-258
Xia, Mingze   I-315, I-494
Xia, Weijie   II-215
Xia, Zhimou   I-545
Xiao, Jingting   I-221
Xie, Jian   I-326
Xie, Linjie   II-273
Xie, Wei   II-558
Xie, Weihao   II-482
Xie, Xufen   I-417, I-444
Xie, Yaqin   II-428, II-612
Xin, Yizong   II-333
Xu, Enwei   II-43
Xu, Ershi   I-271
Xu, Han-yang   II-124, II-132, II-169
Xu, Hongguang   II-381
Xu, Lei   II-472
Xu, Tianliang   I-555
Xu, Xiaolin   I-355
Xu, Yao   I-76, I-85, II-622
Xu, Yu   I-373, II-371
Xu, Yuhua   II-546
Xu, Zhijiang   II-96
Xue, Tong   II-410
Xuguang, Yang   II-233

Yang, Fulong   I-158
Yang, Hongjuan   I-382
Yang, Huamin   II-498
Yang, Jiuru   II-333
Yang, Lu   II-142
Yang, Mingchuan   I-394
Yang, Songxiang   I-626, I-692
Yang, Wenchao   II-622
Yang, Ye   I-300
Ye, Liang   I-682
Ye, Xiaolin   II-647
Yin, Chen   II-537
Yin, Xudong   I-475
Yin, Yanxin   I-195
Yu, Changjun   II-351
Yu, ChangJun   II-509
Yu, Dingfeng   II-482
Yu, Xiaohan   II-225
Yu, Xin-yong   II-53
Yv, Changjun   II-206

Zhai, Xiangping   I-271
Zhang, Cheng   I-648, I-657
Zhang, Haijun   II-418
Zhang, Hailin   II-343
Zhang, Honggang   II-188
Zhang, Jiangxin   II-8
Zhang, Kun-feng   II-53
Zhang, Min   I-505
Zhang, Qi   I-326
Zhang, Qinyu   II-381, II-455
Zhang, Qun   II-132, II-150, II-160, II-169,
      II-198
Zhang, Ruoyu   I-221
Zhang, Song   II-117
Zhang, Tiantian   II-455
Zhang, Tingting   II-381
Zhang, Wenbin   I-181
Zhang, Wenhan   I-122
Zhang, Wenrui   I-405
Zhang, Xiao   I-122
Zhang, Xiaofei   I-247
Zhang, Xin   I-22, II-402
Zhang, Xinyu   I-516
Zhang, Yanchao   I-434
Zhang, Yanfeng   I-423
Zhang, Yao   II-304
Zhang, Yin   II-160
Zhang, Yu   I-355, II-273, II-603

Zhang, Yuli   II-546
Zhang, Yumeng   I-394
Zhang, Yuncui   I-417, I-444
Zhang, Yuxuan   I-417
Zhang, Zijian   II-71, II-106
Zhao, Bing   II-585, II-595
Zhao, Donglai   I-76, I-85, I-205
Zhao, Honglin   I-221
Zhao, Jiang   II-160
Zhao, Kanglian   I-339, I-347, I-405, I-666,
    II-528, II-658
Zhao, Kongrui   II-351
Zhao, Nan   I-516
Zhao, Sichen   II-658
Zhao, Weiguang   I-641
Zhao, Xue   I-122
Zhen, Jiaqi   I-598, I-606
Zheng, Hongxu   I-57

Zheng, Liming   I-30, I-76, I-85, I-205, II-490
Zheng, Yaxin   II-33
Zhong, Weizhi   II-472
Zhou, Changling   II-179
Zhou, Feng   II-124
Zhou, Gang   I-423
Zhou, Ji   I-212, II-254
Zhou, Jianjiang   II-215
Zhou, Mu   I-112, I-133, II-8
Zhou, Ruofei   II-622
Zhou, Tao   II-343
Zhou, Xunzhi   II-537
Zhou, Yanguo   II-343
Zhou, Ying   II-215
Zhu, Feng   II-142
Zhu, Yalin   II-179
Zhuang, Peidong   I-635, I-641
Zou, Nianyu   I-444

Printed in the United States
By Bookmasters